Macmillan Interdisciplinary Handbooks

Religion

Beyond Religion

Macmillan Interdisciplinary Handbooks

Religion

Jeffrey J. Kripal, SERIES EDITOR
April D. DeConick and Anthony B. Pinn, ASSOCIATE EDITORS

Religion: Sources, Perspectives, and Methodologies
Jeffrey J. Kripal, editor

Religion: Social Religion
William B. Parsons, editor

Religion: Beyond Religion
Phil Zuckerman, editor

Religion: Just Religion
Anthony B. Pinn, editor

Religion: Material Religion
Diane Apostolos-Cappadona, editor

Religion: Embodied Religion
Kent L. Brintnall, editor

Religion: Secret Religion
April D. DeConick, editor

Religion: Mental Religion
Niki Kasumi Clements, editor

Religion: Super Religion
Jeffrey J. Kripal, editor

Religion: Narrating Religion
Sarah Iles Johnston, editor

Other Macmillan Interdisciplinary Handbooks series:

Gender

renee c. hoogland, SERIES EDITOR
Iris van der Tuin and Nicole Fleetwood, ASSOCIATE EDITORS

Philosophy

Donald M. Borchert, SERIES EDITOR
James Petrik and Arthur Zucker, ASSOCIATE EDITORS

Macmillan Interdisciplinary Handbooks

Religion

Beyond Religion

Phil Zuckerman
EDITOR

MACMILLAN REFERENCE USA
A part of Gale, Cengage Learning

GALE
CENGAGE Learning·

Farmington Hills, Mich • San Francisco • New York • Waterville, Maine
Meriden, Conn • Mason, Ohio • Chicago

Religion: Beyond Religion

Phil Zuckerman, *Editor*

Jonathan Vereecke, *Project Editor*
Hélène Potter, *Associate Publisher*
Kristine Julien, *Graphic Design Specialist*

© 2016 Macmillan Reference USA, a part of Gale, Cengage Learning.

ALL RIGHTS RESERVED. No part of this work covered by the copyright herein may be reproduced, transmitted, stored, or used in any form or by any means graphic, electronic, or mechanical, including but not limited to photocopying, recording, scanning, digitizing, taping, Web distribution, information networks, or information storage and retrieval systems, except as permitted under Section 107 or 108 of the 1976 United States Copyright Act, without the prior written permission of the publisher.

For product information and technology assistance, contact us at
Gale Customer Support, 1-800-877-4253.
For permission to use material from this text or product, submit all requests online at **www.cengage.com/permissions**.
Further permissions questions can be emailed to
permissionrequest@cengage.com.

Cover photographs reproduced by permission of © P Nutt/Demotix/Corbis.

While every effort has been made to ensure the reliability of the information presented in this publication, Gale, a part of Cengage Learning, does not guarantee the accuracy of the data contained herein. Gale accepts no payment for listing; and inclusion in the publication of any organization, agency, institution, publication, service, or individual does not imply endorsement of the editors or publisher. Errors brought to the attention of the publisher and verified to the satisfaction of the publisher will be corrected in future editions.

LIBRARY OF CONGRESS CATALOGING-IN-PUBLICATION DATA

Names: Zuckerman, Phil, editor.
Title Religion : beyond religion / Phil Zuckerman, editor.
Other titles: Beyond religion
Description: Farmington Hills : Macmillan Reference USA, a part of Gale, Cengage Learning, 2016. | Series: Macmillan interdisciplinary handbooks | Includes bibliographical references and index.
Identifiers: LCCN 2016000472 | ISBN 9780028663548 (hardcover) | ISBN 9780028663616 (ebook)
Subjects: LCSH: Secularism.
Classification: LCC BL2747.8 .R453 2016 | DDC 211/.6--dc23
LC record available at http://lccn.loc.gov/2016000472

Gale, a part of Cengage Learning
27500 Drake Rd.
Farmington Hills, MI 48331-3535

ISBN 978-0-02-866354-8 (this volume)
ISBN 978-0-02-866349-4 (Macmillan Interdisciplinary Handbooks: Religion set)

This title is also available as an e-book.
ISBN 978-0-02-866361-6
Contact your Gale sales representative for ordering information.

Printed in Mexico
1 2 3 4 5 6 7 20 19 18 17 16

Editorial Board

EDITOR IN CHIEF

Jeffrey J. Kripal

J. Newton Rayzor Professor of Religion
Rice University, Houston, TX

Author of numerous books, including *Comparing Religions: Coming to Terms*, with Ata Anzali, Andrea R. Jain, and Erin Prophet (2014); *Authors of the Impossible: The Paranormal and the Sacred* (2010); and *The Serpent's Gift: Gnostic Reflections on the Study of Religion* (2007).

ASSOCIATE EDITORS

April D. DeConick

Chair, and Isla Carroll and Percy E. Turner Professor of New Testament and Early Christianity, Department of Religion
Rice University, Houston, TX

Her most recent books include *The Gnostic New Age: How a Countercultural Spirituality Revolutionized Religion from Antiquity to Today* (2016); *Holy Misogyny: Why the Sex and Gender Conflicts in the Early Church Still Matter* (2011); and *The Thirteenth Apostle: What the Gospel of Judas Really Says* (2007, 2009).

Anthony B. Pinn

Agnes Cullen Arnold Professor of Humanities
Rice University, Houston, TX

Author and editor of numerous books, including *Introducing African American Religion* (2013); *The Hip Hop and Religion Reader* (edited with Monica Miller, 2014); and *African American Religious Cultures* (2009).

Contents

Preface   xi

Introduction   xv

Chapter 1: Defining That Which Is Other to Religion 1

    Ryan T. Cragun
    Associate Professor, Department of Sociology
    The University of Tampa, FL

SECULARITY IN SOCIETY 17

Chapter 2: Secularization 19

    Stratos Patrikios
    Senior Lecturer
    University of Strathclyde, School of Government and Public Policy, Glasgow, UK

Chapter 3: Lived Secularity: Atheism, Indifference, and the Social Significance of Religion 37

    Isabella Kasselstrand
    Assistant Professor of Sociology
    California State University Bakersfield

Chapter 4: Believing in Belief: Toward the Secularization of Faith in Global Economies 53

    Abby Day
    Department of Religious Studies
    University of Kent, Canterbury, UK

Chapter 5: Apostasy 71

    Jesse M. Smith
    Assistant Professor, Department of Sociology
    Western Michigan University, Kalamazoo

Chapter 6: Secularity and Family Life 93

    Christel Manning
    Professor, Department of Philosophy, Theology, and Religious Studies
    Sacred Heart University, Fairfield, CT

Chapter 7: From Rebels to Everyday Atheists: Women and Secularity 111

    Marta Trzebiatowska
    Lecturer, Department of Sociology
    University of Aberdeen, UK

CONTENTS

Chapter 8: Secularism, Diversity, and Race in the Contemporary United States 129

Juhem Navarro-Rivera
El Instituto: *Institute of Latino/a, Latin American, and Caribbean Studies*
University of Connecticut, Storrs

Chapter 9: Secularism, Secularity, and Community 147

Matthew Loveland
Associate Professor of Sociology and Political Science, Department of Political Science
Le Moyne College, Syracuse, NY

Chapter 10: Separation of Church and State in the American Political Traditions 165

Will Barndt
Assistant Professor of Political Studies
Pitzer College, Claremont, CA

Chapter 11: Religion, Secularism, and the Public Sphere 185

Steven Kettell
Department of Politics and International Studies
University of Warwick, Coventry, England

Chapter 12: Secularism, Secularity, and War 203

Stacey Gutkowski
Senior Lecturer in Conflict Studies
King's College London

PSYCHOLOGICAL AND PHILOSOPHICAL ASPECTS OF SECULARITY 223

Chapter 13: Dislike of and Discrimination Against Atheists and Secular People 225

Maxine B. Najle
Doctoral Candidate, Department of Psychology
University of Kentucky, Lexington

Will M. Gervais
Assistant Professor, Department of Psychology
University of Kentucky, Lexington

Chapter 14: The Psychology of Secularity and Nonreligion 241

Sean E. Moore
Associate Professor of Psychology, Department of Social Sciences
University of Alberta-Augustana Campus

Jaynita Maru
BSc Candidate, Department of Social Sciences
University of Alberta-Augustana Campus

Chapter 15: Atheology 263

John R. Shook
Research Associate, Philosophy Department
University at Buffalo, NY

Chapter 16: New Atheism 281

Teemu Taira

viii   MACMILLAN INTERDISCIPLINARY HANDBOOKS

Senior Lecturer, Study of Religions
University of Helsinki

Chapter 17: Secularism and Morality 301

Ryan Falcioni
Associate Professor, Department of Philosophy, Chaffey College, Rancho Cucamonga, CA
Visiting Scholar, Institut für Hermeneutik und Religionsphilosophie, University of Zürich,
Switzerland

Chapter 18: Atheism, Pacifism, and Anarchism 325

Andrew Fiala
Professor of Philosophy
California State University, Fresno

Chapter 19: Humanistic Judaism and Secular Spirituality 343

Adam Chalom
Dean, North America
International Institute for Secular Humanistic Judaism, Lincolnshire, IL

Chapter 20: Naturalism and Well-Being 363

Thomas W. Clark
Director, Center for Naturalism, Somerville, MA
Research Associate, Institute for Behavioral Health, Brandeis University, Waltham, MA

Glossary 385

Index 395

Preface

The Macmillan Interdisciplinary Handbooks on Religion represent the state of the art in one of the most consistently surprising, inherently fascinating, and shockingly relevant fields of modern thought: the study of religion. You hold in your hands something of this surprise, fascination, and shock.

These ten handbooks bring together well over two hundred gifted writers in order to provide the reader with a broad, generous, next-generation vision of how the study of religion thinks today on the cutting edge of tomorrow. The topics include a history and overview of the field and its major methods (*Religion: Sources, Perspectives, and Methodologies*); the social scientific study of religion in fields such as anthropology, psychology, and history (*Social Religion*); the complex interactions of secularism, atheism, law, and religion within the modern nation-state (*Beyond Religion*); religion and social justice (*Just Religion*); the material, artistic, and architectural dimensions of religion (*Material Religion*); religion and embodiment, race, gender, and sexuality (*Embodied Religion*); esoteric or secret forms of religion throughout Western history and in contemporary scholarship (*Secret Religion*); religion and the brain (*Mental Religion*); new understandings of the possible supernatural or transcendent dimensions of religion (*Super Religion*); and, finally, the narrative aspects of religion in ritual, myth, and literature (*Narrating Religion*).

Each of these ten volumes is strongly interdisciplinary, bringing together a broad spectrum of approaches and models. Each volume is also eminently accessible and reader-friendly, containing a helpful glossary, multiple illustrations, and consistent attempts to make the study of religion come alive for the reader or student with little or no prior knowledge of the field.

Two basic images, which are also two basic values, have guided the project from conception to production: the Big Tent and the Bright Future.

A Big Tent. For whatever else it is, the contemporary study of religion is a big tent, which is to say that it is a robustly *interdisciplinary* enterprise that has involved hundreds of thousands of individuals from around the world who, over the course of the last two centuries, have employed numerous intellectual techniques from the humanities, the arts, the social sciences, and the natural sciences in order to understand and analyze those dimensions of human experience and expression that have collected under the broad umbrella term of "religion." The Big Tent metaphor implies the presence of these different perspectives and people. It also implies real disagreement among those in the tent, a civil conversation, and a basic ethic of engagement.

A Bright Future. The other value that has guided this series is a calm conviction that the study of religion has something profoundly important to contribute to the world. The

xi

handbooks spin out of a positive view of the field's institutional future and global relevance. The range of concerns and crises the study of religion speaks to are impressive indeed: social justice, poverty, economic inequity, the moral failures of capitalism, and the new colonialism of global corporations; gender equity, sexual diversity, and racism; medical ethics and health care; climate change and environmental sustainability; secularism, religious freedom, religious violence, and religious intolerance … the list goes on and on. In each case, the religions are not only relevant to the problems at hand. They often have generated the questions and concerns in the first place, even as they have also been integral parts of the same contemporary concerns and crises. The conclusion is as simple as it is pressing: none of these growing problems can be adequately addressed without also addressing their religious dimensions. I cannot speak for my colleagues, but I personally would go so far as to say that the future of the world hinges—perhaps largely—on how well and deeply, or on how poorly and superficially, the global community comes to terms with and *puts into public practice* the methods and questions of the study of religion.

This is a very odd claim inasmuch as most people have never heard of the study of religion, much less put it into practice. Hence, the importance of accessible handbooks—hence this series.

There is another, equally profound reason to ponder and practice the study of religion. It comes down to the fact that the religious traditions encode humanity's consistent attempts to answer the most fundamental questions that human beings can ask. Who are we? What are we? Why are we here? What is the nature of the cosmos in which we find ourselves? How can we flourish as part of a much larger web of life and being? Why do we suffer? Why is there so much injustice in the world? What happens to us when we die? What is the point of all of this? Is there a point? To put the matter in a single word, religion is about *meaning*.

For anyone interested in such questions of meaning—and who, in a full life cycle, will not be?—the study of religion is a resource without equal. Assumptions aside, however, the religions, of which there have been hundreds of thousands in human history, have not given the same answers to these questions. The study of religion, then, can never be about parroting the answers of any particular religion, or even a half dozen "world religions," as if *any* historical religion is the "right" or "correct" one. The study of religion is not a multiple-choice question: "Choose A, B, C or D."

For sure, the study of religion is about "stepping into" the traditional religious answers and worldviews in order to examine and ponder them from within, as it were. But it is also about "stepping out of" the religious framework entirely and asking new questions, including those that suggest that the religions themselves are a part of our problems. Think of it this way. Contemporary moral values that most of us take for granted today—values such as the rule of law, religious tolerance, religious freedom, gender equity, human rights, and now ecological sensibilities—did not fall out of the sky. They arose very gradually, often over centuries, through the intellectual labor and very real social risks of individual writers, activists, readers, and brave religious (and brave irreligious) leaders who dared to step out of their cultural assumptions and imagine new ways of being human. These new humanities rose into public prominence because people dared to imagine them, think them, write them, and put them into public practice.

So, too, with our present problems and their future answers. The same deep engagement or "stepping into," the same brave "stepping out of," and the same daring imagination are called for again. If, on the one hand, we seek a future that is bright and positive instead of dark and violent, we will do well to engage "religion" as fully, as honestly, and as radically as possible. If, on the other hand, we are more interested in the ultimate nature of reality, in the nature and limits of consciousness, and in the meaning of life (and death), we would do well again to take up the study of religion, particularly in its more extreme experiences and expressions.

Whether one conceives of the study of religion as a pressing moral task or as a philosophical search for meaning, such an enterprise cannot be taken up lightly or superficially, for this is not something that we can do in a neutral, distant, or objective way. There really is no way around it: once understood and activated, these ideas and practices will change us. We will become how and what we know. In the process, we will be surprised. We will be fascinated. And we will be shocked. We will also become *more*. This is the Big Tent and the Bright Future of the study of religion.

So come on in, read on, and be more.

Jeffrey J. Kripal
Rice University
July 2015

Introduction

According to the Pew Research Center (2015), there were 1,131,150,000 nonreligious people in the world in 2010, and that number is expected to increase to 1,230,340,000 by the year 2020, a number that will comprise over 15 percent of the world's total population. Some of these billions of people are atheists who don't believe in God. Some are agnostics who aren't sure about God; they remain unconvinced one way or another about the plausibility or implausibility of God's existence. Others are indifferent; they simply don't give all that much thought to God and couldn't care less about anything religious. Many seldom or never go to church, synagogue, mosque, temple, or shrine. Many don't engage in religious rituals or rites. For whatever reason, religious faith, activity, and involvement are not meaningful or important parts of their lives. These people have, for the most part, moved beyond religion.

HISTORICAL ROOTS OF IRRELIGION

Of course, there have always been secular men and women throughout history (Thrower 1980 and 2000; Hecht 2003; Bremmer 2007). Even thousands of years ago, there were individuals who doubted religious teachings, were suspicious of priests, pastors, rabbis, gurus, and imams, and felt downright uncomfortable in pews; people who heard about miracles and questioned their veracity; people who were dubious about the efficacy of prayers, rituals, and sacrifices; individuals who read the Bible or the Qur'an and concluded that these were works written by people, not deities; men and women who were not keen on following saviors and prophets; people who required compelling evidence to believe the extraordinary; and individuals who wandered across bogs and valleys at night, looked up at the stars, and thought to themselves: what a big, grand mystery it all is—and left it at that.

Antiquity. The oldest evidence of such nonbelievers is the body of writings concerning the Carvaka, also known as the Lokayata. The Carvaka were a group of philosophers who lived in India some 2,800 years ago, during the seventh century BCE. They were materialist thinkers who rejected the supernaturalism of ancient Hindu religion and were essentially atheists who saw no evidence for the existence of God or karma or any afterlife. They argued that only that which is perceivable exists and that this material, physical world is the only world there is. Ardent naturalists, they looked at life and saw no magical god behind it all. As they reasoned, "Who paints the peacocks, or who makes the cuckoos sing? There exists here no cause excepting nature" (Hecht 2003, 98).

There is also evidence of secularity in the ancient Middle East of biblical times. For example, the statement in Psalm 14 of the Old Testament, "The fool says in his heart, 'There is no God,'" is clear evidence of the existence of atheism thousands of years ago. Also from the Bible, the ancient Jewish philosopher known as Kohelet (third century BCE) gave voice to existential angst and earnest doubt in the Book of Ecclesiastes. Kohelet suggests that all life is ultimately meaningless and there is no life after death, yet we should not stop enjoying what we can while we can, loving those around us and doing good.

Additional evidence of irreligious orientations from long ago comes from ancient China. The philosopher Xunzi, of the third century BCE, taught that there is no heaven and that morality is socially constructed, not something that comes from God but something humans themselves establish. Other protosecular voices from ancient China include Wang Ch'ung and Hsun Tzu, who lived some 2,000 years ago. Both Wang Ch'ung and Hsun Tzu declared that there is nothing spiritual or supernatural behind the natural wonders of the world, that fortune and misfortune are the mere result of chance alone, and that immortality is impossible.

Later Centuries. Antireligious sentiments and various forms of skepticism were abundant during the classical period in Greece and Rome. Protagoras (fifth century BCE) gave voice to nascent agnosticism, stating that it was simply impossible to know, one way or the other, whether gods existed. Democritus (fifth century BCE) rejected the existence of anything divine and believed that an individual's morality must stem from his or her own sense of self-respect. Epicurus (fourth century BCE) taught that death is a nothingness that need not be feared, that praying was useless, and that there is no divine interest in the affairs of humans. Carneades (second century BCE) debunked standard arguments for theism and theories of divine creation. Lucretius (first century BCE) argued that there was no life after death, that the gods did not exist, and that everything we experience, even the most wondrous, is essentially natural. And these individuals are but a handful among many other voices from ancient Greece and Rome who criticized the truth claims of religion and espoused a nascent secular worldview (Thrower 1980 and 2000; Hecht 2003).

Moving up through the centuries into early Islamic civilization, one finds an impressive array of irreligious thought and argumentation. Muhammad al-Warraq, of the ninth century, doubted the existence of Allah and was dubious of religious prophets. Muhammad al-Razi, of the early tenth century, was an early freethinker who criticized religion and worked hard to advance the sciences of physics, chemistry, and medicine. Ibn al-Rawandi, also of the tenth century, was an outspoken critic of Islam and of religion in general. Omar Khayyam, who lived in the eleventh century, wrote that "men talk of heaven," and yet "there is no heaven but here." According to Khayyam, this life is all there is. "Look not above," he said, "there is no answer there." And prayer is futile, "for no one listens to your prayer" (Hitchens 2007, 8).

Ever since such early articulations of irreligion from long ago, there has been a continual stream of individuals, here and there, throughout the centuries, who have expressed a worldview or orientation that was beyond religion in varying degrees.

Middle Ages and Renaissance. Admittedly, the stream of secularity was fairly small during the Middle Ages, when voices of irreligion are relatively hard to find. But they are there. For example, one of the Icelandic sagas written in the thirteenth century tells of a character named Hrafnkell who, after experiencing various misfortunes, declares that he no longer believes in the gods. Also in the thirteenth century, the Roman Catholic Church issued a condemnation of 219 theses, or propositions it found unacceptable or sinful (Hecht 2003, 259), that included those stating that theological discussions are based on fables, that Christianity is an obstacle to learning, and that only self-evident truths ought to be believed.

The fact that the church had to explicitly forbid these assertions is evidence of their existence—perhaps even popularity—at the time.

Closer to the Age of Enlightenment, nonreligious voices become more abundant, more noteworthy, and more confident. In the sixteenth century, two Italians expressed decidedly irreligious orientations. The first was a peasant known as Menocchio (1532–1599), who publicly declared that it was impossible for Jesus to have been born of a virgin mother, that Jesus was not divine, that much of the Gospel stories were fabrications, that immortality was impossible, and that God may be no more than a figment of human imagination. Menocchio was eventually tried for heresy and convicted as an atheist; he was burned at the stake by the Roman Inquisition. Giulio Casare Vanini (1585–1619), an Italian philosopher, denied the immortality of the soul, believed that humans evolved from apes, and insisted that religious teachings were false. Like Menocchio, he was persecuted for his irreligious views and was eventually arrested; he had his tongue cut out, was strangled, and then was burned to death.

In the seventeenth century, the philosopher Baruch Spinoza (1632–1677) was expelled from his synagogue and the Jewish community of Amsterdam for his skepticism concerning the existence of God (at least as typically understood in his day), his lack of belief in immortality, his criticisms of the rabbis, and his failure to attend Sabbath services. The English philosopher Thomas Hobbes (1588–1679) wrote critically of religion and was labeled an atheist by his adversaries. Matthias Knutzen (1646–1674), a teacher in northern Germany, wrote various pamphlets declaring that God does not exist, that the Bible is not to be believed, and that all the churches and their ministers ought to be rejected. Casimir Liszinksi (1634–1689), a Polish nobleman, was harshly critical of priests, argued that the Bible was false, and wrote a treatise called *The Nonexistence of God*. As a result of his atheism, Liszinksi was tried and executed; his tongue and mouth were burned with hot irons, his hands were burned over a slow fire, and finally his whole body was torched.

The Enlightenment. In the eighteenth century, Scottish philosopher David Hume (1711–1776) doubted standard arguments for the existence of God, applied skeptical reasoning to the notion of miracles, and wrote several philosophical works containing various articulations of agnosticism and atheism. French philosopher Denis Diderot (1713–1784) wrote numerous works that also contained atheistic viewpoints and was a central member of Baron D'Holbach's (1723–1789) circle of nonreligious friends in Paris; D'Holbach was one of the most prominent atheists of his day, and his book *The System of Nature* (1770) argued against the existence of God and in favor of a naturalistic view of the cosmos. On the other side of the Atlantic, American patriot and deist Thomas Paine (1737–1809) published *The Age of Reason* (1794), a sharp critique of institutional religion, the plausibility of miracles, and the veracity of the Bible. Ethan Allen (1737–1789), hero of the Revolutionary War, published *Reason: The Only Oracle of Man* in 1785, a treatise that railed against Christianity, critiqued the Bible, and expressed a host of naturalistic views.

The Nineteenth Century. Although still a heavily stigmatized, maligned, and often illegal enterprise, secularism truly began to bloom in the nineteenth century, as more and more individuals began expressing irreligious views. Not only did they condemn what they saw as irrationalities of religion and inhumanities of religious authorities, but they also articulated and supported the values of rationalism, scientific inquiry, and freedom of thought. The English poet Percy Bysshe Shelley (1792–1822) was expelled from Oxford University for

INTRODUCTION

writing *The Necessity of Atheism* in 1811. John Stuart Mill (1806–1873), the English philosopher, political theorist, abolitionist, and feminist who himself was raised without religion, went on to write and speak about his lack of faith with great candor. British activist George Jacob Holyoake (1817–1906) edited secularist magazines such as *The Reasoner* and *Secular Review* and in 1871 helped found the British Secular Union; he coined the term *secularism* in 1851 and wrote and spoke extensively about positive secular values and ethics. Other leaders of British irreligion included outspoken atheist and politician Charles Bradlaugh (1833–1891), who founded the National Secular Society in 1866, and Annie Besant (1847–1933), who was a prominent advocate of atheism and secularism before she embraced theosophy and moved to India.

Charles Darwin (1809–1882), whose famous writings on evolution challenged traditional views of creation and humanity's origins, also wrote publicly about his own personal loss of faith. The German philosopher Ludvig Feuerbach (1804–1872), in his book *The Essence of Christianity*, argued that God did not make humans in his image; rather, humans invented God and constructed him in their image. Karl Marx (1818–1883), also from Germany, described religion as a man-made opiate that soothes those suffering from exploitive conditions and also keeps them from understanding the real economic sources of their oppression. Friedrich Nietzsche (1844–1900), a third German philosopher, became famous for declaring the death of God and writing numerous scathing critiques of religion.

In the United States, the famous African American leader Frederick Douglass (1818–1895) offered bold, blunt condemnations of American Christianity, and Civil War veteran Robert Ingersoll (1833–1899) wrote and spoke extensively about the implausibility of religious claims, the barbarity of the Bible, and the validity of agnosticism. American feminist leaders Frances Wright (1795–1852), Elizabeth Cady Stanton (1815–1902), and Ernestine Rose (1810–1892) all spoke out against religion and advocated freethinking values and secularist ideals. The well-loved American humorist Mark Twain (1835–1910) was a notable nonbeliever and vociferous critic of religion who mocked it with sharp sarcasm.

The Twentieth Century. Shining lights of secularism from the twentieth century include Margaret Sanger (1879–1966), who fought for women's reproductive rights and whose publication *The Woman Rebel* bore the slogan "No Gods, No Masters"; German psychologist Sigmund Freud (1856–1939), whose classic book *Future of an Illusion* offered a piercing deconstruction of theism; British philosopher Bertrand Russell (1872–1970), whose book *Why I Am Not a Christian* was an unabashed expression of secular skepticism; and the founder of modern Turkey, Kemal Atatürk (1881–1938). The American sociologist and social activist W.E.B. DuBois (1868–1963), one of the founders of the National Association for the Advancement of Colored People, wrote eloquently about his loss of faith in God and eschewal of religion, and he leveled numerous attacks on religious hypocrisy. Anarchist Emma Goldman (1869–1940) advocated atheism in her speeches and writings, as did Jawaharlal Nehru (1889–1964), the first prime minister of India.

Coming up to the present, leading thinkers and writers most recently advocating various forms of secularism include the philosopher Paul Kurtz (1925–2012), the writer Christopher Hitchens (1949–2011), the evolutionary biologist Richard Dawkins (1941–), the neuroscientist Sam Harris (1967–), and two thinkers critical of Islam—the anonymous writer Ibn Warraq (1946–) and the activist Ayaan Hirsi Ali (1969–).

xviii

MACMILLAN INTERDISCIPLINARY HANDBOOKS

SECULARITY TODAY

Despite the importance of these individual expressions of, and advocacy for, secular sensibilities, what has been far more historically and sociologically significant has been the demographic explosion of nonreligious men and women the world over. Today, numerous societies have significant secular populations. This is historically unprecedented. Secularism has grown from some ideas, assertions, and arguments found in the halls of philosophy departments, European salons, and/or posthumously published papers to a lived reality for vast swaths of humanity.

North America. In the 1950s, only about 3 percent of American adults claimed to have no religion, but today somewhere between 25 and 30 percent make this claim. This amounts to approximately 58 million men and women (Baker and Smith 2015). About half of them are atheists or agnostics (ARIS 2009). Rates of secularity among younger Americans are even higher; 35 percent of Americans between the ages of eighteen and twenty-nine say they have no religion (Pew Research Center 2015). Whereas in the 1980s there were twice as many evangelical Americans in their twenties than there were nonreligious twenty-somethings, today nonreligious twenty-somethings outnumber evangelicals in that age range by a ratio of two to one (Putnam and Campbell 2010).

Interestingly, the vast majority of nonreligious Americans are content with their current identity; among those individuals today who claim "none" as their religion, nearly 90 percent say that they have no interest in looking for a religion that might be right for them (Pew Research Center 2012). Additionally, more and more Americans are being raised without religion; of Americans born between 1925 and 1943, less than 4 percent were raised with no religion; of those born between 1956 and 1970, 7 percent were raised with no religion; and of those Americans born between 1971 and 1992, almost 11 percent were raised with no religion (Merino 2012).

In sum, as sociologist Darren Sherkat has recently observed, across the last five birth cohorts in the United States, religious participation, identification, and belief have been on the decline, and "the most substantial trend in religious identification [among Americans] is the rejection of religious identity" (Sherkat 2014, 181).

In Canada, half of adults are secular, and a third reject the idea of God altogether (*National Post,* December 19, 2014). In 1970 about 7 percent of Australians claimed to be nonreligious, but that figure is up to 56 percent today (Nixon 2014; Baker and Smith 2015), with one-third of Australians now being nonbelievers in God; among younger Australians, those born between 1976 and 1990, less than half believe in God (*Daily Telegraph,* April 11, 2009). And nearly a third of New Zealanders are now nonbelievers in God (Keysar and Navarro-Rivera 2013), with half claiming no religious identification (Baker and Smith 2015). These are the highest rates of secularity ever seen in the Anglophone world.

Europe and Britain. In Italy, where several centuries ago the peasant Menocchio and the philosopher Giulio Casare Vanini were executed for their lack of faith, about 13 percent of the population is now atheist or agnostic; that's over 6.5 million Italian adults who lack an affirmative belief in God (Keysar and Navarro-Rivera 2013). Rates of nonbelief in the rest of Europe are even higher: 41 percent of the French, 39 percent of Swedes, 36 percent of Germans, 34 percent of Belgians, 32 percent of Norwegians, 30 percent of the British, 27 percent of Hungarians, and 21 percent of the Spanish do not believe in God (Keysar and

Navarro-Rivera 2013). In addition, 34 percent of Slovenians, 24 percent of Bulgarians, and 23 percent of Russians are nonbelievers in God (Borowik, Ančić, and Tyrala 2013). According to one recent Dutch study, there are now more atheists in the Netherlands than theists (Savela 2015). Atheism is also the majority orientation in the Czech Republic and Estonia, with 64 percent and 52 percent atheist, respectively (Borowik et al. 2013). As for religious identification, according to the World Values Survey, 66 percent of Swedes, 58 percent of Spaniards, 54 percent of the Dutch, 52 percent of the French, and 47 percent of Germans claim none (Baker and Smith 2015).

The situation in Great Britain is particularly noteworthy: in the 1950s, only 2 percent of British adults said they did not believe in God, but today nearly 40 percent of British adults are atheist or agnostic (Bagg and Voas 2010). According to the World Values Survey, 49 percent of British adults claim no religious identification (Baker and Smith 2015). British historian Callum Brown has documented the degree to which "a formerly religious people have entirely forsaken organized Christianity in a sudden plunge into a truly secular condition" (Brown 2001, 1). Such secularizing trends show no sign of abating; according to sociologists David Voas and Siobhan McAndrew, "British society is becoming progressively more secular as each generation emerges and remains less religious than the one before" (2012, 32).

Asia. To be sure, some select societies have seen an increase in religiosity in the past few decades, such as Russia, Israel, and various parts of the Middle East. But these cases are exceptions. Most of the world is secularizing. For example, about 70 percent of the Japanese claimed to hold personal religious beliefs sixty years ago, but today that figure has dwindled to about 20 percent (Reader 2012), and nearly 30 percent of the Japanese are currently atheist or agnostic in orientation (Keysar and Navarro-Rivera 2013).

In addition, only 13 percent of Japanese adults maintain a faith in spiritual beings such as Shinto gods (*kami*), and only 16 percent maintain a belief in other spiritual entities, such as ancestors or animal/folk spirits (Reader 2012). According to Ian Reader, professor of Japanese studies, "statistical analyses, whether of institutional belonging, religious faith or popular practice, all appear to indicate a one-way pattern towards an increasingly secularized Japan.... This tendency has gone hand-in-hand with Japanese modernity, and increases the more population becomes urbanized and educated.... Religion may not yet be dead in Japan but it is dying" (Reader 2012, 31).

In Taiwan, nonbelievers in God constitute 15 percent of the population (Keysar and Navarro-Rivera 2013). In South Korea today, over 55 percent of the population is nonreligious (Baker and Smith 2015; Eungi 2002), with nearly 30 percent being nonbelievers in God (Keysar and Navarro-Rivera 2013). Some estimates of atheism in China place it at 50 percent of the population (WIN-Gallup International 2012), and the World Values Survey reports that 87 percent of Chinese adults are secular (Baker and Smith 2015).

Other Areas. Secularity is also on the rise in Latin America, where nearly 40 percent of Uruguayans, 20 percent of those in the Dominican Republic, and 16 percent of Chileans are nonreligious (Pew Research Center 2014). And although only 8 percent of Brazilians claim to be nonreligious and only 6 percent of Mexicans are atheist or agnostic, that still amounts to tens of millions of people living without religious faith or involvement (Keysar and Navarro-Rivera 2013). As for Mexico, whose founding was steeped in anticlerical secularism, about 6 percent of adults are nonbelievers in God (Keysar and Navarro-Rivera 2013).

Small, notable pockets of secularity in Africa and the Middle East are also growing. For example, an Associated Press investigation recently documented the emergence of over sixty Arabic-language atheist Facebook groups. "Sudanese Atheists" has over 10,000 followers alone (Hadid 2013). Finally, one in ten citizens in both Gabon and Swaziland claims to have no religion (Trinitapoli and Weinrub 2012).

Many other countries—from Azerbaijan to Vietnam—have significant nonreligious populations, but whether irreligious individuals constitute a tiny minority, as in Yemen or Rwanda, or a majority, as in Scotland or Slovenia, they represent a significant chunk of humanity. And that chunk warrants scholarly attention.

STUDYING THE SECULAR

Religion has been studied for a long time. Social scientists, historians, and philosophers have explored almost every aspect of religious life—from religious music to how religious people raise their children, from religious coping mechanisms to how religion intersects with nationalism, from religious charity to religious dietary habits. Indeed, hardly any aspect of religious life has not been studied. That's a very good thing. Religion is such a significant, pervasive, and influential aspect of the human experience—greatly affecting individual life, society, and culture—that it should continue to be studied doggedly, relentlessly.

But what about secular people? What about secular culture? What about the secular experience? What about the growing proportion of men and women who have rejected religion or were never religious to begin with? In recent years, more and more scholars have started to turn their gaze to secular life in its varied articulations and contexts (Baker and Smith 2015; Lee 2015; Cimino and Smith 2014; Manning 2015; Zuckerman 2014; Quack 2012). Secular studies is thus an emerging interdisciplinary field that focuses on manifestations of the secular in societies and cultures, past and present (Zuckerman, Galen, and Pasquale 2016). It entails the study of nonreligious people, groups, thought, and cultural expressions, with an emphasis on the meanings, forms, relevance, and impact of political secularism, philosophical skepticism, and personal and public secularity.

It is hoped that in the years ahead the study of secularity and secularism will develop and grow and that the future research, theory, and data it stimulates will bolster and broaden the understanding not only of irreligion, but also of religion. For if religiosity and secularity only fully make sense when understood in dialectical relation to each other, then they both should be studied with equal rigor. It is in this spirit of seeking to illuminate secular life, particularly in its relation to religious life, that this volume has been conceived.

THE CHAPTERS AHEAD

This volume offers a "state of the art" look at secular life that is focused mainly on, although certainly not limited to, the contemporary American context. Leading scholars within the emerging field of Secular Studies provide rigorous explorations of various aspects of life beyond religion, employing innovative theoretical frameworks and drawing from the best available data.

Chapter 1, "Defining That Which Is Other to Religion" by Ryan Cragun, begins by clearly explaining what relevant terminologies and common designations mean: *religion*, *irreligion*, *secular*, *secularity*, *secularism*, *secularist*, *secularization*, *atheism*, *agnosticism*, *apostasy*, *humanism*, and so forth. Although authors in subsequent chapters may use these terms somewhat differently, as is unavoidable whenever different scholars attempt to make sense of complex phenomena, the definitions put forth by Dr. Cragun provide a solid foundation for analyzing contemporary secular life. To better understand the change from a largely religious to a largely secular world, Chapter 2, "Secularization" by Stratos Patrikios, critically lays out the empirical and historical underpinnings of secularization theory, the idea that as society becomes more advanced—technologically and otherwise—religion becomes less visible and significant.

Chapter 3, "Lived Secularity: Atheism, Indifference, and the Social Significance of Religion," by Isabella Kasselstrand, examines the meanings and expressions of secular life in contemporary northern Europe, arguably the most irreligious region of the world today, by looking at secular life in societies where religious rhetoric is nearly absent from politics and the public sphere and where levels of religious belief and participation are markedly low. Abby Day also examines contemporary secular culture, but her analysis hones in on the nature of belief. In Chapter 4, "Believing in Belief: Toward the Secularization of Faith in Global Economies," Professor Day shows that our understanding of, and discourse surrounding, belief in modern societies has been secularly refashioned, with significant social consequences.

Although understanding societal aspects of secular culture is necessary, it is equally important to understand the individuals who reject religion and embrace a secular identity or orientation. In Chapter 5, "Apostasy," Dr. Jesse Smith explores the process whereby men and women lose their religion. Keeping the focus at the micro level of individual, personal secular experience, Chapter 6, "Secularity and Family Life," by Christel Manning, looks at how secular identity plays out in families and among parents and children. Much research has been done over the decades on the role of religion in family life, and thus Dr. Manning's chapter illuminates a truly neglected area of related study: family life where religion is largely absent. Much has also been written about religion and gender, specifically in relation to women's lives, and here too a significantly underexamined aspect of the human experience is how women's lives, identities, and experiences intersect with secularity. In Chapter 7, "From Rebels to Everyday Atheists: Women and Secularity," Marta Trzebiatowska analyzes various aspects of irreligion, with a particular focus on women.

Race is a central construct and fissure of American society, and many scholars have looked at race and its relation to religion; in Chapter 8, "Secularism, Diversity, and Race in the Contemporary United States," Juhem Navarro-Rivera looks at race and its relation to secularity. As the size of the secular population in this country grows, so too does its racial and ethnic diversity, with important social and political consequences. But racial and ethnic diversity are certainly not the only social phenomena changing, and being changed by, the growth of irreligion. Community in America is in a state of flux, strain, and also innovation. In Chapter 9, "Secularism, Secularity, and Community," Matthew Loveland explores the ways in which nonreligious men and women find a sense of shared experiences, identities, and communal engagement. Given that religion has traditionally been a major source of community for Americans, it is essential to explore how secular men and women meet their needs for communal attachment.

For many, secularism is less about God or God's nonexistence than about the relationship that ought to exist, or not exist, between religion and government. In Chapter 10, "Separation of Church and State in the American Political Traditions," Will Barndt examines some of the key myths, realities, theories, and developments concerning the role of religion in politics and public life. Steven Kettell, in Chapter 11, "Religion, Secularism, and the Public Sphere," broadens the discussion of this important matter, elaborating on this polarizing, contested issue of religion's role in public life and how secularism is part of that debate. And moving beyond debates over the separation of church and state and religion's place in the public sphere, in Chapter 12, "Secularism, Secularity, and War," Stacey Gutkowski broaches new theoretical ground by looking at how secular people, movements, governments, and ideologies are related to violence, conflict, and international struggles.

How do people feel about atheists or other nonreligious individuals? Not kindly. As Maxine Najle and Will Gervais present in Chapter 13, "Dislike of and Discrimination Against Atheists and Secular People," hostility toward, and unsavory stereotypes of, the nonreligious are rife, and the consequences are sociologically and psychologically significant. But what about the minds, emotions, and personalities of secular men and women? In Chapter 14, "The Psychology of Secularity and Nonreligion," Sean Moore and Jaynita Maru lay out and discuss existing scholarship concerning various psychological aspects of irreligion—yet another understudied topic.

Undoubtedly central, when it comes to life beyond religion, are the philosophical arguments justifying a lack of belief in God. In Chapter 15, "Atheology," John Shook identifies and analyzes the reasons underpinning and justifying atheism and criticisms of religion, thereby illuminating the ongoing, dynamic debate between theology and atheology. Within the last ten years, at the forefront of this debate has been the slew of best-selling books critical of religion; in Chapter 16, "New Atheism," Teemu Taira discusses this latest wave of popular secularist rhetoric, examining and interpreting the themes, ideas, and approaches of the leading authors.

Any philosophical or popular discussion of atheism almost always leads to the issue of morality: how can people be good if they are not religious and lack a belief in God? In Chapter 17, "Secularism and Morality," Ryan Falcioni plumbs the hills and dales of this issue, exploring challenges and solutions regarding ethics, morality, and their relation to the secular life. Finishing off a focus on the philosophical in Chapter 18, "Atheism, Pacifism, and Anarchism," Andrew Fiala links these three radical positions to one another, revealing how they inform one another and together point the way toward potential human progress.

The book concludes with two chapters that suggest possible alternative visions to strict irreligious living or atheistic worldviews, both of which still fall squarely within secular culture. For example, many religions have secularized over the centuries or have seen secular versions developed in which certain traditional aspects of a given religion are upheld but others, such as supernatural beliefs, are jettisoned. In Chapter 19, "Humanistic Judaism and Secular Spirituality," Rabbi Adam Chalom discusses Jewish congregations that no longer believe in God or anything other-worldly, illustrating one concrete example of how secular men and women have reimagined religious life and spirituality. And in Chapter 20, "Naturalism and Well-Being," Thomas Clark explores a secular worldview that is characterized by knowledge, science, wisdom, inquiry, wonder, and reality, and to these ends, positively contributes to humans' well-being.

Phil Zuckerman

Professor of Sociology and Secular Studies
Pitzer College, Claremont, CA

BIBLIOGRAPHY

ARIS. "American Nones: The Profile on the No Religion Population." 2009. http://commons.trincoll.edu/aris/files/2011/08/NONES_08.pdf.

Bagg, Samuel, and David Voas. "The Triumph of Indifference: Irreligion in British Society." In *Atheism and Secularity*, Vol. 2: *Global Expressions*, edited by Phil Zuckerman, 91–112. Santa Barbara, CA: Praeger, 2010.

Baker, Joseph, and Buster Smith. *American Secularism: Cultural Contours of Nonreligious Belief Systems.* New York: New York University Press, 2015.

Borowik, Irena, Branko Ančić, and Radoslaw Tyrala. "Central and Eastern Europe." In *The Oxford Handbook of Atheism*, edited by Stephen Bullivant and Michael Ruse, 622–637. Oxford: Oxford University Press, 2013.

Bremmer, Jan N. "Atheism in Antiquity." In *The Cambridge Companion to Atheism*, edited by Michael Martin, 11–26. New York: Cambridge University Press, 2007.

Brown, Callum. *The Death of Christian Britain*. London: Routledge, 2001.

Cimino, Richard, and Christopher Smith. *Atheist Awakening: Secular Activism and Community in America*. New York: Oxford University Press, 2014.

Daily Telegraph. "Faith No More—Atheists in the City of Churches." April 11, 2009. http://www.dailytelegraph.com.au/faith-no-more-atheists-in-the-city-of-churches/story-e6freuy9-1225698664255.

Eungi, Andrew Kim. "Characteristics of Religious Life in South Korea: A Sociological Survey." *Review of Religious Research* 43, no. 4 (June 2002): 291–310.

Hadid, Diaa. "Arab Atheists, Though Few, Inch out of the Shadows." *Jakarta Post*, August 3, 2013. http://www.thejakartapost.com/news/2013/08/03/arab-atheists-though-few-inch-out-shadows.html.

Hecht, Jennifer Michael. *Doubt: A History*. San Francisco: Harper, 2003.

Hitchens, Christopher, ed. *The Portable Atheist: Essential Readings for the Nonbeliever*. 3rd ed. Philadelphia: Da Capo Press, 2007.

Keysar, Ariela, and Juhem Navarro-Rivera. "A World of Atheism: Global Demographics." In *The Oxford Handbook of Atheism*, edited by Stephen Bullivant and Michael Ruse, 553–586. Oxford: Oxford University Press, 2013.

Lee, Lois. *Recognizing the Non-religious: Reimagining the Secular*. New York: Oxford University Press, 2015.

Manning, Christel. *Losing Our Religion*. New York: New York University Press, 2015.

Merino, Stephen. "Irreligious Socialization? The Adult Religious Preferences of Individuals Raised with No Religion." *Secularism and Nonreligion* 1 (2012): 1–16.

National Post. "Even in This Golden Age of Secularism, Vast Majority of Canadians Count Themselves as Members of a Religion: Study." December 19, 2014. http://www.bullfax.com/?q=node-even-golden-age-secularism-vast-majority-canadians-coun.

Nixon, Alan. "New Atheism as a Case of Competitive Postsecular Worldviews." PhD diss. University of Western Sydney, 2014.

Pew Research Center. "The Future of World Religions: Population Growth Projections, 2010–2050." April 2, 2015. http://www.pewforum.org/2015/04/02/religious-projections-2010-2050/.

Pew Research Center. "'Nones' on the Rise." October 9, 2012. http://www.pewforum.org/2012/10/09/nones-on-the-rise/.

Pew Research Center. "Religion in Latin America." November 13, 2014. http://www.pewforum.org/2014/11/13/religion-in-latin-america/.

Putnam, Robert, and David Campbell. *American Grace: How Religion Divides and Unites Us*. New York: Simon and Schuster, 2010.

Quack, Johannes. *Disenchanting India: Organized Rationalism and Criticism of Religion in India*. New York: Oxford University Press, 2012.

Reader, Ian. "Secularisation, R.I.P.? Nonsense! The 'Rush Hour Away from the Gods' and the Decline of Religion." *Journal of Religion in Japan* 1, no. 1 (2012): 7–36.

Savela, Taneli. "More Atheists than Believers, but 60 Pct on the Fence." *NL Times*, January 16, 2015. http://www.nltimes.nl/2015/01/16/atheists-believers-60-pct-fence/.

Sherkat, Darren. *Changing Faith: The Dynamics and Consequences of Americans' Shifting Religious Identities*. New York: New York University Press, 2014.

Thrower, James. *The Alternative Tradition: A Study of Unbelief in the Ancient World*. The Hague: Mouton, 1980.

Thrower, James. *Western Atheism: A Short History*. Amherst, NY: Prometheus, 2000.

Trinitapoli, Jenny, and Alexander Weinrub. *Religion and AIDS in Africa*. New York: Oxford University Press, 2012.

Voas, David, and Siobhan McAndrew. "Three Puzzles of Non-religion in Britain." *Journal of Contemporary Religion* 27, no. 1 (2012): 29–48.

WIN-Gallup International. "Global Index of Religiosity and Atheism." 2012. http://www.wingia.com/web/files/news/14/file/14.pdf.

Zuckerman, Phil. *Living the Secular Life*. New York: Penguin, 2014.

Zuckerman, Phil, Luke Galen, and Frank Pasquale. *The Nonreligious: Understanding Secular People and Societies*. New York: Oxford University Press, 2016.

CHAPTER 1

Defining That Which Is Other to Religion

Ryan T. Cragun
Associate Professor, Department of Sociology
The University of Tampa, FL

As is the case with most areas of research, scholars studying that which is other to religion have wrestled with terminology and the definitions of terms. Of course, all definitions are conditional and scholars can mold and shape them to fit their particular research objective. Even so, a general level of agreement on the definitions of terms can be helpful in clarifying the focus of a field of inquiry. Shared definitions also can help ensure that scholars are talking with each other rather than past each other.

This chapter has two primary aims: (1) to provide definitions of the key terms that are common in the study of what is considered "other" to religion, and (2) to attempt to provide some context regarding the definitions of the key terms, illustrating why definitions are not always universally agreed upon by those employing them. The definitions proposed in this chapter will, no doubt, have more appeal to some scholars than others, and not everyone will agree with every definition. Those disagreements have been addressed in discussing the various terms employed.

Before discussing the terms employed by those who study this topic, it may be helpful to discuss briefly what is meant by *religion* so what is mean by religion's *other* is also more clearly elucidated. There have been many definitions of religion proposed over the years, ranging from the overly broad to the overly specific. To date, no field of scholarly study that takes religion as its focus (e.g., anthropology, psychology, sociology, and religious studies) has coalesced on a single, universal definition of religion. This means that the study of what is other to religion is also difficult to define, because it is difficult to study anything that is other if that central thing is ill defined. Even so, there are a few well-known and widely employed definitions that are worth mentioning.

Émile Durkheim (1858–1917) proposed one of the most famous but also most problematic definitions of religion. For Durkheim, religion was that which is sacred in society. Superficially, this definition seems to work well, as most of the organizations that are generally considered to be religions do, in fact, have sacred components to them. However, there are many other aspects of society that are considered sacred that are not typically considered religious, such as flags, families, and for some, sports teams. Thus, Durkheim's definition is overly broad because sacred things are found outside the context of what most people would consider religious.

Chapter 1: Defining That Which Is Other to Religion

A different approach has been to suggest that religion is context specific. Such definitions consider *religion* to be a signifier that may or may not mean the same thing in different contexts. Thus, what religion is in Japan is different from what religion is in Jordan or in Jamaica. This definition could also be overly broad in that it would include whatever people in a given context consider religion, but it's also overly specific in that it is difficult to offer a comprehensive definition of religion other than to say, "Religion is whatever people in society X say it is." Although technically precise, and useful in illustrating the diversity of religion, this approach fails to offer a general definition that might encompass what most people would consider religion.

A third and fairly popular approach to defining religion stems from the work of Max Weber (1864–1920) who suggested that religions were collective beliefs (and often rituals) relative to the supernatural. There are two key components to this definition. The first component is that the beliefs are relative to the "supernatural." *Super-* means "above" or "beyond." When applied to *-nature*, "supernatural" refers to that which is above or beyond nature or that which we are unable to sense using our five senses or tools that we have developed to enhance those senses. The supernatural would include gods, demons, ghosts, angels, jinni, fairies, and spirits. The second key component is that religion has to be collective beliefs. Some examples should help illustrate the importance of this component of the definition. A pregnant woman who believes she is going to give birth to a demon would likely be considered insane. However, if thousands of people believe that a virgin gave birth to a god, that is not collective insanity; it is a religion. This definition works well to capture most of those institutions and organizations we consider religions (e.g., Catholicism, Hinduism, and Shintoism), but excludes those we do not (e.g., families and football teams).

There are many other definitions that have been proposed for religion other than these three. The point of offering these three definitions is not necessarily to suggest that there is one, absolute, universal definition of religion, but rather to show there is some general agreement on the domain that should be considered religion yet debate continues on precise definitions and terminology. The same is true when it comes to definitions and terms in the study of what is other to religion.

SECULAR AND SECULARITY

The word *secular* is perhaps the most neutral of all the terms that will be discussed in this chapter. The English words *secular* and *secularity* both come from the Latin *saecularis*, which means, variously, "worldly," "temporal," or "of a generation, belonging to an age." The word *secular* was introduced into Christian thought by theologians as a reference to that which is not religious. In other words, secular is an adjective that describes things that are not religious in orientation. For example, sleeping would typically be considered a secular activity, as would exercising. In contrast, praying to a god or burning incense to one's dead relatives would typically be considered religious activities. Thus, secular is a reference to that which is not religious. Secularity is the state of being secular or apart from religion.

It is common today for the word *secular* to be applied as a descriptor to many aspects of social life. For instance, a secular government would be a government that is not attached to or affiliated with a specific religion (though this does not necessarily mean that the government does not privilege or favor a religion). A secular university would be a university that is not affiliated with a religion. Many early universities in the United States, such as

Chapter 1: Defining That Which Is Other to Religion

Yale University, began as religious institutions. Yale University was originally founded to train Congregationalist ministers, and the governance of the university was tied to that denomination. However, over time, Yale University administrators distanced the governance of the university from the denomination to the point that the university is, today, almost exclusively secular in orientation.

It is important to note that *secular* and *secularity* imply no particular perspective on religion; they are essentially neutral terms. The neutrality of these terms is apparent in light of the fact that many religious people engage in secular activities, such as visiting amusement parks or watching sporting events. In those instances, people who consider themselves religious are engaged in secular activities that are unrelated to religion. This does not make them hostile toward religion. It only indicates that they engage in activities that are apart from religion.

SECULARISM

Building on the same root as secular, *secularism* is primarily viewed today as a political philosophy that advocates a separation between religion and government. The "-ism" suffix turns the word *secular* into a philosophy or ideology rooted in the idea that there should be distance between that which is religious and that which is secular when it comes to government.

Jacques Berlinerblau argues in *How to be Secular* (2013) that secularism advocates for two primary interests: "(1) the individual citizen's need for freedom of, or freedom from, religion, and (2) a state's need to maintain order" (xvi). I'll discuss each of these in turn. Although widely accepted today in many countries around the world and enshrined in the Universal Declaration of Human Rights, the idea that individuals should have a right or the freedom to choose their religion is a relatively recent development in world history. For instance, when Martin Luther broke away from the Roman Catholic Church in the sixteenth century, leading to the Protestant Reformation, in a short time span millions of Europeans were forced to become Protestants at the behest of their governments when those governments adopted Lutheranism as the state religion. For instance, in Sweden, the transition of the state religion from Catholicism to Lutheranism took place between 1523 and 1527. During that time, the King, Gustav Vasa, was able to take control over the national church and convert it from Catholicism to Lutheranism. As a result, Swedes began to be instructed in Lutheranism and became Lutherans. Swedes did not have the right to choose their own religion at that time. Similarly, despite suffering persecution over their religious views in England, Puritans did not grant freedom of religion in their colonies in the United States and instead persecuted religious dissenters, such as Mary Dyer, who was hanged in Boston in 1660 for being a Quaker in Puritan Massachusetts. Similar intolerance and persecution of religious dissenters has occurred in predominantly Muslim societies, as well as in Hindu, Buddhist, and Jewish societies (and continues in many of these today).

The idea that humans should have the right to choose their religion or no religion has precursors in Greek and Roman thought, but was formulated more recently by Enlightenment thinkers such as Thomas Paine, Thomas Jefferson, and Voltaire. The term *secularism* itself was coined by George Jacob Holyoake in the nineteenth century, though his use of the term was less political than the modern understanding of secularism and more along the lines of humanism and freethought.

RELIGION: BEYOND RELIGION

3

Chapter 1: Defining That Which Is Other to Religion

The second component of secularism outlined by Berlinerblau, the state's need to maintain order, is a counterbalance to the first. One of the key functions of any government is to develop a system of laws that maintain order in a society. Laws, of course, are not always objectively neutral or devoid of favoritism. To the contrary, many laws are written to benefit specific groups of people. For instance, in the United States, the Constitution originally enfranchised just land-owning White men. In France, the secular government funds both secular public schools but also Catholic and Jewish private schools. This funding reflects a favoritism toward secularism, and also two specific religions (Catholicism and Judaism). It was not until 2008 that the French government began funding a single, private Muslim school in France. When there is not a separation between religion and government, government can be used to privilege or show favor toward specific religions. This is the case in many countries around the world where the divide between government and religion is unclear or nonexistent, such as in Saudi Arabia. In Saudi Arabia, which is a monarchy, the king must comply with Sharia or Islamic law and the Qur'an, and the laws in the country are Islamic laws. There is also no freedom of religion, as individuals who leave Islam in Saudi Arabia can be executed for apostasy (apostasy is discussed in more detail later in the chapter).

Of course, the challenge is finding an appropriate balance between the need of the government to maintain order and simultaneously allowing individuals the right to choose their religion or no religion. Achieving this balance can be a challenge because religion can be an effective extension of the government to regulate behavior. Religion has been (and in some places continues to be) used on behalf of the government to maintain order by proscribing certain behaviors. In order for religion to be an effective extension of government control, it helps if everyone in the society has the same religion. The presence of multiple religions in a society has the potential to undermine religious credibility and can also lead to hostility among religions. Thus, finding an appropriate balance between individual rights and government control is challenging.

However, advocates of secularism generally argue that secularism is the philosophical and political approach that is most effective at finding a balance between these two competing interests because a secular government should not, theoretically, show any favoritism toward any specific religion or religious group. To the contrary, all religions should be viewed and treated as equal before a secular government. As a result, individuals have the right to choose their own religion or no religion, the government guarantees and protects this right, and does not elevate any one religious perspective above any others or privilege any particular perspectives. Thus, secularism is rooted in the idea that the best way to balance the competing interests of religious freedom (or freedom from religion) with the government function of maintaining order in society is for there to be a separation between the government and religion such that the government is secular and does not privilege any one religion over others.

Organizations that advocate for secularism are sometimes labeled *secularist*. Examples of such organizations would be the Secular Coalition for America or the British Humanist Association. Both strongly advocate for secularism, discouraging any involvement of religion with the government. The aim of such organizations is generally to reduce the privileging of religion in those societies. For instance, in the United States, although there is a separation or wall between the government and religion in theory, in practical effect the wall is rather porous. Religions are given a number of tax benefits, including paying no property or income taxes, and religious clergy are allowed to deduct their housing expenses from their taxes (i.e., the parsonage exemption). Although these benefits are given to all institutions that are recognized as religions by the government, in effect they elevate religion over nonreligion.

With a discussion of secularism as it relates to the separation of church and state comes a type of secularism that focuses less on politics and more on criticism of the privileged position of religion in society. Many publications, such as Sam Harris's bestseller *The End of Faith: Religion, Terror, and the Future of Reason* (2004) or Richard Dawkins's 2006 work, *The God Delusion*, as well as several organizations, including the International Humanist and Ethical Union and the Council for Secular Humanism, criticize the position of religion in society and point out some of religion's detriments to society as a whole. The aim of this collective movement is to diminish the privileged position of religion in society—often regarded as a manifestation of politics or power relations—and to create a safe and egalitarian space for nonreligious or secular people.

SECULARIZATION

Also based on the same root term as *secular* is another term widely used by those who study religion and its other: *secularization*. Secularization can refer to two ideas that are closely related. The first idea referenced by secularization is the process of change occurring over time that involves the transformation of aspects of society from religious to secular. This transformation can occur at multiple levels. For instance, at a broader or more macro level, governments can secularize over time. This process would involve removing the influence of religious institutions from the political process. This does not mean that religions do not influence the values and beliefs of politicians involved in political decision making, but rather refers to the direct control or influence of religious institutions on governance. This transition from religiously influenced or controlled government to secular government can be seen in the transition of the former British colonies in North America into the United States. Of the thirteen original colonies, most of them had an established religion that was closely involved in the governance of the colony (the official religions were either Anglican/Church of England or Congregationalist). When the colonies came together to form a new country, not all of the colonies had the same established religions. The solution that developed was to have no official religion for the new country: it was to be a secular government. Over the next decades, each of the original colonies that had an official religion slowly disentangled that religion from the state government. This took hundreds of years in some of the colonies turned states, such as Maryland. The Anglican religion was the official state religion when Maryland was chartered as a colony in 1632, and remained the official religion of the state until 1867, when a new version of the constitution removed the religious requirement for holding political office in the state. This process of disentangling and removing a religion's involvement in government is a form of secularization.

Secularization can also take place at an institutional level. This was described previously in the case of Yale University, which began as a school to train Congregationalist ministers. Over time, the university has removed the influence of the Congregationalist religion from the governance of the university to the point that the religion has virtually no influence on the governance of Yale University today. Similar processes have occurred with hospitals, charities, book publishers, and many other types of organizations.

Chapter 1: Defining That Which Is Other to Religion

Secularization can also take place at the individual level, as people who are raised religious move toward lower levels of religiosity. An example of this at the individual level would be Ayaan Hirsi Ali, a Somali-born activist who now has dual Dutch and American citizenship. She was raised Muslim in various countries in Africa and migrated to the Netherlands in 1992. It was during her time in the Netherlands that she began to encounter ways of thinking that ran counter to what she had been taught as a Muslim. These alternative perspectives eventually led her to leave Islam and ultimately arrive at atheism in 2002. This process of disenchantment with religion is an individual-level manifestation of secularization. Secularization, then, can refer to the process by which different aspects of society (e.g., governments and institutions) and individuals differentiate or diverge from religion. This process has been observed in many societies, in many institutions, in many organizations, and in many people over time.

Secularization can also refer to a well-known theory among those who study religion and its other. The basic argument of secularization theory is that societies will grow less religious as they modernize. Early advocates of secularization, such as Max Weber, referred to this as "the disenchantment of the world." The basic idea is that modern understandings of the natural world (such as the cause of earthquakes or an understanding of what the sun is and how the earth is related to the solar system, the galaxy, and the universe and so on) result in people no longer needing to rely on religious explanations for how the natural world works. People, instead, rely on naturalistic or scientific explanations. As naturalistic understandings of the world replace supernaturalistic understandings, people rely less and less on religion, becoming less religious (or disenchanted) over time. The end result is people's lives are spent almost entirely if not entirely in the secular realm and not in the religious realm.

ATHEISM AND ATHEISTS

At the simplest level, the word *atheism* can be separated into its constituent parts. The *a*-prefix means "without" or "lacking." The root of the rest of the word, *-theism*, is the Greek term, "theos" (θεός), which means God or a god. Theism is the belief in a god or God. The most common understanding of the term *atheism* today is, therefore, without belief in a god, God, or gods. Atheists are individuals who are without belief in a god, God, or gods.

The distinction between *God* with a capitalized *G* and *god* with a lower case *g* is an important one. When capitalized, as in *God*, this is typically a reference to the Judeo-Christian deity, YHWH, the god of the Hebrew scriptures or the Christian Old and New Testaments. When not capitalized, as in *god*, this can refer to any deity, as in Zeus, Thor, Shiva, or Quetzalcoatl. This distinction is important because it introduces an extension to the definition of the term *atheism*. Atheism is not exclusively limited to not believing in the Judeo-Christian deity, though in most Western countries this is often what people understand atheism to mean (i.e., they think that an atheist does not believe in God or YHWH). This understanding is a reflection of Judeo-Christian privilege in countries that are or were predominantly Jewish or Christian because it assumes that there is only one god in which someone does not believe, YHWH or God. In fact, the existence of millions of gods has been asserted by believers, and most people do not believe in most or all of those gods. Additionally, most Jews and Christians who believe in God or YHWH are simultaneously atheists toward all other gods, though typically they do not self-identify as such and are

6   MACMILLAN INTERDISCIPLINARY HANDBOOKS

unaware of this fact. This, again, is a reflection of religious privileging as, for most of these people, they are so unaware of the claimed existence of other gods that they do not realize that they are atheists toward the many other claimed gods.

This raises an important extension of the term *atheism*. As noted, the most common understanding of atheism is to be without a belief in a god or gods. But there are at least two ways that people can be without belief in a god or gods. People can be aware of the claimed existence of a god and deny the existence of that deity. This is typically referred to as positive atheism, meaning the individual is making a positive assertion about the nonexistence of a deity. Many people in Western countries have heard about Aphrodite and Thor, meaning they have some knowledge about these gods, but they do not believe these gods exist. Thus, they are positive atheists toward Aphrodite and Thor; they are making a positive assertion about the nonexistence of these two deities. However, people can also be unaware of the claimed existence of a god and therefore be without belief in that god. This is likely the case for most readers of this chapter regarding the god Jörð, the Norse goddess of the earth. Until now, most readers of this chapter had probably never heard of Jörð and therefore were without belief in Jörð. Readers without any knowledge of Jörð were, in fact, atheists toward Jörð, but in a negative fashion. Negative atheism is being without belief in a god or gods because of no prior knowledge of the claimed existence of that god or those gods. It is in this fashion that most people alive today are atheists: they are unaware of the claimed existence of the millions of gods of, for instance, Hinduism, or the many other gods of the many other extant or defunct religions. They are therefore atheists toward those gods (i.e., without belief), but in a negative fashion. Likewise, it is in this sense that all babies are atheists; until they are taught about a god, they are negative atheists toward all gods.

This discussion of atheism is generally how people understand atheism and atheists today, but this has not always been the case. Historically, things were different. It is likely that there have been atheists for as long as there have been theists or believers in a god, gods, or God. However, the label *atheist* was not used until relatively recently (perhaps the last three to four hundred years) to describe individuals who were without belief in any gods. Instead, *atheist* was used as a pejorative or epithet to describe anyone who did not believe in the claimed god or gods of those in power or was a label applied to someone who held heretical or nonorthodox views of a god or gods. It was in this second sense that Socrates was accused of being an atheist, as he held nonorthodox views of the Greek gods. Early Christians were called atheists by Romans, because they denied the existence of the Roman pantheon. Later, pagans, who believed in many gods, were called atheists by Christians, because pagans did not believe exclusively in the existence of the Christian monotheistic deity, YHWH or God. In all of these cases, the groups targeted with the label *atheist* were labeled as such not because they did not believe in any gods but rather because they did not believe in the god or gods of the dominant social groups or conceived of them differently from how those in power did. The label *atheist* continued to be used to describe those who did not adhere to orthodox views of God or gods of the dominant social groups up until the sixteenth and seventeenth centuries, when the modern understanding of the term developed. One of the earliest atheists in the modern sense was the French Catholic priest Jean Meslier, whose posthumously published writings revealed that he did not believe in any gods. Today, when people self-identify as atheist, they typically (but not universally) mean that they are without belief in any gods. Thus, the modern understanding of *atheism*, without belief in a god or gods, was not how the term was understood historically.

There is one additional extension of the term *atheism* that is worth noting. In recent years, there has been extensive discussion among atheists as to whether atheism is simply a

Chapter 1: Defining That Which Is Other to Religion

negative referent (meaning it only describes what someone does not believe in, i.e., a god or gods) or whether it can also be a positive referent (meaning it indicates what someone does believe in, such as skepticism, humanism, equality, or critical thinking). This discussion has led to a revised understanding of the term *atheist* such that it can be a largely empty signifier, similar to one of the previously discussed definitions of religion. An empty signifier is a label that is applied, whether by the individual or to the individual, that indicates that the individual may belong to a certain category or group of people, but precisely what is meant by membership in that category is not perfectly clear. In this understanding of the term, anyone can identify as an atheist, just as anyone can identify as being religious, but the specific meaning of the term can only be determined by combining the context in which the labeling occurred and what the specific individual understands the term to mean. There is some utility in this approach, but it is also somewhat problematic. The utility lies in the fact that it accurately reflects the many ways that people use language and conceptualize the terms *atheism* and *atheist*. Additionally, it also illustrates the important contextual nature of atheism, as the god or gods toward which someone is without belief are context specific. In other words, an atheist in Saudi Arabia is likely without belief in a different god or gods than is an atheist in India or an atheist in a tribal group in the Amazonian basin in Brazil. Thus, using *atheism* as a largely empty signifier allows for greater variability in how the term is used and what it means. The problem is that it could result in methodological reductionism, meaning that the terms *atheism* and *atheist* can only be understood relative to specific individuals. In other words, the general definition of atheist offered in this section could serve as a sort of generic component of the *atheist* signifier, but just as with religion, precisely what any given individual means by *atheist* would have to be situated in that person and that person's context. There would, therefore, be no universal definition of atheism—just a placeholder for something that is related to being without belief in a god or gods.

AGNOSTICISM AND AGNOSTICS

Like atheism, agnosticism is, at its simplest, understood relative to the constituent parts of the term. The prefix *a-* means "without" or "lacking." The rest of the term, *-gnosticism* is based on the root word, *gnosis*, which also comes from the Greek, gnōsis (γνῶσις), which means "knowledge." Combining the two, *agnosticism* is "without knowledge." Of course, in the context of this chapter, agnosticism is a referent to a god or gods. Thus, agnosticism is "without knowledge of a god or gods." What is meant by knowledge can, of course, be debated, but typically it is understood to be justified true belief, or beliefs that have empirically verifiable evidence to support them.

Readers will note that this definition is similar to that of negative atheism. However, there is a way in which it can be understood to differ. Agnosticism need not be exclusively about having or not having knowledge about the existence of a god or gods. Agnosticism can also refer to whether or not it is possible to obtain knowledge about the existence of a god or gods. In other words, agnosticism can refer not just to whether or not someone has knowledge about a god or gods, but also to whether or not one thinks it is possible to obtain such knowledge. This, of course, is contingent upon how a god is defined or described. For instance, if someone asserted that god was a one pound rock inside a backpack, it would be fairly easy to ascertain whether or not that rock existed through the use of our empirical senses (i.e., touch, sight, taste, and so on). But if someone asserted that god was a rock that was infinitesimally small and invisible, it would no longer be possible to obtain knowledge about the existence or nonexistence of this god-rock as we could neither find it nor sense it. In the first case, we could obtain knowledge about the existence of the rock and would therefore not be agnostic toward the existence of the rock because we would have knowledge. In the second case, we would have no knowledge about the existence of the rock because the claim of the person asserting its existence would be based on a belief, not knowledge. Therefore, we would have no ability to gain knowledge about its existence given the characteristics of the god-rock. Likewise, certain gods are more or less amenable to empirical verification. If someone were to assert that god was a statue that occasionally bled from carved wounds in its wrists and feet, we could empirically verify the existence of the statue and could investigate the source of the blood. We would not have to be agnostic about the existence of the statue or, potentially, the cause of the bleeding. But if someone were to assert the existence of a god that is not omnipotent, nor omniscient, nor just, nor engaged with humans or even with the unfolding of the universe, but is supernatural and undetectable by any human senses or any tools that extend human senses (i.e., a deistic god), this makes obtaining knowledge about the existence of such a deity impossible. It would be impossible to assert whether or not such a god exists based on knowledge of that god and it would be impossible to gain any knowledge of such a god because it is defined and described in such a fashion that there is no way to gain knowledge about the existence of that god. This, of course, does not mean that someone cannot assert that such a god exists. People can assert and have asserted the existence of deities of a great many varieties. But, given the characteristics of the god, there is no way to obtain knowledge about that god, resulting in agnosticism toward this deity. Philosophically, this raises numerous questions concerning epistemology, the characteristics of deity, and whether logic can be used to determine whether a specific deity can or cannot exist, among other concerns. But for our purposes here, this extends the definition of agnosticism to mean something like, "not having knowledge of a god or gods and potentially believing that such knowledge cannot be obtained."

This is not, however, how many people understand the term *agnosticism* today. Many people understand agnosticism to mean that someone is unsure of the existence of a god or that the individual has doubts about the existence of a god. Not being sure about the existence of a god could still qualify as agnosticism if, for instance, one believed in a god but recognized that there was no evidence for the existence of that god. If the basis for the doubts or lack of surety of belief in a god is based on a person's lack of knowledge of those gods, then such individuals would be agnostic theists. But if individuals who are unsure about their belief in a god but believe they have knowledge or can obtain knowledge about the existence of the target god or gods, then this would not qualify as agnosticism using a strict definition of the term. Instead, this would be theistic uncertainty, not agnosticism.

The term *agnosticism* was coined in 1869 by Thomas Henry Huxley (1825–1895), an English biologist, to describe what basically amounts to a side argument between those asserting the existence of a god or gods (i.e., theists) and those asserting the nonexistence of a god or gods (i.e., positive atheists). In Huxley's words, "Agnosticism, in fact, is not a creed, but a method, the essence of which lies in the rigorous application of a single principle.... Positively the principle may be expressed: In matters of the intellect, follow your reason as far as it will take you, without regard to any other consideration. And negatively: In matters of the intellect do not pretend that conclusions are certain which are not demonstrated or demonstrable" (768). For

Chapter 1: Defining That Which Is Other to Religion

Thomas Henry Huxley (1825–1895), English biologist, 1866. *Huxley coined the term* agnosticism *to describe an argument between theists (those asserting the existence of a god or gods) and positive atheists (those asserting the nonexistence of a god or gods). For him, agnosticism was a philosophical position that recognized the limitations of empiricism and logic.* **PRINT COLLECTOR/ GETTY IMAGES.**

Huxley, agnosticism was a philosophical position that recognized the limitations of empiricism and logic. If something cannot be measured empirically or demonstrated logically, then the safest position philosophically is to neither assert nor deny its existence. It's safest to simply assert, "we don't know," and perhaps, "we can't know."

Astute readers will note that the definitions of atheism and agnosticism are not mutually incompatible. Because atheism is without belief in a god or gods and agnosticism is without knowledge of a god or gods, one can be both simultaneously: for example, an agnostic atheist. This would indicate that someone does not believe in a god or gods based on one's lack of knowledge of the god or gods. It could also mean that someone is without belief in a god or gods because one does not believe that it is possible to obtain knowledge about a god or gods. Readers may be interested to note that one of the most well-known atheists today, Richard Dawkins (1941–), would likely describe himself as an agnostic atheist given these definitions. Although Richard Dawkins rejects the existence of the Judeo-Christian God or YHWH, he does not reject the possibility that some sort of deity could exist, contingent upon the characteristics of that deity. Thus, Richard Dawkins is a positive atheist toward some gods as he understands them and rejects their existence, but he is also an agnostic atheist in that he does not believe in any gods but recognizes that it is possible that some god or gods might exist (depending on their characteristics) but we have no knowledge of them and have no way of gaining knowledge about them.

APOSTATES AND EXITERS (AND OTHER TERMS FOR THOSE WHO LEAVE RELIGIONS)

Perhaps the most widely used term to refer to those who leave a religion is *apostate*. This term also comes from the Greek, *apostasia* (ἀποστασία), which means "to defect or revolt." This term can be used in a relatively neutral fashion to simply describe those who leave a religion, but often it is not used that way. Although there has been an attempt in recent years to reappropriate the term *apostate* by those who have left religions similar to how homosexual men reappropriated the term *gay*, it is still generally the case that the label apostate is applied externally to those who leave a religion and is done so by those who remain members of the religion. In this fashion, the label apostate is pejorative and is meant to reflect the sense of betrayal felt by those who remain members of the religion. As a result,

10   MACMILLAN INTERDISCIPLINARY HANDBOOKS

individuals who are labeled apostates by those who remain members of the religion they left are subject to derision and scorn.

Realizing the way apostate is often used, some sociologists studying apostates have illustrated the politicization of the term. As a result, scholars such as David Bromley in *The Politics of Religious Apostasy* (1998) have argued that those studying religion and its other should use the term only in the specific case of individuals who leave religions and then actively work against those religions. Given that the root of the term focuses on defection from a religion, this understanding and application of the term *apostate* makes sense. This also makes sense in light of the millions of people around the world who have left the religions in which they were raised but do not actively work against those religions and are not particularly critical of those religions. Many people who leave are largely indifferent toward or uninterested in religion. Labeling as apostates those who leave a religion but do not actively work against it once they have left is, perhaps, a bit extreme. Considering such individuals apostates or defectors from religion when, in reality, they are indifferent toward religion is again a reflection of religious privileging. Labeling such individuals apostates suggests that all that is required in order for someone to be assigned a deviant and subordinate identity is for them to leave a religion, automatically privileging those who do not leave religions. According to Bromley, then, the term *apostate* is best reserved only for those who leave a religion and then actively work against the religion they left.

Other scholars, such as Cragun and Hammer (2011), have argued that even this moderated use of the term apostate still reflects a privileging of a religion. Because apostate is a pejorative term, these scholars have argued that it should only be used to describe those people who leave a religion when scholars are attempting to capture the attitudes of those who remain members of the religion. It is, of course, accurate to report that those who remain members of a religion think of those who leave as apostates. Thus, using apostate in that sense is an accurate reflection of reality. But referring, generally, to those who leave religions as apostates in any other context except perhaps when such individuals use apostate as a self-reference reflects the privileged and normative status of religion in society. Because privileging religion necessarily subordinates that which is other to religion, to prevent such privileging, those who leave religions should not be labeled using the terminology of the religious. They should be allowed to self-identify and self-label.

Even though apostate is a pejorative term that privileges religion, it continues to be used widely among those who study religion. This reflects, at some level, the contentious nature of scholarship on religion. As Cragun and Hammer (2011) illustrated in their discussion of this term, much of the research on religion in the social sciences has been conducted by individuals who are personally religious. Their bias has been reflected in the language that has been used to describe individuals who leave religions. Apostate is just one of the many pejorative terms that has been used to describe those who leave. Other terms that have been used in reference to such individuals include: defectors, dropouts, disaffiliates, disengagers, and deserters. All of these terms negatively depict those who leave. What's more, these terms are often used in other contexts to do the same thing, such as military deserters or school dropouts. In all of these contexts, the terms suggest deficiencies in those who leave, as though they are somehow morally inferior to those who remain members of the religions. Given the contentious and pejorative nature of these terms, Cragun and Hammer suggest that a more neutral term would be *religious exiter* as it reflects only the fact that someone left a religion and implies nothing else about where that person went, whether the person is now

Chapter 1: Defining That Which Is Other to Religion

critical of the religion left behind, and minimizes the privileging of religion. It may still privilege religion to a small degree in that it necessarily sets religion as being that which someone leaves, rather than inverting that relationship and reflecting the fact that the natural state of all humans is both atheism and secularity. Yet, if people were at some point affiliated with a religion and then leave it, considering such people religious exiters accurately reflects what they have done vis-a-vis religion without unnecessarily suggesting that they are deviant or deficient in some fashion for having done so.

Another common term used by social scientists to refer to those who leave religions is *switcher*. This label is used for those who leave a religion but then join another religion. It is generally used in a more neutral fashion to reflect the relatively common practice in religiously open and pluralistic societies of people changing religions at different points in their lives. It is not, however, typically used in reference to those who leave a religion but do not join another religion. There is not, to date, a term specific to that scenario (though some have suggested "dones" as a possible term), as apostate and the other terms noted do not specify whether individuals who have left a religion joined another religion or left religion altogether.

NONRELIGION, IRRELIGION, AND ARELIGION

Those who study that which is other to religion have increasingly begun to refer to this field or topic of study as the study of nonreligion. *Nonreligion* is, like religion, a problematic term, precisely because it includes religion within the term. One of the most well-known proponents of the term, Lois Lee (2012), suggested that this is perhaps the best term for the field of study focused on that which is other to religion because, unlike secular, secularity, or secularism, nonreligion specifically notes that it is interested in that which is not religion but is related to religion. For instance, *secular* refers to everything that is not religion. Thus, a clown performance at a circus is secular, but so, too, is an atheist who actively works to diminish the influence of religion in a given society. Secular is broad and encapsulates everything that is not religion. *Nonreligion*, as proposed by Lee, is that which is other to religion but is still, in some fashion, related to religion. Thus, those studying nonreligion would not be interested in studying clowns at circuses, but would be interested in studying atheists working against religion. Presumably, the clowns are unrelated to religion, whereas the atheist working against religion is secular but related to religion. Thus, nonreligion refers to that which is other to but related to religion.

Extending this understanding of nonreligion, Johannes Quack (2014) noted that what is both other to and related to religion is culture and context specific. Thus, nonreligious studies or the study of nonreligion will vary based on the culture and context under investigation. Whereas the atheist working against organized religion would likely always be included in the domain of nonreligion, in some contexts, such as India, skeptics working against magicians would also be the study of nonreligion because magicians in India often claim religious and supernatural powers (unlike most magicians in Western countries). Thus, for Quack, nonreligion shifts relative to culturally variable conceptions of religion, allowing the domain of nonreligion to encapsulate both that which is other to religion but still related to religion regardless of what religion is in a given culture or context.

There are two terms closely related to nonreligion that also warrant discussion here. *Irreligion* is generally understood to be a reference to that which is opposed to religion, following Colin Campbell's (1971) definition of the term. Technically, the prefix *ir-* is a variant of the prefix *in-* and simply means "not." Thus, *irreligion*, based on the components of the term, is just that which is not religion. However, among those who study nonreligion, "irreligion" is generally used as Campbell suggested to refer to that which is in opposition to religion. Thus, secularist organizations working against religious influence in society would be considered irreligious, as would the writings of well-known religious critics, such as Sam Harris (1967–) or Daniel Dennett (1942–).

Areligion is different. As has been noted multiple times, the prefix *a-* means without. Thus, areligion refers to that which is without religion. Areligion refers to those things that are devoid of religion. Therefore, unlike nonreligion, which is other to but related to religion, areligion would be that which is other to religion but unrelated to religion. An example of something that is areligious would be most modern airline companies, which are devoid of religion (though there are exceptions).

HUMANISM

To this point, most of the terms discussed that refer to nonreligious individuals have primarily focused on what those people are not. For instance, atheists are without belief in a god or gods and secular individuals are not religious. What these labels do not reflect is the values nonreligious individuals may hold.

Humanism is a philosophical perspective that posits a number of principles not rooted in supernatural or religious beliefs that people can use to guide their behaviors and decisions. Precisely what those principles are varies somewhat based on the specific pronouncement of humanist principles. Pronouncements of humanist principles tend to include ideas such as: ethical and moral principles need not rely on the supernatural or religion, but rather can be based on human experience, logic, and reason; all humans are of equivalent worth and value; working toward the equal treatment of all humans and a world free of discrimination is desirable; science is superior to religion as a method for discerning how the natural and social worlds work; humans have a responsibility to protect all life, human and nonhuman, which necessarily means protecting the environment; each individual can develop meaning and purpose. This list is not inclusive of all such humanist principles, as many such pronouncements have been issued.

That many statements of humanist principles exist warrants some discussion of the history of humanism. The term has been used at various points in time, potentially including in antiquity (e.g., humanista). However, the term first rose to prominence during the Renaissance when it was used to describe a body of knowledge and method of instruction (forming the root of the modern *Humanities*). The basic idea according to scholars at the time was that, during the medieval period in the West there had been something of a regression in knowledge and understanding. Advocates of humanism in the Renaissance believed that the solution to increasing knowledge and understanding was to study the classics (Greek and Roman writings, but also early Christian ones) and to use that knowledge to better understand the world. This understanding of humanism is not entirely unrelated to the modern sense of the term, as it was likely this form of education that gave rise to the modern understanding of humanism.

Humanism as a philosophical system of guiding principles divorced from religion and the supernatural developed later, in the eighteenth and nineteenth centuries. This stemmed from Enlightenment thinking that came to the conclusion that morality and ethics could be developed outside the context of religion. These ideas were developed in various parts of Europe, including France and the United Kingdom, leading to ideas such as those of Auguste Comte (1798–1857) who proposed a religion of humanity. Humanist organizations working toward the betterment of humanity were founded during this time. One of the first humanist organizations with a focus on the modern philosophical understanding was the British Humanistic Religious Association founded in 1853.

Humanist ideas were present in the United States during the eighteenth and nineteenth centuries, but it was in the early twentieth century that the first well-known statement of humanist principles was produced. A critical mass of supporters of humanism developed in various regions, including in New York and Chicago. These early advocates eventually drew up a collective statement of humanist principles that they labeled "A Humanist Manifesto" and published in 1933. This first manifesto was not irreligious or secularist; it allowed for religious humanists. Over time, humanist ideas have shifted and a divide has grown between religious and secular humanists. These shifts eventually led to reformulations of the original manifesto, including versions published in 1973 and 2003 by the American Humanist Association. Other organizations and individuals have also proposed statements of humanist principles. Today, most people who identify as humanist are secular, as in *secular humanism*, but there are still many religious humanists as well.

LESS COMMON TERMS

There are a number of additional terms that are a bit more obscure but are occasionally observed in the research on that which is other to religion. Given that these terms are less common, the definitions offered in this section will be rather brief.

Two terms that are closely related are *freethinker* and *skeptic*. Freethinker is the label applied to individuals who engage in *freethought*, a philosophical approach that argues that truth should be based on logic, reason, and scientific inquiry. Skepticism is a similar approach to questions of knowledge and belief, arguing that all knowledge should be based on empirically verifiable evidence. Skeptics are individuals who adhere to skepticism. Both of these have rather long histories, with roots dating back to the classical eras of Greek and Roman thought, but becoming formalized in Western thought in the last four hundred years or so. Freethinker is generally seen as being more directly related to religion, as the label was adopted in the seventeenth century by those who questioned the need for organized religion for morality, truth, and knowledge. Skepticism can be and often is applied to religion, but is generally seen as applicable to all sources of knowledge and all beliefs (e.g., pseudoscience, psychics, homeopathy, etc.). Thus, although the basic idea behind the two terms is similar, in practical use skepticism is more broadly applied than is freethought.

As noted previously, one of the difficulties atheists and secular individuals have faced is in trying to develop terminology and labels of their own that are not applied to them externally and are implicitly either indicators of what they are not or are derogatory (such as apostate or dropout). One attempt to address these concerns was the creation of the term *bright*. Bright was developed specifically as an alternative to *godless* (a synonym of atheist) by Paul Geisert in 2002 and was meant to portray atheists in a positive light rather than a negative one. Despite support from a number of well-known atheists and humanists, the term does not appear to have become widely used for self-identification among the nonreligious, secularists, and others sympathetic to the ideas it represents.

Another set of terms that are occasionally used to describe and label those who are other to religion are *nonbeliever* and *unbeliever*. Both of these terms position those so labeled in contrast to believers. The general sense of the terms, which are often used interchangeably, is that nonbelievers reject not just belief in a god, gods, or God, but also all supernatural truth claims. As a result, these two terms are similar to freethinker and skeptic.

Two terms have attempted to extend *atheism* in unique ways. The first is *New Atheism,* a label coined by Gary Wolf (2006) to describe the wave of atheist writers who rose to prominence in the early 2000s. Although the philosophical arguments these authors have employed to criticize religion are not particularly novel or new, New Atheists have suggested that what makes them unique is the combination of three key characteristics: the rejection of all supernatural beliefs, advocacy for science, and their open criticism of religion. These characteristics are also not particularly novel, as many early atheists and agnostics held similar views. The second noteworthy attempt to extend atheism was the effort of Jen McCreight and others in 2012 to develop a term related to atheism that indicates more of what those who use the label do believe rather than what they don't believe. The term chosen was Atheism+, suggesting that those who self-labeled as Atheist+ were atheists but also advocates for gender and sexual equality, scientific inquiry, skepticism, and other generally progressive ideas. Both New Atheism and Atheism+ have seen limited adoption by those who are other to religion.

Summary

This chapter has provided definitions for the most commonly used terms in the study of that which is other to religion. It has also tried, in the process, to illustrate that definitions in this area are still in flux. This is due, in part, to the varied definitions of religion, which make defining that which is other to religion somewhat difficult. This is also due to the relatively new nature of this area of research. As research in this area matures, it is likely that these definitions will change and new terms will probably be introduced. Even so, this chapter lays a foundation for those new to this area to have a better understanding of what scholars studying that which is other to religion mean when they use specific terms.

Bibliography

Ali, Ayaan Hirsi. *Infidel.* New York: Atria Books, 2008.

Berger, Peter L. *The Sacred Canopy: Elements of a Sociological Theory of Religion.* New York: Anchor, 1990.

Berlinerblau, Jacques. *How to Be Secular: A Call to Arms for Religious Freedom.* Boston: Mariner Books, 2013.

Bremmer, Jan N. "Atheism in Antiquity." In *The Cambridge Companion to Atheism,* edited by Michael Martin, 11–26. New York: Cambridge University Press, 2006.

Bromley, David G. *The Politics of Religious Apostasy: The Role of Apostates in the Transformation of Religious Movements.* Westport, CT: Praeger Publishers, 2008.

Bruce, Steve. *Secularization: In Defence of an Unfashionable Theory.* Oxford: Oxford University Press, 2013.

Campbell, Colin. *Toward a Sociology of Irreligion.* London: Macmillan, 1971.

Cliteur, P. B. *The Secular Outlook: In Defense of Moral and Political Secularism.* Chichester, West Sussex: Wiley-Blackwell, 2010.

Chapter 1: Defining That Which Is Other to Religion

Comte, Auguste. *The Catechism of Positive Religion*. Cambridge: Cambridge University Press, 2009.

Cragun, Ryan T., and Joseph H. Hammer. "'One Person's Apostate Is Another Person's Convert': Reflections on Pro-Religion Hegemony in the Sociology of Religion." *Humanity & Society* 35 (February–May 2012): 149–175.

Cragun, Ryan T., Stephanie Yeager, and Desmond Vega. "Research Report: How Secular Humanists (and Everyone Else) Subsidize Religion in the United States." *Free Inquiry* (2012): 39–46.

Dawkins, Richard. *The God Delusion*. Boston: Houghton Mifflin, 2008. First published 2006.

Dobbelaere, Karel. *Secularization: An Analysis at Three Levels (Gods, Humans, and Religions)*. New York: Peter Lang Publishing, 2002.

Durkheim, Émile. *The Elementary Forms of Religious Life*. New York: Free Press, 1995. First published 1912.

Eller, Jack David. "What Is Atheism?" In *Atheism and Secularity: Vol. 1: Issues, Concepts, and Definitions*, edited by P. Zuckerman, 1–18. Santa Barbara, CA: Praeger, 2010.

Harris, Sam. *The End of Faith: Religion, Terror, and the Future of Reason*. New York: Norton, 2005. First published 2004.

Huxley, Thomas Henry. "Agnosticism." *The Popular Science Monthly* 34, no. 46 (April 1889): 768.

Josephson, Jason Ānanda. *The Invention of Religion in Japan*. Chicago: The University of Chicago Press, 2012.

Lee, Lois. "Research Note: Talking about a Revolution: Terminology for the New Field of Non-Religion Studies." *Journal of Contemporary Religion* 27, no. 1 (2012): 129–139.

Marsden, George M. *The Soul of the American University*. New York: Oxford University Press, 1994.

Quack, Johannes. "Outline of a Relational Approach to 'Nonreligion.'" *Method & Theory in the Study of Religion* 26, no. 4–5 (2014): 439–469.

Shiner, Larry. "The Concept of Secularization in Empirical Research." *Journal for the Scientific Study of Religion* 6, no. 2 (1967): 207–220.

Smith, George H. *Atheism: The Case Against God*. Buffalo, NY: Prometheus Books, 1980.

Sommerville, C. J. "Secular Society Religious Population: Our Tacit Rules for Using the Term 'Secularization.'" *Journal for the Scientific Study of Religion* 37, no. 2 (1998): 249–253.

Von Stuckrad, Kocku. "Discursive Study of Religion: Approaches, Definitions, Implications." *Method and Theory in the Study of Religions* 25, no. 1 (2013): 5–25.

Weber, Max. *The Protestant Ethic and the Spirit of Capitalism*. New York: Routledge, 2001. First published 1905.

Wolf, Gary. "The Church of the Non-Believers." *Wired*. 2006. http://archive.wired.com/wired/archive/14.11/atheism.html.

FILM AND TELEVISION

An Honest Liar. Dir. Justin Weinstein and Tyler Measom. 2014. A feature documentary covering the life and career of magician James "The Amazing" Randi that publically exposes paranormal fakes and con-artists.

Letting Go of God. Dir. Julia Sweeney. 2008. A humorous monologue about Sweeney's search for God.

Religulous. Dir. Larry Charles. 2008. A documentary put-down of religion by Bill Maher.

The Richard Dawkins Collection (*The Genius of Charles Darwin, The Enemies of Reason, and The Root of All Evil?*). Dir. Russell Barnes. 2009. Three of Dawkins's television documentaries exploring the intellectual battleground between scientific reason and religion.

Secularity in Society

CHAPTER 2

Secularization

Stratos Patrikios
Senior Lecturer
University of Strathclyde, School of Government and Public Policy,
Glasgow, UK

The presence and function of religion in society is foundational in Western thought. Since the first attempts by thinkers such as Plato (427–347 BCE), more than two millennia ago, to define the good life, the good citizen, the good judge, and the good ruler, a negotiation between the absolute and revealed, on the one hand, and the rational and relative, on the other, has been the central pursuit of philosophical debate (Tarcov and Pangle 1987). As part of the absolute and taken for granted, religion has played a constant and central part in that negotiation. Centuries after Plato, St. Augustine (354–430 CE), who made explicit the distinction between a religious domain and a separate secular domain, argued that salvation and happiness could come only from divine grace and revelation, rather than from human justice and reason as recommended by the pagan Greek philosophers (Fortin 1987, 197). In the nineteenth century, along this longstanding normative debate between those for and those against religion's influence in human affairs, a second question crystallized. The question asked whether modern life would push religion to the brink of extinction, and the anticipated answer was affirmative. This is known as the secularization thesis.

What follows is an introduction to the various ways of analyzing the second question from a positive, social scientific perspective. The chapter will not touch on the first, normative debate. It begins by providing a basic understanding of the evolution of social scientific attempts to study the proposition described by the secularization thesis as an empirical hypothesis, although this is not its main aim. Most textbooks in the sociology of religion contain valuable literature reviews on the history of the secularization thesis (e.g., see Davie 2007; Hamilton 1995; Lundskow 2008; McGuire 2002). The primary aim of the present text is to provide a road map of the alternative ways available for studying the secularization thesis against some concrete reality—that is, as a testable proposition. Following this aim, the chapter contains detailed sketches of the research designs and data sources that can be used in empirical applications of secularization theory. Apart from the obvious relevance of scholarship produced by sociologists of religion, the text also draws on the work of political scientists, social and cultural anthropologists, media researchers, and the students of organizations.

The focus of the discussion is on organized religions (churches)—that is, as Meredith B. McGuire defines them in *Religion: The Social Context* (2002), on institutions built around a system of beliefs and rituals that regulate the means of grace or the relationship between a community of individuals and what these individuals perceive as a divine, supernatural being. Therefore, the chapter adopts a substantive definition of religion rather than a functional one, which would treat as religious any phenomenon that uses rituals and symbols and that provides meaning and order in participants' lives. As Steve Bruce explains in *God Is Dead: Secularization in the West* (2002), the latter would allow one to treat football and nationalism as religions, making unfeasible any focused discussion of a specific field of scholarly research.

THE BASIC IDEA

In its purest form, the secularization thesis expects that as society becomes more advanced—technologically and otherwise—religion becomes less important in terms of visibility and significance. The thesis expects a linear process that leads to religion's evanescence. The works of Auguste Comte (1798–1857), David Émile Durkheim (1858–1917), Friedrich Wilhelm Nietzsche (1844–1900), Max Weber (1864–1920), Karl Marx (1818–1883), and later Sigmund Freud (1856–1939) and others are central in this way of thinking, although in certain cases, such as Comte, Marx, and Freud, the normative (all the negative things that ought to happen to religion) and the positive/scientific seem to collude. The second half of the twentieth century brought several attempts to make the secularization thesis more systematic and precise, by combining the different expectations under a unified framework. Sociologists began producing detailed accounts of the phenomenon through the works of Peter Berger (1967), Thomas Luckmann (1967), and Bryan Wilson (1976), and in more recent decades, with those of Olivier Tschannen (1991), Mark Chaves (1994), David Yamane (1997), Steve Bruce (2002), and Karel Dobbelaere (2002).

Figure 2.1. Linear trend. STRATOS PATRIKIOS. ADAPTED FROM PATRIKIOS, 2016.

In a schematic presentation, the typical study in secularization research examines the impact of modernity on religion. Although modernity can be defined in multiple ways—including technological advance, the rationalization of knowledge, and the bureaucratization of social interactions—the easiest type of empirical test conducted takes time (i.e., its progression) as a proxy for modernity and the key explanation of the anticipated religious decline. The assumption is that as time progresses from past to present, societies become more advanced. On the other hand, of the proposed causal relationship, we encounter religion as an abstract phenomenon.

In sum, the simplest expression of the secularization thesis is that of an evolutionary, linear trend: modernity leads to the decline and eventual demise of religion. One now simply has to find indicators or observations of religion as a phenomenon over many time periods, and then examine whether religion actually becomes weaker, or less prominent, or less important as time goes by. Figure 2.1 illustrates this type of approach, with the cause (independent variable) on the left, and the outcome (dependent variable) on the right.

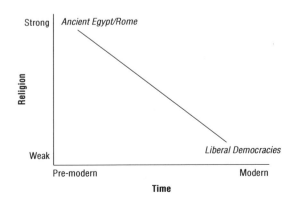

Figure 2.2. Inverse relationship: religion and time. STRATOS PATRIKIOS. ADAPTED FROM PATRIKIOS, 2016.

The relationship is a negative one. The more modern and advanced a society, the less religious it is expected to become. Figure 2.2 captures this postulated inverse relationship.

In the absence of information that is available over multiple time points (past and present), an alternative but suboptimal way to study the secularization thesis empirically is to examine young individuals and compare them with older ones, either in the present or looking at the comparison, and any changes in the generational gaps, across different decades. The assumption is that the young have been socialized in a more modern environment, and therefore they would exhibit the influence of that environment more explicitly, for instance, by being less religious. There are various problems with this approach, mainly the applicability of alternative explanations that have nothing to do with secularization, but with typical lifecycle changes, as Glenn Firebaugh and Brian Harley (1991) suggest. Figure 2.3 illustrates the relationship.

Another alternative type of analysis, in the absence of information from various time points, employs indicators of modernization that vary across countries. The assumption here is that religion in more advanced countries—for instance, those with a higher gross domestic product per capita or with more educated populations—will be weaker than in less advanced countries. Figure 2.4 illustrates this type of approach, and Figure 2.5 stresses the negative character of the postulated connection between modernization and religion.

Figure 2.3. Comparison by age. STRATOS PATRIKIOS. ADAPTED FROM PATRIKIOS, 2016.

Figure 2.4. Comparison by country. STRATOS PATRIKIOS. ADAPTED FROM PATRIKIOS, 2016.

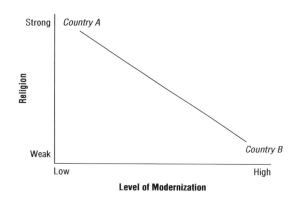

Figure 2.5. Inverse relationship: religion and modernization. STRATOS PATRIKIOS. ADAPTED FROM PATRIKIOS, 2016.

THE CAUSAL LINK

Two urgent questions arise from the previous schematic presentation. First, what is "modern"? Does it have something to do with technological progress? Is it about material prosperity? It is about being a less rural economy and society? Is it about a more participatory way of governing? Is it about a greater degree of pluralism? Is it a way of thinking? Answering this question will help to explain the expectation of religious decline in modernity (for overviews, see Davie 2007; Fox 2013; Hamilton 1995; Norris and Inglehart 2004).

Scientific advance is almost synonymous with modernity. It builds rational accounts of the existence of numerous natural phenomena that once were attributed to supernatural forces. Widespread literacy would also characterize a modern society. Being able to read for oneself, rather than rely on priests, who were traditionally the literate members of a community, weakens the ability of religion to monitor and filter the acquisition of knowledge. A more prosperous and egalitarian world, and the existence of the safety net of the welfare state, at least when compared with past societies, are also thought to diminish the existential anxiety that led impoverished populations to turn to the consolation of

Chapter 2: Secularization

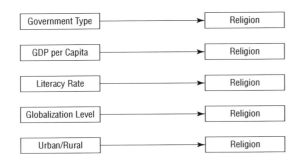

Figure 2.6. Comparison by various indicators of modernity.
STRATOS PATRIKIOS. ADAPTED FROM PATRIKIOS, 2016.

religion. Industrialization and urbanization have taken individuals out of the dense social network of the local community, where members interacted directly with each other and were subject to stronger conformity pressures, depriving on the way churches from an ideal social basis. Globalization and the increased mobility of people and ideas also expose individuals to competing frames of reference and a relativist way of thinking about the world, making any institution that claims to hold the absolute truth sound less credible. The wider participation of ordinary citizens in the political process, another feature of modernity, is also thought to diminish the hold of various elites, secular and religious alike, on individuals.

Depending on how one defines a modern or advanced society, there are numerous ways of measuring modernity. Various indicators of modernity are readily available from the research conducted by large international organizations, not to mention various academic programs that produce their own measures. The World Bank and the United Nations, for instance, provide access to economic and social development information about countries. Organizations such as the Economist Intelligence Unit, Freedom House, Polity, the World Bank and the Central Intelligence Agency provide details on the type of government that operates in each country. So, the diagrams in Figures 2.4 and 2.5 become a little more concrete in Figure 2.6, because "country type" is more specific now.

LEVELS OF ANALYSIS

The second question we need to answer is the following: what is *religion* exactly? To find measures or observations of the religious phenomenon one has to first know what to look for. A useful conceptual tool suggested by Chaves (1994) and Dobbelaere (1999, 2002) is to think about religion, and by extension secularization, as a phenomenon that exists at three levels of analysis.

SOCIETIES AND STATES

First, there is the presence and influence of religion at the societal or macro level. This includes the significance of religion as reflected in a society's norms and its institutions. The degree of differentiation or autonomy between religious and state authority, that is, the church-state arrangements that characterize a political system (Lipset and Rokkan 1967; Rokkan 1970; Martin 1978), is a popular concept in this type of research. The secularization thesis would expect that in a more advanced society—compared with the same society in the past or with a less advanced society of the present—religion would be less visible as a public influence.

American Austrian sociologist Thomas Luckmann (1927–) describes the process in the following manner: "[t]he more 'complex' a society, the more likely it is to develop distinct institutions supporting objectivity and social validity of the sacred cosmos" (1967, 63). Once institutions like education, the military and government have been separated from the "sacred canopy" of the church (Berger 1967), they can then begin to seek legitimacy from sources other than God and to function according to nonmetaphysical criteria: science, rationality, productivity, liberalism, and profit. The religious sphere eventually becomes another institutional domain, without a predominant grip on other spheres of human interaction. This differentiation can be interpreted as the first act in the distancing of social institutions from religious control. It is evident that this type of grand institutional differentiation of religion from other domains of social activity has taken place in most advanced societies in the world. One simply has to think of whether education remains the exclusive remit of clerical personnel (it does not) or whether most countries in the world enforce the formal separation of government and religion (they do) (Fox 2008).

Apart from this general phenomenon of societal secularization as institutional separation and differentiation, or once this development has taken place, other kinds of secularization pressures may be of interest at the macro level. These would involve the waning or increasingly contested presence of religious symbols in public spaces (courtrooms and public squares); the disappearance of religious cues from important (constitutions) and less important texts (party manifestos, the media, and the publishing industry); and the further weakening of the influence of religious institutions, their personnel, and their values over public bodies (the justice system, education, health, and social services).

It is easier to find indicators and concrete information for some of these domains than others. For instance, the Comparative Constitutions Project and its sister Constitute project provide access, with searchable terms, to the content of these documents for most countries in the world. Quantitative data sets (see American political scientist Jonathan Fox's Religion and State Data Set, and Brian Grim and Roger Finke's International Religious Freedom Data Set) provide information on whether a country's legal system makes special religious provisions and on the nature of the relationship between states and organized religions. International organizations, such as the United Nations, can even provide access to the more specialized cross-national indicators, such as the annual production of religious titles by the publishing industry (see Wuthnow 1977). Various online search tools of published content, such as Google Ngrams, facilitate the systematic analysis of general cultural trends in the use of religious terminology in a society's corpus of books, as recorded by Google Books. In addition, as Birgit Meyer and Annelies Moors explain in *Religion, Media, and the Public Sphere* (2006), even though studies of the religious presence in the media usually rely on in-depth, qualitative case studies, tools are available that make possible more systematic comparisons of published news content, both over time and cross-nationally. The Lexis database allows the collection and analysis of information on specific phenomena, such as reporting on controversies that surround the presence of Nativity scenes in public spaces.

As a recent example of a macro-level analysis of the secularization thesis, Fox has compiled and analyzed the cross-national Religion and State Data Set (version 1). In *A World Survey of Religion and the State* (2008), he found stability over time in the bonds that connect governments and organized religion. These bonds cover dimensions such as religious discrimination, regulation, and legislation, and they do not seem to be weakening over the time period covered by the Religion and State Data Sets (1990–2008). One should note, however, that the classic secularization thesis describes a more glacial, slow erosion of the state-religion connection, one that takes place across centuries rather than decades.

In a different type of analysis, studies that take a long-term, historical perspective (e.g., see Lipset and Rokkan 1967; Madeley 2003; Martin 1978; Rokkan 1970) have documented the changing nature of the church-state relationship in Europe, which has

Chapter 2: Secularization

been particularly affected by two critical events: the Reformation and the French Revolution. The evolution of the relationship is in line with the predictions of secularization theory at the macro level: although government allegiance to a single organized religion was more or less the rule until the late nineteenth century, a more neutral stance by the state toward all organized religions or even a negative stance toward religion in general started to become more prominent in the twentieth century.

The following list provides details of some relevant religious indicators that are ideal for this type of analysis:

- The Constitute Project. The Culture and Identity topic includes a Religion category, which allows the user to assess what a country's constitution has to say about the role of God and organized religion in state affairs.

- The Religion and State Data Set. The data set codifies information from human rights reports, academic research, and news content to create information across various countries and over two decades (1990–2008, version 2) on the legal aspects of the religion-state relationship, including formal church-state arrangements, religious observance, the link between citizenship and organized religion, conversion and proselytizing, clerical and faith-based education, clerical appointments, marriage, blasphemy, censorship, religious holidays, and courts.

- The International Religious Freedom Data Set. This is a source that codifies annual reports on the religious situation of various countries (2001–2008) produced by the State Department on religious freedom, discrimination, violence, prejudice, persecution, forced migration, and general favoritism and harassment by the state and other collective actors.

- Google Ngrams. This online search engine allows the user to search for the frequency of appearance of specific terms in the corpus of books available in the Google Books collection. It provides both an online graphic tool that shows the frequency of the term on a yearly basis, covers a few languages, and provides access to the raw data. This is an ideal quick solution for documenting the religious presence in public discourse. As an example, the frequency of the term *God* among publications written in British English between 1800 and 2008 is declining over time, with a dramatic drop in the mid-nineteenth century and another one in the 1960s, as a percentage of all terms found in British English publications. Since the late 1990s, the frequency seems to have picked up slightly. The Google Trends tool allows a similar type of investigation of online search terms over time.

RELIGION AS AN ORGANIZATIONAL PHENOMENON

At the organizational or meso level of analysis, religion can be thought of as an institution, usually an ecclesiastical bureaucracy or church. Because of the difficulties in accessing the relevant information, especially from a perspective that would allow contrasts either over time (longitudinal) or across countries and organizations (comparative), this is the most under-researched level of analysis in secularization studies (e.g., see Berger 1969; Chaves 1994; Dobbelaere 1999; Luckmann 1967). Internal secularization, the meso-level version of the thesis, is seen as an organizational transformation of religious institutions. These are expected to become more *worldly* and *businesslike* over time as a consequence of exposure to various "pressures of scale, complexity, markets, resource (fllig;)ows [and] environmental uncertainty" (Hinings and Raynard 2014, 166).

Empirical applications of the internal secularization thesis are heavily influenced by the view that all large, complex organizations that want to survive, including religious ones, have to adopt external models of bureaucratic and management structures, which have little to do with the original (nonprofit) purpose or the theological orientation of the religious organization (see neoinstitutional theory in DiMaggio and Powell 1983; see also Hinings and Raynard 2014; Weber 1949). Investigations of secularization tendencies would look at the extent to which churches allow nonclerical (lay) personnel to rise to positions of power or the degree to which church bureaucracies become similar to commercial firms in the way they operate and interact with the outside world.

In an example of this type of empirical analysis titled "Intraorganizational Power and Internal Secularization in Protestant Denominations," American sociologist Mark Chaves applies organization theory to the study of personnel dynamics within American Protestant denominations. He treats personnel trends in these denominations as an indicator of internal secularization processes. Adapting theoretical expectations regarding intraorganizational power struggles between personnel subunits in the corporate world, in "Denominations as Dual Structures: An Organizational Analysis," Chaves highlights two key subunits that compete for resources within American Protestant denominations: the value-oriented authority structure ("priests") that controls access to religious goods, and the economy-driven administrative structure ("managers") that is in charge of the more mundane function of religious institutions, such as health services, publishing, and public relations. His analysis of the career backgrounds of top religious officials finds that these come increasingly from the administrative structure with a parallel decline in officials originating from the authority structure (active clergy, such as bishops and pastors).

In another rare study of the phenomenon titled "Professionalization and Secularization in the Belgian Catholic Pillar," Dobbelaere (1979) employs the insider-outsider distinction to study the increase of lay teachers and principals in Belgian Catholic schools, and the parallel decrease of clerical personnel (see also Canavan's 1999 article "The Transformation of Catholic Schools in Australia"). These findings can be viewed as evidence of ongoing internal secularization processes, in which religious organizations begin to emulate the workings and structures of secular, particularly for-profit, organizations. In a sense, the internal secularization thesis posits an increasing isomorphism between religious and secular organizations, with the universal adoption of the latter's form and content (DiMaggio and Powell 1983; Weber 1949).

INDIVIDUALS AND PUBLICS

The individual or micro level of analysis refers to religion as experienced by the individual. This is the most popular level of analysis in recent research. Religion here simply means religiosity. The abundance of census and social survey data sets, from the General Social Survey, the National Election Studies, and the Pew Research Center surveys in the United States, to comparative programs, such as the International Social Survey Program, the World/European Values Survey, and the Eurobarometer series in Europe, provides access to a wealth of individual-level measures of belief (in God, heaven and hell, the afterlife, the inerrancy of the Bible), religious attendance (frequency of church going), and membership or affiliation (belonging to or identifying with a religious tradition). The triptych "believing, behaving, belonging" is a common way of defining religiosity in empirical research.

Using such empirical information, the researcher would then set out to demonstrate whether believing, behaving, and belonging trends—either over time or across countries or comparing the young and the old—are indeed influenced negatively by the pressures of modernization. Evidence of this can be twofold. In the classic sense, one would have to

Chapter 2: Secularization

analyze trends over time in these indicators to establish whether, for instance, the percentage of frequent (typically, weekly) church attendance among the population is declining. In an alternative approach, the analysis would compare the overall level of attendance in more advanced societies compared with less advanced societies, anticipating a lower religiosity level in the former. Both of these findings would suggest the presence of advancing secularization at the individual level.

Numerous examples of empirical studies examine the secularization thesis at the individual level as a question of religiosity trends over time. In "How Secular Is Europe?" (2006), Dutch sociologists Loek Halman and Veerle Draulans analyzed survey data from the European Values Study program to find that indeed religiosity (belief and practice) is declining in European countries, although the speed of decline depends on factors such as a country's religious tradition. In *Sacred and Secular: Religion and Politics Worldwide* (2004), American political scientists Pippa Norris and Ronald Inglehart analyzed survey data from consecutive waves of the World Values Study (1981–2001) and Eurobarometer surveys (1970–1998) to document a general decline in religious attendance across countries, particularly in predominantly Catholic ones, although they found some exceptions to the overall trend (most notably, the United States). In addition to the comparison of religiosity trends over time, the two authors also conducted a comparison of religiosity indicators by country type, focusing on the level of development of each country. They first categorized countries into three groups based on levels of socioeconomic development, using information from the United Nations Human Development Index (HDI). The HDI is a standard measure of societal modernization, and scores countries based on their literacy, life expectancy, and prosperity rates. Norris and Inglehart came up with three country types: agrarian, industrial, and postindustrial societies. They found that the latter group was the more secularized in terms of overall religiosity rates.

This, however, is only one type of evidence that can test the secularization thesis at the individual level. In a variation of the standard expectation, which was developed by Chaves in his 1994 article "Secularization as Declining Religious Authority," religiosity per se may not be the best focus for an empirical assessment of the validity of secularization propositions. It would be more interesting to examine any changes in the influence of religiosity on various individual preferences and practices.

To clarify the usefulness of this alternative approach, which is known as the "declining religious authority" thesis, consider a country where the percentage of frequent church goers (or believers in God or identifiers with a particular denomination) remains stable over time. At face value, this would challenge the validity of the secularization thesis, which expects that over time religiosity would decline. This is the example of the United States at the time of Chaves's contribution—that is, a modern country with historically stable religiosity levels. His argument was that stability in religiosity levels is misleading as evidence of secularization and that the actual focus of secularization research should be on religious authority, that is, whether and to what extent religiosity shapes people's beliefs and practices beyond the religious realm.

These beliefs and practices can include the following: sexual preferences (if your religion forbids premarital sex, do you engage in it anyway?), dietary habits (if your religion allows the consumption of certain foods only on particular days, do you consume them outside those days?), and political preferences (if your church is closer to the Republican Party, do you vote for some other party; if your church is against worldly habits such as voting in elections, do you vote anyway?). An affirmative answer to these questions would be in line

26   MACMILLAN INTERDISCIPLINARY HANDBOOKS

with the "declining religious authority" version of the secularization thesis, despite the presence of stable, healthy levels of religiosity.

In a detailed example of Chaves's reformulation of the secularization thesis, consider the following research question: has the influence of religiosity on party choice become weaker over time? The erosion of the bond that connected American Catholics with the Democratic Party in national elections would serve as evidence of secularization tendencies from the "declining religious authority" perspective, irrespective of the fluctuation of religiosity levels. This approach effectively allows one to examine the relationship between religiosity and a whole host of social and political preferences, and to use any changes in the strength of the relationship over time as evidence of secularization or declining religious authority. Figure 2.7 illustrates the basic idea in Chaves's thesis. Notice that religion now appears on the left-hand side and is treated as an independent variable. The diagram describes an interaction between religiosity and time, meaning that the effect of religiosity on party choice is expected to decline over time. In other words, time is likely to mitigate the ability of religion to affect political preferences.

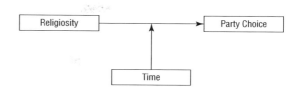

Figure 2.7. Interaction between religiosity and time in affecting party choice. STRATOS PATRIKIOS. ADAPTED FROM PATRIKIOS, 2016.

Studies that set out to test explicitly the religious authority variant of the secularization thesis are not common (e.g., see Hoffmann 1998; Kleiman, Ramsey, and Palazzo 1996; Patrikios 2009). However, any study of the relationship between religiosity and social or political behavior, also known as "the religious cleavage," can serve as a test of the secularization thesis (e.g., see Kotler-Berkowitz 2001; Lijphart 1979; Raymond 2011; Tilley 2015). A useful example is "Belonging, Behaving, and Believing: Assessing the Role of Religion on Presidential Approval" (2008) by Laura Olson and Adam Warber on the influence of religiosity indicators on presidential approval in a series of US presidential elections. The authors utilized survey data from the American National Election Studies program to find that religious affiliation was a weaker influence on presidential approval than belief and attendance. The work by American sociologists Jeff Manza and Clem Brooks in "The Religious Factor in US Presidential Elections, 1960–1992" (1997) and *Social Cleavages and Political Change* (1999) is equally relevant, as they are able to show a fading effect of religious affiliation on presidential vote choice over time. In their cross-national study, *Sacred and Secular: Religion and Politics Worldwide* (2004), Norris and Inglehart find a similar pattern of overall decline in the strength of the relationship between religiosity and support for right-wing ideology and religious parties among developed countries.

The following list provides details of relevant religious indicators that are ideal for this type of analysis. All data sets rely on nationally representative samples of each population. Most data sets cover several decades and include the standard questions on religious practice (church attendance or prayer), religious preference (tradition), and religious belief:

- The General Social Survey. These surveys began in 1972 and continue to the present. The questionnaires on which the data sets are based record responses on the following: degree of respondent's confidence in organized religion, religion in which respondent was raised, whether respondent considers herself as a religious person, evangelical or born-again status, and attitudes toward religious freedom.
- The American National Election Studies. These surveys began in 1948 and continue to the present. The questionnaires on which the data sets are based record responses on the

Chapter 2: Secularization

following: the importance of religion or God in respondent's life; individual stances on Biblical literalism, that is, the authority of the Bible as God's or man's word; and evangelical or born-again status.

- The Pew Research Center Surveys. These surveys record responses on the following: religious knowledge; religion in which respondent was raised; partner's religion; prayer habits; religious identification; religious experiences, such as exorcisms and divine healings; attitudes toward the public display of religious symbols and religious involvement in public life; attitudes toward the factual accuracy of holy texts; and attitudes toward religious extremism and violence. The center also conducts cross-national surveys.

- The International Social Survey Program. This cross-national program has conducted surveys dedicated to religion (in 1991, 1998, and 2008). The questionnaires on which the data sets are based record responses on the following: partner's religion, parental religion, born-again experiences, confidence in organized religion, attitudes toward the presence and influence of religion in politics, attitudes toward modern science, Biblical literalism, position on religion's contribution in peace or conflict, religion's role in interpersonal relations, attitudes toward religious extremism, spiritualism, and subjective images of God (as a mother, master, judge and the like).

- The World/European Values Survey. These surveys began in 1981 and continue to the present. The questionnaires on which the data sets are based record responses on the following: whether the respondent thinks that churches can solve various problems (family, social, and moral), confidence in religious institutions, various attitudes toward the presence of religion in politics, and the role of religion in parenting.

- The Eurobarometer Series. These surveys began in 1970 and continue to the present. The questionnaires on which the data sets are based record responses on the following: importance of religion in respondent's life, along with the other standard measures of religiosity.

A note of caution is in order at this junction. This discussion has reviewed mostly quantitative strategies in the study of religion and secularization at the individual level. Qualitative attempts, which are usually narrower in scope and time span, but afford a closer, more meaningful look at the content of individual beliefs and practices, are also abundant in this scholarly field. The interested reader may want to consult a variety of collective works and academic journals, which cover topics that range from everyday expressions of religiosity (e.g., see Ammerman 2007) to the changing nature of funeral preferences (the *Mortality* and *Omega* journals, published by Taylor & Francis and SAGE, respectively).

CRITIQUES OF THE SECULARIZATION THESIS

This section reviews some of the challenges to the validity of the secularization thesis. As a theory with a long history, the thesis has been criticized from various perspectives. Quite often, secularization trends take place only at some levels of analysis and are not present at others. In addition, as mentioned in the introduction, there are definitional questions regarding what counts as *religion*. Adopt a definition that is too broad, and you can gain in scope and flexibility as you are able to transcend understandings of religion that are too context and period specific, but you can also risk studying any social phenomenon as *religious*. A major critique of the thesis is that it is unable to explain the continuing strength of religion in one of the most advanced societies in the world, the United States. Competing explanations have been put forward to account for this discrepancy. In another challenge,

MACMILLAN INTERDISCIPLINARY HANDBOOKS

Chapter 2: Secularization

the thesis appears to downplay the ability of religious actors to react against the advance of secularization. Too much secularization seems to trigger a religious backlash in many cases. Last, perhaps what is described in the secularization paradigm is not about religion per se, which is able to adopt and survive, but rather is about formal membership to hierarchical organizations.

ONE OR THREE?

Secularization trends on the three levels may not move in a uniform fashion. José Casanova (1994) and Dobbelaere (2002) have noted several plausible scenarios conceivable in which secularization takes place on one of these levels but not on others. The position of the Church of England in Britain is a good example. The church operates in a state that is undergoing clear secularization at the individual level (for information on decline of church attendance, belief, and affiliation, see Bruce 1995; Voas and Crockett 2005). The church, however, still remains the official, established religion of the nation (England), despite the religious decline taking place among the population (see also the concept of "vicarious religion" in Davie 2007).

In addition to this independent movement of trends on the various levels, there is the possibility of connected but diverging trends across levels. For instance, a religious organization that transforms the content of its teachings, and their packaging, to render them more similar to their secular counterparts (e.g., a carefree night out at the movies) and therefore more appealing, could trigger an influx of converts. In other words, secularization tendencies at the meso level could trigger the opposite development at the individual level, by energizing the religious base.

According to Donald Miller in *Reinventing American Protestantism* (1997), an illustration of this type of cross-level relationship, in which organizational or meso-level secularization is followed by the inverse trend at the micro level, can be seen in the rise of megachurches in the American religious landscape. These institutions are large Protestant congregations with 2,000 or 3,000 followers, and they are close to the evangelical family. American sociologist Scott Thumma has studied extensively this relatively recent phenomenon. In "Megachurches of Atlanta" (1996), he defines megachurches as mall-like congregations targeting the baby-boomer generation. In their attempt to attract mainly the unchurched population, these institutions tend to follow a more consumer-friendly approach to worship. Entertainment-oriented activities take place in their facilities, which often include gyms and cafeterias. These rapidly and massively growing nondenominational congregations made the following impression on a visitor, which may explain their success and growth:

> You pull into a mall-sized parking lot and an attendant directs you to a special visitor parking section near the church entrance … You immediately recognize the church looks more like a corporate office park or mall than a traditional church. There is no steeple, no stained glass window, no cross … You enter through one of a series of smoked glass double doors and walk into a large atrium full of people milling about café tables and numerous informational kiosks which remind you of the food court area at your local mall. You are directed to the worship center and are surprised when you enter a space that looks like a theatre and must seat well over 1,000 … On a large stage that juts out into the seating area, a rock band is playing softly. You notice two large video screens high on the back wall of the worship center. (Ellingson 2009, 16)

In "Globalization and Religious Nationalism: Self, Identity, and the Search for Ontological Security" (2004), Catarina Kinnvall writes about a different type of cross-level development:

Chapter 2: Secularization

a state that decides to sever ties with a historically dominant church could trigger a defensive, backlash reaction from individual believers. In this case, secularization tendencies at the macro level could lead to the opposite move at the individual level. In "Identity Crisis: Greece, Orthodoxy, and the European Union" (2003), Lina Molokotos-Liederman suggests that the crisis that erupted between church and state in Greece in 2000–2001 is an illustration of this type of phenomenon. The Greek state had previously introduced Law 2472/1997 on the Protection of Individuals with Regard to the Processing of Personal Data, which prohibited the inclusion of religious affiliation on national identification cards. The Greek state's decision was an attempt by a member state of the European Union to create some separation between church and government. But this took place in a country where approximately 95 percent of the population identify as members of the (Orthodox) Church of Greece, the country's established religion, and where the country's constitution makes explicit reference to the dominance of Orthodox Christianity. It was inevitably seen by the church and a large part of the population as a move toward church-state separation. Analytically, it can be interpreted as a move in the direction of greater secularization at the macro level. The move was quickly followed by the strong reaction of the church and a large part of its membership. The reaction involved the organization of a church referendum against the government's decision, which collected more than three million signatures in a country of ten million, and the staging of massive public rallies against the government. In other words, the macro-level development seems to have triggered the opposite move, by stimulating the religious base, among individual believers.

CONCEPTUAL ISSUES

There is another type of challenge to the expectations of secularization theory (for a critical overview, see Bruce 2011). These expectations may not hold at all if we adopt a functional definition of religiosity, focusing on phenomena that seem to serve similar functions as religion used—for instance, to provide meaning in one's life by explaining one's place in the world as part of a greater scheme (e.g., communism or Marxism and its eschatological promise of a socialist revolution); to create a feeling of collective effervescence (e.g., yoga or other type of recreational exercise); to promote causes and treat their symbols as "sacred" (e.g., nationalist movements, their notion of "fatherland," and their use of flags); to involve the regular repetition of rituals and the use of religion-related words such as *miracle, sacrifice*, and *devotion* (the coverage of sports events and the hymns of sports fans). It is not hard to see how such a broader definition of religion allows one to treat any collective phenomenon that involves enthusiasm, symbolism, and repetition, topped with a message that transcends the mundane character of everyday life—and these are in abundance—as evidence against secularization theory.

Using the example of sports fans, *Los Angeles Times* religion editor Russell Chandler once reported the following quotation by social scientist Charles Prebish: "For many, such sporting events have taken on a religious quality, conferring meaning and cohesiveness upon their lives … For growing numbers of Americans … sport religion has become a more appropriate expression of personal religiosity than Christianity, Judaism, or any of the traditional religions" (Chandler 1986). To take the argument even further, a quick look at the most watched televised events of all times would rank the opening ceremonies of recent Olympic Games quite highly. Similarly, in the United States during the past decade, the numbers of television viewers of the Super Bowl has grown noticeably, making it the most watched broadcast in the country's television history. Taken at face value, such observations could be interpreted as evidence of religious vitality instead of secularization.

A simple online search of news content that contains the terms "quasi-religious experience," "almost religious," or "a religion?" also reveals a wealth of results that cover various aspects of human existence beyond sports. A quick online search, for example, returned results that referred to coffee drinking, using Apple gadgets (the term *cult* was employed), buying a particular model of car, attending a rock concert, being an atheist or a humanist, visiting an exhibition of musical instruments (likened to attending a *shrine*), or believing in equality of opportunity. These practices and beliefs are definitely not in decline compared with past decades, but they do not seem to qualify as definitions of religiosity in the substantive sense of a structured system of interactions between humans and a supernatural entity. What is more, most of them usually are not covered in the major national and cross-national survey programs, which are the main sources of empirical information in this field of study.

NOT PROVEN

Another typical critique of secularization theory raises the question of an idealized, supposedly religious past (e.g., see Martin 1969). For instance, William Williams's 1956 ethnographic study of an English village suggests that the local parishioners were clearly apathetic to religion for centuries. Yet, it was "widely believed that the poor attendance at Church dates from the arrival of the present Rector and that it would immediately improve on the induction of a new incumbent. This is symptomatic of a general tendency to use the shortcomings of the parson as an excuse for the worldliness of his flock" (Williams 1956, 183). It is fortunate that records existed for this particular village. It is usually the case that official statistics and other concrete accounts of past religiosity rates either do not go deep enough in the past, or do not cover geographic areas wide enough to be useful for generalizable comparisons between the present and the distant past. As a counterargument to this critique regarding a fictitious golden religious past, survey evidence from Norris and Inglehart (2004) that begins in the second half of the twentieth century suggests an overall decline of religious participation and belief across most advanced societies, with exceptions.

One of these exceptions presents a serious challenge to the validity of the thesis regarding the decline of individual religiosity over time, and religiosity's influence on other social and political preferences. Secularization theory seems unable to explain the religious vitality present in the United States, one of the most advanced countries in the world. If modernity creates secularization tendencies, then the hypothesized decline is apparently not taking place in a country where advanced modernity—reflected in church-state separation, scientific advance, urbanization, and intense social and physical mobility—coexists with persistently high levels of religious commitment, and the high visibility of religion in politics and public life. This is what the rational choice theory of religion, or religious economy-markets approach attempts to explain (e.g., see Finke and Stark 1988; Iannaccone 1991; Stark and Finke 2000). The approach is a prominent theoretical challenge that has emerged from the failure of secularization theory to explain the strength of American religiosity.

The religious economy approach argues that contrary to the expectations of secularization theory, religious pluralism and the separation of church and state do not lead to the decline of religion. Instead they represent a market mechanism, with positive consequences for churches and believers alike. The mechanism pushes churches to become more active in looking for members, if they want to survive in a competitive religious marketplace. It also provides a greater amount of choice that can cater to the diverse needs of individual worshippers. These rational choice expectations are able to explain the vitality of

Chapter 2: Secularization

religion in a pluralistic religious marketplace, such as the American one. They also can explain the decline of religion in European countries, where many dominant churches are historically linked with and reliant on state subsidies, and do little to attract believers, who in turn, have a limited amount of choice. In a nutshell, the degree of competition, and not of modernization, is the relevant explanation of religious growth and decline.

To look at this from a different perspective, the previous distinction between Europe and the United States may suggest that context matters when evaluating the empirical accuracy of the predictions of secularization theory. According to David Martin in *A General Theory of Secularization* (1978), the historical legacy that shapes the relationship between church and state determines the presence and extent of secularization pressures. This, says the British sociologist Grace Davie (1946–) in *Europe: The Exceptional Case: Parameters of Faith in the Modern World* (2002), supports the position of "European exceptionalism" with reference to secularization trends. Religious decline in Europe could be seen as an outcome of the closeness of church and state, which sustained the lazy religious "monopolies" largely responsible for the decline. Europe, then, cannot be treated as a typical situation, although it formed the basis of most theorizing behind the secularization thesis.

REVERSIBLE AND NOT LINEAR

Some of the most prominent events and actors that have appeared in the international political terrain in the post-Soviet era seem to disconfirm the expectations of secularization theory. The rise of religious fundamentalism in recent decades, and of various nativist movements fueled by religious concerns, is a fitting example. Research on the fundamentalist phenomenon explains the growth of these religious movements as a response to advanced modernity and the marginalization of religion (e.g., see Almond, Appleby, and Sivan 2003; Kinnvall 2004; Patrikios and Xezonakis 2016). As discussed by Peter Beyer in *Religion and Globalization* (1994) and Peter Berger in *The Desecularization of the World* (1999), as the pressures of modernity, exemplified in complex phenomena such as globalization, create a state of anxiety and insecurity (see the post-2007 global financial troubles), individuals are likely to turn to sources of guidance that offer renewed certainty and a stable point of reference. In this view, modernity triggers positive developments for churches, as it makes the absolute truths they espouse more appealing. Therefore, contrary to the predictions of secularization theory regarding the decline of religion for individuals and societies, it seems that advancing modernity has led to the exact opposite reaction from certain populations and in certain parts of the world. A similar reading by Philip Jenkins in *The Next Christendom: The Coming of Global Christianity* (2002) applies to other cases of religious resurgence and other types of religious growth that accompany the advance of modernization in Latin American, Asia and Africa.

A recent instance of this backlash trend might be found in the profile of the estimated thousands of Western-born individuals that have joined the Islamic State (ISIS) group in Iraq and Syria. A typical analysis of the phenomenon usually opens with a question that implies disbelief: "Why would Westerners ever want to support and fight for a theocratic regime"? As these fighters are born and raised in the most advanced and liberal societies of the West—for instance, France, Belgium, and Britain—they are exposed to a strong version of societal modernization. And yet, they feel estranged from it, looking for a more "traditionalist" way of life, particularly one focused on Islam. The question posed in those analyses summarizes quite neatly the inability of the secularization thesis, which expects negative outcomes for religion in modernity, to explain such developments.

ONLY ABOUT ORGANIZED RELIGION

Concepts such as "implicit religion," "believing without belonging," and "belonging without believing" (e.g. "cultural" Catholics) privatized religiosity, or spirituality outside the church can serve as yet another critique of the secularization thesis. This type of argument has been adopted by Davie, among others. Her "believing without belonging" thesis builds on statistical trends that make it clear that the indicators of individual religiosity more closely related to "institutional" forms of religion, namely attendance and membership, are declining in Britain and in many other European countries. It is then argued that this does not signify the disappearance of religion and confirmation of secularization theory, but simply the decline of specialized, institutional forms of religion, and its transformation and survival outside the institutional domain. Faith's survival in this postsecular age seems to be about individuals retaining a belief in God or some other supernatural entity, which is held in private or in unconventional settings rather than within an orthodox, organized context.

Although, according to British sociologists David Voas and Alasdair Crockett in "Religion in Britain: Neither Believing nor Belonging" (2005), the available statistics seem to contradict the idea that religious belief survives outside churches, this is an interesting critique of the secularization thesis as it makes the distinction between organized-hierarchical (declining) and private forms of faith (growing). It belongs to a larger body of research dealing with unconventional and new religious movements that promote more individualized versions of faith and have become popular in many advanced societies. It is noteworthy, however, that even this critique of the secularization thesis at the individual level accepts the presence of secularization tendencies at higher levels of analysis. One of the explanations for the decline of institutional religion rests exactly on the weakening of the church's ability to transmit its values from one generation to the next because of the modern pressures of individualization, pluralism, educational attainment, and mobility.

Summary

A proposition with a long pedigree, the secularization thesis revolves around a positive statement about the relationship between modernity and religion. The thesis expects that material and intellectual advances will weaken religion's influence in society at large, in the way religious organizations operate, and in individuals' lives. In classic versions of the thesis, this is usually seen as a linear, irreversible trend. By extension, the end point of the process may lead to the disappearance of religion from modern life.

It is possible to discard the thesis on various grounds. Even a quick inspection of today's newspapers shows that it would be misleading to expect the theory to apply uniformly at all levels (societies, organizations, individuals) and across all countries. This might be interpreted as advice to study the thesis empirically only on one level of analysis. Such a decision would probably provide a "clean" solution and permit straightforward conclusions. Specifically, one would find that religiosity trends are either going up, remaining stable, or declining (micro-level analysis); that a church is either changing internally to become more customer friendly or is retaining the structure and content it had in the past (meso-level analysis); and, finally, that religion either persists as an influence in society, for instance, in public debates regarding life and death issues, or is retreating from that space (macro-level analysis).

This narrow focus on a single level of analysis, however, would be misleading. A final example, the case of American religiosity and how to approach it analytically, will illustrate

Chapter 2: Secularization

why this might be the case. Despite the most recent surveys, which according to the Pew Research Center (2015) reveal a decline in the Christian population in the United States and the rise of the nonreligious, almost four out of five Americans still report some type of religious affiliation. Yet, this individual-level picture ignores some interesting observations about the content of religious affiliation in America, which seems to carry a heavy nonreligious load.

Robert Bellah's "civil religion" concept (1967) is particularly relevant here as an illustration of the content of American religiosity. American civil religion is an expression of national culture and values. It is not merely an application of individual piety, or devotion to God, or even an affiliation with a particular ethnic group. The rituals of this public theology are not restricted within the church, but also extend to Independence Day celebrations and the inauguration of a new president (the original work used as its primary source Kennedy's inaugural speech; see Bellah's "Civil Religion in America" 1967). In *Civil Religion and the Presidency* (1988), Richard Pierard and Robert Linder note the office of president is the focal point of this American civil religion: citizens see the president as a "high priest" who provides guidance in times of suffering.

With this in mind, a visit to the Washington National Cathedral in Washington D.C., an Episcopal congregation, reveals some interesting elements of the worship environment to which the American believer is exposed. Most notably, the worshipper is encountered by statues of presidents Abraham Lincoln and George Washington, stained glass window portrayals of Confederate generals Robert E. Lee and Stonewall Jackson, a carving that depicts the Magna Carta signing, not to mention references to popular culture—particularly, the Star Wars movie series. Therefore, the high religiosity rates that surveys document among the American population are not exclusively a matter of religion in the traditional definition of the phenomenon but are partly about being American. This "natural melding of religion and nationhood" (Demerath 1998, 30), which is a piece of the societal-level picture, provides a plausible explanation to the apparent conundrum of the survival of religious vitality in the United States. It also illustrates the problems of studying the secularization thesis as a uniform phenomenon, by focusing too narrowly on one level of analysis, while ignoring the others.

Bibliography

Almond, Gabriel R., R. Scott Appleby, and Emmanuel Sivan. *Strong Religion: The Rise of Fundamentalisms around the World*. Chicago: University of Chicago Press, 2003.

Ammerman, Nancy T., ed. *Everyday Religion: Observing Modern Religious Lives*. Oxford: Oxford University Press, 2007.

Bellah, Robert. "Civil Religion in America." *Daedalus* 96 (1967): 1–21.

Berger, Peter. *The Desecularization of the World: Resurgent Religion and World Politics*. Washington, DC: Ethics and Public Policy Center, 1999.

Berger, Peter. *The Sacred Canopy: Elements of a Sociological Theory of Religion*. Garden City, NY: Doubleday, 1967.

Beyer, Peter. *Religion and Globalization*. London: Sage, 1994.

Bruce, Steve. *God Is Dead: Secularization in the West*. Oxford: Blackwell, 2002.

Bruce, Steve. *Religion in Modern Britain*. Oxford: Oxford University Press, 1995.

Bruce, Steve. *Secularization: In Defence of an Unfashionable Theory*. Oxford: Oxford University Press, 2011.

Canavan, Kelvin. "The Transformation of Catholic Schools in Australia." *Journal of Religious Education* 47 (1999): 19–24.

Casanova, José. *Public Religions in the Modern World*. Chicago: University of Chicago Press, 1994.

Chandler, Russell. "Team Spirit: U.S. Sports Mania Called Folk Religion." *The Los Angeles Times*, December 31, 1986.

Chaves, Mark. "Denominations as Dual Structures: An Organizational Analysis." *Sociology of Religion* 54 (1993a): 147–169.

Chaves, Mark. "Intraorganizational Power and Internal Secularization in Protestant Denominations." *American Journal of Sociology* 99 (1993b): 1–48.

Chaves, Mark. "Secularization as Declining Religious Authority." *Social Forces* 72 (1994): 749–774.

Davie, Grace. *Europe: The Exceptional Case: Parameters of Faith in the Modern World.* London: Darton, Longman and Todd, 2002.

Davie, Grace. *Religion in Modern Britain: A Memory Mutates.* Oxford: Oxford University Press, 2000.

Davie, Grace. *The Sociology of Religion.* London: Sage, 2007.

Demerath, Nicholas Jay. "Excepting Exceptionalism: American Religion in Comparative Relief." *Annals of the American Academy of Political and Social Science* 558 (1998): 28–37.

DiMaggio, Paul J., and Walter W. Powell. "The Iron Cage Revisited: Institutional Isomorphism and Collective Rationality in Organizational Fields." *American Sociological Review* 48 (1983): 147–160.

Dobbelaere, Karel. "Professionalization and Secularization in the Belgian Catholic Pillar." *Japanese Journal of Religious Studies* 6 (1979): 39–64.

Dobbelaere, Karel. *Secularization: An Analysis at Three Levels.* Bern: Peter Lang, 2002.

Dobbelaere, Karel. "Towards an Integrated Perspective of the Processes Related to the Descriptive Concept of Secularization." *Sociology of Religion* 60 (1999): 229–248.

Ellingson, Stephen. "The Rise of the Megachurches and Changes in Religious Culture: Review Article." *Sociology Compass* 3, no. 1 (2009): 16–30.

Finke, Roger, and Rodney Stark. "Religious Economies and Sacred Canopies: Religious Mobilization in American Cities, 1906." *American Sociological Review* 53 (1988): 41–49.

Firebaugh, Glenn, and Brian Harley. "Trends in U.S. Church Attendance: Secularization and Revival, or Merely Lifecycle Effects?" *Journal for the Scientific Study of Religion* 30 (1991): 487–500.

Fortin, Ernest L. "St. Augustine." In *History of Political Philosophy*, edited by Leo Strauss and Joseph Cropsey, 3rd ed, 176–205. Chicago: Chicago University Press, 1987.

Fox, Jonathan. *An Introduction to Religion and Politics: Theory and Practice.* Abingdon: Routledge, 2013.

Fox, Jonathan. *A World Survey of Religion and the State.* New York: Cambridge University Press, 2008.

Greeley, Andrew. *Religion in Europe at the End of the Second Millennium.* New Brunswick, NJ: Transaction, 2003.

Halman, Loek, and Veerle Draulans. "How Secular Is Europe?" *British Journal of Sociology* 57 (2006): 263–288.

Hamilton, Malcolm B. *The Sociology of Religion: Theoretical and Comparative Perspectives.* London: Routledge, 1995.

Hinings, Christopher R., and Mia Raynard. "Organizational Form, Structure, and Religious Organizations." *Research in the Sociology of Organizations* 41 (2014): 159–186.

Hoffmann, John. "Confidence in Religious Institutions and Secularization: Trends and Implications." *Review of Religious Research* 39 (1998): 321–343.

Iannaccone, Laurence. R. "The Consequences of Religious Market Structure." *Rationality and Society* 3 (1991): 156–177.

Jenkins, Philip. *The Next Christendom: The Coming of Global Christianity.* Oxford: Oxford University Press, 2002.

Kaufmann, Eric P., Vegard Skirbekk, and Anne Goujon. "The End of Secularization in Europe? A Socio-demographic Perspective." *Sociology of Religion* 73, no. 1 (2012): 69–91.

Kinnvall, Catarina. "Globalization and Religious Nationalism: Self, Identity, and the Search for Ontological Security." *Political Psychology* 25, no. 5 (2004): 741–767.

Kleiman, Michael, Nancy Ramsey, and Lorella Palazzo. "Public Confidence in Religious Leaders: A Perspective from Secularization Theory." *Review of Religious Research* 38 (1996): 79–87.

Kohut, Andrew, and Bruce Stokes. *America against the World: How We Are Different and Why We Are Disliked.* New York: Times Books, 2006.

Kotler-Berkowitz, Laurence. "Religion and Voting Behaviour in Great Britain." *British Journal of Political Science* 31 (2001): 523–554.

Lijphart, Arend. "Religious vs. Linguistic vs. Class Voting." *American Political Science Review* 73 (1979): 452–458.

Lipset, Seymour M., and Stein Rokkan, eds. *Party Systems and Voter Alignments: Cross-National Perspectives.* New York: Free Press, 1967.

Luckmann, Thomas. *The Invisible Religion: The Problem of Religion in Modern Society.* New York: Macmillan, 1967.

Lundskow, George. *The Sociology of Religion: A Substantive and Transdisciplinary Approach.* Thousand Oaks, CA: Sage, 2008.

Madeley, John. "A Framework for the Comparative Analysis of Church-State Relations in Europe" *West European Politics* 26 (2003): 23–50.

Manza, Jeff, and Clem Brooks. "The Religious Factor in US Presidential Elections, 1960–1992." *American Journal of Sociology* 103 (1997): 38–81.

Manza, Jeff, and Clem Brooks. *Social Cleavages and Political Change*. Oxford: Oxford University Press, 1999.

Martin, David A. *A General Theory of Secularization*. Oxford: Blackwell, 1978.

Martin, David A. *The Religious and the Secular: Studies in Secularization*. London: Routledge, 1969.

McGuire, Meredith B. *Religion: The Social Context*, 5th ed. Belmont, CA: Wadsworth, 2002.

Meyer, Birgit, and Annelies Moors, eds. *Religion, Media, and the Public Sphere*. Bloomington: Indiana University Press, 2006.

Miller, Donald. *Reinventing American Protestantism*. Berkeley: University of California Press, 1997.

Molokotos-Liederman, Lina. "Identity Crisis: Greece, Orthodoxy, and the European Union." *Journal of Contemporary Religion* 18 (2003): 291–315.

Norris, Pippa, and Ronald Inglehart. *Sacred and Secular: Religion and Politics Worldwide*. Cambridge: Cambridge University Press, 2004.

Olson, Laura, and Adam Warber. "Belonging, Behaving, and Believing: Assessing the Role of Religion on Presidential Approval." *Political Research Quarterly* 61, no. 2 (2008): 192–204.

Patrikios, Stratos. "Religious Deprivatization in Modern Greece." *Journal of Contemporary Religion* 24 (2009): 357–362.

Patrikios, Stratos, and Georgis Xezonakis. "Globalization, Religiosity and Vote Choice: An Empirical Test." In *Globalization and Domestic Politics: Parties, Elections, and Public Opinion*, edited by Jack Vowles and Georgis Xezonakis. Oxford: Oxford University Press, 2016.

Pew Research Center. *America's Changing Religious Landscape*. 2015. http://www.pewforum.org/2015/05/12/americas-changing-religious-landscape/.

Pierard, Richard, and Robert Linder. *Civil Religion and the Presidency*. Grand Rapids, MI: Zondervan, 1988.

Raymond, Christopher. "The Continued Salience of Religious Voting in the United States, Germany, and Great Britain." *Electoral Studies* 30 (2011): 125–135.

Rokkan, Stein. *Citizens, Elections, Parties: Approaches to the Comparative Study of the Processes of Development*. Oslo: Universitetsforlaget, 1970.

Stark, Rodney, and Roger Finke. *Acts of Faith: Explaining the Human Side of Religion*. Berkeley: University of California Press, 2000.

Tarcov, Nathan, and Thomas L. Pangle. "Epilogue: Leo Strauss and the History of Political Philosophy." In *History of Political Philosophy*, edited by Leo Strauss and Joseph Cropsey, 3rd ed., 907–938. Chicago: Chicago University Press, 1987.

Thumma, Scott. "Megachurches of Atlanta." In *Religions of Atlanta: Religious Diversity in the Centennial Olympic City*, edited by Gary Laderman, 199–214. Atlanta, GA: Scholars Press, 1996.

Tilley, James. "We Don't Do God?' Religion and Party Choice in Britain." *British Journal of Political Science* 45 (2014): 907–927.

Tschannen, Olivier. "The Secularization Paradigm: A Systematization." *Journal for the Scientific Study of Religion* 30 (1991): 396–415.

Voas, David, and Alasdair Crockett. "Religion in Britain: Neither Believing nor Belonging." *Sociology* 39, no. 1 (2005): 11–28.

Weber, Max. *The Theory of Social and Economic Organization*. Glencoe, IL: Free Press, 1949.

Williams, William M. *The Sociology of an English Village: Gosforth*. London: Routledge, 1956.

Wilson, Bryan. *Contemporary Transformations of Religion*. Oxford: Oxford University Press, 1976.

Wuthnow, Robert. "A Longitudinal, Cross-National Indicator of Cultural Religious Commitment." *Journal for the Scientific Study of Religion* 16 (1977): 87–99.

Yamane, David. "Secularization on Trial: In Defense of a Neosecularization Paradigm." *Journal for the Scientific Study of Religion* 36 (1997): 109–122.

WEBSITES

American National Election Studies. http://www.electionstudies.org/.

Constitute Project. http://www.constituteproject.org.

Eurobarometer Series. http://www.gesis.org/eurobarometer.

General Social Survey. http://www3.norc.org/Gss+website/.

Google Ngrams. https://books.google.com/ngrams.

Google Trends. https://www.google.com/trends/.

International Religious Freedom Data Set. http://www.thearda.com/Archive/CrossNational.asp.

International Social Survey Program. http://www.issp.org/.

Pew Research Center Surveys. http://www.pewresearch.org/.

Religion and State Data Set. http://www.thearda.com/ras.

World/European Values Survey. http://www.worldvaluessurvey.org.

CHAPTER 3

Lived Secularity: Atheism, Indifference, and the Social Significance of Religion

Isabella Kasselstrand
Assistant Professor of Sociology
California State University Bakersfield

Most of the Western world, including the United States, is becoming increasingly secular. In essence, *secularity* refers to the absence of religious beliefs, religious practices, and religious influence in the public space. As a result of this shift, scholarly attention to secular culture and *lived secularity*—that is the experiences, values, attitudes, beliefs, and behaviors of nonreligious individuals—is more timely than ever.

This study explores the meanings and expressions of secular life in northern Europe, which is often considered the most secular region of the world. Examining secular life in societies where religious rhetoric is nearly absent from politics and the public sphere, and where levels of religious belief and participation are low, provides important insights into global patterns of secularity and into what the future might hold for religion in the United States as well.

As a native of Sweden and then a graduate student in Scotland, I spent twenty-five years in northern Europe, experiencing what it means to live a secular life in cultures where secularity is in fact the norm. As part of my pursuit of a deeper understanding of secular northern Europeans' approach to day-to-day life, family decisions, social relationship, life-cycle ceremonies, religion, and life purpose, I conducted thirty-two semistructured in-depth interviews with Scottish and Swedish couples. The findings from these interviews, which took place during the summer of 2012, are presented throughout this chapter.

Additionally, in order to provide an account of lived secularity, two misconceptions are addressed in the interest of better understanding the nature of *advanced secularity*—a term used here to describe societies where a majority of individuals are secular and where religion has a very weak, if any, role in public discourse. The first misconception is the notion that for a society to be regarded as highly secular, there has to be a large number of people who are outspoken atheists and members of various secular groups. The second misconception is that if churches serve significant functions in a society, then the society is not *really* secular. To counter these misconceptions, this chapter presents and discusses two paradoxes of lived secularity.

- *Paradox of Secularity and Atheism:* The most secular countries in the world have *low* levels of self-identified atheism and organized secularity.

Chapter 3: Lived Secularity: Atheism, Indifference, and the Social Significance of Religion

- *Paradox of Secularity and Church Belonging:* Some of the most secular countries have *high* levels of church membership, church support, and participation in rituals—and yet can still be considered secular.

SECULARIZATION IN NORTHERN EUROPE

The secularization of northern Europe is a powerful and fascinating sociological and historical phenomenon. *Secularization* can be defined as a decline in the social significance of religion. Along with Bryan Wilson's (1982) idea of secularization, the *social significance of religion* refers to the importance of religious beliefs and actions to social institutions and the individual.

Phil Zuckerman, commenting on the diminishing social significance of religion in northern Europe, observes that "[m]any people living in open, democratic societies simply stop finding religious beliefs sustainable or compelling, they lose interest in participating in religious organizations, and they maintain values, exhibit virtues, find meaning, and develop a sense of identity outside the canopy of religious faith" (2014, 53). With the exception of Northern Ireland, the northern European, Protestant nations are characterized by low levels of church attendance, whereas Southern, Catholic Europe has maintained much higher levels. Similar but less drastic differences can be seen on measures of belief in God.

In relation to the study of lived secularity, Charles Taylor (2007) and Steve Bruce (1992) argue that supernatural beliefs should be considered above other indices when exploring what it means to be secular. As will be discussed further later in this chapter, several functional aspects of religion can be observed in otherwise secular societies with low levels of belief in the supernatural. In this context, Bruce makes a crucial point that "[a]lthough it is possible to conceptualize it in other ways, secularization primarily refers to the beliefs of people. The core of what we mean when we talk of this society being more secular than that is that the lives of fewer people in the former than in the latter are influenced by religious beliefs" (1992, 6).

Examining Scotland and Sweden as two national case studies from northern Europe provides us with a deeper understanding of processes of secularization and lived reality of secular culture, including the shaping of meanings, realities, and life experience. These two, relatively small, northern European nations adopted Protestantism during the Reformation in the sixteenth century and experienced a long history of a state church that has since been disestablished. Both nations show declining levels of church attendance, religious identification, and participation in religious rituals and relatively low levels of religious beliefs. Clearly, then, evidence suggests that both Scotland and Sweden are in fact secularizing nations.

Data from the International Social Survey Program (2008) suggest that less than half of Scots and an even lower proportion of Swedes believe in God, life after death, Heaven, or Hell (however, there is a small sample of Scots in this data ($N=173$)). In terms of church attendance, roughly 1 in 5 Scots and 1 in 20 Swedes claim to attend at least monthly. On the global scale, both of these nations are remarkably secular, particularly when contrasted with a society such as the United States with relatively low levels of secularity.

STUDYING LIVED SECULARITY

How to study the secular presents a methodological dilemma that has received surprisingly little attention in the literature. Zuckerman considers this problem a key concern:

> Many scholars have been aggressively debating secularization for years, and yet despite all of the books and articles that have been written on the subject, all of them—at least that I'm aware of—are generally theoretical and broadly historical in nature, and don't examine secular life as it is actually lived by non-believing men and women in the here and now, or the nuances of the secular worldviews of actual individuals who are irreligious. (2008, 96)

Zuckerman discusses the difficulties in researching the absence of something. How do you study secular life choices and experiences when one cannot simply do so by attending a church and thereby, to some extent, participate in the lived experiences as one can with religion at a place of worship? Grace Davie mentions this concern in relation to *vicarious religion*, which describes the type of religious affiliation of people who do not want to participate in religious practices regularly themselves but who would like the church to remain for their own potential use and that of others and the nation as a whole. Davie asks, "how can a sociologist document a phenomenon which almost by definition remains stubbornly below the radar, at least in its 'normal' manifestations?" (2007, 112). She calls for new approaches to grapple with this issue and states that "[t]he crucial point to grasp in terms of sociological method is the need to be attentive to episodes, whether individual or collective, in or through which the implicit becomes explicit" (Davie 2007, 128).

The dilemma of studying a "lack of something" is intriguing and an issue worth contemplating. Clifford Geertz (1968) argues that the most appropriate and accurate studies of religion involve researching and describing how religion is experienced in the moment that it is practiced rather than through memories or opinions of it. It is undoubtedly a challenge to conduct an in-depth ethnographic study of lived experiences of secular life in the same manner as is done within a religious community. Nevertheless, this is not the aim of this research, for the focus is not on secular practices per se, but rather on life choices, values, and beliefs held by nonreligious individuals living in a society with low social significance of religion. Furthermore, this study is not focused simply on the secular isolated from the religious. Instead, in order to understand the secular, one has to explore remnants of religion, including rites of passage, which are largely tied to religious and civil institutions that carry out such practices.

THE PARADOX OF SECULARITY AND ATHEISM

In my attempt to address the first misconception—that secular societies ought to have high levels of self-defined atheism and organized secularity—I contemplated my own experience of moving from Sweden to the United States. Ironically, it took relocating to what is arguably the most religious country in the industrialized world before I met someone who called herself or himself an atheist. At the same time, I had also only met a handful of people in my life who had professed a belief in God. On the basis of both my own personal experience and the interviews I conducted, I have found that, in northern Europe, religion is very rarely, if ever, a topic of conversation. This was also the case for my own grandparents. Although they were born in the 1920s, religion was never an important part of their lives or identities. In fact, they had been married for nearly sixty years when my grandmother first found out that my grandfather did not believe in God. "It just never came up" was the explanation they gave me when I asked why they had not talked about it earlier.

My grandparents' experience highlights the reality that secularity in Sweden is displayed as indifference toward religion, and not atheism. Several scholars, such as Davie (1994), Paul Heelas (2001), Rodney Stark (2000), and Roger Finke (2000), have equated low levels of atheism with low levels of secularity and have assumed that when few people define themselves as atheist, it means that they are implicitly religious or "somewhat religious." For example, Davie uses the fact that only 4 percent of Britons are atheists as an indicator of enduring belief. However, we can question whether people of Britain do in fact *believe*. Davie states that "few people have opted out of religion altogether" (1994, 2). Yet it is questionable whether the fact that only 4 percent are convinced atheists means that the remaining 96 percent *believe*. This notion effectively assumes that all individuals who are uncertain, who simply do not contemplate religion, or who for various reasons are nonreligious but refrain from identifying as atheist in fact *believe*.

By contrast, the present study shows that the lack of the *need* to define oneself as an atheist is instead an indicator of advanced secularity. In line with this position, Bruce states that "[m]ost people did not give up being committed Christians because they became convinced religion was false. It simply ceased to be of any great importance to them. They became indifferent" (2002, 235). He further explains that secularization involves religion becoming less and less important and people losing interest or not being socialized into it by increasingly indifferent parents. In other words, looking at the number of people who express that they are atheist will present a distorted picture of secularity. Rather, advanced secularity is associated with a larger number of people who are what John Shook (2010) calls *apatheists*: that is, they are neither religious nor outspoken atheists, but rather indifferent to or uninterested in religion. Consequently, in order to provide a more thorough account of the paradox that advanced secularity involves low levels of atheism, the next three sections explore three interrelated aspects of the social significance of religion: religious indifference, opinions on atheism, and organized secularity.

RELIGIOUS INDIFFERENCE: "I DON'T CARE ENOUGH ABOUT RELIGION"

Interestingly, this complete unawareness of the fundamental religious beliefs of one's spouse came across in several of my interviews, and not just from my interview with my grandparents. Particularly in the Swedish context, but also in Scotland, my experience was largely similar to Zuckerman's (2008) in that although a majority were not interested in the topic of religion, they agreed to be interviewed for my research in order "to be nice." In the end, very few people actually declined, but they often stated that they "usually don't think about religion at all." Before I even conducted any interviews, I came across a profound indifference in matters related to religion.

Bertil, seventy-seven, is a retired chief of finance, and Birgitta, seventy-five, a retired chef, married in a civil ceremony, even though both are members of the Church of Sweden. Neither Bertil nor Birgitta believes in God, but this lack of belief is not something they think or talk about. Bertil explained that prior to the interview, they had never discussed religious beliefs with each other. Eager to find out why, I asked them if they saw it as a deeply private matter. Bertil answered that "[r]eligion never comes up. It is not because it is private. You just don't think about it. It is not interesting."

In line with this thinking, Zuckerman (2008) speaks of religion in Sweden as a *nonissue*, as unimportant and uninteresting. This sentiment characterized every one of my interviews in

Sweden, as well as many of the interviews in Scotland. Swedish couple Noah and Lydia are a typical example. Noah is a twenty-four-year-old university student who married his wife, twenty-nine-year-old speech therapist, Lydia, in a civil ceremony at the registrar's office. He states that "I don't ever talk about religion with friends and family. It doesn't come up. There is nothing to discuss because everyone believes in exactly the same thing, or I should say don't believe. What is there to talk about?" In other words, religion comes across as an uninteresting topic because almost everyone has the same attitude about it and you typically do not debate a topic on which most people are in agreement. Zuckerman (2008, 7) quotes Ole Riis who describes this attitude as "lukewarm and skeptical." Most Swedes appear to be rather indifferent to religion, and it typically does not arouse any strong feelings one way or the other.

Some of the Scottish interviewees indicated that the younger generation in particular has no interest in religion and that it no longer stirs up powerful emotions. Pamela, thirty-six, asserts that "I don't think there is anyone with strong enough views really." Similarly, Andrew, thirty-seven, a draughtsman, who does not believe in God, states: "I'm open to the idea that there is something out there. I just don't ever think about it. I don't worry about it. If it's there, it's there, but I just get on with my life." In other words, as a society secularizes, it will likely display an increasingly weaker interest in religion.

OPINIONS ON ATHEISM: "ATHEISM IS A PROACTIVE STATEMENT"

Although many northern Europeans lack religious beliefs, that is not an indication that self-identified atheism is any more common there than elsewhere. Few study participants would call themselves atheist, even though many of them recognized that, technically speaking, they *were* atheists. Alice, for example, is a twenty-eight-year-old librarian who married Ludvig, thirty-one, an office manager, in a Church of Sweden ceremony. She is a nonbeliever who holds no supernatural beliefs whatsoever but who does not call herself atheist.

I.K: Would you call yourself atheist?

Alice: No it sounds so ...

Ludvig: But you <u>are</u>!

Alice: Yes ...

I.K: So what does that mean to you then? When someone says they are atheist?

Alice: I think of someone who is against religion. I know it isn't like that but .... It's not like I don't think religion should exist. And that's what I think when I hear atheist.

Similar to Alice, Lydia has no religious beliefs. She agrees with Alice that the word "atheist" holds a different meaning than simply a belief that there is no god.

I.K: Since you don't believe, would you call yourself atheist?

After a long pause:

Lydia: It sounds so harsh. I know you can select it on Facebook, but I have chosen to not do that.

I.K: Why is that?

Lydia: I feel that when you meet people who say that they are atheists, they're typically not very sympathetic people.

Chapter 3: Lived Secularity: Atheism, Indifference, and the Social Significance of Religion

As my interview with Alice and Lydia illustrates, using self-defined atheism as a measure of levels of secularity or nonbelief in a given society is a poor approach, inasmuch as many nonbelievers simultaneously reject the identity or label of *atheist*. In other words, just asking people whether they are atheists tends to underrepresent actual levels of nonbelief in God. Furthermore, rather than being a requisite for secularization as Davie (1994) argues, a need to identify as atheist indicates that religion still has a prominent role in social life.

Similar to the Swedish interviews, there was a sense that Scots perceived the word "atheist" as rather confrontational. Many Scots are atheists in orientation, given that they believe that there is no god, but at the same time, they do not define themselves as such. As mentioned earlier, levels of atheism may be less useful measures of nonreligiosity, in line with Bruce's (2002) assertion that atheism often has a negative connotation. Olivia expressed this notion when she stated: "I think atheist is a bit hard lined. They seem a bit anti-God rather than … I would prefer to accept other people with their own god or faith. On the other hand, I'm not confused about it. I don't think there is any form of god." Ellie, twenty-nine, a research assistant, and Henry, twenty-nine, a househusband, were of the same opinion.

Henry: People used to think that atheist is someone who strongly believes there is no god, as opposed to agnostic where you don't know. But I think now because of Dawkins, and Hitchens, and people like that, I think people now think that atheists have got a problem with religion. And they are intolerant, and …

Ellie: I think that's why I'm so reluctant to say I am an atheist, and even when I hear the word I picture Christopher Hitchens, and just aggressive…. I just prefer to say that I don't believe in God rather than the word atheist.

Ben, 47 works with property rentals, and his wife Pamela, thirty-six, is an optometrist. They are both nonbelievers, but they married in the Church of Scotland to honor the wishes of Pamela's mother. Even though he is a nonbeliever, Ben dislikes atheism, and he perceives it to be an active form of disbelief.

Ben: I'm not religious, but I'm certainly not an atheist. To me, atheism is no different than religion. It's just a belief in something else. As soon as you put a name on it, it's going to become something. I don't have a name for what I am. To me, atheism is more a proactive thing … about stating your case. Rather than not saying anything, you're instead saying "yeah I am an atheist" and in that case you are just religious but in a different way. Atheism is attention seeking. It's just like naming religion—like you want to have a conversation about it.

James, thirty-seven, a minister in the Church of Scotland and his wife Lily, thirty-four a stay-at-home mom, had a similar idea of atheism as a more active stance.

Lily: A lot of the time, atheists I do know are quite angrier or antagonistic. And they see believers as a threat and are annoyed with religion.

James: If you say atheist to me, I think of someone who has sat down and thought about it and rejected God. But when someone says they are not religious, maybe they just haven't really thought about it.

These accounts may serve as examples of Bruce's (2002) argument that secularization does not lead to atheism but to the declining social importance of religion. This is also why nonreligious Swedes and Scots at the same time have relatively positive feelings about religion, in line with Zuckerman's notion that "in a society where most non-religious people are simultaneously anti-religious … that indicates that religion is still a social or cultural force to be reckoned with" (2008, 106).

ORGANIZED SECULARITY: "I'M ONLY A MEMBER BECAUSE I WANTED THE WEDDING CEREMONY"

With a steep increase in Scottish *nones*—meaning those who do not identify with a religion—many Scots are choosing to have a nonreligious ceremony, such as a civil option or a humanist ceremony (which has been legally recognized in Scotland since 2005). Even though such ceremonies are becoming increasingly popular, few of the interview participants felt that it was important for them to be formal members of the Humanist Society. In fact, most of them only became members because membership was required in order to have a humanist wedding ceremony. As Lucy mentioned, "We joined up for the wedding, but our membership lapsed and we didn't renew because we had to pay."

Susan and John are both thirty-eight years old and are both lawyers. Like Lucy, Susan did not see humanist membership as important.

Susan: We are no longer members and I suspect a lot of people aren't. For a lot of churches, collective worship is a core element in expressing your beliefs, and there is no suggestion that we humanists have to hang around other humanists and talk about other humanist stuff.

Jonas, a thirty-three-year-old opera singer, and his wife Gabriella, thirty-two, a violin teacher, are both Swedes, but reside in Glasgow, Scotland. They married in a Scottish humanist ceremony and are both atheists and active humanists. They explain that organized secularity attracts few Swedes.

Gabriella: It's interesting that even though both sides of our families are all atheists, no one is comfortable speaking about it or calling themselves humanist. And when we had our wedding celebration in Sweden, we arranged for some humanist pamphlets to be handed out to anyone who might be interested but of course our families who were supposed to bring them "forgot them at home."

Jonas: Yes, they think we are aggressive in a way. It is so Swedish. The idea that you're not supposed to be anything at all.

This sentiment arguably relates to secularization and the social significance of religion. Many Scots and Swedes do not feel so strongly about these matters that they see the need to gather around this common set of values. Most of the interviewees who married in a humanist ceremony simply wanted a nonreligious option. If religion still played a significant role in Scottish and Swedish societies, it is likely that more individuals would encourage a more active stand on matters of faith and be involved in humanist and atheist groups. If secularity is the societal norm, there is little need for people to organize around their non-belief.

THE PARADOX OF SECULARITY AND CHURCH BELONGING

Although I grew up in a secular family in a small town in southeastern Sweden, the church was very present in my life. During the month of December, we lit candles in the classroom and read stories from the Bible. One year I was given the honor of playing the part of the Virgin Mary in the Nativity play at my school's Christmas ceremony in the church; I was baptized and confirmed in the Church of Sweden; my mom sang in the church choir; and all the funerals and weddings I have been to in Sweden have all been held in the church.

Chapter 3: Lived Secularity: Atheism, Indifference, and the Social Significance of Religion

This exemplifies the second paradox of secularity—that advanced secularity does not necessarily mean that churches are marginalized. Although many Swedes are indifferent to religion—and specifically the supernatural beliefs of religion—they generally like *the church*. In this fashion, many nonbelieving Swedes use the church for baptisms, weddings, funerals, confirmations, school graduations, and the occasional Christmas ceremony. In accordance with Émile Durkheim's (1912–1995) theory on religion and social cohesion, these rituals doubtless have a special cultural place in the lives of many secular Swedes and indeed signify something *sacred*. That is, they carry extraordinary significance set apart from the material realm of everyday life. Yet these rituals are largely secular practices.

It is unconvincing to deem as nonsecular a nation that scores low on measures of religious belief, but that nevertheless has high levels of what is typically considered *objective religiosity*, such as religious participation, membership, or identification. Wilson discusses this idea:

> Loyalty to a specific religious group, even if commitment to its creed has become largely notional, may continue to evoke response, and these generalized, perhaps at times nostalgic, dispositions might continue to provide the basis for voluntary associations to promote particular causes in the field of social welfare, but they do not in themselves show sustained religiosity as such. (1992, 202)

Churches may hold a secular meaning to nonbelievers, suggesting that in some circumstances, church attendance and a sense of belonging may not in fact be a measure of religiosity but of something entirely different. In many aspects, that something may well be secular; that is, it may not be concerned with the supernatural at all. To address this paradox further, the following five sections explore *cultural heritage, rituals, solidarity, community,* and *values,* as five different secular purposes of churches in northern Europe.

CULTURAL HERITAGE: "EVERYONE WANTED TO GO BACK TO THE CHURCH"

The Scottish and Swedish interview participants shared a strong appreciation for a cultural heritage signified by historic church buildings. Many participants mentioned that there is a special atmosphere in the church. In Scotland, the many historical church buildings that have been converted into pubs, hostels, various businesses, shops, and community centers exemplify the declining popularity and authority of religion. Yet, it was very important to most Scots whom I interviewed that the buildings be maintained, even if their purpose has changed.

In Sweden, church buildings are used for school graduations and end-of-term ceremonies. Natalie, forty-eight, a science teacher, and her husband Per, forty, an engineer, discussed the significance of church buildings. Though both are nonbelievers, they were married in their garden by a minister from the Church of Sweden.

> **Natalie:** Three or four years ago they had to do repairs on the church ceiling and we couldn't use it for the school's end of spring term ceremony. Instead, we had it in the gym. They tried to make it nice with balloons and all, but it just wasn't the same. I don't know why. There is a special atmosphere in the church. It feels more special.... The next year we discussed whether we should keep having it in the gym, since we no longer have a state church. But no, *everyone* wanted to go back to the church. The parents all agreed. No one said anything negative about it.

Even if they do not believe in God and even if they rarely—if ever—attend Sunday services, the interview participants did not avoid entering churches. Indeed, they often described the church building as a place to find emotional well-being, without finding God. Caroline, forty-two, who works in clothing sales, is married to Magnus, also forty-two, a musician. They are both nonbelievers, but Caroline explained that the church is a good place to reflect upon oneself. She stated: "The feeling you get in church might be that you find yourself. You believe in yourself. It is something deeper than what you get elsewhere."

Several others agreed with Caroline. Per and Natalie highlighted the atmosphere and the sense of peacefulness to be found in the church.

Natalie: I think everything the church does is really important. To enter a church, for me always gives a sense of peace.

Per: That would be the reason I don't leave the church. That my church money goes to the building. I get the same feeling when I enter some other buildings too, so it's not the Church in itself. It's the church as a physical phenomenon.

Natalie: No, for me there is a spiritual feeling in the building but I can't say what it is. But it doesn't make me religious. I don't go there and pray to god—"oh dear god, make sure it doesn't rain tomorrow." No.

Even though several Swedish interview participants disliked the supernatural elements of a service, they still felt compelled to attend on certain occasions. This is because to the typical Swede, the Church of Sweden represents important historical and cultural traditions, in line with Jay Demerath's (2000) concept of *cultural religion*, which can be defined as identification with a religion and participation in its traditions and rituals without holding supernatural beliefs. Not surprisingly then, among the Swedes that I spoke to, many attend church at Christmas for the purpose of recognizing cultural traditions. Alice and Ludvig described this sentiment.

Alice: We went to midnight mass sometimes. Maybe because we lived next to the church. It wasn't important. But it was nice and relaxed.... And we always read the Gospel of Luke. Every Christmas.

Ludvig: We do that too. We can't open the presents until it's done.

Alice: Midnight mass, reading from the Bible. It's just a tradition.

Ludvig: It's to remember why we celebrate Christmas.

I.K: But does anyone in your family believe in the religious part?

Ludvig: No, no …

This form of *belonging* is nonetheless not to a *religion* per se, but to a social group in a Durkheimian sense and a recognition of a cultural heritage in line with what Danièle Hervieu-Léger (2006) calls a collective, shared memory. This idea was clearly illustrated by Malin, thirty-two, an English teacher in southeastern Sweden. She does not believe in God but stated that "I think what moves me when I go to church is that you feel part of something bigger.... I almost start to cry because I think everyone in the room is there because we believe in something more … but I can't say it's religious."

RITUALS AND CEREMONIES: "A SECULAR CHURCH WEDDING WOULD HAVE BEEN IDEAL"

The concept of cultural religion can also explain why many secular Swedes prefer the church as a site for life-cycle ceremonies such as weddings, funerals, baptism, and confirmation in the church. As I spoke to Swedish participants about weddings and other rituals, many

Chapter 3: Lived Secularity: Atheism, Indifference, and the Social Significance of Religion

stated that anything but a church ceremony would feel incomplete. For example, Markus, twenty-eight, asserted: "I think baptism is important, but I don't know why. Without it, it feels like the child doesn't get a name."

Furthermore, none of the interviewees who find church rituals and traditions important attend church regularly and most of them do not believe. The notion that religious rituals are not performed for supernatural reasons is highlighted with data presented by Anders Bäckström and colleagues (2004, 61–62). Only 29 percent of respondents relate the purpose of baptism predominantly to Christianity or to being part of a religious community. Interestingly, 71 percent see it as an alternative form of *belonging*, namely, as becoming part of society or the church like "everyone else." Similarly, only 23 percent see a church funeral primarily as having a religious purpose, whereas 77 percent view it either as an important tradition or as giving the deceased a dignified departure without attaching a religious meaning to it.

The wish to have a meaningful, traditional, and yet secular church ceremony was a common sentiment in the interviews. Natalie and Per mentioned that until they had agreed to take part in the interview, they had never even considered the fact that they had a Church of Sweden wedding as conflicting with their (lack of) beliefs. Their wedding took place in their garden with a minister from the local area.

> **Natalie:** We had an idea of what we wanted the day to look like. We wanted it to be on Midsummer Eve, musicians playing, and all of that. Of course with the food and drinks, herring and the alcohol. Just like a normal midsummer. We wanted everyone to dance around the midsummer pole and barbecue.... We told the minister about it and he said "that sounds perfect!" Of course he wanted to say something religious, and we were like "we want music, but no hymns."

> **I.K:** And that was okay?

> **Natalie:** Yes, he really deemphasized religion a lot because he must have understood what we wanted, what our wishes were, and he chose his words according to that. He was very willing to make alterations.

In other words, the minister was willing to accommodate to the fact that they were nonbelievers. Along these lines, many couples who had a civil ceremony, some of whom had made an active decision to leave the Church of Sweden, said that they did not personally feel comfortable with the idea of a secular church wedding, but understood why others make this choice. Olof, a school principal, and Rebecka, a guidance counselor, both thirty-two years of age, married in a civil ceremony, but recognized that even if you do not believe, you can still marry in the church out of tradition.

> **I.K:** Why do you think that so many nonbelievers still choose to marry in the church?

> **Rebecka:** Tradition ...

> **I.K:** Do you understand their choice?

> **Rebecka:** Yes I understand it because you don't reflect over it. You don't think about it.

> **Olof:** It's like funerals that we talked about before.... You don't reflect over whether to be in a church or not or what it means.

> **Rebecka:** And yes, "We need to have three hymns during the ceremony. Which hymns should we choose that are the least hallelujah?" So it doesn't get too religious.

Olof: We have heard that from friends that got married.

Rebecka: You want the wedding there but not the religious part.

These secular church traditions demonstrate yet another facet of *cultural religion*: for many Swedish nonbelievers, the church provides rituals that are sacred but to a large extent secular. However, church ceremonies feel special because of their association with tradition and heritage rather than with faith or belief in the supernatural. This sentiment is illustrated by my conversation with Alice.

Alice: My thought is that humans create meaning and the church is a place that creates meaning. But I don't think there is a god in that house.… Even if nothing happens after death, you can create a similar meaning in your life. Traditions are generally more important than religious faith. For me, traditions create the meaning that others might get through religion.

The fact that ceremonies in the church carry a largely secular meaning as cultural practices further shows that just because Swedes value these church traditions, it does not necessarily mean they are *religious*. Stark and Finke (2000), along with Davie (2002), cite the high prevalence of church rituals in the Nordic countries as evidence of the enduring importance of *religion*, when this may instead be an expression of a *cultural heritage*. Along with the Durkheimian perspective, in Sweden, a church wedding offers a ceremonial sense of occasion serving to recognize a collective identity and "something bigger" even for the nonbeliever.

COLLECTIVE SOLIDARITY: "WE CAN ALL HELP PAY FOR THE CHURCH"

Given the roles of the strong welfare states in northern Europe, another aspect of secular church belonging revealed in the Swedish interviews was the collective responsibility for other people's religious needs. Per and Natalie do not want to leave the Church of Sweden despite their lack of beliefs and regular attendance. Per mentioned that he is "closer to exiting the church than Natalie." She mentioned on multiple occasions that she felt like the church "does good things," so I asked her more specifically what this meant.

Natalie: I'm thinking like this: I'm almost political now but in today's society there is not much solidarity anymore … and the only part in today's Sweden where I feel like we still have that is in a way the Church of Sweden. Everyone has … there is this sense of solidarity. It doesn't matter who enters the church. Everyone is welcome. The church still nurtures this sense of solidarity and I feel like that's important. All children get to be baptized, all couples can marry, and all humans get to be buried. It's a humane feeling I don't see anywhere else.

Similarly, Caroline and Magnus would never consider leaving the church despite a lack of belief and attendance. One reason for this feeling is a collective solidarity, in line with Natalie's thoughts.

Magnus: I do believe the church serves a purpose. Even if things are okay for us it can be of an enormous help. It is a safety net in a way.

I.K: So now that you pay part of your salary to the Church, do you think you get your money's worth?

Magnus: Yes, I think so. Yes.

Caroline: I don't question it.… I don't know what my money goes to. But I like the Church. The building in itself is a cultural heritage … and then I think that there are many people that need to go there and we can all help pay for that. We all have different needs.

THE CHURCH AS COMMUNITY: "I WOULDN'T SAY IT'S ABOUT RELIGION"

Two additional reasons for the secular church affiliation in northern Europe emerged in the Scottish data. First, the church often serves as an important source of *community*. Helen recognized the social aspect of the Church of Scotland. She is now an outspoken atheist, but she mentioned that during her years at university she joined a religious group in search of meaning, belonging, and community. Ben and Pamela had similar thoughts on religion as community. However, they also emphasized that not only are religious beliefs and active attendance in decline in Scotland, but so is religion as belonging to a social group.

> **Pamela:** That's another thing…. It is a community thing as well, not a religious thing. That's why my parents pay quite a lot to the church. They give them a lot of money.

> **Ben:** Yeah those two things often get confused: Religion and community.

> **Pamela:** Usually in the past the church was the center of the community. It is not so much of that anymore. But some people still have that connection.

This decline can also be observed in the diminishing, but still somewhat present, role of religion as *cultural defense*. This theory, proposed by David Martin (1978) and Bruce (2002), suggests that in an "us versus them" situation when a religious identity is questioned or challenged, it can strengthen the sense of community, the attachment to that specific group. Many interview participants shared their thoughts on the relations between Scottish Protestants and Catholics. Most of them were aware of a historical tension between adherents of the two religious groups. Nevertheless, few of them had personally experienced any conflicts. Most interview participants believed this was an issue only in the west of Scotland, particularly in Glasgow. Similar to what Michael Rosie (2004) has argued, the interviewees suggested that this tension was generally weak and certainly was not about religion per se.

> **Helen:** I wouldn't say it's about religion. It's a cultural community. They very much identify themselves as Catholic because their grandparents are Irish. There was a big Irish Catholic community in Glasgow, and they were very much, "We are Catholic and we support Celtic and the Protestants support Rangers." And you know, being Irish and going to Catholic schools, it was very much about this self-identification, but I don't think they were really genuinely Catholic in the sense that they genuinely lived their lives according to the Catholic Church and many of them don't actually believe. It definitely is a social and cultural, ehm … community association much more than religious.

Religion often serves as a social institution around which different ethnic and social groups gather. With secularization, the religious element gradually fades away, but individuals continue to identify with these groups or communities. This illustrates how religion can remain relevant longer or appear to have a stronger place in a secular society.

CHRISTIAN VALUES: "CHRISTIANITY IS ABOUT GOODNESS AS OPPOSED TO GOD"

In addition to its role as community, many couples I interviewed in Scotland linked Christianity to *values*. Pamela and Ben discussed the ambiguity of the term *Christian*.

> **I.K:** If people asked you if you are religious, would you say yes or no?

> **Pamela and Ben:** No.

> **I.K:** What about if they ask you if you're a Christian?

Ben: If you want to take that conversation into context then I would say I have Christian values but I still call them commonsense values, if you call them Christian values, then yeah.

Pamela and Ben further explained that many Scots associate *Christian* with *being a good person*. Ben, who only agreed to a religious wedding for Pamela's (or maybe Pamela's mother's) sake, mentioned that when they got married, he searched for parts of Christianity that he agreed with and focused on those parts rather than the religious element. For him, this meant Christian values.

I.K: When you married in the church and they talked about God, what did this mean to you?

Ben: I interpreted those words as goodness as opposed to God. It makes sense to me, and for that reason it was really interesting. I do think some churches know that as far as attendance, it's a problem, but that's not to say people don't attend their own church so to speak, and I don't mean that they are religious.

I.K: So what do you mean then?

Ben: It's more about the values.

Nicole, forty-six, who works in the banking industry, mentioned the importance of Christian values in much the same vein as Pamela and Ben.

Nicole: To me, being a Christian is about treating others the way you want to be treated, and have respect for people, and all that, you know it's more about values actually than a true religious belief.

I.K: It's more about how you act?

Nicole: Yes.

Although religious beliefs are decreasing, a remaining function of Christianity in Scotland is to teach morality. Callum Brown describes this idea.

> The conundrum may perhaps be best understood by seeing "Christian" as a claim not so much to religious belonging as to "niceness"—a statement of attachment to personal moral qualities which, while not necessarily Christian, are nonetheless best expressed, in the cultural absence of a better rhetoric, by that word. To proclaim oneself to be a 'Christian' is, in British culture, to make a claim to human goodness. (2007, 471)

The notion that Christianity is about being a good person rather than holding certain religious beliefs suggests that Scotland is becoming increasingly secular. Christianity in Scotland seems to have strayed far from its orthodox interpretation, in line with Bruce's (1996, 26) claim of secularization as "the erosion of the supernatural" and a continuous decline in traditional beliefs. This, again, suggests that nonbelievers in increasingly secular societies can—without attaching a supernatural meaning—support and embrace certain aspects of religion in everyday life. Secularity does not necessarily mean a clean break from all aspects of religion.

SECULARITY IN THE UNITED STATES

At the age of twenty-one, I left Sweden for the United States. As I adjusted to my new life as an undergraduate student in California, I was compelled to examine and reconsider the assumptions I had arrived with: I noticed immediately that religion played a very different, and much more significant role in American society than in northern Europe. Whether I encountered Christians, Muslims, or atheists, people spoke passionately about their own beliefs. Religion was present in the media, in politics, and around the dinner table. For the first time in my life, I had friends, and sometimes strangers, ask me what I believed in. My perception of religion in the United States is that most people are firmly aware of their religiosity or secularity, contrary to what I experienced in Scotland and Sweden.

Unlike the case in Sweden, where secularity is the norm, Americans are expected to be religious and active church going is considered the norm. Data from the General Social Survey 2012 (Smith et al. 2013) suggest that around 46 percent of Americans claim to attend church at least monthly and 91 percent believe in God or a higher power. Furthermore, as described by Jesse Smith (2010), in the United States there is a stigma associated with atheism and nonbelief. Some secular Americans do "come out" as nonbelievers to friends and family, but others hide it out of fear of social exclusion.

Even though the United States remains highly religious, it has also experienced a decline in various aspects of religion. For example, according to the Pew Research Center (2015), the percentage of Americans that are religiously unaffiliated has increased from 16.1 to 22.6 between 2007 and 2014. Additionally, there has been an increase in the proportion of theses unaffiliated Americans that explicitly state that they are atheists or agnostics. Furthermore, the percentage of Americans who claim to "never" attend church has risen from 9 percent in the early 1970s to 25 percent today (Zuckerman 2014). Based on our knowledge of lived secularity in less religious societies, we can therefore gain a better understanding of what the future of secularity may look like in the United States. It is clear that the United States is still highly religious, despite becoming increasingly secular. In fact, during the earlier stages of secularization, we will arguably see an *increase* in the number of self-identified atheists as well as individuals who participate in organized nonreligion. However, based on the Swedish and Scottish cases, I argue that a society that is profoundly secular with low social significance of religion will actually see a *decrease* in the number of self-identified atheists and the "need" to associate with various secular groups. Although most religious nones in America are not active atheists (Zuckerman 2014), secularization in the United States has not yet reached the point of normative secularity.

SCOTLAND AND SWEDEN: CONTEXTUAL DIFFERENCES

Both Scotland and Sweden are remarkably secular, but they display important contextual differences in the characteristics of secularity. Sweden is arguably more secular than Scotland; indicators consistently point to lower levels of belief in Sweden than in Scotland. Thus, Sweden exemplifies more advanced secularity, whereas Scotland may serve as a crucial middle ground between the highly secular Sweden and societies such as the United States, with relatively low levels of secularity.

Along with a profound indifference toward religion seen particularly in Sweden but also in Scotland, most of the Swedish interviewees were under the impression that the norm was to *not* believe. Openly religious Swedes were described as "odd" (Noah, twenty-four) or "unique" (Lydia, twenty-nine). This did not come across as strongly in the Scottish context, particularly not in the older generations. More advanced secularization in Sweden may explain why many of the Swedish, but few of the Scottish, participants mentioned a social norm of nonbelief. This also explains why being openly religious, particularly among older Scots, is not perceived as "odd," as was the impression gleaned from the Swedish interviews.

Furthermore, although most participants related atheism to an active standpoint, Scots felt more comfortable defining themselves as atheists and displayed a much stronger awareness of their nonreligiosity than did the Swedes. It often came across as something the Scots had contemplated at length. As such, they were also more likely to associate themselves with secular organizations and to be married in a secular ceremony. At the same time, they were not particularly interested in being active members of any church.

It is also clear that there are key differences in how secularity has developed in these two nations. As seen in the section on the paradox of secularity and church belonging, the remaining functions of churches differ in secular Scotland and Sweden. A majority of Swedes still identify with the Church of Sweden and the religious traditions, such as baptism, church weddings, and funerals that mark key points in the life cycle. By contrast, Scots have ceased to identify with the Church of Scotland altogether and no longer participate in its rituals, although they still see the church as part of Scotland's historic heritage, sense of community, and carrier of values.

Despite such differences, Scotland and Sweden amply serve as northern European case studies illustrating the two paradoxes of secularity. Both peoples hold similar perceptions on atheism, and both are largely indifferent to religion, in accordance with the first paradox of secularity. Although the remaining roles of churches differ in the two nations, they both highlight the second paradox of secularity: the paradox that secular nations can have widespread church support and that church belonging may sometimes be considered a secular matter.

Summary

The perceived importance of religion in people's lives can reveal a lot about contemporary secularity. One reason often offered in support against secularization is that few people are atheists or have rejected all aspects of religion. On the contrary, as this study shows, the lack of the *need* to define oneself as atheist is instead an indicator of advanced secularity. Advanced secularity is associated with a sharp decline in the perceived importance of religion. Thus, in a secular culture, religion fails to generate any strong reactions or interest: People stop talking about religion, they stop thinking about it—they become indifferent.

Furthermore, secularity does not mean hostility toward religion or a complete rejection of all aspects of religion. In a society with low levels of tension and polarization between the religious and the secular and with most people being merely indifferent to religion, there will be little incentive to reject the church entirely. Instead, nonreligious individuals may embrace secular aspects of religion, such as community, life-cycle rituals, cultural identification, and its teachings of morality and solidarity.

From my own experience of living a secular life in three different nations, I ironically sensed a weaker social significance of religion at my own Confirmation in the Church of Sweden than at various meetings with atheists, skeptics, and humanists in the United States. Bruce ably and succinctly sums up the arguments presented in this chapter: "In so far as I can imagine an endpoint, it would not be self-conscious irreligion; you have to care too much about religion to be irreligious" (2002, 42).

Bibliography

Bäckström, Anders, Ninna Edgardh Beckman, and Per Pettersson. *Religiös Förändring I Norra Europa. En Studie av Sverige. Från statskyrka till fri folkkyrka. Slutrapport [Religious Change in Northern Europe. The Case of Sweden. From State Church to Free Folk Church. Final report]*. Stockholm, Sweden: Verbum Förlag, 2004.

Brown, Callum G. "Secularization, the Growth of Militancy and the Spiritual Revolution: Religious Change and Gender Power in Britain, 1901–2001." *Historical Research* 80, no. 209 (2007): 393–418.

Bruce, Steve. *God Is Dead*. Oxford: Blackwell Publishing, 2002.

Bruce, Steve. "Introduction." In *Religion and Modernization: Sociologists and Historians Debate the Secularization Thesis*, edited by Steve Bruce, 1–8. Oxford: Oxford University Press, 1996.

Bruce, Steve. *Religion in the Modern World: From Cathedrals to Cults*. Oxford: Oxford University Press, 1996.

Davie, Grace. *Europe: The Exceptional Case: Parameters of Faith in the Modern World*. London: Darton, Longman, and Todd, 2002.

Davie, Grace. *Religion in Britain since 1945: Believing without Belonging*. Oxford: Blackwell, 1994.

Davie, Grace. *The Sociology of Religion*. London: SAGE, 2007.

Demerath, Nicholas Jay. "The Rise of 'Cultural Religion' in European Christianity: Learning from Poland, Northern Ireland, and Sweden." *Social Compass* 47, no. 1 (2000): 127–139.

Durkheim, Émile. *The Elementary Forms of Religious Life*, translated by Karen. E. Fields. New York: Free Press, 1995. First published 1912.

Geertz, Clifford. *Islam Observed*. Chicago: University of Chicago Press, 1968.

Heelas, Paul. "*The Spiritual Revolution: From 'Religion' to 'Spirituality.'*" In *Religions in the Modern World: Traditions and Transformations*, edited by Linda Woodhead, Paul Fletcher, Hiroko Kawanami, and David Smith, 357–377. London: Routlege, 2002.

Hervieu-Léger, Danièle. "The Role of Religion in Establishing Social Cohesion." In *Religion in the New Europe*, edited by Krzysztof Michalski, 45–63. Budapest, Hungary: Central European University Press, 2006.

International Social Survey Program Research Group. International Social Survey Program (ISSP): Religion. Cologne Germany: GESIS [distributor], 2011.

Martin, David. *A General Theory of Secularisation*. Oxford: Blackwell, 1978.

Pew Research Center. "America's Changing Religious Landscape," May 12, 2015. http://www.pewforum.org/2015/05/12/americas-changing-religious-landscape.

Rosie, Michael. *The Sectarian Myth in Scotland: Of Bitter Memory and Bigotry*. Basingstoke, UK: Palgrave Macmillan, 2004.

Shook, John R. *The God Debates: A 21st Century God for Atheists and Believers (and Everyone in Between)*. Hoboken, NJ: Wiley-Blackwell, 2010.

Smith, Jesse M. "Becoming an Atheist in America: Constructing Identity and Meaning from the Rejection of Theism." *Sociology of Religion* 72, no. 2 (2010): 215–237.

Smith, Tom W. Peter Marsden, Michael Hout, and Jibum Kim. *General Social Survey, 2012* [data file]. Chicago: National Opinion Research Center [producer], 2013.

Stark, Rodney, and Roger Finke. *Acts of Faith: Explaining the Human Side of Religion*. Berkeley: University of California Press, 2000.

Taylor, Charles. *A Secular Age*. Cambridge, MA: Belknap Press of Harvard University Press, 2007.

Wilson, Bryan. "Reflections of a Many Sided Controversy." In *Religion and Modernization: Sociologists and Historians Debate the Secularization Thesis*, edited by Steve Bruce, 195–210. Oxford: Oxford University Press, 1992.

Wilson, Bryan. *Religion in Sociological Perspective*. London: Oxford University Press. 1982.

Zuckerman, Phil. *Living the Secular Life: New Answers to Old Questions*. New York: Penguin, 2014.

Zuckerman, Phil. *Society without God*. New York: New York University Press, 2008.

CHAPTER 4

Believing in Belief: Toward the Secularization of Faith in Global Economies

Abby Day
Department of Religious Studies
University of Kent, Canterbury, UK

It seems so simple. The question on the survey is clear: "Do you believe in God?" Yes or no? It would be easy to mark an answer on the survey, but you pause. Maybe, you think, it depends on what they mean by "believe." And, what they mean by "God."

In practice, belief tends to refer to something that is unproven: it is a provisional statement incorporating both faith and doubt. It's not such an easy question after all, although the people who invent the surveys hope you won't notice. They may be the same people who write academic articles using words like *believer* or *unbeliever*, as if readers will understand what they mean. But what do they mean by *believer*, written without further qualification? Belief may be the main word in Christianity's creed, but it is also one of the five *pillars*, or foundational elements, of Islam. When written or spoken in most Euro-American countries, the term *believer* is implicit and coyly Christian: of course, it means "believe in the Christian God." That it is left without explanation only indicates the way Christian thinking has dominated the West and the academia within it. But, as this chapter will argue, something is changing. *Belief* is a loaded word, usually undefined, and yet it forms survey questions, book titles, and now the latest ad for a soft drink and t-shirts for a political party. If you're like many people, you may look at that survey question again, shrug, and put a tick for "yes." Hedge your bets. Occasionally, a survey may pose the question more richly, inviting you to score your belief from weak to strong—as if it would not vary by the time of day or circumstances: belief has a way of strengthening when, for example, a loved one falls ill. One survey team (Abercrombie et al. 1970, 106) tried to qualify the standard question about belief in God by asking if respondents believed in a God who could change the events on earth. One person replied: "No, just the ordinary one."

In this chapter, the genealogy of how belief is understood and deployed in the social sciences will be traced and some of its current problems in academic discussion will be examined. Meanwhile, as academics tussle over what it should mean and when it should or should not be used, *belief* has been turned into a global commodity in the service of capitalism and into sly political code. One aspect of its meaning becomes clear: *belief* is the word to use when something sacred is at stake. And, in an increasingly secularizing world, it is becoming detached from its religious roots and is put to service for more everyday, secular purposes.

Chapter 4: Believing in Belief: Toward the Secularization of Faith in Global Economies

This chapter reviews examples of some of the theories that try to explain what belief means and how it should or should not be used. But belief actually has a variety of meanings, some of which are deeply embedded in Christian tradition, theology, and imagination—and some that are not.

Looking outward to the lived, everyday world of people in both Christian-dominated and non-Christian countries, this chapter will explore how belief is part of the language of everyday conversations and communications from a variety of sources. Examination shows that belief is a strong identity marker tagging what is held to be sacred by the "believer" and his or her intended audience, expressing doubt, certainty, faith, hope, allegiance, love, and loyalty. Because belief is so important in everyday discourse, capitalist enterprises appropriate it in their search for customers and profits. The chapter concludes by suggesting that the rise of a secularized, global economy liberally acquires popular, emotional, rational, and relational forms of belief in processes that may be replacing both institutional and civil forms of religion in Euro-American and other contexts.

SCHOLARLY SCHISMS ABOUT BELIEF

A turning point in the scholarly understanding of religion in the United States was Stephen Warner's (1941–) seminal paper proposing a "new paradigm," whereby religion was to be understood as transforming rather than declining. Citing numerous sources, Warner pointed to evidence that people who self-identify on surveys as believing in God but not attending church should be viewed as "unchurched" (Warner 1993, 1053) rather than unreligious or secular.

A similar move was made in Britain by Grace Davie (1946–) in her groundbreaking book *Religion in Britain Since 1945: Believing without Belonging* (1994). Her text was, and remains, standard reading for students in religious studies and sociology of religion. The now widely received argument claims that people maintain a private belief in God or other Christian-associated ideals, without attending church or participating in other Christian rites. Confirmations have drastically receded over the last four decades, as have, albeit more slowly, other forms of Christian participation, such as baptisms, funerals, and weddings, but this does not necessarily mean that people have abandoned their Christian faith altogether.

Davie's claim is striking in its simplicity and ramifications: as surveys show that the majority of British people believe in God but do not regularly attend church, it is more accurate to describe them as "unchurched" rather than secular (1994, 12–13). If that were true, it would put to rest arguments that suggest societies have become more secular than religious, and instead, it would re-establish Christianity as a dominant and not dying form of religion, with the majority of the population in Euro-American countries seen as passively religious. The general lack of critical opposition to her theory indicates the relief with which academics in religious studies and the sociology of religion accepted it. In contrast, David Voas (1955–) and Alasdair Crockett (c. 1968–2006) have argued that it was not enough to judge religiosity by an answer to an unweighted survey question: "unless these beliefs make a substantial difference in their lives, religion may consist of little more than opinions to be gathered by pollsters" (2005, 14). Although they, at least, attempt to nuance belief somewhat, they do not offer any particular set of definitions to help scholars move forward with the meaning of belief.

54   MACMILLAN INTERDISCIPLINARY HANDBOOKS

Chapter 4: Believing in Belief: Toward the Secularization of Faith in Global Economies

Just as Warner suggested religion was not declining, only transforming, and the future for religion seemed bright, embedded in Davie's and Warner's theory was a single, remarkable silence: what did they mean by belief? Although Davie writes that although church attendance had declined "some sort of belief persists" (1994, 107), she never defines in her book what she means by belief. The words "some sort" allow for a wide margin of interpretation, as does one footnote: "The term 'belief' is, of course, a wide one, it does not imply the acceptance of particular credal statements" (Davie 1994, 115). By not defining the term and linking it specifically to churched or unchurched behaviors, she implicitly conveys the meaning of belief as belief in God or belief in Christianity. Although Davie is not alone in her implicit Christianization of belief, her work became significant because her countersecularization claim was so strong.

TROUBLE IN ANTHROPOLOGY

Within anthropology, belief has a long and troubled history. Anthropologists like the word *trouble*, not because it means something bad, or antisocial, but because it signifies an undertaking to work out, or deconstruct, as anthropologists like to say, what is often taken for granted. It took anthropology as a discipline the better part of a century to cohere in its opposition to using the term *belief* in anthropological study. This trouble had its roots in the work of the first professor of social anthropology, Edward Burnett Tylor (1832–1917). Tylor was not an anthropologist in the contemporary sense of the word. Although modern-day anthropologists invariably conduct fieldwork, usually in places far removed from the anthropologists' everyday milieu, Tylor read the reports of other people, notably missionaries, who had ventured far from European societies and encountered people they described as *primitives* or *savages*. Many took it for granted that those unfamiliar societies were less advanced than European societies, and Tylor was no exception. In *Primitive Culture* ([1871] 1958), Tylor argued that the roots of all religion lay in a fundamental mistake. He interpreted accounts of ancestor worship and, from there, developed a theory of *animism*, meaning a belief that everything, sentient or otherwise, has a soul. He argued that religion sprung from people's need to explain such uncanny phenomena as seeing someone's spirit. Although Europeans would know, he argued, that such visions were merely part of a dream, less developed people, in his view, mistakenly thought they were actually seeing their deceased relatives returning from the dead. Those false beliefs were, he suggested, similar to the beliefs held by children in his Victorian society that they one day, through the benefit of scientific reasoning, would discard. His view of belief was that it provided a rational, if incorrect, view of the world. It was not only mistaken but also embedded in a typically Victorian view of the progress of mankind (and most definitely of "man"). That idea was profoundly influenced by emerging notions of evolution in which ideas like belief could be seen as understandable within a model that showed—and favored—an apparently universal improvement in people's thinking and physical adaptations. Tylor's definition of religion as "a belief in spirits" and his related theories form the basis of most academic and popular views about religion in the twenty-first century. And yet, it still leaves the word *belief* undefined, although it is linked implicitly to a false view as opposed to, for example, the apparent truth of science. It does much to explain, nevertheless, how dependent on an idea of belief disciplines have become, particularly those who favor using large-scale surveys to measure whether or not people are religious. Scholars sometimes use the term *propositional* to describe beliefs that represent a debatable truth-claim about reality. Agreeing with a statement like "I believe in God" seems to assert a position without indicating what kind, or to what extent, one may believe.

RELIGION: BEYOND RELIGION

MEANING AND BELIEF

Along the scale of belief would be people whose beliefs lend their lives an important sense of meaning. This mode of belief is particularly salient for those in the business of convincing people they need a certain religion or a certain product. The view that people everywhere and at all times have been searching for meaning was central to Max Weber's (1864–1920) theories of religion, stemming from his view that people are driven to reflect on "ethical and religious questions, driven not by material need but by an inner compulsion to understand the world as a meaningful cosmos and to take up a position toward it" (Weber [1922] 1978, 117). The sociologist of religion Peter Berger (1929–) later accepted the same proposition, assuming that a need to "impose a meaningful order upon reality" (1967, 22) is universally instinctive.

Émile Durkheim (1858–1917) analyzed belief from a different perspective and influenced the future of anthropology as strongly as Weber influenced sociology. Like Tylor, Durkheim gained his ideas about religion from reading other people's accounts, most significantly the observations of aboriginal people in what became known as Australia. Durkheim theorized that belief was produced through the ecstasy of collective human ritual action. In celebrating together, the people, erroneously, according to Durkheim, projected a source of their joy onto an image of their particular *totem*. They were in fact he argued, worshipping themselves, as a collective, or, he concluded, as a society. Although, like Tylor, he assumed an error on behalf of the people being studied, he made three important moves that would influence how belief would be interpreted by academics and appropriated by politicians and capitalists.

1. He stressed the importance of embodied practice. Belief had a performative value. In other words, it could exert a force, even a change, on the society that created and adopted it.

2. Belief was emotional rather than intellectual or propositional. What was felt and collectively experienced as joy or, in his term *collective effervescence* was not an unnecessary adjunct to religion but its source.

3. He removed the need for a supernatural, transcendent object of worship. Unlike Tylor, he allowed that a belief in a religion was not necessarily linked to a spirit, or to a rational intellectualist statement, but rather it was "a unified system of beliefs and practices relative to sacred things" (1915, 47). His argument that societies distinguished between the "sacred" and the "profane" opened the way forward for other, more secular forms of belief and replacements for divine-based religions.

One of the legacies of Durkheim's definition was a continuing question as to what was meant by *sacred*. From a social-scientific disciplinary standpoint, sacrality is socially created and contingent. This view contrasts with, for example, theologians, and philosophers who often describe "the sacred" as preexisting humanity. Just as they treat belief, scholars often betray their Christian-centric roots by not only varying in how they use "the sacred," but they often leave it unmarked, as if they and their readers all know that it refers to something made by God.

Once beliefs were understood as being not universally dependent on supernatural beings, they could be powerfully and creatively harnessed to classify that which was sacred and profane. A study about witchcraft among the Azande in Africa by Edward Evans Evans-Pritchard (1902–1973) convincingly demonstrated that people's witchcraft beliefs helped them explain the otherwise inexplicable. The example he used was of a granary, or grain

Chapter 4: Believing in Belief: Toward the Secularization of Faith in Global Economies

store, that might collapse at any given moment and kill or injure people resting in its shade. Just as in the twenty-first century someone might ask why a young, good person is killed in a traffic accident, or contracts an incurable disease, the problem is the same: why do bad things happen to good people? Why would someone just happen to be in the wrong place at the wrong time? One now might hear people talk about the notion of "fate" or that "everything happens for a reason." In 2007, a survey by Cancer Research UK found that a quarter of people believe cancer is caused entirely by fate.

Evans-Pritchard observed that the Azande explained such misfortunes through the curse of a witch: "Witchcraft explains the co-incidence of these two happenings" ([1937] 1976, 23). The recourse was to identify the witch and resolve whatever dispute might exist that caused the witch to lay a curse. Although beliefs could create socially cohesive actions, they could also serve to exclude and discriminate against anything, or anyone, deemed to be threatening to the status quo.

The observation that beliefs could be produced through differing views of what was sacred and profane influenced the anthropologist Mary Douglas (1921–2007) in her work on what was sacred, or pure, and what was "polluted." Douglas's revisiting of Durkheim further distanced the anthropological view of belief as supernaturally referenced. She worked to show that beliefs satisfy a social concern in which "the metaphysic is a by-product, as it were, of the urgent practical concern" (1966, 113). This furthered Durkheim's argument that beliefs are not static or universal, but rather are created collectively to respond to changing circumstances.

MOVES AGAINST BELIEF

Shortly after Douglas published her work on purity and danger, the anthropological distrust of the term *belief* arose through the work of Rodney Needham (1923–2006) who pointed out that anthropologists had failed to account for how they were using the term *belief*. Through a review of mainly philosophical literature, Needham argued that the term should not be used, as it did not have "a natural resemblance among men" and it did not belong to "the common behaviour of mankind" (1972, 188). Overlooking for a moment the universalizing tone, it is important to credit Needham with shaking from anthropology an unspoken assumption that belief would mean the same, and be equally important, anywhere and everywhere. This kind of assumption was deeply embedded in anthropologists' own cultural backgrounds in societies dominated by Christianity.

The Christian-centric nature of belief was interrogated by one of the few religious studies scholars to ever problematize it, Wilfred Cantwell Smith (1916–2000), who examined at length how belief appeared and changed in Christianity over time. He argued that belief was initially a term of love (from *beloved*), trust, and loyalty and then developed into the more recent sense of incorporating ideas of membership, proposition, and doubt (Smith 1979). Later in this chapter, the idea of earlier forms of belief will become more important as its connections with loyalty are explored.

An anthropologist close to Needham later focused on Smith to move Needham's discussion forward. In "Christians as Believers" (1982), Malcolm Ruel (1927–2010) followed Needham to some extent, but created a stronger critique of how the term *belief* was used to mean different things to different people at different times. Here, he described strong versus weak forms of belief, arguing that an everyday weak version of belief generally refers to a sense of expectation or assumption, either of oneself or others. The

RELIGION: BEYOND RELIGION

57

strong form relates to categorizations that usually draw on its Christian use. Ruel concluded that anthropologists ought to dispense with the term and use *faith* instead as this would be more compatible with non-Christian religions. One of the most significant formulations Ruel proposed was to think of belief when used in practice to either mean a "belief that," followed by some propositional statement such as "belief that God exists" or, quite differently, "belief in," as in "I believe in God by which I mean I trust and love him" (1982, 103).

Thus far, anthropologists stayed with the idea that belief was directly related to religion, particularly Christianity, and concerned people's feelings, practices, and ideas. In *Genealogies of Religion* (1993), Talal Asad (1932–) created a new direction of particular relevance to the discussion that follows here. He argued that the style and form of religion, and its related beliefs, were determined by powerful leaders. These leaders, at various points in history, decided what certain forms of belief would be legitimate and what would not. His work shifted the anthropological gaze from one based on ideas about meaning and order to one that would become temporally and spatially contingent. In the Middle Ages, he argued, the practice of religion was situated in forms of knowledge and related practices. This knowledge was threatened during the Enlightenment and the rise of science, which demanded forms of evidence and reason. In response to that threat, he argued, religious leaders stressed the invisible, hidden, nature of belief. Religious belief was given a separate, private, domain removed from the demands of empiricists. Thus, according to Asad, an "emphasis on belief meant that henceforth religion could be conceived as a set of propositions to which believers gave assent" (1993, 40–41).

Joel Robbins (1961–) also worked to reposition belief as something that would change over place and time. In "Continuity Thinking and the Problem of Christian Culture" (2007), he drew on the distinction Ruel made between "believing in" and "believing that" to discuss how the meaning of belief varies. He proposed that the phrase "to believe in" represents a cross-culturally acceptable concept of having faith or trust in the object being believed. Robbins argued that expecting people to convey conveniently their beliefs in "belief that" propositional statements ignores how belief varies across place and time. Robbins urged anthropologists to find out whether people were "really Christian" by examining their actions. A range of actions might be construed as "really Christian" and many of these actions may have more to do with delineating boundaries than with more obvious holy acts.

RATIONALITY AND BELIEF

The idea of propositional belief can be understood more widely within the framework of *rationality*. Terms like *rationality* and *belief* are concepts held together in a relationship, often conceived and sometimes spoken as opposites, dichotomous, in implicit contradiction. Although the word *rationality* has no single accepted definition and may be viewed in a number of ways, the key formulations of interest center on two qualities of what rationality may mean in theory and practice: as a description of a reasonable, evidence-based mode of thinking, and as a practice, or means to an end. The famous seventeenth-century declaration of René Descartes (1596–1650) that "I think therefore I am" provided a sense not only of the importance of rational thought but also of its intrinsic link to the essence of human identity. There was, of course, a corollary: if someone was not "rational," could he or she be human? The human/nonhuman or civilized/primitive dichotomy has had a long and problematic history throughout the study of religion, most markedly in the process of

58   MACMILLAN INTERDISCIPLINARY HANDBOOKS

colonization. Missionaries, explorers, and colonial masters studied indigenous people in the areas they wanted to conquer and considered a common question: are "they" like "us"? The answer to this question had significant ramifications in terms of how easy it would be to conquer and control the "natives." How well were they organized, and along what lines, and how adaptable would they be to change? Given that the "Western" colonial powers were self-styled rationalists, it was not a difficult process to frame the "primitive" others as irrational "believers." This process has ramifications to this day.

Privileging rationality over belief created issues that continue to tax scholars, who typically argue in their critique of rationality that there is no *truth*, or if there were, then there would be multiple truths depending on multiple contexts. A propositional belief is one that may be subject to interrogations about its reasonability and evidence. The second most widely used form of *rational* refers to how it corresponds to achieving desirable objectives or outcomes. Weber's discussion of rationalization in *Economy and Society* ([1922] 1978) related to processes of efficiency or bureaucratization being inevitable, and mutually constitutive, processes of modernization. The problem, as Weber described it, was that those continued processes lead people to experience "disenchantment" and entrapment within what he described as the "iron cage" ([1922] 1978).

So far, academic discussions about belief have been reviewed, with the main point being that there is little agreement about how and when the term is best used. What is clear, however, is that belief is a word so rich and varied in meaning that it needs to be understood in specific contexts of time, place, and people. The next section gives examples of how academics have done just that—with the help, notably, of laypeople who actually use the word in their everyday experiences.

BELIEF TALK

This section explores examples from a 2013 longitudinal research project examining how the term *belief* is used in everyday language and for what purpose. The project's objectives were to explore how beliefs may be defined and how they have changed over time, particularly among young people who had been interviewed five years earlier, when they were as young as fourteen and fifteen years old. The years between fourteen and twenty are some of the most significant in a person's life, mainly because of the rapidity of change, such as leaving school, entering the workplace or further education, leaving home, forming and ending relationships, and becoming less dependent on parents. That period is often marked by changes in religious behavior, with many young people withdrawing from the habits of regular attendance for worship. Mark D. Regnerus and coauthors (2004) found that adolescents withdrew from regular church attendance in most cases, unless they had close friends who attended. The 2013 longitudinal study wanted to discover why that might be the case, and what it could reveal about belief.

To investigate those potential changes within young, and also older, people, and their impact on developing their ideas about beliefs, further research was carried out by revisiting a sample of the population that had been explored as a *snapshot* during initial fieldwork in 2003–2005. That initial phase of research by Abby Day ([2011] 2013) concluded with the finding that belief could be both religious and nonreligious in people's thoughts and behaviors. In keeping with much of the discussion referred to in the previous section, the word *belief* often triggered Christian-based responses among those people who self-identified as practicing Christians. Others described their beliefs in terms of a faith, or trust, in nonreligious ideas and people. It also became apparent that their beliefs were closely held and guarded, prompting another conclusion that those truth claims are important means of creating and communicating identities. The main finding of the project's first phase was to elaborate and enrich definitions of *belief* to include both religious and nonreligious forms, and to demonstrate that when nonreligious people claim a religious identity, on a survey or other instrument such as a national census, they often do so to mark significant social identities. Those occasionally religious people are often described by scholars as *nominal* or *marginal*, but their religious identifications are important to signify forms of social beliefs and a sense of belonging:

- "Natal nominalists" are people who may self-identify as Christians to signal their earlier, family-associated roots, either because they had been baptized or raised in a church-attending family. They conveyed a feeling that being Christian was an identity that had been imposed on them as a result of their baptism or upbringing. As one young man told the interviewer, "I was christened so that means I'm a Christian but not by choice."

- "Ethnic nominalists" are those who had a strong sense that their cultural or national identity was essentially Christian by history or by relation to a specific group. Some people rely on what they perceive to be specific attributes of identity to mark boundaries. The reliance on an "ethnic" category shows "ethnicity" can be a selected, rather than inherent, identity. Weber noted that "ethnic membership does not constitute a group; it only facilitates group formation of any kind" ([1922] 1978, 389). That kind of identity is particularly important in political discourse, as will be described. In research about why people would selected "Christian" as an option on the national census question about identity, one of Day's informants explained why he selected that category although he had already described himself as not religious: identifying as Christian would be "the British way, isn't it? If people are not religious, they're C of E. Church of England. Weddings, funerals, and christenings" ([2011] 2013, 181). Such a tendency to associate with a religion on cultural grounds is not exclusive to Christianity. For example, Jasjit Singh (1972–) found in his 2010 study of young British male Sikhs that many were wearing the turban as a symbol of ethnic identity and belonging.

- "Aspirational nominalists" associate with Christianity because they cognitively and emotionally connect it with a moral component of being a better person. Although they do not attend church or participate in other Christian rites, they may slightly envy those who do. Christian is often a term denoting the "right" way to behave, as expressed by saying "it is the Christian thing to do" or "believing in Christian values." That those values, often described as the Ten Commandments, are not exclusively shared by Christians (or, as in the case of the Ten Commandments, did not originate with Christianity) is not an issue of concern for those nominalists. What matters is the glossed presentation of something good, and often representing progress, that resonates with the idea of being Christian. A curious lacuna in the literature on religion and crime speaks to the normative, taken-for-grantedness that religious people are good. These assumptions ignore the way religion actually works in practice. Globally, conflicts and war crimes are often driven by ethno-religious claims and aspirations. In the Middle East and Africa, current wars and violence are often justified with religious rhetoric; in Europe, the January 2015 attack on the offices of a satirical magazine and a kosher supermarket provoked a confusing array of commentary and analysis. These claims often lead to processes of labeling and *othering*.

MULTIDIMENSIONAL ANALYSIS

Those nominalists and others who did not self-identify with any religion all had strong thoughts and feelings that they described as their beliefs: in their families, in social justice, and in fairness, for example. A multidimensional approach to the analysis expanded the category of belief from a core meaning as propositional or content-based to one that considered other qualities and applications, such as its practices, sources, salience, and function (Day [2011] 2013). This meant that interviewees discussed not just the content of beliefs, such as one girl's comment, "I believe in spirituality," but the practice of that belief (she felt her grandmother watching over her, and often confided in her) and the salience of it (it gave her the strength to live after a suicide attempt). Recalling the example earlier of a survey question about God-belief, the multidimensional approach allows belief to be more widely understood. The importance of belief changes on a scale from weak to strong, ranging from people who might say they believe in God simply because they think everyone else does, so they may as well go along with it, to people whose beliefs affect every action and thought in their daily lives. The findings from this research problematized the conclusions of scholars discussed earlier who maintained that people who answered survey questions to confirm that they believe in God but do not attend church should be understood as "unchurched" rather than secular. On the contrary, considering the salience of beliefs rather than simply their content revealed important variations. An example of that distinction was found during the project with the benefit of qualitative research. Some people, such as Jane, a church-attending woman in her sixties, talked of belief in God as being central to her life. Jane said that God gave her a reason for being and she "could not contemplate life without him" (Day [2011] 2013, 125). This response appeared to contrast with others for whom the existence or not of God played little importance in their lives. In answer to a question about the origins of the universe, Gemma, a fourteen year old, said that she thought that God probably created it, but added in a sharp, derisory tone, "I don't, like, worship him or anything" (Day [2011] 2013, 159). People like Gemma might add to the statistics about how many people believe in God, but it would be inaccurate to suggest that belief made much difference to her or that she could be classified as an unchurched believer. As Asad (1993) predicted, it may be convenient for those promoting religion to argue that beliefs are private and hidden among those who, presumably secretly, harbor deep religious sentiments. Yet the evidence from in-depth discussions suggests a different conclusion: other than being an occasional social marker, the unchurched members of society likely do not hold religion to be important in their daily lives.

Drawing on the first and later phases of the study, a major finding was that the most important variable that helped explain why people believed in different propositions or believed in different people, ideals, or institutions, was the "source" in which they did or did not trust. The study concluded that young people were not drifting through an amoral universe or finding themselves unable to cope with life's challenges in the absence of grand metanarratives, as, for example, other researchers have argued (e.g., see Smith and Snell 2009; Smith et al. 2011). On the contrary, young people were informed and sustained by the social relationships and contexts in which they felt they belonged and in which they believed. The study concluded with a model providing a three-part, interconnected grammar proposing a "trinity of belief" (with a deliberate secularizing of the term "trinity"): propositional (cognitive-rational); felt (both emotional and material, embodied); and performative (created through and creating social action). Rather than seeing different modes of belief as separate or in competition with each other, the "trinity of belief" reveals the way different modes of belief may play a part in people's lives either solely or while

Chapter 4: Believing in Belief: Toward the Secularization of Faith in Global Economies

overlapping. Gemma, for example, accepted a propositional belief in God while rejecting any felt or performative characteristics.

The purpose of the model was not to restrict forms and expressions of belief into only three types, but to propose an analytical tool to help researchers understand the complexity of belief experienced by different people at different times. This may help reprise belief from its near-forbidden status in anthropology as an object of study, following, for example, the advice of Needham and Ruel. A richer interpretation of belief, combined with a multidimensional approach, may allow it to be embraced for cross-comparative purposes. In any case, a term used so frequently in everyday conversation, capitalist endeavors, and political discourse means it cannot be dispensed with simply because it does not share a universal meaning. Indeed, that it varies and produces multiplicities of meaning in different contexts demands scholarly attention.

During the past decade, the aversion to discussing religion in terms of belief has continued among anthropologists, unless it has been thoroughly deconstructed and reassembled. Scholars now engage with belief through broadening its boundaries to include materiality, emotion, discourse, and power (e.g., see Day [2011] 2013; Lindquist and Coleman 2008; Morgan 2010; Vasquez 2010). The old rationality-belief juxtaposition has been replaced by discussions of power relations, intersectionality, performance, and relationality. Those studies specifically show how belief is expressed differently, in different places and times, rather than acting as a single, universal idea.

The academic discussion of belief has been restricted to studies about religion and spirituality. What about the way belief is used and understood in nonreligious environments, and what can that tell us about its place in contemporary, secularizing society?

SELLING THE BRAND OF BELIEF: THREE CASE STUDIES

This section discusses the various interpretations of belief in consumer brand communication to explore how belief is being torn from its religious roots to convey similar, secularized sacred ideals of faith and trust. The goal of advertising is to build awareness of a brand. Brands are goods that have been created, packaged, and promoted in such a way as to differentiate them from the generic product. Often, the core ingredients of a brand and a generic version are indistinguishable. Consider, for example, porridge oats. In an average supermarket, five different versions of porridge oats may be all packaged and sold under different names. People shopping for pain relief may be confronted by more than ten different brands, all of which contain the same ingredients. Some will sell better than others will, mainly because the seller has spent time and money targeting the brand to a specific group of people using a particular message.

Considering how much money is involved in building and sustaining brands (Coca-Cola is on target to spend nearly US$1 billion in 2016 on marketing), decisions taken about advertising are well-researched and carefully created. Behind the advertisements are professionals who conduct detailed market research to understand the needs and identities of their target audience so that they are able to connect their product with the buyer's identity. Writing about building brands, Jean-Noël Kapferer says that brands "that maximise satisfaction will survive [...] It is the end of hollow brands, without identity" (2008, 3).

Chapter 4: Believing in Belief: Toward the Secularization of Faith in Global Economies

A strong identity marker is belief. The following sections examine different ad campaigns from three different companies featuring *belief* to illustrate how the term is adapted and repackaged in ways that mirror how belief is being understood in contemporary scholarship, particularly with an emphasis on *faith*.

COCA-COLA: REASONS, AND PROOF, TO BELIEVE

The drink Coca-Cola, commonly known as "Coke," was invented by American pharmacist John Pemberton (1831–1888) in 1886. He sold nine glasses a day in its first year; by 2015, the company had expanded its range to four hundred different products available in more than two hundred countries, with 1.9 billion servings consumed worldwide every day. In 2012, the Coca-Cola Corporation in a campaign called "Reasons to Believe" appealed to customers around the world to turn from their worries about life's hardships and remember that "despite ongoing economic uncertainty, political unrest, natural disasters and more, the good in today's world far outweighs the bad." The message was adapted differently depending on the national context, but each reflected the central goal to remind people that "for every reason to doubt, there are countless reasons to believe in a better tomorrow" (Coca-Cola 2012). This rational, aspirational, and politically directed use of belief was also directed toward Egypt, for example, in 2011 with a goal of "reinforcing the greater good of humanity in a post–Arab Spring environment" (Coca-Cola 2012). At the same time, the campaign was adapted for Greece, Italy, and Spain to lighten the mood amidst economic hardship. The ad created for Africa was titled "There are a billion reasons to believe in Africa" (YouTube 2008) and featured star Steve Kekana (1958–) singing about loving, praying for, trusting, and believing in Africa. The footage depicted people singing and dancing while slogans ran across the screen, ending with a picture of a child drinking a bottle of Coke against the words: "While the world worries about the future, a billion Africans are sharing a Coke" (YouTube 2008).

The ad campaign plays on two particular modes of belief discussed earlier: felt and performative. These modes are designed to connect with the faith-based, aspirational identities that Coca-Cola assumes is held by the target market. Another distinctive quality of the ad campaign is its global context. In contrast to the arguments of anthropologists cited earlier, *belief* is assumed to have a universal meaning capable of resonating in similar ways in different countries and global contexts. The adaptation to localized circumstances gives a twist, shifting slightly the focus but retaining in general a sense of belief meaning faith, hope and loyalty.

This emotive, embodied rendering of belief is in stark contrast to another campaign targeted toward young people who apparently did not "believe" that the sugar-free version of Coke, "Coke-Zero," tasted just like the regular version. Through a series of campaigns, such as hiding a cup of Coke Zero inside regular Coke cups at a Singaporean cinema, the advertisers appealed to the sense of taste, combined with a rational, empiricist turn on belief. The tagline was "Tasting Is Believing" (Cream).

This cognitive form of belief relates to a propositional mode—that is, an intellectualist, rational form of belief. The core of rationality, as discussed, is reason based on evidence. The brand has been targeted specifically at a young, male demographic (Coca-Cola 2015), which makes the empiricist, rational approach potentially attractive. Research into religion and gender reveals that men are more likely than women to be atheists (Trzebiatowska and Bruce 2012). Although explanations for this are still debated, a common stereotype that men are

RELIGION: BEYOND RELIGION

more rational and women more subjective circulates widely and seems to be an idea that could be plausible for Coke's approach to the male market.

SKY TELEVISION: BELIEVING IN BETTER

Sky Television is the UK provider of satellite television. Its slogan "believe in better" is not only part of its intensive advertising campaign, but also, according to its 2014 annual report, part of its company ethos to encourage its staff to progress and improve.

The need to progress is a characteristic of the capitalist conditions of modernity, argued Anthony Giddens (1938–), who drew attention to the "restless, mobile character of modernity" being a consequence of the capitalist cycle of investment-profit-investment, bringing "a constant disposition for the system to expand" (1990, 11). That need is felt not just in the boardroom of multinational organizations, but also in the homes of consumers contemplating the latest paint colors or window coverings for their living rooms. Television programs focusing on interior design, gardening, cooking, and other domestic enterprises all stress the desire for continuous improvements in personal and family lifestyle. The television is the medium for communicating those desires and, through related advertising, becomes the conduit to acquiring the means to satisfying them by purchasing consumer goods. One phrase marketers use to capture the method of appealing to consumers' apparent, or created, desire for constant improvement is *aspirational marketing*. Marketing professionals (e.g., see Saviolo and Marazza 2013) argue that people need myths to provide security and meaning in their lives (e.g., as anthropologist Bronislaw Malinowski [1884–1942] argued more than a century ago). Those myths are reflected in their values, which will evolve and change, providing companies with new opportunities to sell their products. Those values, and their fluid nature, are examples of beliefs that are emotional, embodied, and performative. Not primarily subject to cognitive, or "propositional," interrogation, they act as identity markers for people whose identity is closely linked as being associated with other people or things that confer certain values. In her 1997 study of working-class women in the North of England, Beverly Skeggs identified patterns of desire for respectability that manifested themselves through constantly aspiring to improve and to "pass" as middle class—to, in other words, "become better."

Marketing theory proposes that all products have a lifecycle, following a pattern of customers' progress through discovering the products, using them, and eventually tiring of them as they seek something new or different to match their changing needs. Change itself becomes fetishized to satisfy the kind of capitalistic restlessness to which Giddens referred earlier. Reinforcing the consumer desire to progress, to become "better" is central to successful advertising.

Advertising revenue is key to Sky Television's success. Sky's operating profit in 2015 climbed 20 percent to more than £1 billion, with revenue from advertising increasing by 6 percent (Oakes 2015).

SONY: UNIVERSAL BELIEF

In 1946, the Tokyo Telecommunications Engineering Corporation was created in Japan to specialize in electronic and telecommunications equipment; in 1958, it changed its name to Sony Corporation. A glance at its company history quickly shows that it has been a company of firsts, often a leader in research and development in the electronics industry. Inventing, producing, and selling (or making) imaginative and innovative products is core to its success and identity. Its wide range of consumer products and businesses, from cameras to music, means it targets itself to a variety of market segments.

The "Make.Believe" campaign was launched in 2009 as Sony's first global campaign (Ramsay 2009). The first advertisement (YouTube 2011) plays on ideas of make believe, or, as the ad forms it, "Make.Believe" (pronounced "make dot believe"). The ad shows a teenage boy wandering through a fantasy world in which he becomes part of a research lab, a film, and a pop concert, pushing a large, illuminated button to progress to the next place. The ad ends with a male voice saying, "Believe that anything you can imagine you can make real. Make dot believe."

In an interview with the campaign designers, the function of the dot was explained as "playing a pivotal role in joining two different elements—make, representing action, and believe, a frame of mind [...] The dot in the brand message is the spark that brings the two elements together, the flash point when new value and experiences are created" (MacManus 2010). Relating this explanation to the previous discussion on belief, the dot can be imagined as representing the action that brings a belief into being: its performative moment. From its pilot in 2009, the image with the words make.believe is now part of all of Sony's advertising. The designers make the point in the interview that the image and its related animated versions need to be used everywhere: "The organization and images are simple, because it was intended to be used by many group companies. No matter what Sony business the logo promotes, it must convey the message clearly and consistently" (MacManus 2010). Contrary to anthropological theories discussed earlier, *belief* has a universal meaning and resonance. It can further be argued, following Giddens, that such universality is both a feature and consequence of global capitalism.

The examples from Coca-Cola, Sky Television, and Sony Corporation show how belief can be used to assist capitalist endeavors, and also how the particularity and context can be sometimes subsumed and sometimes embraced depending on the need of the company accessing it. The constant reminder that the brand is to be trusted and "believed in" provides a secularized version of faith. Just as religions explain, guide, and comfort, so too do new versions of the sacred found through Coca-Cola, Sky, or Sony. This is particularly salient in such current times described as late capitalism, or late modernity, when uncertainty can be reduced by believing in the right brand.

The ability to manage temporal and spatial dimensions to avert the crisis of overaccumulation is one way that capitalism continues to innovate and affect every part of the world. Those movements are not without consequences. As Giddens argued, such ceaseless movements and changes produce a restlessness characteristic of late modernity. Ulrich Beck (1944–2015) has discussed the same problem and argued that it led to several individual and societal problems of increased individualization, loss of community, over-reliance on rationalization, and a constant generation of risk, with its attendant anxieties. Stressing a shared belief in a common product changes the meaning of "common good" from a transcendent value to a tangible, material object.

This supports the view of some scholars who have argued that the increasing modernity would lead to an inevitable decline in religion. This has been central to secularization theories, first substantially addressed by Bryan Wilson (1926–2004). Wilson argued that processes that transferred agency from the supernatural to the secular would lead to decreased religious beliefs and, as a consequence, decreased religious practices as beliefs and practices failed to be incorporated into people's daily lives or consciousness. He assumed this was a global process, "in which the notion of a world order created by some supernatural agency has given considerable place to an understanding of a man-made and man-centred world" (Wilson 2001, 40). Steve Bruce (for a summary of Bruce's many works, see Bruce 2011) argued that secularization would increase as modernity, and indifference toward religion, increased.

Although billions of people around the world are religious, with many adhering to their faith's key tenets and rituals, many others experience and sometimes explicitly use religion primarily to show their belief, or faith, in social structures that affect power relations. The current rise of the Far Right in the United Kingdom and Europe, with attacks on synagogues and mosques, for example, likely is due partly to its success in mobilizing ethno-national-religious sentiments. The key is context: while certain religions are dying out, other forms are growing. In modern cities and states such as London, Egypt, Iran, Brazil, and China people are witnessing pockets of what some theorists, such as Jürgen Habermas (1929–) in "Religion in the Public Sphere" (2006), describe as the postsecular. To understand that requires critically reviewing the role of religion in the modern world by examining how religion is being re-asserted in public. Looking at just a few cases, we can see there is no strict separation: the rise of the European Far Right is arguably a response to perceived encroachments on land and a struggle for resources in which the category of religion becomes a quick way to scapegoat an other; the rise and fall of the Muslim Brotherhood in Egypt demonstrates struggles about religion, the "deep state," and power; the Church of England's continued influence in national politics, education, and the House of Lords, despite falling membership and participation, speaks to established networks and management of wider discourse.

The next section discusses how societies, and in particular their political leaders, respond to such anxieties by seeking to create a sense of belonging through "believing in" a common vision. As Benedict Anderson (1936–) notes in *Imagined Communities* (1993), these ideas then circulate in the media to create a fiction of a nation state.

POLITICS OF BELIEF

Unlike the United States, Britain and other European countries generally have kept public discussion of religion away from politics, with leaders usually distancing themselves from affiliating with any religion. It is interesting to reflect on the conditions that may have prompted such reversals.

During the British 2015 national election campaign, the question of belief informed both advertising and news stories. Writing in the conservative-leaning daily newspaper, the *Telegraph*, UK 2015 election hopeful Nigel Farage (1964–) appealed to voters to "Believe in Britain." Putting immigration at the center of his campaign, the leader of the UK Independence Party (UKIP) urged voters to help remove the current government who continue to occupy the main seat of power: "At what cost to the confidence and belief in the values that underpin British civil society?" (Farage 2015). During the election, Farage told the left-leaning daily newspaper, the *Guardian* that immigration was affecting health and education services, but also damaging towns and cities where it is "difficult to recognise the place being the same as it was 10 to 15 years ago" (Mason 2015).

Throughout his campaign, Farage made references to Christianity, aligning it with his vision to "Believe in Britain." In April 2015, as the crisis of migrants drowning in the Mediterranean captured news headlines, Farage said that Britain should accept a few thousand refugees, but only if they were Christian (BBC 2015). His interviews on other topics were often peppered with references to Christianity. In the *Guardian* interview, for example, he spoke of his party's ability to "turn the other cheek to insults and negativity" (Mason 2015), a clear biblical reference to Jesus.

Given that the Western colonial powers were self-styled rationalists, it was not a difficult process historically to frame the *primitive* others as irrational *believers*. Such phrases and characterizations were once again appearing as migrants from former colonies began to arrive in unprecedented numbers. Commenting on the introduction of Romania into the European Union, Farage warned that many Romanians are "living like animals" and want to move to a "civilised country" like the United Kingdom (Bienkov 2013).

Summary

This chapter began by reviewing how scholars of religion generally use the terms *belief* and *faith*. Their embedded assumption that belief relates to a dominant Christian understanding is in sharp contrast to how belief is actually understood and practiced by people in their everyday lives. Examination of interviews and media (particularly advertising) show how *belief* is a term more related to human understandings of faith and trust than to notions of the divine. Three modes of belief were highlighted: propositional, felt and embodied, and performative. The different degrees to which belief matters in people's lives were discussed to help move the discussion along to re-engage with belief as a term of significance to many people.

Case examples from Coca-Cola, Sky Television, and Sony Corporation showed how the appropriation of belief from a religious context provided a multiplicity of meanings that helped corporations access different populations globally. This all takes place, it was further discussed, in the context of late capitalism that arguably exerts a destabilizing effect on people's lives.

Linked to the rise of late capitalism, late modernity, and globalization, more emotional, rational, secularized forms of belief are arguably significant evidence of nonreligious modes of belief replacing both institutional and civil forms of religion in Euro-American contexts.

Bibliography

Abercrombie, N., J. Baker, S. Brett, and J. Foster. "Superstition and Religion: The God of the Gaps." In *A Sociological Yearbook of Religion in Britain*, edited by D. Martin and M. Hill, 93–129. London: S.C.M., 1970.

Anderson, Benedict. *Imagined Communities*. London: Verso, 1993.

Asad, Talal. *Genealogies of Religion: Discipline and Reasons of Power in Christianity and Islam*. Baltimore, MD: Johns Hopkins University Press, 1993.

BBC. "Election 2015: Turn Migrants Boat Back, Says Farage." April 22, 2015. http://www.bbc.co.uk/news/election-2015-32409901.

Beck, Ulrich. *Risk Society: Towards a New Modernity*. London: Sage Publications, 1992.

Berger, Peter L. *The Sacred Canopy: Elements of a Sociological Theory of Religion*. New York: Doubleday, 1967.

Bienkov, Adam. "Nigel Farage: Romanians Want to Move to a 'Civilised Country'." Politics.co.uk. September 6, 2013. http://www.politics.co.uk/news/2013/09/06/nigel-farage-romanians-want-to-move-to-a-civilised-country.

Bruce, Steve. *Secularization, in Defence of an Unfashionable Theory*. Oxford: Oxford University Press, 2011.

Cancer Research UK. "More Than a Quarter of Britons Think Cancer Is a Matter of Fate." January 3, 2007.

http://www.cancerresearchuk.org/about-us/cancer-news/press-release/2007-01-03-more-than-a-quarter-of-britons-think-cancer-is-a-matter-of-fate.

Coca-Cola. "Coca-Cola Offers Consumers 'Reasons to Believe'." December 17, 2012. http://www.coca-cola company.com/stories/coca-cola-offers-consumers-reasons-to-believe.

Coca-Cola. "How Coke Zero Became a Hero." June 30, 2015. http://www.coca-colacompany.com/stories/how-coke-zero-became-a-hero-10-facts-to-mark-the-brands-10th-birthday.

Coca-Cola. "Our Story 2000 to Now: Living Positively 128 Years On." http://www.coca-cola.co.uk/stories/history/heritage/our-story-2000-to-now-living-positively-125-years-on/.

Cream. "Tasting Is Believing." http://www.creamglobal.com/case-studies/latest/17798/33963/tasting-is-believing/.

Davie, Grace. *Religion in Britain Since 1945: Believing without Belonging.* Oxford: Blackwell, 1994.

Day, Abby. *Believing in Belonging: Belief and Social Identity in the Modern World.* Oxford: Oxford University Press, 2013. First published 2011.

Day, Abby. "Varieties of Belief over Time: Reflections from a Longitudinal Study of Youth and Belief." *Journal of Contemporary Religion* 28, no. 2 (2013): 277–293.

Day, Abby, and Mia Lövheim, eds. *Modernities, Memory and Mutations: Grace Davie and the Study of Religion.* Farnham, UK: Ashgate, 2015.

Douglas, Mary. *Purity and Danger: An Analysis of Pollution and Taboo.* London: Routledge. 1966.

Durkheim, Émile. *The Elementary Forms of the Religious Life.* London: George Allen and Unwin, 1915.

Evans-Pritchard, Edward Evan. *Witchcraft, Oracles, and Magic Among the Azande.* Oxford: Clarendon Press, 1976. First published 1937.

Farage, Nigel. "Nigel Farage's Appeal to Britons: Believe in Britain." *The Telegraph.* February 11, 2015. http://www.telegraph.co.uk/news/politics/nigel-farage/11406632/My-appeal-to-Britons-believe-in-Britain.html.

Harvey, David. *The Condition of Postmodernity.* Oxford: Blackwell, 1990.

Habermas. Jürgen. "Religion in the Public Sphere." *European Journal of Philosophy* 14, no.1 (2006): 1–25.

Kapferer, Jean-Noël. *Strategic Brand Management: Creating and Sustaining Brand Equity Long Term.* London and Philadelphia: Kogan Page, 2008.

Lindquist, Galina, and Simon Coleman. "Introduction: Against Belief?" *Social Analysis* 52, no. 1 (2008): 1–18.

MacManus, Christopher. "Conversation with the Designers of Sony's Make.Believe Campaign." *Sony Insider.* August 20, 2010. http://www.sonyinsider.com/2010/08/20/conversation-with-the-designers-of-sonys-make-believe-campaign/.

Malinowski, Bronislaw. *Argonauts of the Western Pacific.* New York: E. P. Dutton, 1961. First published 1922.

Mason, Rowena. "Nigel Farage: Immigration Has Left Britain Almost Unrecognizable." *Guardian.* March 31, 2015. http://www.theguardian.com/politics/2015/mar/31/nigel-farage-ukip-immigration-britain-unrecognisable-general-election-poster.

Morgan, David, ed. *The Matter of Belief.* London: Routledge, 2010.

Needham, Rodney. *Belief, Language and Experience.* Chicago: Chicago University Press, 1972.

Oakes, Omar. "Sky Profits Surge 20% as Ad Revenue Climbs." *Campaign.* April 21, 2015. http://www.campaignlive.co.uk/article/1343517/sky-profits-surge-20-ad-revenue-climbs#jRQkyVtS8csiXO8U.99.

Ramsay, Fiona. "Sony to Roll Out 'Make.Believe' Activity." *Marketing Magazine.* March 11, 2009. http://www.marketingmagazine.co.uk/article/950113/sony-roll-makebelieve-activity.

Regnerus, Mark D., Christian Smith, and Brad Smith. "Social Context in the Development of Adolescent Religiosity." *Applied Development Science* 8, no. 1 (2004): 27–38.

Ritzer, George. *The McDonaldization of Society.* Newbury Park, CA: Pine Forge Press, 2010.

Robbins, Joel. "Continuity Thinking and the Problem of Christian Culture." *Current Anthropology* 48, no. 1 (2007): 5–17.

Ruel, Malcolm. "Christians as Believers." In *Religious Organization and Religious Experience*, Asa Monograph 21, edited by J. Davis, 9–32. London and New York: Academic Press. 1982.

Saviolo, Stefania, and Antonio Marazza. *Lifestyle Brands: A Guide to Aspirational Marketing.* London: Palgrave Macmillan, 2013.

Skeggs, Beverley. *Formations of Class and Gender: Becoming Respectable.* London: Sage, 1997.

Sky Television. "Annual Report." 2014. https://corporate.sky.com/documents/annual-report-2014/annual-report-2014.pdf.

Singh, Jasjit. "British Sikh Youth: Identity, Hair and the Turban." In *Religion and Youth*, edited by Sylvia Collins-Mayo and Pink Dandelion, 131–138. Aldershot, UK: Ashgate, 2010.

Smith, Christian, and Patricia Snell. *Souls in Transition.* Oxford and New York: Oxford University Press, 2009.

Smith, Christian, Kari Christoffersen, Hilary Davidson, and Patricia Snell Herzog. *Lost in Transition: The Dark Side of Emerging Adulthood.* Oxford and New York: Oxford University Press, 2011.

Smith, Wilfred Cantwell. *Faith and Belief*. Princeton, NJ: Princeton University Press, 1979.

Sony Corporation. "Corporate History." http://www.sony.net/SonyInfo/CorporateInfo/History/history.html.

Trzebiatowska, Marta, and Steve Bruce. *Why Are Women More Religious Than Men?* Oxford: Oxford University Press. 2012.

Tylor, Edward Burnett. *Primitive Culture*. New York: Harper, 1958. First published 1871.

Vásquez, Manuel. *More Than Belief: A Theory of Religion*. Oxford: Oxford University Press, 2010.

Voas, David, and Alasdair Crockett. "Religion in Britain: Neither Believing nor Belonging." *Sociology* 39, no. 1 (2005): 11–28.

Warner, Stephen R. "Work in Progress towards a New Paradigm for the Study of Religion in the United States." *American Journal of Sociology* 98, no. 5 (1995): 1044–1093.

Weber, Max. *Economy and Society*. Berkeley: University of California Press, 1978. First published 1922.

Wilson, Bryan. "Salvation, Secularization, and De-moralization." In *The Blackwell Companion to Sociology of Religion*, edited by Richard K. Fenn, 39–51. Oxford: Blackwell, 2001.

YouTube. "A Billion Years to Believe in Africa." March 28, 2008. https://www.youtube.com/watch?v=PITDaB84BhE.

YouTube. "Sony—Make.Believe Advertisement." February 18, 2011. https://www.youtube.com/watch?v=_s6vMyBb6Ks.

CHAPTER 5

Apostasy

Jesse M. Smith
Assistant Professor, Department of Sociology
Western Michigan University, Kalamazoo

Apostasy has a long and consequential history. As a human construct, it has been conceptualized and applied in a variety of social situations, in different cultural contexts, and across historical periods, always with important personal, institutional, and societal implications. The word *apostasy* itself carries much weight and can invoke the starkest of human emotions ranging from hatred, to pity, to pride. Even in the twenty-first century, apostasy "is a strong word" (Sherkat 2014, 69), and it most often carries negative connotations. And although, as we will see in this chapter, the word is flexible, can have shades of meaning, and can lead to ambiguity when invoked in different contexts, it does seem to have a core to its meaning that has remained more or less constant over centuries.

This is not to suggest society's relationship to, or understanding of, apostasy has remained unchanged, or that society's treatment of apostates in the twenty-first century is the same as it was during the classical or medieval era. Apostasy and its construction as a social problem has evolved considerably over time, and the severity of the consequences for apostasy in individuals has changed dramatically in most societies. Likewise, in most cases, the application of the label *apostate* to individuals and social groups, whether self-imposed or by outside authorities, has shifted over time.

DEFINING APOSTASY

The word *apostasy* is derived from both Latin and Greek references, *apostasia* and *apostasis* respectively. The former refers to "defection" and the latter to "revolt." *Apo*, being the prefix for "separate," "not," or "away from" is joined with *histanai*, which means, "to stand in place." So the most literal rendering of apostasy is something to the effect of "to separate away from a place or position." Over the course of its etymology, and in its broadest sense, the word has come to refer to the abandonment of a once held belief or position.

Most dictionary definitions converge on this central idea. For example, the unabridged *Webster's Dictionary* defines apostasy formally as, "A total desertion of or departure from one's religion, principles, party, cause etc." (2003, 99). Thus, apostasy can technically and generically refer to the repudiation of almost any idea or practice. The essence of apostasy in this sense is the act of "total desertion" itself. At issue is the desertion component, with the actual object of desertion being secondary.

Chapter 5: Apostasy

Theoretically then, the professor who values unions, believes supporting her local union chapter is the best way to protect her academic freedom and job security, and participates in pubic demonstrations organized by union members, but later disengages all union activity having come to reject the idea of unions altogether, has apostatized. This example is not the typical usage, however, and most historical and contemporary applications of the word *apostasy* refer to one's desertion of religion specifically. David Bromley's simple definition of the apostate, "[An individual] who held a religious identity at one time, but who now has rejected that identity" (1988, 69), represents how most of modern social science scholarship has conceptualized apostasy as an object of empirical research. This is the basic sense in which the word will be used here.

This chapter will discuss the nature of apostasy, broadly incorporating relevant historical, sociological, and psychological factors. The discussion is aimed at the features, qualities, and processes of apostasy in general. As we will see, however, apostasy is less a static category applicable only to known (and often infamous) historical examples than it is a fluid concept that represents dynamic processes involving real people in the modern world.

The first part of this chapter discusses the basic features, types, examples, and consequences of apostasy, followed by a brief outline of closely related and overlapping concepts that provide better context for understanding apostasy in the contemporary world. The last part builds on the first by way of discussing apostasy as a social process. That is, rather than viewing apostasy exclusively as a problem of psychology—an "event" or state of mind—we will examine it as a social phenomenon by exploring the interactional, political, and experiential forces that give life to apostasy and make it a useful concept for empirical study. Understanding apostasy in its own terms has merit, but as early advocates of its study suggest, understanding why people reject religion will also lead to greater insight regarding religion itself, as well as society's relationship to it.

THE NATURE AND FEATURES OF APOSTASY

What is apostasy? It depends on the person or group who refers to it, and the person or group to whom it refers. Historically, the term has been used by the monotheisms—Christianity and Islam in particular—to point to those who have abandoned the church or the faith. It has a powerful negative connotation in this use. In contrast to the previous definition and the usual sense in which it is employed in current use, however, apostasy often refers not to a loss of religious belief per se but to the abandonment of the "true" religion or faith for a false or corrupted one.

The *great apostasy* was a phrase used by various religious groups to suggest the idea of the corruption of true Christianity, largely from pagan or other non-Christian sources and from corrupted religious leadership. In this case, it was the Church itself that had "fallen" into apostasy. The term, therefore, has been used not just to refer to individual apostates, those who have defected from true belief and membership, but to entire organizations or even whole societies that are perceived as having fallen into moral decline. Apostasy can be a general reference to the perceived materialism and societal lack of interest in religious matters, to the sinful state of society at large, or to the public "turning its back" on religion. Indeed, this is why some religious leaders and observers characterize modern secular society as *apostate*.

Chapter 5: Apostasy

From the perspective of *schismatic* religion, that is, the splintering or sectarianism that follows from criticism or claims of corruption in an existing religious body, the evolution of religious organizations over time can be viewed as a succession of either awakenings or apostasies, depending on who's perspective is being assessed (see Carpenter 2001). For example, in early nineteenth-century America, during the so-called Second Great Awakening, what eventually came to be Mormonism, was born out of the broader restorationist movement.

The restorationist view was that all Christian churches, to varying degrees, had undergone apostasy from doctrinal divisions, disputed successions of religious authorities, and too much accommodation of worldly and material concerns. Joseph Smith (1805–1844), the founder of the Mormon Church, claimed to receive a revelation from God wherein Joseph was informed of the waywardness of the various churches and was instructed to re-establish Christ's original church in the "latter days." From a historical perspective, religious organizations and even established faith traditions remain always open to being characterized by other religious individuals and groups as being in or heading toward a state of apostasy.

SOCIOLOGY OF APOSTASY

Apostasy has been studied across a number of disciplines, from history and the humanities, to religious studies. But sustained empirical research into the social processes and meaning of apostasy for individuals and groups in the contemporary world has been concentrated in sociological research. Whereas religious leaders and organizations historically used the term as a pejorative, and as way of discrediting those to whom they applied it, sociologists frame apostasy in more neutral terms and from an empirical framework of understanding.

This is analogous to the way in which sociologists came to use the term *cult*, not as a negative label for deviant religion, but as a way to describe in neutral terms, a particular religious *form* based on charismatic leadership, tightly controlled doctrine, and a state of separateness and tension with regard to mainstream religion. As sociologists argue, what makes apostasy distinct as a conceptual category is not just defection from religion, but the *way* in which the person defects (see Bromley 1998). Primarily this refers to the oppositional quality to apostasy.

Sociologists distinguish different social roles (i.e., behavioral expectations) for different kinds of religious defection. In categorical terms, apostasy is simply one specific kind of what is referred to in the literature as the broader process of religious leave-taking or role exit (Ebaugh 1988). Some religious *leave-takers* exit their religious groups on personal grounds of conscience. A church member who leaves her congregation because she holds a different view from her pastor on an issue like abortion or gay marriage has left for political and personal reasons. If she simply quietly stops attending services at this congregation, she has undergone a generic exit. She is not challenging the core religious claims or narrative of Christianity. She has not come to doubt the divinity of Jesus, does not challenge her former pastor, or make public criticisms of his congregation. In short, her exit does not, "seriously challenge the organizational legitimacy" (Bromley 1998, 5) of the congregation. She is also likely to simply find another congregation that is led by someone who shares her views on these issues. In contrast, the apostate undergoes a different exit process. Although the discontent with a particular doctrine or position may be the same as the generic leave-taker, the apostate vocalizes concern with others, challenges specific beliefs or practices, comes to criticize the leadership, or in some other way constructs an oppositional relationship with the religious group.

RELIGION: BEYOND RELIGION

73

Thus, the simple definition of apostasy offered at the opening of this chapter—the "desertion of religion"—belies its more complex nature. The question of why one would abandon a religious organization or faith position, or a description of the process of how this unfolds, is not suggested by this general definition. Apostasy can mean different things to different people, and it can be used in different ways depending on context and the parties involved. For instance, it has been used loosely to refer to those who are indifferent to religion or as a way of critiquing society's moral decline. In the research literature, however, the concept has more technical meanings, has narrower parameters, and is not used as a catchall word to describe undesirable aspects of people or societies.

Sociologists have developed the concept of apostasy for empirical examination by distinguishing it from other forms of religious leave-taking, and they have deployed additional terms to capture its essence. For example, disaffection, alienation, and repudiation each suggest different social and emotional dimensions to apostasy. Disaffection and alienation imply an emotional estrangement with former religious beliefs, whereas repudiation embodies the active side of openly rejecting or opposing a former religious belief system or organization.

Whatever the vocabulary, what is common in the literature are the dual themes of both loss and repudiation of faith (see Zuckerman 2012). The relationship of these together constitutes a key ingredient for apostasy. From this view, the person who quietly loses religious faith without anyone finding out (perhaps he or she continues with religious participation) cannot be construed as an apostate. Awareness of loss of faith by others, and a degree of open repudiation, is essentially a prerequisite for the label apostate to be meaningfully applied. It is in this way that apostasy is social and relational; it is a product of interaction rather than simply (or only) a psychological condition.

As such, those who study apostasy tend to focus on two interrelated components: *identity* and *community*. The former involves cognition and belief (or disbelief) patterns. The latter deals with the social relationships of the individual. Combined, we are presented with apostasy as a social psychological issue. It requires conscious acknowledgment and usually self-identification with having lost or rejected religion, and there are a number of ways one can do this. Those who claim atheism, for instance, clearly signify that they do not accept or adhere to beliefs about God. Atheists may be apostates in an abstract sense because of this, but the relationship of apostasy and a nonreligious identity requires an important distinction. Atheism and agnosticism at base simply indicate a position regarding propositions about the existence of a deity. An atheist need not have ever believed in God or subscribed to a religion, and so the idea of desertion, loss, or rejection is not unambiguously applicable to all nonbelievers.

As Darren Sherkat observes in his study of patterns of religious identification in the United States, "apostasy [relates] to rejecting religion … [and] obviously if you are raised without a religious identification, you cannot have rejected religion" (2014, 69). And yet, as we will see, even the idea of not having the opportunity to reject religion because one was not raised with it, is not quite as obvious as one might think. This chapter will help reveal why the research-related conceptualization of apostasy, and the discussion of what qualifies a person to be an apostate, can be challenging.

In Bruce Hunsberger's application of social learning theory, he limited his definition of apostasy to include only those, "individuals who report being raised in a religious denomination, but who later change their religious orientation to 'none'" (1983, 21). He did this, he argued, because there are important differences, including the socialization experience, between apostates and religious switchers, converts, and the unchurched (those who were not raised with any religion). Likewise, in Phil Zuckerman's phrasing, apostates are those who, "have lived on both sides of the fence: they've been religious, and they've been secular" (2012, 122).

The situation, however, may not be quite as simple as this. Some research has argued that in highly religious societies such as the United States, where religious competition within a varied religious marketplace is strong, that even those raised without religion nevertheless confront it in public life and feel compelled to make an identity choice that signals their rejection of the *theist-centric* norms of US culture (Smith 2011). Does this imply that people such as self-identified atheists have learned about and contended with religion in such a way as to imply they are apostates, whether or not they were "raised" with religion?

In a study of the American public's perception of atheists, Penny Edgell, Joseph Gerteis, and Douglas Hartmann (2006) found that Americans are distrustful of unbelievers, and that although acceptance of religious diversity in general has increased over recent decades, this acceptance has not been extended equally to those who claim no religious belief at all. This highlights the importance of cultural context. That is, even though the "always atheist" does not meet our academic definition of apostasy (not having disaffected *from* religion), the connotations of the word, in practice, sometimes are applied loosely to all those who make their unbelief explicit through the use of identity labels. This point should be considered by students of apostasy as it has implications regarding how apostasy is studied.

When apostasy is tied to self-identification and some aspect of the public sphere, the related component of community comes to the fore. And so a major feature of typical apostasy is that it involves not just a loss or rejection of faith—a state of unbelief on some particular religious precept or claim—but also "rejection of affiliation with a religious category based on an ascribed status" (Caplovitz and Sherrow 1977, 33). In other words, the nature of apostasy involves identity, and identity itself is embedded in, and in reference to, social groups and communities. Therefore, apostasy is represented not only by the loss and repudiation of cognitive beliefs but also by the loss or repudiation of identification with a particular religious group.

TYPES OF APOSTASY

The question, "Who are apostates?" seems to be complicated by the preceding discussion of the nature of apostasy itself. Are all apostates of the same ilk? Is there something at core that makes a person prone to apostasy? A review of the research suggests the answer to these questions is no. As we have seen, the meaning of apostasy is variable and the unit of analysis ranges from the individual apostate, to whole groups of people, and even to the totality of cross-national historical developments involving religious reformations, and various other religious movements, restorations, and revivals over centuries.

Apostasy can be the historical product of successive defections from particular religions, as individuals or groups come to join or create other religions, and it may involve religious grand narratives about the past and claims about the future through prophecy and

Chapter 5: Apostasy

revelation. This all points to the historical dimension of apostasy and its structural and institutional processes. In other words, social forces beyond the individual play an important role in "deciding" who apostatizes. For instance, some research shows that those raised in mainline Protestant denominations, when compared with Catholics and evangelical Christians, and those who have more liberal political views, are more likely to become apostates (e.g., see Brinkerhoff and Mackie 1993).

Similarly, race, class, age, gender, and other social variables are connected to apostasy in meaningful ways. For example, as David Williamson and George Yancey note in *There Is No God* (2013), white, young adult men with high levels of education are at greater risk of leaving religion and adopting overtly nonreligious identities, such as secularist or atheist. A 2015 study by Janet Eccles and Rebecca Catto used Zuckerman's typology of apostasy (to be discussed) to examine the relationship between age and apostasy among women, finding that, among other social factors, holding a feminist perspective plays an important role in leaving religion. In short, there are important sociodemographic correlates and causes of apostasy. According to Merlin Brinkerhoff and Kathryn Burke in "Disaffiliation: Some Notes on Falling from the Faith" (1980), beyond the intellectual and cognitive processes at play in motivating apostasy, external social conditions and structural "locations," including these ascribed statuses, themselves act as "push factors" toward apostasy.

But important micro-level processes also are at play that undergird and produce these broader conditions. Specific patterns of social interactions, particular symbolic features, and social boundaries add deeper understanding of apostasy and its consequences. The remainder of this chapter discusses this aspect of apostasy by examining its social psychological components: the emotional aspects, belief (or disbelief) patterns, narrative qualities, and other group dynamics that underlie apostasy as a social process. Differentiating *types* of apostasy is a useful way to begin.

A number of typologies have been developed in the literature, and related studies suggest that apostates can be meaningfully classified. This is based on the view that those who abandon religion are unlikely to make up a homogenous group that undergo identical processes, or that a single version of apostasy fits all cases. One of the earliest empirically based typologies of apostasy was offered by Brinkerhoff and Burke in "Disaffiliation: Some Notes on Falling from the Faith" (1980). They examined what they referred to as the *communality* (religious participation and identification) and *religiosity* (commitment to specific religious beliefs) of individuals, arguing that previous studies of religious leave-taking had failed to account for the relationship of both. For them, to get at "true apostasy" scholars must incorporate (or cross-tabulate) both dimensions into their analyses of people who leave religion.

Brinkerhoff and Burke (1980) offer a three-part typology of apostates, set apart from a reference category they identify as "fervent followers," who, as the phrase implies, strongly adhere to both the identification and belief components of being religious. The first type of apostate is the *ritualist*. Ritualists are not properly disaffiliates, because they maintain identification and communality with religion. They participate in religious activities such as worship services and community prayer, and they even partake in important symbolic practices such as sacrament and other rituals. However, they do all this without believing in all (or any) of the doctrines espoused by the religion.

76   MACMILLAN INTERDISCIPLINARY HANDBOOKS

Ritualists can be seen as expressing the inverse of Grace Davie's (1946–) well-known phrase, "believing without belonging," based on her 1994 study of secular Britain. In the United Kingdom and elsewhere in secular Europe, Davie argues, many people continue their commitment to religious beliefs and values without participating in conventional religious practices. Ritualists are engaged in the opposite. They make for an interesting type of apostate because they defy the convention in Western religion that people's religious behaviors are the *outcome* of their religious beliefs. A belief in the divinity of Jesus, as an example, would come before the practice of taking the sacrament for the remission of sins.

Outsiders are the second type of apostates. They maintain their religious beliefs, but they no longer identify with a religious organization. A member who notices hypocrisy in his church group, dislikes the pastor, or has some other interpersonal issue regarding his religious identification, may simply disengage from religion without discarding religious beliefs. Becoming an outsider does not always result from personal problems with a religious group. Sometimes it is the result of practical issues such as moving or marrying someone with a different religious identification.

Finally, a person who both loses belief, and completely disengages from religious affiliation, is a *true apostate*. The total disavowal of former beliefs of this third type of apostate suggests not the quiet slide into religious inactivity that many other disaffiliates experience, but a conscious and verbal rejection of the religious identity. This kind of apostasy is "true" because it aligns with the identity and community components defined above. According to Brinkerhoff and Burke, the problem with other studies of religious defectors is that apostates, outsiders, and ritualists (or any other terms used) had been ineffectively, "lumped together and theoretically treated as a homogeneous type" (1980, 44). Parsing meaningful differences between disaffiliates in this simple three-part typology has helped clarify subsequent studies of apostasy.

In "Dimensions of Religious Defection" (1969), an earlier, more complicated study, Armand Mauss offered an eight-celled typology, the product of different combinations of three distinct dimensions of religious defection. Although I do not outline the whole matrix here, I will highlight the three primary dimensions Mauss discussed, including intellectual, social, and emotional dimensions. All of these social psychological factors conspire in patterned ways to produce the apostate role. *Intellectual* apostasy deals with the contents of the defectors' cognitions. It is based on, "disbelief in the central tenets of a religion, accompanied presumably by a belief in rival secular doctrines" (Mauss 1969, 129). Mauss identifies atheism and agnosticism as the most common expressions. This is most like the true apostasy classification, as it suggests not just defection from a particular religion, but total intellectual repudiation of the claims of religion per se.

Next, *social apostasy* points to a kind of anomie for the individual, or the disintegration of important social bonds. This type relies on basic assumptions, rooted in the work of sociologist David Émile Durkheim (1858–1917), about the social functions of religion—that religion is an institutional response to meeting certain needs of human beings. Social apostasy, then, is the product of a break in social ties within one's religious community. Changing status positions that result, for instance, from educational attainment or a new occupation may cause a shift in social networks and ties and can influence social mobility such that relationships with coreligionists change or dissolve.

Chapter 5: Apostasy

Finally, *emotional apostasy* results from a disruption of emotional bonds, or of an emotional or attitudinal disposition toward religious associates, friends, and even family members. Guilt over sinful behavior, an unhappy family life, observed religious hypocrisy, or a ruined relationship with a fellow churchgoer can erode one's relationship with religion in general. In this way, emotional apostasy is akin to the religious outsider category, in which specific religious beliefs may stay intact, while distance between the self and religion grows.

Early research on apostasy relied primarily on survey methods, and these typologies were developed out of this research context. In contrast, *Faith No More* (2012), Zuckerman's in-depth interview-based study of eighty-seven individuals who rejected their religion, represents one of the most recent typologies of apostasy. His analysis contributes to the research by observing the relevance of the life course and noting there is a spectrum regarding the intensity of one's rejection of religion. At what point in life a person rejects religion is key. Zuckerman distinguishes between *early* and *late* apostasy. As Lori Peek notes in "Becoming Muslim: The Development of a Religious Identity" (2005), children who are raised in a religious home and experience religious socialization do not have much choice about their religious identities and beliefs. Their religious identity is ascribed (placed on them) rather than achieved. When these children reach a level of autonomy as teenagers and young adults, and come to reject their religious socialization, they have become *early* apostates.

This is different from those who arrive at apostasy much later in life after working out their own religious preferences as adults. This describes *late* apostates, who leave religion after having adopted a religious identity, not because it was imposed on them as children, but after experiencing their own conversion or making a conscious choice. Zuckerman notes that early apostasy appears to be much more common than late apostasy, at least in the United States where most children experience overt religious socialization in the home.

In addition to when a person leaves religion, there is the question of the depth of their rejection. An eighteen-year-old who questions her religious upbringing, stops going to church after entering college, and comes to consider herself "spiritual, not religious" is quite different from the fifty-five-year-old pastor who comes to fully repudiate the religious doctrines of his church, and leave behind a religious career to become a secular activist. The first case represents *shallow* apostasy, and the second, *deep* apostasy. Finally, Zuckerman distinguishes between *mild* and *transformative* apostasy. The depth of a person's rejection of religion is often a function of how religious he or she was in the first place, so the meaning of the rejection varies accordingly. In Zuckerman's words, "Not everyone [is] as strong in his or her religious convictions or religious identification to begin with—so the withdrawal from religion [takes] on greater or lesser significance depending on how religious the person originally had been" (2012, 7). Mild apostates have less to lose socially, psychologically, and spiritually than transformative apostates, who undergo a wholesale shift in their worldview and often a reconfiguration of important relationships.

Finally, "Casting of the Bonds of Organized Religion" (1993), a study by Merlin B. Brinkerhoff and Marlene Mackie, although not itself a typology of apostasy, is relevant because it connects a number of the previous ideas and provides a baseline for conceptualizing apostasy as a distinct process centered on the interconnections of identity, belief, and community. Like other studies, part of the goal was to show that for apostasy to be a relevant concept for the social sciences, it had to be "distinguished theoretically from other phenomena" (Brinkerhoff and Mackie 1993, 235), such as the much more studied "religious switching." The authors acknowledged apostasy is complex and historically has been "ambiguously conceptualized and measured" (1993, 238) in the social science literature. They developed a model of religious disengagement that examined the stages of respondents' experiences with religion over time—that is, a "religious careers" perspective (1993, 238).

Brinkerhoff's and Mackie's research confirmed many of the assumptions about religious disaffection and "dropouts" generally and continues to have relevance for newer typologies, such as the one offered by Zuckerman. Namely, the formative socialization in family life and school was found to be a significant predictor of apostasy. For instance, citing an earlier study by David Caplovitz and Fred Sherrow (1977), Brinkerhoff and Mackie reiterated that the religious teachings parents bestow on their children play a critical role on later defection. They found education to be equally important and echoed Hunsberger's 1983 study that suggested the college experience for young adults functions as a "breeding ground" for apostasy. More recent studies of atheists and other nonreligious likewise demonstrate the influence of a college education, both in terms of intellectual development, and for identity formation and autonomy, generally (e.g., see LeDrew 2013; Smith 2011).

The primary contribution of the Brinkerhoff and Mackie study was to disentangle apostasy from other kinds of religious leave-taking using empirical data. The study offered a straightforward conceptualization of apostasy by way of contextualizing it among comparative groups, including both non-apostates and other categories of disaffiliates that on first glance may look similar to apostasy. From their survey-based data of young Canadians and Americans, they proposed four categories of religious careers: (1) *stalwarts* were those who stayed with the religion in which they were raised; (2) *converts* were not raised with organized religion, but joined one later on; (3) *switchers* simply changed from one religion to another; and (4) *apostates* were those raised with religion but who later affiliated with no religion. Their analysis suggested that apostates experience doubts about their religious upbringing more frequently and at an earlier age than other groups and that they eventually stop identifying with religion because of this. This is unlike religious switchers who may temporarily disaffiliate, but maintain religious belief, and affiliate once again.

These typologies share the common themes of identity and community. They address various social psychological dynamics of religious defection and direct attention to important differences among those who leave religion. We learn that not all apostasy is the same. Although every type involves rejecting religion and religious belief, the when, where, why, and how of this rejection can vary considerably. Different situations, meanings, and motives underlie each type, and taken together, this work yields important insights about the nature of apostasy.

Constructing a typology of apostasy, as with any typology, has limitations, however. For instance, attempts at accounting for *all* the variables involved—intellectual, emotional, structural, the degree of apostasy, and so on—inevitably will fail to do so. There are many consistencies across the different typologies, but integration of each into a generic theoretical model of apostasy seems unlikely. Rather, future understanding of apostate types likely will continue to rely on a more "bracketed" situation: reasoning different types based on changing social, historical, and research contexts. Additionally, as with many typologies, their usefulness lies mostly in their descriptive nature, not their predictive power. These apostate types are developed from survey responses,

Chapter 5: Apostasy

observations, and interviews that cannot capture future beliefs and behaviors in the life of the apostate. Just as apostasy can follow religiosity, so too can renewed religious commitment grow out of previous states of apostasy. Simply classifying apostasy does not tell us much about the consequences of apostasy for those who actually experience it. It is to this topic we turn next.

CONSEQUENCES OF APOSTASY

The consequences of apostasy vary dramatically. They can be as wide-ranging as having almost no perceivable negative effect (or even cause for positive celebration among those who embrace the label) all the way to having mob-like deadly violence and capital punishment. Perhaps the most obvious difference on average is historical and at the level of the nation-state. In the twenty-first century, open democratic societies with secular governments not only allow for apostasy but also are generally—and legally—indifferent to the individual's rejection of religion. In such societies, even in the context of the most conservative religious organizations, dramatic ostracism, labeling, or punishment meted out to the apostate are rare when compared with historical apostates.

In the first century, for instance, Judas Iscariot's treachery toward Jesus was said to have ended in suicide, and the term "Judas" is still invoked today as a general reference to betrayal and apostasy. Or consider the act of second century Jewish Priest Mattathias, slaying a Jewish apostate. Moreover, the anti-Christian views of fourth-century Roman Emperor Julian landed him the immortal epithet, *Julian the Apostate*. He is depicted in a dream by Saint Basil the Great. In the dream, Saint Basil was sent by Christ to stab Julian to death for his apostasy. From antiquity and throughout the middle ages, the charge of religious apostasy meant serious and often life-threatening consequences, regardless of whether the apostate truly was repudiating and undermining religion or was simply and wrongly accused of this.

These examples involve infamous individuals who possessed status and power. Their positions meant that they were viewed as legitimate threats to religion or society. The meaning of apostasy in these historical contexts was such that they are remembered many centuries later. The idea of imposing severe consequences for apostasy in these contexts would seem rational and justified. This is obviously different from those in the contemporary scientific literature who are

The Dream of St. Basil the Great, *by Paul Lacroix, c. 1880. Because of his anti-Christian views, the fourth-century Roman emperor Julian acquired the epithet Julian the Apostate. In Saint Basil's dream, he is sent by Christ to stab Julian to death.* **UNIVERSAL HISTORY ARCHIVE/GETTY IMAGES.**

labeled apostates. For instance, Caplovitz and Sherrow's 1977 study of apostasy among American college graduates clearly signals a historical change regarding the meaning and consequences for the apostate.

Despite continued negative connotations concerning what the study authors identified as the "personal traits" of apostates such as poor parental relationships and social maladjustment, it is clear that the late-twentieth-century social, political, and religious landscape imbued apostasy more with the ideas of personal freedom of choice, conscience, and lifestyle when compared with the past. Apostasy, they argued, was the product of the countercultural movement of the 1960s, of the general distrust in traditional (and perhaps especially) religious institutions, and of the liberal education students were receiving in college campuses across the nation. Given this different historical context, even a high-status individual holding antireligious views would not likely acquire, as Julian did, an appellation that included the words "the apostate."

And yet, in many parts of the world, into the twenty-first century, apostasy continues to carry tremendous symbolic weight and can produce dire consequences. Some continue to incur terrible social and personal costs at having been labeled an apostate. In theocratic nations, or other societies in which religious

Mattathias and the Apostate, *by Gustave Doré, 1866.* *In 1 Maccabees, when Mattathias, a Jew, refuses a Greek official's order to offer sacrifice to the Greek gods, another Jew comes forward to perform the act, only to be slain by Mattathias.* PRISMA ARCHIVO/ALAMY.

fundamentalist and extremist groups have significant influence, apostasy may continue to be regarded as sinful, evil, and worthy of severe punishment. In Bryan Turner's study of the relationship between contemporary Islam and sovereign states, he writes that, "Islam has regarded apostasy as sinful when it results in actions that are damaging to the community" (2007, 413) and that the customary view in Islam in the twenty-first century makes apostasy, particularly for Muslim women, especially difficult. This is often the case even when, in such societies, "the ability to exit from a community has [officially] been defined as a basic political right" (Turner 2007, 415).

At various points in history, each of the world's major religions have held apostasy from the true faith as one of the most grievous possible sins, as indicated by specific scriptural references in religious canons. But it is not just official doctrines that make apostasy such an egregious error; it is again, the oppositional component to apostasy: when a religious group or institution encounters a challenge or threat from someone previously committed to the religion, the threat seems especially subversive. In this way, religious groups' conflict with secular institutions or authorities actually would be—at least psychologically—less threatening because the opponent did not once share allegiance with the group.

Contemporary apostates, especially those of high public profile, face sanctions or severe punishment for their religious defection through public reaction, or sometimes officially through a religious *fatwa*: a decree issued by a religious leader. In one of the best-known

Chapter 5: Apostasy

examples to the West, author Salman Rushdie (1947–) had an order of assassination placed against him by Ayatollah Khomeini (1902–1989), the Supreme Leader of Iran, in 1989 for his book *The Satanic Verses* (1988). More recently, Ayaan Hirsi Ali (1969–) has been the subject of controversy for her criticism of Islam (see Hirsi Ali 2007, 2015). Before leaving the religion, Hirsi Ali was a devout believer and originally had condoned the fatwa placed on Rushdie. Her apostasy led to a number of death threats for which she went under police protection. Saudi Arabia provides an example of contemporary government-sanctioned punishment for apostasy. Raif Badawi, a young Saudi Arabian author and activist, was sentenced to prison and up to a thousand lashings, fifty of which he received in early 2015, for his comments critical of Islam. This was followed by considerable international controversy, concerns about free speech, and public condemnation of such punishment from various organizations and individuals.

There are other "everyday" apostates not given such media attention, but whose first-person stories are put to writing. Ibn Warraq, in his edited book *Leaving Islam: Apostates Speak Out* (2003), collected essay accounts from former Muslims. In its preface, he explains why many of those who provided their testimonies of apostasy used pseudonyms to protect their identities:

> Apostasy is still punishable by long prison sentences and even death in many Islamic countries such as Iran and Pakistan, and as many of our authors have relatives in those countries, whom they regularly visit, it is common sense and simple prudence not to use their real names. Others still do not wish to unnecessarily upset husbands, wives, parents, and close relatives who, for the most part, remain ignorant of their act of apostasy. (2003, 11)

This suggests a strong stigma associated with leaving the faith, so much so that some apostates choose to keep even family members in the dark. This is not unique to Islam: many former Christians and people of other faiths selectively disclose their rejection of religion because of fear of stigma or reprisal. Some studies (e.g., Smith 2013) show that even atheists involved in secular activism, when they come from religious backgrounds, sometimes will conceal their apostate status from religious family members despite being open about their unbelief in other contexts. The role of the apostate, then, stands as a particularly useful example of the management of a stigmatized identity. In Mauss's 1998 analysis of former Mormons, he argues that apostates undergo a "struggle with the self" as they simultaneously negotiate their unbelief and role as an apostate, while also trying to maintain a positive self-image and moral identity with family and friends who continue as believers in the church.

Lesser-known cases of apostates have been the subject of academic research, which show that the label is not always applied only to those who reject their religion completely. Intellectuals and others who promote liberal versions of the faith can incur similar consequences. An example is Ulil Abshar Abdalla (1967–), who in December 2002, "received a fatwa authorizing his death on grounds of apostasy" (Turner 2007, 415) in connection with a group he led called the Liberal Islamic Network. Moreover, in some cultures one can be accused of apostasy, not only for abandoning faith altogether but also for adhering to a different one. A recent case that received much media attention was that of Mariam Ibrahim (1987–), a Sudanese woman who was accused of apostasy from Islam in 2014 for marrying a Christian.

Excommunication is another potential consequence for apostasy and is much more common than issuing death warrants against religious defectors. Historically, this was the method used by religious institutions such as the Catholic Church for purposes related to punishment, controlling doctrinal issues, maintaining organizational power and control, and protecting against unbelievers corrupting the Church. Many religious groups still formally excommunicate members or have some equivalent for expelling individuals from their organizations. The Mormon Church, for instance, has recently excommunicated prominent members who have challenged the organization. Kate Kelly (1980–) was excommunicated in 2014 for her advocacy for the ordination of women. In the Mormon Church, only men hold the priesthood, and her direct challenge to this doctrine through the feminist group she organized in 2013, Ordain Women, brought enough attention to the issue that she was formally expelled from the church. The literature on new religious movements (NRMs; see Bromley 1998) is replete with examples of members undergoing religious expulsion for a variety of reasons, including questioning leaders, challenging doctrines, and advocating reform, or simply for having lost faith in the group or its teachings. Mutual ostracism between apostate and organization often follows such religious expulsion.

The underlying theme to excommunication is that a force external to the individual—the established religious organization—is challenged, needs to maintain its authority, and does so by expelling the individual. Those who simply become inactive, or lose their faith without protest, often are not excommunicated because they do not challenge or publicly oppose the group. In this case, the religious organization is more likely to seek to recommit lost members rather than threaten them with expulsion. Excommunication, like apostasy itself, affects individuals differently. After a long embattled relationship with a religious organization, some apostates may welcome excommunication, treating it as final symbolic closure on their complete repudiation of the organization. This suggests a kind of excommunication by consent, and the individual may proudly accept the label apostate. Others may be excommunicated against their wishes. They may continue as believers and may desire to remain affiliated with the group, but they are expelled regardless. This involuntary excommunication likely is coupled with the ex-member's denial that they have apostatized at all.

In addition to formal punishment for apostasy, like excommunication—an essentially one-time event—there are also more practical everyday consequences for apostates. Brinkerhoff and Mackie (1993) studied the consequences of "ordinary" apostates by examining the "concomitants of apostasy," which include happiness, life satisfaction, self-esteem, social and political attitudes, and gender traditionalism. Citing a body of literature related to the general question of life satisfaction and overall well-being, they note, "[t]he consistent finding is that … religious persons tend to be somewhat happier and more satisfied with life than nonreligious individuals" (Brinkerhoff and Mackie 1993, 237).

Kirk Hadaway and Wade Roof (1988) used results from the General Social Survey to suggest that apostates, when compared with the religious, are less satisfied and happy. This does make some sense, especially in the context of societies that place a high value on religion. We might expect that apostates, having left behind the benefits of religion, combined with the social stigma associated with nonbelief, would be particularly vulnerable on the question of happiness. Indeed, the psychological stress related to abandoning faith has been documented quite recently, given renewed scholarly interest in the nonreligious, and ranges from mild anxiety about others becoming aware of one's status as an unbeliever, to concern about losing a job or close relationship, to outright fear for one's physical safety (e.g., see Hammer et al. 2012; Weber et al. 2012).

The research is not completely consistent on this question, however, and it is possible to misread the connection between happiness and religiosity. It is quite possible, for

Chapter 5: Apostasy

instance, that it is not one's rejection of religious beliefs and communities per se that is the source of lowered life satisfaction, but rather the kinds of social relationships that are produced by the act of rejecting the norms of religious belief and practice. As Edgell, Gerteis, and Hartmann (2006) found in their study of the American public's attitude toward those who reject religion, nonbelievers (specifically self-identified atheists) are seen as an essential "other." That is, they exist for the public as the symbolic representation of those who would reject the very moral foundation of the good society. Those who received this religious socialization, only to later repudiate it—*apostates*—are seen as particularly guilty of this moral failure.

If, however, morality, meaningfulness, and finding purpose in life are central to what we mean by well-being and happiness, then there must be more to this story. This is the argument of several scholars who research the nonreligious. In a study that summarizes the most recent literature on the health and well-being of affirmative atheists (many of whom left religion), Karen Hwang (2013) argues that the traditional literature suggesting the positive effects of religion on well-being, and the implied negative effects for those who eschew religion, is misleading. In part, the way researchers examine this relationship through use of self-reported data in so-called religion/spirituality (R/S) scales is problematic. As Hwang explains,

> Studies looking at the relationship between R/S and health/well-being often rely on self-report measures of religiosity or spirituality that measure the construct of R/R simply as global indices on a range from "low" to "high".... These assessment methodologies offer little or no information with regard to affirmatively secular individuals, and may lead researchers to assume that individuals who disavow religious or spiritual beliefs must be lacking in some essential dimension of human experience. (2013, 529)

In other words, the problem with researchers arguing that being an apostate or nonbeliever generally "is bad for you" (Hwang 2013, 529) is both conceptual and methodological. Many apostates positively *affirm* their newfound secular views, and find meaning, value, and satisfaction in their nonbelief and repudiation of religion. Although some evidence (e.g., see Smith 2011) clearly does suggest that apostates can experience social and psychological stressors related to their apostasy, this struggle itself can be an important source of meaning.

As Kimberly Blessing stated concisely in her study of meaningfulness, a common misconception, especially in highly religious societies, is that apostates, atheists, and other nonreligious must "lead empty, meaningless, selfish, self-centered lives" (2013, 104) because they lack the purpose and direction offered by religious belief. She goes on to discuss how those without god or religion can and do lead meaning-rich, purpose-driven lives. Perhaps not surprisingly, this is accomplished through much of the same kinds of normative practices that embody cultural values at large: family life, fulfilling work, and meaningful connections with friends and community.

Evidence is strong that at the societal level, some of the least religious nations, such as those in Scandinavia, are also some of the "best" with regard to the overall health and well-being for its citizens. For instance, Zuckerman's (2008) work summarizes the findings of various national measures of societal health (e.g., the United Nations *Human Development Report*) and argues that the nonreligious can in fact experience very high levels of contentment. This is due to the relationship of the secular with social factors, such as gender equality, health care, education, and other important measurements of societal health. Of course, this is not to say that, for example, Denmark and Sweden are filled with apostates per se, given our

Chapter 5: Apostasy

discussion of what constitutes apostasy, but it does clearly suggest that those without religion—including apostates—are not *necessarily* at greater risk for an unhappy life.

APOSTASY AS SOCIAL PSYCHOLOGICAL PROCESS

All the foregoing has implied apostasy as both a multifaceted concept and social psychological process. Rather than demarcating a single event, or strictly a mental state internal to the individual, apostasy often unfolds over time and always in social and historical context. Both in the past, and in modern scholastic use, apostasy is a word meant to capture a phenomenon more complex than a face-value encounter with the term would suggest. We have seen it can be used loosely, and superficially, as a generic reference to those who leave, avoid, or reject some religious, political, or other social organization once important to an individual; it can refer to the state of an entire institution or even society; or it can have a more technical and theoretically grounded meaning, wherein it applies to some but not other kinds of specific relationships between people and broader religious groups. To fully appreciate apostasy as a complex social process, it is useful to connect it to other related concepts that themselves signal significant social processes surrounding religion and its rejection.

APOSTASY AND RELATED CONCEPTS

One reason for the ambiguity regarding apostasy is its relationship, or entanglement, with other related concepts and processes. The nouns heretic, blasphemer, and infidel often circumscribe or link directly to apostasy, and occasionally they are used interchangeably with the term apostate. Taking the first, *heresy* is perhaps the most closely related idea, as it shares considerable overlap with apostasy. This concept has been and continues to be, in several ways, important to all of the world's major religions. It has been of particular interest historically for theologians and scholars in the Christian tradition. From the Greek *haeresis*, the most literal meaning is, "the act of choosing." In Christianity, it came to refer to a specific kind of choice, such that the heretic is one, "who holding perverse dogma, draw[s] apart from the Church of their own free will" (Evans 2003, xii). The seventh-century Spanish Archbishop, Saint Isidore of Seville (560–636 CE), in his work *On Heresies,* stated that heretics are not just those who think wrongly but are those who persist with "determined wickedness in thinking wrongly" (as cited in Evans 2003, xii). The drama of this sentence is not often found in twenty-first-century accusations of heresy, but the core idea remains.

The open "wrong thinking" of the heretic—from the point of view of the faithful— might seem synonymous with the rejection of both religious belief and community that defines the apostate. However, as George Zito explains in his sociological study of heresy:

> Apostasy involves losing one's allegiance to the language of the parent group. [The apostate] moves from the in-group to the out-group and may be ostracized as a consequence ... the true apostate speaks some other language, foreign to the parent group. This does not occur in heresy. In heresy, the speaker employs the *same* language as the parent group, retains its values, but attempts to order its discourse to some other end. (1983, 125)

Put differently, apostates have sufficiently removed themselves from the beliefs and practices of their former religion (even as they actively challenge it), whereas heretics retain important elements of the religion, but do so "wrongly." In this way, heresy can occupy a more deviant status than apostasy. This is not just an issue of semantics applicable only to ancient or

RELIGION: BEYOND RELIGION

85

Chapter 5: Apostasy

medieval history. In a 2014 study of contemporary Indonesian Muslim society, Ahmad Najib Burhani makes use of this distinction in his analysis of mainstream Muslims' views of Ahmadiyya, a late-nineteenth-century "heretical" Islamic religious movement.

Blasphemy, or acute irreverence toward things considered sacred, is another evocative word meant to convey the severity of an individual or group's offense against some religious doctrine or principle. In Judaism and Christianity, the penalty for blasphemy was once punishable by death, in accordance with the book of Leviticus (see Leviticus 24:10–23). Islam, too, has many scriptural references to this sin. Blasphemy often is bound up with apostasy, sometimes as the underlying reason for its indictment. Individuals, like Salman Rushdie, and organizations, such as the publishers of the French magazine *Charlie Hebdo* and the Danish newspaper *Jyllands-Posten*, have each encountered accusations of blasphemy for their writing or depictions of the prophet Muhammad.

Infidel has meaning in both Christianity and Islam, and generally it refers to all unbelievers and others who lack faith in the core teachings of each religion. In the twenty-first century, it most often is associated with Islam, given the recurrent warnings of unbelief in the Qur'an, and the discourse surrounding political Islam (i.e., Islamism) in general. The infidel's experience as such can be coextensive with the process of apostasy. And like "apostate," it can be a self-adopted label, a way of countering the negative connotations intended by those who would apply it to others. This is the case for the controversial ex-Muslim feminist Hirsi Ali, who authored an autobiography provocatively titled *Infidel* (2007), wherein she recounts her own apostasy from Islam. This is now one of two books authored by Hirsi Ali that is directly relevant to the contemporary conversation about apostasy. Her second book, published in 2015, is titled *Heretic*.

Each of these related terms generally point to the concrete behaviors or views of individuals. Conversely, religious schism and NRMs suggest a more abstract and diffuse set of related processes that are broader in scope, and they do so at the collective level. They represent types and forms of religious change over time. By definition, *religious schism* implicates apostasy in that new religious groups or NRMs usually derive from parent religions because of some kind of dissent or discontent among members. Usually this takes the form of an increasing list of grievances with the parent religion, and a desire for a return to a more pure or correct version of the religion. This is where the notion of religious fundamentalism comes from—that is, a return to the "fundamentals" of the religion.

NRM is an academic rephrasing of the idea of the religious *cult*, and these religious bodies, combined with religious sects, reflect a significant portion of religious change in any society. Although both cults and sects are influenced by the religious environment in which they are embedded, cults generally originate more spontaneously, are often more radical in their doctrines when compared with the religious mainstream, and are lead by charismatic authorities. Sects share many characteristics of cults, but their origins can be traced more clearly back to a parent religion from which it spun off.

Religious change is important for the study of apostasy, not only for the obvious reason that this change involves contesting and rejecting traditional religious doctrines and practices, but because a portion of the contemporary research on apostasy itself is derived from the literature on NRMs. For instance, it was interest in the proliferation of cults, most notably out of the countercultural movement of the 1960s and 1970s, that lead to more systematic study of the characteristics and functions of religious groups that were rejecting traditional religious institutions. Public fascination with cults and their leaders emerged throughout these and subsequent decades and produced the anticult movement—made up of both mainstream religionists and secular academics. The Peoples Temple led by Jim Jones (1931–1978) and Heaven's Gate led by Marshall Applewhite (1931–1997) stand as notorious examples of the "cult problem" in the United States. In the twenty-first century, Scientology founded by L. Ron Hubbard (1911–1986) has come under scrutiny for similar reasons. It was interest in the causes and consequences of deviant religious groups that helped spur research into different kinds of religious leave-taking. The biographies and narratives of those who joined and later abandoned cults—cult "survivors" and religious "ex-ers"—informed the developing research on apostasy in important ways (e.g., see Bromley 1998).

The study of religious conversion has shaped the way in which apostasy is understood in the social sciences. As Brinkerhoff and Mackie put it, "By conceptualizing apostasy as the antithesis of conversion, one may turn to the conversion literature to shed light on [it]" (1993, 247). Put simply, apostasy can be seen as reverse conversion, or *deconversion*. Studies of deconversion have examined both those who leave long-standing traditional religious institutions and those who abandon NRMs. Respective examples include Helen Ebaugh's *Becoming an Ex* (1988), which explores the process of religious role-exit among former Catholic nuns, and Janet Jacobs (1989) analysis of deconverts from new religious movements, including those with origins in Hinduism, Buddhism, and Charismatic Christianity.

Although such studies do not always offer explicit models of deconversion, common themes do underlie it as a social psychological process. These include the importance of belief and the cognitive dimensions associated with a change in worldview and the identity dynamics that unfold in group contexts as individual's religious commitments coalesce and then dissolve. At the center of these and related studies is the role of *narrative*. Narratives involve the biographically grounded stories that people tell based on their interpretation of their experience. According to Stuart Wright (1998), in the case of apostates of NRMs, many of these narratives are shaped within a "captivity narrative" framework, wherein participants understand their former religious selves as having been manipulated and controlled by the religious group. The social scientific conception of apostasy has been influenced by the finding in NRM studies that apostates often make efforts to discredit their former religions, thereby developing the oppositional character of their new apostate identity.

More broadly, this literature reveals narrative patterns among apostates, including expressing doubts about religion, challenging specific religious teachings and authorities, and constructing new nonreligious identities (e.g., see Jacobs 1989; Smith 2011). Studies of deconversion map on rather well to the development of the apostate types discussed previously. This is not surprising given that they both explore the interactions between the psychological and social environmental causes of religious defection.

But deconversion is a generic process, and the deconverted may take different paths toward a new identity that may or may not be religious. Recall Brinkerhoff and Burke's (1980) complaint that in the early study of apostasy, too many kinds of disaffiliates were lumped together as though they were a homogenous group. But it is not so much that scholars had been careless or unable to see important differences among varieties of religious leave-takers. Rather, the issue has to do with the fluidity of identity and group process itself. When does one arrive at his or her "true" religious or nonreligious identity? Once one becomes a religious apostate is he or she always such? The answer is no, not necessarily. Not only can a person move between apostate types (e.g., from a ritualist to a true apostate), but he or she may go from apostate to true believer once again. (Discussion of *reconversion* after apostasy will have to be had elsewhere, as it goes beyond the purview of this chapter.)

RELIGION: BEYOND RELIGION

Chapter 5: Apostasy

Importantly, emerging research interest in the nonreligious since the early twenty-first century has yielded fresh analysis relevant for the study of the apostasy. In addition to reiterating important social and demographic patterns of religious affiliation and nonaffiliation, suggesting that variables such as gender and education both push and pull people toward or away from religion, studies (e.g., Sherkat 2014) that focus on identity have offered models of nonreligious identity formation that may inform the apostate process (and vice versa). For instance, Jesse M. Smith (2011) argues that those who come to self-identify as atheists in the United States reveal a simple but generalized pattern:

Starting Point [Ubiquity of theism] > Questioning theism > Rejecting theism > Adopting atheism

He suggests that even those raised without religion, and who never believed in a deity, because they are members of a society that places a high premium on belief in God and the normative practices of religion and have come to *self-identify* with atheism (rather than not identify at all), experience a similar process as those who apostatize from religion. Subsequent studies (e.g., LeDrew 2013) complicate this basic model and show that it may only be one among a variety of different pathways to atheism. Whatever the case, new research on those who embrace and express their unbelief with overt identity labels, such as atheist, both confirm and potentially add new insight into the nature of apostasy in the contemporary religious-nonreligious landscape.

Taken as a whole, the developing literature on atheists, agnostics, the nones (those who claim no religious affiliation, but may hold theistic beliefs), and other nonreligious show the importance of the relationship between religion and nonreligion, belief and nonbelief. An important relationship exists between them; they form and inform each other, or as Richard Cimino and Christopher Smith put it in their 2014 study *Atheist Awakening*, at the level of discourse and practice, atheists *need* the religious, and the religious *need* atheists. This highlights the constructed social and symbolic boundaries between those who adhere to religious beliefs and practices, and those who reject them.

It also appears the numbers of those in Western democratic nations who openly reject religion, and who would accept the label apostate, are increasing. This paints a different picture from a time when the word likely would be avoided at high cost. The shifting patterns of religious affiliation, particularly in the United States, and the fact that, according to Zuckerman (2012), the nonreligious now make up the fastest growing "religious" group in America, must mean a corresponding shift in the meaning of apostasy. Perhaps it has and will continue to lose some of its long historical stigma. The 2012 Reason Rally in Washington, D.C., the so-called Woodstock for Atheists, was reported to be the largest gathering of secularists in the nation's history. No doubt composed of many religious defectors, those holding signs proudly declaring their unbelief and rejection of religion demonstrate how the apostate role can be embraced and incorporated into a positive identity and sense of belonging within a wider community of fellow apostates.

Summary

This chapter has explored the concept of apostasy, including its nature, features, and types, from a primarily social psychological framework. Relevant historical aspects were discussed, and the multifaceted nature of apostasy, both as a social phenomenon and as conceptualized in the social science literature, was underscored throughout. The basic theme and focus was on apostasy as a social process constructed through particular interactions embedded in larger social and historical contexts. Caplovitz and Sherrow's (1977) study examined the relationship between social characteristics and apostasy. "Social origins and apostasy" was the phrasing they used to explain how some come to abandon religion. On the basis of the discussion in this chapter, apostasy *itself* can be viewed as a social process, rather than merely an *outcome* of a set of social characteristics. From this view, the phrasing should be, "social origins *of* apostasy."

Over centuries, the concept of apostasy has varied in both its meaning and application: from religious groups that invoke it doctrinally to label, discredit, or punish those to whom they believe it applies, to secular scholars who employ it technically to describe a particular kind of modern religious leave-taking in religiously pluralist societies. Because of this varied meaning, the consequences of apostasy likewise vary dramatically across time and place. In some corners of the world, it is still seen as a grave sin that is punishable by death, whereas in others, it may be viewed as simply one more option among a growing number of personal "religious preferences."

As was shown, there are different kinds of apostasy, and different ways in which people arrive at that apostasy. Much has been learned about this phenomenon, and researchers now have a better idea of why people would reject religion despite the social costs, and the benefits it affords. Yet, we stand to learn a great deal more by closely examining apostasy and its relationship to other social processes and institutions. There is now a broader literature on those who repudiate faith, and far from being an antiquated notion, the necessity of understanding apostasy in the twenty-first century has grown more, not less relevant.

The drop in the numbers of believing, committed Catholics and the recent apostasy in the Mormon Church are illustrative. Regarding the latter, several "rescues" have been initiated by church leadership. In 2013, for instance, the Mormon Church's upper leadership began intervening with special "firesides" meant to recommit members in the midst of their apostasy from the church. Most notable was the "Sweden rescue," which began with a (now former) Swedish Mormon bishop and "area authority" who oversaw the Church in Europe and who was publicly voicing his disillusion with certain doctrines of the Church. Moreover, in October 2015, the Mormon Church officially labeled same-sex couples as apostates (see Starr 2015). Most of the ensuing controversy, however, came from the new policy in the same declaration which stated that the children of same-sex couples cannot be blessed or baptized until they are legal adults, and they must disavow their parents' relationship in order to receive these ordinances. Any number of other contemporary examples in Christianity, Islam, and beyond demonstrate the continued relevance of this centuries-old idea. As future research on both religion and the secular advances, and as the debate about secularization and the meaning of religion for modern society continues, the study of apostasy will prove useful.

Bibliography

Blessing, Kimberly A. "Atheism and the Meaningfulness of Life." In *The Oxford Handbook of Atheism*, edited by Stephen Bullivant and Michael Ruse, 104–118. New York: Oxford University Press, 2013.

Brinkerhoff, Merlin B., and Kathryn L. Burke. "Disaffiliation: Some Notes on Falling from the Faith." *Sociological Analysis* 41, no. 1 (1980): 41–54.

Chapter 5: Apostasy

Brinkerhoff, Merlin B., and Marlene Mackie. "Casting of the Bonds of Organized Religion: A Religious-Careers Approach to the Study of Apostasy." *Review of Religious Research* 34, no. 3 (1993): 235–257.

Bromley, David G., ed. *Falling from the Faith: Causes and Consequences of Religious Apostasy.* Beverly Hills, CA: Sage, 1988.

Bromley, David G. *The Politics of Religious Apostasy: The Role of Apostates in the Transformation of Religious Movements.* Westport, CT: Praeger Publications, 1998.

Burhani, Ahmad Najib. "Hating the Ahmadiyya: The Place of 'Heretics' in Contemporary Indonesian Muslim Society." *Contemporary Islam* 8, no. 2 (2014): 133–152.

Caplovitz, David, and Fred Sherrow. *The Religious Dropouts: Apostasy among College Graduates.* Beverly Hills, CA: Sage, 1977.

Carpenter, John B. "The Fourth Great Awakening or Apostasy: Is American Evangelicalism Cycling Upwards or Spiraling Downwards?" *Journal of the Evangelical Theological Society* 44, no. 4 (2001): 647–670.

Cimino, Richard, and Christopher Smith. *Atheist Awakening: Secular Activism and Community in America.* New York: Oxford University Press, 2014.

Davie, Grace. *Religion in Britain Since 1945: Believing without Belonging.* Oxford: Blackwell Publishers, 1994.

Ebaugh, Helen R. F. *Becoming an Ex: The Process of Role Exit.* Chicago: University of Chicago Press, 1988.

Eccles, Janet Betty, and Rebecca R. Catto. "Espousing Apostasy and Feminism? Older and Younger British Female Apostates Compared." *Secularism and Nonreligion* 4, no. 5 (2015): 1–12.

Edgell, Penny, Joseph Gerteis, and Douglas Hartmann. "Atheists as 'Other': Moral Boundaries and Cultural Membership in American Society." *American Sociological Review* 71, no. 2 (2006): 211–234.

Evans, G. R. *A Brief History of Heresy.* Malden, MA: Blackwell, 2003.

Hadaway, Kirk D., and Wade Clark Roof. "Apostasy in American Churches: Evidence from National Survey Data." In *Falling from the Faith: Causes and Consequences of Religious Apostasy,* edited by David G. Bromley, 29–46. Beverly Hills, CA: Sage, 1988.

Hammer, Joseph H., Ryan T. Cragun, Jesse M. Smith, and Karen Hwang. "Forms, Frequency, and Correlates of Perceived Anti-Atheist Discrimination." *Secularism and Nonreligion* 1 (2012): 43–58.

Hirsi Ali, Ayaan. *Heretic: Why Islam Needs a Reformation Now.* New York: Harper, 2015.

Hirsi Ali, Ayaan. *Infidel.* New York: Free Press, 2007.

Hunsberger, Bruce. "Apostasy: A Social Leaning Perspective." *Review of Religious Research* 25, no 1 (1983): 21–38.

Hwang, Karen. "Atheism, Health, and Well-Being." In *The Oxford Handbook of Atheism,* edited by Stephen Bullivant and Michael Ruse, 525–536. New York: Oxford University Press, 2013.

Isidore of Seville. *The Etymologies of Isidore of Seville,* edited and translated by Stephen A. Barney. New York: Cambridge University Press, 2010.

Jacobs, Janet. *Divine Disenchantment: Deconverting from New Religions.* Bloomington: Indiana University Press, 1989.

LeDrew, Stephen. "Discovering Atheism: Heterogeneity in Trajectories to Atheist Identity and Activism." *Sociology of Religion* 74, no. 4 (2013): 431–453.

Mauss, Armand L. "Apostasy and the Management of Spoiled Identity." In *The Politics of Religious Apostasy: The Role of Apostates in the Transformation of Religious Movements,* edited by David G. Bromley, 51–74. Westport, CT: Praeger, 1998.

Mauss, Armand L. "Dimensions of Religious Defection." *Review of Religious Research* 10, no. 3 (1969): 128–135.

Olsson, Susanne. "Apostasy in Egypt: Contemporary Cases of Hisbah." *The Muslim World* 98, no. 1 (2008): 95–115.

Peek, Lori. "Becoming Muslim: The Development of a Religious Identity." *Sociology of Religion* 66, no. 3 (2005): 215–242.

Rushdie, Salman. *The Satanic Verses.* London: Viking, 1988.

Sherkat, Darren. *Changing Faith: The Dynamics and Consequences of Americans' Shifting Religious Identities.* New York: New York University Press, 2014.

Smith, Jesse M. "Becoming an Atheist in America: Constructing Identity and Meaning from the Rejection of Theism." *Sociology of Religion* 72, no. 2 (2011): 215–237.

Smith, Jesse M. "Creating a Godless Community: The Collective Identity Work of Contemporary American Atheists." *Journal for the Scientific Study of Religion* 52, no. 1 (2013): 80–99.

Starr, Alexandra. "Mormon Church Declares Same-Sex Couples to be Apostates." National Public Radio. November 6, 2015. http://www.npr.org/sections/thetwo-way/2015/11/06/455014520/mormon-church-declares-same-sex-couples-to-be-apostates.

Turner, Bryan S. "Islam, Religious Revival and the Sovereign State." *The Muslim World* 97, no. 3 (2007): 405–418.

Warraq, Ibn, ed. *Leaving Islam: Apostates Speak Out.* Amherst, NY: Prometheus Books, 2003.

Weber, Samuel R., Kenneth I. Pargament, Mark E. Kunik, James W. Lomax, and Melinda A. Stanley. "Psychological Distress among Religious Nonbelievers: A Systematic Review." *Journal of Religion and Health* 51, no. 1 (2012): 72–86.

Webster's New Universal Unabridged Dictionary. New York: Random House, 2003.

Williamson, David A., and George Yancey. *There Is No God: Atheists in America.* Lanham, MD: Rowman and Littlefield, 2013.

Wright, Stuart A. "Exploring Factors that Shape the Apostate Role." In *The Politics of Religious Apostasy: The Role of Apostates in the Transformation of Religious Movements,* edited by David G. Bromley, 51–74. Westport, CT: Praeger, 1998.

Zito, George V. "Toward a Sociology of Heresy." *Sociological Analysis* 44, no. 2 (1983): 123–130.

Zuckerman, Phil. *Faith No More: Why People Reject Religion.* New York: Oxford University Press, 2012.

Zuckerman, Phil. *Society without God: What the Least Religious Nations Can Tell Us about Religion.* New York: New York University Press, 2008.

FILMS

Letting Go of God. Dir. Julia Sweeney. 2008.

Night of the Iguana. Dir. John Huston.1964.

Winter Light. Dir. Ingmar Bergman.1963.

Young and Wild. Dir. Marialy Rivas. 2012.

CHAPTER 6

Secularity and Family Life

Christel Manning
Professor, Department of Philosophy, Theology, and Religious Studies
Sacred Heart University, Fairfield, CT

The study of secularity and family life is a fascinating and important area of research, yet it is one that remains underinvestigated in the wider field of secular studies. There are several reasons why looking at family life is important. First, family functions as the primary socialization agent that shapes whether and how people acquire and maintain secular or religious beliefs, behavior, and identity. Studying secularity in family life helps scholars understand why some people become religious or secular, how these socialization processes work and how effective they are, and it helps predict the growth or decline of secularity in future generations.

Second, a focus on family life offers a window into the practical, day-to-day aspects of living without religion. Historically, religion has been deeply embedded in family life, governing sex, marriage, and procreation as well as relationships between parents and children and extended family. Families look to organized religion to mark important life transitions such as marriage, the birth of a child, or the loss of a loved one. Religion also provides symbols and ceremonies to remember a family's cultural heritage and a framework for morality and values that can be transmitted to children. Thus, studying secularity and family life illuminates how people find meaning and structure without religion, or with less religion, and what they create to replace the functions of religion.

Finally, a better understanding of secularity in family life is necessary to fully explain the secularization process. Secularity (nonreligion or nonreligiousness) is of course related to secularization (the process by which religion loses influence over society, organizations, and/or individuals). However, it is not entirely clear what their relationship is. It is common to think of secularity as the outcome of secularization. As church and state become separated, the government ceases to enforce the laws of the majority religion, removing traditional sanctions against nonreligious behavior. Religious teachings are no longer disseminated in schools, causing decline in religious knowledge. Furthermore, skeptics and members of minority religions can publically express their views, relativizing the truth claims of religion. The long-term result is that individuals become less religious. They are less likely to believe in God, attend church, celebrate religious holidays in their families, or transmit religions to their children. In other words, the process of secularization goes from public to private.

The notion that secularization facilitates secularity does seem to apply to the United States and many European societies. However, in other cases, the sequence may be the reverse, especially when public institutions prohibit secularization. If the state enforces commitment to one particular religion, then the private sphere of family may be the only safe space where secularity can be expressed. For example, Iran is often described as a

93

Chapter 6: Secularity and Family Life

religious society because its major institutions are not secular. In this context, the place to look for secularity is family life, where some individuals are privately experimenting with behaviors and beliefs that are not permitted by the religious regime. It is possible that as such secularity in the private realm grows over time, there may be increasing pressure for secularization of the public sphere. In short, we need much more attention to secularity in family life if we want to explain the secularization process.

Given its significance, it is curious that family life remains underinvestigated compared with other foci within secularity research. The study of secularity has tended to follow the intellectual framework established by the study of religion, and the academic study of religion has long favored study of public institutions (what happens in church or synagogue, the relations between church and state, the interpretation of official religious texts and scripture) over private religion such as family life. Part of the reason may be sexism. As feminist critics have pointed out, family life in many cultures is women's domain, and until recently that just was not interesting to the male academic establishment. However, another reason is practical and methodological. Because it is private, family life is more difficult to access, observe, and study.

Fortunately, a growing number of scholars are willing to devote the time and effort to such studies and are expanding our understanding of secularity and family life. It should be noted at the onset that much of what we know about secularity and family life is based on research conducted in Western, mostly European and North American societies. This chapter will describe what scholars are learning, the debates among them, and what remains to be researched.

DEFINING SECULARITY AND FAMILY LIFE

The first step in exploring any subject is defining our terms. In the case of secularism and family life, this poses some interesting theoretical questions that are not fully resolved. Let us start with family life. The concept of what constitutes a family is contested, reflecting ideological, legal, and cultural differences within and among various societies. Some would say that a gay couple who is not married but living together raising a child are a family, even if the child has no blood relationship to either of them and is not legally adopted. Others would disagree. There are also different types of families such as single-parent, nuclear, or extended families. However, one need not reach consensus on defining *family* to establish a working definition of *family life*. Most readers can probably agree that *family life* refers to the private realm of life and those interactions and relationships that people have with partners, children, relatives, and whomever else they deem to be members of their family.

It is more difficult to pin down secularity. *Secularity* refers to nonreligion or the quality of being nonreligious; therefore, it can only be understood in reference to religion. Because scholars do not agree on what religion is or what it means to be religious, there are varying definitions of secularity. Our discussion will focus on defining secularity as it pertains to family life. There are several distinctions that are helpful here.

SECULAR BELIEF, BEHAVIOR, AND BELONGING
Barry Kosmin and Ariela Keysar (2002) propose that, similar to religion, secularity can be observed and measured in terms of belief, behavior, and belonging. Using conventional

measures of religion, secular belief would be evidenced by rejection of God or the supernatural, secular behavior by nonparticipation in prayer or religious services, and secular belonging by being unchurched or joining an atheist organization. What complicates the picture is that secular belief, behavior, and belonging do not always go together. This is particularly true in family life. Consider an atheist scientist who attends church with his Catholic wife and children; he is only secular in terms of belief. Alternatively, consider a Swedish family who are members of the Lutheran church and had their children baptized, but they do not believe in God or attend services. They appear religious by belonging but are secular in belief and behavior. A growing number of Americans are unchurched and rarely or never pray or attend services; however, many of them claim to believe in God. They are secular in terms of behavior and belonging but not in belief. The reverse tends to be true in Europe, where people tend to belong but not believe.

AFFIRMATIVE VERSUS PASSIVE SECULARITY

As the above examples indicate, secularity is generally conceptualized in terms of what people are not believing, or doing, or joining. This kind of passive secularity in family life is widespread and is fairly well understood. For example, we know that even among families who identify as being Catholic or Jewish, church attendance is down; intermarriage is up; and people are less likely to say grace, read scripture, or enroll their children in religious education than they were in the past (Putnam and Campbell 2010). We also know that families who identify as having no religion (i.e., the "Nones") tend to be more secular by all of these measures (Kosmin and Keysar 2008). However, we can also think about secularity in terms of what people come to believe or do or join in place of religion. When families identify as atheist or humanist, when they raise their children to believe in science and the natural order of the universe or the ethical principles of the Humanist Association, when they practice meditation or gather with other secularists for a ceremony to mark the death of a loved one, we might call this affirmative secularity. This type of secularity is only beginning to be studied. For example, in her research on families who identify as "None," Christel Manning (2015) distinguishes between philosophical secularists, who have affirmatively adopted an alternative identity, worldview, and sometimes even a community, and indifferents, who have not. Richard Cimino's and Christopher Smith's (2014) book on atheist efforts to organize as a movement includes a chapter addressing how seculars ritualize important life transitions. However, much remains to be done.

DEGREES OF SECULARITY

Similar to religion, secularity manifests to varying degrees. For example, we might say that an individual who does not believe in God, never engages in religious behavior such as prayer or attending services, and does not belong to a religious organization is more secular than an individual who is unchurched but still believes in God. However, real life is often not that clear cut, especially when it comes to family life. Consider the example given earlier of the atheist scientist who attends church with his Catholic wife and children. Is he more or less secular than his colleague who still identifies as Christian and claims to believe in God but is disengaged from any kind of religious practice with his family? Kosmin argues that it is misleading to think of religion and secularity as binaries, especially in societies such as the United States where government does not clearly define religion and individuals and families are free to choose (and mix and match) from various options.

Chapter 6: Secularity and Family Life

CULTURAL DIFFERENCES

The distinctions outlined above help us attend to the diverse ways that secularity may manifest in family life. However, these concepts are drawn mostly from research on Western societies and may not apply as well to other cultures. The default definition of religion in Europe and the United States is based on Christianity, which is characterized by theism, communal prayer and worship, and membership in organizations. Hence, measuring secularity in terms of nonbelief in God, nonparticipation in rituals, or nonmembership is mostly effective. But not all religions are like this. For example, many Buddhists do not believe in God or supernatural beings and do not affiliate with an organization. Does this mean that Buddhists, by definition, are more secular than Christians?

How scholars think about secularity is also shaped by the fact that most Western societies afford some degree of religious freedom. Even countries with established state churches, such as Sweden or the United Kingdom, do not enforce religious laws, and although atheists in America may be viewed with suspicion, they are not burned at the stake. Hence, secularity is often affirmative and public. However, not all societies are like this. In theocratic societies such as Iran or Saudi Arabia, openly expressing secular beliefs (e.g., denial of God or the truth of the Qur'an) or secular behavior (e.g., drinking alcohol, women not covering) can put individuals at risk of running afoul of the law. In such a context, the private sphere of family life may be the only safe space to express one's secularity. Yet researchers are only beginning to explore how it manifests in this context.

METHODS OF RESEARCH

Researchers use various approaches to gather empirical data about secularity and family life.

ANALYSIS OF PRINT AND INTERNET RESOURCES

There is a growing body of popular books and blogs related to secular family life. Many of these sources are directed at parents, offering advice on how to raise children outside religion. Some are affirmatively secular, such as atheist Dale McGowen's book, *Parenting Beyond Belief: On Raising Ethical, Caring Kids Without Religion* (2007). Other books have a more spiritual focus, such as *Planting Seeds: Practicing Mindfulness with Children* by Thich Nhat Hanh (2011) or Wendy Russell's, *Relax It's Just God: How and Why to Talk to Your Kids about Religion When You're Not Religious* (2015). Some authors have also set up websites (e.g., Parenting Beyond Belief Blog; Atheist Parent Forum) directing parents to other resources. By analyzing the content of these sources, researchers have identified common concerns that are shared by secular parents, such as navigating relationships with family members or friends who are religious, teaching morality and ethics to children, and dealing with rituals and celebrations. A more recent topic showing up on secular parent blogs that warrants research is advice for homeschooling, a subject long dominated by religious families. It would also be fruitful for researchers to investigate which sources are the most popular (e.g., in terms of book sales or hits on websites) and why.

QUANTITATIVE RESEARCH

Quantitative research refers to gathering and study of data that can be coded numerically so that results can be mathematically analyzed. The most common way to gather such data is by surveys with fixed response options (e.g., yes or no, agree or disagree on scale of 1–5, and so forth). Surveys can be conducted by phone, mail, or over the Internet. In general, large surveys based on random selection from a given population are considered the most representative. However, such surveys are expensive and, because of the definitional issues we discussed above, it can be difficult to identify secular respondents. Because most people are religious, major national surveys tend to focus on religion and identify secularity mainly in terms of "no" responses to questions about religion. However, recent reports by various polling organizations (e.g., the Pew Research Center's American Religious Landscape Surveys or the Institute for the Study of Secularity in Society's American Religious Identification Surveys) showing dramatic growth in religious Nones in the United States have led to follow-up studies that further investigate some aspects of secular family life, such as demographics, the transmission of moral values, and psychological outcomes of a secular compared with a religious upbringing. A good example is Vern Bengston (2013), whose research originally focused on how families transmit religion but who recently added secular families to his study. We still lack good quantitative data on affirmative secularity in family life, such as how atheist, humanist, or other free-thinker parents are transmitting moral values to their children and whether or not and how they engage in rituals and celebrations.

QUALITATIVE RESEARCH ON SECULARITY IN FAMILY LIFE

Qualitative research involves direct interaction by the researcher with families who identify as secular, including personal conversations and long-term observation of subject behavior. This method is well suited to study secular families. Longer term engagement can help build trust, facilitating insight into more personal feelings or relationships. Observation can provide important data about family interactions that a respondent might not mention in an interview or reveal inconsistencies between stated beliefs and behavior. It also draws our attention to the material culture of secular family life, such as the presence of a Christmas tree in an atheist home or secular books on the shelf of an Iranian family, which may lead an interview in new directions. Personal conversations allow secular people, who occupy a minority in many societies, to articulate their own concerns and worldviews rather than scholars imposing categories that were derived from religion research. Qualitative research takes a great deal of time, so samples tend to be smaller and may or may not be representative of the secular population at large. However, it has the advantage of revealing information about secular families that we would otherwise miss.

METHODOLOGICAL CHALLENGES

Researchers of secularity in family life are exploring a new field that poses unique challenges. One is construct validity, or our ability to accurately define what it is we are trying to understand, in this case secularity. As noted previously, the process of defining secularity in family life is still ongoing, and there is not yet a consensus about what the best measures are. Therefore, it is particularly important for researchers in this field to be clear and explicit about the definitions and measure they are applying.

A second problem is access, meaning how you locate and connect with secular families. Researchers seeking access to religious families will often begin by contacting religious organizations. They may ask leaders for permission to conduct a survey, or to distribute information about the study inviting families to participate. This method has limited utility for accessing secular families. Although there are secular counterparts to organized religion, such as the American Humanist Association (AHA), the Unitarian Universalist Association (UUA), or the Sunday Assembly, most secular individuals tend not to affiliate at all. Because

Chapter 6: Secularity and Family Life

An image used in bus and train ads for the American Humanist Association. *Although there are secular counterparts to organized religion, such as the American Humanist Association, secular individuals tend not to affiliate, making it difficult for researchers exploring secularity to locate and connect with secular families.* **THE WASHINGTON POST/GETTY IMAGES.**

seculars have developed a growing Internet presence, some researchers have tried recruiting research subjects online. This can work well, especially for surveys, but such searches do not reliably yield representative samples. Those using qualitative approaches face the additional challenge of gaining direct access to respondents' private space (e.g., to conduct an interview or to observe a secular wedding or funeral). It can take time to build trust, especially in cultures with high degrees of gender segregation where family life is off limits to outsiders. However, these challenges can be overcome, as the growing number of studies in this field attest.

AREAS OF RESEARCH

As researchers present and publish their findings, several subfields are beginning to emerge within the field of secularity and family life.

RITUALS AND RITES OF PASSAGE

One emerging area of interest is the role of ritual and rites of passage in secular family life. Historically, this has long been a major function of organized religion. Most religions have seasonal holidays commemorating important aspects of a community's history or identity; Passover, Ramadan, Christmas, and Pagan solstices are examples. Religions also conduct ceremonies that provide meaning to important events such as marriage, the birth of a child, or the death of a loved one. The symbols, words, and performance of ritual actions express the family's identity and their shared values concerning transitions to a new life stage. For example, the ritual circumcision for an infant Jewish boy symbolizes his entry into a chosen community that began with Abraham thousands of years ago. In a Christian wedding, the bride's white dress and veil symbolize her virginity, the vows of "love until death do us part" express the ideal of marriage as an eternal bond, and the priest's pronouncement at the end that "you are now husband and wife" asserts their new status as a couple to the assembled community. Rituals also provide formal structures that gather individuals from the community to support individuals dealing with strong emotions such as joy, anger, or grief. Thus, funeral ceremonies in various religions typically involve family members speaking before the assembled community and assurances that the deceased has gone to be with God.

How do secular people navigate life's transitions without the supportive structures of religious belief and ceremony? Research suggests there are two main patterns.

Using Religion. Some secular families simply "use" religion, drawing on established practices, rituals, and ceremonies and giving them new, nonreligious meanings. Meditation rituals are perhaps the most common practice because they are less explicitly linked to God and religion. Although many meditation techniques have their roots in Eastern religions such as Buddhism or Hinduism, the growing popularity of mindfulness meditation as an exercise to reduce stress and improve focus and efficiency in the workplace has secularized meditation. Thus, Sam Harris, one of the best known among the New Atheists, has long advocated meditation as a means of fostering awareness of consciousness that is not inconsistent with a secular and scientific outlook.

However, secular families also make use of more explicitly religious rituals, especially if there are young children in the home. Many atheists celebrate Christmas with a tree, gathering with extended family to exchange gifts and eat traditional foods such as ham or cookies to mark the season. Secular Jewish families may light a menorah at Hanukah to symbolize their historic and cultural identity or build a tabernacle in their backyard to mark the bounty of the harvest. Other families will borrow seasonal ceremonies from various religions, combining Pagan Halloween in fall with solstice celebrations in winter and spring and secular Passover or Easter in the spring.

Some secular families self-consciously assign new, nonreligious meanings to these rituals, asserting that Passover connotes the historic Jewish struggle to overcome adversity or that Christmas is about showing love and appreciation for your family. Manning (2015) reports on a humanist family who put a Mickey Mouse doll on top of their tree (instead of an angel) to express their view that Christmas is an American rather than a religious holiday. Other seculars see no need to reinterpret and are comfortable participating in rituals as part of a cultural tradition that does not require belief in God. This attitude is common in Scandinavian societies where levels of secularization are high but most families rely on churches to celebrate rites of passage. One study documents how Swedish couples approached a clergy member before a church wedding ceremony to make sure there would be minimal references to God (Kasselstrand 2015).

The secular use of religious rituals has led to some debate among secular individuals and among the scholars who study them. Critics assert that such use is hypocritical or that families

Chapter 6: Secularity and Family Life

who engage in such practices are not truly secular (Flynn 2012, Myers 2011). Those who defend the practice argue that communal celebrations are an important part of culture that is not owned by religion (Cornwell 2011, De Botton 2013). They point out that some of the most popular symbols and practices of religious ritual (trees with lights, bunnies and eggs, harvest celebrations) did not originate with religious traditions but were adopted from other cultures and assigned new meanings by religious authorities. Why shouldn't atheists do the same?

Creating Secular Ceremonies. Other seculars, particularly those who affiliate with secular organizations, are beginning to develop their own distinct rituals and ceremonies to mark the seasons or transitions in the life cycle. Organizations such as the American and British Humanist Associations or the Universal Life Church (ULC) will train and certify secular celebrants to conduct ceremonies for events such as weddings, funerals, or the birth of a child for families who are not religious. These rituals resemble religious ones in structure but without religious language or symbolism.

Secular weddings will often begin with opening words about the meaning of marriage or partnership, a reading of literature or poetry chosen by the couple, exchange of vows and rings, the lighting of a unity candle to symbolize sharing of love, and a pronouncement by the celebrant that they are now married. Sociologist Dusty Hoesly, who researches such weddings, finds that the celebrant is usually a friend or family member who has acquired the license to conduct the wedding from an organization such as ULC. In the United States, ULC has become the primary licensing organization for personalized nonreligious weddings and has ordained over 20 million people since 1962. ULC thrives because nonreligious couples seek an alternative to the bureaucratic ceremony at city hall or traditional religious rites, an alternative that is personalized and does not use religious language.

The same is true for secular funerals. Similar to religious funerals, secular ones often feature opening words about the meaning of life and death, reflections commemorating the deceased, burial or cremation, and closing thoughts. Such rituals play an important role in helping grieving families deal with the loss of a loved one; however, they do so without invoking concepts of God or an afterlife. Anthropologist Matthew Engelke (2015, 30–31) gives a striking example of a funeral celebrant trained by the British Humanist Association who opened the ceremony with the following words:

> Dear Dave, Dad and Granddad
> We rejoice that you lived
> We cherish the memory of your words
> We cherish your friendship
> We cherish your love
> And with our love
> We leave you in peace.

The celebrant briefly paused, then continued:

> Without fuss and without fear, Dave has left this world in the
> same way that he entered it. For the same passage that we
> all must make from timelessness to life, we must all take—
> from life back to timelessness. This is the natural order of
> things and it belongs to the life of the world....
> And Dave is now free from all harm, pain and suffering.
> Please be seated.

Finally the celebrant walked over to the coffin "and touched it, very gently, as he might touch the shoulder of a person." Engelke comments on the skill of the celebrant in composing and delivering ritual speech and his attention to the importance of materiality by physically acknowledging the presence of the dead body in the room. The example illustrates the power of ritual, which lies not only in the words that assign meaning to the event being celebrated, but in the performance of actions that signify acceptance and commitment to that meaning.

The role of ritual in secular family life is a rich and fascinating subject that is only beginning to be understood. More empirical data are needed describing the various ways that families celebrate. There is also a need for theory explaining how ritual functions in secular family life. Does it create moral unity and reinforce identity as religious ritual does? How effectively does it help families manage difficult emotions? The power of religious ritual to give comfort and guidance in difficult periods of life derives in large part from the perceived authority of tradition. However, seculars tend to be highly individualistic, free thinkers who question authority; therefore, we cannot assume that ritual will function in the same way.

RAISING CHILDREN IN SECULAR FAMILIES

Another important area of investigation is the question of how secular parents are raising their children. Religious parents will usually raise their children within their own tradition. They may display religious symbols and celebrate major holidays in the home, and they frequently enroll their children in religious education programs such as Sunday school or Hebrew school. By contrast, secular parents do not necessarily raise their children to be secular. Although there are some families that seek to transmit an explicitly secular worldview such as atheism, many do not. Rather, the overriding concern for many secular parents is that their children should choose for themselves.

There are various ways that parents go about this. One study that looked at a wide range of family secularity was conducted by Manning (2015). She found that secular parents in the United States raise their children in many different ways, among which five approaches stood out: *conventional, alternative, self-providing, outsourcing, or non-providing.*

The *conventional* approach refers to parents who raise their children within a particular religious tradition, typically one connected to their family history. They may enroll children in a weekly religious education program, occasionally attend services with children, and engage them in at least nominal celebration of major holidays in the home. Surprisingly, even parents who are affirmatively secular may choose this path, especially if they are married to a religious spouse.

Secular parents who go the conventional route explain that decision in pragmatic terms. They may view religion as a good way to teach morality and values, they wish to connect children to a particular family history and tradition, or they feel their kids should experience rituals such as communion or bar mitzvah that the parent enjoyed in their own childhood. They may also value the youth programming offered by organized religion (e.g., afternoon care, summer camps, volunteer opportunities).

The *alternative* approach refers to secular parents who raise their children within an affirmatively secular tradition by affiliating with an organization such as the AHA, the UUA, or more recently the Sunday Assembly. In an effort to meet the needs of secular families, some of these organizations have developed programs for children that promise not to indoctrinate them into any particular tradition. These include summer camps, afterschool care, and weekend social justice work. UUA and AHA offer formal "worldview education" programs, a kind of secular Sunday school that teaches kids about many different religions as well as humanist and atheist philosophies and encourages the child to choose. UUA's education program was established decades ago, so it is comprehensive, offering various age-appropriate levels, and is available in most of their local chapters. The AHA's program started more recently and has been implemented to various degrees in different locations. Secular parents will often supplement such worldview education by activities within the home. These may include talking or reading to children about humanistic ethics, involving children in social justice activism, or celebrating holidays from several different religious and secular traditions (e.g., Hanukah, a Pagan summer solstice, and Darwin's birthday).

Parents who choose the alternative path usually emphasize the value of a pluralistic upbringing, which they see as particularly well suited for today's world (it fosters tolerance of diversity, provides cultural literacy, and expands the pool of wisdom a young person can draw on). Many also allude to the minority status of secularism and the need for support from a community of like-minded secular families.

The term *self-providers* refers to those parents who do not enroll their children in any kind of formal education program but take it upon themselves to transmit a particular secular worldview within the home. They will often buy self-help secular parenting books or go on Internet blogs to get help teaching their kids about various religions or about secular morality. They use various modes of transmission, including reading to children, conversations, engaging children in creating their own unique family rituals (e.g., inventing a secular blessing to say before meals), or teaching them about rituals that pertain to their family heritage but imparting new meaning to them (e.g., Christmas as solstice signifying the return of natural, rather than divine, light to the world).

Self-providing parents may struggle to maintain commitment to the process of worldview instruction because children lose interest or the parent feels he or she lacks appropriate expertise. These parents may complain about lack of support, yet they stay outside of organized community. This often comes from deep suspicion of any organized philosophy, religious or secular, because they have experienced such institutions as hypocritical or shallow. In some cases, these parents are seeking community but are unable to find a suitable institution in their local area.

Outsourcing refers to secular parents who enroll their children in a religious education program provided by a church or synagogue, but they do not themselves affiliate with that organization or attend services with their child, and they do not intentionally engage in any religious activity in the home. For instance, a secular Jewish family might send their son or daughter to Hebrew school on Sunday mornings, but they do not maintain membership in a temple or attend even on high holidays. They might celebrate Hanukah with presents and sweets, but they view this as a secular holiday that affirms their family history and cultural identity.

Outsourcing parents do so because they see value in learning about religion, even when they themselves have left it behind. Many see religious education as a wholesome activity similar to music or sports that children ought to be exposed to. They often feel an obligation to impart a traditional family heritage, especially when religion expresses a particular culture or ethnicity (e.g., Jews, Irish Catholics). In addition, a few parents will outsource religious education in response to a child's expressed interest in spiritual matters.

The term *nonproviders* refers to those parents who do not engage in a conscious effort to transmit any particular worldview to the child. They do not enroll their child in a secular or religious education program, and their home life does not involve any systematic effort to transmit a religious or secular philosophy to their children. They celebrate holidays, but they do so without reference to any particular "ism"; that is, there are gifts at Christmas or Hanukah, and bunnies and eggs at Easter, but children learn nothing about the religious history of these events, nor do parents substitute secular meaning such as solstices or mark explicitly secular events such as Darwin Day. These families do impart moral values, but these are grounded in the parents' personal experience rather than adherence to a religious or secular tradition. Parents who are nonproviders do not wish to impose any worldview on their child, religious or otherwise. They feel that when they are old enough, children will do so for themselves.

Which approach a family chooses will depend on various factors. One is how secular the parents are; for example, parents who identify affirmatively as atheists are more inclined to self-provide or affiliate with an alternative community than parents who are passively secular or indifferent. The influence of religious spouses or extended family plays a role; thus, secular parents married to religious spouses are more likely to use a conventional approach or to outsource religious education. Geographical location also matters; for instance, secular parents living in regions where evangelical Christians dominate the public culture are more motivated to affiliate with an alternative institution.

To further complicate the picture, parents show considerable movement among the various options over time. A family may experiment with self-providing a humanist upbringing and only later join a humanist community. They may outsource religious instruction, and then after several years the secular parent may be persuaded by a religious spouse to attend religious services with her and the children. They may briefly rejoin organized religion to have a child baptized or circumcised and then soon get turned off, drop out again, and do nothing with their children.

The various ways that secular families raise their children illustrate the difficulties in defining secularity that we discussed earlier in this chapter. Religion and secularity are opposites in theory. However, in real life, especially family life, the boundaries between religiousness and secularity are highly porous, and they are frequently shifting.

THE IMPACT OF SECULARITY ON CHILDREN

The growing number of parents who are raising families without religion has led scholars to pay closer attention to the impact of secularity on children. It is widely assumed in popular and academic discourse that religion is good for children and by implication that a secular upbringing puts children at risk. However, the evidence supporting that assumption is decidedly mixed.

There is a huge literature attesting to the benefits that families may confer upon their children by raising them with religion (see Smith, 2005, for a good overview). Such research typically compares adolescents who are highly engaged in organized religion with those who are not and controls to varying degrees for other factors such as income, education, and so forth. Results suggest that teens involved in religion are less likely to use alcohol and drugs, engage in risky sexual behavior, and have lower rates of depression and suicide. They have

Chapter 6: Secularity and Family Life

closer ties to parents and siblings and do better in school. They have lower rates of media use (e.g., watching TV during school week, downloading Internet porn) and are more engaged in volunteer work to help others. Although all results are correlations, some scholars conclude that religion, organized religion in particular, plays a causal role. One reason is the sheer number of such positive correlations. Another is that organized religion has certain structural characteristics that would seem to facilitate these outcomes. It offers a clear framework to teach ethical values to children: there are compelling narratives that help them remember these messages, regular interaction with peers and adults who share the same values reinforces their plausibility, and a community of caring adults offers opportunities for positive mentoring and networking beyond the young person's immediate family.

However, there is also evidence that religion can be harmful to children. Children raised in highly religious households are more likely to be subjected to emotional and physical abuse and to suffer guilt and anxiety, especially over sexual feelings (Capps 1992, Cooper 2012). In addition, studies purporting to show religion's benefits do not demonstrate that religion itself, rather than membership in an organization or community, is what benefits children. Secular worldviews such as humanism can and do provide clear moral frameworks for teaching morality to kids, and there are plenty of nonreligious narratives that can help parents drive those points home. Secular families can interact with other like-minded families and provide their children with an extended community of caring adults. As the secular movement continues to organize and institutionalize, it is building more of the kinds of communities that support families in similar ways as religion has.

Even if the evidence for religion's benefits is compelling, it would be wrong to draw conclusions about children raised in secular families. First, these studies do not adequately sample secular individuals. A recent review of the literature (Weber 2012) suggests that too many studies linking religion with health and well-being rely on volunteer samples who may or may not reflect the general population. Worse, few studies include respondents who are affirmatively secular. They typically compare people who are highly engaged with organized religion with those who are disengaged or indifferent to religion, ignoring those who have replaced religion with something better, such as faith in humanity, nature, or oneself. As Karen Hwang and colleagues (2011) have pointed out, there is a near universal absence of atheist control groups; therefore, we cannot draw valid conclusions.

In the few studies that do sample affirmatively secular individuals, the benefit of religion often goes away. One study (Bengston 2013) found nonreligious parents to be just as effective in imparting strong ethical standards as religious ones and in teaching children to live a purpose-filled life. Zuckerman (2012, 2014) has argued that a secular upbringing may actually be more likely to help kids grow up into ethical adults. Religion teaches children to obey a set of external rules given by a powerful authority, God, and sometimes enforced by corporal punishment. By contrast, secular families encourage children to think for themselves; they are encouraged to question authority, to rationally solve problems, and to empathize with others. As a result, secular teens are less likely than religious teens to succumb to peer pressure and grow up into adults who are less authoritarian, less racist, and more tolerant of others.

At the present time, the debate over the impact of secular child-rearing remains unresolved. It appears that religious and secular upbringing can have benefits and risks for children. Growing up with religion may cause a teenager to refrain from drinking alcohol and wait longer before having sex, but the secular teen may be less conformist and more tolerant of others. Which is a better outcome may ultimately be a value judgment.

THE ROLE OF FAMILY IN SHAPING SECULAR IDENTITY

Family plays a powerful role in shaping an individual's religious or secular orientation. Most people raised in religious families remain religious as adults, and people raised in secular families are more likely to stay secular. However, as the growing number of secular individuals illustrates, family is not destiny. Despite a family's best efforts to raise their children as good Christians or Muslims, some kids never fully buy into religion. Even when religious socialization is initially successful, adolescents may come to question and eventually reject their families' religion. By the same token, it is not uncommon for a committed atheist to affiliate with religion once he marries and begins a family of his own. Scholars have long been interested in understanding the process by which individuals enter or leave secularity over the course of the life cycle.

Childhood: Could Secularity Be Natural? Some social scientists believe that children are naturally inclined to be religious in the sense of believing and wanting protection from supernatural powers and/or of seeking a transcendent meaning of life. One version of this argument is made in humanistic psychology. Humanistic psychologists believe that all humans have basic needs that include not only food, shelter, and love but also the desire for self-realization. People turn to religion and spirituality to meet those needs. Some researchers such as Robert Coles assert that children take naturally to religion because it speaks to their imagination and desire to find meaning; they have questions about the original causes of nature and time, about why we are here and what happens when people die, and they look to religion to answer those questions. His research shows that children raised with religion do not merely parrot what their parents have taught them and that those raised without it still have questions about God, supporting the idea that some degree of spirituality is inherent.

Another version of the "religion is natural" argument is found in evolutionary psychology. Some scholars see religiosity as a product of evolution; for example, religion promotes cooperation and group cohesion through rites of passage that assign particular roles to adults or children and through moral commandments that prohibit murder and incest and encourage helping others. As a result, religious humans were more likely to survive and reproduce. Other evolutionary psychologists view religious beliefs and behaviors as a byproduct of other evolved traits. Most humans are inclined to overattribute phenomena; that is, they assume an event is caused by purposeful action of an intelligent agent even when that may not be the case. This tendency motivates humans to take preventive action when they are unsure of the presence of an intelligent agent (a tiger in the bushes, a vengeful god in the heavens), making it more likely for religious humans to survive. Whether product or byproduct, religiosity evolved over time into a trait that is probably hardwired in the human brain. This has led some researchers such as Justin Barrett (2012) to speculate that most children would become religious even without parental influence.

Other researchers dispute the argument that children are born religious. Children learn religious beliefs and behaviors from their families, and there are no studies proving they would become religious without this influence. Indeed, it may be impossible to empirically test this hypothesis on children because by the time they are old enough to answer research

Chapter 6: Secularity and Family Life

questions, they have already been socialized into either a religious or secular outlook. Studies on adults suggest that an individual's inclination to be secular can be predicted by variations in personality (e.g., individualism vs. conformity, or a preference for logical reasoning over intuition) independent of family influence (Caldwell-Harris 2012). Thus, either religiousness or secularity may be natural variations in human beings.

The question is an important one. If an inclination toward either religiosity or secularity is inherent, then this suggests that there are limits to the effectiveness of socialization. This challenges the arguments made by Sam Harris and others that religious folks are merely brainwashed. If religiosity is indeed the default setting of the human brain, then it implies that children who resist family efforts at indoctrination are somehow exceptional. Such exceptionality may be viewed as a negative (as in atheists are deviant and abnormal). However, the available evidence (Kanazawa 2010, Lynn 2009, Zuckerman 2009) suggests instead it could be taken as a sign of unusual intelligence or courage.

Adolescence and Young Adulthood: Diverse Paths to Secularity. Secularity is increasingly common, especially in Western society, yet religion is still the norm. Thus, most people who identify as secular were not raised that way but adopt that identity later in life. Secularity is an identity they choose, rather than one that was imposed on them, or what social scientists call an acquired or achieved identity rather than an ascribed one. How and why do individuals make that choice, and what impact does it have on their relationship with family?

Apostasy Versus Discovery. Numerous scholars (Altemeyer and Husberger 2006, Smith 2011, Zuckerman 2012) describe the path to a distinct secular identity as one of apostasy. Most seculars were raised with religion, and apostasy refers to the process by which an individual comes to reject that religion. Apostasy often begins in adolescence or young adulthood when people leave their family home to attend college or work in another location.

Jesse M. Smith (2011), who studied atheists in the United States, describes that process as having four components. The first is the ubiquity of theism. Most atheists view their religious upbringing as something that was imposed on them. Similar to gendered expectations of behavior, belief in God is a default position that one internalizes and is not supposed to question. Smith found this to be the case even among atheists raised in more secular families because they typically encountered high levels of religiosity among their extended family, in their community, or in American culture at large.

The second stage is questioning theism. Individuals experienced doubts about God, usually when they left home to attend college. In this new environment, the family influence recedes as individuals develop new relationships with others who may have similar doubts. College education also tends to increase their skepticism about religion as they learn about other religions with different truth claims and about scientific challenges to religion. They discover that morality is not tied to religion, especially not the Bible, but is an outgrowth of society.

When individuals finally come to reject religion, they enter the third stage. Smith describes the atheist identity as one that is only possible in the context of theism. To be an atheist means not believing in God and rejecting what the individual now sees as irrational belief or practice. The fourth stage is publicly claiming the atheist identity. Smith describes this as a kind of coming out experience akin to that of gays and lesbians. Like them, atheists face negative stigma and are marginalized in society; therefore, there is often a lag time between accepting the new identity and going public with it. For example, this might begin with Internet interactions, such as putting "atheist" in the box that asks about one's religion when registering for a site such as Facebook. Other atheists might start by telling their friends and only later their families, especially if the family is religious. In short, coming out as atheist constitutes an important step of self-acceptance, independence, and empowerment.

Others such as Stephen LeDrew (2013) have questioned this linear model of apostasy, suggesting that the path to secularity is more heterogeneous. Individuals raised in secular families may not experience apostasy from religion but rather "discover" an atheist identity as a coherent way to formulate what they already believe or practice or values they already hold. Discovering atheism may also be more applicable to individuals who never bought into the religion their family tried to socialize them into. The recent development of atheist communities on the Internet provides emergent secular individuals with new support structures that are available long before college and even while they are still living with their families. Because these structures were not available to previous generations, people of different ages may have different experiences of coming to atheism.

Tension Versus Acceptance. Whether the process is apostasy or discovery, most young people who become atheists are adopting an identity that sets them apart from their families. The evidence on what that coming out process is like is mixed. In the United States in particular, atheism still carries a strong social stigma. A study of college-aged US atheists found that many felt ostracized by their families or experienced conflict with their relatives because of their nonbelief (Altemeyer and Hunsberger 2006). A survey of atheists or agnostics in the general American population found nearly 13 percent reported discrimination from their family within the previous five years. The atheists in particular reported negative experiences, with 25 percent "being rejected, avoided, isolated, or ignored by family because of [their] Atheism," almost 30 percent "being asked by family or friends to pretend that [they are] not an atheist," and nearly 38 percent "being advised by family or friends to keep [their] atheism a secret" (Hammer et al. 2012, 54). However, there are also more encouraging signs. A study looking specifically at the process of coming out finds more atheists to have positive than negative experiences (Zimmerman et al. 2015). They report that some atheists experience tension with family as a result of revealing their new identity, with religious parents refusing to accept the new identity or dismissing it as a phase the individual will outgrow. However, most atheists reported that family members were eventually able to adapt and give love and acceptance.

The trajectory by which young people adopt a secularist identity and the impact this has on their relationships with family is likely to change in the future. Cimino and Smith (2014) have described a movement toward secular organization, or Atheist Awakening, in which seculars begin to articulate distinct and substantive belief, behavior, and institutional structures. If this movement is sustained, then atheism and secularity, like homosexual or transgender identities, may become a more widely accepted alternative lifestyle, and the process of entry or exit into that identity may be less fraught with tension.

The Impact of Marriage and Family Formation on Secular Identity. Young adults are far more likely to be secular than children or older adults. In the United States, 35 percent of millennials (those born between 1982 and 1996) claim no religion, compared with 23 percent of the general population (Pew Research Center 2015). However, this can change

Chapter 6: Secularity and Family Life

when they start a family of their own. Studies suggest that marriage and family formation lead many unaffiliated individuals to join a church or synagogue and raise their children there. Yet there is also evidence that these life transitions can consolidate and strengthen a secular identity.

There are several reasons why starting a family may lead a secular individual to affiliate with religion (Ecklund and Lee 2011). One is accommodation to a religious spouse. Although religious individuals tend to have a partner who is also religious, the nonreligious are more often not married to another secular person. Studies show spousal accommodation to be among the most important reasons why secular individuals join a church. However, even when both partners are secular, they may wish to provide children with exposure to religion, perhaps because of a family tradition or because they value the youth programming offered by the local church or synagogue.

However, family formation can also play an important role in the process of building and maintaining a secular identity. Self-identity formation is an interactional process; individuals define themselves as secular or religious, Jewish or Catholic, or liberal or conservative in relation to the other people who claim those labels. That is why an orthodox Jew may perceive a reform Jew to be secular whereas someone raised only ethnically Jewish would see the reform Jew as religious. It also explains why a young person raised without religion may not identify as atheist until he makes new friends who claim that label. Manning (2015, 58) argues that starting a family, "creates new and/or more frequent interactions with significant others that challenge or confirm a young adult's secular identity, causing him or her to reflect and evaluate it in ways they may not have before. Those others include their partner (often not secular), extended families (usually not secular), and the children." She finds that as families negotiate how to raise the children, secular parents learn to articulate the boundaries of their worldview and to determine how important it is in their lives. The children themselves can also play an important role, asking questions that probe what the parent really believes and drawing attention to discrepancies between what adults practice and what they preach. Thus, a person previously indifferent to religion may come to realize and accept that he is an atheist as he thinks about what he wants to teach his kids or as he pushes back against in-laws who want the children baptized. A nonreligious person may discover that secularity is not a central part of her identity and that it is okay to attend church with her husband because it seems to make him happy.

Much of what we know about the role of family formation in shaping secular identity comes from relatively small, qualitative studies. Although these yield important insights, we need a great deal more empirical data to confirm and expand what we have learned. In particular, scholars should pay attention to how children affect that process.

Summary

This chapter has explored the various ways that secularity plays out in family life. We have learned that understanding secularity in this context presents unique challenges. There is not yet a consensus on what secularity is, and a good definition should take into account the various dimensions of secularity (belief, behavior, belonging), the difference between affirmative and passive secularity, degrees of secularity, and cultural differences. The boundaries between secularity and religiousness are often unclear, particularly in family life.

Scholars use various methods of investigating secularity and family, including the analysis of primary sources directed at secular parents, quantitative research, and qualitative studies. Each approach has advantages and disadvantages for learning about particular aspects of family life.

Existing studies show secularity and family life in dynamic and fluid relation to each other. Children may be born with a secular or religious inclination, but family plays a powerful socializing role, pushing an individual in one direction or the other. Most people become secular as adults, and this process can create varying levels of tension with their family of origins. The process of starting one's own family leads some secularists back to religion, but for others it strengthens their commitment to secularity. Some secular families feel comfortable using religious rituals to mark important life events; others create their own secular rites. Unlike churched families, secular parents do not necessarily raise their children to be secular but want to encourage them to become free thinkers and make their own choices about religion. These families use various strategies to transmit their values to children, including reaffiliating with conventional religion, joining an alternative secular community, outsourcing religious education while maintaining a secular home, self-providing transmission of a particular worldview, or doing nothing in particular. The impact of a secular upbringing is unclear; both religious and secular child-rearing appears to result in some positive outcomes for youth.

Although these findings are interesting and provocative, many of them are based on relatively few or small studies (at least compared with what we know about religion and family life). Moreover, all of these findings are drawn from research in Western, usually English-speaking nations, where secularity and family life take particular forms. Therefore, the conclusions may not carry over into other cultures where people often live in close proximity to extended family or where the state enforces a particular worldview, religious or secular. More research is necessary to confirm and expand our knowledge of secularity and family life.

Bibliography

Altemeyer, Bob, and Bruce Hunsberger. *Atheists: A Groundbreaking Study of America's Nonbelievers.* Amherst, NY: Prometheus Books, 2006.

American Religious Identification Surveys. http://commons .trincoll.edu/aris/.

Atheist Parent Forum. http://www.atheistparents.org/.

Barrett, Justin L. "Born Believers." *New Scientist* 213, no. 2856 (2012): 38–41.

Bengston, Vern L., with Norelly Putney and Susan Harris. *Families and Faith: How Religion Is Passed Down Across Generations.* New York: Oxford University Press, 2013.

Caldwell-Harris, Catherine L. "Understanding Atheism/Non-Belief as an Expected Individual-Differences Variable." *Religion, Brain and Behavior* 2, no. 1 (2012): 4–22.

Capps, Donald. "Religion and Child Abuse: Perfect Together." *Journal for the Scientific Study of Religion* 31, no. 1 (1992): 1–15.

Cimino, Richard, and Christopher Smith. *Atheist Awakening: Secular Activism and Community in America.* New York: Oxford University Press, 2014.

Coles, Robert. *The Spiritual Life of Children.* Boston: Houghton Mifflin, 1990.

Cooper, Chase. "Confronting Religiously Motivated Psychological Maltreatment of Children: A Framework for Policy Reform." *Virginia Journal of Social Policy & the Law* 20, no. 1 (2012): 1–42.

Cornwell, Elizabeth. "A Very Atheist Christmas." December 21, 2011. http://www.faithstreet.com/onfaith/2011/12/21 /a-very-atheist-christmas/10622.

Cragun, Ryan T., Barry Kosmin, Ariela Heysar, et al. "On the Receiving End: Discrimination Towards the None-Religious in the United States." *Journal of Contemporary Religion* 27, no. 1 (2012): 105–127.

De Botton, Alain. *Religion for Atheists: A Non-Believer's Guide to the Uses of Religion.* New York: Vintage Press, 2013.

Chapter 6: Secularity and Family Life

Dennett, Daniel. *Breaking the Spell: Religion as a Natural Phenomenon*. New York: Penguin Books, 2006.

Ecklund, Elaine Howard, and Kristen Schultz Lee. "Atheists and Agnostics Negotiate Religion and Family." *Journal for the Scientific Study of Religion* 50, no. 4 (2011): 728–743.

Engelke, Matthew. "The Coffin Question: Death and Materiality in Humanist Funerals." *Material Religion* 11, no. 1 (2015), 26–49.

Flynn, Tom. "Good without God." (Review). *Free Inquiry* 30, no. 2 (2012): 57.

Garrison, Becky. "Preaching to the Nones: How Two British Comedians Started a Popular Atheist Church." *The Humanist* 73, no. 5, (2013).

Hammer, Joseph H., Ryan T. Cragun, Jesse M. Smith, and Karen Hwang. "Forms, Frequency, and Correlates of Perceived Anti-Atheist Discrimination." *Secularism and Nonreligion* 1 (2012): 43–67. doi:10.5334/snr.ad.

Hanh, Thich Nhat. *Planting Seeds: Practicing Mindfulness with Children*. Berkeley, CA: Parallax Press, 2011.

Harris, Sam. *The End of Faith: Religion, Terror, and the Future of Reason*. New York: Norton, 2004.

Hoesly, Dusty. "'Need a Minister? How About Your Brother?' The Universal Life Church between Religion and Non-Religion." *Secularism and Nonreligion* 4, no. 1 (2015): 1–13. doi: http://dx.doi.org/10.5334/snr.be.

Hwang, Karen, Joseph H. Hammer, and Ryan T. Cragun. "Extending Religion-Health Research to Secular Minorities: Issues and Concerns." *Journal of Religion and Health* 50 (2011): 608–622.

Kanazawa, Satoshi. "Why Liberals and Atheists Are More Intelligent." *Social Psychology Quarterly* 73, no. 1 (2010): 33–57.

Kasselstrand, Isabella. "Nonbelievers in the Church: A Study of Cultural Religion in Sweden." *Sociology of Religion* (2015): 1–20. doi:10.1093/socrel/srv026.

Kochhar Humanist Education Center. *Establishing Humanist Education Programs for Children*. 2011. http://khec.americanhumanist.org/.

Kosmin, Barry A., and Ariela Keysar. *American Nones: The Profile of the No Religion Population*. Hartford, CT: Institute for the Study of Secularity in Society, 2008.

Kosmin, Barry A., and Ariela Keysar, eds. *Secularism & Secularity: Contemporary International Perspectives*. Hartford, CT: Institute for the Study of Secularism in Society and Culture, 2002.

Lawton, Graham. "Losing Our Religion." *New Scientist* 222, no. 2967 (2014): 30–35.

LeDrew, Steven. "Discovering Atheism: Heterogeneity in Trajectories to Atheist Identity and Activism." *Sociology of Religion* 74, no. 4 (2013): 431–453.

Lynn, Richard, John Harvey, and Helmuth Nyborg. "Average Intelligence Predicts Atheism Rates Across 137 Nations." *Intelligence* 37, no. 1 (2009): 11–15.

Manning, Christel. *Losing Our Religion: How Unaffiliated Parents Are Raising Their Children*. New York: New York University Press, 2015.

McGowan, Dale, ed. *Parenting Beyond Belief: On Raising Ethical, Caring Kids without Religion*. New York: AMACOM, 2007.

Myers, Paul Zachary. "Atheist Church? NO THANK YOU." Freethought Blogs: Pharyngula. 2011. http://freethoughtblogs.com/pharyngula.

Parents Beyond Belief Blog. http://parentingbeyondbelief.com/parents/.

Pew Research Center. American Religious Landscape Survey. 2015. http://www.pewresearch.org/fact-tank/2015/05/13/a-closer-look-at-americas-rapidly-growing-religious-nones/.

Putnam, Robert, and David Campbell. *American Grace: How Religion Divides and Unites Us*. New York: Simon & Schuster, 2010.

Russell, Wendy. *Relax It's Just God: How and Why to Talk to Your Kids about Religion When You're Not Religious*. Long Beach, CA: Brown Paper Press, 2015.

Smith, Christian, with Melinda Lundquist Denton. *Soul Searching: The Religious and Spiritual Lives of American Teenagers*. New York: Oxford University Press, 2005.

Smith, Jesse M. "Becoming an Atheist in America: Constructing Identity and Meaning from the Rejection of Theism." *Sociology of Religion* 22, no. 2 (2011): 215–237.

Weber, Samuel, Kenneth I. Pargament, Mark E. Kunik, et al., "Psychological Distress among Religious Nonbelievers: A Systematic Review." *Journal of Religion & Health* 51, no. 1 (2012): 72–86.

Zimmerman, Kevin J., Jesse M. Smith, Kevin Simonson, and W. Benjamin Myers. 2015. "Familial Relationship Outcomes of Coming Out As an Atheist." *Secularism and Nonreligion* 4, no. 1 (2015): article 4. doi:10.5334/snr.aw.

Zuckerman, Phil. "Atheism, Secularity, and Well-Being: How the Findings of Social Science Counter Negative Stereotypes and Assumptions." *Sociology Compass* 3 (2009): 949–971.

Zuckerman, Phil. *Faith No More: Why People Reject Religion*. New York: Oxford University Press, 2012.

Zuckerman, Phil. *Living the Secular Life: New Answers to Old Questions*. New York: Penguin Press, 2014.

CHAPTER 7

From Rebels to Everyday Atheists: Women and Secularity

Marta Trzebiatowska
Lecturer, Department of Sociology
University of Aberdeen, UK

> *My head was full of misty fumes of doubt … Neither could I understand the passionate declarations of love for a being that nobody could see. Your family, your puppy and the new bull-calf, yes. But a spirit away off who found fault with everybody all the time, that was more than I could fathom.*
>
> —Zora Neale Hurston (1891–1960)

We cannot study secularity without studying religion. They are two sides of the same coin as both reflect human beings' relationship to the supernatural. Historically, secularity emerged both out of the cultural context of religion and as a reaction to it. As Laura Schwartz puts it in *Infidel Feminism* (2013), when being religious is the unquestioned norm, leaving faith, or *counterconversion* to nonbelief is a process necessarily shaped by one's existing beliefs and practices. Neither can we study secularity without paying attention to gender. Gender is one of the most powerful markers of human identity. It is present in all interactions, but we tend to internalize it to the extent that we no longer notice it. In this sense, as Cecilia L. Ridgeway explains in *Framed by Gender* (2011), gender is a background identity, a ghostly presence always combined with other traits, that at times becomes central to our lives, depending on which elements of identity are contextually prioritized. Gender comes with a host of expectations and prescriptions, a lot of which have a strong basis in religious texts and rituals. All religions have something to say about how women and men ought to behave and live their lives. This is partly why subverting or rejecting religious norms have historically been intrinsically associated with challenging norms of femininity and often leads to wider structural changes in the social roles and status of women. But rejecting dominant norms and expectations is a risky endeavor, and social sanctions usually follow. Any study of gender and secularity will inevitably be an exploration of rebellion and its consequences, which is what this chapter is largely about.

Little is known about female *nones*. The extant publications on the subject have focused on the debate around the gender gap in religiosity (e.g., see Brewster 2013; Mahlamäki 2012) or the compatibility between feminism and atheism (e.g., see Overall 2007). Some authors rightly note that the existing (and scant) research on gender and nonreligion is simply an excuse to explore the religiosity of women. A more productive approach, suggested by Melanie E. Brewster in "Atheism, Gender, and Sexuality" (2013), would be to analyze women and men's accounts of leaving religion and of atheism as a choice, rather

111

Chapter 7: From Rebels to Everyday Atheists: Women and Secularity

than a default option in the aftermath of apostasy. Although this is a valid point, the study of nonreligion generally, and of gender and nonreligion more specifically, is a relatively young (though fast-growing) field. Aspiring students of gender and secularity thus will need to create a novel framework of reference for their work and decide which resources are the most appropriate for them to draw on.

This chapter has eight sections. It begins with a brief clarification on the use of terminology in the text, followed by examples of how female nonbelievers have defined religion and nonreligion for themselves, and the uneasy fit between atheism and the traditional model of femininity. The subsequent section moves on to examine gender differences in religiosity as a starting point for the exploration of the other side of the coin: secularity. It looks at some attempts to explain women's greater attachment to, and detachment from, religion and spirituality. But to understand the present, one needs to develop a methodological strategy, as well as look to the past to create a point of comparison. This is why the next section outlines the basic rules of conducting sociological research and the role of history in making sense of gendered experiences of nonreligion. The penultimate section of the chapter examines three examples of women who rejected organized religion. These historical portraits are used to demonstrate the complex intersection of gender, secular orientation, and political views. The aim of this exercise is twofold. First, it shows that despite ongoing changes in gender norms and expectations in the West, nonbelief remains riskier for women than for men. Second, it highlights the other end of the spectrum at which even female nonbelievers or atheist activists tend to remain invisible unless they make themselves noticed by, for example, publicly condemning sexism within the atheist movement (e.g., see the Elevator Gate in 2011; Green 2011). With these points in mind, the chapter ends by discussing the implications of living a secular life as a woman in the twenty-first century world in light of the legacy of the atheist rebels of the previous eras.

TERMINOLOGY

Throughout the chapter a number of terms are used to denote individuals and organizations critical of religion as an institution, as a set of principles, and as a belief in the supernatural. As will become evident, defining nonreligion is far from straightforward. Terms such as *secular*, *nonreligious*, *atheist*, *infidel*, and *freethinker* are applied interchangeably with the caveat that they originated in particular sociohistorical circumstances and their meanings have altered accordingly. Wherever possible, an explanation is provided to flesh out the subtleties of the phrase. Although scholars have been squabbling over definitions of what constitutes religion for many decades (e.g., see Bruce 2009; Dobbelaere 2011), serious attempts to define nonreligion are a recent development. For in-depth discussions of trouble with definitions, one could do worse than read Lois Lee's article (2012) or Stephen Bullivant's chapter on the subject (2013). Bullivant suggests a working definition of atheism as "an absence of belief in the existence of a God or gods" (2013, 20), whereas Lee argues for more clarity and precision in using terms such as nonreligion, atheism, and secularity. The key point is that both the more specific notion of *atheism* and the umbrella term of *nonreligion* have emerged gradually and mostly as a reaction to monotheistic religions. Any study of these concepts needs to be conducted through the lens of the historical periods that

ATHEIST WOMEN DEFINING NONBELIEF

gave birth to them to establish the objective conditions and subjective actions that brought them to life and altered their essence in the process.

Making sense of people's nonbeliefs is just as complicated as attempting to understand their beliefs. After all, the common misconception about nonbelievers is that there is nothing about them that is worth studying. Undergraduate students often look puzzled when first exposed to nonreligion as a topic in its own right. This is another reason why historical comparisons come in handy. Definitions of nonbelief continue to transmogrify in the constantly shifting cultural and historical circumstances. For example, it is no accident that the Freethought movement emerged and developed in the overwhelmingly Christian era when organized religion had an ideological and palpable stronghold over the population; it was something to rebel against. Nonetheless, American freethinkers (a term coined by the English philosopher John Locke [1632–1704]) of the nineteenth century did not object to religion as a whole. Rather, they had a problem with "irrational religion" (Kirkley 2000, 9). Freethinking women were mostly anticlerical, not anti-God, or antireligion per se, with a few notable exceptions. Although they prized a secular government and morality (understood as human, not religion driven), their actual views on the existence of the supernatural varied greatly and are still hard to pinpoint. Similarly, British female freethinkers' perspectives on religion were far from homogenous. In nineteenth-century England, "secularism was by no means a rigidly defined ideology and although its tone and style were probably more appealing to confirmed atheists, it was also home to some deists and pantheists" (Schwartz 2013, 12). Some expressed aggressively rationalist antireligion attitudes, whereas others leaned more toward agnosticism, varieties of theism, or even, like Annie Besant (1847–1933), spiritualism. Having said that, like their American counterparts, they unanimously rejected "all forms of orthodox religion, especially Christianity" (Schwartz 2013, 41).

The more militant and outspoken female atheists in different historical periods unapologetically equated religion with "nothing more than an error, a set of untrue beliefs founded upon ignorance and superstition" (Schwartz 2013, 75). The English activist Harriet Teresa Law (1831–1897) described religion as "the mental faculty which, independent of, nay, *in spite of sense and reason*, enables man to apprehend the Infinite" (Schwartz 2013, 14). Another Englishwoman, Eliza Sharples (1803–1852), stated in 1828 upon her full switch to atheist standpoint: "I have been full of superstition, but I trust that I have ceased to be so" (Schwartz 2013, 77). Frances Wright (1795–1852), a Scottish-born pioneer of atheist activism, wrote that she was "no Christian, in the sense usually attached to the word. I am neither Jew nor Gentile, Mahomedan not Theist; I am a member of the human family" (Schwartz 2013, 45). The American feminist and author of the feminist Freethought encyclopedia, Barbara G. Walker (1930–) found religion problematic as a young child and proclaimed that "to be locked into a religious mold is slavery to the mind" (Gaylor 1997, 533). The actress Katharine Hepburn (1907–2003) firmly declared in an interview on the *Dick Cavett Show* in 1973 that she did not believe in religion but rather in being kind to one's fellow humans here and now: "If you are totally dedicated to someone else, you can rise above all pain." In 1991, she explicitly referred to herself as an atheist in *Ladies Home Journal.* Madalyn Murray O'Hair (1919–1995) summed up religion as a "collective madness" (Stephens 2014, 249). Taslima Nasrin (1962–), a Bengali atheist who

Chapter 7: From Rebels to Everyday Atheists: Women and Secularity

lives in exile after several fatwas have been issued against her, has called religion the "great oppressor" (Gaylor 1997, 614). Female atheists of the early twenty-first century have tended to be more measured in their choice of words but defining nonbelief continues to cause some confusion for the speakers and listeners alike. As Paul Heelas and Linda Woodhead note in *The Spiritual Revolution: Why Religion Is Giving Way to Spirituality* (2005), cultural context constantly evolves and with alternative spiritualities seemingly on the rise in Western societies, such outspoken and definitive atheism in women does not go unchallenged. Nineteenth-century freethinking women were often put off by the religious institutions and their fellow Christian. For example, an English freethinker Emma Martin (1811/1812–1851) "discovered a petty, unsympathetic and narrow-minded community," while Law, Martin's ideological descendent, described her devout youth as "absorbed in the gloom of religion" (Schwartz 2013, 79). By contrast, in the twenty-first century, churchgoing or participation in rituals is not communally enforced, but it is still considered in good taste to believe in "something out there." For instance, in 2013 Oprah Winfrey (1954–) interviewed the long-distance swimmer Diana Nyad (1949–). Nyad claimed to be "an atheist in awe of nature and humanity"— something akin to what the sociologist Phil Zuckerman (1969–) refers to in his 2014 book *Living the Secular Life* as "aweism." Winfrey told her she could not possibly be an atheist if she felt spiritual, but Nyad insisted that "you can be an atheist who doesn't believe in an overarching Being who created all of this and sees over it." This tableau illustrates the importance of letting nonbelievers, female and male alike, create their own definitions of what it means to be an atheist, not necessarily in relation to religion. In the nineteenth century, women who defied the edifice of Christianity in the West were regularly attacked in newspapers, compared with prostitutes and accused of forgetting their own sex and contravening their Creator's ordinances (see Daniels 1840). In the twenty-first century, female atheists continue to be pigeonholed as "at least spiritual" because the association of atheism and femininity remains somewhat uncomfortable for many.

GENDER, RELIGION, AND NONRELIGION: THE VEXING PUZZLE

Although the central topic of this chapter is the study of gender and secularism, we still need to begin with a discussion of gender and religiosity. According to Tony Walter (1948–) and Grace Davie (1946–) in "The Religiosity of Women in the Modern West" (1998), gender as a distinct subject of study entered the orbit of the sociology of religion relatively late. On the one hand it is astonishing, if we consider that by that point, in the 1980s, the majority of those filling in the pews in Christian churches were women. On the other hand, the omnipresence of a phenomenon can make us blind to it as we are more likely to notice the exception, rather than a rule. Whatever the reason, once sociologists of religion began to pay attention to the female experience, a certain paradox became apparent. It turned out that although, in theory, women constituted the majority in Christian churches, in practice, they were invisible and relatively powerless. Numerous studies of the gender gap in religiosity published since the 1980s have highlighted the quantitative as well as qualitative differences between men and women (for an overview, see Trzebiatowska and Bruce 2012). The framework for thinking about (non)religiosity and gender is simple. In a religious society, everyone is equally religious because religion permeates the fabric of society in that it is present in rituals, daily interactions, and holidays. Religion governs eating habits, sexual mores, and every aspect of life imaginable. But where a discernible gender difference exists,

114   MACMILLAN INTERDISCIPLINARY HANDBOOKS

women tend to be more religious than men. Gender differences in religiosity seem universal across religions and cultures, but the explanation does not lie in biology. Rather, the explanation consists of small differences that overlap and reinforce one another. The following two components are central to solving the puzzle of gender gap in religiosity and, by extension, nonreligiosity:

1. The power relationship between men and women in the context of the changing status of religion and the growing presence of secularism in its various guises;

2. The relative persistence of the gendered division of social roles.

Both points require a detailed explanation because they are highly relevant to the discussion of gender and secularity.

DIFFERENT GENDERS, SIMILAR LIVES

Although shifts in gender relations have been slow and uneven across cultures, Pippa Norris (1953–) and Ronald Inglehart (1934–) find plenty of evidence in their 2003 book *Rising Tide: Gender Equality and Cultural Change around the World* that shows that women and men's lives are gradually becoming more similar in the most affluent postindustrial societies. Some may take umbrage at the implication that women are "catching up" with men by entering domains hitherto reserved for men, but the fact is that the women's social status and opportunities have improved dramatically over the past century or so. The point is about systemic contingencies, not the failure or success of either gender. If secularity is partly caused by the rejection of divine authority and control of religious institutions, then women joined the party later than men purely because of their structural position, not personal, or gender-based inability to do so. Men generally were affected earlier than women by the secularizing forces that reduced the plausibility of religious beliefs and turned religious rectitude from a necessary condition for citizenship into a personal preference. In the social and historical process known as *secularization*—by which we mean that religion gradually lost hold over the public sphere in the West over the past 150 years—men happened to be affected first. In the nineteenth century, society became divided into two spheres: the private (home) and the public (work). These two domains were gendered. Women were thought more suited to the private sphere where they could use their natural caring and nurturing skills, and men were believed to belong in the public sphere, which was characterized by rationality and efficiency. This division of social space meant that as the secularizing forces swept through the public life and men happened to be the ones more involved in it, they also became more secular. As this rigid division became fuzzy over time, women have begun to participate in the public sphere to a similar degree as men. As the lives of women become more similar because of the erosion of traditional gender roles, so the gap in religiosity might diminish or disappear altogether. For the time being, in some contexts, men continue to encourage women to be religious on their behalf: for example, in some societies, to be a good mother, wife, and daughter means to be pious on behalf of the men in the family.

Religion's loss of power, popularity, and prestige in the modern world has been slow and uneven, but it has occurred nonetheless. And so by the same token, the growth in nonbelief has a strong gendered element to it. Undoubtedly, the gender gap in nonbelief has diminished in the past hundred years. As the British social historian Callum Brown (1953–) points out, although in the mid-twentieth century those with "no religion" were overwhelmingly male, the ratio of female to male nones became almost even by the 2000s in modern Western democracies, with the exception of the United States (2011, 58). The

Chapter 7: From Rebels to Everyday Atheists: Women and Secularity

point is that in some cultures in which religion retains enough social prestige and heritage heft to give those who are ambivalent reasons to retain some sort of residual attachment, the gender difference will probably persist. But in societies in which faith is viewed as an entirely private matter—something individual and thus respected as personal and intimate—the gender gap has diminished and may disappear altogether, which means that on the whole women might become as secular as men.

TRANSFORMATION OF GENDER ROLES

The social changes that have weakened organized religion in the West have also reduced some of the differences in life circumstances of men and women. Although the domestic and the public spheres have become less gendered, as well as less strictly separated (e.g., men and women work from home, and men are more likely than before to take paternity leave while their partner goes back to work), when we look at women's social roles, the story is quite different. This is where biology matters a bit more than sociologists would like to admit; women remain the ones capable of giving birth, which subsequently structures their social lives. On average, women remain chiefly responsible for raising children; looking after the elderly, the sick, and the dying; and caring for others more generally. These jobs bring them into contact with religious officials, institutions, and other religious individuals because all religions center on love and caring for fellow humans. So, coincidentally, women's social roles keep them closer to religion than men. Whenever we perform any social role, we also develop a particular attitude to the world around us. The more time women spend caring for others, especially at crucial moments in the life course, such as birth, death, and other rites of passage, the more sympathetic they are to religion in general, and organized religion in particular. According to this piece of the puzzle, women are more religious than men because their "lay" caring attitudes coincide with the professional attitudes of most religious bodies. However, enough women are now free of the social roles that coincidentally brought them into the orbit of organized religion to destroy the web of expectations that disposed them to be more favorable, as a class, to religion. Despite these shifts, the religious foundations that have contributed to creating and strengthening the dominant model of femininity remain influential. In the nineteenth century, the notion of a female atheist was abhorrent to male commentators. According to Evelyn Kirkley in *Rational Mothers and Infidel Gentlemen* (2000), the scarcity of atheist women was attributed to their biological predispositions to credulity, and when allowing for even the possibility of nonbelievers who were women, these commentators recoiled in disgust. Atheism was the antithesis of the notion of "femininity as godliness," which subsequently lead to a stigmatization of female atheists. In the twenty-first century, the disgust is no longer as evident but femininity and atheism may appear an uneasy match. Sam Harris (1967–), one of the founding fathers of New Atheism, claimed in one of his blog entries: "I believe that a less 'angry,' more 'nurturing' style of discourse might attract more women to the cause of atheism" (2014). This theme is explored in more detail later in this chapter.

Minority within a Minority: Gender Differences in Nonreligion. We do not have a great amount of numerical data from the nineteenth century, but we do know that the gender ratio in the golden age of Freethought (1860–1900) was also skewed toward men. In the United States, the percentage of women ranged between 11 and 38, depending on the source of the date; but according to Kirkley (2000), it is safe to assume that around 20 percent of freethinkers in that period were female. In the United Kingdom, women accounted for about a fourth of the audience at Secularist public meetings and only

12 percent of the members between 1881 and 1891, but according to Schwartz (2013), almost half were related to male members in some fashion. Even in the era of surveys, locating the data on the number of female atheists worldwide is challenging, especially when self-identified atheists constitute a relatively small percentage of nonbelievers worldwide (Gallup 2015). On average, according to Ariela Keysar and Juhem Navarro-Rivera in "A World of Atheism: Global Demographics" (2013), men make up the majority of nones across countries and cultures. The gender gap narrows, however, in societies such as France and Germany where atheism is more prevalent, whereas in former communist states like Russia, it has increased, even though the percentage of atheists has declined overall. Nonetheless, these are exceptions and most surveys confirm the general rule in the studies of gender gap in religiosity that the difference is smallest at the extremes of religiosity and secularity.

The Practicalities of Researching Gender and Nonreligion. It is useful to say a few words about how we could approach a study of gender and nonreligion as an intrinsically social phenomenon. In *A Treatise on Social Theory* (1983), British sociologist Walter Garrison Runciman (1934–) suggests four stages of a social scientific investigation: reportage, explanation, description, and evaluation of human behavior. The role of a researcher consists of these four elements: collecting information in as many ways and places as possible; producing an understanding of the data and, if possible, establishing correlation and causation (with the important caveat that the first does not automatically imply the second); attempting to see the point of view of those one describes (seeing the world through their eyes, or "putting oneself in their shoes"); and, finally, the most pragmatically oriented aspect, that is, judging the phenomenon under scrutiny with a view toward designing social policy or helping "those involved to a course of action leading to political transformation" (Runciman 1983, 40). Empiricists are less concerned with description and evaluation. Neither is useful for their purposes, as "no methodological conclusions can be drawn from this" apart from the fact that researchers get the opportunity to "subject the objects of their studies to verbal questionnaires" (Runciman 1983, 40). All four elements are of equal importance and relevance in the task of studying the relationship between gender and nonreligion, but it is crucial not to conflate them. To simplify this recipe even further, two general guidelines are worth noting. First, the increasingly diverse sources of evidence we have the better. Second, it is imprudent to make too much of infrequent and unusual patterns. For instance, it may well be the case that a behavior or belief initially seems commonplace, or popular, but it needs to be scrutinized in the wider context against other factors that are present. Searching historical materials to construct comparisons is one way of conducting such a scrutiny. The importance of history cannot be emphasized enough. The Roman philosopher and politician Cicero (107–43 BCE) wrote as early as 64 BCE:

> To be unacquainted with what has passed in the world, before we came into it ourselves, is to be always children. For what is the age of a single mortal, unless it is connected, by the aid of History, with the times of our ancestors? Besides, the relation of past occurrences, and the producing pertinent and striking examples, is not only very entertaining, but adds a great deal of dignity and weight to what we say. (*Brutus, or the History of Eloquence*)

In other words, to be ignorant of history and to reduce our analysis of any subject to the present-day framework is naïve and short-sighted. Therefore, developing a comprehensive understanding of the intersection of gender and nonreligion requires an acute awareness of historical complexities that create the setting under investigation. Although certain aspects of the research phenomenon will be similar across different historical periods, others will be

Chapter 7: From Rebels to Everyday Atheists: Women and Secularity

unique to the particular moment in which researchers are situated. For instance, our reflexivity regarding gender as an organizing principle of social relations is much greater than it was in the nineteenth century, but this does not necessarily lead to greater gender equality. In some societies, coming out as nonreligious can be a non-event, but in others, the consequences are severe. Placing our own research subjects within wider historical context gives us an opportunity to demonstrate the uniqueness of the historical moment in which we live, as well as its debt to the past. Scholars have ignored nonreligion until relatively recently. Perhaps part of the reason for this lack of attention is the taken-for-granted secularization of the modern West and nonreligion becoming the norm, and hence not exotic enough as a research subject. This lack of attention also could be due to the basic understanding of nonbelief as an absence rather than as a standpoint in its own right. Some commentators (e.g., Baker and Smith 2009) attribute this lacunae to the fact that nonbelievers are simply hard to recruit because they are unaffiliated. Whatever the reason, the field is developing fast, and gender dynamics play a key role in nonreligion. Uncharted pathways toward new knowledge require "creativity and determination" (Baker and Smith 2009, 730), and in light of limited resources for the twenty-first century, history helps to situate the subject in a wider context. To put it briefly, sometimes we need to look back to see the way forward.

WOMEN AND ORGANIZED NONRELIGION

The nineteenth century provided female doubters a fertile ground for involvement in social reform, and the Freethought movement in particular gave them a platform to combine their passion for the active promotion of the freedom of thought. The uniqueness of the Freethought movement lay in its roots in the utopian socialist tradition, as well as its support for a wide array of reform movements, which made it more like a "moral culture" (Kirkley 2000, 156) than a single-minded and goal-oriented organization. In general, freethinkers' understanding of gender was the product of their cultural milieu, so although they were radical in their critique of religion, their views on women closely resembled those of their Christian counterparts. Throughout the Victorian era in Britain, "serious Christianity" dictated the rules of "moral, intellectual, social and political life" (Schwartz 2013, 15) and with that came dominant ideas on what womanhood ought to be. These ideas were riddled with contradictions. First, although women were thought of as intellectually and physically weaker, they were simultaneously believed to be morally superior to men. This domestic ideology was in fact useful for freethinking feminists because the contradiction meant that women's moral superiority and caring nature also predisposed them to regenerate society, and thus to act in the public sphere traditionally labeled as masculine. For example, in 1847, Elizabeth Cady Stanton (1815–1902) moved from Boston to Seneca Falls, a provincial town near New York, with her husband and sons. According to Susan Jacoby in *Freethinkers: A History of American Secularism* (2004), domesticity, isolation, and boredom prompted her to seek intellectual company of like-minded women, which in turn lead to the start of what later became the organized women's rights movement. Second, the consequences of women's disproportionate involvement in religion were bittersweet. On the one hand, it was assumed that women were drawn to religion because they were susceptible to the strong emotions that it involved, but on the other hand, the feminization of religion was not welcomed by Christians or freethinkers. Feminized Christianity put men off, according to the church professionals, and it enslaved women while stalling the rational revolution on a societal scale, according to the secularists. Femininity, characterized with quiet conformity on the one hand, and uncontrollable sexuality on the other, posed a problem for atheist and religious men alike.

Still, although the religious majority thought of female piety as a good thing, American freethinkers saw feminine predisposition to religiosity as a major problem. Women "were the noose of Christianity's stranglehold on the country" (Kirkley 2000, 28). In other words, women liked religion a little too much, which in freethinkers' eyes made them chiefly responsible for the persistence and power of Christianity. Yet again, women were a problem because of their commitment to Christianity, which enslaved them. The Freethought movement was split into two camps. Some freethinkers saw innate sexual differences as the main reason for women's susceptibility to religion. Women were naturally more emotional (and irrational), and so was religion. This made femininity and piety a natural fit. Others were social constructionists of their era in that they believed that human nature was pliable—if external conditions changed, so would women's attitude toward religion. While acknowledging these natural and environmental factors, many female freethinkers were bewildered, not unlike secular feminists of the twenty-first century, by women's willingness to put faith "in a creed which places them in a position which, in many instances, is scarcely above the level of the brute" (Schwartz 2013, 134). Overall, freethinkers, both male and female, could be misogynistic in their assessment of women's suitability for independent thinking as they blamed "women's own stupidity [...] for their inability to recognise Christianity as their oppressor" (Schwartz 2013, 135). Whether this predisposition was thought to be natural, or socially imposed, women were urged to develop their own critical faculties and rebel, just like men had done. Kirkley notes that freethinkers went as far as to argue that men attended church only because women ordered them to and for practical reasons, such as avoiding negative social sanctions and maintaining the higher community status churchgoers enjoyed. Free-thinkers saw male believers as ignorant; accordingly, they were described as "mentally castrated little Willies" (Kirkley 2000, 44). Despite this call to arms, freethinkers were conflicted between their ideological agenda and the objective conditions under which they pursued it. For instance, they did not necessarily want to attract too many women to their movement as it would diminish its status. Whatever the internal disagreements on gender among freethinkers, Kirkley explains, ultimately they believed that the victory of rational thought over religious superstition would unite men and women and consequently alter gender relations. The secularization of society then was intimately tied up with improvements in women's status. But seemingly the burden of instigating this transformation was placed solely on women's shoulders: they had to become rational. In other words, they had to become more like men. Thus, there were two sides to becoming a freethinking woman. The discovery of a new way of functioning in the world could be exhilarating in its emancipatory potential, but at the same time, Freethought was based on science and reason, culturally coded as masculine and as such strictly opposed to the emotional and ethereal qualities traditionally assigned to women. Some female converts to Freethought joined in with the critics of feelings as the enemy of the rational world, but others argued that emotions need to have a place in the new secular society to attract women who were "naturally" more emotionally driven. According to Kirkley, freethinkers did not necessarily achieve gender equality, but they did engage in heated debates over gender roles that we continue to struggle with in the twenty-first century. Arguments over rationality versus emotions, and the gendering of the private and public, continue to rumble on in all dimensions of social life, both off- and online.

Chapter 7: From Rebels to Everyday Atheists: Women and Secularity

NONRELIGION AND RESPECTABILITY

Religion, with its prescriptions and rituals, serves as a perfect tool of control and monitoring. Although it places the same expectations on women and men, women are held responsible for upholding dominant social mores, particularly the ones associated with sexuality, such as desire, modesty, and respectability. The nonconformists who challenged these rules of conduct automatically defied not only religious authority, but also dominant notions of femininity. Contesting religious culture was intrinsically associated with the development of women's rights ideology and movement in the nineteenth and early twentieth centuries, even though few feminists of that time identified as atheists. Those who did explicitly fused their abandonment of faith with rejection of patriarchal authority in all its guises. Some female freethinkers explicitly claimed to have rejected religion because it was a tool men used to control women. All in all, freethinking women combined two hazardous activities: an attack on Christianity with the fight for women's rights. For instance, Wright believed that "truth has no sex" and as "teachers of the public," freethinking women had "to encourage intellectual development of others and themselves according to the rules of unemotional, rational and fact-based investigation" (Schwartz 2013, 119). Public speaking was a male-dominated activity, and when taken up by women, it signified something akin to cross-dressing according to the fiercest critics. Church officials saw it as the equivalent of wearing trousers or a beard. As noted in Annie Laurie Gaylor's edited volume *Women Without Superstition* (1997), mob violence against female public speakers was a frequent occurrence, especially because their style was highly confrontational and they defied the Christian model of proper femininity. According to Schwartz, as women's public speaking became more common in the twentieth century, there was less scope for freethinkers to challenge the norms of femininity by adopting an adversarial style. Public speaking and public writing meant that freethinking women broke out of the domestic sphere and entered this hitherto masculine domain. This fact combined with the use of rational and scientific arguments meant that freethinking feminists "appropriated a distinctively masculine narrative" as independent intellectuals rebelling against authority (Schwartz 2013, 88). Atheism was by definition unfeminine but not inevitably so. By renouncing religion, women were showing there was nothing ineluctable about the much-lauded association between femininity and enthusiastic religiosity. Moreover, secularity constituted a middle-ground where women had more potential for creativity because apart from renouncing religion and patriarchy, they had no one movement agenda to draw upon.

Rebellion against traditional femininity was also equated with immorality, particularly of the sexual kind. The atheist feminist Ernestine Rose (1810–1892) was famously described as "a thousand times below a prostitute" by a newspaper editor (Kolmerten 1999, xvii) and such language was not uncommon when referring to many of her sisters in arms. In the second half of the nineteenth century, secularists were determined to prove that morality was independent from religion, so the question of sex was central to their mission. As a movement, they needed to appear respectable to be accepted. Although approaches to the question of marriage and free love varied among the members, freethinking feminists were expected to remain conventional and conservative in their gendered behavior. So while in the 1830s and 1840s freethinking feminists cohabited with men, in the 1870s, the two leading feminists were married. Similarly, in their deconversion stories, many freethinking women emphasized the strength and sincerity of their former Christian faith to demonstrate their integrity. The large majority hailed from devout Christian backgrounds, and they did not want to give the impression that their atheism was fueled by disillusionment with religion. Rather, they turned away from faith as a result of dedicated and lengthy intellectual journey. As Schwartz writes, they also presented themselves as respectable (rather than freelovers in search of sexual freedom) to show that despite being serious about their faith, they could not continue to believe because of their intellectual awakening. Freethinking women were at pains to demonstrate that their infidelity developed despite strong commitment to religion. It was not their lack of effort that made them into unbelievers, but rather it was the reality of organized forms of religiosity that they found oppressive and stifling. To put it simply, they tried but intellect and reason won.

BADLY BEHAVED WOMEN MAKING HISTORY

The exact levels and quality of religious adherence in different historical periods is a debated subject. The proponents of the secularization thesis—the argument that religion declines as societies modernize and industrialize—would argue that the Middle Ages was a profoundly religious period in Western history, especially when compared with the twentieth century (e.g., see Bruce 2011). The advocates of the rational choice theory in the study of religion—the idea that humans are hardwired for religion and a wealth of religious choices available increases religiosity among a population—would argue that there was never a golden age of religiosity in Europe and that high levels of religious activity are cyclical and determined by the supply and demand forces in the religious marketplace (e.g., see Stark and Finke 2000). It is certainly the case that when religious institutions are in a position to dictate the norms to the population, deviating from these norms is a brave move. If the norm implies a belief in the supernatural of some sort, without necessarily specifying its denominational features, nonconformism is easier to conceal but abnormal nonetheless.

Long-term historical dynamics are important when we consider different forms of atheism that had existed long before the phrase was coined in sixteenth-century France (from Ancient Greek *atheos*) must be understood in their sociohistorical context. For example, in the medieval period, the term *unbelievers* referred to "members of other religions, enemies outside one's own secular system of loyalty or rebels from the inside" (Weltecke 2013, 166). Alternative beliefs constituted more of a threat than lack of beliefs and "atheism was considered as an immorality, a sign of ignorance, or as a spiritual problem" (Weltecke 2013, 176). Fast-forward to the nineteenth century and we have the term *freethinkers* applied to an organized movement of nonbelievers and antireligionists in Britain and the United States. Adding gender to the mix complicates the picture further because women traditionally have been cast in the role of moral guardians and beacons of virtue to the point of being held responsible for the honor of not only family members but also whole nations. A good example is the mythology surrounding women and national pride, the instances of honor killings, or the disproportionate vilification of female miscreants historically. As Laurel Thatcher Ulrich notes, "[w]ell-behaved women seldom make history," (1976, 20) while rule-breakers are remembered for challenging the status quo. But female rule-breakers commit a double crime: against the commonly accepted rules of social conduct and against gender expectations. The consequences can be severe. For example, the freethinker Besant's husband denied her custody of their daughter "on the grounds that her views made her unfit to be a mother" (Schwartz 2013, 53). As we have scarce numerical data for the proportion of atheist women before the twentieth century, we

Chapter 7: From Rebels to Everyday Atheists: Women and Secularity

need to rely on widely publicized historical accounts of female nonreligion, or more accurately, instances of women's rebellion against organized religion. The following sections describe the cases of three women who gained notoriety as troublemakers for overtly rejecting religion, among other things. All three publicly declared atheism and fought for the freedom of thought.

HYPATIA OF ALEXANDRIA (350–415 CE)

"Badly behaved" women who challenge the normative order of their time tend to be visible. This in turn means they are more likely to become scapegoats in larger social conflicts. The fate of Hypatia, a female philosopher, mathematician, and astronomer in ancient Alexandria, and the martyr patron of female atheists, is a case in point. Alexandria was the cultural hub of the ancient world but by 364 the city had become a site of conflict between Christians, Jews, and pagans, which created a precarious political climate that partly contributed to Hypatia's tragic demise. Schooled by her philosopher father, Hypatia developed a passion for science and philosophy and soon surpassed her teacher in knowledge and intellectual curiosity. She devoted herself to the study of mathematics and astronomy, and became a well-respected teacher of Neoplatonism. Hypatia's public lectures attracted

The death of Hypatia (350–415), mid-nineteenth-century illustration. *Hypatia, a philosopher, mathematician, and astronomer in ancient Alexandria, and the martyr figure of female atheists, was beaten to death by an angry mob.* PRINT COLLECTOR/GETTY IMAGES.

Chapter 7: From Rebels to Everyday Atheists: Women and Secularity

large audiences, and people traveled from afar to listen to her speak. She wore a scholar's cloak, moved freely around the city, and attended male gatherings—not a lifestyle typical for a woman of her time. Her wisdom and civic virtue were admired by many, including Alexandria's Roman governor, Orestes. Orestes controlled the civil government of the city while the archbishop Cyril was in charge of its main religious institution. Rumor had it that Orestes refused to relinquish his control over the city to the church because of his association with Hypatia. Orestes was not easy to get rid of, but Hypatia, an unorthodox woman and his close friend, constituted the next best target for Cyril's fanatic followers. An angry mob ambushed her carriage, dragged her into a church where she was stripped naked and beaten to death with roof tiles, and her remains subsequently torn apart and burned. This gruesome death demonstrates that Hypatia symbolized a threat to Christianity, patriarchy, and masculinity in more ways than one. Like many female atheists who came after her, she was ahead of her time and she paid the price. The murder of Hypatia also marked the beginning of the end of secular philosophy in the Roman Empire (Hecht 2003). The Spanish movie *Agora* (2009) about Hypatia's life and work has been both criticized and celebrated for its depiction of early Christians as ignorant and bloodthirsty thugs—a reception that underscores the ongoing debates between believers and nonbelievers. Hypatia broke the rules, but she was also a victim of the accident of timing whereby the intricate web of historical events and individual relationships lead to her death. The next female atheist under the spotlight happened to live in a safer time and suffered fewer consequences of her difference.

ERNESTINE L. ROSE (1810–1892)

Needless to say, Rose's story is just as remarkable as that of Hypatia's, although with a happier ending. Rose was born in Poland in 1810. Her father was a rabbi and even though Rose rejected all religion, her Jewish background inevitably shaped her subsequent life path in multiple ways. She developed an interest in "the Judaic ethic of repairing and restoring the world through acts of charity" and her father taught her to appreciate the art of argument as an interactive quest for understanding and knowledge (Dorres-Worter 2008, 2). Rose's upbringing gave her the tools to question the world around her and made her into a rule-breaker. She began to test the boundaries of her cultural and religious milieu at a young age, and was quickly labeled as a heretic and a rebel. When she was sixteen, after her mother's sudden death, her father arranged for Ernestine to marry, but she refused. This resulted in a potential loss of the inheritance from her mother, which was meant as a dowry in the arranged marriage. In an act of defiance, Ernestine appealed her own case in the secular court and won. She only kept a small amount of the inheritance and moved to Berlin when she was seventeen. There she faced another challenge. At the time Jews were not allowed to live in Berlin unless

Ernestine L. Rose (1810–1892), Polish-born American social reformer. As a public speaker advocating for social reform in the United States, Rose was a multiple outsider: she was a woman, a foreigner, a Jew, and an atheist. **HULTON ARCHIVE/GETTY IMAGES.**

RELIGION: BEYOND RELIGION

Chapter 7: From Rebels to Everyday Atheists: Women and Secularity

they had substantial capital behind them. Yet again, Ernestine presented her case to the authorities and finally to the King of Prussia, Frederick William III (1770–1840). He promised to relax the law on the condition that she be baptized as Christian. Ernestine did not conform on the grounds that her atheism covered all religions. Remarkably, the king granted her the right to remain in Berlin despite her refusal to convert. Ernestine subsequently spent some time in London where she got involved in the Owenite movement and met her English husband, William Rose (1813–1882). They arrived in New York in 1836, and Ernestine immediately became a spokeswoman for social reform. Rose was also a multiple outsider in her capacity as a public speaker: she was a woman, unmistakably foreign because of her strong accent, and she was a Jew and an atheist (Jacoby 2004, 97). In addition, because a lot of female activists were Christians at the time, she was not uniformly accepted by women either.

Rose was sarcastic and her speeches punchy. She identified as an atheist in a public lecture given in Boston, in 1861. She questioned the veracity of the Bible and God—a risky endeavor. Rose realized that she challenged the "forbidden ground, too holy and sacred for mortals to approach" (Dorres-Worters 2008, 295). She drew a clear distinction between belief and knowledge, and demonstrated that the latter cannot as yet give us any evidence for the existence of God:

> It was a great mistake to say that God made man in his image. Man, in all ages, made his God in his own image; and we find that just in accordance with his civilization, his knowledge, his experience, his taste, his refinement, his sense of right, of justice, of freedom, and humanity, so has he made his God. (Dorres-Worters 2008, 297)

In the spirit of prioritizing rational thinking over the spiritual and supernatural, she also proclaimed that "Ignorance is the mother of Superstition. In proportion to man's ignorance is he superstitious—does he believe in the mysterious" (Dorres-Worters 2008, 297). She illustrated her point by examining the story of Creation and Noah's ark and subjected it to a stringent point-by-point criticism based on logical and rational thinking. Most important, Rose finished that particular speech by addressing believers from the point of view of an atheist: "Though I cannot believe in your God whom you failed to demonstrate, I believe in man; if I have no faith in your religion, I have faith, unbounded, unshaken faith in the principles of right, of justice, and humanity" (Dorres-Worters 2008, 300). If nonbelievers are still commonly associated with immorality in the twenty-first century, as Penny Edgell et al. write in "Atheists as 'Other': Moral Boundaries and Cultural Membership in American Society" (2006), it is not hard to imagine the disapproval Rose must have faced. She was well aware of this and pre-empted any accusations by adding: "Whatever good you would do out of fear of punishment, or hope of reward hereafter, the Atheist would do simply because *it is* good; and, *being so*, he would receive the far surer and greater reward, springing from well-doing, which would constitute his pleasure, and promote his happiness" (Dorres-Worters 2008, 300). In this simple exhortation, she encapsulated the underlying principle of "being human" and detached it from a religious belief while also highlighting the centrality of the individual's happiness and well-being.

Rose never denied her religious roots but equally insisted that her struggle for equal rights for women transcended birthplace, race, and nationality—it was universal (Dorres-Worters 2008, 40). Moreover, unlike many of her contemporaries in the fight for equal rights, Rose did not claim that special virtues were associated with femininity but rather that women deserved universal rights because they were human beings. Atheism certainly drove her political activism, but she combined it with the overall concern for human, not simply women's rights. Her life demonstrates the complexity of professing an overtly atheist identity as a woman, both in the nineteenth century and in the present-day. As a freethinker, she believed that religion was dangerous because it occluded individuals' minds and rational thinking. Alongside her radical freethinking peers, she argued passionately for the freedom of the human mind as the basis for freedom more generally. Rose suffered from ill health in later life and died in 1892 in England. She remains the least known and the most outspoken atheist of her era.

MADALYN MURRAY O'HAIR (1919–1995)

The public face of nonbelief and atheism in 1960s America was Murray O'Hair. She gained such notoriety with her antireligious views that in 1964 *Life* magazine labeled her as "The Most Hated Woman in America" (Seaman 2005). Like other female nonbelievers, Mitchell Stephens writes in *Imagine There's No Heaven: How Atheism Helped Create the Modern World* (2014), Murray O'Hair felt strongly about the imposed presence of religion in her family's life and demanded her son be exempt from school prayer. When she wrote a letter to the editor of the local newspaper and her case was covered soon after, she suffered severe community backlash. Her tires were slashed, her windows broken, her cat was killed, and her son was abused and threatened. Despite these silencing attempts, she persevered and eventually won a court case to stop compulsory prayer in American schools. Murray O'Hair took to lawsuits as her main weapon against organized religion and later tried to force Maryland's churches to pay taxes but lost the court case. She even sued NASA, following footage of an astronaut praying for peace, but also lost. Undeterred, she remained a committed atheist activist, setting up a number of organizations, including the Freethought Society of America, the Society of Separationists and the American Atheists, as well as a publication, *American Atheist*. Her unwavering dedication to the atheist cause was driven by the conviction that "once a person is bitten by the Atheism bug, that person stays an Atheist for the rest of his or her life" (Stephens 2014, 255). This scenario did not ring true for Murray O'Hair's own son who became a devout Christian. Her life was remarkable but, like many controversial figures, she met a gruesome end. In 1995, Murray O'Hair, her younger son, and her granddaughter all disappeared along with more than $600,000 from the American Atheists' bank account. It later transpired they had been murdered. Paradoxically, the killer was not her enemy per se but a former employee of American Atheists and an ex-con who sought revenge after Murray O'Hair had written an article about his criminal activity. Although she may not have achieved as much as her nineteenth-century predecessors, she certainly behaved badly enough to make history by publicly challenging religion.

Madalyn Murray O'Hair (1919–1995) at the American Atheist Bookstore. In the 1960s O'Hair was the public face of atheism in the United States. Her antireligious views earned her the label "The Most Hated Woman in America" in *Life* magazine. **JOHN PREITO/GETTY IMAGES.**

Chapter 7: From Rebels to Everyday Atheists: Women and Secularity

FROM REBELLION TO INDIFFERENCE?

So why is the apostasy of women so much more threatening than that of men? It may be partly because it is much more than the loss of one more soul. It is the loss of the family transmission of the faith. In most times and places, women have taken the lead in teaching children the faith and ensuring their compliance with ritual requirements. And in most times and places, women have had sole responsibility of teaching girls. Even the most pious father would not, until recently, have felt comfortable educating his infant daughters. Another reason is that female noncompliance often threatens the status quo and signifies larger changes on societal level. Leaving religion and God behind is a symptom of independence because women's lives had been dictated by religions until not so long ago. According to Gaylor, the churches have always opposed every right women have won, no matter how trivial it may seem to subsequent generations. For women, atheism signifies more than just an escape from religious authority; it is bound up with nonconformism more generally. As the journey to nonbelief primarily consists of independent study and unconventional approach to the world, the women who undertook it in the nineteenth century often felt liberated not only from religion but from the more general sense of oppression as a class. A turn to atheism inadvertently put women in charge of their lives and relationship with the world around them. Many realized that "a world that had previously been defined according to the teachings of some higher authority, was now theirs to judge, participate in, and seek to change as only they saw fit" (Schwartz 2013, 94). In 1911, Robert G. Ingersoll's (1833–1899) daughter envisioned the rise of a new woman who "will belong to no church, [...] will be fettered by no senseless formula or puerile dogma" (Kirkley 2000, 69). The new woman will be an agnostic but tolerant and open. Most important, she will be "sovereign of herself," "free and fearless" in "thought, word and deed" (Kirkley 2000, 69). In the words of another poster girl for nonreligion (and an early sociologist), Harriet Martineau (1805–1876), she would be "a free rover on the broad, bright breezy common of the universe" (Peterson 2007, 13). This prophesy has since come true to a certain extent. As the number of female nonbelievers keeps growing, the atheist woman is no longer stigmatized as a symbol of antifemininity and immorality. In most Western societies, nonreligious women do not stand out and they could be described as "everyday atheists," unlike the rebels of the previous historic periods. It is entirely possible, of course, that many other female contemporaries of Hypatia or Rose had similar thoughts with regard to religion but never voiced them for fear of repercussions.

The study of gender and secularism in the twenty-first century needs to take into account the vast array of historical complexities that do not simply pre-date the status quo but have contributed to its creation. The process of apostasy, or deconversion, will not occur in settings where secular upbringing is the norm, but where religion remains strong, it will always be gradual and associated with higher levels of education. For example, Besant went from finding contradictions in the Bible, testing Christian dogmas against reason, through declaring herself a theist, to finally in 1874, publicly taking on an atheist identity, after she had met the renowned secularist Charles Bradlaugh (1833–1891). Losing one's religion does not happen overnight, and women continue to face more severe social sanctions as a result of abandoning their faith. The more religious the culture, the more empowering and risky atheism is for women both in the personal and the social dimension. In such circumstances, loss of faith causes anxiety as it can be tied up with the loss of status, and with social ostracism. A life devoid of any direct contact with religious ideas and behavior is also becoming an increasingly common scenario among the younger generations of women in the United Kingdom as well as in some European and Scandinavian countries.

Summary

The main goal of this chapter is to demonstrate the complexities of studying nonreligion and atheism in the context of gender relations. In many ways, those interested in the subject are working with a relatively blank canvas. If they dig deeper, they may discover novel ways of approaching the question, be it through historical comparisons, through analogies with existing studies of gender and (non)belief, or through re-setting the sociological compass entirely by redefining the conceptual framework in light of the twenty-first-century realities of women's lives. This chapter sets the scene for such endeavors by first outlining the basic debate on gender differences in religiosity. This argument points to the possibility of a gradual and uneven decrease in this gap as the lives of women and men become more similar on average. A brief analysis of the female experience and public demonstration of atheism testifies to the highly contingent nature of attitudes toward gender and religion. Two strong themes emerge. First, in religious societies, women's nonreligion tends to be labeled as rebellion against their nature, gender-specific duties, and the normative order more generally. In contexts in which religious beliefs are perceived as a private matter, female infidels fall into the ordinary category of "everyday atheists" who only voice their views when directly confronted with orthodox religious individuals or beliefs in public life. Second, even in the absence of formal social sanctions for atheist women, a certain unease persists about the pairing of femininity and lack of belief in the supernatural. This unease has roots in the history of gender relations and particularly in the nineteenth-century depictions of female freethinkers. Although the objective conditions that gave birth to the vivid image of what Lori D. Ginzberg calls the "Red Harlot of Infidelity" (1994, 195) are long gone, her ghost still haunts our collective consciousness.

Bibliography

Baker, Joseph O'Brian, and Buster Smith. "None Too Simple: Examining Issues of Religious Nonbelief and Nonbelonging in the United States." *Journal for the Scientific Study of Religion* 48, no. 4 (2009): 719–733.

Besant, Annie. *An Autobiography*, 2nd ed. London: Theosophical Publishing Society, 1893.

Brewster, Melanie E. "Atheism, Gender, and Sexuality." In *The Oxford Handbook of Atheism*, edited by Stephen Bullivant and Michael Ruse, 511–525. Oxford: Oxford University Press, 2013.

Brown, Callum. "The People of No Religion: the Demographics of Secularisation in the English-Speaking World since c. 1900." *Archiv für Sozialgeschichte* 51 (2011): 37–61.

Bruce, Steve. "Defining Religion: a Practical Response." *International Review of Sociology* 21, no. 1 (2009): 107–120.

Bruce, Steve. *Secularization: In Defence of an Unfashionable Theory*. Oxford: Oxford University Press, 2011.

Bullivant, Stephen. "Defining 'Atheism.'" In *The Oxford Handbook of Atheism*, edited by Stephen Bullivant and Michael Ruse, 11–21. Oxford: Oxford University Press, 2013.

Daniels, C. F. "Female Irreligion." *The Ladies' Companion* 13 (1840): 111–113.

Dobbelaere, Karel. "The Contextualisation of Definitions of Religion." *International Review of Sociology* 21, no. 1 (2011): 191–204.

Dorres-Worters, Paula, ed. *Mistress of Herself: Speeches and Letters of Ernestine Rose, Early Women's Rights Leader*. New York: The Feminist Press CUNY, 2008.

Edgell, Penny, Joseph Gerteis, and Douglas Hartmann. "Atheists as 'Other': Moral Boundaries and Cultural Membership in American Society." *American Sociological Review* 71, no. 2 (2006): 211–234.

Gaylor, Annie Laurie, ed. *Women without Superstition: "No Gods—No Masters."* Madison, WI: Freedom from Religion Foundation, 1997.

Ginzberg, Lori D. "'The Hearts of Your Readers Will Shudder': Fanny Wright, Infidelity, and American Freethought." *American Quarterly* 46, no. 2 (1994): 195–226.

Chapter 7: From Rebels to Everyday Atheists: Women and Secularity

Green, David Allen. "Sharing a Lift with Richard Dawkins: The Rationalist Champion Compares Propositioning a Woman with Chewing Gum." *New Statesman*, July 6, 2011. http://www.newstatesman.com/blogs/david-allen-green/2011/07/richard-dawkins-chewing-gum.

Harris, Sam. "I'm not the Sexist Pig You're Looking For." September 15, 2014. http://www.samharris.org/blog/item/im-not-the-sexist-pig-youre-looking-for.

Hecht, Jennifer Michael. *Doubt: A History*. New York: HarperCollins, 2004.

Heelas, Paul, and Linda Woodhead. *The Spiritual Revolution: Why Religion Is Giving Way to Spirituality*. Oxford: Wiley-Blackwell, 2005.

Jacoby, Susan. *Freethinkers: A History of American Secularism*. New York: Owl Press, 2005.

Keysar, Ariela, and Juhem Navarro-Rivera. "A World of Atheism: Global Demographics." In *The Oxford Handbook of Atheism*, edited by Stephen Bullivant and Michael Ruse, 553–587. Oxford: Oxford University Press, 2013.

Kirkley, Evelyn. *Rational Mothers and Infidel Gentlemen: Gender and American Atheism, 1865–1915*. New York: Syracuse University Press, 2000.

Kolmerten, Carol. *American Life of Ernestine Rose*. New York: Syracuse University Press, 1999.

Lee, Lois. "Research Note: Talking about a Revolution: Terminology for the New Field of Non-religion Studies." *Journal of Contemporary Religion* 27, no. 1 (2012): 129–139.

Mahlamäki, Tiina. "Religion and Atheism from a Gender Perspective." *Approaching Religion* 2, no. 1 (2012): 58–65.

Norris, Pippa, and Ronald Inglehart. *Rising Tide: Gender Equality and Cultural Change Around the World*. Cambridge: Cambridge University Press, 2003.

Overall, Christine. "Feminism and Atheism." In *The Cambridge Companion to Atheism*, edited by Michael Martin, 233–250. Cambridge: Cambridge University Press, 2007.

Peterson, Linda, ed. *Autobiography: Harriet Martineau*. Peterborough, ON, Canada: Broadview Press, 2007.

Ridgeway, Cecilia L. *Framed by Gender: How Gender Inequality Persists in the Modern World*. New York: Oxford University Press, 2011.

Runciman, Walter Garrison. *A Treatise on Social Theory*, Vol. 1. Cambridge: Cambridge University Press, 1983.

Schwartz, Laura. *Infidel Feminism: Secularism, Religion and Women's Emancipation, England 1830–1914*. Manchester, UK: Manchester University Press, 2013.

Seaman, Ann Rowe. *America's Most Hated Woman: The Life and Gruesome Death of Madalyn Murray O'Hair*. London: Bloomsbury, 2005.

Stark, Rodney, and Roger Finke. *Acts of Faith: Explaining the Human Side of Religion*. Berkeley: University of California Press, 2000.

Stephens, Mitchell. *Imagine There's No Heaven: How Atheism Helped Create the Modern World*. Basingstoke, UK: Palgrave Macmillan, 2014.

Trzebiatowska, Marta, and Steve Bruce. *Why Are Women More Religious Than Men?* Oxford: Oxford University Press, 2012.

Ulrich, Laurel Thatcher. "Vertuous Women Found: New England Ministerial Literature, 1668–1735." *American Quarterly* 26 (1976): 20–40.

Walter, Tony, and Grace Davie. "The Religiosity of Women in the Modern West." *British Journal of Sociology* 49 (1998): 640–660.

Weltecke, Dorothea. "The Medieval Period." In *The Oxford Handbook of Atheism*, edited by Stephen Bullivant and Michael Ruse, 164–179. Oxford: Oxford University Press, 2013.

Zuckerman, Phil. *Living the Secular Life: New Answers to Old Questions*. New York: Penguin, 2014.

FILM AND TELEVISION

Agora. Dir. Alejandro Amenábar. 2009. Historical drama about the life and death of Hypatia.

Dick Cavett Show. 1968–1974. A talk and variety show hosted by Dick Cavett.

CHAPTER 8

Secularism, Diversity, and Race in the Contemporary United States

Juhem Navarro-Rivera
El Instituto: *Institute of Latino/a, Latin American, and Caribbean Studies*
University of Connecticut, Storrs

As the size of the secular population in the United States grows, so too has the racial and ethnic diversity of the secular population. Once a small segment of the population, and mostly white in its racial composition, secular Americans have increased to become one of the largest "religious" subgroups and the largest non-Christian group in the American religious landscape.

One of the interesting traits of its new secular population is its growing racial and ethnic diversity. As this chapter demonstrates, racial and ethnic minorities are becoming important segments of the secular population. Among the youngest cohort—people under thirty years of age—roughly half of secular Americans are people of color: African Americans, Latinos, Asian Americans, and other groups. In the secular population at large, about one-third are people of color.

These changing racial characteristics are part of a larger trend of an increasingly diverse American population. The US Census Bureau, the government agency in charge of demographic and economic statistics, expects that by the middle of the current century the white population of the United States will no longer be a majority. Instead, the new majority will consist of a diverse group of people with heritage principally from Africa, Latin America, and Asia, rather than from Europe, as has been the case since the beginning of the United States.

This process is occurring among the secular population, a group loosely defined by its rejection of traditional religion. They may be atheists, agnostics, humanists, or they may just not prefer any religion and call themselves *nones* (a short for the preference "nothing in particular" usually offered in public opinion surveys). The importance of this process of racial diversification among secular Americans stems from the new challenges its brings, challenges that will be discussed throughout this chapter.

Once upon a time, the secular population was relatively homogeneous. As recent as 1990, the National Survey of Religious Identification (NSRI) found that four-in-five secular Americans identified as racially white. Thus, an increasingly diverse population brings to the fore issues of class, inequality, and representation that have been mostly absent from a community that was much smaller and homogeneous in the not so distant past.

To articulate how racial and ethnic diversity is changing the secular population, and the challenges and opportunities this diversity brings, this chapter has three main sections: (1)

secularism and diversity, (2) secularism and race at a glance, and (3) racial diversity: a unique opportunity of American secularism.

The first section discusses the growth of the secular population in the United States. The main feature of this section is a comparison of the secular population with the Christian population in the United States. The reasoning for these comparisons is that secular Americans' growth has come mostly at the expense of the defections from the dominant religious group in the nation.

The main sources of comparison are demographic (age, sex, and race), social (education and income), and political (party preference and ideology). These include comparisons of Christian and secular Americans to the general population and to major subgroups (or traditions) of the secular and Christian populations. The social, demographic, and political differences show how race and other characteristics shape these particular subgroups' cultures. The purpose is to show how secular Americans are distinct from the general population and from the dominant Christian groups.

The second section discusses the social, demographic, and political differences between secular Americans by racial and ethnic background. The purpose of this section is to show how secular Americans' racial differences could become a source of contention in the future as their social statuses vary, mostly replicating the existing racial structures, but there is a major opportunity to create a community because of important similarities, particularly on political matters.

The chapter concludes with a discussion of the challenges and opportunities that this racial diversity brings. This is particularly important in terms of the social cohesion of the group as well as for its potential future political impact.

SECULARISM AND DIVERSITY IN THE UNITED STATES

The growth of the nonreligious population in the United States has become a major subject of discussion among journalists and scholars. As the most religious major industrial democracy, the United States has been an outlier in terms of the extent to which its population belongs to religious congregations, claims affiliations with a particular faith or belief, and attends religious services.

The nonreligious in the United States, for a long time, accounted for a small fraction of the population. According to John Clifford Green (1953–) in *Religion and the Culture Wars* (1996), some survey estimates dating back to the 1960s calculated that just 5 percent (or one in twenty Americans) had no religious affiliation. According to Barry A. Kosmin (1946–) and Ariela Keysar (1955–) in *Religion in a Free Market* (2006), just twenty five years ago, in 1990, the NSRI recorded that only 8 percent of adults in the United States identified as nonreligious.

Kosmin and Keysar also reported that a major source of growth occurred in the 1990s when the nonreligious population nearly doubled from 8 percent to 14 percent according to the 2001 American Religious Identification Survey (ARIS), a study that continued the work of the 1990 NSRI. The third survey in the series, the 2008 ARIS, detected a smaller growth level between 2001 and 2008, when the nonreligious population was estimated at 15 percent of American adults. Since the release of the ARIS 2008, the population without religious affiliation has continued to grow.

Chapter 8: Secularism, Diversity, and Race in the Contemporary United States

Recent surveys by the Pew Research Center's Religion in Public Life Project and Public Religion Research Institute (PRRI) find that now more than one in five Americans do not identify with a religion. This nonreligious cohort now rivals Roman Catholicism as the largest "religious" tradition in the country.

The main source of growth in this major secular boom comes from young people. As Robert P. Jones, Daniel Cox, and Juhem Navarro-Rivera report in their *2012 Pre-Election American Values Survey*, public opinion surveys that measure religious identification consistently find that young people, especially those of the millennial generation (primarily those under the age of thirty years), are more likely to identify as nonreligious. But this group is not the only source of growth; as Kosmin and Navarro-Rivera (2012) demonstrate, between 1990 and 2008, a significant portion of members of generation X (born between 1965 and 1980) also left organized religion.

What makes the young cohort a distinctive one is the extent to which this secular cohort is also racially diverse. The United States is currently undergoing a major demographic transformation. Members of groups belonging to racial and ethnic minorities are becoming more visible in the population, and collectively, are expected to become a majority of the country by 2050.

This racial diversity is crucial for understanding the future of secularism in the United States. People of color, particularly young ones, are becoming increasingly secular; a major source comes from the growth of Latino and Asian Americans in the population.

To show the diversity of the secular population, this chapter draws on the 2013 American Values Atlas (AVA). This is the first survey in an annual series conducted by PRRI tracking religious affiliation in the United States. The 2013 AVA consists of more than 44,000 interviews conducted in 2013 by the polling firm SSRS. The surveys were conducted in English and Spanish among adults eighteen years of age and older in the continental United States.

The survey collects demographic information including age, sex, education, income, and race. The main question of the project is: "What is your present religion, if any? Are you Protestant, Roman Catholic, Mormon, Orthodox such as Greek or Russian Orthodox, Jewish, Muslim, Buddhist, Hindu, atheist, agnostic, something else, or nothing in particular?" I define the secular population as those who answer any of these three choices: "atheist," "agnostic," or "nothing in particular."

According to the 2013 AVA, more than one in five (22%) Americans identify with any of the three secular options in the religious identification question of the survey. One interesting feature of the AVA project is that it includes a question probing among those who identify as "nothing in particular" whether they consider themselves to be "secular," "religious," or "spiritual but not religious."

The AVA 2013 shows that most (77%) secular Americans identify their religion as "nothing in particular," compared with "atheist" or "agnostic" (22%). When those who have no particular religious identification are asked about their secular or religious status, however, two-thirds (67%) respond their identity as being secular while about one in five (22%) identify as religious. Just 7 percent say they are "spiritual but not religious." Taking into account the one-fifth of secular Americans who identify as atheist or agnostic, this means that nearly three-quarters (74%) of all secular Americans are, indeed, secular. But as the next few paragraphs show, substantive demographic, social, and political differences exist within the secular population.

RELIGION: BEYOND RELIGION

131

Chapter 8: Secularism, Diversity, and Race in the Contemporary United States

Demographic, Social, and Political Characteristics of Selected Christian and Secular Subgroups (2013)

	All Americans	All Christians	Mainline Protestants	Evangelical Protestants	Catholics	All Seculars	Atheist	Agnostic	None
Age									
18–29	22	18	18	15	19	33	41	42	31
30–49	35	33	31	33	36	38	35	32	39
50–64	26	28	27	29	27	19	15	16	20
65+	18	21	23	22	18	19	10	9	9
Sex									
Men	48	45	44	43	48	57	70	63	54
Women	52	55	56	57	52	43	30	37	46
Race/Ethnicity									
White	65	65	75	66	57	68	75	76	65
Black	11	13	14	20	3	9	3	3	10
Latino	15	16	5	8	35	12	11	9	13
Asian	3	2	1	1	2	5	4	7	5
Mixed/Other	4	3	3	4	2	5	6	3	5
Education									
High school or less	45	47	41	49	50	45	31	29	49
Some college	26	26	27	28	22	26	28	31	24
College graduate	28	27	31	23	27	29	40	40	26
Income									
$50,000 or less	74	75	73	78	74	74	67	72	75
More than $50,000	13	13	15	10	14	15	23	18	14
Political Party									
Democrat	32	32	33	30	33	32	42	36	30
Independent	37	34	35	32	37	49	44	52	49
Republican	22	26	24	32	21	10	8	8	11
Other	9	8	7	7	9	9	6	5	9
Political Ideology									
Liberal	26	21	26	16	25	40	59	51	35
Moderate	28	28	31	24	30	29	22	29	30
Conservative	37	43	36	53	38	22	13	16	24
Other	9	7	7	6	7	9	6	3	18

SOURCE: American Values Atlas. Public Religion Research Institute. 2013.

Figure 8.1. *Demographic, social, and political characteristics of selected Christian and secular subgroups (2013).* © **GALE, CENGAGE LEARNING.**

Figure 8.1 shows the current social, demographic, and political composition of the secular population. The table compares the general adult population of the United States, religious Americans, Christian Americans, and secular Americans by age, sex, education, income, and race. Christians are defined as those who identify with any Christian denomination, including several Protestant traditions, Catholics, Mormons, Orthodox Christians, and Jehovah's Witnesses.

In addition to the overall Christian population, the three major Christian traditions in the United States (mainline and evangelical Protestants and Roman Catholics) are included for comparison purposes. Mainline and evangelical Protestants are the two major groups in the Protestant tradition. Mainline churches are part of the reform away from Roman

Chapter 8: Secularism, Diversity, and Race in the Contemporary United States

Catholicism and include Anglican or Episcopalian, Congregationalist, Quaker, Lutheran, and Methodist denominations.

The evangelical traditions are those with a focus on revival and a belief in biblical inerrancy. The main denominations are the Baptist churches, whereas more recent denominations, such as the Assemblies of Christ, also fall under this tradition.

American Catholics belong to the Roman Catholic Church, the dominant Christian tradition in the world. Secular Americans are those who identify as atheist, agnostic, or as belonging to no religion in particular.

Substantial differences exist between those identifying with the dominant Christian and those who identify with no particular religion, especially in the distribution of sex, race, and age. Yet, these groups are not monolithic, and major differences also exist between the major Christian traditions and the three main secular cohorts.

DEMOGRAPHIC CHARACTERISTICS

The three demographic characteristics discussed in this section are age, sex, and race. Secular Americans are notably younger than the American population and the Christian population. Secular Americans and Christians have major gender gaps. Secular Americans tend to be men, while a majority of Christians are women. Finally, although Christians, especially Catholics and evangelical Christians have large portions of the population which are people of color, secular Americans are less diverse, though their racial diversity has been on the rise.

AGE

Secular Americans are much younger than Christians. Seventy-one percent of secular Americans are under the age of fifty years. This number includes 33 percent of secular Americans who are under the age of thirty years. Only 18 percent of Christians are younger than thirty years of age and 51 percent are younger than fifty. Christians are more than twice as likely as seculars to be over the age of sixty-five (21% versus 10%). Indeed, Christians are slightly older than the American population as a whole.

Looking at the Christian and secular subgroups also yields important differences. Among Christians, the Catholic cohort is slightly younger than the mainline or evangelical Protestants. Fifty-five percent of Catholics are under the age of fifty, while 48 percent of evangelicals and 49 percent of mainline Protestants are under this age-group.

Secular subgroups also vary by age but more than seven in ten of seculars, regardless of cohort, are under the age of fifty. The "nothing in particular" or "none" cohort is the relatively oldest group because only 31 percent of the group is under the age of thirty years. More than four in ten atheists (41%) and agnostics (42%) are twenty-nine years old or younger.

These differences in age corroborate findings from previous studies such as the ARIS and the Religious Landscape Surveys by the Pew Research Center's Project on Religion in Public Life. The growth of secularism in the United States has been the result of gains at the expense of the dominant Christian traditions.

RELIGION: BEYOND RELIGION

133

SEX

One of the major characteristics of the secular population has been its gender gap. In the ARIS series surveys, as well as in the Pew and PRRI surveys and other studies men are more likely to identify as secular than women. The reverse is true for religious identification, as women are more likely to identify as religious than men. The AVA data show that this secular-religious gender gap is still a reality.

The majority of American adults are women (52%). The majority of Christians are women as well (55%), including 56 percent of mainline and 57 percent of evangelical Protestants. Catholic Americans' gender ratio is similar to the general population's gender ratio.

A majority of secular Americans are men (57%), although this percentage has declined since the 2008 ARIS found that 60 percent were men. The ARIS 2008 also found, and the 2013 AVA confirms that there are major differences among secular Americans depending on their identification. Atheists are the most likely to be men. Currently, 70 percent of self-identified atheists are men, as are 63 percent of agnostics. Those who identify as "nothing in particular" have the largest percentage of women identifying as such (46%), although a majority are men (54%).

RACE AND ETHNICITY

Recent surveys from the Pew Research Center and Public Religion Research Institute find that in terms of their racial diversity, secular Americans are improving and growing more similar to the general population. Currently, the racial composition of secular Americans includes a larger cohort of the dominant racial group, white Americans. More than two-thirds (68%) of secular Americans identify racially as white, a slightly higher percentage than the population overall or the Christian population (65% for both).

The differences between Christian traditions and secular subgroups show how history and outreach affect affiliation and membership. The mainline Protestant churches have the whitest membership in terms of racial composition (75% white), while the evangelical Protestant tradition has the largest African American cohort (20% of evangelicals are black Americans). Catholic Americans have the least racially white cohort because more than one-third (35%) have a Latino background.

According to Philip Barlow (1950–) and Mark Silk (1950–) in *Religion and Public Life in the Midwest* (2004), mainline tradition churches are dominant in the northeastern and midwestern United States among Americans who descend from English colonists and other colonists or later immigrants from the Netherlands, Germany, and northern Europe. This explains its skewed racial profile as membership is concentrated among those with European descent.

Evangelical tradition churches are concentrated in the southern United States, with the Southern Baptist Convention being the largest denominational organization in the tradition (Wilson and Silk 2005). Because of this regional dominance and history, the Baptist tradition is the Christian tradition to which most black Americans affiliate. Most African Americans are descendants of slaves brought to the United States and the English colonies before the dawn of the Republic from Africa between the sixteenth and nineteenth centuries. Over time their descendants made the church one of the few spaces in which they could debate and discuss their issues. As Melissa Victoria Harris-Lacewell writes in *Barbershops, Bibles, and BET* (2004), the Black Church, as these institutions are collectively

Chapter 8: Secularism, Diversity, and Race in the Contemporary United States

known, is one of the pillars of the community. In addition, according to the Center of Religion and Public Life Project in *The Shifting Religious Identity of Latinos in the United States* (2014), evangelical churches have made inroads in Latin America, particularly Puerto Rico and Central America where their descendants or members of the diaspora in the United States have converted to or continued membership in this tradition.

The Catholic churches tend to have the largest Latino population because of the historical link between the Roman Catholic Church and the Spanish Crown in its American colonies. Forced conversion of the natives and an official church status created a captive audience that has lasted five centuries.

Among secular Americans, the racial differences are also stark. Atheists and agnostics have the whitest populations in the secular cohort. About three-quarters of atheists (75%) and agnostics (76%) are white Americans. The nones are the most racially diverse. Although the vast majority are white (65%), about one in ten are African American (10%) or Latino (13%) and an additional 5 percent are Asian American.

This section described the demographic characteristics of secular and Christian Americans. Secular Americans are notably younger than most Americans, and all secular groups are substantially younger than Christian Americans, a characteristic that bodes well for the growth of secularism in the near future. Secular Americans and Christians have inverse gender gaps in which the majority of seculars are men and women account for a majority of Christians. Christian and secular populations despite having similar percentages of the dominant white population have varying distributions of people of color in their memberships. Evangelical Christians historically have been denominations of African Americans and an increasing cohort of Latinos and Asian Americans. The nones have the most racially diverse secular population, something that may be related to the strong religious communities that people of color, particularly African Americans and Latinos, come from. The following section describes the social characteristics of Christians and secular Americans.

SOCIAL CHARACTERISTICS

Education attainment and income are two characteristics that are closely correlated. As Keysar notes, among secular Americans, high education attainment is a particular characteristic, especially among atheists and agnostics. Daniel Cox (1979–) writes in "Is Atheism Only for the Upper Class?" (2013) that the assumption of upper-class bias also has been placed among atheists, as they tend to have higher levels of income than other Americans.

EDUCATION

About three in ten Americans (28%) report having a college degree and about one-quarter (26%) say they have no degree, although they attended college at some point. More than four in ten (45%) earned a high school diploma or received less education. The Christian population and the secular population have similar education profiles to those of the general population.

Among Christian groups, mainline Protestants have the highest college graduation rate (31%) while evangelicals have the lowest (23%). The Catholic and evangelical cohorts have the lowest education profiles. About one-half of Catholics (50%) and evangelicals (49%) report having a high school education or less.

RELIGION: BEYOND RELIGION

135

Chapter 8: Secularism, Diversity, and Race in the Contemporary United States

High education attainment has been considered one of the reasons for rising secularism in the American population. In the case of atheists and agnostics, this rings true. Similar to mainline Protestants, four in ten atheists and agnostics have a college degree or higher. The nones' education profile suggests that higher education attainment is not necessarily the key to increasing secularism, given that many of the new secular Americans are of the *none* variety.

INCOME

According to the US Census Bureau (Noss 2014), the median household income in 2013 was roughly $52,000. According to the AVA, nearly three-quarters (74%) of Americans had an income of $50,000 or less, whereas 13 percent reported an income of more than $50,000. In terms of income, Christians and secular Americans do not vary much from each other. Among Christians, there are no major differences, but there are significant differences among secular Americans. Nearly one-quarter (23%) of atheists and about one-fifth (18%) of agnostics report an income of $50,000 or higher.

There seems to be an educational and income bias toward atheism and agnosticism. These two groups tend to have household incomes higher than the median American income and higher rates of education attainment as measured by college completion rates. The nones, however, have education rates closer to those of the general population and members of major Christian traditions. This may be due to the nones' mostly coming from Christian traditions, and the racial composition of the group. Nones have the most diverse racial profile of the secular population, and people of color in the United States are often at a disadvantage in terms of education and economic opportunities.

POLITICAL CHARACTERISTICS

Politics is an area where religious groups have distinct profiles. In American elections, there are significant differences in voting patterns by religion and race. According to Jones, Cox, and Navarro-Rivera (2012), white Christians are more likely to vote for Republican candidates, whereas Christians of color, such as African American Protestants or Latino Catholics, prefer Democratic candidates. Navarro-Rivera (2012) reports that Democratic Party candidates are also preferred by secular Americans.

POLITICAL PARTY

According to the Public Religion Research Institute's 2014 American Values Atlas, a plurality of Americans identify as political independents (37%), whereas an additional 9 percent say they identify with another minor party or refuse to state a preferred political party. The Democratic Party is preferred by Americans over the Republican Party by 9 percentage points (32% versus 23%). Christian Americans have a partisan affiliation similar to the general population, whereas secular Americans have a distinct skew toward independent and nonpartisan affiliations.

Among Christians, mainline Protestants and Catholics have profiles similar to Americans overall. Evangelicals have the most Republican-leaning profile as 32 percent identify as Republicans, although overall Evangelicals have a balanced partisan profile: roughly three in ten are Republicans, Democrats, or independents.

Secular Americans have a more consistent profile. They are marked both by a preference for the independent label and a rejection of the Republican Party. Nearly half

Chapter 8: Secularism, Diversity, and Race in the Contemporary United States

(49%) of secular Americans identify as independent, including 52 percent of agnostics, 49 percent of nones, and 44 percent of atheists.

Although secular Americans overall prefer the Democratic Party at a similar rate to the population as a whole, there are important differences among them. More than four in ten atheists (42%) identify as Democrats. The rates are lower for the other two groups: more than one-third (36%) of agnostics and three in ten (30%) of nones prefer the Democratic Party.

Aside from their strong identification as independents, what also distinguishes secular Americans is their rejection of the Republican Party. Overall, just one in ten secular Americans identify as Republican, half as many compared with the general population. This low preference is shared by all secular groups.

POLITICAL IDEOLOGY

Another aspect of the politics of the United States is its political ideology. Conservatives tend to prefer lower spending on government functions and market-based solutions to problems, a strong military, and restrictions on behavior stemming from religious beliefs. Liberals tend to prefer government-based solutions to problems and are more likely to oppose restrictions on behavior based on religious beliefs.

Figure 8.1 shows that a plurality (37%) of Americans identify as conservative, whereas the moderate (28%) and liberal (26%) cohorts are roughly of equal size. Similar to the partisan affiliation gap, major ideological differences exist between Christians and seculars in the United States.

More than four in ten (43%) Christians identify as conservative, a higher rate than the general population, whereas half as many (21%) are liberals. The conservative advantage is present in the three main Christian subgroups but is more pronounced among evangelical Protestants, of which a majority (53%) identifies as conservative. Only 16 percent of evangelical Protestants identify as liberal.

Among secular Americans, the opposite is true. Secular Americans are nearly twice as likely to call themselves liberal compared with Christians (40% versus 21%) and are much less likely to prefer the conservative label. Just about one in five (22%) secular Americans call themselves conservative.

Although at least a plurality of all secular subgroups call themselves liberal, there are significant differences. Atheists are the most likely to call themselves liberal, while the nones are the least likely. Nearly six in ten (59%) atheists say they are politically liberal compared to about half (51%) of agnostics and more than one-third (35%) of nones.

Secular Americans' political profile is distinct from that of most Americans and Christians in the United States. Secular groups tend to prefer an independent label over partisan labels, but when they chose a party, they prefer the Democratic Party over the Republican Party by wide margins. This is not the case among Christians who tend to slightly prefer the Democratic Party. Another important distinction of secular Americans is that they are the most likely to identify as liberal. In fact, about one-third of liberals are secular, meaning that secular Americans are overrepresented in this political constituency. Jones, Cox, and Navarro-Rivera (2012, 2013) find that, although secular Americans have historically preferred the Democratic Party candidates and have held liberal views on relevant policy, the addition of secular people of color who hail from groups that have

RELIGION: BEYOND RELIGION

137

Chapter 8: Secularism, Diversity, and Race in the Contemporary United States

historically voted for Democrats may be the basis of a new secular multiracial secular left in the United States.

Major differences are evident between Christian and secular Americans in their population composition. For secular Americans, the future seems bright because their population is younger, especially the growing segment of nones. This group also happens to be the more racially diverse within the secular cohort, as well as the one with a more equal gender ratio. The influx of women and people of color, as well as their lower levels of income and education attainment, may also influence political views, skewing the secular population toward the Democratic Party and liberal ideological views. The next section explores how these characteristics vary by race.

SECULARISM AND RACE AT A GLANCE

Once identified as a group that was overwhelmingly white, male, and wealthier than the population in general, secular Americans are becoming, in the twenty-first century, more racially and socially diverse. For example, a recent analysis of racial diversity among religious groups in the United States by the Pew Research Center shows that the nones have a racial composition that most resembles the US population in general, which corroborates the information described in the previous section.

This section describes the demographic, social, and political composition of the secular population. It shows how secular people of color have a distinct social, demographic, and political profile from the general secular population. Understanding the sources and potential consequences of these differences is important for the future of the secular community. In the United States, issues of race are salient for understanding political debates and conflict. There are major social and economic difference between the dominant white Americans (of European descent) and those whose ancestry lies elsewhere, particularly Africa and Latin America.

RACIAL AND ETHNIC GROUPS

In the general population, African Americans and Latinos tend to have lower incomes and lower levels of education attainment, among other hardships stemming from a history of colonialism and discrimination. The increasingly African American, Latino, and Asian American secular cohorts share the histories and disadvantages of the groups at large in American society. The four main racial groups are explored in the following sections.

White Americans. The dominant racial group in American society are those who identify as white. This group originally included the descendants of European colonists to North America (as well as more recent immigrants to what is known in the twenty-first century as the United States). Membership in this group has expanded over time. Initially, as Michael Omi and Howard Winant explain in *Racial Formation in the United States* (1994), those considered to be white were those of English or northern European background, whereas those of Irish or southern European backgrounds were not considered to be white.

Religion was a major source of these differences. The English and northern Europeans were Protestants, whereas those from Ireland and southern Europe, such as Italians, were Catholic. In addition, those who were not Christians, such as Jews, were not considered

Chapter 8: Secularism, Diversity, and Race in the Contemporary United States

white. As their intermarriage with other Americans of European descent, and their economic status improved, these Americans were considered white (see e.g. Ignatiev 1995). For this reason, whiteness is considered a marker of class as well as of race.

African Americans. African Americans are to a large extent the most religious of American racial groups. A majority claims affiliation in Christian Churches of evangelical bent.

Starting with their history of enslavement, African Americans have suffered from a history of discrimination in the country. After the Emancipation Proclamation was issued on January 1, 1863, laws were put in place and other practices developed to ensure their diminished status as citizens, and strict racial codes defined the membership in the community. This pattern of discrimination continues well into the twenty-first century. Although some legal and legislative victories in the mid-twentieth century granted African Americans legal and social protections, the community still faces major problems as the result of historical neglect and discrimination. These problems include lower education and income status, lower life expectancy rates, and higher levels of poverty, among other problems.

Latinos. Latino Americans account for nearly 20 percent of the American population, and this population is expected to continue to grow. Some population estimates by the government predict that Latinos will account for nearly one-third of the population by the middle of the twenty-first century. Most Latinos trace their roots to Mexico.

The large Mexican population can be attributed to its proximity to the United States. In addition to the shared southern US-Mexican border, a large part of the territory that currently is part of the US southwest was formerly part of Mexico. In recent years, because of economic crises, many Mexicans migrated to the United States seeking better economic opportunities.

In addition to Mexican immigration and the large cohort of Americans of Mexican descent already living in the country, other Latino groups currently live in the United States. Caribbean groups, such as Cubans, Dominicans, and Puerto Ricans, have major enclaves in the northeastern United States. Similar to Mexican immigrants, many of these Caribbean Americans came for economic or political reasons. Another major group of Latinos come from Central America. Mostly from Guatemala, Nicaragua, and El Salvador, these Latinos have come to the United States fleeing civil strife and economic uncertainty, becoming one of the fastest-growing groups of Latinos in recent years.

The largest source of growth in recent years among the nones comes from Latino Americans. Once a mostly Catholic group, toward the end of the twentieth century, many Latinos started abandoning their parents' faith in favor of primarily Pentecostal Protestant churches. In the twenty-first century, the move toward Pentecostalism has slowed, and Latino Catholicism is undergoing a similar change as global Catholicism, where, especially in Europe, the religion is being abandoned in favor of no religious affiliation.

Asian Americans. Another growing segment of the population, Asian Americans have also been in the United States for a long time, particularly in the western part of the country. Chinese immigrants were employed in mining, construction, and other dangerous occupations (Dearinger 2016). According to Andrew Gyory in *Closing the Gate: Race, Politics, and the Chinese Exclusion Act* (1998), people from Asian descent were legally

RELIGION: BEYOND RELIGION

139

Chapter 8: Secularism, Diversity, and Race in the Contemporary United States

excluded from migrating to the country for a century. Although Asian Americans have made great social and economic advancements, it is worth noting that many of the studies mostly include English-speaking Asian Americans and that some vulnerable immigrant populations are excluded because of language barriers. Asian Americans have a less cohesive religious profile than Latinos, who can at least pinpoint a common Catholic colonial history. Instead, Asian Americans have a diverse religious history that ranges from nontheistic traditions, such as Buddhism, to Christian and Muslim traditions.

RACIAL DIFFERENCES AMONG SECULAR AMERICANS

The statistics in Figure 8.2 show how different racial and ethnic groups within the secular American population vary according to their social, demographic, and political characteristics. Some of the differences between members of the groups by race can be attributed to actual differences present among Americans of these particular racial groups. As

Demographic, Social, and Political Characteristics of Secular Americans by Racial and Ethnic Identification (2013)

	Secular Americans	White	African American	Latino	Asian American
Secular Groups					
Atheist	11	12	4	10	8
Agnostic	11	13	5	9	16
None	78	75	92	82	75
Sex					
Men	57	56	54	59	57
Women	43	44	46	41	43
Age					
Percent under age 30	33	28	35	48	56
Education					
High school or less	45	40	59	65	33
Some college	26	27	24	20	24
College graduate	29	33	16	14	43
Income					
Less than $50,000	74	72	83	81	72
More than $50,000	15	18	8	7	19
Political Party					
Democrat	32	31	51	30	31
Independent	49	49	40	51	50
Republican	10	13	3	8	7
Other	9	7	7	12	12
Ideology					
Liberal	40	40	35	41	41
Moderate	29	29	31	26	32
Conservative	22	22	24	24	19
Other	9	9	10	10	8

SOURCE: American Values Atlas. Public Religion Research Institute. 2013.

Figure 8.2. *Demographic, social, and political characteristics of secular Americans by racial and ethnic identification (2013).* © GALE, CENGAGE LEARNING.

noted in Figure 8.1, the vast majority (68%) of secular Americans identify as white, while 12 percent are Latino, 9 percent are African American, and 5 percent are Asian American.

In terms of their secular identification, African Americans are the most likely to identify as nones. More than nine in ten (92%) secular African Americans say their religion is "nothing in particular," whereas among Latinos the figure is 82 percent. Three-quarters of secular Asian Americans and whites identify as none. These two latter groups are, conversely, the most likely to identify as atheist (whites 12%) and agnostic (Asian Americans 16%), respectively.

The sources of these differences may come from the religious traditions that are dominant in each group. African Americans are the most religious group in the United States, and the pressures of denying being secular are the highest for this group. Latinos also come from highly religious backgrounds, which may affect the extent to which they are willing to admit doubt in the divine as part of their religious identity. As noted, many Asian Americans have nontheistic religious backgrounds, which may explain why they have the highest proportion of agnostics in their community.

Sex and Age. The secular population is well-known for its gender gap, which is male dominant. This gap is replicated across all racial and ethnic groups. The fact that the gap is similar across race and ethnicity suggests that the religious expectations of women in the United States are similar for all groups. In other words, lack of religion among men may have less of a stigma than among women.

Although there are no major differences in terms of the sex distribution of the secular population, there are important age differences. This is especially true in the youngest cohort. Although the overall secular population tends to be young (33% under the age of thirty), this youth is not similarly distributed across racial groups.

A majority (56%) of Asian Americans and nearly half (48%) of Latinos who identify as secular are under the age of thirty. The percentage of African Americans (35%) under thirty is similar to that of the secular population, whereas only 28 percent of white secular adults are younger than thirty. The age patterns of these groups are consistent with population growth patterns in the United States. Asian Americans and Latinos are the fastest-growing racial and ethnic minorities in the country and could pave the way for a future of American secularism that has a more diverse and racially equitable community.

Sexual diversity is a major issue for all racial subgroups in the secular population. As discussed, the nones have a substantially more diverse population regarding gender, but these differences do not necessarily translate to a major improvement in social and economic status particular racial groups. On the other hand, the young age of Asian Americans and Latinos in the secular community indicates that these groups will become important for the continued growth of the group. The inclusion of these groups in the community may well depend on their education, economic, and political characteristics.

Education and Income. The need for more racial inclusion becomes more relevant when looking at the differences between racial and ethnic groups in terms of social characteristics. There is a wide education gap between Asian American and white seculars, and African

American and Latino seculars. The former groups have much higher levels of education attainment. More than four in ten (43% of Asian Americans) and one-third (33%) of whites report having a college degree. These rates are much higher than African Americans (16%) and Latinos (14%). These differences in education attainment may explain the different ways in which these groups identify as members of the secular community, as the more educated members prefer the atheist and agnostic labels. According to Kosmin and coauthors in *American Nones* (2009), the latter label, in particular, is preferred by people with higher levels of education.

These education differences are also related to the income differences in the community. Atheists and agnostics are more likely than most Americans to report incomes greater than $50,000. These income differences are reflected in racial differences among secular Americans. Nearly one in five white (18%) and Asian Americans (19%) report an income of more than $50,000. This represents more than twice the percentage of African American (8%) and Latinos (7%) reporting these higher than average incomes.

Secular Americans replicate the education and income disparities in the general population. African Americans and Latinos have lower incomes as well as lower levels of education attainment. These differences are related to the lower levels to which these groups identify as atheist or agnostic, which tend to have an upper-class bias. Given the prominent size of the Latino cohort in the growing secular population, and the historical importance of African Americans, it becomes imperative for secular Americans to address these disparities to improve the overall well-being of their community. Whether there is political will to make these improvements is a question to be answered next.

PARTY PREFERENCE AND IDEOLOGY

Despite the differences in education and income characteristics, the political profile of secular Americans varies little by race. In terms of political party preference, all groups are more likely to report a preference for the Democratic Party over the Republican Party, but only among African American seculars a majority identify as Democrat (51%) and also are the least likely to identify as Republican; only 3 percent of African American seculars prefer the Republican Party.

A majority (51%) of Latinos prefer to identify as independent, although Democrats (30%) widely outnumber Republicans (8%). These affiliation patterns are also true for Asian Americans. Half of secular Asian Americans identify as politically independent, whereas 31 percent prefer the Democratic Party and just 7 percent identify as Republican. Whites mostly follow this pattern as well, although they are the most likely to identify as Republican. Nearly half (49%) of white seculars are independents, 30 percent are Democrats, and 13 percent are Republicans.

There are also few differences in their ideological profile. Roughly four in ten white (41%), Latino (40%), and Asian American (40%) seculars consider their political views as liberal, whereas more than one-third (35%) of African Americans say they are liberal.

There is major agreement on political matters among secular Americans by race. The advantage of the Democratic Party over the Republican Party in the overall group's partisan preference is reflected in all the major racial subgroups in the community. This is also true as it relates to ideology. Secular Americans account for a large segment of the population identifying as *liberal* and the liberal label is distributed across all racial groups. The level of

Chapter 8: Secularism, Diversity, and Race in the Contemporary United States

agreement in terms of partisanship and ideology bodes well for the creation of a cross-racial secular coalition.

Secular Americans share some similarities but also have some major racial disparities in their midst. The disparities mainly relate to socioeconomic status, with African American and Latino seculars having much lower levels of income and education attainment. These patterns reflect the general population's patterns and are further evidence that as secularism becomes an increasingly attractive identity category, the population will begin to resemble the general population. Secular Americans have similar political views, and the ideological and partisan profiles of secular Americans are similar regardless of race. The next section discusses the potential impact of a multiracial secular cohort and identifies building blocks for a major secular realignment of American politics.

Summary

One quote attributed to the late, great African American civil rights leader Dr. Martin Luther King Jr. (1929–1968) says that "Sunday morning at 11 am is the most segregated hour in America." Dr. King was, of course, referring to the racially segregated way in which American Christians worship their God.

The descriptions in the first section of this chapter show that Christian communities tend to have slightly more members of color. Christian traditions are more racially diverse than the atheist and agnostic communities. This was even more true in the past, before the secular explosion beginning in 2010 started, including young Latinos and Asian Americans leaving their ancestors' religious traditions.

The racial diversification of secular Americans, rapidly occurring in recent years, carries within it the racial disparities of America at large. There are no major racial gaps in the gender distribution of secular Americans, and these groups tend to be skewed toward males. In terms of education attainment and income distribution, they reflect the country in which they live.

The years of 2014 and 2015 brought a newfound attention on the issue of race and racism in the United States. The attention gathered by the #BlackLivesMatter movement to bring to justice the police officers who killed unarmed African American men in the cities of Ferguson, Missouri; New York; and Baltimore, Maryland—among other cities—has placed systemic racism at the forefront of public debates in the country. The focus on systemic racism, in combination with the increasingly activist rhetoric coming from some sections of the population, have brought issues of race, racism, and discrimination to the forefront of American politics.

As race becomes, once again, one of the major overt issues in our political debates, secular Americans need to understand that these issues are occurring in their own communities. This is where politics becomes an important tool and works as a guide for understanding how secular Americans could succeed where Christians have not.

Dr. King may have referred to worship, but Christians are not just racially divided by place, but also by politics. Political research consistently finds that African American and white Protestants have major political differences reflected in their voting patterns. For example, although the African American vote is nearly unanimous for Democratic Party

Chapter 8: Secularism, Diversity, and Race in the Contemporary United States

candidates (more than 90% in recent elections), the opposite is true for white Protestants. The latter mostly vote for Republican Party candidates, including more that three-quarters of white evangelical Protestants.

The same is true for the other major Christian group: Catholics. White Catholics and Latino Catholics have different views of society and politics, which also are reflected in their voting preferences. Latino Catholics vote overwhelmingly for Democratic Party candidates. White Catholics have preferred Republican candidates, albeit by smaller margins.

Compounding these differences since 2010 is the most prominent issue in the United States regarding racism and the role of the state and society in adopting formal and informal institutions that exacerbate social and economic differences between the majority of whites and the rest of the population. Politics and race is an area in which secular Americans can succeed in creating a unified community in ways that Christians could not achieve. The political similarities among secular Americans are greater than their social and economic differences.

Public opinion surveys by PRRI and the Pew Research Center have tracked the thoughts of Americans from different religious traditions regarding American society and culture. What these surveys tend to find is that on cultural issues, such as same-sex marriage and abortion, two of the major behavioral and moral issues debated in the twenty-first century, secular Americans (regardless of race) agree on the legalization of these two issues. This is not surprising as attitudes on these issues are shaped by religious belief. These are issues in which Christians have shown the strongest opposition.

Yet, on cultural matters such as immigration, in which Americans are divided by race, secular Americans are on the side of inclusion and tolerance. Secular Americans favor a path to citizenship for undocumented immigrants and tend to agree that the influx of immigrants enriches American society and culture. Once again, most opposition comes from white Christians.

Finally, on racial matters, secular Americans also have more liberal positions. On issues like police abuse and criminal justice reform that have wide racial gaps with people of color and white Americans standing on opposite sides of the issue, secular Americans stand on the liberal side as well.

These are good signs about the future of the secular community because one of the major issues facing the secular community that will affect the future directions of American secularism is the one of race. On paper, secular Americans seem to be in the right place for creating a racially diverse community if we take their opinions on racial issues of economic and social justice at face value.

The success of a multiracial secular enterprise will be determined by how those in the dominant racial group, white seculars, are willing to become allies and partners of the people of color in their communities. Is the secular American leadership ready to expand their issues base beyond matters of separation of church and state and of religious freedom to include issues of social, racial, and economic justice as part of a secular agenda? The political strength and cohesion of the secular movement depends on not just accepting people of color and saying the right things in public opinion surveys, but in acting on those thoughts of racial and social equality. Acceptance of the growing groups of people of color into the secular community will determine how much the size of the group will matter when enacting social and political change, and how much secular Americans will affect the future of American society in a meaningful way.

144   MACMILLAN INTERDISCIPLINARY HANDBOOKS

Bibliography

Barlow, Philip, and Mark Silk, eds. *Religion and Public Life in the Midwest: America's Common Denominator?* Lanham, MD: Rowman AltaMira, 2004.

Cox, Daniel. "Is Atheism Only for the Upper Class?" *The Huffington Post.* 2013. http://www.huffingtonpost.com/daniel -cox/is-atheism-only-for-the-upper-class-socioeconomic -differences-among-the-religiously-unaffiliated_b_31468 94.html.

Dearinger, Ryan. *The Filth of Progress: Immigrants, Americans, and the Building of Canals and Railroads in the West.* Oakland: University of California Press, 2016.

Gonzalez, Juan. *Harvest of Empire: A History of Latinos in America.* New York: Penguin Books, 2001.

Green, John Clifford. *Religion and the Culture Wars: Dispatches from the Front.* Lanham, MD: Rowman & Littlefield, 1996.

Gyory, Andrew. *Closing the Gate: Race, Politics, and the Chinese Exclusion Act.* Chapel Hill, University of North Carolina Press, 1998.

Harris-Lacewell, Melissa Victoria. *Barbershops, Bibles, and BET: Everyday Talk and Black Political Thought.* Princeton, NJ: Princeton University Press, 2004.

Jones, Robert P, and Dan Cox. *Beyond Guns and God: Understanding the Complexities of the White Working Class in America.* Washington, DC: Public Religion Research Institute, 2012. http://publicreligion.org/research/2012/09 /race-class-culture-survey-2012/.

Jones, Robert P., Daniel Cox, and Juhem Navarro-Rivera. *2012 Pre-Election American Values Survey: How Catholics and the Religiously Unaffiliated Will Shape the 2012 Election and Beyond.* Washington, DC: Public Religion Research Institute, 2012. http://publicreligion.org/site/wp -content/uploads/2012/10/AVS-2012-Pre-election-Report-for -Web.pdf.

Jones, Robert P, Daniel Cox, and Juhem Navarro-Rivera. *Hispanic Values Survey: How Shifting Religious Identities and Experiences Are Influencing Hispanic Approaches to Politics.* Washington, DC: Public Religion Research Institute, 2013. http://publicreligion.org/research/2013/09 /hispanic-values-survey-2013/.

Jones, Robert P, Dan Cox, and Juhem Navarro-Rivera. *A Shifting Landscape: A Decade of Change in American Attitudes about Same-Sex Marriage and LGBT Issues.* Washington, DC: Public Religion Research Institute, 2014. http://pub licreligion.org/research/2014/02/2014-lgbt-survey/.

Keysar, Ariela. "Who Are America's Atheists and Agnostics?" In *Secularism and Secularity: Contemporary International Perspectives*, eds. Barry A. Kosmin and Ariela Keysar, 33–40. Hartford, CT: Institute for the Study of Secularization in Society and Culture, 2007.

Kosmin, Barry A., and Ariela Keysar. *American Religious Identification Survey (ARIS 2008) Summary Report.* Hartford, CT: Institute for the Study of Secularism in Society and Culture, 2009. http://www.scribd.com/doc /17136871/American-Religious-Identification-Survey -ARIS-2008-Summary-Report.

Kosmin, Barry A., and Ariela Keysar. *Religion in a Free Market: Religious and Non-Religious Americans Who, What, Why, Where.* Ithaca, NY: Paramount Market Publishers, 2006.

Kosmin, Barry A., Ariela Keysar, Ryan T. Cragun, and Juhem Navarro-Rivera. *American Nones: The Profile of the No Religion Population.* Hartford, CT: Institute for the Study of Secularism in Society and Culture, 2009. http://www .scribd.com/doc/26619711/American-Nones-The-Profile -of-the-No-Religion-Population.

Navarro-Rivera, Juhem. "The Evolution of the Religiously Unaffiliated Vote, 1980-2008." *Faith in the Numbers.* 2012. http://publicreligion.org/2012/10/the-evolution-of -the-religiously-unaffiliated-vote-1980-2008/.

Navarro-Rivera, Juhem, Barry A. Kosmin, and Ariela Keysar. *US Latino Religious Identification 1990–2008: Growth, Diversity & Transformation.* Hartford, CT: Institute for the Study of Secularism in Society and Culture, 2010. http://www.scribd .com/doc/28995963/US-Latino-Religious-Identification -1990-2008-Growth-Diversity-Transformation.

Noss, Amanda. *Household Income: 2013.* Suitland, MD: US Census Bureau, 2014. https://www.census.gov/content /dam/Census/library/publications/2014/acs/acsbr13-02.pdf.

Omi, Michael, and Howard Winant. *Racial Formation in the United States: From the 1960s to the 1990s.* New York: Routledge, 1994.

Pew Research Center Religion and Public Life Project. *The Shifting Religious Identity of Latinos in the United States.* Washington, DC: Pew Research Center, 2014. http:// www.pewforum.org/2014/05/07/the-shifting-religious -identity-of-latinos-in-the-united-states/.

Public Religion Research Institute. *American Values Atlas.* 2013. www.ava.publicreligion.org.

Wilson, Charles Reagan, and Mark Silk. *Religion and Public Life in the South: In the Evangelical Mode.* Lanham, MD: Rowman AltaMira, 2005.

CHAPTER 9

Secularism, Secularity, and Community

Matthew Loveland
Associate Professor of Sociology and Political Science, Department of Political Science
Le Moyne College, Syracuse, NY

Up early on a Sunday morning, Jill only has time to get dressed and head out the door. Like many others, she's running late for church. Her coffee will have to wait until the regular social held after service. But, that's better anyway, she thinks, because getting up early like this is as much for the fellowship as it is for the inspiration. The inspiration comes from the words of the charismatic leader of the group she feels so much a part of, the thoughtful readings that help her make sense of the trials and tribulations of modern life, and the joyful songs the congregation sings together. It helps her to remember she's not alone in her convictions and gives her the opportunity to share her beliefs with like-minded folks who become dependable friends. The hour she sets aside on Sunday morning gives her the energy she needs to get through the week, so she doesn't mind waking up early to attend the service.

Jill's story, while fictional, is like that of many other Americans who devote regular time to a local religious congregation. However, Jill's group is a little different. Although it has many of the familiar routines and rituals of the churches that dot the landscape of modern America, Jill's is an "atheist church." More accurately, it is what is known worldwide as Sunday Assembly—a global movement of secular congregations that intend "to live life as fully as possible" (Sunday Assembly 2015). More so than any time in recent history, nonbelievers are working to create stable, lasting communities where they can be themselves without feeling like outsiders. As of 2015, there are about sixty-eight Sunday Assemblies around the world, including thirty-one in the United States, with more planned to be founded soon (Sunday Assembly 2015).

Although atheists reject theism—belief in god—many nonetheless enjoy life in community. For example, Pippa Evans, one of the two founders of the Sunday Assembly movement, is a former Christian who eventually stopped believing in God. Although she felt she no longer needed religious faith, she missed the sense of community that comes from being part of Christian congregation, the volunteering for a common goal, and the joy of celebrating life together with others who shared her beliefs (Sunday Assembly 2015). Sunday Assembly is a somewhat unique movement of atheists trying to build worldwide community, but nonbelievers and secularists work in many other ways to develop active social lives and to live their beliefs with others.

This chapter examines how and why nonbelievers are working to build community. We will begin by learning how sociologists conceptualize and operationalize community.

Chapter 9: Secularism, Secularity, and Community

Sunday Assembly, Conway Hall, London. *The Sunday Assembly movement incorporates ritual into secular community. Groups of nonbelievers join in singing, reading, and thoughtful reflection on what is important to them.* © **DAVID LEVENE.**

Our definition of community will shape how we think about secular communities and will allow us to see that secularists are a diverse group with different approaches to forming bonds with other nonbelievers. Throughout the chapter, you will notice that secular community sometimes takes the form of "real-life" meetings, and very often, it takes shape via the Internet. Next, the chapter explores values that are common among secularists, as well as conflicts among different factions of nonbelievers about how best to build community and relate to believers. Although the popular image of atheists is often that they are contentious and disagreeable, there are also those who choose to be less confrontational and to frame atheism as a positive contributor to human progress. We will learn about secularist organizations with global, national, and local presences, and we will consider the rituals of secular community.

WHAT IS COMMUNITY?

Before learning about atheist community, it is essential to know what scholars mean when using the term *community*. The word is probably meaningful to you even if you have trouble defining it. You likely think of the town you grew up in and the friends and acquaintances you know there. To some extent, then, community can be a function of place. In this place, there are some people you know well and are close to, and there are others you only recognize as familiar without knowing much, if anything, about their day-to-day lives. As such, sociologists argue that communities can exist among people with strong social ties as well as among people whose connections to one another are relatively weak.

You might also think of communities that are not defined by geography as much as by common interests or goals. For example, if you are a college student, you might consider other students at your school part of the college community. A college may be considered a community to the extent that students, faculty, and staff are bound together in the interest of teaching and learning. Maybe you get together with these other students at sporting or social events, and perhaps you publicly express your shared membership in the community with sweatshirts or baseball caps bearing a stylized logo. Still another way we sometimes think about community is to identify with others who share a common interest in cultural or social commitments. In this case, people can be members of a community that is fully independent of place. For example, *gamers* may think of themselves as members of a community even if they do not know one another personally and interact only virtually via computer networks. Christians who live on different continents may think of themselves as part of a worldwide community of believers whose connections to one another exist only in an imagined sense.

Although the term *community* often is used in everyday conversations, by the media, and by social scientists, you may be surprised to learn that it is not necessarily an easily defined concept, and its use in research can be sometimes contentious (e.g., see Beckford 2015, 225). Early sociologists, for example Ferdinand Tönnies (1855–1936) and David Émile Durkheim (1858–1917), gave careful attention to the dynamics of community, whereas later social scientists like Robert Bellah (1927–2013) were deeply concerned about the loss of community in modern times. Relevant to our exploration of atheism and community, many sociologists see religion as vital to community, and scholars of religion such as James A. Beckford (1942–) in "'Community' in the Sociology of Religion" (2015) regularly use terms like *religious community* to write about religious movements. Furthermore, research by Penny Edgell, Joseph Gerteis, and Douglas Hartmann in "Atheists as 'Other'" (2006) has documented that religious believers find it difficult to accept atheists as members of their own.

Modern notions of community have been made more complex. In fact, rather than discussing only one or two forms of community, social scientists instead identify several types of communities. Steven Brint argues in "Gemeinschaft Revisited: A Critique and Reconstruction of the Community Concept" (2001) that eight different forms of community can be identified by considering the context of social interaction, the motivation for and frequency of the interaction, and whether the interaction is face to face or computer mediated. Among Brint's types of communities are those based on place, those based on engaging in common activities, and those based on common beliefs, imagined communities, and virtual communities. Each of these types of communities are common among atheists and other nonbelievers, and reflection on these characteristics of community will help us to understand how nonbelievers relate to one another as well as to believers. For example, some atheists groups are international and include thousands of members who may never meet one another, whereas others are local and meet regularly in coffee shops and libraries. Some atheist groups organize volunteer events and perform charity in their communities, whereas others may come together only online to discuss their beliefs.

WHAT DO WE CALL THE ATHEIST COMMUNITY?

One of the more complex aspects of atheist social life is the wide range of terms that is often used to describe nonbelievers, by themselves and others. An atheist, of course, is one who does not believe in any god. According to the 2014 General Social Survey (GSS) about 3.5 percent of Americans do not believe in god. There are, however, other kinds of nontheists as well. Agnostics do not rule out the possibility that gods are real, but rather believe that knowledge of such gods is unattainable—about 5.3 percent of 2014 GSS respondents say there is no way to find out if god is real. Other people, while rejecting traditional notions of god, may believe in a so-called higher power (13% of 2014 GSS respondents) and many believers even experience significant doubts (20% of 2014 GSS respondents). What seems clear is that a relatively wide net must be cast to capture the range of people who reject traditional religious belief. For example, although some people do identity as atheist, in many countries this is a small population. Once one includes secular humanists, freethinkers, or skeptics, the size of the community begins to rise. It can be difficult to draw boundaries around identifiable groups of nonbelievers, a term that itself is more a residual category than a clear set of people who share a common set of norms and beliefs. Instead, we must recognize the diversity of nontheists and secular groups. The alliances and divisions within this large group will tell us much about what community looks like among nonbelievers.

WHAT DO SECULARISTS VALUE?

Brint's approach to identifying communities includes considering whether groups are based on shared belief or common action. Although we will consider some common actions of atheist and secularist communities, belief, or rather lack of belief in gods, is central to atheist community. It may seem obvious that what binds some atheists to one another is a common rejection of religious explanations about the world, but many nonbelievers would prefer to build community around a set of positive shared values rather than simply the rejection of what religious people believe. The choices that atheist groups make about this question have important implications for the sort of community that can emerge. If an atheist group decides to orient itself around the rejection and critique of religion, it likely will find itself in high tension with religious groups that are dominant in most societies. On the other hand, a secularist movement that works to develop a set of ethical guidelines about how to live in the world, and make it a better place, may be able to exist alongside religion without much overt conflict. In fact, we can see examples of each of these types of atheist movements in contemporary society.

For many secularists, the core values of atheism are rationality and the scientific method, and through their promotion, social progress. This is certainly the case with the New Atheist movement (a loosely organized movement of vocal atheists like Richard Dawkins (1941–) and Sam Harris (1967–) making public proclamations of their irreligion). Although it does not have any formal leadership or organization, one of its most public proponents is the evolutional biologist Dawkins. Dawkins is not shy about his own secular beliefs, nor has he been reluctant to openly criticize religious beliefs or those who hold them. His widely read and discussed book *The God Delusion* (2008) makes clear his stance that belief in any god runs counter to human intelligence and scientific knowledge about the world. Dawkins started the Richard Dawkins Foundation for Reason and Science, and on the foundation's website he writes clearly that its mission "is to promote scientific literacy and a secular worldview." Dawkins explains that he wishes to promote evidence-based responses to the world's problems, like climate change and overpopulation and that religion is the primary opponent of using science to improve human life. He writes that "[c]ritical thinking is the real savior of human kind," a phrase that many secularists would agree is a fundamental tenet of secularism.

Dawkins is not alone in his public criticism of religion, and many secularists actively denigrate religious faith. Examples of popular culture atheists who often harshly critique religious belief include comedians Bill Maher (1956–), Penn Jillette (1955–), and Ricky Gervais (1961–). Ricky Gervais makes critical jokes about religion to his nearly 10 million Twitter followers and has become a focal point for average secularists looking for like-minded nonbelievers in mainstream culture. Maher and Gillette have each made videos for the Openly Secular Campaign, a project founded to encourage average nonbelievers to be open about their atheism so that, as part of a community, discrimination might end. The mission of Openly Secular reads as follows: "The mission of Openly Secular is to eliminate discrimination and increase acceptance by getting secular people—including atheists, freethinkers, agnostics, humanists, and nonreligious people—to be open about their beliefs."

The series of videos available on the website of Openly Secular provides examples of how people from many backgrounds came to identify as secularists, whether they are atheists, freethinkers, agnostics, humanists, or simply nonreligious. Many of the videos show average nonbelievers telling of their experiences of discrimination for their nonbelief, but also revealing how being open has allowed them to find community. The comedic team of Penn Jillette (1955–) and Teller (1948–) delivers the message that being honest and forthright about one's atheism is a choice that is up to the individual, but that a community of nonbelievers of which one will become a part is available when they do speak up. Their video assures closeted nonbelievers that it is easier to be openly atheist than it once was and that they will be accepted by mainstream culture. Maher's video is more aggressive in its critique of religious belief and believers, and it is not the only one that openly refutes religious teachings. These videos reflect the tension that many atheists feel between their own groups and wider society, and help us understand why some atheists choose to build a community of nonbelievers united around debunking faith and the promotion of rationality and science.

For others, for example nonbelievers who identify first as secular humanists, and for whom atheism is just one aspect of their worldview, the secularist community is built around a set of prosocial ethical teachings. To see an example of what is sometimes called "positive atheism" (Cimino and Smith 2015, 87) you can read "The Humanist Manifesto III" on the website of the American Humanist Association (AHA). The manifesto does not dwell on criticizing religious teachings or faith, but rather it outlines a positive and secular view of human potential and social progress. It opens as follows: "Humanism is a progressive philosophy of life that, without supernaturalism, affirms our ability and responsibility to lead ethical lives of personal fulfillment that aspire to the greater good of humanity."

Later, the manifesto offers a vision of a secular and just society grounded in global community:

> Working to benefit society maximizes individual happiness. Progressive cultures have worked to free humanity from the brutalities of mere survival and to reduce suffering, improve society, and develop global community. We seek to minimize the inequities of circumstance and ability, and we support a just distribution of nature's resources and the fruits of human effort so that as many as possible can enjoy a good life.

Chapter 9: Secularism, Secularity, and Community

The Humanist Manifesto, then, offers a less aggressive approach to building secular community than what is seen by proponents of the New Atheism. Instead of harshly critiquing religion, many nonbelievers would rather not antagonize the faithful because they fear it makes secularism look uninviting and intolerant.

In this latter camp of nonbelievers who choose to focus on popularizing a positive version of secularism is Greg Epstein (1977–). Epstein is the Humanist Chaplain at Harvard University, as well as the executive director of the Humanist Hub. The Humanist Hub was founded in 1974 to serve Harvard's humanists, atheists, and agnostics, but it has grown to be the center of community life for secularists in Boston. The Humanist Hub's mission statement states plainly that it is "a center for humanist life — a nonreligious community committed to the power of connection to help us do good and live well." Epstein, who is ordained as a humanist rabbi, could be viewed as a popular culture counter to aggressively antireligious celebrities like Maher or public scholars like Dawkins. Epstein's 2010 book *Good without God: What a Billion Nonreligious People Do Believe* starts from the premise that there are many nonbelievers in the world, and they are good people who live lives that benefit others. The book traces the development on secularist morality, outlining the basic values that many members of the imagined secular community share. In addition to providing a positive version of atheism for nonbelievers to bond over, Epstein's book is meant to help build connections with nonbelievers. In this regard it is an excellent example of the Humanist Hub's mission to "use reason and dialogue to determine our highest ethical values, … act on those values with love and compassion, and [to] help one another evolve as individuals, as we work to improve our world."

ATHEISM AND MAINSTREAM SOCIETY

There is room for debate about how accepted nonbelievers are in mainstream society. Certainly, as Darren E. Sherkat notes in "Beyond Belief: Atheism, Agnosticism, and Theistic Certainty in the United States" (2008), the number of seculars in America is growing, and as Phil Zuckerman (1969–) writes in *Society without God* (2008), around the world many countries are much more secular than the United States. According to Nicholas Vargas in "Retrospective Accounts of Religious Disaffiliation in the United States" (2012), as the numbers of nonbelievers grow, and more people identify as atheist or have secularists as friends, communities may become more accepting of those who reject religious belief. The New Atheism has given many individual atheists the confidence to speak up. As Richard Cimino and Christopher Smith write in "The New Atheism and the Formation of the Imagined Secularist Community" (2011), new media (e.g., blogging and social networking) provide nonbelievers with the opportunity to connect and find others who share their way of thinking. Atheist identity historically has been stigmatized, and atheists usually have been more focused on defending "against persistent religious influence" rather that advancing a secular worldview (Cimino and Smith 2011, 25). Scholars of irreligion and secularity, however, are beginning to document ways that nonbelievers are being more proactive in forming their own communities.

It is not only well-known scientists and writers like Dawkins, Harris, or Christopher Hitchens (1949–2011), or celebrities like Maher and Brad Pitt (1963–) who are making their atheism public. A recent example of a well-known public figure "coming out" as a nonbeliever is that of American Football star Arian Foster (1986–). Profiled in *ESPN The*

Magazine (Keown 2015), Foster tells how he grew up Muslim but found the courage to tell his devout father of his doubts during high school. Religion had been a significant feature of Foster's life not only through his family, but also via football. During his college career at the University of Tennessee, he studied philosophy and spent a lot of time discussing his views with his religious teammates. In fact, because he was the only nonbeliever on the team, Foster felt like an outsider. The team would regularly pray together before games, even making church attendance mandatory. This experience is quite common for atheists from all walks of life in the United States who often transition from religious belief to irreligion. As Jesse M. Smith explains in "Becoming an Atheist in America: Constructing Identity and Meaning from the Rejection of Theism" (2011), even those who are not raised in religious families are exposed to religious belief through other institutions like schools, friends, or sports because it is a common part of American life. Foster, like many nonbelievers, didn't have the built-in sense of community that many religious faithful do. Scholars who study atheist community would argue that Foster being open about his lack of religious belief may help to create imagined community for other atheists—although they may never come together to talk about their belief systems, they know others think like they do.

Building this sense of community is undoubtedly important, and not only so that atheists have people with whom to discuss their beliefs. Will M. Gervais, Azim F. Shariff, and Ara Norenzayan note in "Do You Believe in Atheists?" that atheists are less trusted than believers and do experience discrimination, and as Edgell and coauthors write in "Atheists as 'Other'" (2006) many in America reject atheism as a dangerous belief system. The study by Edgell and coauthors provides valid evidence that atheists are not accepted into the imagined communities of many in America. The results of a nationally representative survey show that many Americans are uncomfortable with atheists, do not want them in their families, and think that nonbelievers reject the norms of American life and are therefore difficult to trust. In this environment, it is not surprising that atheists work to create their own communities. It is not only a matter of having friends, but also of creating a safe space to be who they are, and to achieve political and social recognition.

ATHEIST COMMUNITY AND ATHEIST IDENTITY: SOCIOLOGICAL INVESTIGATIONS

It is a basic sociological insight that who we are as individuals is very much a function of the social groups to which we belong and the networks of others with whom we interact. To self-identify as Christian, for example, is to claim membership in a global tradition that dates back many centuries. Think about religious identity, or lack thereof, from the perspective of the Christian or atheist. When someone learns that you are a Christian, they are likely able to think of other Christians they know and Christian organizations (i.e., churches) with which they are familiar. This helps them make sense of who you are and gives them a guide about how to interact with you. Conversely, if you tell someone you are an atheist, it is fairly likely that they will not be aware of any atheist organizations or traditions. Because atheists are quite rare in most places, they may not know other nonbelievers. As discussed, they may even be suspicious of you and your rejection of religious norms. In this latter case, then, your identity is much harder to communicate. Many atheists, therefore, are seeking to build communities so that their presence and identity become more well-known and understood.

Sociological research, in fact, suggests that "becoming an atheist" is very much about finding a community with which to identify. Smith (2011) writes that atheist identity is produced via social interaction and that the stories of those who "come out" as nonbelievers share many common features. Many who identify as atheist began their lives in religious environments. Belief in god is common and being socialized to share that belief is typical for young people in religious societies. Importantly, while family, church, and school are important in exposing children to religious faith, religion is "deeply entrenched" in American culture (Smith 2011, 220). Even those born into nominally or nonreligious families are exposed to religious socialization beyond their immediate experience, and they often have little choice about participating in religion to some degree. In a religious society like the United States, belief in god is the default position (Smith 2011, 222).

For some who eventually lose their faith, or even publicly criticize religious teachings, it begins with personal and private questions about beliefs that are held widely in their existing community. Leaving the family of origin, perhaps for college, presents an opportunity to meet people with different beliefs and to critically question religious dogma (Smith 2011; Uecker, Regnerus, and Vaaler 2007). In fact, according to Sherkat (2014), even for most lifelong believers, changes in religiosity are related to joining new social networks or other significant life events like education, marriage, or childbirth. The transition to atheism is a "slow progression," which may include a period of doubting while still being religiously active. Eventually, doubt may turn into a "generalized and non-descript discontent with religious beliefs" and deeper questions about what it means to be a moral person (Smith 2011, 223–224). In "Discovering Atheism: Heterogeneity in Trajectories to Atheist Identity and Activism" (2013), Stephen LeDrew notes that such self-examination may result in a fundamental tension between a long-standing religious identity and a newly discovered sense that one can live without faith in god.

Atheist identity is more than simply not believing in a god. For many nonbelievers, it is an active rejection of religious teachings and the construction of a new sense of self that involves finding a new community to join. Like most religious conversion experiences, Sherkat (2014) explains that social networks are important, but Smith (2011) emphasizes the internalization of a scientific and rational worldview. Atheism is, then, explicit rejection of supernatural explanations and construction of symbolic boundaries between theism and nonbelief. The last step in Smith's model of becoming an atheist is to "come out"—to publicly claim the identity as an atheist. Not only are the disruptions of coming out as an atheist symbolic, but also in a country in which many people are less likely to trust that atheists share their vision of community, these disruptions have social consequences as well. Although research shows that friendships between believers and nonbelievers are relatively common, many atheists actively seek out fellowship with like-minded, thus limiting their ties with believers. Most of the atheists interviewed in Smith's study faced little resistance from friends and family. Not unlike Muslim women who understand discarding the veil as a rejection of religious, atheists who publicly self-identify may experience a sense of liberation.

Smith's model of becoming an atheist is generally accepted, but in "Discovering Atheism" (2013), LeDrew questions how often one's path to atheism follows such a clear path. Essentially, Smith's model is the same as a well-known model of how one might join a religious movement presented in 1965 by John Lofland and Rodney Stark. Rather than converting to a new religious movement, Smith argues that the atheist convert rejects religion and adopts a rational and scientific worldview. LeDrew questions the degree to which claiming an atheist identity is a function of adopting a new rational, nonsupernatural perspective, and adds two other ways that atheists may "discover" their new identity, rather than rejecting a past identity. Some who become atheists may have been raised in a thoroughly secular environment and thus do not experience any period of questioning deeply held religious convictions. Instead of a somewhat radical conversion, these folks become atheists through a process of socialization similar to how anyone might become religious. Others may have been raised secular, and at some point in their lives seek religion, but end up finding faith unsatisfying. Rather than someone who has rejected religious belief, these atheists were always nonbelievers who had never found a way to publicly be what they already knew they were. In LeDrew's model, it is the communal life of atheism—which is early in its development—that must be. Although New Atheists get much attention with their strident criticism of religious belief, many average atheists do not learn about the belief system from them. Instead, what the New Atheist movement may do is to make atheism more public and raise awareness of the possibility of living as an open atheist and finding others who share one's beliefs.

MODERN AND TRADITIONAL WAYS TO BUILD SECULAR COMMUNITY

The books that symbolize the New Atheist movement, as well as media coverage of the growth of nonbelief, help to spread awareness of atheism. Potential atheists are perhaps converted after reading Dawkins or learning about nonreligion groups in their hometown, but this does not automatically lead to a growing sense of community among atheists. A question that likely comes to mind when one thinks about atheist community is "where do atheists meet other atheists?" The short answer is that atheists meet each other in ways similar to any common interest group. Certainly, for organized religious groups, there are straightforward ways to meet others who share your way of thinking. For example, a member of the Church of Jesus Christ of Latter-day Saints, commonly referred to as Mormons, could move across the country, if not around the world, and look up the nearest church as a way to meet fellow believers in a new hometown.

Although movements like Sunday Assembly mean that atheist churches are increasingly available to nonbelievers, most communities do not have such an option. What is available to most nonbelievers is access to the Internet, and according to Smith and Cimino (2012), it has become a vital source of secular community and political mobilization. Because of the wide availability of communication technology like blogs and social media, nonbelievers are able to produce personalized spaces to express their identity and to transform what it means to be a nontheist. Via the narrow-casting capabilities of the web, nonbelievers can produce and consume content tailored specifically to their interests. Some examples of successful secularist websites are PZ Myers blog, Pharyngula, and the YouTube channel Thunderfo00t. Beyond these popular outlets, smaller communities use the Facebook group Black Atheists and active conversations regularly occur on the Atheist Forums website. The Internet is a powerful tool for individual secularists to communicate with one another, to be open about their beliefs, anonymously if they choose, and to create the shared sense of identity that defines community. A more traditional organizing tool, but one that also has a large presence on the Internet, are voluntary associations and nonprofit organizations.

One way to begin to identify community among those who reject traditional religious beliefs is to look at the formal organizations taking root among the secularist movement. One of the longest-lived freethought organizations in the United States is the American Humanist Association. The group's website explains its defining values as such:

> Humanism encompasses a variety of nontheistic views (atheism, agnosticism, rationalism, naturalism, secularism, and so forth) while adding the important element of a comprehensive worldview and set of ethical values—values that are

Chapter 9: Secularism, Secularity, and Community

grounded in the philosophy of the Enlightenment, informed by scientific knowledge, and driven by a desire to meet the needs of people in the here and now. (American Humanist Association 2015)

From this description, it is clear that the humanist movement is relatively inclusive while rejecting certainty in the existence of any gods. The passage answers questions that many religious communities also address—"who are we?" and "what do we do?" (Becker 1999, 267).

Furthermore, using the website, an interested surfer can relatively easily identify a local group affiliated with the national organization. As I wrote this chapter, in fact, I used the search capability to identify a local organization located only a few miles from my home. Although I did not previously know of the barely year-old organization, I had soon looked through its calendar to find meetings I would be able to attend. The group hosts regular book club meetings, speakers, and discussions. One of the planned events was titled "Humanism in Daily Life: Practical Aspects of Secular Living." Before I left the website I had found the organization's Twitter account, and after following, I was presented with options to follow similar accounts from around the United States and other countries. Here, then, is a nationally affiliated local community of humanists who gets together regularly to discuss what they believe and learn how to practice their beliefs, as well as using modern communication technology to reach out to potential new members. With only a few clicks of my mouse, I had become aware of a group of people who share atheist beliefs and had become electronically involved in their community.

Another well-known national nontheist organization is American Atheists. Founded in 1963, American Atheists prioritizes working for the civil rights of nonbelievers. Primarily an organization working to establish and protect the legal rights of atheists, American Atheists strongly defends its understanding of the "separation of church and state." Similar to the American Humanist Association, it also maintains a large network of locally affiliated chapters. Like many atheist groups, individuals affiliated with American Atheists see themselves as activists who educate about atheism, establish networks, and defend communities of nonbelievers. On the organization's website, a page is devoted to the formation of atheist community. It is described as follows: "As America's premiere atheist organization, American Atheists is dedicated to developing and supporting a healthy, thriving, and respected atheist community in the United States. By providing access to resources, leadership, and organizational support, American Atheists partners with more than 150 local organizations to build and maintain a vibrant community." To support the growth of atheist community, American Atheists publishes a newsletter and the *American Atheist* magazine, hosts a streaming television channel, and holds annual conferences around the United States.

A newer atheist organization is the Secular Student Alliance (SSA). The SSA works to build and protect space on college and university campuses for secularism and freethinkers, engaging in local and national political activism. It is also active on Facebook, Twitter, and YouTube. The organization was founded by eight college students in 2000, and held its first major event at the University of Minnesota in August of the same year. SSA claims cooperation as one of its core values, and in that spirit, it is partnered with other nontheist organizations around the world. With more than 270 affiliates at many US colleges and universities, as well as in high schools, SSA makes it possible for young people to see themselves as part of a vital community of nonbelievers. When we consider the future of secularism, these organizations that help young nonbelievers meet each other may be particularly important. How do members come to learn about their college atheist clubs, what sorts of activities do the clubs do, and what do they mean to their members?

FOSTERING COMMUNITY VIA THE SECULAR STUDENT ALLIANCE

The Openly Secular website includes a number of videos from college students and recent graduates who discovered their own nonbelief and a new community of like-minded secularists while at school. There are many common themes in the stories of how college students find and build atheist community on campus. For many students, this is the first opportunity they have been given to think about religion and religious practice outside of the control of their parents. Many come to college with strong religious beliefs and continue to practice as they had while living at home. Learning about world religions or simply other versions of their own faith leads some to reconsider what they believe. Once these beliefs are tested, many college students look to find others with whom to ask questions and find new answers.

One college student on the Openly Secular website describes coming to college after being raised by a Jewish mother and a Christian father in a relatively nonreligious household. At college she joined a Catholic student organization and became involved, even being baptized into the faith. What she liked most about the organization was the music, the volunteering, and the sense of community. During her junior year she attended a meeting of the freethinker club, not knowing that it was part of the SSA. She enjoyed the debate and open conversation encouraged by the group, and eventually became the club president. An important moment for her transition into a secular identity was seeing a debate about evolution between Bill Nye ("the science guy"; 1955–) and creationist Ken Ham (1951–). Nye's expertise in refuting creationism solidified her commitment to secularism. Like many other atheists who become active members of their communities, she cites the superiority of science and reason over religion as a primary value. Had she not first felt at home in the student freethinker club, she may not have experienced the debate in the same way.

Although this is just one student's experience, sociological research about college atheist clubs, as well as news stories and opinion pieces about atheist experiences on college campuses provide further verification of the role community plays in the development of atheist identity, as well as the stigma that may come with being openly secular. An excellent study of secular community on college campuses is an essay by religious studies scholar Steven Tomlins of a university atheist club in Canada. The Atheist Community of the University of Ottawa (ACUO) is "dedicated to the promotion of the irreligious community" (Tomlins 2015, 119) and the promotion of secular values on the university campus. The club is as much a social group, however, as it is an activist club. One member of the group is quoted as saying, "We're a drinking club with an atheism problem" (Tomlins 2015, 119). Like many student clubs, ACUO also hosts campus events like movie nights and awareness weeks.

The students interviewed by Tomlins joined the club for several reasons. A very common answer to the question "why did you decide to join an atheist community?" was "to meet like-minded people." Although the group does do advocacy work to spread a secular message or to debate religious student groups, individual students often join simply for the social connections. Another reason that students join the group has to do with what we can call "getting along." It is one thing to share a worldview, but without a sense of fellowship, it is unlikely that many groups could last. For one student, it was finding others who shared his sense of humor that led to joining ACUO. For many secular people, religion is often the butt of the joke. In polite, religious society, this can often lead to scorn. Secular groups provide a safe space within which to express one's ideas without being judged. As can be seen throughout this chapter, humor is a common theme among atheist community. Whether it is professional comedians making jokes about religion and believers, or if it is a group of friends bonding over "impolite" conversation, humor gives secularists a chance to build friendships and have fun—not unlike the experiences of religious people who enjoy the fellowship of religious community. In fact, when asked what the ACUO means to them, many students directly referred to the sense of community they have found. So, it is not simply the basic values of reason and the scientific method that hold the group together, but instead the comfortable human relationships that can be built on top of shared beliefs.

CONFLICT AND COMMUNITY

The ACUO formed on a diverse university campus in a country that is relatively accepting of the nonreligious. Most of the students did not report feeling significantly unwelcome in wider society, but rather an attraction to a group of people with a common interest. In other countries, like the United States, atheism is less well accepted by mainstream society. As Edgell and coauthors have noted (2006), many Americans are suspicious of atheism and worry that secularists do not share their vision of American values and community life. Edgell and coauthors use the theory of "symbolic boundaries" to explain the social marginalization of secularists. Symbolic boundaries are the categories we use to identify the groups to which we belong and those who are outsiders. The idea can be traced back to Durkheim's work on the solidarity of communities, with those who are symbolically excluded being considered morally inferior. These cultural boundaries that exist between atheists and believers are not solely expressed via attitudes, but sometimes have real consequences for atheists who choose to be public and organize around their beliefs.

For example, an article in the *Catholic Education Daily* (Scharfenberger 2015), a web-based publication of the conservative Catholic organization The Cardinal Newman Society, argued that Catholic campuses should not welcome atheist student clubs. Some leaders of Catholic campus believe that such clubs conflict with the mission of Catholic education and are dangerous. Dr. Douglas Flippen, a philosophy professor at Christendom College, argues that accepting freethinker clubs on campus will "disrupt and undermine the community" of Catholic colleges (Scharfenberger 2015). Although some Catholic universities like Georgetown and Loyola Chicago have officially recognized chapters of the SSA, others, for example the University of Dayton, Duquesne University, and the University of Notre Dame, have denied the formation of atheist student organizations. In these cases, campus leaders worry that allowing a secular student organization would "contradict the University's mission and compromise its Catholic identity" (Scharfenberger 2015). These real controversies help to validate the expectations of the theory put forth by Edgell and her colleagues. If a college believes that atheism is dangerous, then secular students are likely to feel less a part of the campus community than students who are believers. Of course, this may be the case even at secular or public universities and colleges because religion is the norm in American society. How do you think secular students feel in your community?

SECULAR RITUALS AND HOLIDAYS?

Rituals are central to religious life. Durkheim's analysis of religion argues that it is participation in these shared activities, and the common understanding of their meaning, that creates communities of religious believers who agree on what is sacred and profane. It is somewhat strange, then, to think of secularists engaging in ritual behavior. Sociologists, as noted by Cimino and Smith (2015), have documented the growing presence of ritualistic behavior among atheist groups, even if some atheists reject the notion of ritual as too much a part of a religious worldview and opposed to secular values of freethinking and individualism. The growing Sunday Assembly movement is the best example of incorporating ritual into secular community. During these meetings, groups of nonbelievers join one another in singing, reading, and thoughtful reflection on what is important to them. As Cimino and Smith (2015) point out, this ritualized behavior can create solidarity and make secularity more legitimate in the eyes of wider society.

The Center for Secular Inquiry works to promote the acceptance of secular humanism in mainstream society. One way to do this is to provide humanists with resources similar to those that churches, mosques, or synagogues provide believers. An example is the secular celebrant program which "provide[s] officiates for non-religious weddings and other rites of passage" (Cimino and Smith 2015, 88). To meet the demand of humanists looking to celebrate the common rituals that mark major life events, the Humanist Ceremonies website provides numerous tips for finding celebrants and conducting ceremonies. A humanist funeral, for example, consists of opening music and words of welcome, thoughts on life and death from a secular point of view, a tribute to the deceased, readings of poetry or prose, and a time for loved ones to reflect on the life of the person who has died. This is followed by "the committal—when the curtains are closed or coffin lowered," closing words, and final music.

Secular rites of passage are not the only time that nonbelievers participate in ritual. Cimino and Smith (2015) report that 32 percent of the secularists they studied should have a part in their regular meetings. These included baby-naming ceremonies, de-baptism, and winter-solstice celebrations. Other ritualized behavior common to meetings of nonbelievers include moments of silence for personal reflection, meditation, listening to music, and listening to a speaker. Secular rituals, write Cimino and Smith, are like "low church" practices common to many protestant Christian congregations, and have a strong focus on the material, rather than the spiritual, world (Cimino and Smith 2015, 90). Many of those interviewed said the rituals produced only weak emotional responses, but sociologists nonetheless point out that ritual performance can help build solidarity and communicate a sense of commonality to outsiders. As we have seen before, Cimino and Smith also point to the role of humor in secular community. Joking about those who do not share insider status among secularists is a way to create a sense of "us and them" that is a part of most, if not all, identifiable communities, and the notion that conflict with outsiders can create solidarity is not new to sociology.

Finally, some secularists celebrate holidays of their own. Two that Cimino and Smith discuss are celebrations of the winter solstice and Darwin Day. Winter solstice, which occurs near the Christian celebration of Christmas, is often celebrated with parties and are popular with former believers who want to continue celebrating the traditional holiday season. Darwin Day may be the most unique secular holiday. Celebrated by various secularist communities since the early 1990s, and most common on college and university campuses, Darwin Day is for many a day to celebrate science. Darwin, perhaps, takes on the role of a secular saint who dedicated his life to the values nonbelievers cherish. The spirit of Darwin Day, write Cimino and Smith, ranges from strongly worded attacks on religious faith to more subdued events meant to share science and secularism with interested believers.

SECULAR POLITICAL COMMUNITY?

Some countries are more secular than others. For example, sociologist Zuckerman has profiled the northern European countries of Denmark and Sweden where a majority of

Chapter 9: Secularism, Secularity, and Community

citizens live day to day lives that are nearly entirely secular. Although not all of the Danes and Swedes interviewed by Zuckerman self-identify as atheists, few people regularly participate in religious rituals or communities. Zuckerman was surprised to find that many of those he interviewed were neither proudly atheist nor privately religious under the surface. Instead, religion appeared to be a relative nonissue for the average person. Sweden and Denmark are nonetheless quite healthy societies when evaluated by common measures of quality of life. For example, they each rank favorably compared with other countries on measures of literacy, life expectancy, income inequality, education attainment, and other markers. Denmark and Sweden also enjoy relatively low crime rates, and the populations score highly on standard measures of happiness as well. These northern European countries serve as a great example of how predominantly secular countries can be well-functioning, moral communities.

The United States, on the other hand, is a quite religious country relative to the rest of the world. In fact, although the first amendment prohibits the government from establishing a common religion that all citizens must support, religion is very much a part of public life. Consider that our money reads "In God We Trust," or that presidents regularly end important political speeches by saying "God bless America." You can likely think of several other examples of how religion becomes a part of public life in America. In fact, scholars have pointed out that American civil society—the public space that exists between the government and business—is quite religious. Religious people, for example, are often active volunteering in their local communities and participating in political activity. A secular person who decides to engage the public sphere is likely to end up part of community prayer breakfasts or being involved in a group prayer before a city council meeting or a community-wide day of volunteering. Critical scholars have pointed out that the American civil society is very much a religious space, many going so far as to claim that America has a civil religion that promotes belief in God and looks skeptically upon those who refuse to express such a belief because they may threaten the solidarity that is essential for living together as citizens.

Perhaps this close mixing of public life and religious belief is nowhere more common than in America's Bible Belt. This is an informally defined region in the United States that includes the southeast and stretches into the Midwest. Here, it is generally accepted that religion plays more of a role in public life than in other regions of the United States. For that reason, scholars, such as Christopher Garneau, have paid particular attention to the public participation and acceptance of nonbelievers and many secularists have made it a point to organize in defense of their right to freedom from religion. A good example of secular activism in the face of an overly religious political community comes from Oklahoma, and the group Oklahoma Atheists, or AOK. The nonprofit organizes more than twenty-eight meetups every month and claim to be the fifth largest atheist community on Meetup.com. In fact, a great way to see how atheists use the Internet to create community is to go to Meetup.com and search for atheist meetups.

AOK, of course, meets in Oklahoma which is, according to sociologist Garneau, one of the most evangelical Christian states in the United States. The state is currently involved in a political controversy about whether a monument such as the Ten Commandments can be placed on the grounds of the state capitol. Although the state's Supreme Court ruled that the statue violates the state constitution, the attorney general is fighting that decision. Regardless of how the controversy is finally resolved, the case illustrates how Christianity is very much a part of public life in Oklahoma. For nonbelievers, sociologist Garneau says,

Chapter 9: Secularism, Secularity, and Community

living secretly as an atheist can create psychological tension and the need to find a community of other secularists with whom to share the burden. Many atheists first find community via the Internet on social media sites like Facebook or Atheistforum.com. Members of AOK, and others that Garneau interviewed, would very often transform these online get-togethers into face-to-face meetings. It may be just a few times a year, or it may be as often as AOK's nearly daily meetings, but spending time in community with others who share your experience and understand your sense of stigma helps to alleviate the stress of living outside the rules of America's religious public sphere.

Summary

This chapter has presented a broad overview of how social scientists think about secularism and community. This discussion should make it clear that many nonbelievers value connections with others and want to join with their fellow secularists in friendship and to explore, and defend, their own beliefs. In this way, secular community is not very different from religious community. From Sunday Assembly meetings that are very much like typical religious celebrations, to secular rites of passage, to celebrations of holidays like Darwin Day, nonbelievers live their lives just like most believers. In fact, as much research has documented, it is hard to imagine how any individual atheist could maintain such an identity without forming some degree of community with others who share beliefs and values. Groups like SSA and American Atheists provide the organizational context needed to meet other atheists and have opportunities to express secular identity. For those nonbelievers who may not want to participate in ritual or communal behavior similar to that of believers, the Internet provides numerous virtual meeting rooms to connect with others and discuss basic values or even common hobbies and popular culture.

Unfortunately, as similar to believers as many secularists are, a lot of nonbelievers continue to feel stigmatized in societies that remain quite religious. Secular community often forms in direct response to this marginalization. The stress of being an outsider leads many nonbelievers, young and old, to want to share their burden with like-minded nonbelievers. We should expect secular communities to persist, and perhaps to grow, as long as mainstream society retains its religious character. Political controversies about religious monuments on public ground, as well as the fear of losing close friends and family by coming out as an atheist, will compel nonbelievers to form their own spaces. Of course, public opinion polls are regularly finding growing numbers of religion nones—those who have no religious affiliation—so, although not all of the nones are atheists, perhaps secular organizations will find a growing profile in public life. If that is the case, we may see the specialized secular organizations fade as individual atheists feel more accepted in the wider community.

The study of secularism is a relatively new subfield in sociology and the other social sciences. It is certain that scholars will continue to learn about how secularists live in modern multicultural societies, so this chapter should be considered an invitation to learn more about secular community rather than a definitive statement. Perhaps as a function of its relative youth, its values of individualism, skepticism, and free thought, or the many tools available to construct it, the secular community is constantly evolving. Nonbelievers are actively creating new ways to live with one another in the modern world, and this rapid change and fundamental diversity mean that social scientists must continue to learn about secular life in community.

RELIGION: BEYOND RELIGION

161

Bibliography

American Atheists. http://athiests.org.

American Humanist Association. "The Humanist Manifesto III." https://www.americanhumanist.org.

Atheist Forums. Atheistforums.com.

Becker, Penny Edgell. *Congregations in Conflict: Cultural Models of Local Religious Life*. Cambridge; New York: Cambridge University Press, 1999.

Beckford, James A. "'Community' in the Sociology of Religion: The Case of Britain." *Social Compass* 62, no. 2 (2015): 225–237.

Black Atheists. https://www.facebook.com/BlackAtheists/.

Bokemper, Daniel. "It's Gonna be AOK: Weathering the Secular Struggle in Oklahoma." 2015. http://www.oxford-karma.com/culture/its-gonna-be-aok-weathering-the-secular-struggle-in-oklahoma/.

Brint, Steven. "Gemeinschaft Revisited: A Critique and Reconstruction of the Community Concept." *Sociological Theory* 19, no.1 (2001): 1.

Cimino, Richard, and Christopher Smith. "The New Atheism and the Formation of the Imagined Secularist Community." *Journal of Media and Religion* 10, no. 1 (2011): 24–38.

Cimino, Richard, and Christopher Smith. "Secular Humanism and Atheism Beyond Progressive Secularism." *Sociology of Religion* 68, no. 4 (2007): 407–424.

Cimino, Richard, and Christopher Smith. "Secularist Rituals in the US: Solidarity and Legitimization." In *Atheist Identities–Spaces and Social Contexts*, edited by Lori G. Beaman and Steven Tomlins, 87–100. Switzerland: Springer International Publishing, 2015.

Dawkins, Richard. *The God Delusion*. Boston: Houghton Mifflin, 2008.

Dawkins, Richard. "A Letter from Richard Dawkins." Richard Dawkins Foundation for Science and Reasoning. https://richarddawkins.net/aboutus/.

Edgell, Penny, Joseph Gerteis, and Douglas Hartmann. "Atheists as 'Other': Moral Boundaries and Cultural Membership in American Society." *American Sociological Review* 71, no. 2 (2006): 211–234.

Epstein, Greg. *Good without God: What a Billion Nonreligious People Do Believe*. New York: Morrow, 2009.

Garneau, Christopher. "Stigma Management by Midwestern Secularists." In *Religion and Political Tolerance in America*, edited by Paul A. Djupe. Philadelphia: Temple University Press, 2015.

Gervais, Will M., Azim F. Shariff, and Ara Norenzayan. "Do You Believe in Atheists? Distrust is Central to Anti-Atheist Prejudice." *Journal of Personality and Social Psychology* 101, no. 6 (2011): 1189.

Green, Rick. "Pruitt Fighting Decision to Remove Ten Commandments Monument." *The Oklahoman*. 2015.

Humanist Ceremonies. https://humanism.org.uk/ceremonies/.

Humanist Hub. www.humanisthub.org.

Keown, Tim. "The Confession of Arian Foster." *ESPN the Magazine*. 2015.

LeDrew, Stephen. "Discovering Atheism: Heterogeneity in Trajectories to Atheist Identity and Activism." *Sociology of Religion* 74, no. 4 (2013): 431–453.

LeDrew, Stephen. "Reply: Toward a Critical Sociology of Atheism: Identity, Politics, Ideology." *Sociology of Religion* 74, no. 4 (2013): 464–470.

Lofland, John, and Rodney Stark. "Becoming a World-Saver: A Theory of Conversion to a Deviant Perspective." *American Sociological Review* 30, no. 6 (1965): 862–875.

Oklahoma Atheists. www.oklahomaatheists.com.

Openly Secular Campaign. www.openlysecular.org.

Pharyngula. P. Z. Myers blog. http://freethoughtblogs.com/pharyngula/.

Scharfenberger, Kimberly. "Atheist Clubs Don't Belong at Catholic Colleges, Experts Say." 2015. http://www.cardinalnewmansociety.org/CatholicEducationDaily/DetailsPage/tabid/102/ArticleID/4323/Atheist-Clubs-Don%E2%80%99t-Belong-at-Catholic-Colleges-Experts-Say.aspx.

Sherkat, Darren E. "Beyond Belief: Atheism, Agnosticism, and Theistic Certainty in the United States." *Sociological Spectrum* 28, no. 5 (2008): 438–459.

Smith, Christopher, and Richard Cimino. "Atheisms Unbound: The Role of the New Media in the Formation of a Secularist Identity." *Secularism and Nonreligion* 1, no. 1 (2012): 17–31.

Smith, Jesse M. "Becoming an Atheist in America: Constructing Identity and Meaning from the Rejection of Theism." *Sociology of Religion* 72, no. 2 (2011): 215–237.

Sunday Assembly. 2015. http://sundayassembly.com/.

Thunderf00t. YouTube. https://www.youtube.com/user/Thunderf00t.

Tomlins, Steven. "A Common Godlessness: A Snapshot of a Canadian University Atheist Club, Why its Members Joined, and what that Community Means to them." In *Atheist Identities–Spaces and Social Contexts*, edited by Lori G. Beaman and Steven Tomlins, 117–136. Switzerland: Springer International Publishing, 2015.

Uecker, Jeremy E., Mark D. Regnerus, and Margaret L. Vaaler. "Losing My Religion: The Social Sources of Religious Decline in Early Adulthood." *Social Forces* 85, no. 4 (2007): 1667–1692.

Vargas, Nicholas. "Retrospective Accounts of Religious Disaffiliation in the United States: Stressors, Skepticism, and Political Factors." *Sociology of Religion* 73. no. 2 (2012): 200–223.

Vargas, Nicholas, and Matthew T. Loveland. "Befriending the 'Other': Patterns of Social Ties between the Religious and NonReligious." *Sociological Perspectives* 54, no. 4 (2011): 713–731.

Zuckerman, Phil. *Society without God: What the Least Religious Nations Can Tell Us about Contentment.* New York: New York University Press, 2008.

FILM AND TELEVISION

Atheism: A Rough History of Disbelief. Jonathan Miller. Dir. Richard Denton. BBC, 2004. Television mini-series documentary.

Beautiful Minds. "Richard Dawkins." Season 2, episode 3, 2012. Dir. Jacqui Farnham.

Religulous. Dir. Larry Charles. 2008 "Comic documentary" mocking religious beliefs, hosted by American comedian Bill Maher.

CHAPTER 10

Separation of Church and State in the American Political Traditions

Will Barndt
Assistant Professor of Political Studies
Pitzer College, Claremont, CA

America has not one tradition of separation of church and state, but two. Of the two, the most commonly understood is the newer: a tradition of considering religion to be a private matter, an activity that is inappropriate for the state to support and ought be free from state interference. This is the tradition established by the country's founding documents, particularly the Constitution, which keeps the religious life of citizens at a distance from the federal government. Since the mid-twentieth-century, the US Supreme Court has regularly turned to this tradition as it has ruled on church-state issues.

Yet most scholars agree that this is not the only American tradition of church and state. Parallel to the privatizing tradition of the country's founding documents runs a different older tradition, a tradition that encourages Americans to turn outward in their religion, as participants in a political community seeking to identify and pursue shared public goals. This more public tradition of church and state has been most visible in the ways that American churches (and other religious congregations) have become actively involved in—indeed, sometimes built their own—civic associations, welfare institutions, social movements, and political parties.

TWO RELIGIOUS TRADITIONS

Paradoxically, these two American traditions point in different directions. Our public Constitution suggests that Americans ought understand religion as a private interest. Yet, historically, private associations like churches have pointed Americans toward considering religious life as a foundation of the public sphere. This chapter explores how exactly this American paradox has informed the country's centuries-long wrestle with the idea of "separation of church and state."

RELIGIOUS LIFE AS PRIVATE

The origins of the privatizing American tradition can be found in the work of English political philosopher John Locke (1632–1704), whose ideas were widely discussed among the American founders. In his *Two Treatises of Government and A Letter Concerning Toleration*, Locke argued that religion and government were fundamentally different. Churches were devoted to heavenly ends: to *convincing* people of the truth of God and

Chapter 10: Separation of Church and State in the American Political Traditions

religious revelation. Government, on the other hand, was committed to changing the way the earthly world worked—ultimately, for Locke, through the use of *force*. In Locke's theory, that is, churches and governments had both different goals and different ways of achieving those goals: religion devoted itself to heavenly ends via convincement, while government devoted itself to earthly ends via force.

This difference was critical to Locke. Because, he believed, no one could ever really be convinced of religious truth by force, any attempt by a government to do so would be futile. Consequently, Locke argued, the state should tolerate different sects—any attempt to convince people of religious truth through government means was doomed to failure. Religious belief, for Locke and the Americans who would follow him, was thus a *private* interest, a matter that ought to remain between individuals and God. It was not a concern for the state. (Note that Locke did not believe that the state had to tolerate Catholics, arguing that their loyalty to the pope made their loyalty to civil government suspect.)

John Locke (1632–1704), English political philosopher. For Locke and the American Founders, on whom he was profoundly influential, religious belief was a private interest and not a concern for the state—a matter that ought to remain between individuals and God. **FINE ART IMAGES/HERITAGE IMAGES/GETTY IMAGES.**

RELIGIOUS LIFE AS PUBLIC

In contrast with this Lockean vision, American religious congregations have consistently provided an avenue by which citizens have sought to transcend their private interests and to enter the public sphere. As will be discussed, the Puritan world of New England exemplified this tradition. Yet the tradition extends far beyond that sect, place, and time. As Robert D. Putnam (1941–)—and Alexis de Tocqueville (1805–1859) before him—have argued, historically in America,

> Churches provide an important incubator for civic skills, civic norms, community interests, and civic recruitment. Religiously active men and women learn to give speeches, run meetings, manage disagreements, and bear administrative responsibility. They also befriend others who are in turn likely to recruit them into other forms of community activity. In part for these reasons, churchgoers are more likely to be involved in secular organizations, to vote and politically participate in other ways, and to have deeper informal social connections. (Putnam 2000, 66)

It is through their churches and other religious congregations, that is, that many Americans have oriented themselves toward and entered public life. This public orientation of American churches has not always been liberal, nor democratic, but it has certainly been participatory. Time and time again, churches have provided the foundation from which Americans have launched new civic associations, social movements, and political parties. They have been one foundation of the American public sphere. And although this chapter focuses primarily on Christian denominations, the dynamics it describes are broadly found within American communities of faith.

LOOKING FORWARD

In pursuit of understanding these American traditions, this chapter focuses on three main areas of church-state relations, all of which in different ways have been present since the American colonial era:

1. The myriad ways in which churches have oriented Americans toward public causes;

2. The struggle within the US state to ensure that this religiously inspired public activity impinges neither on the private interests nor on the public life of other citizens; and

3. The persistent tension between these two American traditions.

By exploring these phenomena as they have developed over the past four centuries, this chapter provides guideposts for understanding the paradoxes, the terrors, and the possibilities of these different traditions of separation of church and state in the United States. And, in doing so, it asks us to consider what might become of each of these two American traditions as the country appears to move "beyond religion."

COLONIAL ESTABLISHMENTS

Religion and public life were deeply intertwined from the beginning of the American experiment. In the first half of the eighteenth century, a time when the Atlantic coast was composed almost entirely of British colonies, a large percent of the settler population attended churches.

ESTABLISHED CHURCHES IN THE COLONIAL ERA: THEORY AND THE CHURCH OF ENGLAND

Residents of most colonies did not simply attend *any* church. Many colonies had an established church: a church recognized and supported by the colonial government as the official church of that government. In practice, this meant that the overlap between church and state was both apparent and real throughout most colonies. Colonial courts enforced religious law. Churches were the places where people gathered publicly. Voting, office-holding, and other forms of participation in government were usually restricted to those who professed the established faith. And colonial governments transferred tax revenues to financially support their churches.

The governments of Virginia, Georgia, the Carolinas, and eventually Maryland all established the Church of England as their official colonial church. (The Church of England, or Anglican Church, was so named because it was the established church of England.) In establishing the Church of England these colonial governments simply imported the English model to new English territory in the American colonies. In Virginia after the 1660s, for example, churches were established at public expense, minister's salaries were paid at public expense, church attendance was mandatory, and churches were recognized as official repositories of births, deaths, and marriages. As Michael W. McConnell (1955–) writes in "Establishment and Disestablishment at the Founding" (2003), non-Anglicans—particularly Quakers and Puritans—and their churches were at various times banned from the Anglican colonies.

Chapter 10: Separation of Church and State in the American Political Traditions

OTHER ESTABLISHED CHURCHES IN THE COLONIAL ERA: THE DISSIDENTS

Not all colonial governments established the Church of England as their official religion. In fact, religious dissidents founded several American colonies: Puritans in Massachusetts, Connecticut, and New Hampshire; Quakers in Pennsylvania and New Jersey; and Catholics in Maryland. These colonies—chartered or otherwise founded with the permission of the English Crown—quickly became havens for English (and other northwestern European) dissidents. They became places of refuge for Calvinists, Lutherans, Catholics, and Anabaptists, sects that regularly had been oppressed for their religious differences by the established churches of the European polities from which they emigrated.

Upon founding new colonies many of these dissidents created established churches of their own. Perhaps most prominently among these was Puritan Massachusetts, where the establishment of churches happened not at the level of the whole colony, but at the level of individual towns. There, ministers were selected in town meetings, effectively establishing local official churches, which were supported at public expense.

This New England establishmentarianism was rather different than that of the Anglicans in the southern colonies. Although the Puritans insisted on separate leaderships for church and state, they also believed that both these organizations had divine tasks that must be communally supported. For the Puritans, the political community must work together to support the (separate, but equally divine) ends of the state and the ends of the church. Unlike Locke, the Puritans believed that religion should pull people together into the public sphere. To be clear, these participatory Puritans regularly participated in illiberal—as in the banishment of Roger Williams (1603–1680), the founder of Rhode Island who argued forcefully against established churches—and sometimes murderous—as in the case of the Salem witch trials—activities. As McConnell writes, through this belief that they were religiously ordained to work together to build what John Winthrop (1587–1649) called a "city upon a hill," these New Englanders pioneered a tradition of religiously informed American political participation.

NONESTABLISHED AND INFORMALLY ESTABLISHED COLONIAL CHURCHES

Of course, not all the American colonies had established churches. A Catholic member of the English nobility, Lord Baltimore (Cecil Calvert, 1605–1675) founded Maryland as a haven for religious dissenters. Delaware, too, lacked an established church. Yet of the nonestablished colonies, Rhode Island deserves particular mention. The founder of Rhode Island, Williams, was a devout Puritan (although his theology evolved in complex ways) who rejected the idea of an established church in Massachusetts, arguing that close relations between state and church were unnecessary to good government. Predictably, this led to conflict with authorities in Massachusetts and eventually to Williams's founding of a new colony. In accord with Williams's theology, the new government of Rhode Island was thus founded without an established church.

Pennsylvania, too, became famous for its more tolerant approach to religious minorities. As in Rhode Island and Delaware, residents of colonial Pennsylvania could practice most faiths without state interference. William Penn (1644–1718), the Quaker founder of the colony, committed its government to absolute religious tolerance in his *Frame of Government of Pennsylvania* (1682) and *The Charter of Privileges* (1701), Pennsylvania's constitutions until Independence. Consequently, religious dissidents flocked to Pennsylvania: not just Quakers, but Lutherans, Calvinists, Mennonites, and other Anabaptists.

MACMILLAN INTERDISCIPLINARY HANDBOOKS

Yet the absence of an established church in Pennsylvania was perhaps more theory than practice. Quakers dominated colonial government in Pennsylvania. Many colonial legislators were Quaker, bringing with them to public office a coherent set of religious beliefs about how they ought to govern. Indeed, the famously tolerant Pennsylvania colonial government in practice operated on the same principles as the Quaker church. Quaker colonial political theorists and legislators, for example, believed that the constitution was a sacred document—that it came directly from God—and that it would be unfaithful to break it. When non-Quakers assumed office, they were expected to work within this framework. According to Jane E. Calvert (1970–) in *Quaker Constitutionalism and the Political Thought of John Dickinson* (2009), opponents of the dominant faction in the Pennsylvania assembly even referred to it as "the Quaker Party," foreshadowing future religious participation in partisan politics. Pennsylvania thus presents yet another version of colonial church-state relations in America: an informally established church operating alongside a formally tolerant state.

Given the religious diversity of the colonial population—a diversity that only increased with the rise and vitalization of Baptists, Methodists, and Presbyterians during the First Great Awakening of the 1730s and 1740s—these colonies remained important havens for religious dissidents until Independence.

COLONIAL DIVERSITY: THE BEGINNINGS OF PARADOX

The American colonies thus represented a diverse lot before Independence: some with established Anglican churches, some with (formally or informally) established dissenting churches, and some carefully avoiding any establishment whatsoever. In all the colonies, however, the language of public life was suffused with the language of (Christian) religion. As Barry Allen Shain (1950–) writes in *The Myth of American Individualism* (1994), although debates about establishment churches raged, they raged almost exclusively in the language of Calvinists, Anglicans, Quakers, Baptists, and Catholics. Even Williams wrote in these terms: "When [the Church] has opened a gap in the hedge or wall of separation between the garden of the church and the wilderness of the world…. [If] He will ever please to restore His garden and Paradise again, it must of necessity be walled in peculiarly unto Himself from the world" (Williams 1644). Yet this colonial tradition was to be challenged at Independence.

THE FOUNDING: DISESTABLISHMENT AND ITS DISCONTENTS

It is but one of the many ironies of the intertwining of religious and public life in America that the country's two most important founding documents—the Constitution and Declaration of Independence—are all but silent on the question of religion. Religion was mentioned only once in the Constitution as originally ratified, in Article VI, where religious tests for public office are prohibited. And, Danielle Allen's (1971–) *Our Declaration* (2014) notes that although Thomas Jefferson's (1743–1826) Declaration of Independence refers to God in four instances, the references are vague at best—and were inserted not by Jefferson but by others as the document was collectively revised.

ANTISECTARIANISM: RELIGION, THE FOUNDING DOCUMENTS, AND THE FOUNDERS

This near absence has been understood by scholars, in large part correctly, as evidence that the signers of the Declaration and the Constitution sought to distance first the newly

Chapter 10: Separation of Church and State in the American Political Traditions

independent states and later their new federal government from any particular religious sect. In this sense, the documents are clearly anti-establishmentarian. They suggested, following Locke, that the government should keep aloof from religion, allowing belief to remain a private matter between citizens and their gods.

Most of the signers of these founding documents had, in fact, been exposed to (and often read extensively on) new theologies and ideas that downplayed not only sectarianism but even religion itself. To take one example, natural religion drew on Enlightenment ideas to suggest that religious truth could be discerned by uncovering laws of nature: as God had created nature, the laws that governed it were his laws. Closely related, Deism suggested that God was no longer active in the world and that the Bible was not evidence of his revelation. At the same time, many founders were enthralled with the possibility of rationalism, the idea that scientific experiment and reason were at the core of understanding not only nature but also politics itself.

Driven by these ideas, many founders believed that the new nation was leading the way into a postsectarian world, a world in which religious conflict would be a thing of the past. Virginia was at the forefront of this movement during this period. Influenced by Locke, Jefferson introduced a "Bill for Establishing Religious Freedom" in Virginia in 1779. A few years later, James Madison (1751–1836) penned his "Memorial and Remonstrance against Religious Assessments." Together, these documents made a remarkably strong case for both religious liberty and disestablishment in Virginia. As the founding era unfolded, it seemed clear that a Lockean spirit, rather than a Puritan one, was informing the constitution of the new nation.

It is important to insert three cautionary notes here. First, Gregg L. Frazer has convincingly argued that the dominant approach to religion among the founders was theistic rationalism. Opposed both to natural religion and to pure rationalism, theistic rationalists sought a middle way between the two: "Adherents were willing to define God in whatever way their reason indicated and to jettison Christian beliefs that did not conform to reason. Theistic rationalism was not really a religion or denomination per se but rather a religious belief system and an approach to religious belief" (Frazer 2012, 14). Many founders in effect found their religious home in this system. Even Jefferson, who published a revised version of the Bible in which he excised references to the miraculous or supernatural, seems to have subscribed to a version of theistic rationalism.

Second, many founders believed that some sort of religious belief was a necessary support for good government. Even if they were not devoutly religious themselves, founders like George Washington (1732–1799) were civic republicans: they believed that political life depended on virtue and that religion was a useful way to make (or keep) people virtuous. For civic republicans, it was not the truth of religion that mattered—it was its value in directing people toward the public good.

Third, these founders—in their religious beliefs—represented a rather small elite segment of the American population. In other words, the silence on religion in the Constitution and Declaration should not be confused with secularism among the still-religious majority of the American population. Indeed, the United States at Independence was on the cusp of an explosion of popular religious activism, the Second Great Awakening.

These caveats notwithstanding, for a medley of reasons and beliefs, the Declaration of Independence and the Constitution that was sent to the states for ratification remained all but silent on the question of religion. This deafening silence did not go unnoticed.

THE CREATION OF THE FIRST AMENDMENT

When the Constitution passed to the states for ratification, debate broke out on whether religion ought be more explicitly treated in the document. From one perspective, Henry Abbott (1740–1791), a delegate to the North Carolina ratifying convention, was particularly concerned that "pagans, deists, and Mahometans [Muslims] might obtain offices among us" (Waldman 2009, 134). From another perspective, religious leaders like Baptist minister John Leland (1754–1841) worried that Article VI of the Constitution did not do nearly enough to protect freedom of religion. Despite these debates, the US Constitution was ratified without amendment in 1788.

Three years later, the First US Congress adopted new amendments to the Constitution (ten of which were ratified the Bill of Rights). The first of these amendments, eventually, would become central to American understandings of the separation of church and state. Based in no small part on Jefferson's and Madison's contributions in Virginia, the first two clauses of the First Amendment read as follows "Congress shall make no law respecting an establishment of religion, or prohibiting the free exercise thereof." While the first clause enjoined the federal government not to establish religion, the second enjoined it not to interfere in citizens' private religious lives. These two clauses, respectively, came to be known as the establishment clause and the free exercise clause.

Even with the First Amendment, however, the Constitution remained all but devoid of religious references. Given the colonial history of established churches, this was a remarkable point of agreement—and an apparently remarkable departure from longstanding colonial traditions of publicly oriented religious life. The founding documents clearly created a new nation whose federal government would treat religion as a private manner.

THE CONTRARY STATES: CONTINUED ESTABLISHMENTS AND THE LIMITS OF THE FIRST AMENDMENT

In line with Lockean principles, the First Amendment delineated basic parameters of church-state relations for the new federal government. It is critical to remember that the Bill of Rights, including the First Amendment, *initially only curtailed the powers of the federal government: it did not apply to the states.*

Even under the Lockean US Constitution, states could keep—legally at least—their official established churches alive. Well into the nineteenth century, state churches continued to be partially funded by state revenues. Moreover, many states continued to require public officeholders to swear religious oaths. As famously tolerant Pennsylvania moved from colony to state, for example, a debate broke out between Benjamin Franklin (1706–1790) and the Lutheran Reverend Henry Muhlenberg (1711–1787) over whether Pennsylvania Assembly members had to acknowledge God. Franklin thought no. Muhlenberg said yes. Franklin lost.

In the first years of the new Republic, the American paradox of separation of church and state was already in full view. The country contained two seemingly irreconcilable ideas about how church and state ought be related. One, as expressed in the Lockean Constitution, viewed religion as a largely private matter, an area in which the government ought not interfere. The second viewed religion as a potential wellspring of public life, an institution worthy of public support, as expressed in the persistence of established churches in some states and localities.

RELIGION: BEYOND RELIGION

Chapter 10: Separation of Church and State in the American Political Traditions

CHURCH AND STATE IN THE NEW REPUBLIC: THE FIRST 150 YEARS

The years between 1790 and 1940 witnessed tremendous transformations in American political life: the rise of mass political parties, the expansion of suffrage, the emergence of a Supreme Court empowered by judicial review, the Civil War (1861–1865) and end of slavery, Reconstruction and the emergence of a legally segregated South, the explosion of industrial capitalism, the expansion of military armament with powerful new technologies, the rise of new imperial ambitions, the geographic expansion of the United States to the Pacific Ocean and beyond, and many more. Indeed, the United States in 1940 was all but unimaginable at the outset of the Republic.

Across this time of enormous change the balance between the two American political traditions of separation of church and state remained remarkably stable. Formally established state churches would fall by the wayside, but congregations would develop new ways of remaining actively engaged in public life: through voluntary associations, social movements, and political parties. At the same time, the Lockean approach to church-state relations, embedded in the Constitution, continued to hover over this sea of publicly involved religious organizations. For nearly 150 years, this represented the way in which the two competing traditions of church and state in America unfolded together.

THE SECOND GREAT AWAKENING AND THE COMPLETION OF DISESTABLISHMENT

Established state churches did persist into the new Republic—yet they would not last for long. By the turn of the nineteenth century only three states would retain established churches (Green 2010): uncoincidentally, these were the historically Puritan Connecticut, New Hampshire, and Massachusetts. Given this trend, it seemed to many that Jefferson and his fellow founders might well have succeeded in uprooting the place of religion in public life. The Lockean spirit of the Constitution, it appeared, was permeating the new Republic. For example, the United States ratified in 1797 The Treaty of Peace and Friendship of Tripoli, which proclaimed that "the government of the United States of America is not in any sense founded on the Christian Religion... [and] has in itself no character of enmity against the laws, religion or tranquility of Musselmen [Muslims]." A few short years alter, President Thomas Jefferson in 1802 wrote a letter in reply to the Danbury [Connecticut] Baptists Association in which he restated Rogers Williams's idea of a "wall of separation" between church and state. Though this letter restated arguments Jefferson had already made in Virginia and was in part motivated by baser partisan concerns, its repurposing of Williams's language would come to have enormous implications for debates about church-state relations.

Nonetheless, these postsectarian hopes were being dashed even as they were being formed. Beginning in about 1790, the religious life of the newly independent states began to change dramatically. The early nineteenth century witnessed a renewed religious fervor— what came to be known as the Second Great Awakening. This revitalization and evangelization of existing sects (especially Baptists and Methodists) created a newly popular alternative to longstanding American denominations like Anglicans, Quakers, and Congregationalists. In so doing, the Second Great Awakening unleashed an individualized, freeing, populist religious politics: a politics that insisted that all people had free will and could choose to be saved, a politics that used new communication and organization

172   MACMILLAN INTERDISCIPLINARY HANDBOOKS

Chapter 10: Separation of Church and State in the American Political Traditions

techniques to create mass Christian movements. It represented, as Tocqueville observed and Nathan Hatch (1946–) later argued, "the democratization of American Christianity."

The emergence of this new religious fervor, ironically, represented the final nail in the coffin of established church projects. Societal pressures—including the diversification of Protestant sects—drove a wedge between established churches and the states, leading to their rapid disappearance. In New England, as Donald L. Drakeman (1953–) writes in *Church, State, and Original Intent* (2010), Baptists and other dissidents pushed hard to disestablish state churches, a dynamic foreshadowed in Virginia in the 1770s when Presbyterians and Baptists successfully pressured to disestablish the Anglican Church there. In 1833, Massachusetts became the last state to stop publicly funding established churches.

The Second Great Awakening did not simply push for disestablishment: it suggested an alternative. And it was through that alternative that the Puritan idea of connections between religion and public life was kept alive.

RE-INVENTING PUBLICLY DIRECTED RELIGIOUS LIFE: ORGANIZING FOR THE PUBLIC GOOD

In the early 1800s, American churches faced an apparent dilemma. State governments were ending religious establishment—a historically full-fledged means of reinforcing connections between religion and public life. Yet with the Second Great Awakening, many Americans were becoming not only more religious but also more concerned about the implications of their religious beliefs for public life. This produced a paradox. Despite the privatizing Lockean Constitution, American churches and their adherents searched for new ways to turn their religious beliefs outward to the public sphere.

In place of formal connections with the state, many churches moved to create new kinds of organizations dedicated to public life. Evangelical Methodists and Baptists, for example, worked to bring religion to the American popular classes, establishing camp meetings where people could come and talk together about religion. Out of this work came the creation of vast numbers of new religious schools and missionary societies. The fervor also bubbled over into electoral politics: when Thomas Jefferson ran for president, his partisan opponents accused him of being a "howling atheist"—foreshadowing religious partisanship in decades to come. It was through this kind of religious organizing, built on and directed by particular congregations, that the second American tradition of church-state relations persisted into the new Republic: religious Americans continued to organize publicly for what they perceived to be the public good.

Churches and Voluntary Societies: Poor Relief and Education. Perhaps the most widespread way in which churches remained oriented to the public sphere was through their creation of reform and voluntary societies (Green 2010). These societies worked to establish new kinds of organizations that would both serve growing public needs—and bring new adherents into their denominational folds.

Take, for example, the response of religious voluntary societies to the growing dislocation and impoverishment of the mid-nineteenth century. After 1815, the vast majority of Americans experienced both an economic and physical uprooting. Although many moved west along the frontier—contributing to the genocide of Native Americans as they went—others found themselves at the mercy of emerging new economies. As state policy makers encouraged industrialization and promoted the full-fledged geographic

RELIGION: BEYOND RELIGION

173

Chapter 10: Separation of Church and State in the American Political Traditions

expansion of the country, Americans found themselves ripped out of family and religious communities in the countryside and tossed into unfamiliar worlds of the city and factory. Moreover, vast populations of new immigrants were arriving on American shores.

It was into this context—moral, economic, and geographic upheaval—that many churches stepped in the first half of the nineteenth century. Drawing on re-invented ideas of Christian charity, evangelical Christians formed a myriad of voluntary organizations that served the needs of America's poorest, including the American Tract Society, the Female Missionary Society for the Poor, and the Young Men's Missionary Society, to name a few. At the same time that evangelical Christians were building organizations to deal with the crisis, Catholics—a population growing with immigration—re-invented charitable organizations for the poor in their new country: the St. Vincent de Paul Society, parish societies, orphanages, schools, hospitals, and women's homes. Such charitable organizations often appeared (relatively) more survivable than the grim state-sponsored poorhouse that dotted cities and counties. American religious institutions thus became regular public purveyors of poor relief and education.

In this sense, even after disestablishment, religious congregations played a critical role in serving—and in fact constituting—the American public. They were organizations through which religious citizens turned outward to the world, transcending their private, personal interests and working toward their (often illiberal) visions of the public good. It was in these organizations that the publicly oriented tradition of American church-state relations persisted.

Connections and Linkages: Churches, Social Movements, and Political Parties. Yet this religious organizing was not just about voluntary societies, poor relief, and schools. It also bled into new social movements and political parties.

Most prominently, many churches quickly became fully involved in the most contentious political issue of the nineteenth century: slavery. Churches and preachers became public advocates in this debate, as it played out at the state and national levels, helping to found organizations such as the American Anti-Slavery Society. At the same time, Baptist, Methodist, and Presbyterian clergy were key players in forging secessionist attitudes among their congregations in the run-up to the Civil War. Through this debate, moreover, African American churches further solidified their role as a foundation of black political life in the country. As Frederick C. Harris argues in "Black Churches and Civic Traditions" (2001, 140), out of these churches grew "a civic tradition that nurtures a sense of charity for the poor and an active concern for political life."

As in earlier periods, churches also became actively involved in partisan politics. During the 1840s, anti-Catholic sentiment swept through Protestant communities in response to recently increased German and Irish immigration: from the pulpit, Protestant ministers preached against the rise of Catholic influence in schools. By the late 1840s, secret voluntary societies—such as the American Protestant Association—were advocating concerted action to keep anyone but Protestants from holding public office. This trend culminated in the formation of the American ("Know-Nothing") Party, at its heyday in the mid-1850s. Although the American Party collapsed as the country moved toward civil war, anti-Catholic partisanship—present since the colonial era—would remain a recurrent theme of party politics through the middle of the next century. (A similar trajectory led from church organizing to the Anti-Saloon Society to partisan electioneering in the late nineteenth and early twentieth centuries.)

Chapter 10: Separation of Church and State in the American Political Traditions

Although formally established state churches disappeared by the 1830s, Christian (Protestant and Catholic) churches and their affiliated organizations remained directed toward organizing for their versions of the public good. They worked to invent new ways that church and state might work in tandem, in clear keeping with the second American tradition of church-state relations.

PUBLIC ORGANIZING INTO THE TWENTIETH CENTURY

American churches did not stop "organizing for the public good" with the turn of the twentieth century. Just as in the previous century, clear connections persisted between the organizational life of churches, the voluntary societies they sponsored, emergent social movements, and the development of political parties. Although the United States never developed stable European-style confessional parties—political parties centrally organized around religious identity—the religious lives of Americans continued to filter into their party system.

Consider, by way of example, the angst of conservative fundamentalist and evangelical Protestants at the beginning of the twentieth century. By the early 1900s, many believed themselves to be threatened by the rise of scientific reasoning, liberalizing cultural and sexual mores, and the theory of evolution—not to mention growing waves of Catholic and Jewish immigrants. This perceived threat pushed these devout Protestants into the public sphere once more, leading to, as Daniel K. Williams notes in *God's Own Party* (2010), their creation of the World's Christian Fundamentals Association (WCFA) in 1919.

Six years later, all eyes in the nation were turned to Dayton, Tennessee. There a public schoolteacher (John Scopes [1900–1971]) had famously agreed to be prosecuted as a test of a state law that made it illegal for public school teachers "to teach any theory that denies the Story of the Divine Creation of man as taught in the Bible, and to teach instead that man has descended from a lower order of animals" (Butler Act, State of Tennessee, 1925). Unsurprisingly, the WCFA was actively involved in preparing for the case, and even ensured that three-time failed Democratic presidential candidate William Jennings Bryan (1860–1925), an anti-evolutionist Presbyterian, would take part in the prosecution. Although Bryan won—and the Tennessee anti-evolutionist law was not repealed for decades—the trial was viewed as a public relations victory for the pro-evolution camp, increasing conservative Protestant fears for the future.

These fears played out in the 1928 Democratic presidential convention, where Jennings Bryan came to the New York Convention to lead fundamentalist Democrats against the nomination of the Catholic Governor of New York, Al Smith (1873–1944). Smith had also sought the Democratic nomination in the extraordinarily contentious 1924 Democratic convention, where the recently revived Ku Klux Klan worked hard (and successfully) to block his nomination. Although Smith lost overwhelmingly to Herbert Hoover (1874–1964) in 1928, conservative Protestant hopes for the future were dashed by the election of President Franklin Delano Roosevelt (1882–1945) in 1932, and the subsequent repeal of Prohibition and growth of Catholic influence in the Roosevelt administration. Faced with their failure in controlling Democratic politics, these fundamentalist Protestants largely withdrew from party politics—for the moment.

To take another example from this period, Protestants across the political spectrum embraced in the early twentieth century what came to be known as the social gospel, a Christian theological movement centrally concerned with social injustice. Applying what

RELIGION: BEYOND RELIGION

175

Chapter 10: Separation of Church and State in the American Political Traditions

Anti-evolution books on sale in Dayton, Tennessee, where the Scopes "Monkey" trial took place. *In 1925 John Scopes, a public schoolteacher, was tried for violating a Tennessee ban on teaching human evolution. The trial became a public sensation, and the pro-evolution camp emerged with a public relations victory.* **TOPICAL PRESS AGENCY/HULTON ARCHIVE/GETTY IMAGES.**

they believed to be a Christian ethic to the conditions of city neighborhoods, associations like the Federal Council of Churches and the Young Men's Christian Association (YMCA) organized for better working and housing conditions for the urban poor. The rise of the social gospel also fueled more explicitly political organizations, including the Prohibition movement and the American Federation of Labor. And, according to Gary Dorrien's book *The New Abolition* (2015), it deeply influenced Martin Luther King Jr. (1929–1968) and the Southern Christian Leadership Conference, arguably the central organization in the civil rights struggle of mid-century.

The first decades of the twentieth century, in short, replicated a long-standing tradition of American church-state relations: churches and their members continued to organize for their own visions of the public good. Still hovering above this publicly oriented religious activity remained the other, Lockean, constitutional vision of separation of church.

CONSTITUTIONALISM IN THE NINETEENTH CENTURY

Although that Lockean ideal was clearly enshrined in the Constitution, the ultimate arbiter of that document, the Supreme Court, all but ignored connections between religion and public life during the first 150 years of the nation's existence. The three major exceptions to this inattention all occurred in the late nineteenth century: *Reynolds v. United States* (1879),

Chapter 10: Separation of Church and State in the American Political Traditions

Church of the Holy Trinity v. United States (1892), and *Bradfield v. Roberts* (1899). The Reynolds case is discussed in the following, but in both *Church of the Holy Trinity* and *Bradfield*, the Court suggested that it actually accepted an important role for religiously affiliated organizations in constituting the public sphere. *Bradfield* allowed Congress to appropriate funds to reconstruct a nonsectarian hospital run by Catholic nuns. And in *Church of the Holy Trinity*, the Court even suggested—this would be overturned—that the United States was a "Christian nation." At the turn of the twentieth century the practice of a public sphere undergirded by religious organizations had barely been commented on by the Supreme Court. This was soon to change.

SEPARATION OF CHURCH AND STATE IN THE LONG NINETEENTH CENTURY

As established churches came to a Lockean end in the early nineteenth century, new churches—invigorated by the Second Great Awakening—threw themselves into organizing for what they perceived to be the public good. From voluntary and moral reform societies to abolitionist movements to anti-Catholic parties and partisanship, churches and their adherents recovered and re-invented the longstanding American proclivity to wed religious fervor to devotion to the public sphere. For nearly 150 years, the privatizing spirit of the Constitution and the public spirit of churches persisted together across American political life. Separation of church and state in the country remained as paradoxical as ever.

INCORPORATING LOCKE: A CRITICAL JUNCTURE IN THE 1940s

After 150 years of relative neglect, church-state issues finally became central to the Supreme Court's docket in the 1940s. In effect, the Court decided during that decade to evaluate the constitutionality of the two different American traditions of separation of church and state. And by the early 1970s, it seemed the privatizing Lockean tradition had finally gained the upper hand.

Beginning in the 1920s, the Court had been selectively applying particular provisions in the Bill of Rights to the states. (It must be remembered that before incorporation the Bill of Rights only applied to the federal government.) This process, known as incorporation, opened up vast new areas of state politics to federal intervention and regulation. In *Cantwell v. Connecticut* (1940), the Supreme Court applied the Incorporation Doctrine to the free exercise clause. Then, in *Everson v. Board of Education* (1947), the Court incorporated the establishment clause. With these decisions, the Court effectively invented a new and powerful strain of US jurisprudence—a strain squarely located in the Lockean tradition of separation of church and state. (Jurisprudence surrounding the free exercise clause and jurisprudence surrounding the establishment clause are often separated. Yet, as discussed here, the issues attending to each often intersect.)

JEFFERSON LIVES? EVERSON, REYNOLDS, AND THEIR SUCCESSORS

At stake in *Everson* was a challenge to a New Jersey school district's policy of reimbursing parents for the cost of getting their children to and from school—regardless of whether that school was public or parochial. In a five-to-four decision authored by Justice Hugo Black (1886–1971), the Court ruled the policy unconstitutional. Most notably, Black argued that the founders intended that the First Amendment create a "wall of separation" between church and government at the national level—and that incorporation could effectively

RELIGION: BEYOND RELIGION

177

Chapter 10: Separation of Church and State in the American Political Traditions

extend that wall to the level of states. Resurrecting Jefferson's language, Black not only revived the Lockean spirit of the Constitution but also declared that the Court had a responsibility to ensure that the states abided by that spirit as well.

In this regard, Black's decision about establishment in *Everson* reached back to the Court's (arguably only other) important nineteenth-century decision on religion, *Reynolds v. United States* (1878). The *Reynolds* case centered on the free exercise clause in the then-federal territory of Utah, to which members of the Church of Latter Day Saints (Mormons) had migrated in 1847 after confronting significant popular violence in the Midwest. At the time, the Mormon Church accepted bigamy and polygamy as part of Church doctrine, practices that brought it into open conflict not only with the American Protestant establishment, but also with much of non-Protestant America. The US Congress outlawed these practices in 1862: because Utah at that time was federal territory, not yet a state, this federal law applied to its residents.

Under this new law, George Reynolds (1842–1909), a secretary to the Mormon leader Brigham Young (1801–1877), was convicted of having multiple wives, fined, and sentenced. In response, he appealed to the US Supreme Court, claiming that the law infringed on his First Amendment right to freely exercise his religion. The Court ruled against Reynolds, arguing that the intention of the First Amendment was to protect *beliefs, not actions*. With seemingly self-evident connections to Locke, the Court thus differentiated between a person's internal beliefs (which were not subject to state regulation) and a person's actions on behalf of those beliefs (which could be subject to state regulation if they violated the law).

Indeed, in ruling against Reynolds, the Court turned (as it would in *Everson*) to Jefferson's "Bill for Establishing Religious Freedom" and Madison's "Memorial and Remonstrance." As Drakeman (2010) rightly notes, part of what was fascinating about this decision is that its author, Justice Waite (1816–1888), turned to the ideas of the founders for support. In the nineteenth century, the practice of trying to divine the original intent of the founders—judging constitutionality based on what one believes the founders meant while writing the Constitution—was all but unheard of. In *Reynolds* and *Everson*, however, the Court reached back to the founding and wrenched Jefferson's and Madison's words into the present. In so doing, they reinvigorated that privatizing Lockean tradition of the separation of church and state found in the Constitution.

Following *Everson*, the Court would work for many years (and more or less steadily) toward a jurisprudence based on its interpretation of Jefferson's "wall of separation." In *McCollum v. Board of Education* (1948), *Engel v. Vitale* (1962), and *Abington School District v. Schempp* (1963), the Court ruled against voluntary religious classes, nonmandatory theist prayer, and Bible readings by officials in public schools. At the same time, the Court ruled that laws that burden religious individuals must have a "compelling state interest" and be enforced through the "least restrictive means" (Muñoz 2013, 6). By 1963, the Court had effectively created a new line of jurisprudence in which (1) the state could not unduly burden the religious with its laws and (2) religious and state institutions (most notably public schools) must remain separate.

In 1971, this separationist project was further clarified when the Court sought to resolve some of these issues in *Lemon v. Kurtzman*. This decision articulated a three-part test for whether a policy violated the establishment clause: (1) Does it have a secular political purpose? (2) Is its primary purpose to advance or inhibit religion? And (3) does it excessively

Chapter 10: Separation of Church and State in the American Political Traditions

entangle government with religion? Evidently, the most contentious piece of the test was evaluating "excessive government entanglement." Yet these clearly stated (if difficult to apply) criteria expressed the spirit of constitutional separationism.

In three short decades, the Court had decided that the religion clauses of the First Amendment applied to the states and applied those clauses to rule unconstitutional a wide range of activities through which religious organizations had directed themselves toward public life. As the Court worked to build a constitutional "wall of a separation" in the states, the two long-standing traditions of American state-church relations came fully into conflict.

TENSIONS, ACCOMMODATIONS, AND MOBILIZATIONS IN THE LATE TWENTIETH CENTURY

From the mid-1970s forward, US politics underwent a sea change. After a half-century of New Deal policies, a combination of external and internal economic problems—as well as growing opposition to progressive social policy—brought new political ideas and movements to the surface.

Central among these movements were politically organized evangelical and fundamentalist Christians. After the Smith fiasco, these Christians had largely retreated from partisan politics. But they had never stopped organizing: conservative Protestants did not withdraw from the public sphere for long. Already by the early 1940s, fundamentalists had met in St. Louis and formed the National Association of Evangelicals (NAE), which sought "to make sure that the Christian Church will return to a new leadership, producing new statesmen for our government circles, influencing education, and rebuilding the foundations of society" (quoted in Williams 2010, 17). While initially focused on combatting "anti-Christian policies," the organization became closely affiliated to the Republican Party, with which it found clear agreement on anti-Communism during the Dwight D. Eisenhower (1890–1969) administration.

As the Court became increasingly involved in adjudicating church-state issues, however, conservative Protestants found themselves increasingly fragmented, largely over the issue of civil rights. The NAE, for example, experienced a schism when it became clear that its and other evangelical leaders, like Billy Graham (1918–), were willing to discuss civil rights legislation. Segregationist Protestant leaders—like Jerry Falwell (1933–2007) and Bob Jones (1883–1968)—thus defected from the NAE and aligned themselves with politicians like Strom Thurmond (1902–2003). Conservative Protestants came together again to oppose the candidacy of Catholic John F. Kennedy (1917–1963), but it was the cultural and jurisprudential changes of the 1960s that remobilized them into party politics—a remobilization with effects that resonate into the twenty-first century (Williams 2010).

The motivations of individual Christian activists of course varied widely, from evangelism to abortion, from education policy to conversion experiences. At an organizational level, the implications of new Christian activism were quickly apparent: a massive reorganization of the publicly oriented lives of conservative Protestants. Two organizations in particular merit mention. First, fundamentalists began to take over the long-standing Southern Baptist Convention from more liberal and moderate leaders. Second, Falwell founded the Moral Majority, which sought to mobilize fundamentalist Protestants into Republican Party politics. Although the Moral Majority folded by the late 1980s,

RELIGION: BEYOND RELIGION

179

replaced in importance in some ways by Pat Robertson's (1930–) Christian Coalition and James Dobson's (1936–) Focus on the Family/Family Research Council, it clearly indicated a successful remobilization of fundamentalist and evangelical Protestants in the 1980s. Together, these organizations mobilized thousands of conservative Christians into public action. As Jon Shields (1976–) has argued in *The Democratic Virtues of the Christian Right* (2009), this remobilization represented a reschooling of conservative Christians in civic skills—the kinds of civic skills that had long underlain the American tradition of publicly oriented religious life.

Over the course of the 1980s, hundreds of thousands of Christians found a new home in the changing Republican Party. According to Williams, conservative Christian factions controlled Republican parties in a full third of the states during the 1990s. By 1993, nearly 60 percent of fundamentalist or evangelical Christians identified as Republicans—while only a third identified as Democrats. As this occurred, over the course of the 1980s and 1990s, more Republican politicians began adopting the language and espousing the policy priorities of many Christian conservative voters: favoring school prayer, the display of Christian icons (like the Ten Commandments) at public buildings, and vouchers that could be used in religious schools; opposing abortion and same-sex marriage.

This process of party realignment reinvigorated constitutional disputes over state-church issues. But unlike earlier eras, it also brought about highly polarized conflict over nominations to the Supreme Court itself. In 1987, conservative Christians were infuriated when President Ronald Reagan's (1911–2004) conservative nominee to the Supreme Court, Robert Bork (1927–2012), was blocked (a nomination that Christian leaders like Falwell had welcomed). In some ways, this tension was predictable. Having advanced for three decades the idea of a "wall of separation," the Court now faced increased scrutiny and opposition from a well-organized conservative Christian movement, well represented in the Republican Party.

As the composition of the Court—and the interests of social movements and political parties—changed, so too did jurisprudence surrounding issues of church and state. Indeed, the late twentieth century produced contentious and confusing jurisprudence related to the establishment clause. Although some scholars saw nothing but increased conflict, others saw a clear drift toward accommodationism, as noted by Vincent Phillip Muñoz (1972–) in *Religious Liberty and the American Supreme Court* (2013) (accommodationism suggests that the Court should, in certain ways, allow for the state and religion to mutually support one another).

These debates played out in a number of divisive Court decisions, beginning with *Lynch v. Donnelly* (1984). In the *Lynch* decision, Justice Sandra Day O'Connor (1930–) proposed the "endorsement test," which suggested that actions are unconstitutional if they create the perception that the government is either endorsing or disapproving of religion. According to O'Connor, such policies send "a message to non-adherents that they are outsiders, not full members of the political community, and an accompanying message to adherents that they are insiders, favored members of the political community."

Justice William Rehnquist (1924–2005) proposed a quite different approach in 1985. Responding in a dissent to an opinion (*Wallace v. Jaffree*) that used the Lemon test to invalidate a moment of silence in Alabama public schools, Rehnquist argued that the idea of a "wall of separation"—the idea that had been introduced in *Reynolds* (1878), made central in *Everson* (1947), and underlain jurisprudence ever since—should be rejected by the Court. As long as a state action did not favor one religion over another (or over nonreligion), Rehnquist argued, it was constitutional. This doctrine of nonpreferentialism, a version of accommodationism, became an important theoretical alternative to the separationist approach the Court long advanced.

In *Lee v. Weisman* (1992), Justice Anthony Kennedy (1936–) took a different tack, proposing a new test of unconstitutionality: whether an action constituted "psychological coercion" on the part of the state. The case concerned whether religious clergy could lead prayers at high school graduations. Kennedy argued that such an action constitutes coercion insofar as it "places subtle and indirect public and peer pressure on attending students to stand as a group or maintain respectful silence."

In a strong dissent to *Lee*, Justice Anton Scalia (1936–2016) argued that the kind of coercion that was a hallmark of established religion entailed "force of law and threat of penalty." According to Scalia, state action on religious issues was coercive only if it was enforced through law—as had been, for example, the established ministers of New England during the early nineteenth century. In a series of opinions and dissents, Justice Clarence Thomas (1948–) agreed with Scalia—but went even one step farther, arguing at one point that the religion clauses should never have been incorporated in the first place.

Then, in 1997, the Court modified the still-active Lemon test in *Agostini v. Felton*. In effect, the Court combined the second and third parts of the test. Whether a law has the primary purpose of advancing religion would now be evaluated by three criteria: whether the program created state indoctrination of religion; whether it defined its beneficiaries by religion; and whether it created an excessive entanglement. As Muñoz (2013) explains, instead of independently considering whether an action excessively entangled government with religion, the Court would now evaluate it within the context of whether the action's primary purpose was to advance or inhibit religion.

Jurisprudence on church-state issues at the end of the twentieth century thus had become murky. When was entanglement constitutional? If it did not involve state endorsement of religion? If it did not entail psychological coercion? If it did not entail legal coercion? Should the Court approach church-state issues through a separationist lens or an accommodationist lens? These questions about the constitutionality of church-state connections remained hotly debated—as the religiously devout continued mobilizing into the public square. The paradox of the dual American traditions of separation of church and state rolled on into the new millennium.

TOWARD THE FUTURE

In the early twenty-first century, a number of significant events suggested ways in which the American tradition of separation of church and state might be reorganized. Indeed, there were indications that church-state politics in the new millennium might be shifting, as the American state seemed to open itself to new kinds of accommodation—while religiosity among the American public fell sharply. This scenario—a more accommodationist state with a less religious population—raises intriguing questions about the sustainability of the long-standing American traditions of separation of church and state.

SHIFTING JURISPRUDENCE AND FAITH-BASED INITIATIVES

Indeed, the Court in the twenty-first century seemed to shift toward a more accommodationist perspective. In 2007, a five-to-four decision in *Hein v. Freedom from*

Chapter 10: Separation of Church and State in the American Political Traditions

Religion Foundation allowed President George W. Bush's (1946–) administration to establish the White House Office of Faith-Based and Community Initiatives, which sought to help religious and nonreligious organizations to provide federally funded social programs. Although some saw the office as closely tied to Bush's own evangelicalism—and that of his supporters—it did not disappear after he left office. Instead, it persisted, and indeed was reinvigorated, during President Barack Obama's (1961–) administration.

In addition, the Court handed down a related, major jurisprudential change in *Greece v. Galloway* (2014). At stake in the case was whether town board meetings, composed mostly of adults, could begin with a prayer. A majority of the court in effect tossed out the endorsement test in favor of some version of the coercion test, suggesting that such a prayer was not coercive enough to violate the establishment clause. The majority disagreed, however, on whether such an action would be coercive in schools, and indeed, whether the establishment clause ought to have been incorporated at all. Nearly 400 years after the founding of Puritan Massachusetts, the American state was still debating the role of ministers in the public life of towns.

In 2014, the Court decided another major case in *Burwell v. Hobby Lobby Stores, Inc.* Under the Obama administration's new health care initiative, for-profit corporations had to offer certain kinds of contraception to employees through their health plans. (Objections to this initiative among conservative Christian organizations were predictably widespread.) Hobby Lobby, a family-owned and -run business, sued, claiming that these provisions violated its free exercise of religion. A divided court agreed, with a majority arguing that closely held corporations do have rights to freedom of religion. Coming on the heels of *Citizens United v. FEC* (2010), the *Hobby Lobby* decision raised important questions about the ways in which civil rights were accruing to corporations: What might it mean for religious for-profit corporations to take their beliefs into the public sphere? How, if at all, might business participation in publicly oriented religious life shape that American tradition?

DECLINING PARTICIPATORY RELIGIOUS LIFE

As the federal government struggled to delineate church-state relations in the new century, religious life itself seemed to be withering in America. At least a quarter of young Americans claimed no religious belief whatsoever. Moreover, religious affiliation among Americans dropped: a 2015 poll by the Pew Forum found that between 2007 and 2014 the percentage of Americans who identified as Christian declined by nearly eight percentage points—an extraordinary fall in such a short time period. The change was driven almost entirely by a decline in Catholic and mainline Protestant affiliation—and a rise in Americans claiming no religious affiliation whatsoever.

These events have raised the possibility that the American public—if not the American state—may be turning toward a more Lockean understanding of the role of religion in public life. Such a trend, should it continue, promises to raise critical new questions about the American tradition of publicly oriented religion. It could provide an enormous challenge to the old Puritan tradition of organizing for the public good. As the country seems to move beyond religion, the question remains as to what public life may look like in the future.

For the moment, religion and the public square remain intimately intertwined—as evidenced, for example, by President Obama's "A More Perfect Union" speech in 2008; the presence of a Catholic pope addressing a joint session of Congress in 2015; the emergence of the first-ever Supreme Court with no Protestant members in 2010; the continued heated

Chapter 10: Separation of Church and State in the American Political Traditions

rhetoric that surrounds religion in our presidential campaigns; and the growth of other non-Christian faiths (and their publicly directed organizations) in the American population.

Summary

America's two traditions of church and state have evolved together over the past four centuries. The privatizing Lockean tradition found in our public Constitution and the more publicly oriented tradition found in our private religious congregations have long been in tension. From the colonial era through the founding, from the long nineteenth century through the short twentieth, the diverse ideas found in these two traditions have formed a central strand of American political thought—and American political organizing. The question looking forward is, as always, how will these traditions unfold as American society, religious life, and politics continue to shift into the future. What will be the next step in the long American dance between Locke and the Puritans?

Bibliography

Allen, Danielle. *Our Declaration: A Reading of the Declaration of Independence in Defense of Equality*. New York: Norton, 2014.

Ault, James M., Jr. *Spirit and Flesh: Life in a Fundamentalist Baptist Church*. New York: Vintage, 2004.

Calvert, Jane E. *Quaker Constitutionalism and the Political Thought of John Dickinson*. New York: Cambridge University Press, 2009.

Dorrien, Gary. *The New Abolition: W. E. B. Du Bois and the Black Social Gospel*. New Haven, CT: Yale University Press, 2015.

Drakeman, Donald L. *Church, State, and Original Intent*. New York: Cambridge University Press, 2010.

Frazer, Gregg L. *The Religious Beliefs of America's Founders: Reason, Revelation, and Revolution*. Lawrence: University of Kansas Press, 2012.

Green, John C. *The Faith Factor: How Religion Influences American Elections*. Lincoln, NE: Potomac Books, 2010.

Harris, Frederick C. "Black Churches and Civic Traditions: Outreach, Activism, and the Politics of Public Funding of Faith Based Ministries." In *Can Charitable Choice Work? Covering Religion's Impact on Urban Affairs and Social Services*, ed. Andrew Walsh, 140–156. Hartford, CT: Pew Program on Religion and the News Media and the Leonard E. Greenberg Center for the Study of Religion in Public Life, 2001.

Hatch, Nathan O. *The Democratization of American Christianity*. New Haven, CT: Yale University Press, 1989.

Jefferson, Thomas. "Bill for Establishing Religious Freedom." 1779.

Locke, John. *Two Treatises of Government and A Letter Concerning Toleration*. Edited by Ruth W. Grant and John Dunn. New Haven, CT: Yale University Press, 2003.

Madison, James. "Memorial and Remonstrance against Religious Assessments."

McConnell, Michael W. "Establishment and Disestablishment at the Founding, Part I: Establishment of Religion." *William & Mary Law Review* 44 (2003): 2105–2208.

McWilliams, Wilson Carey. *The Democratic Soul*. Edited by Patrick J. Deneen and Susan J. McWilliams. Lexington: University of Kentucky Press, 2011.

Muñoz, Vincent Phillip. *Religious Liberty and the American Supreme Court: The Essential Cases and Documents*. Lanham, MD: Rowman & Littlefield, 2013.

Obama, Barack. "A More Perfect Union." 2008. http://www.npr.org/templates/story/story.php?storyId=88478467.

Penn, William. "The Charter of Privileges, Granted by William Penn, Esq.: to the Inhabitants of Pensilvania and Territories, 1701." Historical Society of Pennsylvania. http://digital history.hsp.org/pafrm/doc/charter-privileges-granted -william-penn-esq-inhabitants-pensilvania-and-territories -1701.

Penn, William. "Frame of Government of Pennsylvania." May 6, 1682. The Avalon Project. Yale Law School. http://avalon.law.yale.edu/17th_century/pa04.asp.

Putnam, Robert D. *Bowling Alone: The Collapse and Revival of American Community*. New York: Simon & Schuster, 2000.

Chapter 10: Separation of Church and State in the American Political Traditions

Shain, Barry Allen. *The Myth of American Individualism: The Protestant Origins of American Political Thought*. Princeton, NJ: Princeton University Press, 1994.

Shields, Jon A. *The Democratic Virtues of the Christian Right*. Princeton, NJ: Princeton University Press, 2009.

Tocqueville, Alexis de. *Democracy in America*. Edited by Harvey C. Mansfield and Delba Winthrop. Chicago: University of Chicago Press, 2000.

Waldman, Steven. *Founding Faith: How Our Founding Fathers Forged a Radical New Approach to Religious Liberty*. New York: Random House, 2009.

Williams, Daniel K. *God's Own Party: The Making of the Christian Right*. New York: Oxford University Press, 2010.

Winthrop, John. "A Model of Christian Charity." 1630.

COURT CASES

Abington School District v. Schempp. 374 US 203 (1963).

Agostini v. Felton. 521 US 203 (1997).

Bradfield v. Roberts. 175 US 291 (1899).

Burwell v. Hobby Lobby Stores, Inc. 573 US ___ (2014).

Cantwell v. Connecticut. 310 US 296 (1940).

Church of the Holy Trinity v. United States. 143 US 457 (1892).

Citizens United v. FEC. 558 US 310 (2010).

Engel v. Vitale. 370 US 421 (1962).

Everson v. Board of Education. 330 US 1 (1947).

Greece v. Galloway. 572 U.S. ___ (2014).

Hein v. Freedom from Religion Foundation. 551 US 587 (2007).

Lee v. Weisman. 505 US 577 (1992).

Lemon v. Kurtzman. 403 US 602 (1971).

Lynch v. Donnelly. 465 US 668 (1984).

McCollum v. Board of Education. 333 US 203 (1948).

Reynolds v. United States. 98 US (8 Otto.) 145 (1878).

Wallace v. Jaffree. 472 US 38 (1985).

CHAPTER 11

Religion, Secularism, and the Public Sphere

Steven Kettell
Department of Politics and International Studies
University of Warwick, Coventry, England

Debates around the role of religion in the public sphere are, it seems, never far away from the headlines. Whether questions of religiously inspired violence, the influence of faith-based organizations in education and welfare systems, religious opposition to legislation on reproductive rights, disputes around end-of-life issues, questions about the limits of free speech, or controversies around equalities on matters of gender and sexual preference, these and myriad other topics all testify to the enduring power of religion to shape contemporary social and political affairs.

Not surprisingly the theme of religion in public life is, for many, a contested and polarizing issue. On one side of the debate, those supporting a role for religion in public life typically argue that religion forms a key part of people's identities, maintain that excluding religion from the public square is illiberal and undemocratic, and claim that religion can provide a uniquely valuable source of social capital that is beneficial to society as a whole. On the other side of the debate, supporters of secularism claim that religion's propensity for sectarianism, prejudice, and conflict means that human rights and freedoms can best be ensured by privatizing matters of faith and by removing them from the public square altogether.

The purpose of this chapter is to examine these issues by considering a variety of questions that are central to the topic of religion, secularism, and the public sphere. The chapter is set out as follows. First, it begins by examining the idea that there has been a *return of religion* to public life from the latter decades of the twentieth century and looks at some of the key ways in which this has been expressed. Second, it examines some of the various ways in which the idea of *secularism* (defined as a broad position of neutrality on the part of the state towards religious affairs) can be interpreted and understood. Third, the chapter discusses the origins of secularism before looking at some of the main ways in which divergent historical trajectories have led to differing varieties of secularism in practice. Fourth, the chapter examines some of the main arguments both for and against secularism, before concluding with a brief discussion of claims that we are moving toward a postsecular world.

THE RETURN OF RELIGION

Assumptions about the role and the future of religion have been a fundamental part of the social sciences ever since they emerged during the course of the nineteenth century. One of

Chapter 11: Religion, Secularism, and the Public Sphere

the most prominent and enduring claims—known as the *secularization thesis*—was that religion would face an inexorable decline (leading, according to some scholars, to its eventual extinction) as the forces of Western modernity, such as industrialization, advances in science and technology, and the development of increasingly sophisticated forms of knowledge, progressed and spread their way around the world. For a long period of time, many scholars were convinced that such predictions were destined to be fulfilled. Throughout the postwar period from 1945 (in industrial Western nations at least), religion did seem to be fixed on a clear trajectory of decline, and its influence over developments in the public sphere appeared to be progressively diminishing. In Western Europe, for example, as Pippa Norris and Ronald Inglehart note in *Sacred and Secular* (2004), the position was stark: church attendances, memberships, and levels of public commitment to religious beliefs and practices all fell simultaneously.

According to the *return-of-religion* thesis, however, these trends began to slow down, or even go into reverse, during the latter decades of the twentieth century. In short: religion began to reassert itself as a key political and social force. High-profile events such as the Iranian (Islamic) Revolution of 1979, the rise of the Christian Right in the United States during the 1970s, the collapse of (formally atheist) Communist regimes in Eastern and Central Europe, and the emergence of religious forms of nationalism in countries, such as Egypt, Nigeria, Turkey, India, Afghanistan, and Pakistan, were said by many commentators to have demonstrated that religion was making a comeback (e.g., see Micklethwaite and Wooldridge 2009; for an overview of the return-of-religion thesis see Hjelm 2015).

Claims of religious decline and resurgence are keenly contested by scholars on either side of the debate. Context remains an important anchor point. Empirical evidence indicates that formal, organized religion is waning considerably in developed (industrial and postindustrial) regions of the world, such as Europe, Australia, and Canada, and is now showing signs of decline in the United States as well. But in less developed (traditional or agrarian) societies, such as Africa, Asia, and the Middle East, religion continues to flourish. These dynamics produce a complex demographic picture in which processes of secularization continue to undermine religion, but in which the overall number of religious adherents in the world continues to rise (on these points, see Norris and Inglehart 2004).

VIOLENCE AND FREE SPEECH

One does not have to look far to find concrete evidence of the way in which religion can shape and influence public affairs. One obvious example here is the theme of religiously inspired conflict and violence. Communal disputes and infighting in places such as Northern Ireland, Yugoslavia, Kashmir, and Israel-Palestine clearly illustrate the ability of religion to set people against each other, as does the ongoing threat of (at least in part) religiously motivated terrorism. This was vividly highlighted by the al-Qaeda attacks on New York and Washington, DC, on September 11, 2001. The resulting global "war on terror," replete with terrorist aftershocks in places such as Bali, Madrid, and London, has profoundly shaped the landscape of international affairs in the first fifteen years of the twenty-first century. In 2016, the rise of the so-called Islamic State across large swathes of the Middle East continues to bring home the problems of religious violence, posing an ongoing and seemingly intractable security threat to countries across the region as well as the wider world beyond.

Issues around free speech and expression (themselves often intersecting with the theme of religious violence) have been a critical flashpoint in debates around religion in the public sphere. A clear illustration of this was the publication of Salman Rushdie's (1947–) novel, *Satanic Verses,* in 1988. The book, which many Muslims considered to be offensive, led to protests from the Muslim community in the United Kingdom and was followed by the issuing of a *fatwa* (a religious edict) by the leader of Iran, Ayatollah Khomeini (1902–1989), which called for Rushdie to be killed. The author was forced to go into hiding for ten years, and the Japanese translator of the novel, Hitoshi Igarashi (1947–1991), was murdered by an Islamic extremist in 1991.

Another high-profile example of tensions in this area was the Danish Cartoons crisis of 2005 and 2006. The incident was prompted by the publication of cartoons of the Muslim prophet Muhammad by the Danish newspaper *Jyllands-Posten,* which were subsequently reprinted by numerous newspapers throughout Europe. Their publication was met with a series of protests around the world in which more than two hundred people were killed. In a similar incident, employees of the satirical French magazine *Charlie Hebdo* were gunned down by Islamic extremists following the publication of similar cartoons in 2014, resulting in a dozen deaths.

Issues surrounding religion and free speech are not limited to Islam. In 2004, a play titled *Behzti* (*Dishonour*) was closed down in the United Kingdom following protests by Sikh groups who found its contents offensive. The following year the play *Jerry Springer the Opera* was also shut down in the United Kingdom following protests by conservative Christian groups. More recently, an art exhibition in Buenos Aires featuring Ken and Barbie dolls transformed into religious figures, such as Buddha, Jesus, and Kali, was canceled in 2014 after protests from Catholic and Hindu organizations.

Less contemporary examples, such as the protests that greeted the release of Martin Scorsese's (1942–) film *The Last Temptation of Christ* (1988) or Monty Python's parody *The Life of Brian* (1979), also illustrate the point.

FREEDOMS AND EQUALITIES

These incidents, and others like them, are said by some scholars to have exposed clear fault lines between the growing assertiveness of religion and the core values of Western liberal democracies, with serious implications for social trust and cohesion. But the significance of these issues extends far beyond the West. According to a survey published by the Pew Research Center, for instance, by the end of 2010 almost a third (30%) of the world's countries had laws or policies prohibiting blasphemy, apostasy, or defamation of religion, with legal punishments including fines, imprisonment, and death (see Pew Research Center 2011). Further research conducted by Pew has shown that the levels of government restrictions on religion have increased around the world in recent years, with almost two-thirds (63%) of the world's population living in countries that are classed as having high or very high levels of restriction (see Pew Research Center 2015).

Another key issue for debates around religion and the public sphere has been the introduction of legislation designed to enhance human rights and equalities. In recent years, the principal focus here has tended to center on issues of gender and homosexual rights. One of the highest profile examples in this respect has been the case of same-sex marriage. Although same-sex unions have been legalized in a number of countries around the world (including France, Norway, Portugal, Spain, Britain, and the United States), the parameters of the debate have in most cases highlighted a clear split along religious lines, with a significant majority of religious adherents being staunchly opposed. Similar divisions can be

Chapter 11: Religion, Secularism, and the Public Sphere

seen in a variety of other public policy areas, especially when they are deemed to involve "moral" themes. High-profile examples here include birth control and abortion (often involving struggles around access and the time limits involved), euthanasia and assisted suicide (involving campaigns around their legalization), and advancements in medical technologies (particularly notable in developments involving the use of human embryos, such as stem cell research).

WHAT IS SECULARISM?

These various issues (and the list is far from exhaustive) have highlighted some of the ways in which the return of religion has fueled debates about the role of religion in the public sphere. These debates often divide and polarize opinion between those favoring a role for religion and those favoring a public square that is free from religious influence. The core principles involved, however, are far from unambiguous. This becomes immediately apparent when considering the concept of *secularism* itself.

The term *secularism* is something of a deceptive one. In one respect, it is a relatively easy and straightforward concept to define. In the modern, conventional understanding of the term, secularism is usually taken to mean some kind of normative commitment to neutrality on the part of the state toward religious affairs. In other words, secularism necessitates that the state should neither favor, disfavor, promote, nor discourage any particular religious (or nonreligious) viewpoint over another. In institutional terms, this understanding of secularism typically is taken to mean a commitment to the separation of church and state.

But debates around secularism are filled with questions about conceptual definition and meaning. One reason for this is because the notion of the secular is inextricably intertwined with its polar opposite notion of the religious. Both of these terms emerged in Western Europe during the Middle Ages and bear the hallmarks of this particular historical context. The term *religion* (deriving from the Latin *religio*), for example, was initially used to refer to the communal life of Christian monks inside their religious orders. In contrast, the term *secular* (deriving from the Latin *saeculum*) was used to refer to the world outside of these monastic communities. Right from the beginning, then, the terms *secular* and *religious* were set in a diametrically opposed relationship to one another, with the *secular* being defined primarily in terms of what it was not. In this case, the term secular referred to those things, places, and ideas that were not religious and that were distinct from the sacred and the realms of religious authority (e.g., see Taylor 2007).

THE SECULAR AND THE RELIGIOUS

The original meaning of the term *secularism*, which was formulated in 1851 by the English secularist campaigner, George Holyoake (1817–1906), was defined in opposition to religious themes. In this case, the term was intended to outline the basis for a moral framework of human life independent of that provided by religion (as well as, in part, to avoid the negative connotations associated with the term *atheism*). As Holyoake himself put it, secularism was hereby to be understood as "the study of promoting human welfare by material means; measuring human welfare by the utilitarian rule, and making the service of others a duty of life…. Secularism is a series of principles intended for the guidance of those who find Theology indefinite, or inadequate, or deem it unreliable" (Holyoake, 1871, 11).

This interlinking between the concepts of the *secular* and the *religious* creates a number of problems. One issue is that the concept of religion itself remains an intensely ambiguous and contested one. A key reason for this also stems from the historical context from which the term emerged, being used here to refer to the specific features of Western European forms of Christianity during the Middle Ages. Other problems derive from the highly diverse nature of religious beliefs and behaviors themselves, which make it difficult even to arrive at a coherent and meaningful definition of what religion actually is. Not all religions, for example, subscribe to a belief in a god or gods (many varieties of folk religion do not), not all religions have a requirement for regular attendance at a place of worship or for belonging to a particular institution or group (Buddhism and Confucianism are good examples here), and not all religions adhere to a divinely inspired set of values or moral code (e.g., hunter-gatherer societies have typically amoral forms of religion with little or no godly interest in the ethical affairs of human beings). Given this variation, there is no agreement among scholars as to whether religion requires or constitutes particular forms of beliefs (such as a belief in supernatural forces or the existence of a god or gods), certain types of behavior and practices (such as active and regular participation in specific rituals or attendance at a place of worship), membership of a particular group or organization (typically some form of church), a commitment to follow a particular set of values (such as a divinely inspired order), or whether it involves some combination of these or other factors.

SOME CONCEPTUAL PROBLEMS

Because the parameters of the secular are defined in relation to the boundaries of the religious, these conceptual issues have important theoretical and empirical implications. Indeed, some scholars argue that the conceptual framework of binary and distinct secular and religious spheres is so historically and culturally specific that the terms cease to have any real use, meaning, or value outside of this particular context. Applying the terms to non-Western cultures and societies that do not make such clear-cut distinctions is said to be misleading and inappropriate, bordering, at worst, on Western intellectual imperialism. Islamic societies, for instance, are often said to have a worldview that permeates both public and private spheres of life such that the idea of separate religious and secular spheres does not apply. Given these issues, some scholars, such as Timothy Fitzgerald (1987) and Talal Asad (2003), have argued that the broad, ambiguous, and ethnocentric nature of the terms *secular* and *religious* are so problematic that they should be abandoned altogether.

These conceptual problems make it important to distinguish between a number of related and often-overlapping terms that often appear in debates around the role of religion in the public square. Some of the key concepts include the secular (generally defined as something for which religion is not the primacy reference point, such as a nonreligious space); secular*ity* (as the state of being secular); secular*ism* (the institutional distinctions between religious and secular spheres, for instance, the advocacy of a secular society); and secular*ization* (referring to processes leading to the general decline of religion as a social force, such as a fall in the number of religious adherents, a diminution of religious influence in the public sphere, or a corresponding loss of religious authority).

Another problem with the term secularism is that there is no consensus on what it actually means. As scholars have pointed out, secularism can be seen in a number of different ways, such as a doctrine, a worldview, an ideology, a normative stance (usually negative) toward religion, or a constitutional approach referring to the specific institutional relationship between religious and nonreligious authority. By the same token, just as the

Chapter 11: Religion, Secularism, and the Public Sphere

concept of secularism can be taken to mean different things, so, too, the *practice* of secularism can be taken in a variety of directions. Although the basic premise of secularism refers to a commitment to neutrality on the part of the state toward religious affairs, the idea of neutrality does not, in any way, provide an all-encompassing prescriptive framework, but it can be interpreted in a number of different ways, yielding a range of possible institutional relationships. These divergent forms of secularism can be said to vary along a continuum according to the extent to which the state maintains a distance *from* religion (namely, a public sphere without any religious influence—or what we might call *exclusivist* secularism), or supports a position of equity *toward* religion (providing equal recognition and access for all religions in the public sphere, in what might be termed *inclusivist* secularism). This distinction is also sometimes described as one between *illiberal* and *moderate* or between *hard* and *soft* forms of secularism (e.g., see Kosmin and Keysar 2009; Modood 2010).

THE ORIGINS OF SECULARISM

Reflecting this adaptability, the exact forms taken by secular institutional arrangements in any given context are shaped by a number of factors. These include a range of social, cultural, and political conditions, such as the extent, forms, and diversity of the religions involved, as well as the particular features of national and historical circumstance.

The originating impulse for the development of secularism appeared in Western Europe and was bound up with a series of historical processes leading to the emergence of the territorially sovereign state, the rise of nationalism, and the growing influence of popular sovereignty. These developments were all set within an overarching context of growing philosophical ideas and debates around the application of rationality and reason in the Enlightenment, as well as ongoing political and religious conflicts from the fifteenth to the seventeenth centuries. Before this point, political and religious sources of authority had been closely and inextricably intertwined. For early human societies (from hunter-gatherer groups to agricultural settlers) the organization of society itself was held to be divinely structured and ordained, forming an integral part of the cosmic order. Religion, for these ancestral groupings, was a way of ordering their social relationships as well as narrating and expressing their place within a deeply *enchanted universe*.

Religious codes and practices became increasingly complex as human societies grew larger and more sophisticated, but they continued to provide a key pillar for social order and cohesion. Important, too, was the role of religion in upholding and reinforcing political legitimacy. Rulers frequently claimed to derive their authority from, or to have been appointed directly by, the gods, and in some cases (such as the Egyptian Pharaohs or later Roman Emperors), even to have claimed to have been divine themselves (e.g., on these themes, see Bellah 2011).

THE PROTESTANT REFORMATION

This close intertwining of political and religious sources of power and authority was broken by historical developments in Western Europe. The critical event here was the sixteenth-century Protestant Reformation, which eroded the dominance of the Roman Catholic Church and produced a series of major religious wars (even if the reality was that these conflicts were as much about politics as they were about religion) between the main European powers. The most significant of these conflicts, the Thirty Years' War, which lasted from 1618 to 1648 and killed more than a quarter of the German population, was

MACMILLAN INTERDISCIPLINARY HANDBOOKS

Chapter 11: Religion, Secularism, and the Public Sphere

brought to an end by the Treaties of Westphalia. The resulting settlement created a new and novel set of ideas about the relationship between spiritual and temporal sources of authority. It prohibited rulers from intervening in the internal affairs of other states (and, importantly, from attempting to impose or influence religious matters beyond their own domain) and led to the emergence of the territorially sovereign state, which was now held to be the primary source of political power and authority. This established the key structures on which modern international politics are still based in the twenty-first century.

But as important as this all was, the Westphalian settlement did not lead to a separation of church and state. The defining phrase underpinning the settlement—*cuius regio, eius religio* (translated as: "whose realm, his religion")—meant that while those in charge of national states were now prohibited from intervening in the internal affairs of other states, they remained free to uphold and enforce a particular religion within their own territory.

Indeed, in many ways, the events of the Protestant Reformation led to an extension of religious power and influence within Western Europe, as both Protestants and Catholics followed the Treaties of Westphalia with intensive efforts to remake society on religious lines (typically involving concerted drives to impose new forms of religious morality on those over whom they ruled). According to Charles Taylor in *A Secular Age* (2007), these efforts were accompanied by the establishment of many national churches, which were seen by political rulers as a key part of the process of establishing territorial unity and for embedding the kind of collective national identities that the new state structures required.

FROM RELIGIOUS TO SECULAR RULE

All the same, the fallout from the Protestant Reformation led ultimately to a decline of religious influence in the public sphere. Over time, new ideas of national sovereignty produced a corresponding shift in the basis of ruling legitimacy itself. Whereas the legitimate political power and authority of monarchs previously had rested with their claim to have been appointed by god (a notion known as *divine right*), secular ideas of political legitimacy as something that was embedded in the idea of the *nation* now began to gain strength. As they did so, the notion that sovereignty was something that derived from (and therefore rested ultimately with) "the people" of that nation also grew in popularity. The spread of these nationalist ideas and programs for constructing nation states on Westphalian principles culminated in a series of nationalist revolutions from the late eighteenth century—the most notable and important of which were the world historic revolutions in America (1776) and France (1789). Taken together, these various developments helped to create a new modern political and social order based around individual citizenship rights, civil liberties, equality, and rule by popular consent (see Himmelfarb 2004; Taylor 2007).

The unique historical trajectory of Western Europe also led to a new set of ideas about the role of religion in the public sphere. This was characterized by the emergence of a largely "exclusivist" form of secularism founded on the notion of religion as a social problem and as a source of oppression and violent conflict. Consequently, this fed into a corresponding view of human liberty and well-being as something that required freedom from religion and led to a form of exclusivist secular neutrality grounded in the institutional separation of church and state.

SECULARISM IN FRANCE

This exclusivist form of secularism was expressed most fully in the case of France. Here, the popular struggle against the power of a strong and repressive Catholic Church with close

RELIGION: BEYOND RELIGION

191

Chapter 11: Religion, Secularism, and the Public Sphere

links to an entrenched and unpopular aristocratic regime led to the events of the French Revolution in 1789 and eventually (following the re-establishing of close links to the Catholic Church by Napoleon Bonaparte [1769–1821] in 1801) to a model of secularism characterized by the privatization of religion and a public sphere free from overt displays of religious expression and influence. This conception of secularism, known as *laïcité*, has come to form a key part of French national identity. Religious elements are not driven out of society (e.g., the French state continues to fund many Catholic private schools), but the state retains a moral capacity to actively intervene to uphold the general social good as defined by the broader values of national citizenship. The French model of secularism was placed on a legal footing in 1905 with the Law on the Separation of the Churches and the State, which prohibited the state from recognizing or funding any form of religion. Challenges to the terms of French secularism have been firmly rebuffed. In 2004, the French government imposed a ban on displays of religious symbols and items of clothing in public schools after a high-profile case in which two Muslim schoolgirls were expelled for wearing the hijab. In 2011, a full ban on wearing the Islamic veil (the niqab and the burqa) in public spaces was also introduced (see Kuru 2009).

SECULARISM IN THE UNITED STATES

An exclusivist (if less forcible) variety of secularism also took root—although for very different reasons—in the United States. A key part of the explanation here is to be found in the high levels of religious pluralism and diversity that were present within the American colonies in the eighteenth century. For many settlers fleeing religious conflict and persecution in Western Europe, the American colonies were considered to be an attractive destination precisely because they would provide a greater degree of religious freedom. In a significant number of cases, however, high levels of religious zeal also led to new forms of persecution, restrictions on religious liberty, and growing tensions between competing religious groups. As Susan Jacoby notes in *Freethinkers: A History of American Secularism* (2004), religious tests and qualifications for public officeholders, for example, were normal and widespread.

Faced with a growing need to secure peaceful coexistence between religious groups and to prevent any single one of them from dominating its rivals, the newly independent American states enshrined constitutional provisions for maintaining a secular system. A key step along this road was Section 16 of the 1776 Virginia Declaration of Rights, overseen by Thomas Jefferson, which stated that "all men are equally entitled to the free exercise of religion, according to the dictates of conscience." Following this, the First Amendment of the US Constitution (which was ratified in 1791) provided the keystone for the new secular arrangements, declaring that "Congress shall make no law respecting an establishment of religion, or prohibiting the free exercise thereof." This amendment created a form of secularism prohibiting the privileging of any particular religion and supporting the strict separation of church and state (the so-called Jeffersonian Wall). As such, although individual citizens are free to express themselves and to use religious language and arguments in the public sphere, the US state is constitutionally prohibited from lending its support, or declaring its opposition, to any particular form of religious (or nonreligious) worldview.

This constitutional separation of church and state has set the framework for a series of legal battles over the role of religion in the public sphere, leading to a number of high-profile court cases around the use of religious symbols and ceremonies in state buildings, land, and offices. High-profile examples here include secular groups opposed to the displaying of a cross-shaped section of steel found in the wreckage of the World Trade Center in the partially state-funded National September 11 Memorial and Museum (the case was eventually lost in 2013), opposition to the displaying of Christian nativity scenes in public parks, opposition to the exhibition and distribution of religious material in public schools (a case in 2012 saw a teenage atheist, Jessica Ahlquist [1995–], successfully file a lawsuit for the removal of a religious prayer banner), and opposition to displays of the Ten Commandments around courthouses (in 2011 an Ohio appeals court ordered Judge James DeWeese to remove a poster of the Ten Commandments from his courtroom, following a similar case involving the same judge in 2000). Long-standing (and as-yet unsuccessful) campaigns for removing the phrase "Under God" from the pledge of allegiance and "In God We Trust" from the US currency (both formally introduced during the 1950s at the height of the Cold War against Communism) are good illustrations of these campaign measures as well.

ILLIBERAL SECULARISM

The kind of exclusivist secularism found in France and the United States can take more authoritarian and illiberal forms too. The rise of Communism during the twentieth century, for instance, saw states such as the Soviet Union and China enforce (at various times) official scientific materialist doctrines for the promotion of atheism and pursue an overtly antireligious agenda that not only kept religion out of the public sphere but also led to the imposition of significant restrictions and inhibitions on religious freedom. The spread of authoritarian models of secularism was further shaped by the variable experiences of imperialism and decolonization. In countries such as Iraq, Egypt, Tunisia, and prerevolutionary Iran, for example, postcolonial nationalist regimes established authoritarian (in some cases, totalitarian) structures of rule that were highly suspicious of (if not overtly hostile to) religious groups, which were seen as potential competitors for political power and authority. In some cases, such as the Muslim Brotherhood (which was founded in Egypt in 1928), religious movements critical of the ruling regimes were banned and driven underground.

The case of Turkey is illustrative in this respect as well. Here, the postwar nationalist ruler, Kemal Ataturk (1881–1938), adopted an exclusivist form of secularism based on the French system as part of a broader project of modernization that was designed to follow the developmental model of the West. Set against the historical backdrop of the Ottoman Empire, in which religion had been a dominant social and political force, the Turkish secular arrangements included a variety of constitutionally enshrined controls and restrictions on religious practices, particularly involving the role of religion in the public arena (such as bans on displays of religious symbols and clothing in state buildings). According to Ahmet Kuru, author of *Secularism and State Policies toward Religion: The United States, France, and Turkey* (2009), the Turkish model of secularism has also been challenged in recent years, not least by the rise of the Justice and Development Party (AKP, in Turkish Adalet ve Kalkınma Partisi), which has been in government since 2002 and which has been seen by many commentators as pursuing an Islamist agenda.

INCLUSIVIST SECULARISM

Although these particular forms of exclusivist secularism are a product of specific historical trajectories, secularism in Western Europe is nevertheless a mixed affair. In contrast to the French model of *laïcité,* for example, most Western European countries have adopted a more open and accommodating position, involving more nuanced, pragmatic, and flexible

Chapter 11: Religion, Secularism, and the Public Sphere

relationships between the state and religion. Article 9 of the European Convention on Human Rights, for example, stipulates (subject to certain limited qualifications) that "Everyone has the right to freedom of thought, conscience and religion; this right includes freedom to change his religion or belief and freedom, either alone or in community with others and in public or private, to manifest his religion or belief, in worship, teaching, practice and observance."

For historical reasons, many European countries also retain a residual accommodation toward Christianity. A good example of this is the case of the United Kingdom. Although the United Kingdom is (by and large) a secular society, it maintains close institutional links to religion, with formally established Churches in both England and Scotland. Moreover, the reigning monarch occupies the position of Head of the Church of England, whose Bishops also continue to hold reserved seats in the upper chamber of the legislature (the House of Lords), a situation that is unique among advanced liberal democracies. More than this, the constitutional basis of the United Kingdom's entire parliamentary system (based on the authority of the Crown-in-Parliament) is itself said to derive from divine warrant as expressed in the coronation oath.

The most accommodating and inclusive model of secularism, however, is found in the case of India. In a similar fashion to the development of secularism in the United States, secularism in India was adopted as a means of dealing with the social dilemmas associated with high levels of religious pluralism and diversity. That said, in contrast to the US model, which requires the state to maintain a clear distance from religion, the chief characteristic of the Indian model is that it upholds a system based on the equality and liberty of religious communities as well as individual rights. According to Rajeev Bhargava in his article "States, Religious Diversity, and the Crisis of Secularism" (2011), the principal aim of Indian secularism is to support a notion of neutrality in which all religions are permitted equal access to, and a role in, the public sphere, but in which the state maintains a position of "principled distance," intervening only to ensure that the overall balance of social values is maintained.

SECULARISM: THE ARGUMENTS FOR AND AGAINST

Although secularism comes in a variety of forms (ranging from "exclusivist" to "inclusivist," or from "hard" to "soft" models), debates around the role of religion in the public sphere tend to polarize between advocates of an exclusivist secular state who favor a public sphere free from religious influence and those who argue that religion should play an active role in public life. The arguments on both sides of this debate are extensive and varied, but their key features focus on a number of core themes: issues of effective democratic governance, participation and fairness, religious freedom, and the extent to which religion serves as a positive or a negative social force.

Arguments for secularism range from overt antireligious sentiments to claims that a secular state offers the best guarantor of civil rights and freedoms (including freedom of religion). In contrast, arguments in favor of a role for religion in the public sphere typically are based on the idea that religion provides a public good and the claim that denying religion a role in the public square is illiberal, undemocratic, and an infringement on religious freedoms. These various arguments are expanded upon in more detail in the following sections.

Chapter 11: Religion, Secularism, and the Public Sphere

THE NEED FOR PUBLIC REASON

One of the most influential arguments in favor of an exclusivist form of secularism was set out by the American political theorist and philosopher John Rawls (1991–2002). The central point of Rawls's case was that political arguments that were made in the public sphere (which he defined principally as covering the courts, the government, and candidates for public office) should be framed in nonreligious terms using what he called public reason. This was a set of criteria for concepts, terms, and language that the vast majority of reasonable citizens (both religious and nonreligious alike) could legitimately accept as a framework for communication. Rawls argued that in a pluralist democratic society in which citizens held a variety of competing and sometimes incompatible worldviews (or what he termed "irreconcilable comprehensive doctrines"), the language of religion—such as Christian doctrines of sin and salvation—was such that it could only be fully and properly understood by religious adherents and therefore was not universally accessible to all citizens. As such, Rawls argued that allowing the use of religious arguments in the public domain would limit the ability of free citizens to engage equally in the processes of open deliberation that were necessary for a democratic society to function effectively. In contrast, public reason would provide a common language of *general* reasons on the meaning of which there was a universal (or at the least an extremely broad) consensus. Public reason, then, offered a form of language that everyone could understand (see Rawls 1971, 1997).

This exclusivist position was somewhat modified in Rawls's later work on the issue, which saw him adopt a more accommodating view toward religion in the public sphere. The substance of his later thinking was that religious arguments should not be excluded from the public realm *per se*, but they could be admissible on the condition that sufficient public reasons to support the claims that were being made would be forthcoming in due course (see Rawls 1997).

RIGHTS, FREEDOMS, AND EQUALITIES

Another common (and related) argument in favor of exclusivist secularism is that a secular state is a necessary condition for ensuring human rights and freedoms, including the freedom of religion (i.e., the freedom to worship and to practice religion freely). The central claim here is that, because secularism protects the state from religion, citizens cannot be subjected to, or forced to abide by, religious imperatives, dictates, or laws. By the same token, because secularism also protects religion from the state, religious citizens themselves (at least in the private sphere) are free from state interference. Supporters of secularism often maintain that secularism requires that citizens have freedom *from* religion and highlight the fact that religious organizations continue to enjoy extensive privileges in politics, culture, and law.

These privileges are said to be unfair and unwarranted because they are not open and freely available to all citizens regardless of their beliefs. Thus, even in largely secular societies, such as the United Kingdom, religious organizations are still able to secure benefits for themselves that are not available to other social groups, such as trade unions or nonreligious charities. Such privileges in the case of the United Kingdom include the involvement of religious authorities in the education system (allowing them to discriminate against students on the basis of their ascribed religion) and a variety of exemptions around issues relating to tax and legal regulations (such as employment law and the provision of public services). One contentious issue for secular campaigners in the United States is the fact that many religious organizations are able to register as charities, enabling them to claim billions of dollars of

RELIGION: BEYOND RELIGION

195

Chapter 11: Religion, Secularism, and the Public Sphere

public subsidy. In Germany, the state automatically deducts a "church tax" from registered members of many religious denominations as part of its public subsidies for religion unless members expressly opt out (and risk losing access to religious services as a result). Similar taxes are in place in a number of other European countries, such as Austria, Italy, and Finland. In short, the overall argument from secular supporters here is that religious views and organizations have enjoyed an excessively privileged and protected status for far too long and that they should be given no more respect or special treatment than any other viewpoint, opinion, or special interest group.

RELIGION AS A NEGATIVE SOCIAL FORCE

Alongside these arguments, supporters of exclusivist secularism also frequently highlight the various ways in which religion can serve as a negative social force. Some of the key arguments here include the role of religion in cases of violence and conflict, including terrorism and intercommunal violence, but also including instances of personal violence, such as the parental withholding of medical treatment for children on religious grounds; instances of discrimination on issues of gender, sexual orientation, and reproduction rights; the role of religion in education systems, such as seeking to ban or distort discussion of scientific topics in the classroom, such as evolution; and high-profile cases of the abuse of religious power, such as the child abuse scandals in the Catholic church.

These views are most forcefully expressed by the so-called new atheists—two exemplars of which are typically said to be Richard Dawkins (1941–) and Sam Harris (1967–). The general new atheist view is that religion should have no role to play in the public square at all and that religious beliefs themselves should be challenged wherever possible. One of the main reasons for this is that religious views are said to be irrational (by definition, relying on "faith" as an absence of evidence) and, in part because of this, are a source of social othering, creating strong in- and out-group dynamics and mentalities, leading to prejudice, intolerance, and violence. On this basis (even if they may not all sign up to the particulars of the new atheist critique), many supporters of secularism argue that allowing religion into public life opens the way to all manner of toxic social divisions and risks generating competitive "arms races" between different religious groups as each seeks to maintain and extend its own specific privileges. A public sphere free from the influence of religion, it is duly maintained, is the only way to promote rational political discourse, and it aids social cohesion, tolerance, and democracy.

In addition to these points, many advocates of secularism also maintain (as Holyoake did) that religion is not needed for moral or ethical behavior and that secular societies can be just as effective (if not, in some cases, more so) at engendering trust and social cohesion as religious communities. Research by the sociologist Phil Zuckerman (1969–), author of *Society without God* (2008), for instance, has found that secular societies tend to be more politically progressive and have lower levels of social inequality, higher levels of happiness, and lower rates of violent crime. Other research (e.g., Kettell 2014) has found that secular countries tend to have higher levels of political freedoms and civil and religious rights than countries that maintain an institutionalized link to religion in the form of an established church.

THE NEED FOR DEMOCRATIC FAIRNESS

In contrast to the previous arguments in favor of secularism, a common argument in favor of a greater role for religion in the public sphere comes from the German social theorist Jurgen

Habermas (1929–). In what, in many ways, is a weaker and more accommodating version of the position taken by Rawls, Habermas argues that although the highest legislative domains of the state should be shaped by public (or what he prefers to call secular) reason, the remainder of the public sphere should be open and accessible to religion views and arguments. One reason for this is that religion is thought to have a moral dimension with the potential to make a valuable contribution to public discourse, such as highlighting issues of injustice, poverty, marginalization, and exclusion. Another reason is that it was said to be unreasonable (if not impossible) to expect citizens for whom religion was an intrinsic part of their identity to exclude their real beliefs from political debates. As such, Habermas calls for a broader "multidimensional concept of reason" (2006, 16) and maintains that nonreligious citizens need to be more open and respectful of religious claims and ideas so that citizens can work together to find ways of reaching a "rationally motivated agreement" (2006, 5).

Following this line, critics of exclusivist secularism frequently contend that excluding religion from the public sphere imposes an unreasonable burden on citizens with religious beliefs because the need to translate arguments into public reason is distributed unequally, falling as it does on religious but not nonreligious citizens. As such, by refusing to allow a space for religious views in public life and by rejecting any basis for communal rights based on religious belonging, exclusivist secularism is said to violate the moral agency of religious citizens, forcing them to behave in ways that run contrary to their deeply held principles and convictions. At the same time, exclusivist secularism also compels religious citizens to act in an inauthentic manner in the course of public debates, requiring that they put their real motivations to one side and instead justify their arguments in terms of public reason (e.g., on these various points, see Asad 2003; Connolly 2000; Wolterstorff 2010).

EQUALITY AND SOCIAL CAPITAL

In a similar fashion, critics of exclusivist secularism also argue that religious discourses or worldviews are no different from (and are therefore just as valid as) political worldviews or ideological perspectives, such as liberalism, socialism, and conservatism. Political frameworks such as these are said to be as equally totalizing and mutually incomprehensible as religious perspectives such that it is unreasonable to single out religion for exclusion from the public sphere. Banning religious arguments from the public domain is therefore said to be profoundly illiberal, undemocratic, and a barrier to the free flow of ideas within society. Moreover, an exclusivist form of secularism is also said to contain intrinsic dangers, because suppressing people's identities in this way risks creating pressures that might lead to growing resentment, potentially driving otherwise-moderate people of faith into more extremist positions than they otherwise would adopt (e.g., see Stepan 2000; Wolterstorff 2010).

A related claim here is that religious views also warrant a space in the public sphere because (and, again, echoing Habermas) they are able to make a valuable contribution in terms of promoting positive social values. At the core of this argument is the claim that religion provides a substantial public good, a national resource, and a repository of values and morality that can be drawn on for the benefit of all. Commonly cited historical examples of this include the role of religious organizations in opposing slavery; their role in developing the civil rights movement in the United States; and the role of the Catholic church in opposing, and ultimately helping to bring down, the Communist regimes of the Soviet bloc.

Aligned to this is the popular assertion that religion provides a beneficial source of social capital, helping to engender the "social glue" of public trust, cooperation, and cohesion that a democratic society needs to function effectively. Key arguments here, for example, are that religious citizens are more likely to become engaged in charitable activities, such as volunteering and making donations to good causes, than nonreligious citizens. This assumption (which secular campaigners vigorously contest) has underpinned a range of public policy measures, including the promotion of faith-based initiatives in the United States under the Presidency of George W. Bush, and the attempt to foster a Big Society agenda in the United Kingdom based on providing religious groups with a greater role in the delivery of public services (on these issues, see Smidt 2003).

MYTHICAL AND MILITANT SECULARISM

Another common argument put forward by opponents of secularism is the claim that the idea of "neutrality" on which secular states are based is a myth. Instead, critics maintain that the relationship between religion and the public sphere will always and invariably reflect underlying power relations within a society, supporting certain values and interests rather than others. From this perspective, secularism is considered to be akin to a political ideology based on antireligious normative foundations. Here, the supposedly neutral secular state reflects a historically specific, ethnocentric Western bias that is rooted in certain ideas about the nature of politics and particular assumptions about the character of religion. This, according to Tariq Modood in "Moderate Secularism, Religion as Identity and Respect for Religion" (2010), views religion as a source of conflict and social tensions and is hostile to non-Christian (for which, read: Protestant) forms of religion—typically Islam—that are unable or unwilling to confine themselves to the private sphere.

Related to this argument is the view that the very concept of reason that has dominated secular Western thought since the time of the Enlightenment (this being rooted in the merits of science and rationality as the handmaidens of progress, and set-up as the antithesis of religion) is itself an ethnocentric worldview. Like religion, the claims of secular reason—such as the view that human beings have certain inalienable rights (e.g., the right to life, liberty, property, and so on)—are also said to be founded on unprovable, nonverifiable assumptions. Moreover, the idea of reason by itself is said to provide no basis for deriving a moral framework for human life and society, but merely—without religion as an anchor—descends into crass individualism, moral relativism, and an impoverished public discourse. On this basis, critics contend that religion has an equally valid and democratic claim to representation in the public sphere as nonreligious perspectives.

In recent years, many critics have complained about what they see as a militant, radical, intolerant, and illiberal form of secularism (usually also linked to a human rights agenda promoted by minority groups) that is determined to marginalize religion and force it out of public life. Some of the most high-profile assertions here have come from the Vatican. Pope Benedict XVI (1927–), for example, warned on several occasions that radical and aggressive secularism was gaining ground in the United States and Europe and that this development posed a grave threat to freedom of expression as well as traditional values. In the United Kingdom, the claim that religion is being driven out of public life has also led to a number of high-profile court cases. In 2012, four such cases involving alleged discrimination on religious grounds were taken to the European Court of Human Rights. Three of the cases were rejected, while the fourth (involving the case of an airline stewardess who wanted to wear a crucifix) was upheld, requiring that the uniform of the airline be amended to allow for reasonable accommodation (a change that the airline had already undertaken, effectively making the ruling a moot one; on the idea of "militant secularism," see Kettell 2015).

Chapter 11: Religion, Secularism, and the Public Sphere

A POSTSECULAR WORLD?

The effectiveness of these arguments are shaped, to a large extent, by the social and political conditions in which they are deployed. The boundary between the secular and the religious spheres is not fixed or immutable, but rather it is variable and contested and open to change. This has been highlighted by the idea of a return of religion, which has challenged assumptions that religion was destined to die out or remain confined to the private sphere. Indeed, for some commentators, these developments have given rise to the notion that we have now entered a postsecular world.

Although the exact contours and features of this new global landscape are not entirely clear, a central claim here is that the public reassertion of religion poses a significant problem for exclusivist models of secularism. One of the main dilemmas confronting secular Western societies at the present time is how to balance a commitment to neutrality toward religion with growing levels of religious pluralism, diversity, and assertiveness driven by the increasingly interconnected nature of the world resulting from processes of globalization. For many scholars, these pressures are likely to prove so great that the only solution will be to adopt more accommodating, inclusivist public spheres.

Just like the concept of secularism, however, the term *postsecularism* remains a contentious one. As yet there is no consensus among scholars as to whether the concept indicates some kind of reversion to premodern, traditional forms of religion, some kind of new coexistence between religious and secular worldviews, or a change in the form of religion itself as well as its relationship to the public sphere. Moreover, not all commentators are convinced that the idea of the postsecular is a useful or meaningful reflection of contemporary developments (on these points, for instance, see Beckford 2012). For some, claims about a return of religion are themselves considered to be problematic. Scholars such as Norris and Inglehart (2004), for example, maintain that processes of secularization are continuing to unfold and that, contrary to appearances, religion is continuing to decline in places where the forces of modernity hold sway. Indeed, in recent years one of the most striking trends in the United States—long held up as an example of how religion can thrive in a technologically advanced and modern society—has been the growth of the so-called nones (a term used to describe the ranks of the religiously unaffiliated). From this perspective, then, the return of religion and the growing assertiveness of religion in public life is not interpreted as the failure of secularization, but rather it is seen as a sign that secularization is still very much under way. The assertiveness of religion is, from this perspective, seen as a rearguard action against ongoing, unabated decline.

Summary

The return of religion during the latter decades of the twentieth century has reinvigorated debates around the role of religion in public life. These debates deal with a range of contentious issues, including religious violence and conflict, issues of free speech, and religious opposition to reproductive rights and equalities legislation. Opinions on this subject tend to be polarized between two antagonistic points of view. On the one side are those who favor a role for religion in public life. On the other are those favoring a public sphere free from religious influence.

Chapter 11: Religion, Secularism, and the Public Sphere

Secularism—defined as a commitment to neutrality toward religion on the part of the state—comes in a variety of forms, both conceptually and in practice. A lack of scholarly consensus around the interconnected terms of the religious and the secular creates problems of definitional clarity, whereas practical differences reflect divergent national contexts and paths of historical development. The key arguments for and against an exclusivist model of secularism center on a number of core themes. Supporters claim that secularism offers the best guarantee of upholding civil rights and freedoms. Critics claim that excluding religion from the public sphere undermines religious freedoms and removes a valuable source of social capital.

Whether the return of religion turns out to be a transformative development toward a postsecular society, or is merely a phase in the course of religious decline, remains to be seen. But whatever the outcome may be, debates over the role of religion in the public sphere look set to continue for some considerable time to come.

Bibliography

Asad, Talal. *Formations of the Secular: Christianity, Islam, Modernity*. Stanford, CA: Stanford University Press, 2003.

Beckford, James. "Public Religions and the Postsecular: Critical Reflections." SSSR Presidential Address. *Journal for the Scientific Study of Religion* 51, no. 1 (2012): 1–19.

Bellah, Robert. *Religion in Human Evolution: From the Paleolithic to the Axial Age*. Cambridge, MA: Belknap Press, 2011.

Bhargava, Rajeev. "States, Religious Diversity, and the Crisis of Secularism." Open Democracy, March 22, 2011. https://www.opendemocracy.net/rajeev-bhargava/states -religious-diversity-and-crisis-of-secularism-0.

Connolly, William. *Why I Am Not a Secularist*. Minnesota: University of Minnesota Press, 2000.

Dawkins, Richard. *The God Delusion*. London: Bantam Press, 2006.

Fitzgerald, Timothy. "A Critique of 'Religion' as a Cross-Cultural Category." *Method and Theory in the Study of Religion* 9, no. 2 (1987): 91–100.

Habermas, Jurgen. "Religion in the Public Sphere." *European Journal of Philosophy* 14, no. 1 (2006): 1–25.

Harris, Sam. *The End of Faith: Religion, Terror, and the Future of Reason*. New York: Norton, 2004.

Himmelfarb, Gertrude. *The Roads to Modernity: The British, French and American Enlightenments*. New York: Knopf, 2004.

Hjelm, Titus, ed. *God Is Back*. London: Bloomsbury, 2015.

Holyoake, George J. *The Principles of Secularism*, 3rd ed. London: Book Store, 1871.

Jacoby, Susan. *Freethinkers: A History of American Secularism*. New York: Metropolitan Books, 2004.

Kettell, Steven. "The Militant Strain: An Analysis of Anti-secular Discourse in Britain." *Political Studies* 63 no. 3 (2015): 512–528.

Kettell, Steven. "State Religion and Freedom: A Comparative Analysis." *Politics and Religion* 6, no. 3 (2014): 538–569.

Kosmin, Barry, and Ariela Keysar, eds. *Secularism and Secularity: Contemporary International Perspectives*. Institute for the Study of Secularism in Society and Culture, 2009.

Kuru, Ahmet. *Secularism and State Policies toward Religion: The United States, France, and Turkey*. Cambridge: Cambridge University Press, 2009.

Micklethwait, John, and Adrian Wooldridge. *God Is Back*. London: Penguin, 2009.

Modood, Tariq. "Moderate Secularism, Religion as Identity and Respect for Religion." *Political Quarterly* 81, no. 1 (2010): 4–14.

Norris, Pippa, and Ronald Inglehart. *Sacred and Secular*. Cambridge: Cambridge University Press, 2004.

Pew Research Center. "Latest Trends in Religious Restrictions and Hostilities." 2015. http://www.pewforum.org/2015 /02/26/religious-hostilities/.

Pew Research Center. "Rising Restrictions on Religion." 2011. http://www.pewforum.org/2011/08/09/rising-restrictions -on-religion2/.

Rawls, John. "The Idea of Public Reason Revisited." *University of Chicago Law Review* 64, no. 3 (1997): 765–807.

Rawls, John. *A Theory of Justice*. Cambridge, MA: Harvard University Press, 1971.

Rushdie, Salman. *The Satanic Verses*. London: Viking, 1988.

Chapter 11: Religion, Secularism, and the Public Sphere

Smidt, Corwin, E. *Religion as Social Capital: Producing the Common Good*. Waco, TX: Baylor University Press, 2003.

Stepan, Alfred. "Religion, Democracy, and the 'Twin Tolerations.'" *Journal of Democracy* 11, no. 4 (2000): 37–57.

Taylor, Charles. *A Secular Age*. Cambridge, MA: Harvard University Press, 2007.

Wolterstorff, Nicholas. *Justice: Rights and Wrongs*. Princeton, NJ: Princeton University Press, 2010.

Zuckerman, Phil. *Society without God: What the Least Religious Nations Can Tell Us about Contentment*. New York: New York University Press, 2008.

FILMS

The Last Temptation of Christ. Dir. Martin Scorsese. 1988.

Monty Python's Life of Brian. Dir. Terry Jones. 1979.

CHAPTER 12

Secularism, Secularity, and War

Stacey Gutkowski
Senior Lecturer in Conflict Studies
King's College London

Since 2011, events in the news have highlighted the role that secular actors, ideas, and institutions play in violent conflicts around the world. For example, following the 2011 Egyptian revolution, the Muslim Brotherhood competed with various conservative, secular, army-backed forces for the control of the state, culminating in substantial street violence and many deaths and injuries on all sides. In 2015, four atheist bloggers were killed in Bangladesh for their outspoken writings against Islam. In July 2015, six participants in the annual Gay Pride parade in Jerusalem, an important forum for political expression by the secular Jewish Israeli community, were stabbed by an ultra-Orthodox Jewish assailant known for his antisecular views. The shooter in the February 2015 killing of three young Muslims in Chapel Hill, North Carolina, in the United States in a dispute over a parking space had previously condemned all forms of religion on social media, describing himself as "antitheist." And in the aftermath of the January 2015 attacks on the Charlie Hebdo cartoonists in Paris, the French media repeatedly condemned the attack on free speech as yet another indication of Islamist intolerance for secular values.

These examples suggest seven things about the role that secular actors and ideas play in violent and nonviolent conflicts across the globe. First, as in the Egyptian revolution example, actors articulating their identities as secular compete with actors articulating their identities as religious for control of governments. The two sides use these identity constructions to garner followers and to demonize the other side even when their motivations and language are similar. One example is Hamas and Fatah. Although in the past these two factions have stressed their Islamist and secular leftist credentials to gain support for their resistance to Israeli occupation, the two Palestinian factions have come to use similar language, a combination of Islamism and secular nationalism.

Second, secular political ideologies have animated revolutionary wars since the late nineteenth century. These include Marxist-inspired postcolonial struggles in Latin America and sub-Saharan Africa, Maoist insurgencies in Asia, the communist revolutions in Russia and China, and the secular nationalist revolution in Turkey following the defeat of the Ottoman Empire in World War I. Third, as in the Bangladesh and Chapel Hill examples, secular political and personal ideologies drive both violence committed against individuals and violence committed by individuals.

Fourth, secular governments have imposed restrictions on religious institutions and actors as part of repressive projects of economic and social modernization and to stem resistance to authoritarian rule. This was particularly the case in the early and mid-twentieth

203

Chapter 12: Secularism, Secularity, and War

century, in the Soviet Union, India, Mexico, Ghana, Indonesia, Iran, Turkey, Kenya, and Egypt. These governments used violence to do so and were met with violent resistance by actors who stressed their religious identities. Fifth, Western secular social and political traditions shape how Western states and societies view "religious violence," as in the Charlie Hebdo case. These secular political traditions have become a lightning rod for those wishing to justify terrorism and violence, such as the assassination of Dutch filmmaker Theo van Gogh (1957–2004) or the attack on the US embassy in Benghazi following the release of an American film. In both cases these attackers justified their actions by arguing that these films insulted the Prophet.

The picture is not all bleak. Sixth, individuals who identify as not particularly religious stress the importance of secular, liberal ideas such as human rights and international law for defining how actors should behave in a conflict. Although some people understand these ideas as grounded in religious ethics, many see them as based on humanist principles. And seventh, secular, power-sharing governments in Lebanon, Bosnia, and Northern Ireland have helped to stem conflict between political factions. In these cases, each sect has a certain number of seats in parliament and control over government ministries. No group is able to dominate the other politically or economically. This has led to imperfect but peaceful coexistence after civil wars in those countries.

STUDYING VIOLENT CONFLICT: WHY DOES SECULARISM MATTER?

Paying attention to the role that secular actors, ideas, and institutions play in conflict allows us to understand more about the social, political, and economic context of some conflicts in three main ways. Specifically, these are conflicts in which one side differentiates themselves as not religious in opposition to an enemy they characterize—or who characterize themselves—as religious.

First, as analysts, we are better able to explain how alliances and enemies are made by understanding how competing political movements within a society construct their identities to gain followers and demonize other groups. Paying attention to how secular and religious groups construct their identities in relation to each other is one example of this. This also helps us to explain in part why violence is triggered between some groups who take different positions on the appropriate role for religion in public life. For example, Islamist actors may use their religious identity to flag up to possible supporters that they are concerned with the development of an ethical society. Liberal or leftist actors in a Muslim majority context might flag up to possible supporters that they are concerned with the preservation of individual freedoms—including from religious encroachment—and the establishment of a political sphere in which clerics do not dominate. However these liberal and leftist actors rarely articulate their politics as antireligious or use the word "secular" to describe their political identity, and the prominence that their position on religion enjoys within the wider context of their political platform varies from case to case.

Second, as analysts, we are better able to explain the underlying structural factors that lead to imbalances of political and economic power within societies, which sometimes spill over into violence. We can do this by understanding how powerful secular institutions such as governments, militaries, and international institutions perceive and behave toward religio-political actors. Third, by understanding how individuals and social groups see their enemies and friends and themselves, we can better interpret how actors understand what it means to behave ethically in the context of the life and death dilemmas posed by war and postwar transitions.

204   MACMILLAN INTERDISCIPLINARY HANDBOOKS

In short, paying attention to the ways in which actors, ideas, and institutions interact with and address secularism cannot help us tell the full story about any given violent conflict. But it can help us to illuminate particular dimensions of certain kinds of conflict. Before we explore this through a series of case studies, it is worth noting what scholars have written about this area so far. Unlike some of the other, more established areas covered in this volume, this is a new and emerging area of scholarship. The conclusion discusses topics that are ripe for new and exciting research.

TWO TRAINS RUNNING ON PARALLEL TRACKS

To understand why there has been less written on the relationship between violent conflict and secularism than many other areas in this volume, it is useful to think about the metaphor of two trains running on parallel tracks. On one track, there has been a great deal written about various aspects of secularism—for example, what the term means, its historical emergence, and manifestation in various geographic contexts; its intersection with ethnicity and gender; and its impact on various spheres of human life, such as the family, the economy, and the arts. On the other track, there has been a great deal written about war and violent conflict—for example, why and when it happens; how it has changed societies, states, and individuals; and how methods for waging war have changed over the centuries.

Why has this parallelism happened? One reason is due to the nature of war and violent conflict. Most objectives in war—gaining and holding territory, killing the enemy, undermining the ability of a military to re-arm or sustain itself—are pragmatic considerations. They may intersect with matters of identity, ideology, or culture—for example, an army may have restricted duties on their holy day and some of its units may be slower than usual to respond to a surprise attack. But this is the exception and far more often war objectives are shaped by pragmatism.

A second reason for this parallelism is that while actors engaged in violent struggles during the twentieth and twenty-first centuries have expressed a variety of secular ideologies and identities—communism, socialism, Marxism, nationalism, liberalism—they have not particularly stressed the secular aspect of these ideologies. Indeed, their ideologies often included both secular and religious components. For example, during the Algerian War of Independence, in which the National Liberation Front (FLN) struggled to free the country from French colonial rule, they used the languages of national self-determination, anti-imperialism, pan-Arabism, socialism, and Islam to articulate and justify their struggle. Further scholarly attention to the secular component *as secular* as well as intertwined with religion in complex ways can illuminate the unexplored history of a conflict. To take the Algerian example again, the FLN was able to mobilize nationalist resistance through the construction of a clear distinction between Muslim Algerians and Catholic and Jewish *pied-noirs*, European descendants born in Algeria and associated with the secular French state.

RELIGION AND CONFLICT: TWO CONVERGING TRACKS

By contrast to this story of parallel tracks, much more has been written about the convergent impact of religious actors, symbols, institutions, and ideas on violent conflict. For example, Ron Hassner, author of "Debating the Role of Religion in War" (2010), has suggested that

Chapter 12: Secularism, Secularity, and War

religion shapes how wars are waged by proving legitimacy for weapons, targets, timing, and location of confrontation; by shaping how soldiers feel about their own soldiering as prescribed by God; by shaping actors' tactical and strategic calculations, such as using the religious sensitivities of the enemy to weaken their morale; by shaping actors' conceptions of victory and defeat as holy and righteous; and in prolonging the duration of conflicts in which soldiers understand that to surrender would be to blaspheme. Scholars have also explored, for example, why groups have fought over sacred sites such as the Old City of Jerusalem; how religious leaders have justified both violence and peace through recourse to religious texts; and how and why religious minorities have been violently targeted by religious majorities, such as attacks on Muslims in Myanmar by the Buddhist majority.

For several reasons, much more been written about the role of religious actors in conflict. First, particularly since the Al Qaeda attacks on targets in the United States on September 11, 2001, there has been an explosion of scholarly and popular interest in the relationships between religion and violence. This has mainly focused on jihadist activity against Western targets and how Western states have pursued the so-called War on Terror. Since the 1990s scholars such as Mark Juergensmeyer had been investigating the intersection of religious fundamentalism, nationalism, and violent and nonviolent political and social conflict around the world, looking at cases such as India, Sudan, Iran, Pakistan, Nigeria, Northern Ireland, Israel, and the United States. Scholars claimed that, contrary to the modernization thesis that had seemed so persuasive to scholars influenced by Western thought, religion had not simply disappeared as states and societies transitioned from traditional to modern ways of living. Rather, in their view, religion was alive and well. In fact, they contend, particularly since the 1970s, there had been a "religious resurgence" in political contexts around the world, sometimes with violent consequences. Some scholars argue that this is an indication that far from the world becoming the secular haven the modernization theory would have us believe, the world is instead becoming more *postsecular* with religion having an increasing social, economic, and political role around the world.

Read in a different light, we can see that secularism is actually a fundamental part of this violent, so-called religious resurgence since the 1970s. This was a backlash against forms of secular nationalism such as Arab nationalism in the Middle East. The year 1979 was a particularly critical turning point for religiously-inspired activism against secular nationalism. The Iranian revolution saw the overthrow of the secular, Western-backed Shah. The Soviet Union invaded Afghanistan to back the communist government there, prompting a Western-backed insurgency that drew in jihadist fighters from across the Middle East and South Asia to fight the "atheist enemy." And a group of jihadist insurgents briefly took over the Grand Mosque in Mecca, condemning the Saudi royal family for being overly influenced by the secular West and insufficiently Islamic.

Second, Western scholars were beholden to another bias, what William Cavanaugh has called the "myth of religious violence." In Cavanaugh's view, Western thinkers and indeed Western societies and governments at large, have long associated religion with violence because of a particular episode in European history, the Thirty Years' War, in which the churches and religious symbolism played a prominent role. In his view, this "myth of religious violence" led Western scholars in the early years of the so-called War on Terror to be overly distracted by Islam, leading them to overlook the larger political and economic forces driving global jihadism. In recent years, scholars have started to reflect on, unpack, and counter these secular biases within the academy and to point out their influence on governments, intergovernmental organizations, nongovernmental organizations, and militaries.

206   MACMILLAN INTERDISCIPLINARY HANDBOOKS

Chapter 12: Secularism, Secularity, and War

Particularly from the 1960s to the 1990s, scholarship within and outside of the West was subject to a series of secular biases about the political roles played by religious actors. This was largely due to the influence of secular, leftist ideologies within Western and non-Western universities from the mid-twentieth century. Marxists, liberals, conservatives, and postcolonial scholars held different versions of these biases, but there were two primary messages. The first message, influenced by the modernization theory, was that religion was a form of traditional social organization and thinking that was gradually losing ground to other ideological forces. According to this message, one example was the influence of leftist and nationalist ideologies on revolutionary struggles to cast off European imperial rule. Among non-Western intellectuals, themselves often working within these leftist, nationalist, and anticolonial ideological paradigms, this bias converged with a second, normative bias: that religious forces were socially and politically retrograde and their influence should be fought against. As part of this fight, these intellectuals chose to focus their scholarships on matters other than religion. The War on Terror catalyzed renewed scholarly interest in the role of religion in violent conflicts around the world, highlighting both contemporary and historical cases.

The next sections explore the complex relationships between secularism, religion, security, and conflict with examples from three regions: the Middle East, Central Asia, and Western Europe. Two examples are explored from each region to show the regional diversity as well as the multiple ways in which secularism and security issues converge around the world.

MIDDLE EAST: TURKEY AND EGYPT

Examples from the Middle East illustrate well the dynamics of competition between secular and religious actors for political control. The label *secular* is highly problematic, in theory and practice, in the Middle East. Actors in the Arab Middle East and Iran are more inclined to use terms such as *leftist*, *liberal*, *Ba'athist*, *communist*, *socialist*, and *Marxist* to describe their orientation, with a critique of Islam's influence implied in the term. In the West, the designations *agnostic*, *atheist*, or *indifferent* tend to refer to someone's personal beliefs rather than one's politics. In the Arab world, there is a public, political, and performative aspect to these labels. Additionally, a person may simultaneously declare a religious affiliation (Sunni Muslim, Christian, etc.) to mark out their political identity in a national context. In Turkey and among Israeli Jews, the label *secular* is more prominent. As in the West, religious practice and discourse run along a spectrum in the Middle East. Individuals situate themselves somewhere along the spectrum but engage in practices and language that are a mix of "religious" and "secular."

In the second half of the nineteenth century, intellectuals in Lebanon, Egypt, and Iran began to articulate secular political and social ideas. These were inspired by, but not reducible to, contemporary European currents of thought. Intellectuals came into contact with these ideas through European occupation but also through their own study and travels to the West. As Paul Salem writes in "The Rise and Fall of Secularism in the Arab World" (1996), the growth of Arab secular outlooks received a boost after World War I, with the collapse of the Ottoman Empire, abolition of the Caliphate (the supreme leadership of Sunni Muslims), and extension of the British and French mandates in the Levant. Saeed Rahnema explains in "Retreat and Return of the Secular in Iran" (2011) that the constitutional revolution in Iran (1905–1911) catalyzed the intellectual and political

RELIGION: BEYOND RELIGION

207

development of the secular left and reformers who advocated the separation of religion and state, leading to both alliances and confrontations with the clerics.

During this period, the originators and proponents of these new secular ideologies (Arab nationalism, Ba'athism, Turkish nationalism, and reformists in Iran) saw important continuities between Islam as heritage and the new, modernizing direction in which they hoped to move their countries. They recognized that Islamic practice would likely continue to be important to their populations. Similarly, in 1948, the secular Zionist leaders of the new state of Israel established the Status Quo arrangement as a way to formally preserve Jewish heritage after the Orthodox religious leadership was decimated in the Holocaust.

Political secularism thus developed along different paths in the region, and its proponents used varying levels of coercion, violence, and reform to achieve their ends. For example, as part of their ideological bans on political pluralism, the secular Ba'ath parties in Iraq and Syria periodically cracked down on Islamist political activity, arresting and executing activists. One famous example of this is the 1982 siege and massacre at Hama, where the secular Syrian government brutally put down a six-year insurgency by the Muslim Brotherhood. After ascending to the monarchy in Iran in the 1920s, Reza Shah (1878–1944) banned religious festivals, preaching in public, and the wearing of religious symbols. His regime also heavily restricted mosque activity.

During the 1940s and 1950s, the new, secular forces of nationalism, communism, and Ba'athism in the Arab world vied both violently and nonviolently with proponents of the traditional Arab monarchies. Western efforts during the Cold War sapped the communist parties in the Arab world and Iran of potential influence. On the margins of this dynamic, two Islamist political projects developed gradually over the course of the early twentieth century, but these projects were not powerful enough to compete on equal terms with secular forces until the 1970s and 1980s. The Muslim Brotherhood was founded in Egypt in the 1920s and spread to other parts of the Arab World. Wahhabist ideology, developed in the eighteenth century, spread through the Gulf with the consolidation of Saudi Arabia as a state. But the humiliating defeat of the Arab powers by Israel in the 1967 war gave oxygen to Islamist political projects and they began to gain followers during the 1970s. Those Islamists understood the secular ideologies, particularly Arab nationalism as a political alternative to Western-backed monarchies, to have "failed" to transform their societies. Instead, they offered religiously inspired alternatives, which they argued would restore dignity and prosperity to the Arab states. In Iran, clerical reformers, clerical fundamentalists, nationalists, and leftists competed with each other and often formed alliances against the Shah. Although these secular forces aligned themselves with Ayatollah Khomeini (1902–1989) to depose the Shah's secular regime by force in the 1979 revolution, they were quickly surpassed by the clerical forces. Thousands of secular intellectuals were killed by the theocratic regime in the late 1980s.

The terms of secular politics and ways of life in the Middle East have undergone some reconfiguration since 2001, under pressure from rejuvenated forms of religiously infused politics. They now have vigorous competition in most states in the Middle East. Secular political and social ideas continue to be held among the middle classes in the Arab Middle East, Iran, Israel, and Turkey, which emerged across the region later in the twentieth century. Arab monarchs justify their rule on the basis of their Islamic credentials, and the societies in these countries are traditional. However, the elites and middle classes in these countries engage simultaneously in secular social practices in private and traditionally Islamic ones in public.

In Turkey, since the early 2000s, the AK Party's conservative democratic program has engaged in the gradual adjustment of state secularism. In Israel, particularly since the 1990s, religious nationalist forces have come to seriously vie with the secular forces that have dominated the state from the time of its founding. The two parts of Jewish Israeli society have achieved a sometimes-uneasy parity, held together by ongoing conflict with the Palestinians and regional threats. Secular power-sharing arrangements in Lebanon between Sunnis, Shiites, and Christians have partially but not completely curtailed the rising influence of religiously inspired, Shi'a party Hezbollah. In post-Baathist Iraq, the trauma of the 2006–2008 civil war briefly led people to support the participation of more secular parties in the power-sharing government. The failed Sunni protests of 2012 and the subsequent rise of the Islamic State, however, led once again to violent sectarianism in the country.

EGYPT

Although the competition between actors in the Middle East has often been articulated in the languages of religion and secularism, this competition has been based on the control of the reins of government and of economic resources. For example, the Egyptian revolution of 2011 opened up political space for a range of secular actors to compete with each other and with a range of Islamist actors. Before that time, since the 1952 revolution, secular forces backed by the army had dominated. They determined where, when, and how religious matters would be dealt with by the state and curtailed their primary competitors, the Muslim Brotherhood. After several decades of assassinations, imprisonment, and exile, President Anwar Sadat (1918–1981) allowed a limited rapprochement with the Muslim Brothers. During the 1990s and early 2000s, President Hosni Mubarak (1928–) allowed some Muslim Brotherhood candidates to compete in the elections, while at the same time imprisoning others. Following Mubarak's resignation in January 2011 and a short caretaker army government, Muslim Brotherhood leader Mohammed Morsi (1951–) was elected as president by a small percentage of the population. His government attempted to radically reform the constitution and the government. They altered the settlements around religion, which had held since 1952, and cracked down violently on secular competitors, particularly those affiliated with the army and the former Mubarak regime.

President Morsi was deposed by the army after one year in office. The army also engaged in a violent cleansing of its Muslim Brotherhood opposition, with the courts sentencing hundreds of Morsi supporters and Morsi himself to death. Levels of street violence and crime have been reduced under authoritarian army rule since mid-2013. The army, however, continues to fight multiple insurgency movements and demonize nearly all Islamist actors, including the Muslim Brotherhood, as a security threat to the state. There are both secular and Islamist insurgency movements. One of these movements, Waliyat Sinai, declared allegiance to the Islamic State in 2014. Liberal and leftist (secular) factions have struggled to organize themselves sufficiently to pose a serious challenge to army rule. This Egyptian case contrasts with Tunisia, which also experienced a largely nonviolent revolution in 2011. After a period of Islamist rule following the 2011 revolution (which overthrew a long-standing secular regime), Tunisian citizens elected a unity government between Islamist and secular parties.

TURKEY

In contrast to Egypt, in Turkey, secularism is state policy and has formal legal status. Following the founding of the Republic in 1923, the new Kemalist government engaged in a series of reforms to modernize the state and do away with the trappings of the Ottoman Empire. These reforms included the prominence of Islam in public life and targeted elements of both the state apparatus (e.g., law, education, political parties, and state institutions) and the lifestyles of citizens (e.g., dress codes and the conduct of family life). The government's abolition of the Caliphate was intended to solidify this modernization process.

The new government led by Mustafa Kemal Ataturk (1881–1938) did not intend to banish religion entirely from the political sphere but rather to harness it for nationalist purposes. The Kemalists established Sunni Islam as the primary state religion and a source of morality and national unity. Through the *Diyanet İşleri Başkanliği*, the Directorate of Religious Affairs established in 1924, the government aimed to bring all religious practice and institutions under the purview of the state. The government restricted the activities of the religious courts and eventually closed them down completely. It closed down autonomous religious seminaries and Sufi lodges. It placed the administrations for holy places (*waqf*) under state control. The *Diyanet* was charged with administering all mosques and with hiring all mosque personnel. It employed and trained many well-respected scholars. It also incorporated numerous research institutes to shape and promote research on Islam. Those who tried to resist this institutionalization of religion in the 1920s and 1930s were driven into exile or put to death as threats to state security.

This process of modernization radically transformed Turkish society. At the end of the 1960s, however, Islamist politics re-emerged in the national arena, participating in the ruling coalitions, in the guise of the Welfare and Virtue parties. This political competition intensified at the start of the 1980s, following a national crisis in the 1970s. In response, the government introduced a ban on the wearing of the headscarf in public places in 1982. This ban stood until the conservative AK Party overturned it in 2013, despite the participation of Islamist parties of varying shades during the intervening years. On February 28, 1997, the army forced the resignation of the prime minister from the Islamist Welfare Party. Although the army has long considered itself to be the defender of the secularist values of the Republic, this was the climax of its activities to securitize Islamism and enforce a secular political agenda. For example, from the 1980s until the 2000s, the army led a campaign to expel 2,000 Islamist officers and to force 3,000 additional personnel to resign. For example, as Hulya Arik writes in "Security, Secularism and Gender: The Turkish Military's Security Discourse in Relation to Political Islam" (2015), whether or not a soldier's wife wore the headscarf was taken as a key marker of Islamism, rendering that family a potential security risk to the state.

CENTRAL ASIA: TAJIKISTAN AND UZBEKISTAN

Examples from Central Asia illustrate the dynamics of secular state suppression of religious competitors. During the period 1927–1941, the Soviet Union engaged in the destruction of Islamic infrastructure across its central Asian republics. According to Adeeb Khalid in "Ulama and the State in Uzbekistan" (2014), the Bolsheviks believed that a cultural revolution in central Asia was necessary to secure the gains of the revolution there. This cultural revolution included replacing old elites (including the Muslim religious leadership, the *ulema*) with new, secular figures and the use of state institutions to transform the traditional society into a secular and "rational" one. This was a period of both violent and nonviolent repression, including the closing of shrines (*mazars*), law courts, educational establishments, publishing houses, and most mosques. Traditional Qur'anic schools *(maktab)* were replaced by a modern, secular, and centralized state education system. The Communist Party banned the wearing of the veil and many women ceased to wear it as a mark of their new secular, modern identity. Many of these Islamic religious leaders in these republics were arrested, assaulted, or executed. In response, others went into hiding or refused to speak out publicly. These efforts to transform society initially were not solely the result of state efforts. During the 1920s, the Jadids, or Muslim modernizers aligned with the Communist Party, competed with the conservative *ulema* for influence. Eventually both groups came under anticlerical attack from the state. They also were both cut off from interacting with foreign clerics or studying overseas. Even when the period of violent suppression ended in 1941, this Islamic infrastructure was not rebuilt. It remained this way for fifty years until the collapse of the Soviet empire.

Once the Soviet Union entered World War II, the state stopped overtly suppressing Islam and instead shifted to ways of controlling its parameters in the names of maintaining state security. Like the *Diyanet*, the Soviets established the SADUM, the Spiritual Administration for the Muslims of Central Asia and Kazakhstan. It trained a small number of *ulema*, while at the same time, the traditional *ulema* carried out some underground teaching for small numbers of students (*hujra*). Still, the Soviet de-Islamization project was largely successful. As channels of socialization, the school and the army were not only secularizing forces but were atheistic. The generations that came of age after the 1950s largely accepted that religion would be absent from the public sphere, unconsciously accepting the Communist Party's contention that secularism was necessary for state security. Krisztina Kehl-Bodrogi notes in *Religion Is Not So Strong Here* (2008), for example, that the absence of mosques was not a major source of grievance for these generations.

In the early 1990s, there was a period of religious revival in the former Soviet states, both within Islam and within the Russian Orthodox Church. From the late 1980s, during the Perestroika years of Soviet liberalization under Mikhail Gorbachev (1931–), the SADUM opened many new mosques and published Islamic literature. Since the late 1990s, post-Soviet governments have revived Soviet suspicions of security threats posed by Islamist actors and institutions to the state. The Soviet education system had long taught that Islam was merely a preliminary stage in human evolution that had been surpassed by the modernizing advances of Marxist-Leninism. The state had an obligation to prevent its citizens from returning to religion, the "opiate of the masses." As recipients of this educational system, post-Soviet elites continued the political tradition of treating Islam with suspicion. As Khalid notes (2007, 2014), citizens have been persuaded by nationalist discourses that construct politicized Islam as "Wahhabist" and the product of subversive foreign influence.

UZBEKISTAN

How states have chosen to construct and manage the "threat" posed by "Islam" has varied between central Asian states, although there are some similarities. In Uzbekistan, after a brief window of leniency, the state came to control and regulate Islam in the name of protecting and preserving the national values of the people. The state has full control of religious education through the re-named Muslim Board of Uzbekistan (MBU), the former SADUM. Unlike Soviet-era attempts to restrict the role of Islam in the public sphere, the state has attempted to co-opt Islam to capitalize on its moral authority to support national values. Still, the state restricts religious expression to those mosques, imams, and publications that support the government. In 2000, the MBU banned any publications that do not conform to state-sponsored Hanafi theological orthodoxy. People are often arrested

Chapter 12: Secularism, Secularity, and War

for possessing "illegal" literature, often from the group Hizb-ut-Tahrir, which the Uzbek government considers a particular threat.

TAJIKISTAN

Although these dynamics have largely curtailed the political influence and organizing potential of the *ulema* in Uzbekistan, in Tajikistan, something different has happened. Following the collapse of the Soviet Union, during the 1992–1997 civil war, the *qoziyyot*, or highest Islamic institution, was transformed into a government-controlled Islamic center along with the High Council of *Ulema*. Islamic practices have thrived outside of these institutions, enjoying much more visibility in the public sphere, with young Tajiks particularly publicly active. In response, explains Tim Epkenhans in "Defining Normative Islam" (2011), the Tajikistani government has both attempted to celebrate and co-opt the Islamic resurgence and curtail it through the introduction of a repressive law in 2009, allowing the Department of Religious Affairs to directly intervene in religious associations. Competition among Muslim actors for influence among the faithful has remained vibrant within the public and political spheres in Tajikistan, despite state efforts to promote what it denotes as "moderate" Islam and restrict "radical" Islam.

During the 2008–2011 Rasht Valley conflict, the largest outbreak of violence since the end of the civil war, the government justified its violent crackdown on economically powerful warlords in the region by painting them as "jihadist terrorists" who posed a threat to the state. Despite its seemingly more accommodationist stance toward Islam in the public sphere, the government reverted to discursive patterns similar to those used by the Bolsheviks during the 1920s to build national support for its response to the insurgency. Edward Lemon explains in "Mediating Conflict in the Rasht Valley, Tajikistan" (2014) that it also attempted to justify its counterinsurgency strategy to the West and gain Western support by framing it in the language of the War on Terror. Thus, as these two cases indicate, post-Soviet states in Central Asia have continued to exercise their secular state sovereignty over Islamic ideas and practices through both violent and nonviolent means, justifying these practices in the name of security for the state and the nation.

WESTERN EUROPE: FRANCE AND THE UNITED KINGDOM

Liberal democracies have dealt with matters somewhat differently. These states take various positions on what the relationship between the state and religious institutions, ideas, and individuals should look like. Some similarities, however, differentiate them from the authoritarian regimes and non-liberal democracies in Central Asia and the Middle East. Historically in Western democracies the principles of liberalism and secularism have been intertwined. Liberal commitments to the individual rights and freedoms—particularly the freedoms of belief, expression, and association; equality before the law; and tolerance—have shaped what states have seen as the appropriate role for religion in public life.

These commitments to the freedom of the individual have acted as some check on state intervention into people's lives. For example, since the terrorist attacks of September 11, 2001, although many Western states have adopted laws to put suspected jihadists under surveillance, the terms of these laws have been limited—although many would argue not nearly enough—by the personal liberties guaranteed under liberal democratic systems. The term *liberal democracy* is somewhat of a misnomer, as most Western democracies contain elements of both liberalism and republicanism. Under these hybrid systems, the rights of the individuals are balanced by the rights of the collective. Since 9/11, many Western states have justified counterterrorism laws and policies that target Muslims under the principle that the rights of the collective trump the rights of the individual in times of emergency. Additionally, as in the Central Asian case, Islam is a minority religion numerically and culturally. A long history of Western, culturally Christian Orientalism helped to pave the way for constructions of Islam as a risk to the West physically and culturally. These constructions gained popularity in Western societies after 9/11, but they also were tempered somewhat in countries with larger Muslim minorities.

FRANCE

Over the past fifteen years, a great deal of media and scholarly attention has been paid to the peculiarities of French secularism or *laïcité* on the one hand and the place of Islam in French society on the other. This media and scholarly attention has emphasized the negative impacts of *laïc* political sentiments on French domestic policies toward its Muslim population. The 2004 law banning the wearing of religious symbols in public schools, the subsequent 2010 ban on the wearing of the full face veil in public places like schools and hospitals, and the January 2015 jihadist attacks on the Charlie Hebdo offices (which the attackers said were due to the cartoonists repeatedly lampooning the Prophet) and November 2015 attacks across multiple sites in central Paris have attracted particular comment. The securitization of Islam—the designation of Islam as a security threat—is not an inevitable outcome of French laws and customs of separating religion and politics. Nor do these instances of securitization tell the full story about how the French government works with and governs its Muslim population.

A 1905 law formally separates church and state in France. *Laïcité,* a principle of the 1789 revolution, was enshrined in the 1958 French constitution. Rhetorically, the principle of separation is vigorously espoused by politicians and citizens alike. John Bowen in "Working Schemas and Normative Models in French Governance of Islam" (2012) has argued that *laïcité* is actually the composite of two ideas that arose in French history, particularly in the nineteenth century. The first is the idea that people should have the freedom to form religious institutions. The second is that the state should have the authority to regulate and govern religious institutions (similar to what we have seen in the examples from Turkey and Central Asia). The rhetorical principle of separation is important in French politics. It historically has been important to the left wing of French politics, but between 2002 and 2007, it came to be the preserve of the right wing. In practice, the combination of these two principles has produced a series of paradoxical state actions. For example, as Murat Akin explains in "Laïcité and Multiculturalism" (2009), the ban on religious symbols in schools came into effect at the same time as the establishment of the first Muslim high school in France. French efforts to formally regulate Muslim institutions began in 1989.

This is not to say, however, that the principle of *laïcité* does not contain within it the sense that religion is something potentially dangerous that should be watched carefully by the state for the purposes of maintaining security and national unity. The 2003 Stasi report recommended that the ban espouse the principle of national unity and noted the need to carefully manage diverse religious expression as a threat to that unity. The French historical experience (anticlericalism during the French Revolution, France's experience in the Algerian War of Independence, social instability in the North African suburbs of Paris from the 1980s onward, and then the spread of the Algerian civil war in the 1990s to France) contributed to

Chapter 12: Secularism, Secularity, and War

popularizing the idea that Muslims particularly may pose a danger to France. From 2002 to 2012 the French government gradually adopted a more right-wing position on Islam for various reasons. According to Jeremy Ahearne in "Laïcité: A Parallel French Cultural Policy (2002–2007)" (2014), this was due to a growing consensus between left and right over a need to legislate against the veil, the 2005 riots in the North African suburbs, and Nicolas Sarkozy's (1955–) bid to woo the right during his first presidential campaign. During this period, measures were taken that reflect the right wing's securitization of Islam. In addition to the veil bans, notes Bowen (2012), immigration officials have denied citizenship to those they deemed to have radical views but who do not belong to proscribed organizations.

UNITED KINGDOM

This Western secular ambivalence toward Islam also had an impact on state foreign policies after 9/11, for both good and ill. The British government, security services, and military faced such challenges in learning how to deal with Muslim populations in the decade after 9/11. There were collective patterns of behavior—influenced by secular habits and political assumptions—that British civilian and military policy makers tried to overcome but never completely managed (Gutkowski 2012, 2013). These secular habits produced paradoxical British policy in Southern Iraq during the Coalition Provisional Authority period (2003–2004). On the one hand, the British initially underestimated the threat posed by the Sadrist militia (key instigators of the 2006–2007 civil war). On the other hand, British habits of political liberalism also led them to work with Islamist politicians to facilitate representative democracy in Iraq (Gutkowski 2011a, 2013).

After the London bombings, the British government, security, and military poured resources into understanding Islam and overcoming their secular biases. This again had contradictory results. On the one hand, UK counterterrorism policy both led to the overt policing of religion—affecting mosques, imams, interfaith dialogue, and religious education in schools. On the other hand, it also made possible overdue support and political recognition for Muslim and other religious organizations. In Afghanistan, advances in cultural analysis, particularly under the auspices of the army's cultural specialist unit from 2009 onward, led the British to appreciate how Islam functions within the Pashtun majority culture. This not only helped North Atlantic Treaty Organization forces to better grasp the cross-border significance of the Pakistani Taliban but also led them to overlook Islam and underestimate the importance of the influx of foreign jihadists and a shift toward Al Qaeda tactics from Iraq (such as improvised explosive devices) after 2006.

Encounters with jihadists, with Muslim-majority states, and with their own Muslim minorities during the post-9/11 wars also left a lasting impression on Western societies and politics. The wars provoked debate around the terms of multiculturalism and the appropriate role of religion in political life in the West. It also prompted widespread discussion of what it means for individuals to live without religion and made many Western policy makers less wary of moderate Islamist political parties.

CONSENSUS IN THE ACADEMIC LITERATURE

To return to our metaphor of the two trains, although these two trains of scholarship on conflict and secularism have run along, largely in parallel, for many years, their tracks have converged at some points. That said, it is a bit more difficult to point to many sustained academic debates in this area, but there have been some noteworthy areas of scholarly consensus.

RELIGION AS DANGEROUS, SECULARISM AS PRODUCING SAFETY

International relations scholar David Campbell has written: "Danger is not an objective condition. It does not exist independently of those to whom it may become a threat" (1992, 2). In a similar vein, several scholars have pointed to an intimate relationship between the parameters of secular politics and how states and societies understand what is dangerous or risky and what is necessary for state security or for the protection of the powerful or the majority (Gutkowski 2011). For example, Pinar Bilgin in "The Securityness of Secularism? The Case of Turkey" (2008) has argued that secular nationalist Kemalist elites in Turkey in the early twentieth century referred repeatedly to Turkish secularism (*laiklik*) as the best political and social arrangement for keeping Turkey safe. The Kemalist elites argued that so long as the Turkish state has control over religious institutions, it could prevent challenges to the state from both inside and outside the country.

Other scholars, particularly of the Turkish and French case, have argued that the headscarf has come to be constructed by secular governments, societies, and individuals as being at odds with the norms of separation between religion and public life. This then poses a security threat to social consensus and stability. Scholars agree that these assumptions have a long historic provenance in European thought. Luca Mavelli in *Europe's Encounter with Islam: The Secular and the Postsecular* (2012) has argued that there has been a secularist myth in Western politics since the 1648 Peace of Westphalia (which brought an end to the Thirty Years' War and established the secular state as a political unit in international politics) that state security requires the separation of religion from political life. Like Cavanaugh (2009), Mavelli has argued that this particular European experience of these wars in which religious symbolism and institutions played a role led to the myth that religion needs to be regulated by the state to provide security for its citizens. For example, by banning the wearing of the *niqab* (face veil) in public places, the French government has hoped to promote social consensus and also to drive what it understands as "Islamist" symbolism out of the political sphere.

As Mavelli, Cavanaugh, Shakman Hurd, and I argue, however, this myth is false for two reasons. First, the public expression of religious symbolism does not by definition produce social dissension or encourage violence against the state. Second, liberal, secular states also engage in behavior that makes their citizens less safe, such as denouncing the private, peaceful expression of Islam and engaging in foreign policies that provoke further threats.

GOVERNMENT SUPPRESSION OF RELIGIOUS DISSENT

Scholars have identified a pattern across states that do not have liberal governments and that also have either a large Muslim minority or a culturally Muslim majority. Governments in Indonesia; the former Soviet republics, including Tajikistan and Azerbaijan; Turkey; and Egypt have engaged in modernizing projects that have curtailed the activities of Muslim religious leaders and institutions, including mosques. Some of the harshest examples of state repression of Islam include China during the Cultural Revolution and following the declaration of Albania as the world's first "atheist state" by Communist leader Enver Hoxha (1908–1985) in 1967 (Khalid 2014, 523).

Chapter 12: Secularism, Secularity, and War

Ahmet Kuru in *Secularism and State Policies towards Religion* (2009) has distinguished between "passive secularism," in which religion plays a role in the context of a secular state, and "assertive secularism," in which the state forcibly restricts the penetration of religion into the political sphere. In cases in which assertive secularism has been enforced, states have tried to control domestic political dynamics and to attempt to curtail alliances between dissident groups and their international backers. These activities have ranged from the near-total destruction of Muslim religious institutions in the central Asian Soviet republics, to the Saddam Hussein–era (1937–2006) assassination of Shi'a Islamist leaders, to the comparatively more gentle regulation of mosques and imam training in Turkey and the ban on head scarves in public places.

This kind of regulation of Islam is not just the preserve of governments who see themselves as secular. For example, the Jordanian government presents itself as moderately Muslim but also regulates its mosques. There is a difference between Muslim states that stand within Islamic discourse and aim to co-opt Islam and use it for nationalist purposes and Communist states that stand outside this discourse and aim to restrict Islamic discourse as a security threat to national cohesion. Additionally, in countries where the regulation of religion is the norm, Islamists are not the only religious groups seen as a threat to the government. For example, in Turkey, evangelical Christianity has been seen as a threatening force by the state because it threatens to split citizens' loyalty between the state and external actors. In 2001, the National Security Council named Christian missionaries as the third largest threat to Turkey.

DEBATES IN THE ACADEMIC LITERATURE

Where debate continues in academic literature, it has focused on the relationship between secularism and politics more broadly, rather than particularly on war, violence, and conflict. The prompt for much of this debate was the War on Terror. Three main areas of debate are related to one another and also are similar to debates that crop up in other areas explored in this book. These are debates over the following: What is secularism? Who are secular people? What do we mean by the label "secular"? How might this label constrain analysis, causing us to miss important dynamics?

DOES SECULARISM REDUCE VIOLENCE?

Particularly since 2001, there has been a rich debate across the social sciences about the compatibility or incompatibility of Islam—or indeed other religious traditions—with democratic values. Political and social theorists have agreed that many Western states, societies, and individuals have fallen for the myth that religion is somehow incompatible with liberal, secular forms of democracy. They have argued in favor of their compatibility. They understand this compatibility in different ways, however. For example, Jürgen Habermas (1929–) has famously argued that both religious and secular forces can and should engage in democratic dialogue in the public sphere so long as the religiously inspired articulate their claims in the secular language of rights and sovereignty. This will, he argues, reduce violent and nonviolent political contention around the world. Conversely, other scholars have argued that what is required to reduce conflict is a move away from a secular public sphere toward a postsecular public sphere in which religious voices play a much larger role (e.g., see DeVries and Sullivan 2006; Petito and Mavelli 2014).

216   MACMILLAN INTERDISCIPLINARY HANDBOOKS

Beyond these theoretical debates, the case study literature also suggests that the answer to the question "does secularism reduce violence?" is far from straightforward. In some cases, political secularism at the state level seems to reduce contention between societal groups and to protect religious minorities from attack. Northern Ireland, Bosnia, and Lebanon are examples of this, as is the protection of Egyptian Copts under secular governments in Egypt and religious minorities in pre-2011 Syria. In other cases, violence occurs between religious and sectarian groups in spite of state-sponsored secularism. For example, India has seen periodic violence between its Hindu majority and Muslim minority, such as the 2002 riots following the Godhra train burning and the 1992 dispute over the Ayodhya mosque.

WHAT DO WE MEAN BY THE WORDS THAT WE USE?

As argued elsewhere in this book, and by Walter B. Gallie (1956), the terms *secular, secularism*, and *secularization* are essentially contested concepts. Scholars looking at issues of violence, security, and conflict similarly disagree over the best way to use these terms. For example, Timothy Samuel Shah and Daniel Philpott in "The Fall and Rise of Religion in International Relations History and Theory" (2011) identified no fewer than nine definitions of secularism that are relevant to the study of global affairs (and, by extension, relevant to the study of violence and conflict). Six of these are as a historic description of activities outside the medieval monastery; as a political process of the differentiation or integration of religion into the workings of the state; as a social state of affairs in which large numbers of people have stopped practicing religion; as a social state of affairs in which people have stopped practicing but still believe; as a political tool to suppress religion; and as a social or political ideology that advocates keeping religion in its own private sphere, away from other areas of life such as the state, economy, or family. Other definitions of secularism abound.

For scholars studying the relationships among religion, secularism, violence, security, and conflict, many follow Talal Asad's famous contention in *Formations of the Secular* (2003) that the distinction between *religion* and *secularism* is a Western construction and ultimately false. Scholars working on cases outside the West have taken broad issue with the term *secular*. They argue that it describes well European history, whereby the Church lost power and the state gained power as the Christian medieval worldview was gradually transformed into one in which spheres of human activity—government, economics, science, the family, civil society—were no longer dominated by individual religious beliefs or by the Church. The term, however, does not accurately describe cases within but particularly outside the West in which religious and secular ideas, institutions, and forces are deeply intertwined. It is not possible in these cases, they contend, to determine where the religious stops and the secular begins. For example, participants in the 9/11 attacks and the London bombings engaged in practices considered un-Islamic and yet they espoused a jihadist political ideology. It may make sense to talk about various heterodox forms of divergence from, for example, Jewish or Muslim orthodox religious beliefs and practice. But it is still up in the air whether the Western-informed concept of secularism is particularly useful for analysts of non-Western cases. This is important as most cases of contemporary violent conflict have occurred outside the West.

This terminological debate has an impact on conflict analysis, including the prescription of political secularism to aid the regulation of conflict in conflicts between religious or sectarian political groups. For example, some may argue that the resolution of

Chapter 12: Secularism, Secularity, and War

the Palestinian-Israeli conflict requires, among many other things, the gradual de-fusion of religio-ethnic ideas about the land through a secularization of mainstream political discourse and the regulation of sacred sites by secular international institutions like the United Nations Educational, Scientific and Cultural Organization. It is hard to see how the imposition of more political secularism would help to resolve issues when religion resonates to some extent for the majority of people on both sides of the dispute, personally and collectively.

NONRELIGION: POLITICAL TRADITION VERSUS THE LIVED EXPERIENCE OF ACTORS

Scholars such as Hurd and Cavanaugh have argued that Western secular political traditions have shaped the thinking of Western governments about how to respond to security threats posed by jihadist actors. Still, the precise social and political mechanisms whereby broad political traditions are absorbed by actors and translated into action are underexplored in the literature, both empirically and theoretically. My own contribution to this debate has been to argue for a more nuanced sociological approach that takes seriously the mechanisms whereby actors mediate these broad political traditions and translate them into action (Gutkowski 2013). We need to pay attention to people's individual and collective habits and lived experiences, which are shaped by secular political traditions. This allows analysts to better see two things. First, it helps analysts to better see more precisely how Western secular assumptions blinded policy makers to the dynamics of political Islamism both within and outside the West. Second, it helps analysts to better see areas in which Western secular assumptions have facilitated an astute response to jihadism, for example, by promoting the inclusion of Islamist politicians in the new Iraqi and Afghan governments.

My own contribution to these terminological debates also has been to argue that we need to pay far more attention to how people who are not particularly religious understand conflicts in which religious nationalism or other forms of religiously inspired politics play a role. By paying more attention to how people who fall further toward the nonreligious end of the religious-nonreligious spectrum think about and act during times of violent conflict, we can shed light on four social and political dimensions of warfare. These are as follows: (1) how people understand what it is to behave ethically during war; (2) how people understand and cope with the existential threats posed by war; (3) how people construct religio-political actors as dangerous or not; and (4) how people think violent conflict should be managed.

AREAS FOR FURTHER STUDY

As noted earlier, this topic is a rich and cutting edge area of study, ripe for further research. What other areas would be interesting for researchers (from undergraduates to professors) to explore? Much has been written on cases in which secular and religious political groups compete within society, but there is still a great deal of scope to explore in empirical detail how secular worldviews intersect with forms of political and social belonging in conflict situations. How do secular ideas about how to behave during war, use violence or wage peace intersect with secular (and also religious) political identities? For example, how has the Syrian Army and

218

MACMILLAN INTERDISCIPLINARY HANDBOOKS

Chapter 12: Secularism, Secularity, and War

government used both its secular Baathist and Alawi identities to maintain support in the face of threats from an ever-changing kaleidoscope of Sunni Islamist and secular militant groups, including the Islamic State? Other interesting cases to explore include Tunisia, Egypt, Palestine, Lebanon, Israel, Iraq, Iran, China, and Uganda, among others.

Additionally, a range of discrete topics brings together issues of secularism, conflict, and security, particularly although by no means exclusively in Western contexts. These include humanist military chaplaincies or how religious chaplaincies serve nonreligious populations; what is distinctively nonreligious about coping strategies and narratives among those who have lived through conflict, including refugees and combatants; what are the relationships between secular humanist ethical convictions and antiwar activism; how do secular perceptions of religion shape how armies or individual soldiers fight and perceive the enemy; how do secular ethical systems and symbols inspire soldiers; the secularization of the just war tradition as it is taught in military academies; public controversies in the West surrounding the visibility of religion in issues of national and international conflict; secular dimensions of burial, mourning, and memorialization practices conducted by national militaries (usually by a religious chaplain); and how secularization processes were driven forward or retarded by violent conflicts other than World Wars I and II. Considerable scope also exists for the further development of research on the interaction between secular and religious actors in the context of wartime humanitarian aid and postconflict development and peace building.

The field will advance theoretically by moving past the "trains on parallel tracks" phenomenon to bring well-established areas of scholarship into dialogue with each other. One example is to bring the established literatures on secularism and secularity into conversation with the established literatures on the ideologies that have driven wars since the nineteenth centuries—nationalism, Marxism, Maoism, fascism, capitalism, imperialism and anti-imperialism. This conversation would shed light on the relationship between the secularization (and desecularization) of societies and the political impact of these social processes. Bringing the literature on atheism and pacifism to bear on case studies of particular conflicts around the world could shed further light on how individuals ethically navigate war and conflict. Bringing the literature on secularism and peaceful dialogue in the public sphere into conversation with that on conflict could enrich the literature on postwar reconciliation. This work will require substantial engagement across the boundaries of academic disciplines and the exploration of comparative cases from around the world. Finally, the literature on violence and liberalism—in which secularism is implied but not explicitly dealt with—could be brought into conversation with the literature on secularism to better theorize the relationships between violence and secularism.

Summary

To conclude, secular actors and ideas play a role in violent and nonviolent conflicts in the following seven ways:

1. In their struggles for control of governments, actors sometimes characterize their politics as religiously-inspired or as democratic and against religious conservatism. They often have much in common but use identity labels to gain followers and demonize other groups.

2. People have been murdered for expressing their secular beliefs and have committed murder in the name of their secular beliefs.

RELIGION: BEYOND RELIGION

Chapter 12: Secularism, Secularity, and War

3. Secular political ideologies have inspired nationalist revolutions.

4. Secular governments have imposed harsh restrictions on religious institutions and actors they have labeled dangerous.

5. Western secular social and political traditions have shaped how the West has seen Islam as dangerous after 9/11; jihadists have justified attacks on civilians as a critique of the secular, decadent West.

6. Individuals' ideas about war and security are shaped directly by their secular beliefs and not just indirectly by the political traditions of their governments.

7. Secular power-sharing governments have prevented a return to civil war between sectarian groups.

Still, it is important that we as analysts do not over-interpret the role of secular ideas, actors and institutions in violent conflict. More often than not, actors in conflict are preoccupied with issues of the distribution of power within or between societies, and issues of religious identity, belief or practice are at best tangential to these. Therefore I have tried to point to the limited circumstances where I think the terms of secularism form a salient part of these violent dialogues over power, so that we may proceed with due analytical caution.

Bibliography

Ahearne, Jeremy. "Laïcité: A Parallel French Cultural Policy (2002–2007)." *French Cultural Studies* 25, no. 3/4 (2014): 320–329.

Akin, Murat. "Laïcité and Multiculturalism: The Stasi Report in Context." *British Journal of Sociology* 60, no. 2 (2009): 237–256.

Arik, Hulya. "Security, Secularism and Gender: The Turkish Military's Security Discourse in Relation to Political Islam." *Gender, Place and Culture: A Journal of Feminist Geography* 22, no. 10 (2015): 1–18. doi:10.1080/0966369X.2015.1034242.

Asad, Talal. *Formations of the Secular: Christianity, Islam, Modernity*. Stanford, CA: Stanford University Press, 2003.

Bilgin, Pinar. "The Securityness of Secularism? The Case of Turkey." *Security Dialogue* 39, no. 6 (2008): 593–614.

Bowen, John R. "Working Schemas and Normative Models in French Governance of Islam." *Comparative European Politics* 10 (2012): 354–368.

Campbell, David. *United States Foreign Policy and the Politics of Identity*. Minneapolis: University of Minnesota Press, 1992.

Cavanaugh, William T. *The Myth of Religious Violence: Secular Ideology and the Roots of Modern Conflict*. Oxford: Oxford University Press, 2009.

Cole, Juan. "Militant Secularism in the Middle East?" Informed Comment. October 4, 2013. http://www.juancole.com/2013/10/militant-secularism-middle.html.

De Vries, Hent, and Lawrence E. Sullivan. *Political Theologies: Public Religions in a Post-Secular World*. Bronx, NY: Fordham University Press, 2006.

Epkenhans, Tim. "Defining Normative Islam: Some Remarks on Contemporary Islamic Thought in Tajikistan—Hoji Akbar Turajonzoda's Sharia and Society." *Central Asian Survey* 30, no. 1 (2011): 81–96.

Gallie, Walter B. "Essentially Contested Concepts." *Proceedings of the Aristotelian Society* 56 (1956): 167–198.

Goldstone, Brian. "Violence and the Profane: Islamism, Liberal Democracy and the Limits of Secular Discipline." *Anthropological Quarterly* 80, no. 1 (2007): 207–235.

Gutkowski, Stacey. "The British Secular Habitus and the War on Terror." *Journal of Contemporary Religion* 27, no. 1 (2012): 87–103.

Gutkowski, Stacey. "It's Not All about Islam: Misreading Secular Politics in the Middle East." Open Democracy. April 25, 2015. https://www.opendemocracy.net/arab-awakening/stacey-gutkowski/it%E2%80%99s-not-all-about-islam-misreading-secular-politics-in-middle-east.

Gutkowski, Stacey. "Misreading Islam in Iraq: Secular Misconceptions and British Foreign Policy." *Security Studies* 20, no. 4 (2011a): 592–623.

Gutkowski, Stacey. *Secular War: Myths of Religion, Politics and Violence*. London: I. B. Tauris, 2013.

Gutkowski, Stacey. "Secularism and the Politics of Risk: Britain's Prevent Agenda, 2005-2009." *International Relations* 25, no. 3 (2011b): 346–362.

Hassner, Ron. "Debating the Role of Religion in War." *International Security* 35, no. 1 (2010): 201–208.

Jansen, Yolande. "Secularism and Security: France, Islam and Europe." In *Global Politics in a Secular Age*, edited by Linnell E. Cady and Elizabeth Shakman Hurd, 69–86. Basingstoke, UK: Palgrave Macmillan, 2010.

Juergensmeyer, Mark. *Terror in the Mind of God: The Global Rise of Religious Violence.* Berkeley: University of California Press, 2000.

Kehl-Bodrogi, Krisztina. *Religion Is Not So Strong Here: Muslim Religious Life in Khorezm after Socialism.* Berlin: Lit Verlag, 2008.

Khalid, Adeeb. *Islam after Communism: Religion and Politics in Central Asia.* Berkeley: University of California Press, 2007.

Khalid, Adeeb. "Ulama and the State in Uzbekistan." *Asian Journal of Social Science* 42 (2014): 517–535.

Kuru, Ahmet T. *Secularism and State Policies towards Religion: The United States, France and Turkey.* New York: Cambridge University Press, 2009.

Lemon, Edward. "Mediating Conflict in the Rasht Valley, Tajikistan." *Central Asian Affairs* 1 (2014): 247–272.

Mavelli, Luca. "Between Normalisation and Exception: The Securitisation of Islam and the Construction of the Secular Subject." *Millennium: Journal of International Studies* 41, no. 2 (2013): 152–181.

Mavelli, Luca. *Europe's Encounter with Islam: The Secular and the Postsecular.* Routledge: London and New York, 2012.

Petito, Fabio, and Luca Mavelli, eds. *Towards a Postsecular International Politics? Changing Patterns of Authority, Legitimacy and Power in a Postsecular World.* Basingstoke, UK: Palgrave Macmillan, 2014.

Rahnema, Saeed. "Retreat and Return of the Secular in Iran." *Comparative Studies of South Asia, Africa and the Middle East* 31, no. 1 (2011): 34–45.

Salem, Paul. "The Rise and Fall of Secularism in the Arab World." *Middle East Policy* 4, no. 3 (1996): 147–160.

Shah, Timothy Samuel, and Daniel Philpott. "The Fall and Rise of Religion in International Relations History and Theory." In *Religion and International Relations Theory*, edited by Jack Snyder, 24–59. New York: Columbia University Press, 2011.

Shakman Hurd, Elizabeth. *The Politics of Secularism in International Relations.* Princeton, NJ: Princeton University Press, 2008.

Psychological and Philosophical Aspects of Secularity

CHAPTER 13

Dislike of and Discrimination Against Atheists and Secular People

Maxine B. Najle
Doctoral Candidate, Department of Psychology
University of Kentucky, Lexington

Will M. Gervais
Assistant Professor, Department of Psychology
University of Kentucky, Lexington

No man will say, 'There is no God' 'till he is so hardened in sin that it has become his interest that there should be none to call him to account.

—Matthew Henry

In an interview with a journalist for American Atheists in 1987, then-presidential candidate George H. W. Bush expressed his dislike for atheists, reportedly saying, "No, I don't know that atheists should be considered as citizens, nor should they be considered patriots. This is one nation under God" (O'Hair 1987). While the veracity of this quote has been debated, similar opinions—that atheists are not citizens or do not have the same rights as citizens—are held by many influential members of the government. Supreme Court Justice Antonin Scalia, for example, gave a speech on October 1, 2014, to Colorado Christian University in which he claimed that the constitutional requirement of separation of church and state does not mean that "the government cannot favor religion over nonreligion." He went on to say: "I think we have to fight that tendency of the secularists to impose it on all of us through the Constitution" (Ashtari 2014). Although the First Amendment protects those who choose to abstain from religion as much as it protects those in minority religions and the dominant religions, Americans seem to assume a sense of "generic monotheism" as a sort of standard in society. For instance, many (perhaps even most) Americans oppose removal of mentions of "God" in the Pledge of Allegiance and on currency, traditions that, though often believed to be quite old, only date back to the Cold War.

BROADER EXAMPLES

Dislike of and discrimination against atheists is both widespread and largely tolerated. For example, several American states still have laws in their state constitutions that specifically allow discrimination against atheists, barring them from public office; these states include Maryland, North Carolina, and Tennessee (Bulger 2012). Beyond the United States, more than fifty other countries have blasphemy laws still on the books, with varying weights and punishments.

Chapter 13: Dislike of and Discrimination Against Atheists and Secular People

Atheism is punishable by death in thirteen countries, and blasphemy carries mandatory jail time in thirty-nine countries, six of which are considered Western countries (Evans 2013; IHEU 2013). Not all of these laws are merely vestiges of older, antiquated laws; Saudi Arabia recently passed legislation categorizing all atheists as terrorists (HRW 2014).

Beyond legal discrimination, atheists also face interpersonal and day-to-day instances of prejudice. Interestingly, social norms render overt expressions of prejudice against most groups socially undesirable, but some groups are still seen as "fair" targets for prejudice (Crandall, Eshleman, & O'Brien 2002), and one may gauge the degree to which a group is viewed negatively by assessing the degree to which overt prejudice against that group is seen as socially acceptable. By that standard, anti-atheist prejudice is still very much in vogue. Atheists are one of the few groups that it is generally considered acceptable to dislike, unlike other historically disliked groups, such as African Americans and homosexuals, that have gained favorability in explicit public opinion polls over the last few decades. For instance, people are much more willing to say they would *not* vote for a presidential candidate who, all else held constant, was an atheist, than they are to say the same about a black, Muslim, Hispanic, gay, or Mormon candidate (Wike and Menasce Horowitz 2007). Atheists are also less likely to be seen as sharing the same vision of American society or as being acceptable romantic partners for respondents' children (Edgell, Gerteis, & Hartmann 2006). These findings simultaneously demonstrate the strength of anti-atheist sentiments and their acceptability in a culture increasingly intolerant of other prejudices. Such prejudicial attitudes may, in turn, motivate prejudicial behavior.

An interesting field experiment tested the impact of anti-atheist prejudice in a real-world setting. A group of artisanal shoemakers from Berlin, named Atheist Shoes for their atheist-branded, handmade shoes, began to notice that their American customers were having uncommonly frequent issues with their shipments arriving late or not at all. Atheist Shoes had a practice of using packaging tape for their boxes that read in large print

Shoes and packing tape from the German company Atheist Shoes. *When American customers had problems with shipments arriving late or not at all, some assumed the packing tape was the cause and requested that Atheist Shoes send future packages without this tape.* COPYRIGHT © THE MEANINGFUL SHOE COMPANY LTD.

Chapter 13: Dislike of and Discrimination Against Atheists and Secular People

ATHEIST. Some of their American customers assumed this was the cause for their shipment delays and requested that Atheist Shoes send future packages without this tape.

To test the effect of the atheist-label tape on their shipments, the shoemakers decided to conduct an experiment with a batch of their American shipments. They shipped 178 packages to 89 people in 49 states: some with their normal atheist tape and others with regular unlabeled packing tape. They found that the atheist-packaged shoes, on average, got to their destination later than their counterparts, that atheist-branded packages were more likely to get lost or go missing, and that in one instance, the atheist package arrived thirty-seven days later than the generic package (AtheistBerlin 2013). These results were limited to their US packages, as compared to their control tests in Germany and Europe. As a result, Atheist Shoes discontinued their use of *ATHEIST* packaging tape for their American customers. Although this example may seem rather trivial, it demonstrates the range of disadvantages and discrimination faced by atheists today.

DEFINING AND EXPLAINING THE ATHEIST STEREOTYPE

An oddity of the stereotyping of and prejudice against atheists is that, as a whole, atheists lack any meaningful sense of cohesion or group membership. For the most part, they are collectively and individually inconspicuous. With some exceptions, they tend to live outside of close-knit congregations or groups centered on their lack of religious beliefs. Even in countries with large numbers of atheists, lack of belief does not tend to be a central part of their identities. As comedian Ricky Gervais put it, "Saying 'Atheism is a belief system' is like saying 'not going skiing is a hobby.'" What, then, drives the strong antipathy many hold toward atheists?

One possibility is that—like many other forms of prejudice (Cottrell and Neuberg 2005)—anti-atheist prejudice may be driven primarily by a negative emotional reaction. White American college students tend, for example, to *fear* African American men but view gay men with *disgust* (Cottrell and Neuberg 2015). Might a common emotional reaction unite anti-atheist prejudice with other forms of interreligious negative perceptions? Preliminary work suggests a possible role of disgust as a core emotional reaction to religious outgroups. In one study (Ritter and Preston 2011), Christian participants were given a mildly disgusting drink before and after reading a passage about either atheism (from *The God Delusion* by Richard Dawkins), Islam (from the Qur'an), or a control passage (from the dictionary). Though the drinks were identical, participants were led to believe they were part of a marketing study to compare the two drinks and rate which one they preferred.

After being exposed to the atheist and Islamic passages, participants rated the second drink as more disgusting than the first. These passages seemed to induce feelings of disgust and revulsion in the participants, which they misattributed to the drink. Because the drinks were identical, the greater the difference in ratings of disgust from the first to second drink, the more disgusted the participants felt toward the second drink, and thus the more disgusting they found the intervening prime passage. Thus, when participants tasted the exact same drink after reading an antireligious passage written by an atheist, and they found it more disgusting than the drink before the passage, they were misplacing their revulsion for the passage by blaming the (identical) drink. This same trend was not observed in the participants who read a passage from the Bible or a control from the dictionary; these two identical drinks were not rated as significantly different in terms of how disgusting

RELIGION: BEYOND RELIGION

227

participants found them, thus ruling out the possibility that *any* religious passage would induce this effect. In this study, results did not seem specific to anti-atheist sentiments, but rather was a general reaction to literature from other—perhaps viewed with hostility—religious groups.

Although disgust characterized reactions to both Islamic and militant atheist texts, it is possible that anti-atheist prejudice does not primarily derive from disgust. Different prejudices have been shown to stem from fundamentally different, often emotional, reactions. For instance, racial prejudices tend to be rooted in fear or anger, whereas anti-gay prejudices tend to be rooted in disgust (Cottrell and Neuberg 2005; Inbar, Pizarro, Knobe, and Bloom 2009; Tapias, Glaser, Keltner, Vasquez, and Wickens 2007). While the aforementioned "disgusting drink" study found that anti-atheist prejudice had a disgust component, other studies have repeatedly found that anti-atheist prejudice differs from anti-gay prejudice, with homophobia being linked to disgust of gays and lesbians but anti-atheist prejudice being linked to feelings of distrust (Gervais, Shariff, and Norenzayan 2011). Atheists have been repeatedly found to be intuitively associated with untrustworthiness and immorality. Thus, while atheist texts may evoke disgust, disgust is plausibly not a primary motivator of anti-atheist prejudice.

ATHEISTS AS UNTRUSTWORTHY

To test intuitive associations between different groups of people and different attributes, participants were given a task known as the conjunction fallacy (Tversky and Kahneman 1983), a task that involves the participant reading a vignette depicting or describing an individual. The classic example from the original Tversky and Kahneman paper gives the following vignette:

> *Linda is 31 years old, single, outspoken, and very bright. She majored in philosophy. As a student, she was deeply concerned with issues of discrimination and social justice, and also participated in anti-nuclear demonstrations.*

Following this vignette, participants are asked:

Which is more probable?
> A. Linda is a bank teller.
> B. Linda is a bank teller and is active in the feminist movement.

Though probabilistically and logically option A is more probable than option B due to B being a subset of A, people nonetheless intuitively associate the description given (liberal, etc.) with the potential group membership in the second choice (feminist), leading people to choose option B. This incorrect judgment of probabilities is known as the conjunction fallacy: in the example, the presence of the feminist movement works in conjunction with the information in the vignette to allow the individual to commit the statistical fallacy. By independently manipulating the contents of the description and the groups implied by option B, researchers can assess the degree to which people intuitively associate groups with descriptions.

By adapting this technique to incorporate atheists into the second option category, researchers have been able to investigate the intuitive associations commonly held about atheists. Gervais and coauthors (2011) used this method to test whether vignettes depicting untrustworthy individuals (e.g., someone hitting a parked car and only pretending to leave insurance information, finding a wallet and stealing the money instead of trying to return it) would be seen as representative of atheists more so than they were of other groups. While these vignettes did not cause people to commit the conjunction fallacy error (i.e., picking

Chapter 13: Dislike of and Discrimination Against Atheists and Secular People

option B) when the second group in option B was Christian or Muslim, it did result in a significant proportion of conjunction errors in the condition that gave Atheists as the option B group. Rapists were the only other group in this study that was seen as representative of the untrustworthy individual; rapists and atheists did not differ significantly in rates of errors made. Thus, while Christians and Muslims were not intuitively seen as untrustworthy, atheists and rapists were, and to a similar degree.

This same technique has been replicated using a series of moral transgressions, ranging from the minor, for example, antipatriotism, to the especially heinous, serial homicide. Atheists are intuitively associated with such moral transgressions as disloyalty, disrespect for authority, dishonesty, cheating, stealing, animal cruelty, incest, cannibalism, serial homicide, and necrobestiality (Gervais 2014a). These transgressions did not trigger conjunction errors with any of the comparison groups used in the study, including religious groups such as Buddhist, Christian, Hindu, Jewish, and Muslim, and ethnic groups such as Asian, black, Hispanic, Native American, and white. One implication of these findings is that people tend to intuitively agree with the sentiment suggested in Dostoyevsky's *The Brothers Karamazov:* without God, everything is permitted. They assume that without God, there is no reason to choose good. Intuitively at least, people seem to assume that religion serves a necessary inhibitory function in preventing immoral conduct. Strikingly, even atheists share this intuitive association with their religious counterparts, albeit to a lesser extent.

Why might people intuitively associate atheists with immorality and untrustworthiness? What is it about not believing in a supreme, supernatural being that would cause atheists to be seen as untrustworthy? This uneasiness about atheism may be unfounded, but it makes a certain amount of sense when we consider other psychological findings about basic human behavior. For instance, when participants are asked in surveys to think about "God," they have increased public self-awareness and answer in more socially desirable ways; this finding suggests that feelings of being watched, as might be induced when thinking about an omniscient god, may produce more socially desirable behaviors (Gervais and Norenzayan 2012b). It is not very surprising that people who feel watched, especially by a god, would be on their best behavior, as people generally suppress their selfish urges when they feel they are being watched (Bateson, Callow, Holmes, Roche, and Nettle 2013; Bateson, Nettle, and Roberts 2006). Thus, by extension, it also makes sense that atheists—who are defined only by their lack of belief in the existence of any sort of god or gods, overseeing deities and deistic ones alike—would be seen as morally suspect to those who assume that inhibition of selfish urges can only be induced by supernatural watchers.

Of course, in reality, belief in a god may not directly translate to better behavior, as is evidenced by the lower rates of crime in less theistic societies as well as by empirical investigations of the matter (Didyoung, Charles, and Rowland 2013; Zuckerman 2013). One major reason for this reality is that the authorities who govern and influence human behavior are not only of the divine sort, but also of the secular variety. Thus, although atheists may not believe that committing a sin will result in divine punishment, they very well understand that committing a crime runs the risk of their suffering corporeal punishment. Theists do not always intuitively consider this objective fact. Actually, the opposite is often true. In 2015 reality television celebrity Phil Robertson from the show *Duck Dynasty* gave a vivid account of what he felt should be done to atheists to prove what he saw as the errors of their ways. He encouraged breaking into an atheist's home and forcing the atheist to watch as his family was brutally raped and murdered in front of him, saying the atheist would have to accept this behavior because, as an atheist, he believed no

RELIGION: BEYOND RELIGION

Chapter 13: Dislike of and Discrimination Against Atheists and Secular People

one (read: no god) could judge the intruder for it and that there is no right and wrong (Mazza 2015a). Robertson went on to say that an atheist in that situation would be forced to acknowledge that some things are objectively wrong. The *Duck Dynasty* crew seems to have many odd beliefs about atheists, as another cast member later gave an interview in which he claimed that in reality there are no *real* atheists, as everyone in modern society who uses the Gregorian calendar, he maintains, implicitly acknowledges Jesus as Christ because the calendar years are based on approximations of his birth (Mazza 2015b). The argument here, presumably, does not apply to the months named after non-Christian gods.

Even when we take Robertson's strawman atheist depiction at face value, we find it difficult to fathom that an atheist would be likely to think that violently brutalizing and murdering a family would have no consequences, given that atheists are still subject to police jurisdiction and must abide by the same laws as theists. Although theists may not intuitively consider this fact, they can be induced to think of it. In this way, reminders of secular authority are effective in reducing anti-atheist prejudice (Gervais and Norenzayan 2012c). Likewise, the increasing perceived prevalence of atheists is decreasing the distrust of atheists, operating under the same notion that an underestimation of the local atheist population indicates that the presence of atheists isn't as calamitous as intuitively might be assumed since they apparently are coexisting peacefully without their notice (Gervais 2011).

Phil Robertson's notion that gods keep theists from committing awful atrocities is the one often cited to explain why atheism is a flawed belief system. Comedian and evangelical atheist Penn Jillette refers to this notion when he is questioned about his nonbelief. In an interview, Jillette said, "The question I get asked by religious people all the time is, without God, what's to stop me from raping all I want? And my answer is: I do rape all I want. And the amount I want is zero. And I do murder all I want, and the amount I want is zero" (Jillette 2012). Jillette goes on to say how terrifying an idea it is that, in the absence of a god, theists *would* be raping and killing people. Fortunately, this is not the case, as is illustrated by a recent study. In this study, predominantly Christian college students at a large southern university were asked to list the five things they would like to do but are prohibited from doing by their religion (Najle and Gervais Unpublished data-a). Among the most commonly listed activities were premarital sex and, as expected, the consumption of drugs and alcohol. Thus, the world of theists unleashed from their gods may not be as bleak as Phil Robertson or many other theists might think it would be.

ATHEISTS AS LACKING MORAL KNOWLEDGE

In addition to their belief in a supernatural being overseeing their behavior, theists also contend that their morals come from their religious teaching and scriptures. This idea of moral knowledge stemming from religious teaching seems to be another element that is at the heart of anti-atheist prejudice. People intuitively judge vignettes about individuals lacking moral knowledge (i.e., they did not know whether or not a moral transgression was wrong) as more representative of atheists than of theists, and vice versa (i.e., when they did know an action was wrong, they were more representative of theists) (Najle and Gervais Unpublished data-b). This finding suggests that people think religious instruction and belief is a prerequisite for proper moral development. Without religion instructing people as to what is wrong and putting the brakes on immoral human impulses, humans, according to this logic, cannot tell right from wrong. This idea is further supported by the fact that people place more personal responsibility on an atheist committing a moral act than on a theist performing the same moral act, with the theist's religious instruction taking some of

Chapter 13: Dislike of and Discrimination Against Atheists and Secular People

the credit in the theist's case (Gervais 2014b). Thus, it appears that people tend to believe that humans are inherently immoral (or perhaps amoral), controlled by impulses that are predominantly selfish and harmful to others. If this were true, we would expect that areas with high-density populations of atheists would have higher crime rates and lower standards of living and security than areas where theists greatly outnumber the atheists. In fact, the opposite is true. Secular nations have lower murder and crime rates than their religious counterparts; the same pattern holds for states, with the less religious states having lower murder rates than the more religious states (Zuckerman 2009). This pattern extends to family values and levels of altruism, both of which tend to be higher in nonreligious countries (e.g., lower divorce rates, higher per capita donations to poorer nations) as well as human rights issues (e.g., higher support for equality for genders, races, and sexual orientation; lower support for the use of torture and capital punishment) (Zuckerman 2009). Therefore, although thinking that atheists lack moral knowledge might make sense on an intuitive, superficial level, in real-world examples, there is little, if any, evidence to support this thought (Bloom 2012).

ATHEISTS AS REMINDERS OF MORTALITY

Another possible contributor to anti-atheist prejudice is the threat the existence of atheists brings to a theist's worldview. By this logic, an atheist's denial of a theist's faith specifically calls into question theism's account of the afterlife, meaning that theists, rather than achieving salvation or any kind of afterlife, would simply cease to exist (Cook, Cohen, and Solomon 2015). This possibility, however, fails to account for the extreme and vitriolic antipathy toward atheists that is not experienced by any other religious outgroup. If anything, by this account other religious outgroups should inspire *more* discomfort than atheists. For instance, a Muslim should be more upset about Christians proclaiming that those who reject Jesus Christ as their god will burn in hell, as compared to atheists who simply don't comment on the afterlife or assert that nothing happens when you die. In a very real and tangible sense, the hellish eternity to be faced by being wrong about Christianity should be more upsetting to Muslims than being wrong about atheism.

VARIETIES OF ATHEISM

In this chapter, we have been treating atheists as a homogeneous group because that is generally how others perceive them. In reality, however, atheists come in a variety of flavors. Atheists do not all have the same reason for their lack belief in a god or gods. There is a significant and meaningful difference between a person who was raised as a fundamentalist Pentecostal Christian who later in life becomes an atheist versus a person who grew up in a secular home, never adopting beliefs about one god or another. Given this distinction, does it make sense to apply the same level of anti-atheist prejudice to all atheists? Does it make sense to consider the Christian apostate and the cultural atheist as ostensibly lacking moral knowledge in the same way? Of course, no stereotype truly captures all members of a group—nor is it really meant to. Although negative prejudice against any group or subgroup is undesirable, it's important to understand the distinctions between the types of atheism if these types are inducing distinct stereotypes or reactions. To date, four types of atheism, stemming from four separate cognitive pathways, have been identified and defined: mind-blind atheism, apatheism, inCREDulous atheism, and analytic atheism (Norenzayan and Gervais 2012).

RELIGION: BEYOND RELIGION

231

Mind-blind atheism refers to people who lack belief in a supernatural deity because they find it difficult to conceive of such an entity. To a degree, an individual's ability to conceive of a god is related to his or her ability to conceive of and understand other humans, to understand their goals and intentions. This concept is known as *mentalizing* or *mind perception*. Being able to mentalize offers obvious benefits for successful human interaction, but research has also suggested that it might be one of the key cognitive processes underlying religious belief (Gervais 2013). Ultimately, mentalizing appears to be a necessary but insufficient element for developing belief in a god or gods. When an individual has normal mentalizing abilities, but still lacks belief, other factors may be contributing to this religious disbelief. Many nonbelievers simply don't find religion particularly motivating.

For these nonbelievers, the term *apatheism* was coined, meaning "a disinclination to care all that much about one's own religion" (Rauch 2003). These nonbelievers can conceive of gods without difficulty, but they lack the motivation to believe that any of them are real. People lack religious motivations for different reasons, but common motivations for believing in supernatural agents include a need for emotional comfort, meaning, or order. Human suffering and existential threats are powerful and common motivators for belief (Gray and Wegner 2010; Norenzayan and Hansen 2006).

For many, scholars and people in general, religion is an inescapable default in humans, with only rare exceptions resulting in atheism (Barrett 2010). Predominantly secular countries like New Zealand, Norway, and Sweden are thriving examples to the contrary. Religious beliefs may be very easy for humans to adopt, but cultural support for these beliefs reinforces it in succeeding generations. When atheism is the result of lacking cultural support for religious belief, then we have *inCREDulous atheists*—a play on the term "credibility enhancing displays," or CREDs (Henrich 2009), a key concept in cultural learning. InCREDulous atheism is straightforward: When visible cultural cues supporting belief in any specific gods are lacking, nonbelief flourishes.

But sometimes atheism occurs within a majority religious culture. Research has found correlational and causal relationships between higher *analytic thinking* and lower religious belief (Gervais and Norenzayan 2012a; Pennycook, Cheyne, Seli, Koehler, and Fugelsang 2012; Shenhav, Rand, and Greene 2012). Thus, for some people, a general tendency to process information analytically, rather than intuitively, leads to nonbelief. Some (fallaciously) interpret this causal link as proof that atheists are significantly smarter than theists because they have "thought their way out of" religion, but in reality, the size of this effect is quite small and explains only a fraction of the variability in belief in gods. Similarly, small correlations between analytic thinking and religious disbelief do not imply—contra some arguments that religion is an intuitive default (Atran and Norenzayan 2004; Barrett 2000; Bloom 2007; Boyer 2001, 2008)—that atheism is cognitively unnatural or requires significant cognitive effort to overcome. Rather, analytic thinking is one factor that, in some contexts, might bias some individuals toward reduced religiosity.

SUMMING UP THE TYPES

To take hold, belief in supernatural agents has many necessary but insufficient factors. That is, without key cognitive mechanisms religious belief may be impossible, but the presence of these cognitive mechanisms does not guarantee belief. Mentalizing and other mental faculties are generally a minimum, but without the right motivational factors and cultural support, belief in a god or gods can still fail to take hold. Even when these areas are satisfied, analytic atheism can result, overriding the intuitive and culturally reinforced beliefs.

No empirical research has yet been conducted to determine if, in fact, these different types of disbelief yield different reactions and stereotypes when compared directly to one another. Thus, it is difficult to say anything definitive about whether tailoring stereotype-reducing techniques to the specific type of atheism would make a difference. Future research on anti-atheist prejudice would benefit by considering the possibility that attitudes toward atheists may differ depending on the type of atheist in question. It is currently unknown, for example, whether religious individuals distrust lifelong Scandinavian atheists as much as they distrust people who opted out of religion at a later age.

CONSEQUENCES OF THE STIGMA

AGGRESSION TOWARD ATHEISTS

Empirical work has shown that people are more aggressive toward atheists. In one study in which participants were given the opportunity to stab a voodoo doll, more proxy violence was directed at atheists than at any other group (Ng, Chester, and Gervais Unpublished data). In this experiment, participants were asked to put 51 pins in the dolls, as indicated on a slider from 0 to 51 on the screen. When shown multiple dolls said to represent a number of different groups, participants were more willing to stick a great number of pins in a voodoo doll representing an atheist than in voodoo dolls representing a religious ingroup (Christian), a religious outgroup (Muslim), and a disliked outgroup (gay men) (Ng, Chester, and Gervais Unpublished data).

In follow-up studies, Ng and his colleagues found that anti-atheist aggression, as measured by the number of pins stabbed into a representative voodoo doll, was highest when the hypothetical atheist in question described to participants was engaging in antireligious activities as compared to when they were engaging in pro-atheist (but not antireligious) activities and the control about campus parking issues. This is an important point: negative reactions to atheists do not seem to stem from, or be exacerbated by, atheists promoting their own worldviews. Rather, the perception that atheists are antireligious spurs negative reactions and potential violence. As atheist social movements gain steam, their ability to effectively reduce stigmatization of atheism will hinge, in part, on the degree to which they can avoid reinforcing negative perceptions of atheists as smug, argumentative, or antireligious.

PRESSURE TO BELIEVE

In view of the stigma associated with lacking religion and the potential discrimination and harm facing those who identify as atheist, it is not surprising that unbelievers may be reluctant to "come out" as such. Despite the decline in belief in gods (Pew 2012, 2015), accurate levels of disbelief are difficult to measure and it is clear that levels of religiosity are being overestimated. In countries like the United States that have religious majorities, there are social desirability concerns about religious beliefs and practices, and people tend to overreport on these topics (e.g., Cox, Jones, and Navarro-Rivera 2014; Hadaway, Marler, and Chaves 1993; Presser and Stinson 1998; Sedikides and Gebauer 2010). For example, when asking people about attending weekly religious services, the self-reported levels of weekly church attendance are anywhere from 83 to 130 percent higher than what churches report their attendance levels are, which in turn are overestimated as well (Hadaway et al. 1993; Hadaway, Marler, and Chaves 1998). Investigations of actual church attendance versus polling self-reports have found that the numbers reported by Gallup are double the actual numbers (Hadaway and Marler 2005).

What accounts for this gap? Why do people feel the need to overstate their level of religiosity and participation in religious services and activities? With topics discussed in this chapter in mind, it becomes clearer why people would feel pressure to give at least the appearance of being fairly religious, even if they are not. If atheists lack moral knowledge because of their lack of beliefs, and furthermore lack motivation to act morally without the reinforcer of a supernatural watcher, doing the opposite (or at least claiming to) might yield the opposite perception from others. Because of this perception that religion and/or belief in a god is required to be good, social desirability motivations will lead people to overclaim these elements of their belief. Thus, when trying to accurately measure religious belief, explicit measures such as self-reports of religiosity or church attendance will often be positively biased.

How, then, can we accurately gauge levels of religious belief? For large-scale polling, a couple of interesting techniques can address this issue. One such technique is the unmatched count technique (UCT; see also Coutts and Jann 2011; Raghavarao and Federer 1979). UCT involves giving two separate groups of people a list of neutral items (e.g., "I own a cat," "I know how to ride a motorcycle"). In one of these groups, an additional sensitive item is included. In both groups, rather than indicating each item that is true for them, the participants give a total count for the list (e.g., "6/10 are true for me"). Then the averages of the two groups are compared. Since the second group has the same list, plus one item, the two averages can be compared to see the base rates of that additional, sensitive item without having any individual participant having to directly disclose whether or not the sensitive item is true of them. This technique has been used on a variety of socially undesirable behaviors, such as illicit drug use, spousal abuse, and other such crimes.

Gervais and Najle employed this technique in a large, nationally representative sample to ascertain levels of religious disbelief in the United States. Preliminary analyses suggest that, as hypothesized, indirectly measured atheism rates using the UCT were considerably higher than straightforward self-reports suggest. Indeed, this data suggests that roughly 30 percent of American adults do not believe in God—a stark deviation from the roughly 11 percent figure generated by self-reports in nationally representative telephone surveys conducted by Gallup and Pew. Additionally, it implies that a large proportion (perhaps 30 to 50%) of Americans who do not believe in God will fail to report this disbelief, even in anonymous online surveys. The UCT measure highlights the importance and utility of an alternative to explicit measures of religious belief. The results above show that even in anonymous surveys and polls, participants and respondents are feeling the pressure to respond in socially desirable ways, despite the inherent anonymity allowed to them. The social pressure to appear religious in America is not just an idle curiosity. Basic theory on the basis of religious cognition advances only inasmuch as it can accurately predict variability in belief and disbelief (Norenzayan and Gervais 2013). If self-reported disbelief drastically understates the actual prevalence of atheism, different methods are needed to obtain estimates of unbiased atheism prevalence.

STEREOTYPE REDUCTION

Atheism involves an interesting form of stigma and prejudice because, like sexual orientation or political ideology, it is a concealable identity. This presents something of a challenge when employing common prejudice-reducing techniques, such as simulated social contact.

Chapter 13: Dislike of and Discrimination Against Atheists and Secular People

In this method, an individual holding a negative prejudice against a certain group is asked to imagine interacting with a member of this group and, most importantly, having the interaction be a positive one. Even just imagining a positive interaction like this can significantly reduce the prejudice originally felt (Crisp and Turner 2009). The positive nature of the interaction is the key to this technique. However, with atheists, this technique does not work in its simplest, most common form. Participants in one such experiment reported being unable to even imagine having positive interaction with an atheist (LaBouff 2014). The concealability of atheism may have been part of the problem, as participants explained that in order to become aware of the individual being an atheist, they must have exposed themselves in some unpleasant way or another as an atheist. Further instructions had to be given to participants beyond the standard used in simulated social contact in order to negate the assumption that knowing someone is an atheist automatically meant that the atheist had been derogatory or inflammatory in some way (i.e., an atheist may only be known to someone after the individual mentions his or her belief in a god and the atheist ridicules the individual for the belief, highlighting their own lack of belief). However, once these elaborated instructions were given, the participants were able to reap the benefits of the imagined interactions, though to a limited extent.

Another potential way to mitigate anti-atheist prejudice is to address the source of the stereotypes. Because much of anti-atheist prejudice stems from a perception of atheists as untrustworthy owing to their lack of moral knowledge, which is in turn due to their lack of religious instruction, perhaps changing the perception that morality is not an innate facet of human development may help break that connection. Rather than being a uniquely human or particularly religious phenomenon, primatologists have shown that (at least proto-) morality is present in our primate relatives (De Waal and Waal 2013). Thus, making this fact salient to individuals may decrease their perception that atheists cannot be moral because of their lack of religion. Unfortunately, participants who read about the origins of morality in primates or innate morality in preverbal infants did not show differences in anti-atheist sentiments despite their increased understanding of how innate morality is (Mudd, Najle, Ng, and Gervais under review). The manipulation had the intended effect on perceptions of the nature of morality, but it did not reduce antipathy toward atheists. One possible explanation for this finding is that the participants experienced a disconnect between what they learned in the lab setting and what they felt about atheists on a more implicit level. Another possible explanation is that learning about the supposed innateness of morality was not enough to absolve atheists. For instance, while a participant may comfortably accept that babies and chimpanzees have some sense of morality, they nonetheless assume that atheists have been corrupted from their originally moral baby selves by the evils of society. More research would be needed before conclusively stating why this method did not help reduce perceptions of atheists as immoral.

One method that has had success involves reminding individuals of the relative prevalence of atheists in the real world. When people are told that atheists are in fact quite prevalent already, anti-atheist prejudice declines as compared to telling people that there are fewer atheists than they might think (Gervais 2011). This seems to stem from the idea that their perception of atheists as inherently and necessarily immoral leads to negative outcomes for individuals and humanity in general. Learning that, in fact, atheists are successfully navigating in their community and peacefully coexisting without wreaking havoc, then perhaps they are considered to be not as bad as originally thought. This method is promising because it would be easy to implement on a wide scale, with the scope of reach increasing as atheists "come out" to their community and friends. That being said, it is understandable

RELIGION: BEYOND RELIGION

Chapter 13: Dislike of and Discrimination Against Atheists and Secular People

that atheists might be reluctant to reveal their religious disbelief before being able to obtain confirmation of their acceptability. Unfortunately, in that respect it can end up being tautological, with atheists remaining in the closet perpetuating the prejudice and discrimination that is keeping them hidden while their coming out might reduce these sentiments. In the meantime, boosting explicit awareness of the civility, cooperation, and lower crime rates existing in largely nonreligious countries like Finland and New Zealand may help hasten the coming out process.

Further research is necessary to explore other ways to reduce stereotypes. One potential avenue for study is to look further into the influences and origins of morality. If theists are reminded that their own morals are based on the "whims" of society and not on religious scripture alone (e.g., they no longer stone people for being gay), will their perception of atheists improve? Additionally, does the type of atheism endorsed by a given individual make a difference in how he or she is perceived? Are apostates more or less trustworthy in the eyes of wary theists? Does it matter what religion the apostates came from before losing faith, or is an ex-Muslim atheist the same as an ex-Baptist atheist? Is a Scandinavian individual raised to be an atheist more or less trustworthy than the ex-theist? These questions invite future research.

Summary

By definition, atheists are no more a group than any other negatively defined label (e.g., people who don't sew, people who don't watch rugby), being more dissimilar than sharing any particular creed or characteristics. Atheism comes in a variety of different types, with different causes and motivations for religious disbelief, making for even less homogeneity. Nonetheless, they are still widely and actively disliked. Laws prohibiting them from pursuing certain positions or punishing their existence with jail time still exist on the books in many countries. Moreover, public opinion polls show widespread antipathy toward them. This antipathy seems to stem from a belief that humans are intrinsically immoral and need religion to correct for their flaws, with atheists being seen as representative of myriad horrendous moral transgressions and as lacking basic moral knowledge. Attempts to reduce this antipathy have had mixed results, with even commonly used stereotype reduction techniques having failed. Still, other methods have had more success, such as reminders of why atheists still face secular consequences along with everyone else and already exist in large, sometimes concentrated numbers without the eruption of total anarchy. Efforts continue in the literature to fully understand and eventually reduce these anti-atheist sentiments, with hopes of eventually improving theist-atheist cooperation and relations.

Bibliography

Ashtari, Shadee. "Antonin Scalia Says Constitution Permits Court to 'Favor Religion over Non-Religion.'" *MSN.* http://www.msn.com/en-us/news/politics/antonin-scalia -says-constitution-permits-court-to-favor-religion-over -non-religion/ar-BB75vV4.

AtheistBerlin. "USPS Discrimination Against Atheism?" http:// www.atheistberlin.com/atheist/?study.

Atran, Scott, and Ara Norenzayan. "Religion's Evolutionary Landscape: Counterintuition, Commitment, Compassion, Communion." *Behavioral and Brain Sciences* 27, no. 6 (2004): 713–730.

Barrett, Justin L. "Exploring the Natural Foundations of Religion." *Trends in Cognitive Sciences* 4, no. 1 (2000): 29–34.

Barrett, Justin L. "The Relative Unnaturalness of Atheism: On Why Geertz and Markusson Are Both Right and Wrong."

Religion, 40, no. 3 (2010): 169–172. doi: 10.1016/j.religion.2009.11.002.

Bateson, Melissa, Luke Callow, Jessica R. Holmes, Maximilian L. Redmond Roche, and Daniel Nettle. "Do Images of 'Watching Eyes' Induce Behaviour That Is More Pro-social or More Normative? A Field Experiment on Littering." PLoS ONE 8, no. 1 (2013): e82055. doi:10.1371/journal.pone.0082055.

Bateson, Melissa, Daniel Nettle, and Gilbert Roberts. "Cues of Being Watched Enhance Cooperation in a Real-World Setting." *Biology Letters,* 2, no. 3 (2006): 412–414.

Bloom, Paul "Religion, Morality, Evolution." *Annual Review of Psychology* 63 (2012): 179–199.

Bloom, Paul "Religion Is Natural." *Developmental Science* 10, no. 1 (2007): 147–151.

Boyer, Pascal "Being Human: Religion: Bound to Believe?" *Nature* 455, no. 7216 (2008): 1038–1039.

Boyer, Pascal *Religion Explained: The Evolutionary Origins of Religious Thought.* New York: Basic Books, 2001.

Bulger, Matthew. "Unelectable Atheists: U.S. States That Prohibit Godless Americans from Holding Public Office." http://americanhumanist.org/HNN/details/2012-05-unelectable-atheists-us-states-that-prohibit-godless.

Cook, Corey L., Florette Cohen, and Sheldon Solomon. "What If They're Right about the Afterlife? Evidence of the Role of Existential Threat on Anti-Atheist Prejudice." *Social Psychological and Personality Science* 6, no. 7 (September 2015): 840–846.

Cottrell, Catherine A., and Steven L. Neuberg. "Different Emotional Reactions to Different Groups: A Sociofunctional Threat-Based Approach to 'Prejudice.'" *Journal of Personality and Social Psychology* 88, no. 5 (2005): 770.

Coutts, Elisabeth, and Ben Jann. "Sensitive Questions in Online Surveys: Experimental Results for the Randomized Response Technique (RRT) and the Unmatched Count Technique (UCT)." *Sociological Methods and Research* 40, no. 1 (2011): 169–193.

Cox, Daniel, Robert P. Jones, and Juhem Navarro-Rivera. "I Know What You Did Last Sunday: Measuring Social Desirability Bias in Self-Reported Religious Behavior, Belief, and Identity." Washington, DC: Public Religion Research Institute, 2014.

Crandall, Christian S., Amy Eshleman, and Laurie O'Brien. "Social Norms and the Expression and Suppression of Prejudice: The Struggle for Internalization." *Journal of Personality and Social Psychology* 82, no. 3 (2002): 359.

Crisp, Richard J., and Rhiannon N. Turner. "Can Imagined Interactions Produce Positive Perceptions?: Reducing Prejudice through Simulated Social Contact." *American Psychologist* 64, no. 4 (2009): 231.

De Waal, Frans, and Frans B. Waal. *The Bonobo and the Atheist: In Search of Humanism among the Primates*: New York: Norton, 2013.

Didyoung, Justin, Eric Charles, and Nicholas James Rowland. "Non-theists Are No Less Moral than Theists: Some Preliminary Results." *Secularism and Nonreligion* 2 (2013): 1–20.

Edgell, Penny, Joseph Gerteis, and Douglas Hartmann. "Atheists as 'Other': Moral Boundaries and Cultural Membership in American Society." *American Sociological Review* 71, no. 2 (2006): 211–234.

Evans, Robert "Atheists Face Death in 13 Countries, Global Discrimination: Study." *Reuters.* http://www.reuters.com/article/2013/12/10/us-religion-atheists-idUSBRE9B900G20131210.

Gervais, Will M. "Everything Is Permitted? People Intuitively Judge Immorality as Representative of Atheists." *PloS one* 9 (4): e92302. doi:10.1371/journal.pone.0092302, 2014a.

Gervais, Will M. "Finding the Faithless: Perceived Atheist Prevalence Reduces Anti-atheist Prejudice." *Personality and Social Psychology Bulletin* 37, no. 4 (2011): 543–556.

Gervais, Will M. "Good for God? Religious Motivation Reduces Perceived Responsibility for and Morality of Good Deeds." *Journal of Experimental Psychology* 143, no. 4 (August 2014b): 1616–1626.

Gervais, Will M. "Perceiving Minds and Gods: How Mind Perception Enables, Constrains, and Is Triggered by Belief in Gods." *Perspectives on Psychological Science* 8, no. 4 (2013): 380–394.

Gervais, Will M., and Ara Norenzayan. "Analytic Thinking Promotes Religious Disbelief." *Science* 336, no. 6080 (2012a): 493–496.

Gervais, Will M., and Ara Norenzayan. "Like a Camera in the Sky? Thinking about God Increases Public Self-Awareness and Socially Desirable Responding." *Journal of Experimental Social Psychology* 48, no. 1 (2012b): 298–302.

Gervais, Will M., and Ara Norenzayan. "Reminders of Secular Authority Reduce Believers' Distrust of Atheists." *Psychological Science* 23, no. 5 (2012c): 483–491.

Gervais, Will M., and Maxine B. Najle. (Unpublished data). "Honest Atheism Rates: Unbalanced Count Technique to Measure Rates of Nonbelief."

Gervais, Will M., Azim F. Shariff, and A. Norenzayan. "Do You Believe in Atheists? Distrust Is Central to Anti-atheist Prejudice." *Journal of Personality and Social Psychology* 101, no. 6 (2011): 1189.

Gray, Kurt, and Daniel M. Wegner. "Blaming God for Our Pain: Human Suffering and the Divine Mind." *Personality and Social Psychology Review* 14, no. 1 (2010): 7–16.

Hadaway, C. Kirk, and Penny Long Marler. "How Many Americans Attend Worship Each Week? An Alternative Approach to Measurement." *Journal for the Scientific Study of Religion* (2005): 307–322.

Hadaway, C. Kirk, and Penny Long Marler, and M. Chaves. "Overreporting Church Attendance in America: Evidence That Demands the Same Verdict." *American Sociological Review* (1998): 122–130.

Hadaway, C. Kirk, and Penny Long Marler, and M. Chaves. "What the Polls Don't Show: A Closer Look at US Church Attendance." *American Sociological Review* (1993): 741–752.

Henrich, Joseph. "The Evolution of Costly Displays, Cooperation and Religion: Credibility Enhancing Displays and Their Implications for Cultural Evolution." *Evolution and Human Behavior* 30, no. 4 (2009): 244–260.

Human Rights Watch (HRW). "Saudi Arabia: New Terrorism Regulations Assault Rights." *Human Rights Watch*. http://www.hrw.org/news/2014/03/20/saudi-arabia-new-terrorism-regulations-assault-rights.

Inbar, Yoel, David A. Pizarro, Joshua Knobe, and Paul Bloom. "Disgust Sensitivity Predicts Intuitive Disapproval of Gays." *Emotion* 9, no. 3 (2009): 435.

International Humanist and Ethical Union (IHEU). "You Can Be Put to Death for Atheism in 13 Countries Around the World." http://iheu.org/you-can-be-put-death-atheism-13-countries-around-world.

Jillette, Penn, interview by Ron Bennington. *Penn Jillette Rapes All the Women He Wants To/Interviewer: R. Bennington*. http://www.theinterrobang.com.

LaBouff, Jordan. *Imagining Atheists*. Paper presented at the Fifteenth Annual Meeting of The Society for Personality and Social Psychology, Austin, TX. Preconference Talk, https://www.youtube.com/watch?v=B-tcCD292vo, 2014.

Mazza, Ed. "Phil Robertson of 'Duck Dynasty' Reveals Bizarre Atheist Rape and Murder Fantasy." http://www.huffingtonpost.com/2015/03/25/phil-robertson-atheist-rape_n_69 36662.html, 2015a.

Mazza, Ed. "Si Robertson, 'Duck Dynasty' Star, Says Atheists Don't Exist." http://www.huffingtonpost.com/2015/07/07/si-robertson-atheists_n_7741006.html, 2015b.

Mudd, Tommy L., Maxine B. Najle, Ben K. L. Ng, and Will M. Gervais. "Priming the Origins of Morality: Automatic Reduction of Implicit Biases Associated with Atheists." Under review, 2015.

Najle, Maxine B., and Will M. Gervais. *Drugs, Sex, and Minor Speed Infractions: Self-generated Lists of Desirable Activities Prohibited by Religious and Secular Laws.* (Unpublished data-a).

Najle, Maxine B., and Will M. Gervais. "Not Knowing Right from Wrong: Perceptions of Atheists as Lacking Moral Knowledge." (Unpublished data-b).

Ng, Ben K. L., Dave Chester, and Will M. Gervais. "Simulated Aggression toward Atheists and Other Outgroups." (Unpublished data).

Norenzayan, Ara, and Will M. Gervais. "The Origins of Religious Disbelief." *Trends in Cognitive Sciences* 17, no. 1 (January 2013): 20–25.

Norenzayan, Ara, and Ian G. Hansen. "Belief in Supernatural Agents in the Face of Death." *Personality and Social Psychology Bulletin* 32, no. 2 (2006): 174–187.

O'Hair, Madalyn. "Can George Bush, with Impunity, State that Atheists Should Not Be Considered Either Citizens or Patriots?" *The History of the Issue*, 2008. http://www.positiveatheism.org/writ/ghwbush.htm.

Pennycook, Gordon, James Allan Cheyne, Paul Seli, Derek J. Koehler, and Jonathan A. Fugelsang. "Analytic Cognitive Style Predicts Religious and Paranormal Belief." *Cognition* 123, no. 3 (2012): 335–346.

Pew. "America's Changing Religious Landscape." Pew Research Center, 2015.

Pew. "'Nones' on the Rise: One-in-Five Adults Have No Religious Affiliation." *Religion & Public Life*. Pew Research Center, 2012.

Presser, Stanley, and Linda Stinson. "Estimating the Bias in Survey Reports of Religious Attendance." *American Sociological Review* 63, no. 1 (1998): 136–152.

Raghavarao, Damaraju, and Walter T. Federer. "Block Total Response as an Alternative to the Randomized Response Method in Surveys." *Journal of the Royal Statistical Society. Series B (Methodological)* (1979): 40–45.

Rauch, Jonathan. "Let It Be." *The Atlantic* (May 2003). http://www.theatlantic.com/magazine/archive/2003/05/let-it-be/302726.

Ritter, Ryan S., and Jesse Lee Preston. "Gross Gods and Icky Atheism: Disgust Responses to Rejected Religious Beliefs." *Journal of Experimental Social Psychology* 47, no. 6 (November 2011): 1225–1230.

Sedikides, Constantine, and Jochen E. Gebauer. "Religiosity as Self-Enhancement: A Meta-Analysis of the Relation between Socially Desirable Responding and Religiosity." *Personality and Social Psychology Review* 14 (February 2010): 17–36.

Shenhav, Amitai, David G. Rand, and Joshua D. Greene. "Divine Intuition: Cognitive Style Influences Belief in God." *Journal of Experimental Psychology: General* 141, no. 3 (2012): 423.

Tapias, Molly Parker, Jack Glaser, Dacher Keltner, Kristen Vasquez, and Thomas Wickens. "Emotion and Prejudice: Specific Emotions toward Outgroups." *Group Processes and Intergroup Relations* 10, no. 1 (2007): 27–39.

Tversky, Amos, and Daniel Kahneman. "Extensional versus Intuitive Reasoning: The Conjunction Fallacy in Probability Judgment." *Psychological Review* 90, no. 4 (1983): 293.

Wike, Richard, and Juliana Menasce Horowitz. "Views of Religion and Morality." *Global Attitudes & Trends.* Washington, DC: Pew Research Center, 2007.

Zuckerman, Phil. "Atheism, Secularity, and Well-Being: How the Findings of Social Science Counter Negative Stereotypes and Assumptions." *Sociology Compass* 3, no. 6 (2009): 949–971.

Zuckerman, Phil. "Atheism and Societal Health." In *The Oxford Handbook of Atheism,* ed. Stephen Bullivant and Michael Ruse, 497–510. Oxford: Oxford University Press, 2013.

CHAPTER 14

The Psychology of Secularity and Nonreligion

Sean E. Moore
Associate Professor of Psychology, Department of Social Sciences
University of Alberta-Augustana Campus

Jaynita Maru
BSc Candidate, Department of Social Sciences
University of Alberta-Augustana Campus

Starting a discussion about the psychology of secularity and nonreligion can be challenging and often misleading because most of the visible and well-known expressions of disbelief are only thin slices of behavior from the otherwise complex lives of individual nonbelievers.

Most people have seen or heard examples of public intellectuals such as Richard Dawkins (1941–) or Christopher Hitchens (1949–2011) or entertainers such as Bill Maher (1956–), George Carlin (1937–2008), and Ricky Gervais (1961–) promoting "public" atheism or criticizing religion. Many have likely heard of high-profile news stories describing buses displaying atheist slogans, opening of atheist churches, protests over the inclusion or exclusion of religious symbols in public and political spheres, and the horrific stories of atheist bloggers being murdered in religious countries. Although powerfully illustrative, these examples are still too limiting and often don't do justice to the complexities and constantly changing interior mental life of the nonbeliever. They are only the moderately representative *public* expressions of psychological belief systems that differ widely between people, are often in flux, and are not necessarily that visible or detectable.

If forced to choose one example of something that attempts to capture this dynamic psychological process, the example one of us often chooses to start this conversation is an episode of the television series *Community*, titled "The Psychology of Letting Go" (2010). Spurred by the death of one of the main character's mother, the rest of the cast discusses nonreligion and religious beliefs, often exemplifying different types of nonreligion (agnostic, antireligious, spiritual but not religious). Most important to the present discussion, over the span of a single episode, several of the characters experience significant shifts in the nonreligious beliefs they espouse, whereas others bolster their beliefs as they confront threats to their existence and changes in the understanding (or meaning) of their lives. It is this kind of complex psychological experience that we will try to capture and distill in the following pages as we describe our approach to the psychology of nonreligion and secularity.

241

Chapter 14: The Psychology of Secularity and Nonreligion

BACKGROUND

Over the past decade, there has been growing academic interest in developing the interdisciplinary study of secularity and nonreligion. This interest partly has been driven by the dramatic population growth in the number of people claiming to have "no religion" in many Western cultures (e.g., see Pew Research Center 2015; Twenge et al. 2015; Zuckerman 2006) as well as by the everyday discourse concerning secularity and the place of religion in contemporary society (e.g., see Dawkins 2008; Hitchens 2008). Scholars from sociological, anthropological, political studies, and religious studies backgrounds have led this charge by developing a common research terminology, founding a research organization devoted to the topic (Nonreligion and Secularity Research Network), starting a journal for publishing academic papers on the topic (*Secularism and Nonreligion*), and publishing several important compendiums on issues concerning secularity and nonreligion (e.g., see Bullivant and Ruse 2013; Kosmin and Keysar 2007; Martin 2006; Zuckerman 2010). A quick survey of the literature points to one major missing or incomplete piece in this scholarly puzzle. The field of psychology, with its primary emphasis on the empirical study of individual mental and behavioral processes, has largely remained on the sidelines of this academic endeavor. For example, a 2014 content analysis by Brewster and coathors titled "Arrantly Absent: Atheism in Psychological Science from 2001 to 2012" of the existing literature on atheism indicated that psychological scientists had only contributed a small percentage of the work and often on a narrow set of topics such as anti-atheist prejudice. Given that the study of secularism and nonreligion often invokes key concepts that are central to psychological science (e.g., perceptions, attitudes, belief, values, self-identity, etc.), we will try to describe how psychologists can become more centrally involved in developing this interdisciplinary field.

This chapter will try to illustrate that psychologists have much to offer in terms of the study of secularity and nonreligion, particularly when it comes to answering questions about why individuals espouse these types of beliefs as well as how these beliefs affect people's day-to-day lives. We begin by describing the approaches psychologists take to conceptualizing and measuring aspects of the individual's mental life that are relevant to personal belief systems (e.g., beliefs, attitudes, values, worldviews, etc.) and discuss how these approaches might be applied to issues of secularism and nonbelief. Next, we describe some of the important historical contributions that psychologists have made to the study of secularity and nonreligion that serve as illustrations of the utility of psychological research methods and then discuss some of the key findings in the emerging psychological study of nonreligion. We then present a brief discussion of how a typological and multidimensional understanding of nonreligion and secularity may assist in augmenting the existing research on the topic. We will conclude the chapter by reviewing some of the promising areas of research in which the greater focus on individual mental life offered by psychological approaches can enrich our understanding of secularity and nonreligion.

DEFINING SECULARITY AND NONRELIGION

To empirically study the concepts of nonreligion and secularity, psychological scientists typically first start the process by defining these phenomena in a way that permits their measurement (i.e., an operational definition). To aid this process, we adopt the terminology

242   MACMILLAN INTERDISCIPLINARY HANDBOOKS

that interdisciplinary researchers have developed to define both nonreligion and secularity as a starting point, but then narrow our focus using the commonly accepted theoretical approaches and methodologies of psychology.

DEFINING NONRELIGION

For the purposes of this chapter, when we use the term *nonreligion*, we are referring to any aspect of mental activity or behavior that is "*primarily* defined by a relationship of difference to religion" (Lee 2012, 131). This broad definition includes active opposition to religion typically reported by antireligious or atheist individuals and also encompasses the beliefs of individuals who structure their worldviews differently but not necessarily in opposition to religion. For example, this definition encompasses agnostic belief systems, in which individuals primarily define themselves in terms of an epistemology in which definitive knowledge of immaterial or supernatural things connected with religious belief (e.g., deities or the afterlife) is considered unattainable, as well as humanists who found their belief system in values that emphasize the importance of equality and justice in the naturalistic world of human relationships, or freethinkers who tend to emphasize libertarian and independent or autonomous values in defining their belief systems (or worldviews). Importantly, this definition also embraces the beliefs of individuals who may self-identify with a religious affiliation label but who may doubt, question, or outright reject some of the orthodoxies of their faith traditions (e.g., unchurched or nonaffiliated individuals who no longer take part in religious activities but still self-identify with a religion). To assess these varying qualities of individual belief systems, we suggest that psychologists start by using the vast repertoire of self-report tools that psychologists have developed to assess other aspects of psychological functioning, and then expand their analysis using some of the emerging methodologies in psychology to gain a more detailed understanding of nonreligion and secularity.

DEFINING SECULARITY

Although *secularity* is a term that is sometimes used interchangeably to describe nonreligion and is sometimes used by individuals to describe their belief system (e.g., *secular* humanist), we suggest one important clarification for assessment purposes. According to L. Lee in "Research Note: Talking about a Revolution" (2012), secularity is an *ideology* that is defined by its difference to religion, which suggests an underlying political or social expression of secularism. For example, secularity often deals with ideas that religion should be separated or not influence the public and political spheres of life. What this definition implies from a psychological standpoint, which distinguishes mental activity from behavioral processes, is that nonreligion is a more broadly encompassing internal or *private* description of a person's belief system, while secularity is the external or *public* expression of that belief system. For the most part, an individual's internal mental life tends to be consistent with his or her expressed behaviors, especially for those beliefs, attitudes, or values that are important or centrally defining to a person's identity; but as social psychologists and sociologists often point out, these outward expressions also can be affected by the social context in which strong roles, norms, or cultural expectations predominate. Given that a strong stigma is associated with public expression of nonreligiosity, it will be important to distinguish how individuals both privately and publicly express their beliefs.

CONTRIBUTIONS OF PSYCHOLOGICAL THEORIES AND APPROACHES

Perhaps the most important contribution psychological scientists offer the study of secularity and nonreligion is their emphasis on the individual mental perspective on the

Chapter 14: The Psychology of Secularity and Nonreligion

topic. Given the fundamentally subjective nature of belief and widespread person-to-person variability in expression of nonreligious or secular beliefs, such a perspective seems absolutely essential to understanding why people adopt and express a nonreligious or secular identity. Specific fields of psychology offer many useful perspectives on the nature of disbelief. For example, neuroscientists and evolutionary psychologists emphasize how the human brain has evolved specific systems that contribute to the construction of belief, mentalizing of others, and other relatively automatic cultural transmission processes (e.g., see Hermann et al. 2007; Norenzayan and Gervais 2013; Spunt and Lieberman 2013). By examining these various brain-based psychological processes, nonreligion researchers may be able to better understand the types of nonbelief that are associated with activation of differing neural networks as well as how evolutionary pressures may have influenced the development and spread of secular cultural values alongside the more prominent religious values. In addition, cognitive psychology, with its emphasis on the analysis of the interior mental life of the individual (e.g., see Smith and Kosslyn 2007), as well as social psychologists who study social cognition, have contributed many innovative assessment techniques for examining the nature of subjective belief systems, especially those that cannot be assessed directly by verbal self-reporting (e.g., see Gawronski and Payne 2010; Klauer, Voss, and Stahl 2011). These techniques can be used to complement the existing array of self-reports that typically are used to examine nonreligion. Integrating perspectives such as these into secularity and nonreligious studies should support and augment the prevalent sociological, anthropological, and philosophical analyses of secularity and nonreligion.

In addition to the focus on the individual, developmental psychologists have devoted extensive resources to addressing questions of how belief systems develop and change throughout the life span (e.g., see Granqvist and Dickie 2006; Longo and Kim-Spoon 2014; Twenge et al. 2015). These research approaches have documented a number of important findings about how scientific and religious beliefs are socially and culturally transmitted as well as some of the critical developmental time periods in which fluctuations in religiosity and religious disidentification can occur over the lifetime of an individual and generationally across different age cohorts. The growing body of work helps to document that belief systems are remarkably stable over the lifetime of an individual but also that predictable cognitive development and social context variables encourage consistency or belief change. These developmental studies also point to some of the underlying psychological motives and goals that contribute to the increasing secularization of Western culture (e.g., individualism; Twenge et al. 2015) as well as the conversion processes that can lead individuals to no longer identify with a religion (e.g., Longo and Kim-Spoon 2014). By integrating these developmental approaches into secularism studies, researchers may be able to better understand how secular and religious cultures develop, change, or stabilize over the lifetime of the individual.

Another important perspective of psychology comes from the social and personality psychology traditions. These disciplines were strongly shaped by theorists such as Kurt Lewin (1890–1947), who emphasized the importance of studying the person in context (i.e., the person in their environment). An important reminder from this approach to mental life is that individual beliefs may be more or less salient in particular social contexts and that this situational salience may influence how people express their beliefs. In other words, an atheist person will not necessarily navigate their social world by constantly thinking about their rejection of a personal god. It is only in situations that direct their attention to this belief (e.g., their employer refuses to fund birth control as part of their health care plan

244

MACMILLAN INTERDISCIPLINARY HANDBOOKS

because of religious objections) that this belief might become top of mind and has greater potential to affect their behavior (e.g., they may be more likely to file a workplace grievance or lawsuit against their employer). Although a great deal of sociological work has been devoted separately to describing either the individual level expressions of nonreligion (e.g., Zuckerman 2012) or the social contexts in which secular values are expressed (e.g., Zuckerman 2008), less research has been devoted to explicitly understanding how these two facets of nonreligious living are linked. We suggest that a social psychological understanding of nonreligion will help illustrate these important linkages and also help researchers understand when and in what kinds of situations they will have a stronger impact on people's everyday experiences. For example, some research indicates that encouraging individuals to adopt analytical mind-sets decreases belief in gods and supernatural agents (e.g., Gervais and Norenzayan 2012) and increases belief in evolution (e.g., Gervais 2015).

Finally, by introducing social and cultural psychological models that describe how the changes in self and larger cultural context mutually influence one another (e.g., Mutual Constitution Model; see Markus and Kitayama 2010), secularity researchers may be better able to explain how values of independence (see Markus and Kitayama 1991; Triandis 1995) commonly connected to secularism can be reinforced by the larger cultural context that supports individualistic freedoms, choices, and expressions. This assumption about the importance of individualism as a cultural value is connected to some of the twenty-first century philosophical analysis of secular values. As C. Taylor pointed out in his expansive historical and philosophical review of the development of secular societies titled *A Secular Age* (2007), the shift from a pre-Enlightenment view of the self as embedded in society that was necessarily connected to religious activities to the more modern view that the individual can exert choice and control over their religious beliefs and participation was likely an intuitive cultural mind-set that was at the core of the development of secular values. What this analysis implies is that in cultures in which this view of the independent self are prominent (i.e., most Western cultures), levels of nonreligiousness also should be higher. Conversely, despite the increasing globalization pressures toward uniformity in cultures, there should be many cultures in which the self and religion still are viewed as embedded within one another. For example, research in the South Pacific island nation of Tonga, where nearly the entire population reports affiliation with some form of Christianity, illustrates how the Tongan emphasis on collectivism, embeddedness, and interconnection in relationships likely precludes the development of the kind of individualistic nonreligion found in Western cultures (e.g., Moore, Young Leslie, and Lavis 2005; Young Leslie and Moore 2012).

The cultural psychological approach to nonreligion encourages researchers to examine the culturally specific values that may contribute to or discourage secularity (e.g., values of laïcité in Québécois culture in Canada; Melançon 2015) as well as to make comparisons between various cultural groups. As M. Farias notes in "The Psychology of Atheism," presently there are very few direct comparisons of cultures that are more or less religious in terms of how atheism or other types of nonreligion develop and are expressed. By examining the group-based processes and intergroup relations involved in the development of nonreligion, researchers will be able to better understand how group identities contribute to tension between religious and nonreligious individuals.

CONTRIBUTIONS OF PSYCHOLOGICAL RESEARCH METHODS

Although the psychological study of secularity and nonreligion is currently in its infancy, a number of more well-developed streams of empirical psychological inquiry related to these concepts (i.e., psychology of religion and spirituality; Hill and Hood 1999; psychology of attitudes; Robinson, Shaver, and Wrighstman 1991) have helped shape our current understanding and point to important theoretical and methodological contributions that psychologists can offer to the developing field. These same approaches, however, also have hindered the development of an independent psychology of secularity because of some of the theoretical assumptions built into the measurement models of belief and attitudes connected to religion (e.g., the assumption that secular beliefs are negatively correlated or the inverse of religious beliefs on a self-report scale). This approach confuses low religiosity as being the equivalent to nonreligion, even though some evidence indicates that these identities are not one and the same (e.g., Hunsberger and Altemeyer 2004). Unfortunately, this confusion may have led some researchers to inadvertently dismiss *all* psychometric approaches as an invalid starting point for a psychology of secularity.

By re-examining these key methods and topics, we contend that psychologists can help deepen the academic understanding of the diversity in secular and nonreligious orientations and identify the aspects of secular belief systems that operate largely independently of religious worldviews (e.g., naturalistic ontologies, libertarian-freethinking values) as well as those beliefs that overlap with religious and spiritual territories (e.g., rejection-opposition to a god concept, belief in an afterlife, etc.).

SELF-REPORT METHODS

Psychological approaches to measuring individual beliefs or attitudes and subjective understandings of experience with perceived religious events have a long history dating back to the establishment of modern psychology. These methods overlap and share many commonalities with those from other social scientific disciplines, such as sociology. Psychologists such as R. Hill and R. W. Hood (1999) who study religiosity, in particular, have reviewed and compiled the varied arsenal of surveys, questionnaires, structured interviews, and other psychometric tools designed to assess a host of beliefs, values, motives, and behaviors connected to religion and spirituality. This methodological toolbox should have provided a wealth of starting points for conceptualizing a psychology of secularity and nonreligion, but as Farias (2013) pointed out, this tradition actually hindered the study of religious nonbelief. For years, researchers assumed that nonreligion was simply the inverse of religiosity and that the zero point on an underlying quantitative psychological dimension of religiosity validly assessed psychology of the nonreligious. At face value, this may seem like a valid assumption, but several researchers have pointed out that religious nones possess heterogeneous belief systems that may be quite independent of religious worldviews (e.g., Farias 2013; Norenzayan and Gervais 2013; Silver et al. 2014). For example, many measures of religiosity do not tap into values of independence and freethinking, social justice and humanism, or other beliefs related to a naturalistic understanding of the world. As a result, it makes the use of such existing psychometric scales of religiosity largely inappropriate for assessing nonreligious beliefs.

Putting aside all issues of *scale content* (i.e., the types of concepts measured) does not invalidate the more general *research method* (i.e., the mode of measurement) of using self-reports to assess the underlying types or qualities of nonreligion. Developing new question content that assesses the presumed unique qualities of nonreligious belief systems should allow researchers to empirically define and differentiate the variety of worldview beliefs connected to secularism. In fact, the development of self-report rating scales that afford a dimensional understanding of the various beliefs and evaluations existing in secular and nonreligious worldviews (i.e., rating scales that imply a quantitative continuum of belief or subjective endorsement) as well as a statistical description of how these evaluation dimensions are related to one another should provide researchers with an even deeper understanding of the breadth and diversity in people's belief systems. It will help researchers determine whether nonreligious outlooks have a common belief or core. Dimensions of nonreligious belief could be directly compared to measures of religiosity, where appropriate, to test the assumption that certain nonreligious beliefs are negatively correlated with religious ones (e.g., the possible connection of atheism to the rejection of Christianity; Greer and Francis 1992, or the connection of agnosticism to a Quest orientation; Batson and Schoenrade 1991).

EMERGING PSYCHOLOGICAL RESEARCH METHODS

On top of the existing self-report methods, psychologists can enrich secularity and nonreligion studies by examining the perceptions, attitudes, and values that are part of these belief systems using emerging and established methodologies developed in the various fields of neuroscience, cognition, developmental, social, and cultural psychology. For example, a major interest in contemporary social psychology research on attitudes and beliefs has been on identifying the nature and connection of implicit (i.e., unconscious) and explicit (i.e., conscious) evaluations of social objects and how these cognitive processes can affect judgments and behavior. Although the explicit components of belief typically are assessed using conscious self-report techniques, implicit attitudes are assessed using indirect reaction time assessments or by priming manipulations of particular concepts (e.g., belief in a god or supernatural agent). A report by J. Jong, J. Halberstadt, and M. Bluemke titled "Foxhole Atheism, Revisited" (2012) using these kinds of implicit reaction time assessments found that while explicit reports of belief in a God differed between self-labeled religious and nonreligious participants, their implicit beliefs did not differ. Thus, by comparing implicit and explicit secular or nonreligious attitudes, psychologists may provide a more nuanced (and potentially less polarizing) answer to some of the questions about how secular and religious worldviews relate to one another.

In addition to these developing novel implicit measures of nonreligion, we can envision a psychology of secularity and nonreligion that incorporates methods from psychological fields such as the cognitive and social neurosciences. Existing neuroscientific methods such as brain imaging or electrophysiological measures could be used to determine the physiological networks or regions of the brain connected to nonbelief or compare individuals with different types of nonreligious belief systems (e.g., atheists, agnostics, apostates) in terms of their neurocognitive functioning. The longitudinal and cross-sectional study of the development of secularity and nonreligion is another promising area of research (e.g., see Longo and Kim-Spoon 2014; Twenge et al. 2015). By examining the developmental context of nonreligious belief systems and identifying individual, interpersonal, and social-contextual variables that may correlate with different types of nonbelief, psychologists will be able to provide answers that augment some of the sociological analyses of the topic and distinguish different developmental trajectories in people's belief systems. Social psychologists have developed many techniques to examine how situational changes in our lives influence the expression of different beliefs that easily could be adapted to issues of nonreligion and secularity. For example, event-related sampling or other everyday experience techniques, in which individuals report on the their mental and behavioral responses over the course of their day, could be used in secularity and nonreligious studies to determine how prominent or influential nonreligious beliefs are in

Chapter 14: The Psychology of Secularity and Nonreligion

the various everyday contexts people encounter. These methods are not meant to be exhaustive but rather should encourage psychologists to think about how their own research approaches and methods that might be used to develop this emerging interdisciplinary field.

PSYCHOLOGY OF SECULARITY AND NONRELIGION: KEY FINDINGS

Although the empirical study of secularity and nonreligion remains on the fringes of academic psychology, there is actually a long history of its investigation, and psychologists established some of the foundational knowledge on the topic. This section as of 2016, describes some of these groundbreaking studies and highlights some of the recent findings about the correlates of nonreligion.

AN EARLY EXAMPLE OF THE PSYCHOLOGY OF NONRELIGION

Despite the common refrain that nonreligion and secularity studies is a new field, psychological studies of this topic can be found dating back to the early twentieth century. For example, G. B. Vetter and M. Green published "Personality and Group Factors in the Making of Atheists" (1931), one of the first empirical self-report surveys of American atheists that helped to document many of the key demographic and personality characteristics associated with this population. The findings also illustrated some of the possibilities about how nonreligious belief systems develop. For example, they found that their atheist respondents were primarily male, white, urban dwellers, and many of these men lived in the northeast and western United States. They also found respondents reported a diversity of labels for their beliefs systems and that a number of their respondents still attended religious services while professing no religion. One of the more surprising findings they reported was that a large proportion of the atheists were World War I veterans, providing some early evidence against the no-atheists-in-foxholes hypothesis. In terms of socialization and development, this research also helped document that individuals from certain faith backgrounds (Jews, Methodists) were more likely to develop nonreligious thinking (i.e., become apostates), that loss of at least one parent before the age of twenty was common in the atheist sample, and that the process of developing nonreligious beliefs was often a gradual process that often began during the early adulthood years (between the ages of twenty and thirty). In addition, Vetter and Green's study documented many of the predictors of nonbelief documented in other contemporary surveys, including intellectual (i.e., education, "wide" reading), moral (i.e., disgust with religious hypocrisy), and motivational and emotional (i.e., death of a family member) perceived causes, to name a few. Finally, consistent with the twenty-first century research documenting a general public distrust of atheists and prejudice toward nonbelievers, many of the respondents to this survey admitted that they did not publicly avow their nonbelief for fear of it affecting their personal or social lives.

A NEW "GROUNDBREAKING" STUDY IN THE PSYCHOLOGY OF NONRELIGION

Despite the promising start offered by Vetter and Green's (1932) approach, the empirical study of secularity and nonreligion never really took flight in psychological science until the past decade. The majority of research done in the interim was primarily conducted by sociologists and population researchers who examined demographic correlates connected to the *religious none* category (e.g., see Veevers and Cousineau 1980; Vernon 1968; Zuckerman 2006). One of the works that inspired much of the renewed interest in the examination of the underlying psychological dynamics of nonbelievers was R. Hunsberger and

B. Altemeyer's 2006 book *Atheists: A Groundbreaking Study of America's Nonbelievers*, which they personally hailed as the first comprehensive psychological study of American atheists. In their work, Hunsberger and Altemeyer adopted a mixed-methods approach involving a series of surveys and interview questions posed to convenience samples of Canadian and American respondents. They examined the nature of their belief systems and how these were connected with self-reported outcomes such as dogmatism in belief systems, endorsement of zealotry in childhood socialization and education practices, and the extent to which they espoused ethnocentric attitudes toward religious and nonreligious groups. Some of their key findings indicated that the nonreligious tended to be less dogmatic, less zealous, and lower in authoritarianism.

Hunsberger and Altemeyer's work also hinted at the diversity in types of nonbelievers with some of their work comparing the psychological outcomes of "public" atheists who belonged to atheist, humanist, and other formal nonreligious organizations with reports of people they categorized as agnostics and inactive believers. Although most of the nonreligious respondents across these types of individuals reported less dogmatism in their thinking than religious respondents, there were also differences between the nonreligious in terms of their ethnocentrism and zealotry, with avowed public atheists showing slightly more ingroup favoritism and zealotry compared with the private atheists. These patterns of differences between types of nonbelievers points to an important conclusion that many secularity researchers have already highlighted—that nonbelief is a family of heterogeneous belief systems and that these differences in belief systems also have important consequences for psychological functioning. It is because of this foundational concern that we suggest that for psychologists to help advance the understanding of nonreligion, they must first participate in work that compares and contrasts the dimensions of beliefs at the core of nonreligious belief systems, examine how these differences manifest in different psychological predictors and outcomes, and compare these belief systems with religious worldviews.

CORRELATES OF SECULAR AND NONRELIGIOUS BELIEFS

Using these two psychological studies of nonreligion as benchmarks, much of the twenty-first century work on the psychology of secularity has been devoted to examining the belief correlates and psychological dispositions connected (or correlated) with reports of secular or nonreligious beliefs. For example, according to M. Farias and M. Lalljee in "Holistic Individualism in the Age of Aquarius" (2008), in terms of values, nonreligious and secular people tend to emphasize greater individualism, independence, and expression of personal freedoms. They tend to value personal achievement, stimulation, self-direction, universalism, and self-satisfying hedonism more highly; report moral concerns that are more strongly founded around fairness and concern for others; and reject magical beliefs and some of the more otherworldly-transcendent beliefs connected to spirituality. In terms of gender identification, most surveys of nonreligion repeatedly show that males are more likely to report having no religion (e.g., see Galen 2009; Kosmin et al. 2009). This correlation should not be unsurprising, given the wealth of psychological research indicating that masculinity is closely tied to expressions of independence (e.g., see Kashima et al. 1995; Triandis 1989).

A second line of research has demonstrated support for the idea that nonreligion tends to be connected with certain patterns of personality or chronic thinking and evaluation styles (i.e., less dogmatism and zealotry; Altemeyer and Hunsberger 2006). For example, in terms of global personality traits, people low in religiosity have been found to be higher on openness to experience (Galen 2009; Galen and Kloet 2011; Silver et al. 2014). This correlation presumably reflects that nonreligious people tend to adopt a thinking style that supports

Chapter 14: The Psychology of Secularity and Nonreligion

nonconformist thought, opposes authoritarianism, and endorses more politically and civically liberal viewpoints. Supporting this idea, other personality research by V. Saroglou on "Religion and the Five Factors of Personality" (2002) has found that nonreligious people tend to be lower on agreeableness and conscientiousness scales of the Big Five personality model. These latter correlations of nonreligion with agreeableness and conscientiousness have not been documented consistently and have been criticized for confusing low religiosity with nonbelief.

Another consistent pattern of findings originally documented in the foundational studies of nonreligion, which has been replicated in several recent studies (as of 2016), is the link of nonreligion with cognitive styles emphasizing analytical thought and a more general connection to intellectual pursuits. For example, a number of surveys have found that secular and nonreligious individuals tend to report higher levels of educational attainment. Other research has found that individuals low in religiosity tend to be more successful at reaction time and general knowledge and trivia tasks as well as in solving analytical thought problems. Together, these patterns of findings indicate an association of nonreligiosity with certain analytical styles of thinking. An important point about interpretation of all of these correlation patterns is that these kind of correlational designs need to be interpreted cautiously because they may be confusing correlation with causation.

A NEW FRAMEWORK FOR DEVELOPING AND REFINING THE PSYCHOLOGY OF SECULARITY AND NONRELGION

Although these initial results are promising, we suggest that to better understand nonreligion, psychologists need to engage in a research program that examines the diversity and dynamics of belief systems underlying the label *religious none*. The current framework that we use to study the psychology of secularity and nonreligion builds on and expands the use of self-report methods that have been used extensively in psychological research. It assumes nonreligiosity is a family of heterogeneous belief systems that are dynamic and develop in response to changes in the individual, their social context, and their cultural background (see Streib and Klein 2013 for a similar dynamic perspective). This research framework is grounded in some of the developing functional analyses of belief systems connected to twenty-first century theoretical innovations in the areas of the psychology of worldviews, experimental existential psychology, and the psychology of meaning. We use these theories to help us provide a framework for understanding the nature, types, and psychological functions of nonreligious thinking. These perspectives offer an overarching framework for understanding how secular and religious belief systems can be understood as independent belief systems that can produce many of the same psychological outcomes as religious belief. Additional insight from functionalist perspectives developed in the psychology of religion provide insight about the psychological motives underlying worldviews that may be shared in common by secular and religious systems. By engaging in this kind of theoretical development, we hope this kind of work will help researchers move beyond the practice of simple self-labeling to examining the underlying predictors as well as the psychological outcomes that are connected to various secular and nonreligious belief systems.

PSYCHOLOGY OF WORLDVIEWS

By connecting the study of nonreligion to research on worldviews, psychologists can assist secularity researchers in better understanding the multidimensional nature of belief systems as well as the purpose of worldview belief systems. A worldview is a complex set of interrelated beliefs and assumptions about how the world works, including a person's subjective view of how they fit into this psychologically constructed world—in essence, an intuitive philosophy of the world containing ontology, axiology, teleology, praxiology, epistemology, and semiotics. Although not explicitly stated by worldview researchers, presumably these knowledge (or inference) systems evolved in humans as a result of our mind-perceiving and purpose-seeking brains, which presumably underlie and motivate individuals to seek out a sense of meaning, purpose, and identity. These subjective assumptions are often not always conscious but rather have important impacts on how an individual expresses their beliefs and the behavioral choices they make. Worldviews involve multiple facets of psychological functioning that serve as the foundation for an individual's belief systems. For example, M. E. Koltko-Rivera's 2004 literature review of the *worldview* concept illustrated that at least seven major groupings of assumptive worldview beliefs pertain to ideas about human nature, will, cognition, behavior, interpersonal functioning, the nature of truth, and how the world operates. Within these groupings, humans presumably develop a number of more specific assumptions to help them better understand the nature of their existence and their reality. These groupings of belief assumptions have important consequences for an individual's thinking and behavior. In general, researchers assume that worldview-relevant beliefs afford humans a subjective sense of value, purpose, and importance. Because of this privileged or valued status, individuals generally will seek to preserve or maintain their worldview-relevant beliefs and avoid adopting positions that their lives are meaningless. This motivational function will be elaborated further in the next section.

By examining some of the groupings of worldview-relevant beliefs, researchers should be able to develop an understanding of the diversity of secular and religious worldviews that fit into the relevant belief groupings, identify common subtypes of belief systems within the larger category of *nonbelief*, and identify the similarities and differences in secular and religious worldviews. For example, W. M. Norenzayan and A. Gervais's (2013) review of some of the presumed evolutionary origins of disbelief illustrate the utility of this approach. They discussed how doubt, feelings of existential security, apathy toward religion or spirituality, and active questioning of religion can result in different pathways (or types) of nonbelief. Although this is a promising start in developing a classification system, it remains to be seen whether these four categories can be assessed empirically in reports of nonreligious and secular beliefs, whether the four types are independent of one another, and finally whether these four types are functionally independent from belief systems reported by religious individuals. To address these important questions, researchers will need to examine more closely the types of worldview-relevant belief categories that connect to some of these origin categories and develop measures to test whether these types of disbelief can be assessed reliably and shown to be independent belief systems.

PSYCHOLOGICAL FUNCTIONS OF DISBELIEF

Although the psychology of worldviews perspective affords an expanded understanding of the *content* of belief systems that structure human understanding of their own existence, innovations in the areas of experimental existential psychology, psychology of meaning making and maintenance, and functional analyses of belief systems should provide a framework for better understanding the *dynamics* of these beliefs. In particular, these approaches can help researchers understand the development, socialization, stabilization, and change process connected to various worldviews. Psychologists who study meaning making (e.g., Markman et al. 2013) as well as the functional aspects of religious belief (e.g., Hood, Hill, and Spilka 2013; Saroglou 2014) contend that the development of human consciousness and self-awareness drives people to seek a coherent and generally *predictable* understanding of themselves, their relationships, and the world in which they live. These "meaning motivations" commonly are reflected in people's subjective goals or desires to achieve things like knowledge, relatedness, mastery or control, transcendence, and a strong sense of identity that form the core of various belief systems (both religious and nonreligious). Importantly, researchers consider these various psychological needs to be *overdetermined*, which means that such needs can be satisfied by any number of effective solutions (e.g., relatedness can be satisfied by developing closeness with a significant life partner, a best friend, a material object, or a personal god). Thus, people are able to achieve similar outcomes connected to meaning pursuits (e.g., esteem, efficacy, moral responsibility, satisfaction, belonging, understanding, purpose) but accomplish them in different manners. This perspective is consistent with the belief replacement hypothesis described by Farias (2013) in which nonreligious people are thought to replace important meaning-related beliefs traditionally espoused by religionists with beliefs that are more consistent with a nonreligious worldview (e.g., explaining events with naturalistic explanations versus supernatural ones).

We suggest that to better understand the nature and diversity in nonreligious and secular belief systems, psychologists should examine how the religious nones fit into the dimensions of human meaning-making pursuits that have been identified by prior functional analyses of belief systems. By doing so, they will be able to identify both the discontinuities and continuities between religious and nonreligious or secular worldviews. For example, some twenty-first century research suggests that nonreligious people tend to prioritize freedom, independence, and liberal values in terms of relatedness goals; that understanding and purpose goals tend to be framed in terms of analytical, naturalistic, and scientific ontological explanations; and that an endorsement of progress beliefs in the natural world are at the core of transcendence needs of nonreligious individuals. In addition to identifying correlates of nonreligious belief, this functional analysis of nonreligion can help point to the kinds of social contexts in which nonreligiosity will guide people's judgments and behaviors as well as areas in which conflict may arise between the religious and nonreligious. For example, control and mastery concerns often are front and center when large-scale tragedies or natural disasters cause widespread loss of life.

MEANING MAINTENANCE PROCESSES IN PSYCHOLOGICAL WORLDVIEWS

In addition to pointing out how individuals attain a sense of meaning, meaning-maintenance (MM) theorists (Proulx and Inzlicht 2012) and experimental existential (EE) psychologists (Greenberg et al. 2004) also have developed theoretical perspectives to explain how people preserve or change their worldview-relevant beliefs in response to perceived situational *threats* and challenges they might experience. In general, people are motivated to preserve or defend their existing worldviews that have developed through socialization and enculturation processes to combat the potential perception of meaninglessness. According to MM theorists, people tend to *defend* the integrity of their worldviews through strategies such as bolstering their beliefs with supporting evidence (i.e., assimilation), indirectly affirming their perceived personal value with other valued identities (i.e., affirmation), or distancing themselves from troubling information (i.e., abstraction). Although speculative, we suggest that reliance on these differing MM strategies also may be at the core of the

Chapter 14: The Psychology of Secularity and Nonreligion

differences that exist among various nonreligious belief systems. For example, active opposition to religion that characterizes the antireligious sentiments expressed by the New Atheist movement often tends to be grounded in more active assimilation and argumentation strategies that are meant to bolster nonreligious beliefs, whereas individuals who report antipathy, distance, or disregard for religious matters may be using more abstraction-based strategies to preserve meaning in their belief systems by emphasizing the separateness and distance of their beliefs.

TYPOLOGY OF NONBELIEVERS

Perhaps the most important question in understanding the dynamics of secular and nonreligious belief systems is attempting to understand the varying content of these diverse worldviews and determining whether a consistent underlying pattern of beliefs or typology that distinguishes some key qualities of differing nonreligious identities as well as whether these beliefs are separate and independent from religious belief systems. To date, most research has relied on self-labeling to study the different types of nonreligion. Although this approach helps move beyond the simple demographic analysis of individuals who report they have "no religion" and sorts individuals into various categories of nonbelief, some problems with this approach limit its utility.

PROBLEMS WITH NONRELIGIOUS CATEGORICAL SELF-LABELING

First, a categorical analysis implies that nonreligious identity is static and the self-assigned categories may not be sensitive to some of the underlying changes in beliefs that influence self-labeling. Second, awareness is widespread that some elements of nonreligious identity are stigmatized or perceived negatively by the general public. As a result, some nonreligious individuals may be unwilling to assign themselves a specific label because of social desirability concerns. These social desirability concerns may explain why generally a greater number of people endorse "no religion" or "nonaffiliation" on surveys of religious identification, such as those by the Pew Research Center (2015), compared with those who self-label with terms like atheist or agnostic. Third, the self-labeling approach often assumes that researchers and respondents share the same understandings of a label and its meanings in terms of self-identification. Although researchers can provide definitions of the belief systems to respondents, this does not necessarily guarantee that respondents agree or identify with the definitions they are provided. Illustrating this problem in *Amazing Conversions* (2006), Altemeyer and Hunsberger showed that a small percentage of people who self-identified as atheists still reported believing in some form of supernatural agent even though this belief seems to contradict the core definition of atheist belief systems (i.e., belief in a god). Finally, the single-label approach reduces a complex worldview belief system with a variety of interconnecting assumptions, attitudes, values, and beliefs to a single label that may be unsatisfactory to researchers and respondents alike in capturing the multidimensionality of nonreligiosity.

EMERGING TYPOLOGIES OF NONBELIEF

Because of these issues with self-labeling, a number of researchers as of 2016 have attempted to develop classification systems or typologies that are more sensitive to the variety and diversity of themes and dimensions underlying nonreligious belief systems using both of inductive and deductive approaches. In "Analytic Thinking Promotes Religious Disbelief"

RELIGION: BEYOND RELIGION

253

(2013), Gervais and Norenzayan used an evolutionary framework to interpret prior research findings and identify how certain evolved cognitive, motivational, and cultural processes in the brain may be responsible for four different types of religious disbelief. On the basis of their literature review, they identified four independent evolutionary origins of nonreligion that presumably are connected to different types of nonbelief expressions (see Figure 14.1). Although a promising theoretical foundation, to date, there have not been any attempts to empirically validate the existence of these categories.

In another recent study, "The Six Types of Nonbelief: A Qualitative and Quantitative Study of Type and Narrative" (2014), Silver and coauthors used qualitative thematic analysis to derive six types of nonreligion from interviews with religious nones and then verified these categories with a larger sample of online survey respondents by asking them to choose one of these six categories to define their belief system (see Figure 14.1). Notably, some of these

Theoretical "Types" of Nonreligion and Secularity

Nonreligion Type & Description	Norenzayan & Gervais (2013)	Silver et al. (2014)	Moore et al. (in preparation) Study 1	Moore et al. (in preparation) Study 2
1. Intellectual nonbeliever				
Actively opposes religious beliefs via embracing analytical thinking	√	√		√
2. Indifferent nonbeliever				
Apathy and general disengagement from religion due to nonreligious upbringing	√	√	√	√
3. Culturally supported nonbeliever				
Strong secular institutions promote disengagement or apathy	√			
4. Uncomprehending nonbeliever				
Inability to mentalize/envision deities or transcendent states	√			
5. Activist nonbeliever				
Promotes humanist values as alternative to religion		√		
6. Seeking unbeliever				
Actively questions religion but embraces spiritual uncertainty		√	√	
7. Antireligious nonbeliever				
Aggressively opposes all forms of religious institutions and beliefs		√	√	√
8. Spiritual but not religious				
Embraces traditions of religion but rejects formal affiliation		√	√	
9. Freethinking nonbeliever				
Prefers forming own opinions and opposes accepting institutionally imposed doctrines				√

Figure 14.1. *Theoretical "types" of nonreligion and secularity.* SEAN E. MOORE. ADAPTED FROM MOORE, 2016.

categories that were empirically derived appear to overlap with Gervais and Norenzayan's categories (e.g., an indifferent category, an intellectual or analytically based category), but a number of important classification types also diverged (see Figure 14.1). In addition to these differing definitions, a number of important empirical questions were not addressed such as the relationship of the types that could not be investigated because the quantitative study participants were forced to choose one label for their belief systems. Because these categories were treated as separate qualitative categories, there is no way to determine how they might be related to one another, nor how they may be connected to dimensions of religious belief. To investigate these kinds of questions, a dimensional approach to assessing nonbelief is likely necessary.

A PROVISIONAL DIMENSIONAL TYPOLOGY OF NONBELIEF

To examine the similarities and differences in worldview-relevant beliefs endorsed by nonreligious individuals, our research attempted to adapt the common psychometric methods and analytical tools developed by psychologists to assess the underlying dimensional qualities of nonbelief and secularity (e.g., Hoyle and Leary 2009). To accomplish this goal, we developed a large pool of self-report statements representing different types of nonbelief (Moore, Toor, and Mushayandebvu forthcoming) based on reviews of the literature as well as through group discussion by the research team about the varying dimensions of beliefs that may account for nonreligious worldviews. We then transformed these statements into rating scales questions (i.e., Likert-types scales). Next, we administered initial versions of these nonreligion questionnaires to large convenience samples of university undergraduates on two university campuses, one sample of students from a large urban-based campus (Study 1), and a second sample from a small, rural-based liberal arts campus (Study 2). The samples consisted of those who self-labeled as nonreligious as well as those who identified a religious affiliation to determine whether there were any expressions of nonreligious beliefs reported by the religiously affiliated. We then used exploratory factor analytic techniques to identify the number of statistical types (or factors) present in the reports and to eliminate questions that did not distinguish these types.

The results of this initial work were to our knowledge the first attempt to assess the multidimensional nature of nonreligion using self-report survey methods (see Figure 14.1 for summary). The analysis not only provided some support for other conceptualizations of nonreligion typologies but also answered questions about the connections between religious and nonreligious belief systems. In terms of the types of nonreligion that emerged in the factor analysis, four distinguishable groupings across both samples were partially or completely independent of one another. Interestingly, the factors that emerged across the two samples were slightly different in structure of the items involved. With the urban campus respondents, the factors appeared to assess antireligious atheism, agnosticism-seeking, nonreligious but spiritual beliefs, and indifferent-inexperienced nonreligiosity. With the rural students, antireligious atheism and indifferent-inexperienced factors also emerged, but the other two factors reflected analytical atheism and independent freethinkers. Explanations for these differences in factor structure currently are speculative. Because this was an initial attempt to assess the multidimensional characteristics of nonreligion, further research on the topic is needed. To better understand the variability in types of dimensions involved, we are currently in the process of collecting a larger, cross-national sample of respondents and are assessing aspects of each respondent's social context that might predict differences in their expression of nonreligion (Moore and Maru, in

Chapter 14: The Psychology of Secularity and Nonreligion

progress). This kind of research opens up a number of important avenues of research that connect this kind of typological analysis to some of the key findings that have been documented with the some of the research on nonreligion.

APPLICATIONS AND EXTENSIONS OF THE DIMENSIONAL-TYPOLOGICAL APPROACH TO NONRELIGION AND SECULARITY

DEVELOPMENTAL STUDIES OF NONBELIEVER WORLDVIEWS

One way in which we envision that this kind of psychological approach can broaden the understanding of nonreligion is by connecting the types of nonreligiousness to existing developmental psychology methodologies that permit examination of the dynamics of worldview development across the life span (i.e., longitudinal studies, cross-sectional studies, event sampling studies). For example, in longitudinal studies, researchers could attempt to examine whether the differing types of nonreligious worldviews have predictable developmental trajectories or could examine how important life events affect the stability or change in the expression of different types of nonreligion. Researchers could seek to determine whether critical events encourage specific kinds of nonreligious thinking (e.g., parental loss and its connection to atheism, agnosticism, humanism).

In addition, developmental studies of the types of nonbelief and secularity can identify the levels of stability and change that may occur across the spectrum of nonbelief types. It may be the case that certain types of nonbelief show greater stability because there is greater worldview defensiveness, especially in belief dimensions involving strong or emotionally arousing convictions (e.g., antireligious atheism). Presumably, as T. Proulx and M. Inzlicht write in "The Five 'A's of Meaning Maintenance" (2012), these desires to hold strong and stable worldviews result in individuals using MM and fluid compensation strategies that work to preserve prior important beliefs. Longitudinal and experimental studies could examine how different types of existential challenges (e.g., mortality salience; Greenberg et al. 1997) or compensation strategies (e.g., instructions to think analytically; Gervais 2015) affect the types of beliefs reported by nonreligious individuals.

PREDICTORS AND CORRELATES OF TYPES OF NONBELIEF

Another important area of nonreligion research that could benefit from integration within this typological approach to nonbelief is research that examines psychological correlates or predictors of belief systems. This type of research approach typically has assessed some other psychological trait or process (e.g., personality, analytical thinking, values, morals) and determined its connection to nonreligious or secular beliefs, with some expectation that the underlying psychological aptitude preceded the development of nonreligiosity. Importantly, this developing body of research has documented many connections between psychological dispositions and expressions of disbelief.

Of greatest relevance to the current discussion in this chapter, the majority of research that has examined these predictors and correlates of nonreligion and secularity has used either categorical self-labeling of nonreligious belief systems or comparisons of people who report having no religion with individuals who profess some form of religion. To date, there have not been any efforts to examine how the multidimensional expressions of nonreligion may affect the patterns of correlations that are observed. This approach to understanding religion and secularity assumes some level of diversity in nonreligious belief systems and

Chapter 14: The Psychology of Secularity and Nonreligion

identifying the association of types of beliefs with various psychological correlates and predictors may provide more fine-grained and conditional understanding of the predictors of nonreligion. Some researchers (e.g., Galen 2009; Galen and Kloet 2011) have noted that some of the previously documented associations do not hold when several categories of nonbelief are examined. These findings also point to specific beliefs that strengthen a general nonreligious or secular worldview. For example, research by Gervais and Norenzayan (2012) has shown that priming or reminding people of specific belief dimensions (e.g., analytical thinking) can strengthen nonreligious convictions. By examining the multidimensional basis on nonbelief, it is hoped that researchers might be able to identify which patterns of beliefs are connected to specific psychological processes. Once identified, specific beliefs could be studied experimentally to determine how they might cause changes in nonreligious self-identification. These kinds of experimental studies would help address the causality problem identified by prior researchers and may also help nonreligious researchers develop greater understanding of the dynamics and development of different nonreligious belief systems.

PSYCHOLOGICAL OUTCOMES CONNECTED TO TYPES OF NONRELIGION

Other correlates of nonreligion and well-being have been treated as consequences or outcomes of adopting and expressing nonreligiosity. The following sections describe some of these key outcomes and explains how a dimensional typology might augment understanding of the topic.

Mental Health, Life Satisfaction, and Well-Being. One important nonreligion research area that may benefit from a more detailed typological analysis is the research that examines the mental health and well-being consequences of nonreligion and secularity belief expression. This work was inspired by the weight of evidence documenting that highly religious people tend to report significant but marginally higher levels of life satisfaction and other forms of positive mental well-being and health outcomes compared with other people who report less religiosity (aka the discontented unbeliever hypothesis; Diener, Tay, and Myers 2011; Hackney and Sanders 2003; Koenig and Larson 2001). Significantly, this work was criticized by nonreligion researchers for conflating and confusing the strength of religious belief with nonreligious or secular beliefs (Galen and Kloet 2011; Mochon, Norton, and Ariely 2011; Weber et al. 2012). These critics often point out that nonreligious people with committed beliefs or strong foundations in their belief systems do not necessarily show the pattern of less psychological adjustment portrayed by prior work. Instead, it is confusion, questioning, or lack of strength and commitment to one's worldview that predicts lower levels of psychological adjustment. This interpretation is consistent with the widely documented effect showing belief inconsistencies tend to result in increased psychological discomfort (i.e., cognitive dissonance; Festinger 1957). Incorporation of dimensional self-report scales in combination with longitudinal designs might allow for a closer examination of the dynamic changes in specific nonreligious beliefs that may be connected to improvements or declines in mental health.

Public Perceptions of Nonbelievers. One final use of this kind of psychological framework for understanding the types of nonreligion that exist is in considering how it might be extended to the growing corpus of research that examines the nature and impact of anti-atheist prejudice (e.g., see Cragun et al. 2012; Doane and Elliot 2015; Gervais 2013; Gervais et al. 2011). Although this research focuses more on public perceptions or metaperceptions of the atheists, future research might consider examining how expressions

RELIGION: BEYOND RELIGION

257

Chapter 14: The Psychology of Secularity and Nonreligion

of different types of nonreligion (i.e., agnosticism, freethinking, humanism) are viewed by the public. Although the specific public expressions of disbelief in a god seems to be at the core of the stigmatization, distrust, and fear connected to these prejudices, it may be the case that other expressions of nonbelief are less stigmatized or even protective to the individual expressing them. For example, perhaps humanism, in its foundational expressions of values focusing on fairness, social justice, and promoting the human condition is a nonreligious belief system that is viewed less negatively and may even promote bonding and the formation of healthy relationships that can enhance a person's well-being.

Summary

In this chapter, we have attempted to describe how some of the psychological approaches to understanding individual thought and behavior can be successfully applied to the topic of nonreligion. We hope that in doing so, psychologists will be able to contribute unique perspectives on the topic that will assist in building and expanding the interdisciplinary study of nonreligion and secularity. The first part of this chapter attempted to provide a thumbnail sketch of how some of the prominent psychological approaches to understanding individual belief systems or worldviews (e.g., cognitive neuroscience, developmental, social, cultural psychological) can enhance our understanding of the content and function of nonreligious beliefs. We also described some of the key findings that researchers have already documented about the psychology of secularity and nonreligion.

In the latter part of this chapter, we described one specific theoretical and methodological approach that we have used in our research. This approach is founded in the psychological theories that attempt to describe the nature and function of psychological belief systems or worldviews. In adopting this approach, we are assuming an underlying dynamic characteristic of all belief (and nonbelief) systems in which an individual's worldview-relevant beliefs develop and change in relation to important social and cultural influences present in their inhabited psychological context. Methodologically, it relies on quantitative self-report scales that permit the assessment of multiple expressions of nonreligious belief that sometimes overlap and are interconnected with one another but at other times are independent or separate expressions of a diverse and subjective view of the world. By using these types of methods, psychologists can help nonreligion researchers grasp a better understanding of the key types of nonbelief as well as an understanding of how multiple belief dimensions help to define these typologies. The final part of the chapter spent some time discussing how this typological understanding has been used in our research and how it might be applied to other topics that have been investigated by nonreligion and secularity researchers.

Bibliography

Altemeyer, Robert, and Bruce Hunsberger. *Amazing Conversions: Why Some Turn to Faith and Others Abandon Religion.* Amherst, NY: Prometheus Books, 1997.

Batson, C. Daniel and Patricia A. Schoenrade. "Measuring Religion as a Quest: 2.) Reliability Concerns." *Journal of Scientific Study of Religion* 30 (1991): 430–447.

Beit-Hallahmi, Benjamin. "Atheists: A Psychological Profile." In *The Cambridge Companion to Atheism*, edited by Michael Martin, 300–317. New York: Cambridge University Press, 2006.

Brewster, Melanie E., Matthew A. Robinson, Riddhi Sandil, Jessica Esposito, and Elizabeth Geiger. "Arrantly

Absent: Atheism in Psychological Science from 2001 to 2012." *The Counseling Psychologist* 42 (2014): 628–663.

Bullivant, Stephen, and Michael Ruse. *The Oxford Handbook of Atheism.* New York: Oxford University Press, 2013.

Cragun, Ryan T., Barry Kosmin, Ariela Keysar, Joseph H. Hammer, and Michael Nielson. "On the Receiving End: Discrimination against the Non-religious in the United States." *Journal of Contemporary Religion* 27 (2012): 105–127.

Dawkins, Richard. *The God Delusion.* New York: Houghton Mifflin Harcourt, 2008.

Diener, Ed, Louise Tay, and David Myers. "The Religion Paradox: If Religion Makes People Happy, Why Are So Many Dropping Out?" *Journal of Personality and Social Psychology* 101 (2011): 1278–1290.

Doane, Michael J., and Marta Elliott. "Perceptions of Discrimination among Atheists: Consequences for Atheist Identification, Psychological and Physical Well-Being." *Psychology of Religion and Spirituality* 7, no. 2 (2015): 130–141.

Farias, Miguel. "The Psychology of Atheism." In *The Oxford Handbook of Atheism*, edited S. Bullivant and M. Ruse, 468–482. New York: Oxford University Press, 2013.

Farias, Miguel, and Mansur Lalljee. "Holistic Individualism in the Age of Aquarius: Measuring Individualism/Collectivism in New Age, Catholic, and Atheist/Agnostic Groups." *Journal for the Scientific Study of Religion* 47 (2008): 277–289.

Festinger, Leon. *A theory of Cognitive Dissonance.* Palo Alto Stanford, CA: Stanford University Press, 1957.

Galen, Luke W. "Profiles of the Godless: Results from a Survey of the Nonreligious." *Free Inquiry* 29 (2009): 41–45.

Galen, Luke W., and Jim Kloet. "Personality and Social Integration Factors Distinguishing Non-religious from Religious Groups: The Importance of Controlling for Attendance and Demographics." *Archive for the Psychology of Religion* 33 (2011): 205–228.

Gawronski, Bertram, and B. Keith Payne, eds. *Handbook of Implicit Social Cognition: Measurement, Theory, and Applications.* New York: Guilford Press, 2010.

Gervais, Will M. "In Godlessness We Distrust: Using Social Psychology to Solve the Puzzle of Anti-atheist Prejudice." *Social and Personality Psychology Compass* 7, no. 6 (2013): 366–377.

Gervais, Will M. "Override the Controversy: Analytic Thinking Predicts Endorsement of Evolution." *Cognition* 142 (2015): 312–321.

Gervais, Will M. and Ara Norenzayan. "Analytic Thinking Promotes Religious Disbelief." *Science* 336 (2012): 493–496.

Gervais, Will M., Azim F. Shariff, and Ara Norenzayan. "Do You Believe in Atheists? Distrust Is Central to Anti-atheist Prejudice." *Journal of Personality and Social Psychology* 101 (2011): 1189–1206.

Granqvist, Pehr, and Jane R. Dickie. "Attachment Theory and Spiritual Development in Childhood and Adolescence." In *The Handbook of Spiritual Development in Childhood and Adolescence*, edited by Eugene C. Roehlkepartain, Peter L. Benson, Pamela E. King, and Linda Wageners, 197–210. Thousand Oaks, CA: Sage, 2006.

Greenberg, Jeff, Sander L. Koole, and Tom Pyszczynski. *Handbook of Experimental Existential Psychology.* New York: Guilford, 2004.

Greenberg, Jeff, Sheldon Solomon, and Tom Pyszczynski "Terror Management Theory of Self-Esteem and Cultural Worldviews: Empirical Assessments and Conceptual Refinements." In *Advances in Experimental Social Psychology*, edited by Mark. Zanna, Vol. 29, 61–139. New York: Academic Press, 1997.

Greer, John E., and Leslie J. Francis. "Measuring 'Rejection of Christianity' among 14–16-Year-Old Adolescents in Catholic and Protestant School in Northern Ireland." *Personality and Individual Differences* 13 (1992): 1345–1348.

Hackney, Charles H., and Glenn S. Sanders. "Religiosity and Mental Health: A Meta-analysis of Recent Studies." *Journal for the Scientific Study of Religion* 42 (2003): 43–55.

Herrmann, Esther, Josep Call, María V. Hernández-Lloreda, Brian Hare, and Michael Tomasello. "Humans Have Evolved Specialized Skills of Social Cognition: The Cultural Intelligence Hypothesis." *Science* 317, no. 5843 (2007): 1360–1366.

Hill, Peter C., and Ralph W. Hood Jr. *Measures of Religiosity.* Birmingham, AL: Religious Education Press, 1999.

Hitchens, Christopher. *God Is Not Great: How Religion Poisons Everything.* Toronto: McClelland Stewart, 2008.

Hood, Ralph W., Jr., Peter C. Hill, and Bernard Spilka. *The Psychology of Religion: An Empirical Approach*, 4th ed. New York: Guilford, 2009.

Hoyle, Rick H., and Mark R. Leary. "Methods for the Study of Individual Differences in Social Behavior." In *Handbook of Individual Differences in Social Behavior*, edited by Mark R. Leary and Rick H. Hoyle, 12–23. New York: Guilford Press, 2009.

Hunsberger, Bruce E., and Robert A. Altemeyer. *Atheists: A Groundbreaking Study of America's Nonbelievers.* Amherst, NY: Prometheus Books, 2006.

Chapter 14: The Psychology of Secularity and Nonreligion

Jong, Jonathan, Jamin Halberstadt, and Matthias Bluemke. "Foxhole Atheism, Revisited: The Effects of Mortality Salience on Explicit and Implicit Religious Belief." *Journal of Experimental Social Psychology* 48 (2012): 983–989.

Kashima, Yoshihisa, Susumu Yamaguchi, Uichol Kim, Sang-chin Choi, Michele J. Gelfand, and Yuku Masaki. "Culture, Gender, and Self: A Perspective from Individualism-Collectivism Research." *Journal of Personality and Social Psychology* 69 (1995): 925–937.

Klauer, Karl C., Andrea Voss, and Christoph Stahl. *Cognitive Methods in Social Psychology*. New York: Guilford Press, 2011.

Koenig, Harold G., and David B. Larson. "Religion and Mental Health: Evidence for an Association." *International Review of Psychiatry* 13 (2001): 67–78.

Koltko-Rivera, Mark E. "The Psychology of Worldviews." *Review of General Psychology* 8 (2004): 3–58.

Kosmin, Barry A. and Ariela Keysar. *Secularism and Secularity: Contemporary International Perspectives*. Hartford, CT: Institute for the Study of Secularism in Society and Culture, 2007.

Kosmin, Barry A., Ariela Keysar, Ryan T. Cragun, and Juhem Navarro-Rivera. *American Nones: The Profile of the No Religion Population*. Hartford, CT: Institute for the Study of Secularism in Society and Culture, 2009.

Longo, Gregory S., and Jungmeen Kim-Spoon. "What Drives Apostates and Converters? The Social and Familial Antecedents of Religious Change among Adolescents." *Psychology of Religion and Spirituality* 6 (2014): 284–291.

Lee, Lois. "Research Note: Talking about a Revolution: Terminology for the New Field of Nonreligion Studies."*Journal of Contemporary Religion* 27 (2012): 129–139.

Lee, Lois. "Secular or Nonreligious? Investigating and Interpreting Generic 'Not Religious' Categories and Populations." *Religion* 44 (2014): 466–482.

Maio, Gregory R., and Geoffrey Haddock. "Theories of Attitude: Creating a Witches' Brew." In *Contemporary Perspectives on the Psychology of Attitudes*, edited Geoffrey. Haddock and Gregory Maio, 425–453. New York: Psychology Press, 2004.

Markman, Keith D., Travis Proulx, and Matthew J. Lindberg. *The Psychology of Meaning*. Washington, DC: American Psychological Association, 2013.

Markus, Hazel R., and Shinobu Kitayama. *"Culture and the Self: Implications for Cognition, Emotion, and Motivation." Psychological Review* 98 (1991): 224–253.

Markus, Hazel R., and Shinobu Kitayama. "Cultures and Selves: A Cycle of Mutual Constitution." *Perspectives on Psychological Science* 5 (2010): 420–430.

Martin, Michael. *Cambridge Companion to Atheism*. Cambridge: Cambridge University Press, 2006.

Melançon, Jérôme. "Reflection after Marcel Gauchet: Laicity and the Inherited Boundaries between Religion and Politics in Quebec." *Religious Studies and Theology* 34 (2015): 85–89.

Mochon, Daniel, Michael I. Norton, and Dan Ariely. "Who Benefits from Religion?" *Social Indicators Research* 101 (2011): 1–15.

Moore, Sean E., Heather Young Leslie, and Carrie A. Lavis. "Subjective Well-Being and Life Satisfaction in the Kingdom of Tonga." *Social Indicators Research* 70, no. 3 (2005): 287–311.

Moore, Sean E., and Jaynita Maru. "Assessment of the Types of Nonreligion in a Cross-National Sample." Forthcoming.

Moore, Sean E., Puneet K. Toor, and Shungu E. Mushayandebvu. *Development and Validation of a Scale to Measure Types of Nonreligion and Secularity*. Forthcoming.

Norenzayan, Ara, and Will M. Gervais. "The Origins of Religious Disbelief." *Trends in Cognitive Sciences* 17 (2013): 20–25.

Pew Research Center. *America's Changing Religious Landscape*. 2015. http://www.pewforum.org/files/2015/05/RLS-08-26-full-report.pdf.

Proulx, Travis, and Michael Inzlicht. "The Five 'A's of Meaning Maintenance: Finding Meaning in the Theories of Sense-Making." *Psychological Inquiry* 23 (2012): 317–335.

Robinson, John P., Phillip R. Shaver, and Lawrence S. Wrightsman. *Measures of Personality and Social Psychological Attitudes*, 1991. San Diego, CA: Academic Press.

Saroglou, Vassilis. "Conclusion: Understanding Religion and Irreligion." In *Religion, Personality, and Social Behavior*, 361–392. New York: Psychology Press, 2014.

Saroglou, Vassilis. "Religion and the Five Factors of Personality: A Meta-analytic Review." *Personality and Individual Differences* 32 (2002): 15–25.

Silver, Christopher F., Thomas J. Coleman, III, Ralph W. Hood, Jr., and Jenny W. Holcombe. "The Six Types of Nonbelief: A Qualitative and Quantitative Study of Type and Narrative." *Mental Health, Religion and Culture* 17 (2014): 990–1001.

Smith, Edward E., and Stephen M. Kosslyn. *Cognitive Psychology: Mind and Brain*. Upper Saddle River, NJ: Pearson/Prentice Hall, 2007.

Spunt, Robert P., and Matthew D. Lieberman. "The Busy Social Brain: Evidence for Automaticity and Control in the Neural Systems Supporting Social Cognition and Action Understanding." *Psychological Science*, 24 (2013): 80–86.

Streib, Heinz, and Constantin Klein. "Atheists, Agnostics, and Apostates." In *APA Handbook of Psychology, Religion, and Spirituality*, edited by Kenneth I. Pargament, 713–728. Washington, DC: American Psychological Association, 2013.

Taylor, Charles. *A Secular Age*. Cambridge, MA: Harvard University Press, 2007.

Triandis, Harry C. *Individualism and Collectivism. New Directions in Social Psychology*. Boulder, CO: Westview Press, 1995.

Triandis, Harry C. "The Self and Social Behavior in Differing Cultural Contexts." *Psychological Review* 96 (1989): 506–520.

Twenge, Jean M., Julie J. Exline, Joshua B. Grubbs, Ramya Sastry, and W. Keith Campbell. "Generational and Time Period Differences in American Adolescents' Religious Orientation, 1966–2014." *PLoS ONE* 10, no. 5 (2015): e0121454. doi:10.1371/journal.pone.0121454.

Veevers, J. E., and D. F. Cousineau. "The Heathen Canadians: Demographic Correlates of Nonbelief." *Pacific Sociological Review* 23 (1980): 199–216. doi: 10.2307/1388817.

Vernon, Glenn M. "The Religious Nones: A Neglected Category." *Journal for the Scientific Study of Religion* 7 (1968): 219–229.

Vetter, Geo B., and Martin Green. "Personality and Group Factors in the Making of Atheists." *Journal of Abnormal and Social Psychology* 27 (1931): 179–194.

Weber, Samuel R., Kenneth I. Pargament, Mark E. Kunik, James W. Lomax, and Melinda A. Stanley. "Psychological Distress among Religious Nonbelievers: A Systematic Review." *Journal of Religion and Health* 51 (2012): 72–86.

Young Leslie, Heather E., and Sean E. Moore. "Constructions of Happiness and Satisfaction in the Kingdom of Tonga," In *Happiness across Cultures: Views of Happiness and Quality of Life in Non-Western Cultures*, edited by Helaine Selin and Gareth Davey, 181–193. New York: Springer, 2012.

Zuckerman, Phil. "Atheism: Contemporary Numbers and Patterns." In *The Cambridge Companion to Atheism*, edited by M. Martin, 47–65. New York: Cambridge University Press, 2006.

Zuckerman, Phil. *Atheism and Secularity*. Santa Barbara, CA: Praeger, 2010.

Zuckerman, Phil. *Faith No More: Why People Reject Religion*. New York: Oxford University Press, 2012.

Zuckerman, Phil. *Society without God: What the Least Religious Nations Can Tell Us about Contentment*. New York: New York University Press, 2008.

TELEVISION SERIES

Community. Created by Dan Harmon. 2009–2015.

Community. "The Psychology of Letting Go." 2010. Dir. Anthony Russo.

Daria. Created by Glenn Eichler and Susie Lewis. 1997–2001.

Extras. Created by Ricky Gevais. 2005–2007.

Family Guy. Created by Seth MacFarlane and David Zuckerman. 1999–.

House M.D. Created by David Shore. 2004–2012.

The Kids in the Hall. Created by Dave Foley, Bruce McCullough, Kevin McDonald, Mark McKinney, and Scott Thompson, 1988–1994.

Orange Is the New Black. Created by Jenji Kohan. 2013–.

Penn and Teller: Bullshit! Created by Randall Moldave and Eric Small. 2003–.

Six Feet Under. Created by Alan Ball. 2001–2005.

South Park. Created by Trey Parker, Matt Stone, and Brian Graden. 1997–.

Star Trek. Created by Gene Roddenberry. 1966–1969.

True Detective. Created by Nic Pizzolatto. 2014–.

The Walking Dead. Created by Frank Darabont. 2010–.

FILMS AND DOCUMENTARIES

Contact. Dir. Robert Zemeckis. 1997.

Creation. Dir. Jon Amiel. 2009.

Crimes and Misdemeanors. Dir. Woody Allen. 1989.

Dogma. Dir. Kevin Smith. 1999.

Flatliners. Dir. Joel Schumacher. 1990.

Going Clear: Scientology and the Prison of Belief. Dir. Alex Gibney. 2015.

The Hitchiker's Guide to the Galaxy. Dir. Garth Jennings. 2005.

The Invention of Lying. Dir. Ricky Gervais and Matthew Robinson. 2009.

Letting Go of God. Dir. Julia Sweeney. 2008.

Monty Python's The Life of Brian. Dir. Terry Jones. 1979.

Paul. Dir. Greg Mottola. 2011.

Philomena. Dir. Stephen Frears. 2013.

Religulous. Dir. Larry Charles. 2008.

Saved! Dir. Brian Dannelly. 2004.

The Unbelievers. Dir. Gus Holwerda. 2013.

CHAPTER 15

Atheology

John R. Shook
Research Associate, Philosophy Department
University at Buffalo, NY

Atheology is the intellectual defense of atheism and the argumentative counterpart to theology. To be effective against theology's efforts to make god-belief reasonable, atheology accurately defines atheism, analyzes theological positions, and methodically constructs arguments why no one should think any god exists. Atheology makes a substantial contribution to secular philosophy. It is also extremely practical. Successful atheology explains why religious beliefs aren't needed for being a reasonable person, a moral individual, and a responsible citizen. These explanations support secular justifications for restraining religion's control over society and the lives of its members. Atheology indirectly assists the effort of political secularism to advocate for limiting the amount of control that religion and government can exercise over each other (Berlinerblau 2012; Blackford 2012), and to defend the rights of individuals to dissent from religion and live their lives as nonbelievers (Marshall and Shea 2011; Dacey 2012; Boyle and Sheen 2013).

IDENTIFYING ATHEOLOGY

Historians confess difficulties with identifying secular philosophical systems. They have a hard enough time even identifying atheist philosophers. "Not before Marx," says one; "Not before Hume," says another. Even twentieth-century philosopher Jean-Paul Sartre (1905–1980) couldn't detect much before his own existentialism: "it seemed to me that a great atheist, truly atheist philosophy was something philosophy lacked" (de Beauvoir 1984, 436). Yet Sartre's own communism should have brought one exemplar to mind. Could communist Karl Marx (1818–1883) mark the start of secular philosophizing? No atheistic philosophy existed before Marx's generation, declares James P. Mackey (2000, 26).

But what about feminist Frances Wright (1795–1852)? Her 1829 public lectures across America delivered a resounding atheist, feminist, and socialist stance against religion and its evils, shocking both sides of the Atlantic and provoking a flurry of theological responses. Minister and Oxford classicist Benjamin Godwin took notice, but his *Lectures on the Atheistic Controversy* (1834) selected a different target for refutation in the name of Christianity. Godwin chose the notorious atheist Mirabaud, whose 1770 treatise *Systeme de la nature* (1770), translated as *The System of Nature* (1889), represented atheism for theologians before they ever heard of Marx. This Mirabaud was the pseudonym of Paul-Henri Thiry, Baron d'Holbach (1723–1789), a completely materialist philosopher, whose audacious atheism astonished Europe before David Hume's (1711–1776) skeptical work,

263

Chapter 15: Atheology

Dialogues Concerning Natural Religion (1779), was posthumously published. Hume wouldn't openly defend atheism, although he denied the possibility of knowing whether any gods exist. Yet Hume knew well the bold materialism and anti-theism of Thomas Hobbes (1588–1679). Another philosophical authority, Bishop George Berkeley, declared Hobbes an unmistakable atheist in *The Theory of Vision* (1732, 374). Cambridge philosopher Ralph Cudworth (1617–1688) agreed about Hobbes, but his own treatise *The True Intellectual System of the Universe* (1678) battled atheist philosophers of ancient Greece, especially the great atomist Epicurus (third century BCE). Epicurus and his devoted Roman poet Lucretius (first century BCE) appear on every list of atheist philosophers assembled by medieval, Renaissance, and Enlightenment historians and theologians. Before Epicurus, the great Greek philosophers Plato and Aristotle (fourth century BCE) designed philosophical systems that included a place for a god knowable to philosophy but not to any religion, because the popular religions are just ignorant myths. They both could also look back further in time to the dawn of philosophy, where cosmologies such as the one framed by Anaxagoras (sixth century BCE) left no place for gods to do anything and gave no reason to be religious.

Although this chapter focuses on atheology as it developed in Western thought, skepticism toward deities and philosophical atheists can be found in the ancient world from Egypt and Persia to India and China. Doubt about the gods is given voice in the earliest Hindu Veda, the *Rig Veda* (King 1999, 201–202). Early Buddhism and Jainism had no interest in a supreme deity, and important schools of Confucian thought made no use of gods, heavens, or immortality (Martin 2007). In Muslim and Hindu regions, minority traditions of freethought and secularity are not unknown to this day (Strousma 1999; Quack 2011).

ATHEOLOGY AND THEOLOGY

Atheology is more than the rejection of gods—atheism does that. Atheology explains what atheism is, and how to effectively defend atheism.

A term ending with *-ology* points to the exploration of something, so atheology is the exploration of individual disbelief and public atheism. More specifically, atheology explores varieties of disbelief in religions, explains how atheists justify and encourage nonreligious views, and defends their secular engagement with religion and religious aspects of society. There are boundaries to atheology. Atheology isn't responsible for describing the lives of nonbelievers in general, or the ways they manifest their secularity in their personal lifestyles, their social responsibilities, or their political stances. Hundreds of millions of people live nonreligious lives all around the world without bothering to engage with religion or explain why they disbelieve in gods. Atheology is specifically concerned with defending disbelief and denials of religious claims about otherworldly matters. Atheology is not concerned with studying how people in the world are disengaging from religious practices or distancing themselves from religious institutions. The field of secular studies is the wider interdisciplinary area of research into the psychological, social, cultural, and political phenomena associated with nonbelief, secularity, and disengagement from religion (Flynn 2007; Zuckerman 2010; Arweck et al. 2013; Beamon and Tomlins 2015). Religious scholars and theologians have a more venerable, but less objective, tradition of investigating kinds and causes of unbelief (Borne 1961; Marty 1964; Caporale and Grumelli 1971; Jossua and Geffre 1983; Habgood 2000).

264 MACMILLAN INTERDISCIPLINARY HANDBOOKS

Atheology is not just opposition to theology, although responding to theological arguments is included in atheology. Atheology and some kinds of theology could converge in a surprising agreement. Liberal theology, postmodern theology, existentialist theology, and radical theology have all been deprioritizing God as a supernatural reality, or having any reality at all. Perhaps *God* should only be a symbol of sacredness, a pointer toward mystery, a label for nature's immensities, a character in a religious narrative, an ideal of moral perfection, a proxy for ethical absolutes, an expression of hope, a heartfelt response to beauty (or other elevated feelings), an encounter with a source of awe, and so on. Atheology can easily agree that any meaning to *God* is reducible to these thoroughly human matters.

Furthermore, a worldview that leaves out God could approve some features of religions. Examples include religious humanism and religious naturalism (Schulz 2002; Stone 2008). A philosophical perspective could agree with religion about the value of uplifting emotions, the benefits of ritual and meditation, the rightness of ethical principles, the high worth of human life, and responsibilities to take care of the planet. Is belief in a god always necessary for these important things?

The investigation of nontheistic religiosity is exemplified by some European thinkers such as Georges Bataille as read in his *L'expérience intérieure* (1943). Simone Weil (1909–1943) and Emmanuel Levinas (1906–1995) also found religiosity in the absence of god. Alasdair MacIntyre (1929–) and Paul Ricœur (1913–2005) explored a "post-theology" in *The Religious Significance of Atheism* (1969). Jacques Derrida (1930–2004) refused to call himself an atheist, because he questioned the philosophical and logical presumptions required for denying existence of God. All the same, God is dead, along with all metaphysics, necessities, and absolute values. An American version of this Death of God movement was established by Thomas Altizer (1927–). Whether this perspective is labeled as a-theology, (a)theology, or a/theology, it deserves close attention from philosophy (Taylor 1987; Westphal 1993).

In America, the term *atheology* was independently used by a philosopher of religion, Alvin Plantinga (1932–). He defined natural atheology as "the attempt, roughly, to show that, given what we know, it is impossible or unlikely that God exists" (1967, vii). Plantinga was probably aware that the term *atheology* was old, brought into wide usage by Ralph Cudworth (1617–1688), the great Cambridge scholar of the seventeenth century. Cudworth vaulted to prominence with his defense of religion, *The True Intellectual System of the Universe, Wherein All the Reason and Philosophy of Atheism Is Confuted and its Impossibility Demonstrated.* Chapter two of the first volume starts with a list of accusations against atheism, and defines a "system of Atheology" as "Atheism swaggering under the glorious appearance of philosophy" (1820, 175). In Cudworth's view, atheism is the denial of religion, and atheology is the effort to rationally justify atheism by constructing an intellectual worldview that lacks a god—or at least the true God.

Writing during the seventeenth century, Cudworth expected that theology could rely on sound philosophy to prove that a God exists. By the end of the seventeenth century, however, dissenters and freethinkers were pondering alternatives to Christianity.

FREETHOUGHT, RELIGIOUS CRITICISM, AND ATHEOLOGY

Freethought supplies the general aims and tactics for questioning and criticizing religion, religious leadership, and any other authority relying on religion. Freethought does not always involve rejecting scripture or defying God's divinity (blasphemy), discrediting

Chapter 15: Atheology

religious authorities (anticlericalism), abandoning the true faith (apostasy), or disbelieving God's existence (atheism). Most of the history of freethought involves core concerns such as philosophizing about God, humanity, and nature (potential heresies), reveling in altered states of intense emotions (promoting spiritualisms), reforming religious practice and religious institutions (risking schisms), and rearranging church-state politics (seeking religious liberties).

Freethought raises critical challenges to conformist and conservative religion, but only a portion of freethought has been devoted to impiety and irreligion: denying all religious claims, abandoning religion, and encouraging disbelief in religion (Robertson 1936; Larue 1996; Israel 2001; Watson 2014). The destination of atheism is not the exclusive destiny of freethought, but fears over apostasy have largely determined the hostile religious agenda against all freethought. It is specifically freethought atheology that can more directly lead toward atheism.

Religion's defenders are not mistaken about the threats to orthodoxy posed by freethinking, religious criticism, and civic dissent. Arguing that religious authorities cannot actually know what they think they know, and are not as holy as they seem, can make others doubt what is knowable and holy about God. Arguing that the stories recounted in scriptures could not be as truthful and testimonial as they appear can make others wonder how much human wit is actually responsible for holy writ. Arguing that scriptural commandments and holy laws are contrary to what people really know is right can make others wonder if anything divine stands behind their edicts. Arguing that God cannot fulfill our expectations about true righteousness and goodness can make others wonder why such a god is worthy of faith. These sorts of criticisms, taken individually, may not suffice to inspire apostasy or produce many atheists. Yet they can be selectively wielded by freethinking reformers who want to remain religious but escape dogma and church. Taken collectively, the religious criticism fostered by freethinking can produce serious questioning, wavering faith, uncaring agnostics, doubting skeptics, and bold atheists, and it may push some trends toward rising secularity and some degree of irreligion across a population (Bruce 2011).

Religious criticism in general is the intellectual effort to justify either certain religious reforms or the entire elimination of religious practices and commitments. Religious criticism, whether undertaken by the faithful or the nonreligious, judges religion against the sensibilities and tastes of most people in the area, the moral standards peculiar to a society, a society's standards of public responsibility, or the prevailing laws in that region or nation. Religious critics communicate with targeted audiences who share some local norms, but these critics don't think about where those norms came from, how they might be objectively valid for all humanity, or whether they could be justified on solely secular grounds. Religious criticism is all the more effective when it has local force, but there it can only have relative force. Atheology, by contrast, holds religious institutions and individuals to objective and universal standards, expecting religious people to rise to those standards by dropping obstructing religious beliefs, at least to the point of admitting skeptical doubt.

Four primary methods of atheology can be distinguished, depending on whether atheology relies on rationality alone; rationality plus science; moral norms of health, personal conduct, and social ethics; or human rights, civil rights, and justice. We may accordingly speak of rationalist atheology, scientific atheology, moral atheology, and civic atheology. The next section explains them in detail.

Chapter 15: Atheology

The four atheologies match up against the four primary kinds of theology:

Numinal theology asks and answers the question, is a god needed to explain numinous experiences? If so, then we should regard the gods with awe as supreme. Rationalist atheology, by contrast, finds no logical way to conclude anything about gods from human experience.

Natural theology asks and answers the question, is a god needed to explain the order and course of the cosmos? If so, then we should revere the gods for our existence. Scientific atheology opposes natural theology because it finds no explanatory role for any gods while exploring and explaining nature.

Moral theology asks and answers the question, is a god needed to ensure a natural and human orientation toward goodness? If so, then we should accordingly harmonize our personal and social lives. Moral atheology, by contrast, finds more ethical options by leaving belief in all gods behind.

Civic theology asks and answers the question, is a god needed to ensure that society conforms to civil order? If so, then we should ensure that everyone in society is properly religious. Civic atheology opposes civic theology by arguing that greater justice and social harmony is achieved by insulating politics away from religious control.

The four primary atheologies, itemized in contrast to the four theologies listed here, were sporadically defended in classical Greece and Rome, and they all were completely revived in the eighteenth century in Europe.

Although these four atheologies can cohere and support each other, it should never be assumed that a freethinker pursing one also endorses the others. For many centuries, the skepticism inherent to rationalist atheology prevented many skeptics from supposing that materialism could be reasonably affirmed. And both skeptics and materialists were torn over whether to abandon religious morality, or call for revolutions of civil order. Each atheist freethinker was free to decide whether a personal intellectual dissent from religion would pair up with the public behavior of impiety. For example, many freethinkers over recent centuries have denied God but upheld religion's ethos as a guide to morality, or encouraged religious observance as beneficial to civic life.

What should be the right relationship between our knowledge of reality and our duty to society? By the late eighteenth century, representative freethinkers had notably occupied four primary options. First, Thomas Hobbes (1588–1679), an English philosopher, defended materialism based on science while also upholding popular religion as a political tool for maintaining social harmony and government stability. Second, Epicurus (341–270 BCE), an ancient Greek philosopher, was known for preferring naturalism (before modern science) but casting scorn against popular religion and urging that people seek their own personal happiness. Third, Michel de Montaigne (1533–1592), a French philosopher, perceived how religion has no basis in reason but he defended each person's duty to maintain faith in God. Fourth, Denis Diderot (1713–1784), another French philosopher, couldn't find where reason could justify religion either, but he regarded blind faith as the enemy of badly needed reforms to society and government.

There is an additional category for atheologians making a place for godly or divine or transcendent matters in their worldviews while denying most everything about the gods worshipped by the world's religions. Prominent thinkers in this additional category include Giordano Bruno (1548–1600), Baruch Spinoza (1632–1677), Voltaire (1694–1778),

RELIGION: BEYOND RELIGION

267

Chapter 15: Atheology

G. W. F. Hegel (1770–1831), Charles Peirce (1839–1914), Martin Heidegger (1889–1976), A. N. Whitehead (1861–1947), and Paul Tillich (1886–1965).

THE FOUR ATHEOLOGIES

The method of atheology appealing only to simple matters such as common sense, simple reasoning, and basic logic can be distinguished first. Because this atheology relies on ordinary rational capacities possessed and understood by (nearly) everyone to justify disbelief toward religious claims, it is labeled as rationalist atheology. By contrast, a second method of philosophical atheology that appeals to both common rationality and specialized scientific knowledge to justify rejecting religious worldviews is scientific atheology. The third and fourth atheologies appeal to established norms and values. Arguments against religion that point out its violations of healthy living and deviations from moral norms are provided by moral atheology. Arguments against religion that point out its violations of social ethics, standards of civic responsibility, and principles of good government are provided by civic atheology. Typical atheological works focus on just one or another of these four atheologies. Essays applying all of these atheologies are collected in two volumes edited by Michael Martin and Ricki Monnier (2003, 2006).

Rationalist atheology applies common rationality and basic logical thinking to support the denial that gods exist (Le Poidevin 1996; Everett 2004; Oppy 2006; Shook 2000). Rationalist atheology skeptically rejects theology's arguments for whatever divine entity it proposes, aiming at doubt, not disproof, of that proposal. Successful rationalist atheology demonstrates that no person is reasonable for thinking that anything godly or divine (supernatural, transcendent, etc.) exists. Rationalist atheology doesn't first define God and then disprove it, so theology cannot complain about misunderstandings or missed targets. If a theology cannot make its own conception of its god(s) comprehensible enough for its own argumentative support, rationalist atheology only need point this out to win by default, because it remains reasonable for anyone to decline to believe in an incomprehensible deity. If a theology could argue for some conception of a god without a single fallacious misstep, then rationalist atheology fails, and anyone would be reasonable for thinking that such a god really exists.

Naturally, theology and rationalist atheology strongly disagree about whether any nonfallacious theological argument can be formulated. Here is one simplified example, following an argument for God made by medieval theologian St. Thomas Aquinas (1997, 22).

1. The things we observe in the world come into existence because they are created by some other thing(s).

2. Trying to imagine anything causing its own creation is a bad explanation for 1.

3. Trying to imagine an endless chain of causes going back into an infinite past is a bad explanation for 1.

4. A First Cause that causes everything else, but wasn't caused itself, is the only other explanation for 1.

5. When other explanations are bad explanations, one must accept any remaining explanation as correct.

6. A First Cause must have caused everything else, due to 4 and 5.

7. Everyone thinks that a First Cause of everything else is basically the same thing as a God.

8. A God is the explanation for everything else, because 6 and 7 are correct. Therefore, God exists.

Rationalist atheology exposes false premises and fallacious gaps in this reasoning.

Premise 1 assumes that everything in and about nature has to be created, but some unchanging things might not have been created, such as fundamental physical energies and the laws they obey. Theology would first have to prove that nothing natural is uncreated. Pointing to the Big Bang can't help, because cosmological science suggests that some forces (quantum matters, for example) prevailed prior to our universe. Theology can argue with scientific atheology about that issue; rationalist atheology only needs to point out that premise 1 hasn't been established. Premise 2 seems plausible, but premise 3 can be disputed. An infinite chain of past causes could conceivably be correct, because that would account for all created things, although an image of something infinite won't arise in the imagination. Conceivability mustn't be confused with imaginability. Just because something can't be imagined doesn't leave it inconceivable, or useless for explanations. Mathematicians work with concepts of infinity without trying to picture them imaginatively, and scientists work with theoretical concepts too complex to be imagined in any detail. Premise 4 may not be identifying the only other explanation, because premise 3 may be wrong. Even if a First Cause had to be the only remaining explanation, that doesn't make it a good explanation. A First Cause has to be conceived as a necessarily existing and uncaused entity, which is so far beyond anything experienced or imagined that it can't seem more plausible than the other options. Besides, even if it could be a good explanation because it is an ultimate explanation, an infinite chain of causes is similarly an ultimate explanation that would necessarily exist in an uncaused way. Furthermore, premise 5 is false—premises 2, 3, and 4 could all be rejected as unsatisfactory. It always remains possible that no good explanation is available, so premise 6 can be rejected and nothing should be believed about the creation of everything, halting this argument at skeptical doubt. Finally, Premise 7 is false. Nonreligious people don't have to presume that this First Cause is God; a primeval creative power might be nothing like a god. Furthermore, even if there really is a First Cause, religious people might not want to assume it has to be their God, either. That entity would be truly powerful but it could also be entirely physical, such as a fundamental energy or force, obeying only natural laws. Even a religious person thinks of a God as something more than a merely physical matter to be understood by science. Premise 8 has nothing to support it because premises 6 and 7 don't have to be accepted, so this argument cannot supply enough reasons to think that God exists.

Scientific atheology is different from rationalist atheology by applying a wider body of knowledge from science, in addition to common sense and rational principles, to skeptically doubt whether any god exists (Stenger 2007; Philipse 2012; Shook 2014). That knowledge needn't exceed the comprehension of most people, if they have some education. Basic information from geology, astronomy, biology, or human physiology can often suffice to show that no religious explanation for worldly matters is required. Science can explain matters once taken to be signs from God, such as earthquakes and comets. No deity had to design the structure of the eye or the brain, arrange the order of our solar system's planets, and place the stars in the heavens. Rarely does scientific atheology have to rely on sophisticated advances of research science, such as quantum physics, big bang cosmology, or neuroscience. The need to use knowledge from those advanced fields usually arises only

RELIGION: BEYOND RELIGION

269

Chapter 15: Atheology

when a theology thinks that it can make god-belief more plausible by appealing to those fields first. For example, if a theological argument asks us to detect a miraculous intervention in the Big Bang's start to our universe, or quantum level randomness, or a quantum holism that connects minds, scientific atheology counters by explaining why divine activity cannot be concluded from the scientific evidence (Stenger 2009).

Scientific atheology's aim is not to demonstrate that naturalism is correct, nor may it presume that naturalism is correct. Modern naturalism is a vaster ongoing project, because it is a type of secular philosophy about the capacity of the sciences to satisfy the intellect, take priority over other sorts of explanations, and have the primary responsibility for knowing what reality ultimately includes and what it does not (Fales 2007). Because naturalism as a complete worldview is not yet part of the established body of human knowledge (although it is growing into that role), scientific atheology cannot directly appeal to the authority of naturalism. Scientific atheology only appeals to the knowledge that the social, biological, and natural sciences have thoroughly (but not infallibly) confirmed, so it constitutes knowledge that all humanity can reliably use. Even scientific theories deemed unacceptable by conservative religions still remain available to scientific atheology, such as biological evolution, because a theory's unacceptability to some religion or another has no intellectual relevance to whether science has firmly established that knowledge. Science alone confirms its growing stock of confirmed knowledge, and nothing other than science controls its experimental methods. (If religion, or philosophy, held veto power over whether science could acquire knowledge, science would hardly flourish.)

Moral atheology criticizes religious institutions, practices, and personal commitments toward God on the basis of normative values that all humanity should respect (Kurtz 1987; Howard-Snyder 2006; Hitchens 2007; Aiken and Talisse 2011). The schematic form to a typical argument is this: "If religion's god is real, then a follower must accept a violation of an important value, but it is unreasonable to accept that violation, therefore belief in that god should be abandoned." Moral atheology specifically appeals to standards for healthy human functioning, basic moral norms, and reasonable social ethics. These standards are those most widely shared by civilized societies. Most of the world's religions, by now, endorse basic standards. Plenty of agreement about right and wrong, and good and evil, is already available even if religious ethics and secular ethics cannot agree about all moral matters. Nor does moral atheology have to wait for ethical theories, such as deontology and utilitarianism, to converge in agreement. The civilized world knows enough about right and wrong. Any deity commanding or encouraging murder, terror, suicide, harm to innocent people, and harm to oneself isn't worthy of anyone's faith.

The problem of evil is an example from moral atheology. No one should have to think that tragic evils are actually good or beneficial events. Knowing the difference between good and evil and hating evil are important moral standards to uphold. However, someone believing that a good God exists, but this God allows evils to happen, must look at evils differently. A good God would only allow good things to happen (if this being can't prevent some events from happening, it is no God at all), so evils must actually be acceptable. The religious believer is caught in a dilemma. If evils are not good, then a good God can't really exist; to affirm a good God is to surrender one's ability to tell good from evil. There are only two ways out of this dilemma: either give up thinking any God exists, or begin to think that God isn't good. Theology can try to evade the dilemma by faulting us humans for choosing evil, but that doesn't explain natural disasters or the consequences of using our freedom. No person chose living on a planet where earthquakes and hurricanes and plagues kill

270   MACMILLAN INTERDISCIPLINARY HANDBOOKS

thousands. When we do choose, and happen to choose sin, God uses hell for punishment, but hell is supposedly a great evil that somehow also must be good for God. Creative religions can avoid moral atheology's condemnations by (1) ensuring conformity with civilized standards for the moral treatment of all people, and (2) changing God's job description to relieve any responsibility, directly or indirectly, for anything evil. Moral atheology cannot disprove every god imaginable; it only urges religions to abandon uncivilized and immoral deities.

Civic atheology appeals to human rights, political rights such as civil rights and liberties, and principles of social justice in order to criticize religion and religious belief (Cliteur 2010; Kurtz 2010). Although the concept of human rights is not yet as universal as could be hoped, most cultures and religions are able to recognize many of them. Civilized societies regard degradations to life, safety, liberty, and property seriously. Complete agreement about human rights is a goal for the future, not an accomplishment. That is why civic atheology doesn't require a presumption that the universalization of a specific set of human rights or civil rights is practically achievable or even theoretically demonstrable. If a demonstrably universal ethics were assured by secular philosophizing, laying moral foundations for human rights, civil rights, and social justice would be greatly facilitated. Secular political philosophy has also tried to justify a few human rights, civil rights, and principles of social justice without presuming a prior moral consensus or a proven universal ethics. Civic atheology cannot accomplish any of these things, nor take them for granted. Only a current consensus among civilized peoples about rights and justice, however minimal, can be included with the body of human knowledge about proper civic affairs. That consensus is a reasonable basis for rejecting religious convictions responsible for any violations. Gods requiring disrespect for human dignity and human rights, or gods that demand social injustice or degrading inequalities, are gods that must be abandoned as unreal. Like moral atheology, civic atheology cannot disprove every kind of deity, but religions are firmly told to abandon uncivilized and unjust gods.

MODES OF ATHEOLOGY

There are three primary modes of pursuing atheology: the pedagogical, practical, and philosophical modes.

Pedagogical atheology is instruction for children and young adults explaining why faith, religion, and quasi-religious beliefs should be avoided (McGowan 2007; McGowen et al. 2009; Hitchcock 2009). This age-appropriate atheology tackles only broad concerns with only mild intensity, without any indoctrination into atheism as if it were a creed to be blindly accepted. Children can be introduced to asking questions and thinking critically about such things as empirical exploration, basic science, exposing superstition and magical thinking, and skeptical inquiry into the paranormal and supernatural. Children can also be introduced to the world's major religions, pointing out all their different gods and notions of afterlives, along with the disagreements about moral expectations that religions perpetuate.

Paired with a cross-cultural and historical interest in religion in general, and humanistic encouragement of respect and toleration, pedagogical atheology needn't inspire anger or hostility toward religious people or any religion. The primary goals are helping children with their critical thinking skills, the confidence to question everything, and the methods of self-guided inquiry. Pedagogical atheology, along with humanist education for children, is a rich field for expansion and enrichment. Future progress will take advantage of developmental and educational psychology, the study of cognitive biases, and research into magical thinking and religious susceptibility.

Practical atheology offers persuasive discussions about atheism designed for adult audiences. It utilizes common sense and logic, a measure of science, moral and civic norms, and a judicious selection of life wisdom to explain religion's failings, recount theology's fallacies, encourage the naturalistic worldview, sustain a lifetime nonreligious stance, and utilize secular ethics such as utilitarianism and humanism (Smith 2000; Grayling 2002; Price 2006; Barker 2011; Rosenberg 2011; McGowan 2013; Ruse 2015). Intellectual history can also introduce a wide audience to the legacy of irreligion (Hecht 2010; Schneider 2013).

This genre of popular practical atheology has been around a long time, going back to nineteenth-century nonbelievers such as Robert Green Ingersoll (1833–1899) in America and Charles Bradlaugh (1833–1891) in England (Turner 1985; Radest 1990; Jacoby 2004). During the first half of the twentieth century, the Little Blue Books series of hundreds of pamphlets published by Emanuel Haldeman-Julius (1889–1951) connected numerous freethinking and atheist writers with a vast readership across America—over 20 million copies sold in the single year of 1927. Publishing over one hundred of his pamphlets in this series, Joseph McCabe (1867–1955) was a leading voice of rationalism, atheism, and irreligion in America (Cooke 2001). In England, Harold Blackham (1903–2009) popularized humanism with his books such as *The Human Tradition* (1953), and he led the British Humanist Association for many years. Paul Kurtz (1925–2012) reinvigorated popular atheism in America, founding the Council for Secular Humanism and its magazine *Free Inquiry* in 1980.

Practical atheology offers well-rounded insights into living without religion and holding a secular worldview, designed for adults wavering away from religion or seeking an affirmative nonbelieving life stance (Kurtz 2000). Practical atheology is also related to counseling for psychological issues and mental trauma that people suffer within religious settings. Helping people obtain access to mental health care and transition their lives away from harmful religiosity can assist people deciding for themselves to become nonreligious (Winell 1993; Ray 2012). Even clergy are admitting disbelief and contemplating how to walk away from their churches (Dennett and LaScola 2013).

Philosophical atheology takes atheology to its highest intellectual level, separating its tasks into rational, scientific, moral, and civic atheologies. It applies anything and everything within the realm of human knowledge, from logic and observation to confirmed science and objective values, to its agenda of showing how nothing godly need be taken as real and nothing religious is needed for life. Philosophical atheology does not primarily aim at persuasively deconverting the religious toward nonbelieving secularity, or exhorting nonbelievers toward firm atheist or humanist commitments. Those are goals of practical atheology, which can speak to wide audiences with straightforward and inspirational language. Practical atheology can rhetorically engage religion and effectively rehearse simpler counterarguments against basic theology, but the sophisticated arguments handling theology's intricacies and novelties are developed by philosophical atheology. In the academic world, philosophical atheology is the application of secular philosophy best equipped to engage in dialogue and debate with theologies.

COMPLETE ATHEOLOGY

The four philosophical atheologies—rationalist, scientific, moral, and civic—offer intellectual challenges capable of showing that worldviews omitting gods or anything supernatural or transcendent can be reasonable. Typical works of atheology fall into just one of these four kinds. Quite rare are thinkers comprehensively covering all four atheologies; rarer still are those coherently uniting all four atheologies to work together.

Comprehensive atheologies are rare because thinkers have their own preferred methods for tackling philosophical and religious issues. The logical skeptic may not be a scientific worldview builder, the scientific mind may not be a sage moralist or a social reformer, and a political revolutionary may have no patience for metaphysical disputations. An even higher standard beyond comprehensive atheology is its coherent unification on entirely rational-naturalistic-secular grounds without internal inconsistencies or lingering hints of reliance, positively or negatively, on religious ideas or sentiments. Coherence is not easily achieved. For example, skeptical reason may deny the scientific realism sufficient for naturalism; naturalism may deny the moral agency required for secular ethics; and political rights may require other foundations besides reason and nature. Appealing to metaphysical necessities, cognitive necessities and a prioris, and fixed absolutes, whether in the guise of reason, science, or ethics, has also remained a powerful secular temptation. If those last temptations can all be avoided, then a comprehensively coherent atheology can become a complete atheology.

Complete atheology had been beyond the grasp of Western atheism for a long time, since the classical era of atomistic materialism from Epicurus and Lucretius. Within a brief period of less than two centuries, the foundations of modern science restored that opportunity. Isaac Newton's theories of motion and gravity and Darwin's theory of evolution eliminated God's jobs of guiding all the heavenly bodies and creating every species of life. With scientific knowledge on the ascendant and natural explanations for our intellectual capacities in development, skepticism began to ally with naturalism by the end of the nineteenth century. The nineteenth century also witnessed dramatic alliances between naturalism and ethics, for example, in the philosophies of Auguste Comte, Karl Marx, John Stuart Mill, and Herbert Spencer. Atheologians sustained the Enlightenment's momentum by forecasting endless human progress thanks to biological evolution and cultural evolution.

Friedrich Nietzsche (1844–1900) announced that "God is dead" at the hands of humanity, yet he doubted evolutionary atheological schemes. He also perceived how atheism may stand transfixed in the "shadows" of god that linger after the death of god, continuing to seek its own necessities, absolutes, and finalities. The four volumes of his middle period represent his great effort at a complete atheology: *The Gay Science* (1882), *Thus Spoke Zarathustra* (1883–1885), *Beyond Good and Evil* (1886), and *On the Genealogy of Morals* (1887). At the start of the twentieth century, there appeared two ambitious attempts to satisfy the highest atheological standards. Italian philosopher Benedetto Croce (1866–1952) published his *Filosofia come scienza dello spirit* (Philosophy of the Spirit) in four volumes from 1902 to 1917, with *Philosophy of the Practical: Economic and Ethic* (1913) as its centerpiece. Spanish-born American philosopher George Santayana (1863–1952) published his five-volume *The Life of Reason: The Phases of Human Progress* (1905–1906). Santayana's philosophy assigns an important role for metaphysical thinking and religious experience, ensuring that secular philosophy can explain religion. That was also true of American philosopher John Dewey's (1859–1952) *Experience and*

Chapter 15: Atheology

Nature (1925) and German philosopher Martin Heidegger's *Being and Time* (1927). Both awarded philosophical priority to the environs of lived experience—this life-world or the realm of human "being-in-the world." For this sort of phenomenology, plenty of earthly religiosity, but no unnatural deity, enlivens the human world.

Forging a complete atheology would evidently be neither automatic nor easy. Could skepticism really be compatible with naturalism? Would ethics really be based only on our human biology? How could politics start from inalienable rights that science can't locate in nature?

The vulnerabilities arising when atheology stays at a level below comprehensiveness and coherence remain on display in New Atheism. Most writings related to this upstart genre, inaugurated by Sam Harris (1967–) and Richard Dawkins (1941–), only engage in religious criticism for public audiences to polemical and political effect, offering an entryway into practical theology. The vulnerabilities of New Atheism aren't about whether it grapples with every twist and turn of academic theology, but rather with its lack of atheological comprehensiveness, much less coherence. New Atheism's criticisms against religion tend to be narrow, leaving broader issues about atheism unanswered. Skepticism is sharply wielded against anything religious, whereas no skepticism is permitted about the capacity of science to explain the world's ways or the ability of a materialistic lifestyle to fulfill human lives. Many books in this genre defend science over religion while ignoring problems establishing naturalism, as if atheism's own worldview was secure (Pigliucci 2013). Others decry religion's irrationalities, and the naïve credulity of the faithful, as if the nonreligious are always paragons of rationality.

Religion has been raising concerns about atheism's values for millennia, but New Atheism as a whole hasn't inspired consistent or coherent answers. Many authors in the New Atheist genre criticize religion's moral failings without accounting for ethics among nonbelievers, as if sound morals or social justice automatically comes with irreligion. Atheists disparaging religion's notion of free will overlook explaining how anyone is morally responsible in a deterministic world. Some atheists do reject moral responsibility, even as they denounce the behavior of religious people. Many writing in this genre are pleased to announce that after religion, no one has to think that there are any worthy values beyond what is personally satisfying, and no one is bound by an objective code of ethics. Yet other atheists blithely announce that scientific research into human genes, or brains, will soon deliver verdicts on what constitutes human happiness, moral value, and ethical duty (Kaufman 2012). This genre agrees that religion's dangers must be exposed to scorn, but can't see any harms to eliminating religiosity in the face of much evidence. In general, authors start from diverse viewpoints and apply all sorts of satirical, rhetorical, and argumentative tactics without much concern for overall clarity or coherence. Religious reactions to New Atheism are similarly disorganized in response (Haught 2008; Mohler 2008; Zacharias 2008; McGrath 2011; Hughes 2013).

Atheology can only improve popular atheism, but it can display its own limitations. Theology's criticism that much of atheology may yet be a misbegotten creature of theology has some merit (Dupré 1999; Onfray 2007). Falling short of comprehensiveness and coherence despite the assistance of secular philosophy can leave an atheology vulnerable due to incompleteness. Few examples of comprehensive atheology are available after Dewey and Heidegger. One was assembled by American philosopher Corliss Lamont in *Humanism as a Philosophy*, later retitled *The Philosophy of Humanism* (1997). Indian socialist and freethinker M. N. Roy composed a set of tracts during the 1940s and early 1950s presenting a broad

Chapter 15: Atheology

philosophical and scientific humanism, including *Science and Philosophy* (1947) and *Radical Humanism* (1952). British philosopher Antony Flew's work *Atheistic Humanism* (1993) offered a single-volume comprehensive atheology. German philosopher Jürgen Habermas developed an entirely secular worldview in major works including *Theorie des kommunikativen Handelns* (Theory of Communicative Action, 1981) and *Faktizität und Geltung* (Between Facts and Norms, 1992), and specifically in *Zwischen Naturalismus und Religion* (Between Naturalism and Religion, 2005). Canadian philosopher Kai Nielsen's two works, *God and the Grounding of Morality* (1991) and *Naturalism and Religion* (2001), together provide a comprehensive atheological philosophy.

Complete atheology sets an even higher standard. Too many atheologians end up unable to adequately ground their own positions, and they leave key tenets at odds with each other, or they ground their views on foundations favorable to religion. Some examples include pursuing their humanism spiritually (yearning for transcendence), resigning themselves to naturalism nihilistically (leaving only subjectivism), bracing knowledge with a priori necessities (leading to platonism), abandoning objective truth methodologically (embracing just relativism), discerning values and ideals existentially (while demoting science), endorsing moral rules traditionally (relying on religion), or grounding their political systems rationalistically or idealistically (ignoring human nature).

Examples of complete atheology since Marx, Büchner, and Nietzsche are rare. It could be argued that Heidegger is one example, in the German language; Habermas is another. In the English language, after Santayana and Dewey, the next complete atheological effort came from philosopher Paul Kurtz. In a trilogy of works—*In Defense of Secular Humanism* (1983), *The Transcendental Temptation: A Critique of Religion and the Paranormal* (1986), and *Forbidden Fruit: The Ethics of Humanism* (1987)—he offered a complete atheology in exclusively secular terms without appeals to transcendence, existentialism, subjectivism, nihilism, moral absolutes, a priori principles, or a God's-eye view of the world.

Summary

Atheology explores what atheists think, why they are not religious, and how they defend the reasonableness of their disbelief in religion. Atheology's defenses of atheism are more sophisticated than the wider genre of religious criticism, which secular people also undertake. Religious criticism provides simpler and practical ways to point out how religion is harming people and societies, and why religion has no reasonable basis in fact or logic. Because religious criticism only appeals to what is already locally taken to be common knowledge and sound morality, it cannot offer justifications why no one, anywhere, shouldn't be religious. Atheology encompasses the intellectual efforts to explain why it would be reasonable for anyone to lack religious convictions and think that no gods exist.

Philosophy provides essential tools for conducting atheology. Atheology borrows philosophy's logical methods, ethical wisdom, and long experience with debating theology. Philosophy itself is neither religious nor antireligious. Indeed, theologies from the ancient world and the modern world, representing major religions all around the globe, have borrowed heavily from philosophy. When philosophy finds that it cannot agree with religious views about ultimate or divine realities, and assists nonreligious worldviews with the tools for constructing atheology, that aspect of philosophizing may be labeled as secular

RELIGION: BEYOND RELIGION

275

Chapter 15: Atheology

philosophy. Secular philosophy and atheology together supply foundational principles for the various kinds of secularisms promoting secularization: the diminishment of religious influences over culture, society, and personal belief.

Four primary kinds of atheology have been conducted across the long history of philosophy: the rationalist, scientific, moral, and civic atheologies. For the purposes of teaching people about atheism, the three modes to atheology handle separate educational levels. Pedagogical atheology is instruction guiding children and young adults away from religiosity toward secular and scientific worldviews. Practical atheology is designed for public adult audiences who want to understand their secularity, find nonreligious answers to the big questions in life, and defend their viewpoint against religions. Philosophical atheology assembles sophisticated intellectual justifications for disbelief in the ultimate realities proclaimed by religions and defended by theologies. The highest achievement for philosophical atheology is complete atheology: a fully secular system of all four atheologies working harmoniously together.

Bibliography

Aikin, Scott F., and Robert B. Talisse. *Reasonable Atheism: A Moral Case for Respectful Disbelief*. Amherst, NY: Prometheus Books, 2011.

Altizer, Thomas. *The Gospel of Christian Atheism*. Philadelphia: Westminster Press, 1966.

Aquinas, Thomas. *Basic Writings of St. Thomas Aquinas*, Vol. 1, translated by Anton C. Pegis. Indianapolis, IN: Hackett, 1997.

Arweck, Elisabeth, Stephen Bullivant, and Lois Lee, eds. *Secularity and Non-Religion*. London and New York: Routledge, 2013.

Barker, Dan. *The Good Atheist: Living a Purpose-Filled Life Without God*. Berkeley, CA: Ulysses Press, 2011.

Bataille, Georges. *L'expérience intérieure*. Paris: Gallimard, 1943.

Bataille, Georges. *The Unfinished System of Nonknowledge*, edited by Stuart Kendall, translated by Michelle Kendall and Stuart Kendall. Minneapolis: University of Minnesota Press, 2001.

Beaman, Lori, and Steven Tomlins, eds. *Atheist Identities: Spaces and Social Contexts*. Berlin: Springer, 2015.

Berkeley, George. *The Works of George Berkeley*, Vol. 1, edited by A. C. Fraser. Oxford: Clarendon Press, 1871.

Berlinerblau, Jacques. *How to Be Secular: A Call to Arms for Religious Freedom*. Boston and New York: Houghton Mifflin Harcourt, 2012.

Blackford, Russell. *Freedom of Religion and the Secular State*. Malden, MA: Wiley-Blackwell, 2012.

Blackham, Harold. *The Human Tradition*. London: Routledge, 1953.

Borne, Étienne. *Atheism*, translated by S. J. Tester. New York: Hawthorne, 1961.

Boyle, Kevin, and Juliet Sheen, eds. *Freedom of Religion and Belief: A World Report*. London and New York: Routledge, 2013.

Bruce, Steve. *Secularization: In Defense of an Unfashionable Theory*. Oxford: Oxford University Press, 2011.

Caporale, Rocco, and Antonio Grumelli, eds. *The Culture of Unbelief*. Berkeley: University of California Press, 1971.

Cliteur, Paul. *The Secular Outlook: In Defense of Moral and Political Secularism*. Malden, MA: Wiley-Blackwell, 2010.

Cooke, Bill. *A Rebel to His Last Breath: Joseph McCabe and Rationalism*. Amherst, NY: Prometheus Books, 2001.

Croce, Benedetto. *Philosophy of the Practical: Economic and Ethic*, translated by Douglas Ainslie. London: Macmillan, 1913.

Cudworth, Ralph. *The True Intellectual System of the Universe, Wherein All the Reason and Philosophy of Atheism is Confuted and its Impossibility Demonstrated*, Vol. 1. London: for Richard Priestly, 1820. First published 1678.

Dacey, Austin. *The Future of Blasphemy: Speaking of the Sacred in an Age of Human Rights*. London: Continuum, 2012.

Dawkins, Richard. *The God Delusion*. London: Bantam Press, 2006.

de Beauvoir, Simone. *Adieux: A Farewell to Sartre*. New York: Pantheon, 1984.

Dennett, Daniel, and Linda LaScola. *Caught in the Pulpit: Leaving Belief Behind*. Durham, NC: Pitchstone, 2015.

Derrida, Jacques. "Ellipsis." In *Writing and Difference*, translated by Alan Bass. London and New York: Routledge, 2001. First published 1967.

Dewey, John. *Experience and Nature*. Chicago: Open Court, 1925.

d'Holbach, Paul-Henri Thiry. *The System of Nature: Or, Laws of the Moral and Physical World*, translated by H. D. Robinson. Boston: J. P. Mendum, 1889.

Dupré, Louis. "On the Intellectual Sources of Modern Atheism." *International Journal for Philosophy of Religion* 45, no. 1 (1999): 1–11.

Erdmann, Johann Eduard. *A History of Philosophy*, 3 volumes, edited by Williston Hough. London: Swan Sonnenschein, 1890. First published 1865.

Everitt, Nicholas. *The Non-Existence of God*. London and New York: Routledge, 2004.

Fales, Evan. "Naturalism and Physicalism." In *The Cambridge Companion to Atheism*, edited by Michael Martin, 118–134. Cambridge: Cambridge University Press, 2007.

Flew, Antony. *Atheistic Humanism*. Buffalo, NY: Prometheus Books, 1993.

Flynn, Tom. *The New Encyclopedia of Unbelief*. Amherst, NY: Prometheus Books, 2007.

Godwin, Benjamin. *Lectures on the Atheistic Controversy*. London: Jackson and Walford, 1834.

Grayling, A. C. *Meditations for the Humanist: Ethics for a Secular Age*. Oxford: Oxford University Press, 2002.

Habermas, Jürgen. *Between Facts and Norms: Contributions to a Discourse Theory of Law and Democracy*, translated by William Rehg. Cambridge, MA: MIT Press, 1996.

Habermas, Jürgen. *Between Naturalism and Religion*, translated by Ciaran Cronin. Cambridge, UK: Polity, 2008.

Habermas, Jürgen. *The Theory of Communicative Action*, 2 volumes, translated by Thomas McCarthy. Boston: Beacon, 1984–1987.

Habgood, John. *Varieties of Unbelief*. London: Darton, Longman and Todd, 2000.

Harris, Sam. *The End of Faith: Religion, Terror, and the Future of Reason*. New York: Norton, 2004.

Haught, John F. *God and the New Atheism: A Critical Response to Dawkins, Harris, and Hitchens*. Louisville, KY: Westminster John Knox Press, 2008.

Hecht, Jennifer Michael. *Doubt, A History: The Great Doubters and Their Legacy of Innovation from Socrates and Jesus to Thomas Jefferson and Emily Dickinson*. New York: HarperCollins, 2010.

Heidegger, Martin. *Being and Time*, translated by Joan Stambaugh. Albany: State University of New York Press, 1996. First published 1927.

Hitchcock, S. C. *Disbelief 101: A Young Person's Guide to Atheism*. Amherst, NY: Prometheus Books, 2009.

Hitchens, Christopher. *God Is Not Great: How Religion Poisons Everything*. New York: Hachette Book Group, 2007.

Howard-Snyder, Daniel, ed. *The Evidential Argument from Evil*. Bloomington: Indiana University Press, 2006.

Hughes, John, ed. *The Unknown God: Sermons Responding to the New Atheists*. Eugene, OR: Wipf & Stock, 2013.

Hume, David. *Dialogues Concerning Natural Religion*. Cambridge: Cambridge University Press, 2007. First published 1779.

Hurd, Elizabeth Shakman. *The Politics of Secularism in International Relations*. Princeton, NJ: Princeton University Press, 2009.

Israel, Jonathan. *Radical Enlightenment: Philosophy and the Making of Modernity, 1650–1750*. New York: Oxford University Press, 2001.

Jacoby, Susan. *Freethinkers: A History of American Secularism*. New York: Henry Holt, 2004.

Jossua, Jean-Pierre, and Claude Geffre, eds. *Indifference to Religion*. Edinburgh, UK: T. & T. Clark, 1983.

Kaufman, Whitley. "Can Science Determine Moral Values? A Reply to Sam Harris." *Neuroethics* 5, no. 1 (2012): 55–65.

King, Richard. *Indian Philosophy: An Introduction to Hindu and Buddhist Thought*. Edinburgh, UK: Edinburgh University Press, 1999.

Kurtz, Paul. *Embracing the Power of Humanism*. Lanham, MD: Rowman and Littlefield, 2000.

Kurtz, Paul. *Forbidden Fruit: The Ethics of Humanism*. Amherst, NY: Prometheus Books, 1987.

Kurtz, Paul. *In Defense of Secular Humanism*. Amherst, NY: Prometheus Books, 1983.

Kurtz, Paul. *Multi-Secularism: A New Agenda*. New Brunswick, NJ: Transaction Publishers, 2010.

Kurtz, Paul. *The Transcendental Temptation: A Critique of Religion and the Paranormal*. Amherst, NY: Prometheus Books, 1986.

Lamont, Corliss. *The Philosophy of Humanism*, 8th ed. Amherst, NY: Humanist Press, 1997.

Larue, Gerald A. *Freethought Across the Centuries*. Amherst, NY: Humanist Press, 1996.

Le Poidevin, Robin. *Arguing for Atheism: An Introduction to the Philosophy of Religion*. London and New York: Routledge, 1996.

Chapter 15: Atheology

Levinas, Emmanuel. *Of God Who Comes to Mind*. Translated by Bettina Bergo. Stanford, CA: Stanford University Press, 1998.

Levinas, Emmanuel. *Totality and Infinity: An Essay on Exteriority*, translated by Alphonso Lingis. Pittsburgh, PA: Duquesne University Press, 1969.

MacIntyre, Alasdair C., and Paul Ricœur. *The Religious Significance of Atheism*. New York: Columbia University Press, 1969.

Mackey, James P. *The Critique of Theological Reason*. Cambridge: Cambridge University Press, 2000.

Marshall, Paul, and Nina Shea. *Silenced: How Apostasy and Blasphemy Codes Are Choking Freedom Worldwide*. Oxford: Oxford University Press, 2011.

Martin, Michael. "Atheism and Religion." In *The Cambridge Companion to Atheism*, ed. Michael Martin, 217–232. Cambridge: Cambridge University Press, 2007.

Martin, Michael, and Ricki Monnier, eds. *The Impossibility of God*. Amherst, NY: Prometheus Books, 2003.

Martin, Michael, and Ricki Monnier, eds. *The Improbability of God*. Amherst, NY: Prometheus Books, 2006.

Marty, Martin E. *Varieties of Unbelief*. New York: Holt, Rinehart, and Winston, 1964.

McGowan, Dale. *Atheism For Dummies*. Mississauga, Canada: John Wiley & Sons Canada, 2013.

McGowan, Dale, ed. *Parenting Beyond Belief: On Raising Ethical, Caring Kids Without Religion*. New York: AMACOM Books, 2007.

McGowan, Dale, Molleen Matsumura, Amanda Metskas, and Jan Devor. *Raising Freethinkers: A Practical Guide for Parenting Beyond Belief*. New York: AMACOM Books, 2009.

McGrath, Alister. *Why God Won't Go Away: Engaging with the New Atheism*. London: SPCK, 2011.

Mohler, R. Albert Jr. *Atheism Remix: A Christian Confronts the New Atheists*. Wheaton, IL: Crossway Books, 2008.

Nielsen, Kai. *God and the Grounding of Morality*. Ottawa, Canada: University of Ottawa Press, 1991.

Nielsen, Kai. *Naturalism and Religion*. Amherst, NY: Prometheus Books, 2001.

Nietzsche, Friedrich. *Beyond Good and Evil*. Translated by Judith Norman. Cambridge: Cambridge University Press, 2001. First published 1886.

Nietzsche, Friedrich. *The Gay Science*, translated by Josefine Nauckhoff and Adrian Del Caro. Cambridge: Cambridge University Press, 2001. First published 1882.

Nietzsche, Friedrich. *On the Genealogy of Morals*. Translated by Douglas Smith. Oxford: Oxford University Press, 1996. First published 1887.

Nietzsche, Friedrich. *Thus Spoke Zarathustra*, translated by Adrian Del Caro. Cambridge: Cambridge University Press, 2006. First published 1883–1885.

Onfray, Michael. *Atheist Manifesto*, translated by Jeremy Leggatt. New York: Arcade, 2007.

Oppy, Graham. *Arguing about Gods*. Cambridge: Cambridge University Press, 2006.

Philipse, Herman. *God in the Age of Science? A Critique of Religious Reason*. Oxford: Oxford University Press, 2012.

Pigliucci, Massimo. "New Atheism and the Scientistic Turn in the Atheism Movement." *Midwest Studies in Philosophy* 37, no. 1 (2013): 142–153.

Plantinga, Alvin. *God and Other Minds: A Study of the Rational Justification of Belief in God*. Ithaca, NY: Cornell University Press, 1967.

Price, Robert M. *The Reason-Driven Life: What Am I Here on Earth For?* Amherst, NY: Prometheus Books, 2006.

Quack, Johannes. *Disenchanting India: Organized Rationalism and Criticism of Religion in India*. Oxford: Oxford University Press, 2011.

Radest, Howard B. *The Devil and Secular Humanism: The Children of the Enlightenment*. New York: Praeger, 1990.

Ray, Darryl. *Sex & God: How Religion Distorts Sexuality*. Bonner Springs, KS: IPC Press, 2012.

Robertson, J. M. *A History of Freethought*, 4th ed. London: Watts and Co., 1936.

Rosenberg, Alex. *The Atheist's Guide to Reality: Enjoying Life without Illusions*. New York: W. W. Norton, 2011.

Roy, M. N. *Radical Humanism*. New Delhi: n.p., 1952.

Roy, M. N. *Science and Philosophy*. Calcutta: Renaissance Publishers, 1947.

Ruse, Michael. *Atheism: What Everyone Needs to Know*. Oxford: Oxford University Press, 2015.

Santayana, George. *The Life of Reason; or, The Phases of Human Progress*, 5 vols. New York: Charles Scribner's Sons, 1905–1906.

Schneider, Nathan. *God in Proof: The Story of a Search from the Ancients to the Internet*. Berkeley: University of California Press, 2013.

Schulz, William F. *Making the Manifesto: The Birth of Religious Humanism*. Boston: Skinner House, 2002.

Shook, John R. *The God Debates: A Twenty-First Century Guide for Atheists and Believers (and Everyone in Between)*. Malden, MA: Wiley-Blackwell, 2010.

Shook, John R. "Scientific Atheology." *Science, Religion and Culture* 1, no. 1 (2014): 32–48.

Smith, George H. *Why Atheism?* Amherst, NY: Prometheus Books, 2000.

Stenger, Victor. *God: The Failed Hypothesis: How Science Shows That God Does Not Exist.* Amherst, NY: Prometheus Books, 2007.

Stenger, Victor. *Quantum Gods: Creation, Chaos, and the Search for Cosmic Consciousness.* Amherst, NY: Prometheus Books, 2009.

Stone, Jerome A. *Religious Naturalism Today: The Rebirth of a Forgotten Alternative.* Albany: State University of New York Press, 2008.

Stroumsa, Sarah. *Freethinkers of Medieval Islam: Ibn al-Rāwandī, Abū Bakr al-Rāzī and Their Impact on Islamic Thought.* Leiden, the Netherlands: Brill, 1999.

Taylor, Mark C. *Erring: A Postmodern A/theology.* Chicago: University of Chicago Press, 1987.

Turner, James. *Without God, Without Creed: The Origins of Unbelief in America.* Baltimore, MD: Johns Hopkins University Press, 1985.

Watson, Peter. *The Age of Atheists: How We Have Sought to Live Since the Death of God.* New York: Simon & Schuster, 2014.

Weil, Simone. *Waiting for God,* translated by Emma Craufurd. London: Routledge and Kegan Paul, 1951.

Westphal, Merold. *Suspicion & Faith: The Religious Uses of Modern Atheism.* New York: Fordham University Press, 1993.

Winell, Marlene. *Leaving the Fold: A Guide for Former Fundamentalists and Others Leaving Their Religion.* Oakland, CA: New Harbinger, 1993.

Zacharias, Ravi K. *The End of Reason: A Response to the New Atheists.* Grand Rapids, MI: Zondervan, 2008.

Zuckerman, Phil, ed. *Atheism and Secularity,* 2 volumes. Santa Barbara, CA: Preager, 2010.

CHAPTER 16

New Atheism

Teemu Taira
Senior Lecturer, Study of Religions
University of Helsinki

In an article titled "The Church of the Non-Believers," published in 2006 in *Wired*, an American monthly magazine, journalist Gary Wolf wrote about the intellectual brothers who are mounting a crusade against belief in God. He called them "the New Atheists [who] will not let us off the hook simply because we are not doctrinaire believers. They condemn not just belief in God but respect for belief in God. Religion is not only wrong; it's evil" (Wolf 2006). Although it was not necessarily the very first use of the term *New Atheism* (Zenk 2013, 251), soon after the publication of Wolf's article it started to circulate in American and European media.

The term created some confusion and, despite the shared minimal understanding that it denoted strong criticism of religion, people persistently questioned what was new in the New Atheism, as if "new" were an analytical attribute. Zenk has suggested that the term not be used at all in scholarly texts, unless it is in quotation marks ("New Atheism") (Zenk 2013, 245), but this depends on the criteria established for definitions. Apparently, no scholar has suggested that it is a clearly defined technical term for scholarly purposes; rather, it was originally a journalistic term, a shorthand term for talking about publicly visible antireligious atheist authors. It is difficult to demonstrate beyond doubt the shared attributes limited to those named as New Atheists, if that is required for the term to have any meaningful use. However, the term has a largely agreed reference point in four thinkers, their writings and their supporters, namely, Richard Dawkins (b. 1941) and his *The God Delusion* (2006), Daniel Dennett (b. 1942) and his *Breaking the Spell* (2006), Sam Harris (b. 1967) and his *The End of Faith* (2004), and Christopher Hitchens (1949–2011) and his *God Is Not Great* (2007).

The ideas of these four authors are far from identical, but they do share some similarities. Furthermore, these authors are networked on the basis of their shared activities and mutual endorsements. Thus, they themselves are in part responsible for the fact that people have started to associate them with each other, while at the same time identifying differences between their ideas. Despite the differences, one typical idea they do share is that Charles Darwin's theory of evolution by natural selection is the best explanation for the origins and development of life. They contrast Darwin's explanation with religious claims for life's beginning, claims that they consider both false propositional statements about the world, and harmful. These four writers refuse to show respect for ideas and practices on the basis that they are regarded as religious. Their criticism is not limited to so-called fundamentalists—despite the fact the New Atheists' characterization of a religious person is reminiscent of fundamentalism—but it also targets so-called moderate religious

281

Chapter 16: New Atheism

people and their beliefs. Furthermore, they want to promote and spread nonreligious and atheistic convictions and strengthen the atheist identity.

This chapter provides an introduction to the key authors labeled as New Atheists, explores their reception, and offers multidisciplinary tools by which to interpret the recent visibility of atheist criticism of religion. Furthermore, it is suggested that local contexts with their specific histories should be taken into account when examining the dissemination and adjustment of New Atheism. Finally, this chapter asks whether New Atheism is already becoming a thing of the past, superseded by other forms and types of atheism.

THE FOUR HORSEMEN

Gary Wolf's article mentions Dawkins, Dennett, and Harris, but not Hitchens, because Hitchens's *God Is Not Great* had not yet been published at the time of the article. Later, all four participated in a roundtable discussion titled *Four Horsemen*—a biblical allusion to the four horsemen of the apocalypse—in September 2007, and it is available on YouTube. Each of their contributions has shaped what has become known as New Atheism.

SAM HARRIS

When *The End of Faith* was published in 2004, Sam Harris (b. 1967) was a PhD student of cognitive neuroscience in the United States. He later completed his degree, but his reputation is not based on academic work. He is, before anything else, an author whose first book's success gave him the opportunity to publish books dealing with many topics, such as free will, science-based morality, and spirituality.

The End of Faith takes Islam and Christianity as its main targets. It is difficult not to read the book against 9/11, and according to Harris himself, he started to write the book after the events that led to the collapse of New York's Twin Towers. Some scholars have criticized Harris's ignorance of Islam and the Middle East (Atran 2010; Dickson 2010; Hedges 2008) as well as his selective use of sources; for example, he relies on pro-Israeli sources (Bradley and Tate 2010, 113). The book is filled with controversial statements and suggestions that Harris has had to later explain. For instance, he has been interpreted as supporting torture, preemptive strikes, and the invasion of Iraq. Although Harris has since qualified his statements, his disdain for Islam is clearly reflected throughout his writings. Indeed, hypothetical examples of Islamic suicide bombers are to be found from the first page of *The End of Faith* to his later work on scientific morality (*The Moral Landscape* 2010, 63).

Although Harris's focus is on Islamic terrorism, he states that "the greatest problem confronting civilization" is not limited to so-called religious extremism. "Religious moderates," he writes, "are, in large part, responsible for the religious conflict in our world, because their beliefs provide the context in which scriptural literalism and religious violence can never be adequately opposed" (2004, 45). The point here is not to suggest that the statement is plausible, but to demonstrate one shared aspect among the four horsemen (even by less provocative Dennett 2006, 297–301)—namely, the claim that moderate believers are somewhat responsible for the more extreme, religiously justified acts.

282   MACMILLAN INTERDISCIPLINARY HANDBOOKS

Harris does not criticize all religious or spiritual traditions equally. In his first book, *The End of Faith* (2004), he makes some positive observations about Eastern spirituality. Ever since, he has been an outspoken defender of spirituality, meditation and his "distilled" version of Buddhism, most substantively in *Waking Up* (Harris 2014). This stance clearly distinguishes him from other bestselling atheist authors. Furthermore, Harris is a strong defender of American and Israeli foreign policies. In addition, at the same time that he highlights the natural sciences as a path to obtain not only knowledge but also morality, he puts much less emphasis on the theory of evolution in explaining religion and human behavior than either Dawkins or Dennett. Moreover, although he has contributed to the consciousness-raising of people who do not believe in God and who are critical of Islam, Christianity, and Judaism, he has been reluctant to speak positively about atheism as an identity. In fact, the word "atheism" cannot be found in the index of *The End of Faith*.

RICHARD DAWKINS

The most famous of the four authors is Richard Dawkins (b. 1941), British ethologist and evolutionary biologist, who was Professor of Public Understanding of Science at the University of Oxford until 2008. In 2006 he published *The God Delusion*, a vehement critique of religion. He had written critically about religion earlier, but this was his first book-length effort. It has sold more than two million copies, and it has been translated into more than thirty languages.

Dawkins's main message in relation to religion is that science and the theory of evolution explain the origins of life and its development. Religions are wrong, he says, and also harmful in their claims about the world and in their doctrines that ultimately aim to control people. One of his most famous positions is that parents should not offer a religious upbringing to their children, but should instead let them decide for themselves when they are old enough. He suggests that the origin of religion might be the by-product of children's habit of learning to obey their parents. As obedience is necessary for survival up to a point, particularly when small kids learn to avoid danger, Dawkins claims that children learn religious beliefs as part of the baggage. His reasoning has achieved far from scholarly consensus because children cannot be taught to believe whatever their parents say (Barrett 2012, 181–185).

But detailing scholarly criticism of Dawkins is not the main purpose here, although it is notable that Dawkins's popular writings about religion claim to be scientifically valid. There are more relevant aspects of his works and efforts that merit attention—namely, Dawkins's aim to promote consciousness-raising among people uncertain about their standpoint or too shy to state openly that they do not believe the teachings of any religion. Dawkins is clear about this aim in his preface: "My dream is that this book may help people to come out" and initiate "a chain reaction" that ends up improving the public image and status of atheists (2006, 27).

Dawkins is a celebrated public intellectual whose work goes well beyond popular books. He lectures around the world and contributes actively to public discussions in newspapers and television. Furthermore, he has presented several documentaries, all of them seeking to further the public status of the natural sciences and some of them taking religion as their primary opponent. Dawkins's celebrated stance notwithstanding, he is also strongly criticized throughout the mainstream media, particularly when he comments on religious issues, claiming religious beliefs to be false and harmful, and suggesting that privileges of religious institutions should be discarded.

DANIEL DENNETT

Daniel Dennett (b. 1942) is a well-known American philosopher who, in addition to his scholarly works, has written popular books about evolutionary biology and cognitive science. His first full-length critique of religion was *Breaking the Spell: Religion as a Natural Phenomenon* (2006). The spell Dennett wishes to break is, first of all, that religion cannot be studied in the same way as any other natural phenomenon and, second, the hold of religion itself. Although Dennett suggests that "natural" in the subtitle of his book is the opposite of "supernatural"—meaning that there is no space for supernatural explanations in the study of religion—in practice it means that religion is studied by means of the natural sciences, particularly from the point of view of the theory of evolution and cognitive science rather than the humanities and social sciences.

Despite locating himself, both problematically and ahistorically, as a pioneer in the naturalistic study of religion, Dennett overall presents a tone and style that are more moderate and cautious than those of the other three authors. In fact, a Christian critic of Dawkins, Alister McGrath, deems Dennett's book a "well-argued, thoughtful, and interesting work, which shows no signs of the rambling and ranting" which he finds in Dawkins's writings on religion (Dennett and McGrath 2008, 28; see also Day 2008, 193).

Although Dennett clearly denies the existence of God and promotes the theory of evolution as the explanatory framework for religion as a natural phenomenon, his overall attitude differs from that of Dawkins, Harris, and Hitchens in at least three ways. First, Dennett has defended teaching about religion in schools. He thinks that children should receive neutral and objective information about religions as part of their education (Dennett and McGrath 2008, 25–26; Dennett 2006, 327–328). Second, he does not argue that religions are simply harmful. He admits that they can be beneficial too; for example, he points out the positive correlation between health and religiosity. At the same time, Dennett wonders whether there are better means to get the benefits of religion and whether the negative side effects of religiosity trump the positive aspects. At least he is willing to say that the issue is complex and that it is wise to postpone judgment until better information becomes available. Third, Dennett demonstrates some interest in the academic study of religion by referring to it more than the other New Atheists do. Although scholars of religion (e.g., Geertz 2008) have heavily criticized his views, at least he finds it relevant to make mention of some scholars whose professional lives have been dedicated to explaining religion.

CHRISTOPHER HITCHENS

Christopher Hitchens (1949–2011) jumped onto the New Atheist wagon a bit later than the other three. As a well-known and respected essayist, he had already published critical works on religious issues. For example, his short but devastating critique of Mother Teresa, *The Missionary Position: Mother Teresa in Theory and Practice* (1995), deserves mention here. His *God Is Not Great,* published in 2007, does not even pretend to be a scholarly work, but Hitchens is content to mock religious beliefs and practices by selecting humorous and horrifying examples. As a Brit who moved to America in 1981, he was able to address readers on both sides of the Atlantic better than Dennett or Harris, who are speaking almost exclusively to American audiences.

God Is Not Great is a collection of anecdotes intended to stack up as an argument against what Hitchens considers the silly and harmful nature of religious beliefs and practices. Furthermore, it suggests that religion gets privileged treatment for no justifiable reason. Hitchens has a point in some of the instances he mentions, such as when he wonders whether demands for male circumcision or prohibition of drawing a certain figure were taken seriously if made by nonreligious mass movements. However, the basic problem with the book is his tendency to reduce complex phenomena to categorical straightjackets consisting of two sides—irrational and barbaric religion on the one side and rational and secular civilization on the other side (Fitzgerald 2011, 110). Hitchens's avoidance of nuance is telescoped in the subtitle of the book's US edition: *How Religion Poisons Everything* (the subtitle of the original UK edition was *The Case Against Religion*). It is notable that Hitchens had earlier used the phrase "poisons everything." In his essay "Against Rationalization," published in his collection *Love, Poverty and War: Journeys and Essays* (2004), he states that it was binladenism (referring to the founder of al-Qaeda, Osama bin Laden) that poisoned everything. The replacement of binladenism for religion suggests that for Hitchens the prototypical form of religion is extremist and violent.

Hitchens's criticism of religion differed from that of the other like-minded atheists in that it was coming from a man with no academic pretensions. He was known and appreciated as a journalist and provocative essayist, but not as a scholar of any area. Furthermore, although he subscribed to the idea of evolution by natural selection and highlighted the importance of the natural sciences, he had other sources that could replace religion. He called for the new Enlightenment, thus locating himself in the tradition of Voltaire (1694–1778) and other eighteenth-century thinkers in critiquing supernatural beliefs and religion on the basis of reason. However, his greatest passion was literature. He wrote extensively about literature in general and his love of it, but, in his writings on religion, he argued that literature offers meaning for life as a replacement for religious meaning-making. In this binary religion, he maintained, is the sphere of rules, orders, and taboos, whereas literature is the sphere of freedom, reason, imagination, questioning, and moral thinking. It is not a surprise that celebrated British fiction writers, such as Ian McEwan, Martin Amis, and Salman Rushdie, whose works have been labeled as representing "the New Atheist novel" (Bradley and Tate 2010), were all personal friends of Hitchens and publicly praised by him. Indeed, *God Is Not Great* was dedicated to Ian McEwan.

ASSOCIATED PEOPLE

In addition to these four authors, there are others addressing the same issue and yet others who are keen to identify themselves with the New Atheists. For instance, American physicist and critic of religion Victor J. Stenger (1935–2014) suggested in his work *The New Atheism: Taking a Stand for Science and Reason* (2009) that he would like to be included as the fifth New Atheist. Another American physicist, Lawrence M. Krauss, is also known for his atheist activism. In *The Unbelievers* (2013), a documentary film, he traveled around the world with Richard Dawkins, spreading the message of science and atheism against religion. British philosopher, author, and well-known public intellectual A. C. (Anthony Clifford) Grayling has published several books arguing against religion and for secular humanist morality. Furthermore, he is a regular contributor to public debates on religion and values in the British media. He joined forces with Dawkins in signing an "atheist protest letter" arguing that the Pope should not have been given the honor of a state visit in September 2010, when Benedict XVI visited Britain (Knott, Poole, and Taira 2013, 168).

It would be possible to continue listing potential New Atheists, as many celebrities from actors to stand-up comedians have joined their cause on one or more occasions.

RELIGION: BEYOND RELIGION

Chapter 16: New Atheism

Furthermore, plenty of people have shared their experiences online and on social media after reading *The God Delusion* or watching the antireligious comic documentary *Religulous* (2008), which was hosted by comedian Bill Maher. Many state that they converted to atheism as a result of reading *The God Delusion* or watching *Religulous*. The boundaries between who is counted as New Atheist and who is not are not clear, and they cannot be, if it is generally agreed that the term *New Atheism* is used loosely to refer to some atheist authors and their supporting network, and is not used as a strictly defined analytical concept.

As should be obvious by now, New Atheism is a gendered phenomenon, and it has been exposed to feminist criticism (Beattie 2007). All key figures associated with it are men. There are female atheist thinkers and activists, such as Somali-Dutch ex-Muslim Ayaan Hirsi Ali, whom Hitchens (2011, 33) named as one of his heroes, and some of them have leading roles in humanist associations, but the most famous ones are men, as are most atheists in general. Surveys demonstrate the gender imbalance. The data based on World Values surveys indicate that only in four out of fifty-seven countries the percentage of atheist women surpassed men (Khan 2010). Global Atheist Census online found that 74 percent of atheists are men (Field 2013). In Finland, longitudinal comparison of a number of surveys shows that only 30 percent of self-avowed atheists are women (Taira 2012b, 25). Furthermore, the key atheist authors are predominantly white men whose education has been in the natural sciences or analytic philosophy. In addition, the most famous authors are either British or North American. However, the ideas of New Atheists have disseminated beyond Britain and North America, and some of the national differences will be addressed later in this chapter.

RECEPTION AND DISSEMINATION

So far the emphasis in this text has been on books and their authors. This is not an insignificant aspect. Even a major part of the reception of these works has revolved around book-length responses written mainly by Christian theologians, both liberal and conservative. Even by a cautious estimation, more than fifty books have been published in the English language as a response to the four New Atheist bestsellers. This total does not include other languages, so the overall number is likely much higher. The responses deal with the Dawkins, Dennett, Harris, and Hitchens in different ways. For instance, many British responses focus solely on Dawkins (Cornwell 2007; Jones 2007; Robertson 2008; Ward 2008). Some leave Dennett out because of his more moderate argument and style (Day 2008; Haught 2008). Most responses do not focus on others apart from the four horsemen. Their content varies from appeals to stop one-sided provocations and attempts to find alliance with unbelievers in a fight against extremism to more straightforward and impassioned judgments of the New Atheists.

In addition to published books, there have been several campaigns criticizing religion and promoting atheist or nonreligious identity. The most famous campaign is the so-called Atheist Bus Campaign that first took place in London and a couple of other British cities in January 2009. The advertisement on the sides of the buses suggested that "There is probably no God. Now stop worrying and enjoy your life."

The idea for the campaign came from British comedy writer and journalist Ariane Sherine as an atheist response to religious advertisements, and it was organized jointly with the British Humanist Association and Dawkins. It was launched with the help of donations.

Chapter 16: New Atheism

British atheists Ariane Sherine, Richard Dawkins, and Polly Toynbee next to a London bus ad, January 6, 2009. *When Sherine, a television writer, proposed an advertising campaign to help bring atheism out into the open, Dawkins, an internationally prominent atheist intellectual, and Toynbee, a newspaper columnist, endorsed it.* LEON NEAL/GETTY IMAGES.

As in many other atheist campaigns, the main point was not about whether many people would see the buses with the advertisements (although I happened to see one in Leeds where I lived then). The media attention it attracted was far more important for the campaign. With the help of the media, the campaign reached far more people than the buses. Furthermore, the photographs taken during the launch of the campaign were promoting the more diverse image of atheism. As a relatively young (she was born in 1980) nonwhite woman, Sherine was a perfect person to stand next to Dawkins in front of one of the buses in pictures that became widespread in the media, thus suggesting that not all atheist activists are angry old white men of the sciences.

Later the campaign was extended to other countries. According to the forthcoming *The Atheist Bus Campaign: Global Manifestations and Responses* by Spencer Bullivant and Steven Tomlins, it took place in fourteen countries in a rather similar manner. There were some differences in how it was organized and in the variety of responses. In many locations it was followed by other consciousness-raising events.

The Atheist Bus Campaign was just the tip of the iceberg. Since then, the topic of atheism has become more visible in the mainstream media (Knott, Poole, and Taira 2013, 101–117; Taira and Illman 2012), and the work of New Atheists has inspired and empowered atheist organizations (Cimino and Smith 2010).

None of these developments means that atheism has become more popular and accepted. The New Atheists have raised atheism to public discussion, but its impact is unclear. As John

Chapter 16: New Atheism

Cornwell writes in his criticism of Dawkins, it may well be that his campaigning does more good than harm to religion: "what an explosion of reviews, viewpoints, newspaper columns, debates, lectures, and seminars he has prompted!" (2007, 18). Similarly, Methodist minister Jenny Ellis was quoted in the British tabloid *The Sun* thanking Dawkins for "his continued interest in God and for encouraging people to think about these issues" (quoted in Knott, Poole, and Taira 2013, 105). Furthermore, the Christian think tank Theos donated £50 to the Atheist Bus Campaign "in the belief that talking about God is a good thing" (quoted in Knott, Poole, and Taira 2013, 106). These comments may be examples of wishful thinking on the part of Christians, but they remind us that the visibility of atheism in public life does not automatically lead to the increased popularity of atheism, but to the situation in which many topics are framed according to religion-related language (rather than, say, emphasizing ethnicity). It should be noted, however, that this is largely an elite debate that does not occupy everyone's thoughts. Despite Dawkins's constant presence in the media, 38 percent of the British sample in the 2010 YouGov poll responded that they did not know who Richard Dawkins was (Taira 2015, 118).

POLITICAL DIMENSION IN INTERPRETING NEW ATHEISM

There are many partial but complementary ways to interpret and explain New Atheism. One considerable aspect is related to political struggles (Kettel 2013, 2014; McAnulla 2012; Taira 2012a). Another is the role of the media, which conditions the possibilities given for atheist activities and frames how their cause comes to be understood by the general population. Finally, a sociological interpretation is needed for interpreting the rise of New Atheism.

THE GROWING INFLUENCE OF RELIGION

The politics of New Atheism is not focused on political parties, but rather on shaping influential opinion through the media. In the United States one of the main worries of New Atheists has been the perceived growing political influence of religion. Feeding this worry are the continued popularity of creationism, the rise of Islamic terrorism, and the close relationship of the Christian right with the George W. Bush administration in the early 2000s. Although New Atheists loathe the Christian Right and Evangelicals more generally, the relationship with the foreign politics of the Bush administration was more ambiguous.

For the four horsemen, Bush's religious identity and its connection with his politics became a negative issue. For instance, Dawkins mocked Bush, who allegedly suggested that God told him to invade Iraq, by responding that it is "a pity that God didn't vouchsafe him a revelation that there were no weapons of mass destruction" in Iraq (2006, 112). In contrast, Hitchens strongly supported US foreign politics and the invasion of Iraq. Harris's writings are full of support for anti-Islamic operations. He suggests that although it is understandable that the "failure to acknowledge our misdeeds over the years has undermined our credibility in the international community," the criticism of the current policy (as of 2004)—as exemplified in the work of Noam Chomsky—is "a masterpiece of moral blindness" (2004, 140–141). For his part, Dennett lamented not that the United States invaded Iraq but that the operation was not "large enough" and not well enough "deployed to reassure people without having to fire a shot" (2006, 282).

IDENTITY POLITICS OF ATHEISM

The political dimension of New Atheism is not limited to support or criticism of state policies. Another, even more significant dimension is what can be called identity politics. This term refers to empowering strategies and procedures that are based on differentiating a group from others on the basis of their socially constructed identity. Such constructed groups often see themselves marginalized and therefore demand greater recognition and attempt to improve their social status (Heyes 2012; Taira 2012a 102–103). This complaint is expressed straightforwardly by Dawkins who writes in the preface of *The God Delusion* that his "purpose is consciousness-raising" (2006, 25) and makes an analogue between atheists and the gay movement. He suggests that "exactly as in the case of the gay movement, the more people come out, the easier it will be for others to join them" (2006, 27). This part of Dawkins's message works in some parts of Europe, but its primary focus is on the United States. Indeed, according to the American Mosaic Project Survey conducted in 2003, 47.6 percent of US citizens said they would disapprove if their child wanted to marry an atheist, whereas only 33.5 percent would oppose their child marrying a Muslim. Similarly, 39.6 percent felt that atheists do not agree with their vision of American society, whereas the equivalent percentage for Muslims and homosexuals was 26.3 percent and 22.6 percent, respectively (Edgell, Gerteis, and Hartmann 2006, 218). The more recent American Trends Panel, conducted in 2014, demonstrates that atheists receive an average rating of 41 in the scale from 0 (cold) to 100 (warm) as a response to the "feeling thermometer." Muslims scored 40, but all other minority groups identified in the survey were seen more positively—between 48 (Mormons) and 63 (Jews) (Pew Research 2014). Although atheists are not considered most warmly in all western European countries, from the atheist point of view the situation is worse in the United States, as comparative value surveys indicate.

The surveys show that a lot of work remains to be done to improve the public image of atheists in the United States. In the New Atheist books, this image altering is done primarily by arguing that religious beliefs are wrong and harmful. The rise of Islamic extremism is as good an enemy internationally as are creationists closer to home. As a counterforce, atheists promote the natural sciences in education and society, combined with the argument—well backed up by some social scientific studies (Beit-Hallahmi 2007; Zuckerman 2009)—that morality and living according to values society holds dear do not require religious beliefs or practices.

Although the New Atheist identity politics has fertile ground in the United States, differences between other localities should not be overlooked. For example, British atheists have their own struggles, which are partly inspired by all four horsemen but not necessarily fully addressed by them. In Britain, atheists typically oppose faith schools, the presence of Church of England bishops in the House of Lords, and the government's interest in forming partnerships with faith communities, to name but a few examples. However, being nonreligious does not carry strong negative associations, and it is not an "impediment to gaining political office" (Bullivant 2010), although being vocally antireligious may not increase one's chances to form political alliance with others.

In Nordic countries, the struggles are slightly different. In Finland, for example, the main issues addressed by atheist activists concern the privileged role of the Evangelical Lutheran Church as guaranteed in law. The Lutheran Church's membership fees are collected directly from taxes, and even companies pay taxes to the church. The presence of Lutheran practices in schools and other publicly funded institutions such as health care, prisons, army, and universities is an issue that is raised constantly in public debate because atheists have to adjust to these practices or opt out of events deemed as religious. Atheists are

Chapter 16: New Atheism

not regarded as a discriminated minority in the sense that individuals are mistreated in private life because of their atheism, but they feel that public institutions do not adequately address their identity and conviction. Because local settings are varied, the New Atheist arguments need some translation. Specifically, they need to be adjusted to local struggles. Therefore, they can be inspirational in politics, but they do not provide any kind of direct guidance for action in all locations.

THE ROLE OF MEDIA

Another relevant aspect of understanding New Atheism is the role of media. More than anything else, the media creates conditions for atheism to get its visibility. News production is global, bringing more information about distant parts of the world faster than ever before. There has been a liberalization of media economies, leading to decreased regulation and less centralized media. Technological development has made new media platforms (such as YouTube and social media) part of everyday life in the modern world.

The same development has contributed significantly to the so-called publicization of religion (Herbert 2011; 2012), so the overall development has contributed to the visibility of both atheism and religion. However, it has been suggested that the development of media as a semiautonomous institution leads to mediatization; that is, other institutions become more dependent on resources controlled by the media, and hence they have to submit to the rules the media operates by in order to become heard and seen in the society (Hjarvard 2013, 23). In practice, this means that although media outlets compete for audience and their attention, they tend to prefer a polarized framing of any debate in seeking clicks and comments. Therefore, the provocative attitude of New Atheism fits well with the way in which contemporary mainstream media operate.

Only some developments are driven by traditional producers of media content. Atheism is flourishing in digital media, helping people to find like-minded others and form an "imagined secularist community" (Cimino and Smith 2011, see also Smith and Cimino 2012; Taira 2015, 114–116). This is mainly because of the possibilities digital media allows for user-generated content in blogs and discussion fora. YouTube has made it possible for people to listen to talks given in a distant location. Twitter has proven influential in its own way. For instance, Dawkins and Harris are active users of Twitter, allowing them to comment quickly without the traditional mediating institutions. Although the published books and mainstream media attention have been crucial in enhancing the visibility of New Atheism, it is hard to imagine it would have received such widespread attention without the development of digital media.

SOCIOLOGICAL INTERPRETATIONS

Finally, the rise of New Atheism is subject to relevant sociological interpretations. As already suggested, most of the writings on New Atheism have been theological responses, but some useful edited volumes dealing with social scientific analyses of the New Atheism have been published (Amarasingam 2010; Cimino and Smith 2015; Taira and Illman 2012). In order to start uncovering social conditions surrounding the recent visibility of atheism, it is necessary to understand what was expected to happen some decades before there was much demand for atheistic campaigns.

Chapter 16: New Atheism

THE "RETURN" OF RELIGION

The intellectual vision had been that secularization was almost linear and inevitable. Soon after the Second World War, but especially in the 1960s, sociologists started to predict convincingly the decline of religiosity in the modern world. Some version of secularization is present in most of the classical social science scholars such as Auguste Comte, Karl Marx, Max Weber, and Émile Durkheim. An updated and more elaborated version of the rise of secularization to the detriment of the social significance of religion in the process of modernization emerged in the 1960s in the works of sociologists of religion Bryan R. Wilson and Peter L. Berger. Their vision became popular among educated elite, as exemplified in *Time* magazine's famous cover from 1966 asking, "Is God dead?" Although *Time*'s story referred primarily to atheism within Christianity, especially in the work of US theologian Thomas J. J. Altizer, it hinted of wider changes in society. Intellectuals were largely convinced of the decline of religiosity.

It is not necessary to suggest any specific year when the tide turned, but two significant publications mapped the changes from the Islamic revolution in Iran in the late 1970s to the early 1990s. First was Gilles Kepel's *The Revenge of God: The Resurgence of Islam, Christianity and Judaism in the Modern World* (1994, French orig. 1991). Kepel's idea of the resurgence of religion relates mainly to the rise of fundamentalism, but he also deals with the idea of the re-Christianization of Europe, especially in Catholic areas. Second was José Casanova's *Public Religions in the Modern World* (1994), which argues that even though secularization may happen on the level of institutional differentiation and decline in beliefs, practices, and membership, the secularization subthesis concerning the privatization of religion is not valid. Instead, religions are becoming—and should become, according to Casanova's (2008, 101) normative statement—more relevant in the public sphere as rational conversation partners, particularly in the United States, developing countries, and Catholic Europe. Later on, many other scholars in sociology, theology, religious studies, politics, and international relations followed this trend of challenging the inherited vision, albeit in very different ways.

The changing narrative does not mean that every single part of the secularization debate is out of date or has been proven wrong. There is much evidence of decline in religious beliefs, practice, identification, and membership, especially in many European countries. What is more important here is to trace the expansion from the scholarly narrative to the mainstream public discourse. In 2009 two journalists, John Micklethwait and Adrian Wooldridge, published a book titled *God Is Back: How the Global Rise of Faith Is Changing the World*. The book's main message is emblematic of the changing intellectual narrative outside narrow scholarly circles: forget secularization, religion is back!

The changing narrative is anchored in many conflicts and controversies. The best known is 9/11 in 2001, but the following bombings in Madrid (April 11, 2004) and London (June 7, 2005) shocked Europe. Furthermore, the assassination of Dutch populist antimulticulturalism politician Pim Fortuyn in 2002, the French headscarf affair (*l'affaire du foulard*) in 2004, the murder of Dutch film director and critic of Islam Theo van Gogh by a Muslim in 2004, the Danish cartoon controversy in 2005, the Swiss minaret ban in 2009, and *Charlie Hebdo* shooting in France in 2015 have kept Islam in the news through controversies and contributed to the awareness of the new presence of religion in public life. All these events have fueled the New Atheist cause and have proved expedient to the claims about the dangers of religion.

It is not an exaggeration to suggest that New Atheism coincides and makes use of the more general trend in which the typical "Other" serving to constitute the imagined identity

RELIGION: BEYOND RELIGION

Chapter 16: New Atheism

of the (supposedly rational) West has changed from previous images exemplified in African black cannibals of colonial times to Nazis and Communists, and further to Islamic extremists/terrorists in the contemporary world. A good example of the Islamic stereotype is the case of Shakeel Ahmad Bhat, better known as Islamic rage boy, whose picture has been in many newspapers and whose face has become a popular Internet meme. The simple image—a stereotype—of a raging Muslim in demonstration is enough to convey the idea that "we" are not supposed to identify with it (Morey and Yaqin 2011, 22–30). "We" are not asking questions about his life history, but we are satisfied with the judgment, given by Hitchens, that he is a "religious nut bag," whose demands—whatever they are—are "impossible to satisfy" (Hitchens 2009). Given such writings, it is not surprising that it has been suggested that New Atheism belongs to the Eurocentric realm of "white male hauteur" (Salaita 2008, 152), whose "Other"—what "we" are not and what is threatening—is the supposed return of religion, particularly Islam.

The aim of atheist campaigners is to diminish the role of religion in society. Because religion has not vanished by itself in an ever-modernizing society, as was predicted, the New Atheists feel a greater need for activism and promotion of a critical attitude toward religion. In this sense, it may be acceptable to suggest that New Atheists "re-sacralize the secularization thesis" (Borer 2010, 134) in opposition to sociologists of religion who have "desacralized" or refined it in recent decades. If religion is seen as a serious threat to society and its rational and scientific planning, then secularization would be the desired development. If the secularization narrative is understood to be in crisis, activism is regarded as an urgent task.

IMAGINED ENEMIES OF MODERN SCIENCE

The rise of atheism, and New Atheism in particular, is partly a reaction to the new visibility of religion. However, this statement needs qualification: it is also a reaction against other imagined enemies of scientific rationality. This notion can be illustrated by making a useful distinction between two kinds of "secular" intellectuals: those who see "the knowledge gained by the advancing natural science as the point of" their life and those who have "lost faith in science with the same thoroughness as the Enlightenment had lost faith in God" (Rorty 1982, 228). Those who have lost faith in science typically include members of the so-called academic left—a shorthand expression for a number of diverse positions and theoretical approaches, such as continental philosophy, relativism, social constructionism, poststructuralism, postcolonialism, postmodernism, and feminist theory. There is no such homogeneous group as the academic left, but in New Atheist discourse, the aforementioned fields of study and theoretical approaches are lumped together as antiscientific (see Dawkins 2006, 388; Dennett 1998; Harris 2004, 179; Hitchens 2011; Stenger 1999).

The construction of the academic left as an enemy of New Atheism can be understood in at least two complementary ways. First, New Atheists represent a new kind of intellectual type and activity in which scientists are speaking directly to the lay public. The development of a new kind of intellectual is known as a suggested solution to the dilemma of "two cultures." In the late 1950s, British chemist and novelist C. P. Snow (2001) lamented the existence of two academic cultures: the traditional humanist-literary culture and the scientific. Those who were called intellectuals were found in the humanist-literary culture. They spoke directly to the masses, whereas members of the natural sciences communicated to larger audiences through traditional intellectuals. One solution to this dilemma has been the development of a new kind of science intellectual who avoids the middleman and writes for the general public using a popular approach and often talks about social issues (morality, politics and religion) despite being educated in the natural sciences. Called the third culture (Brockman 1995), this solution to the dilemma of two cultures comes with criticism of humanist-literary intellectuals for their alleged dismissal of science. In particular, Dawkins and Dennett represent this new kind of science intellectual. Religion is their good enemy but not the only one.

Second, constructing the academic left as an enemy is to be understood sociologically as part of the crisis of modernity. To put it briefly, New Atheism is in many ways a reaction to the implosion of the illusions of modernity, especially to the diminished prestige of science and of white educated men's threatened loss of social status in an increasingly diverse and multicultural society. Linda Woodhead (2012, 8–9) has emphasised the role of the weakened status of science in explaining the visibility of atheism, but it was journalist Andrew Brown who in a personal conversation first suggested that New Atheism be considered as the educated white elite's reaction to their threatened status. However, the issue is both broader as it relates to the general changes in modernity and narrower as it relates to atheists insisting on the superiority of the natural sciences over religious positions and cultural research. Sociologist Zygmunt Bauman has suggested repeatedly that (for him) modernity in its current liquid phase means "modernity minus its illusions" (Bauman and Tester 2001, 75). The implosion of modernity's illusions of an inevitable march toward an ever more rational and perfect society has resulted in a situation in which it has become common to be more modest in claims that increasing knowledge ensures social progress. It is their trust in progress through the rational and scientific organization of society that unites New Atheists as defenders of modernity with its illusions.

THE IMPORTANCE OF NATIONAL CONTEXTS

Although this analysis is not blind to a multiplicity of situations and locations, it is deliberately general. Sociologist David Martin has reminded us that when assessing secularization and potential reasons for the decline of religion, the theorizing "is profoundly inflected by particular histories, which in modern period are national histories qualified in a minor or major way by regional variations" (2011, 7). The situations of dominant religious institutions in the United States, Britain, or Finland are very different, not because the countries are in different stages of modernization, affluence, well-being, and education, but because the roles and functions of dominant churches vary from one nation to another. This holds true for our attempts to understand the role and scope of New Atheism because atheism has particular national histories, too.

The New Atheist message is addressed predominantly (but not exclusively) to American readers. This is explicit in Dennett's preface to *Breaking the Spell*, where he states that "this book is addressed in the first place to American readers" (2006, xi) and in Harris's second book, *Letter to a Christian Nation: A Challenge of Faith* (2007), which is written in a form of a letter to Christians in the United States. It is important, however, to look at other national contexts, for example, two European examples: Britain and Finland (about New Atheism in Germany, see Zenk 2012).

As already suggested, it is not a problem for a top politician to be an atheist in Britain. At the same time, British society does not cherish a direct antireligious attitude. This can be exemplified by examining the newspaper coverage of Dawkins during the papal visit to Britain in September 2010. Although Dawkins is an appreciated, respected author, commentator, and host in science documentaries, the media can give him a harsh treatment when he criticizes religion, particularly if the target is not Islamic extremism, creationism, or value-conservative evangelicalism. This attitude is not surprising for rather conservative and pro-Christian newspapers, which saw Dawkins's actions against the Pope as a "celebrity vendetta" motivated by "empty hatred." But such criticism is found in more left-leaning and liberal papers, too. For example, the *Independent* suggested that atheism could do without Dawkins (Knott, Poole, and Taira 2013, 168–170). This harsh statement does not take anything away from Dawkins's celebrity status, but it shows that even in a country where nonreligiosity is a far from marginalized position, the mainstream media does not strongly support campaigning against religious views.

The situation in Finland with regard to being an atheist is similar to that in the United Kingdom, though there are additional reasons to include Finland in this part of the discussion. In Finland, atheism has been strongly associated with communism and the former Soviet Union, the ruling neighboring country until Finland gained its independence in 1917. The dominant Evangelical Lutheran Church of Finland has historically been involved in the formation of Finnish nationalism, including during the Second World War, when Finland fought against the Soviet Union. Therefore, if atheism is associated with communism, it is also seen as a sign of anti-Finnishness. One aim of local atheist activists who have been inspired by New Atheism has been to break this chain of connections between atheism, communism, and anti-Finnishness. Activists have openly stated that they have tried to get people to associate atheism with Darwinian evolution and the natural sciences. Dawkins's campaign for science and atheism has been especially helpful in this endeavor, but the national history and traditional association of atheism with the threatening enemy explains why, in a rather secular Finland, atheism has been a much less popular identity than in other north European Protestant countries (Taira 2012b).

Another relevant aspect that can be drawn from examining this national setting relates to my personal experience. At the end of 2013, I was invited to give a talk to the Humanist Union of Finland about the new visibility of atheism. During the talk I took questions from the participants regarding New Atheist bestsellers and documentaries such as *Religulous*. As I expected, people were well aware of the basic arguments of the four horsemen. They were willing to criticize them while sharing with them the position of being for science, rationality, and humanist values and being against largely "irrational" religion. To my surprise, however, very few of them had read all four bestsellers, although the books are readily available in the Finnish language. Many had read one of them, some had read two. This suggests that although the most celebrated contemporary atheists are known and can be seen as giving further confidence to activists in local settings, their direct impact can be very limited. Rather, the case is that activists at the grass-roots level want to justify and identify their own activities by emphasizing differences from the four horsemen, despite sharing the wish to associate atheism with the natural sciences and secular humanism rather than communism. This problem may be limited to countries such as Finland where New Atheism is seen as too American in style, but it demonstrates the importance of examining local contexts in addition to the arguments and public role of the most popular atheists.

IS NEW ATHEISM COMING TO AN END?

The New Atheist bestsellers were published between 2004 and 2007. Since then, there have been several publicity campaigns, but the hype surrounding New Atheism has waned.

Chapter 16: New Atheism

Hitchens died in 2011 and Stenger died in 2014. Dennett has not been widely discussed in public in recent years. Dawkins and Harris have continued to stir the public debate, but have a much lower profile than they had some years ago. It is time to ask, what were the achievements of New Atheism, and where is it going, if anywhere?

"ATHEIST AWAKENING?"

As emphasized earlier, evaluation of the achievements and possible future directions of New Atheism has to be contextualized nationally. For instance, Richard Cimino and Christopher Smith see New Atheism as entangled with a wider "atheist awakening" in the United States, connecting it more generally with the rise of the "nones" (i.e., people with no religious affiliation) (Cimino and Smith 2015). It is doubtful whether New Atheism can take credit for people being increasingly less affiliated with religion, but at least its rise coincides with its stated aims. Rather than causing the rise of *nones,* proponents of New Atheism have attempted to provide a narrative frame for the development (Silk 2014)—to the point that campaigning atheists have tried to unify the diverse category of nones and establish themselves as representatives of nones by talking about "we."

One aim of New Atheism has been to divest religion of respect. It is difficult to assess whether its plan has worked. On the one hand, it appears that the overall questioning of religious beliefs and practices has increased in public discussion. On the other hand, this disrespect has contributed to the negative reputation of atheism and made the formation of alliances with moderate or liberal religious people more difficult. However, what has happened is that the most vocal atheists are representing religiously unaffiliated people in the media—whether or not they agree with activist atheists (Taira 2015, 119). For this reason, Jacques Berlinerblau (2012, xxiv), who campaigns for secularism—a political standpoint suspicious of relations between government and religion—complains that New Atheism is hijacking the voice of secularism in the American public, thereby making religiously moderate people suspicious of secularism and driving them into the arms of religious conservatives.

In Finland, atheism has become a more visible topic in the media, thus creating a greater awareness of atheism and nonreligiosity, but this does not mean that atheism as an identity has become much more popular, mainly because of the previously mentioned national history. A telling example from Finland demonstrates that the increasing visibility of atheist debates has led people to state their opinion of atheism in surveys. In 2008, 60 percent had either a neutral attitude toward atheism or responded that they did not know, whereas in 2011 the percentage declined to 52. Still more people had negative than positive attitudes, but the interesting change was that both positive and negative views had increased (positive: 18 percent in 2008, 22 percent in 2011; negative: 22 percent in 2008, 26 percent in 2011) (Taira 2012b). Hence, consciousness-raising has taken place, but again that does not necessarily mean that atheism is more popular or is seen in a more positive light. Nor does it mean that atheists have been able to produce larger social effects.

In addition to attitudes toward atheism, the membership rate in atheistic organizations is another relevant indicator of measuring the success and popularity of atheism. There is evidence that the number of members in such organizations has increased, but in many European countries the growth stopped around 2010. In Finland, for example, the numbers have gone down since then, and in 2015 they were only slightly above the numbers in 2006, when New Atheism was not yet being discussed in public.

RELIGION: BEYOND RELIGION

295

DISMISSING THE DIVERSITY OF ATHEISM

The achievements of New Atheism for society are hard to measure, but so far there is little direct evidence that it can take credit for the continuing statistical decline of religious beliefs, practices, and identification. It is perhaps easier to clarify the impact of New Atheism within the field of atheism. In addition to the empowering effect of New Atheism for atheist organizations, it has influenced the dominant forms of atheism. Historically, there have been different forms of atheism. In the nineteenth and twentieth centuries, the most prominent atheist thinkers were Friedrich Nietzsche (1844–1900), Karl Marx (1818–1883), Sigmund Freud (1856–1939), and Jean-Paul Sartre (1905–1980). Although it is not very common to speak about Freudian atheism, there are specific legacies which we call Nietzschean, Marxist, or—by following Sartre—existentialist atheism. This is not the place for an in-depth discourse on atheism, but it is evident that the above-mentioned thinkers are not the main inspiration for present-day atheism. None of the four horsemen speaks highly about any of them. A telling example is the volume edited by Hitchens—*The Portable Atheist: Essential Readings for the Nonbeliever* (2007). In this book Hitchens presents excerpts from forty-seven critics of religion but includes no texts by Nietzsche or Sartre (Freud and Marx are included, however).

It appears that the two historical atheist forefathers of New Atheism are David Hume (1711–1776) and Charles Darwin (1809–1882), despite the fact that neither identified themselves as atheist. Dennett (2006, 27) states that Hume is his hero, whereas Dawkins (1986, 6) once suggested that Darwin's theory of evolution by natural selection offered an intellectually satisfying justification to atheism. Such statements construct a tradition around New Atheism as if the lineage ran from Hume to Darwin and further to New Atheism. The purpose in this chapter is not to demonstrate the problems involved in putting them in the same group; for example, neither Hume nor Darwin would have accepted the confrontational style of the four horsemen. However, constructing such a narrative about the atheist tradition functions to exclude other prominent atheists and critics of religion from the tradition. Atheism is increasingly associated with the Darwinian theory of evolution and the natural sciences as well as with Dawkins and like thinkers, even in continental Europe where other forms of atheism once were more prominent. In this sense, the rise of New Atheism has lead to a decrease in the visibility of other forms of atheism.

ATHEISM WITH SPIRITUALITY AND COMMUNALITY

At the same time that the forms of atheism have narrowed, one of the unintended consequences of the rise of New Atheism has been a new expansion of atheistic forms. One reason for this expansion is that since the criticism posed by the four horsemen, people have started to ask whether atheism can be more constructive and whether it could be understood as having a positive content that is not reduced to scientific criticism of religion and political campaigns against religion. This possibility has led to a new fragmentation of the field of atheism. There is no ready-made typology available for the forms, but for the sake of clarity at least two prominent options can be identified—atheist spirituality and religion without belief in God—although in practice the difference between the two becomes blurred.

The New Atheists and self-proclaimed atheists who have become known following the publication of the New Atheist bestsellers are distancing themselves from monotheistic beliefs. This is what unites New Atheists and so-called spiritual atheists, or those atheists who see something good in religious traditions and institutions. A closer look at the spectrum demonstrates that authors such as Harris (2014) and Steve Antinoff (2009) deny the existence of God and God-like supernatural beings and have doubts about religious institutions, but they have very positive views on some Buddhist or Zen-Buddhist ideas and practices such as meditation. They can be called proponents of "atheist spirituality" (see Taira 2012c).

Then there are writers such as Alain de Botton (2012) and André Comte-Sponville (2008) who deny the existence of supernatural beings, but who want to preserve many practices of institutional religious traditions, such as rituals and community building. Furthermore, there are atheistic guidebooks for good living emphasizing the beauty of literature and hobbies without making positive references to the importance of Eastern traditions or Western religious institutions (Maisel 2009). These authors, whose books about atheism, spirituality, and religion have been published since the New Atheist bestsellers, take a New Atheist critique of religion as their starting point. They seem to agree that New Atheism was a moment of criticism without a positive, constructive guidance for leading a good and satisfying life as an atheist. In that sense, they can be understood as a next step after the high peak of New Atheism.

What is missing in these books is practical implementation. The Sunday Assembly, initiated by two British stand-up comedians, Sanderson Jones and Pippa Anderson, is probably the best-known example of an atheist congregation. In London in 2013, the organization of nonreligious gatherings in a deconsecrated church began where people sang songs, celebrated community, and listened to short presentations about the cosmos and related topics. Despite its clear atheistic standpoint, it has not been antireligious at any point in its public statements. It has received a lot of curious and mainly positive coverage in the media, but not all atheists have understood why there has to be any kind of worship-like nonreligious gatherings. In any case, the development of the Sunday Assembly and its spread from London to other parts of Britain and further to the United States and Australia have suggested that this might be the next phase in the direction of atheism, thus leaving New Atheism behind. However, as the Sunday Assembly is so recent a formation, it is too early to draw any conclusions. It is likely, however, that there will be small atheist (face-to-face and virtual) groups and networks that take a stand—positive, negative, or neutral—and define themselves in relation to New Atheism.

New forms of atheism have emerged as a reaction to New Atheism, but it does not mean that criticism of religion has vanished. The issues highlighted by the New Atheists have continued and find their ways into headlines every once in a while, often in the form of media debates. Although new voices have suggested that atheism should come with social responsibility and progressive politics, others maintain that criticism of supernatural beliefs and the influence of religion in society remains the only task for atheist activism.

Summary

This chapter has suggested that despite the vagueness of the term *New Atheism*, there are still enough common factors to reasonably speak about authors such as Dawkins, Dennett, Harris, and Hitchens in the same context. These authors have contributed to the recent visibility of atheism and criticism of religion by arguing that religious beliefs are false and harmful. Furthermore, they have suggested that no special respect is to be accorded to religions, protecting them from criticism, regardless of whether religious people are liberal or conservative, moderate or extreme. These claims are entangled with the attempt of New Atheists to make people "come out" and state their atheism (or nonreligiosity) in public.

Chapter 16: New Atheism

New Atheists claim to speak for rationality, reason, and science. Rather than aiming at falsifying or verifying their arguments, it has been demonstrated that political analysis, examination of the role of the media, and sociological studies are needed to provide appropriate understanding of why New Atheism has developed and gained a lot of attention.

New Atheism has received attention for the atheist cause, but has failed to score many measurable and concrete achievements. Rather, many have started to favor a more constructive approach instead of provocative criticisms of religion. These are by no means incompatible quests, but some have regarded the politics of New Atheism as detrimental to the secularist cause and others have actually tried to leave New Atheism behind by emphasizing that spirituality is relevant or that religions may have positive functions beyond supernatural beliefs. This does not mean an end to New Atheism as such because people such as Dawkins and Harris still make headlines and still attract an audience in the public sphere, but the high point of New Atheism has waned and the term itself may soon lose its urgency and usefulness. However, as the whole discourse on New Atheism is relatively recent, only time will tell how the situation is going to develop. Therefore, cautiousness in predictions is recommended. For the same reason, however, there are plenty of questions regarding New Atheism—its rise in general and its adjustment in local contexts—that still need to be properly addressed in future studies.

Bibliography

Amarasingam, Amarnath, ed. *Religion and the New Atheism: A Critical Appraisal*. Leiden, the Netherlands: E. J. Brill, 2010.

Antinoff, Steve. *Spiritual Atheism*. Berkeley, CA: Counterpoint, 2009.

Atran, Scott. *Talking to the Enemy: Faith, Brotherhood, and the (Un)making of Terrorists*. New York: Ecco Press, 2010.

Barrett, Justin L. *Born Believers: The Science of Children's Religious Belief*. New York: Free Press, 2012.

Bauman, Zygmunt, and Keith Tester. *Conversations with Zygmunt Bauman*. Cambridge, UK: Polity Press, 2001.

Beattie, Tina. *The New Atheists: The Twilight of Reason and the War on Religion*. London: Darton, Longmann and Todd, 2007.

Beit-Hallahmi, Benjamin. "Atheists: A Psychological Profile." In *The Cambridge Companion to Atheism*, edited by Michael Martin, 300–317. Cambridge: Cambridge University Press, 2007.

Berlinerblau, Jacques. *How to Be Secular: A Call to Arms for Religious Freedom*. Boston: Houghton Mifflin Harcourt, 2012.

Borer, Michael Ian. "The New Atheism and the Secularization Thesis." In *Religion and the New Atheism: A Critical Appraisal*, edited by Amarnath Amarasingam, 125–137. Leiden, the Netherlands: E. J. Brill, 2010.

Botton, Alain de. *Religion for Atheists: A Non-believer's Guide to the Uses of Religion*. London: Hamish Hamilton, 2012.

Bradley, Arthur, and Andrew Tate. *The New Atheist Novel: Fiction, Philosophy and Polemic after 9/11*. London: Bloomsbury, 2010.

Brockman, John. *The Third Culture: Beyond the Scientific Revolution*. New York: Simon & Schuster, 1995.

Bullivant, Stephen. "The New Atheism and Sociology: Why Here? Why Now? What Next?" In *Religion and the New Atheism: A Critical Appraisal*, edited by Amarnath Amarasingam, 109–124. Leiden, the Netherlands: E. J. Brill, 2010.

Bullivant, Spencer, and Steven Tomlins, eds. *The Atheist Bus Campaign: Global Manifestations and Responses*. Leiden, the Netherlands, E. J. Brill, forthcoming.

Casanova, José. *Public Religions in the Modern World*. Chicago: University of Chicago Press, 1994.

Casanova, José. "Public Religions Revisited." In *Religion: Beyond a Concept*, edited by Hent de Vries, 101–119. New York: Fordham University Press, 2008.

Cimino, Richard, and Christopher Smith. *Atheist Awakening: Secular Activism and Community in America*. Oxford: Oxford University Press, 2015.

Cimino, Richard, and Christopher Smith. "The Empowerment of American Freethinkers." In *Religion and the New Atheism: A Critical Appraisal*, edited by Amarnath Amarasingam, 139–156. Leiden, the Netherlands: E. J. Brill, 2010.

Cimino, Richard, and Christopher Smith. "The New Atheism and the Formation of Imagined Secularist Community." *Journal of Media and Religion* 10, no. 1 (2011): 24–38.

Comte-Sponville, André. *The Book of Atheist Spirituality: An Elegant Argument for Spirituality without God*. London: Bantam Press, 2008.

Cornwell, John. *Darwin's Angel*. London: Profile Books, 2007.

Dawkins, Richard. *The Blind Watchmaker*. New York: W. W. Norton, 1986.

Dawkins, Richard. *The God Delusion*. London: Black Swan, 2006.

Day, Vox. *The Irrational Atheists: Dissecting the Unholy Trinity of Dawkins, Harris and Hitchens*. Dallas, TX: BenBella, 2008.

Dennett, Daniel. *Breaking the Spell: Religion as a Natural Phenomenon*. London: Penguin, 2006.

Dennett, Daniel. "Postmodernism and Truth." 1998. http://ase.tufts.edu/cogstud/papers/postmod.tru.htm.

Dennett, Daniel, and Alister McGrath. "The Future of Atheism: A Dialogue." In *The Future of Atheism*, edited by Robert B. Stewart, 17–49. London: SPCK, 2008.

Dickson, Rory. "Religion as Phantasmagoria: Islam in *The End of Faith*." In *Religion and the New Atheism: A Critical Appraisal*, edited by Amarnath Amarasingam, 37–54. Leiden, the Netherlands: E. J. Brill, 2010.

Edgell, Penny, Joseph Gerteis, and Douglas Hartmann. "Atheists as "Other": Moral Boundaries and Cultural Membership in American Society." *American Sociological Review* 71, April (2006): 211–234.

Field, Clive. "Demographics of Atheism." *British Religion in Numbers*, January 26, 2013. http://www.brin.ac.uk/news/2013/demographics-of-atheism/.

Fitzgerald, Timothy. *Religion and Politics in International Relations: The Modern Myth*. London: Continuum, 2011.

Geertz, Armin. "How *Not* to Do the Cognitive Study of Religion Today." *Method and Theory in the Study of Religion* 20, no. 1 (2008): 7–21.

Harris, Sam. *The End of Faith: Religion, Terror, and the Future of Reason*. London: Free Press, 2004.

Harris, Sam. *Letter to a Christian Nation: A Challenge of Faith*. London: Transworld, 2007.

Harris, Sam. *The Moral Landscape: How Science Can Determine Human Values*. New York: Free Press, 2010.

Harris, Sam. *Waking Up: A Guide to Spirituality without Religion*. New York: Simon & Schuster, 2014.

Haught, John F. *God and the New Atheism: A Critical Response to Dawkins, Harris and Hitchens*. Louisville, KY: Westminster John Knox Press, 2008.

Hedges, Chris. *I Don't Believe in Atheists*. New York: Free Press, 2008.

Herbert, David. "Theorizing Religion and Media in Contemporary Societies: An Account of Religious 'Publicization'." *European Journal of Cultural Studies* 14, no. 6 (2011): 626–648.

Herbert, David. "Why Has Religion Gone Public Again?: Towards a Theory of Media and Religious Re-publicization." In *Religion, Media and Culture: A Reader*, edited by Gordon Lynch and Jolyon Mitchell with Anna Strhan, 89–97. London: Routledge, 2012.

Heyes, Cressida. "Identity Politics." In *The Stanford Encyclopedia of Philosophy*, edited by Edward N. Salta (Spring 2012 edition). http://plato.stanford.edu/entries/identity-politics/.

Hitchens, Christopher. *God Is Not Great: How Religion Poisons Everything*. London: Atlantic Books, 2007.

Hitchens, Christopher. *Hitch-22: A Memoir*. London: Atlantic Books, 2011.

Hitchens, Christopher. "Look Back in Anger." *Slate*. 2009. http://www.slate.com/articles/news_and_politics/fighting_words/2007/06/look_forward_to_anger.html.

Hitchens, Christopher. *Love, Poverty and War: Journeys and Essays*. New York: Nation Books, 2004.

Hitchens, Christopher. *The Missionary Position: Mother Teresa in Theory and Practice*. London: Verso, 1995.

Hitchens, Christopher, ed. *The Portable Atheist: Essential Readings for the Nonbeliever*. London: Da Capo Press, 2007.

Hjarvard, Stig. *The Mediatization of Culture and Society*. London: Routledge, 2013.

Jones, Kathleen. *Challenging Richard Dawkins: Why Richard Dawkins Is Wrong about God?* Norwich, UK: Canterbury Press, 2007.

Kepel, Gilles. *The Revenge of God: The Resurgence of Islam, Christianity and Judaism in the Modern World*. Cambridge, UK: Polity Press, 1994.

Kettel, Steven. "Divided We Stand: The Politics of the Atheist Movement in the United States." *Journal of Contemporary Religion* 29, no. 3 (2014): 377–391.

Kettel, Steven. "Faithless: The Politics of New Atheism." *Secularism and Nonreligion* 2 (2013): 61–72.

Khan, Razib. "Sex Differences in Global Atheism, Part N." *Discover*. November 18, 2010. http://blogs.discover magazine.com/gnxp/2010/11/sex-differences-in-global -atheism-part-n/#.VVCwEmb1cdU.

Knott, Kim, Elizabeth Poole, and Teemu Taira. *Media Portrayals of Religion and the Secular Sacred: Representation and Change*. Farnham, UK: Ashgate, 2013.

Maisel, Eric. *Atheist's Way: Living Well without Gods*. Novato, CA: New World Library, 2009.

Martin, David. *The Future of Christianity*. Farnham, UK: Ashgate, 2011.

McAnulla, Stuart. "Radical Atheism and Religious Power: The Politics of New Atheism." *Approaching Religion* 2, no. 1 (2012): 87–99.

Micklethwait, John, and Adrian Wooldridge. *God Is Back: How Global Rise of Faith Is Changing the World*. London: Allen Lane, 2009.

Morey, Peter, and Amina Yaqin. *Framing Muslims: Stereotyping and Representation after 9/11*. Cambridge, MA: Harvard University Press, 2011.

Pew Research. "How Americans Feel about Religious Groups." 2014. http://www.pewforum.org/2014/07/16 /how-americans-feel-about-religious-groups/.

Robertson, David. *The Dawkins Letters: Challenging Atheist Myths*. Ross-shire, Scotland: Christian Focus, 2008.

Rorty, Richard. *Consequences of Pragmatism: Essays 1972– 1980*. Minneapolis: University of Minnesota Press, 1982.

Salaita, Steven. *The Uncultured Wars: Arabs, Muslims and the Poverty of Liberal Thought*. London: Zed Books, 2008.

Silk, Mark. Explaining the Rise of the Nones. *Religion News Service*, January 7, 2015. http://marksilk.religionnews .com/2015/01/07/explaining-rise-nones/.

Smith, Christopher, and Richard Cimino. "Atheisms Unbound: The Role of the New Media in the Formation of a Secularist Identity." *Secularism and Nonreligion* 1 (2012): 17–31.

Snow, C. P. *Two Cultures*. Cambridge: Cambridge University Press, 2001. First published 1959.

Stenger, Victor J. "An Interview with Particle Physicist." 1999. http://www.positiveatheism.org/crt/stenger1.htm.

Stenger, Victor J. *The New Atheism: Taking a Stand for Science and Reason*. Amherst, MA: Prometheus, 2009.

Taira, Teemu. "Atheist Spirituality: A Follow on from New Atheism?" In *Post-Secular Religious Practices*, edited by Tore Ahlbäck, 388–404. Turku, Finland: Donner Institute for Cultural and Religious History, 2012c.

Taira, Teemu. "Media and the Nonreligious." In *Religion, Media and Social Change*, edited by Kennet Granholm, Marcus Moberg, and Sofia Sjö, 110–125. New York: Routledge, 2015.

Taira, Teemu. "More Visible but Not (Necessarily) More Popular: Atheism (and Atheists) in Finland." *Approaching Religion* 2, no. 1 (2012b): 21–45.

Taira, Teemu. "New Atheism as Identity Politics." In *Religion and Knowledge: Sociological Perspectives*, edited by Mathew Guest and Elisabeth Arweck, 97–113. Farnham, UK: Ashgate, 2012a.

Taira, Teemu and Ruth Illman, eds. 2012. *The New Visibility of Atheism in Europe*. In *Approaching Religion* 2, no. 1 (2012).

Ward, Keith. *Why There Almost Certainly Is a God: Doubting Dawkins*. Oxford: Lion, 2008.

Wolf, Gary. "The Church of Non-Believers." *Wired*, issue 14.11. 2006. http://archive.wired.com/wired/archive/14.11 /atheism.html.

Woodhead, Linda. "Introduction." In *Religion and Change in Modern Britain*, edited by Linda Woodhead and Rebecca Catto, 1–33. London: Routledge, 2012.

Zenk, Thomas. "Neuer Atheismus: New Atheism in Germany." *Approaching Religion* 2, no. 1 (2012): 36–51.

Zenk, Thomas. "New Atheism." In *The Oxford Handbook of Atheism*, edited by Stephen Bullivant and Michael Ruse, 245–260. Oxford: Oxford University Press, 2013.

Zuckerman, Phil. "Atheism, Secularis and Well-Being: How the Findings of Social Science Counter Negative Stereotypes and Assumptions." *Sociology Compass* 3, no 6 (2009): 949–971.

FILMS

Religulous. Dir. Larry Charles. 2008. "Comic documentary" mocking religious beliefs, hosted by American comedian Bill Maher.

The Unbelievers. Dir. Gus Holwerda. 2013. Documentary that follows Richard Dawkins and Lawrence Krauss as they travel around the world and speak for science and against religion.

CHAPTER 17

Secularism and Morality

Ryan Falcioni
Associate Professor, Department of Philosophy, Chaffey College,
Rancho Cucamonga, CA
Visiting Scholar, Institut für Hermeneutik und Religionsphilosophie,
University of Zürich, Switzerland

The philosophical questions that emerge when contemplating the complex relationships between secularism and morality are numerous. For the secularist or the secular-curious, successfully grappling with philosophical questions is essential to constructing a coherent and defensible secular ethic. For nonsecularists, analyzing these questions will help them to understand both the reasons for, and the philosophical difficulties with, secular ethics and secularism more broadly. Six areas will be addressed in the following order: (1) Defining and Using Terms: Some Philosophical and Ethical Dimensions of Secularism and Morality; (2) Can One Be Moral without God, gods, or Religion? (3) Can One Be Moral with God, gods, or Religion? (4) Does One Need God, gods, or Religion to Ground Morality? (5) Assessing Religious Ethics; and (6) Constructing and Assessing Secular Ethics. This chapter will sketch the philosophical terrain of these six areas of interest with the goal of providing the reader with a sense of the historical and contemporary issues and debates surrounding the intersection of morality and secularism.

At this point, a caveat must be issued concerning the nature and scope of the philosophical issues addressed. In addition to being admittedly selective in the topics discussed, this contribution is also selective in focusing primarily on the Western philosophical, religious, and historical traditions. That said, some of the views and the developments from non-Western traditions will be discussed as they arise. It is not within the purview of this text or the expertise of the author to do complete justice to these broader realities and the philosophical literatures involved.

DEFINING AND USING TERMS: SOME PHILOSOPHICAL AND ETHICAL DIMENSIONS

What is the meaning of the terms *secularism* and *morality*? Is secularization the same thing as secularism, secularity, or atheism? Ryan T. Cragun's chapter in this volume explores the varied definitions of, academic understandings of, and relationships between terms such as *secular, secularism, secularization, irreligion, atheist,* and *agnostic*. But ultimately, what the categories of the secular and the religious mean to different people are, well, different. And this reality must be addressed. The upcoming discussion will shed some light on this complicated business of getting clear on what secularism is, or can be, and how it relates to morality.

301

Chapter 17: Secularism and Morality

DEFINING *SECULARISM* AND *MORALITY*

One helpful way to frame the issues raised in this discussion is to consider two interrelated dimensions of secularism. First, there is a macro-level secularism wherein social and political structures are, or become, less influenced by religion. Related to this is the micro or personal dimension, wherein individual beliefs and practice are or become less traditionally religious. There is a broad historical trend in the West (and many would argue, around the globe) of increased secularization on both fronts. In light of these secularizing trends, many important figures since the Enlightenment have championed the emergence of a new secular age that will replace the age of religiously blinded ignorance. This supersessionist view is often called the secularization thesis. This thesis is often itself a moral vision for the world and the moral questions and dimensions stemming from it are numerous: Is this really happening? Are secularism and religion really fixed epochs (or even categories) that are perennially at odds? Is increased secularization a good thing for individuals, societies, or the world?

In *A Secular Age* (2007), Canadian philosopher Charles Taylor (1931–) describes the first, macro-level type of secularism as a social and political phenomenon wherein the major institutions of a state operate independently from the religious institutions. Taylor also elaborates on the second or micro-level type of secularism wherein there is a decline in individual expressions of traditional faith. In this second sense, the focus is on the changes and decline in personal religious belief and practice. To assess this type of secularism, Taylor recommends looking at things like attendance rates at houses of worship, rates (and degrees) of belief in, or commitment to, traditional religious doctrines and teaching, and other forms of personal expressions of faith. And as seen with the first form, this type of secularism is increasing in many ways in the modern world. To be sure, fundamentalist revivals and new forms of religiosity are emerging all over the world as these words are being written. The spread of evangelical and charismatic forms of Christianity in Latin American and Southeast Asia and the rise of Islamic fundamentalist groups are but a couple of examples of the myriad ways that religious individuals and traditions push back against the increasing secularization in both public and private life. That said, as Phil Zuckerman (1969–) writes in "Atheism: Contemporary Numbers and Patterns" (2007), there is a progressive, measurable increase in secularism in both of these senses across the globe. For a particularly revealing portrait of the increase in secular attitudes, beliefs, and behaviors in America, see the detailed data at Pew Research Center's Religion and Public Life Project. Taylor ultimately points to a third approach to analyzing secularism as a social phenomenon that is inclusive of the first two but focuses on "conditions of belief" (2007, 3). This perspective seeks to address the changes and developments that have occurred over the past few hundred years wherein individuals in many modern societies can choose to believe or disbelieve, practice, or not practice, their faiths. Even for devout religious believers, it is generally possible for them to consider, and genuinely contemplate, not believing. There is the social and personal space to contemplate such a decision. It has become an option among options, as with so many other things in life. To use William James's (1842–1910) term, secular ways of belief and life have become *living options* for many people in the modern world in a way that was virtually impossible just a few centuries ago. Much of the discussion in this chapter will address questions that occur in this space. The focus will be on particular reasons, arguments, and options for secular ethics that have emerged in the modern era.

COMPLICATIONS WITH DEFINING MORALITY

The term *morality* has been used in different ways in different contexts. For the purposes of this chapter, morality refers to the realm of human (and potentially some animal) experience

302

MACMILLAN INTERDISCIPLINARY HANDBOOKS

Chapter 17: Secularism and Morality

that deals with values. There is both a public and a personal dimension to morality. On the one hand, there are the views and values of our social systems that often are codified in law or are at least implicit in a social contract. On the other hand, there are our individual perspectives and ways of developing moral views and identity in the world. And the two are, undoubtedly, related.

The enterprise of figuring out what people value, developing systems to embody and enforce those values, and navigating our own perspectives within such systems, seems to capture what many philosophers think of as morality. At this point, a question emerges involving how, or if, this is different than what is meant by ethics. And, indeed, some philosophers hold that there should be a distinction between these terms, wherein ethics refers to macro systems or objective ethical frameworks and morality refers to individual or even subjective ethical experiences or claims. That said, in *Ethics for Life A Text with Readings* (2010), Judith Boss (1942–) explains that in common usage and in the philosophical literature, these terms increasingly are used interchangeably. For example, if we say that someone did something that was unethical, this generally means the same thing as saying that what they did was immoral. It is at least fairly difficult to imagine a significant difference between these two judgments. Could one say (with any legitimacy), "That was horribly immoral … but at least it wasn't unethical" or vice versa? It is difficult to know what to make of such a claim. The separation of such terms is also difficult to maintain in light of their etymology. According to Boss, the Latin term *moralis*, from which the term *morality* is derived, and the Greek term *ethos*, from which the word *ethics* is derived, both generally refer to the cultural customs or habits of a people group. In light of such concerns and keeping with the trend in the academic literature, this chapter will use the terms synonymously and will refer to both the macro-level dimension of ethics involving the codes and norms of a given domain of public life, as well as the individual understandings and expressions of value that operate within these public frameworks.

CAN ONE BE MORAL *WITHOUT* GOD, GODS, OR RELIGION?

Although this question has a deeper philosophical and theological significance, this is one that, at least at an empirical level, can be clearly answered: Yes. This reality can be seen even given the moral claims of virtually any given tradition. For example, can an atheist abide by the biblical commandments not to murder, steal, or commit adultery, or the admonishment to love one's neighbor as oneself? Of course. Not only can this happen, but as sociologist Zuckerman writes in *Society without God* (2008) and others have shown, the nonreligious often do a better job of abiding by or fulfilling the moral commandments of the religious than do the religious themselves. And, at the societal level, Zuckerman has shown that societies that have high degrees of organic atheism (atheism, or secularism that developed internally and without state-sanctioned coercion) generally have greater degrees of societal health (e.g., gender equality and low poverty rates), individual and societal security, and otherwise ethical treatment. Unfortunately, religious societies do not fare so well and the correlation goes the other way. With few exceptions, societies with lower rates of organic atheism and higher degrees of religiosity have lower levels of societal health. The goal is not to argue for or against religious or secular ethical systems but rather is to point out that data confirm the possibility and reality of people behaving ethically (by virtually all available measurements) without belief in God, gods, or religion. And thankfully, this is not generally a seriously debated issue. Most religious ethicists agree that people from other religions and

RELIGION: BEYOND RELIGION

303

Chapter 17: Secularism and Morality

secularists alike can and do act morally and are also capable of having good reasons for doing so. The lingering part of this issue involves whether there are distinctive religious reasons or motivations that are superior to secular ones.

CAN ONE BE MORAL *WITH* GOD, GODS, OR RELIGION?

Just as some religious people think that it is not possible to be moral without God, it is a hallmark of many types of secular ethical systems that not only do they see religious systems of ethics as unnecessary but also as obstacles to more authentic morality. In this way, secular ethicists have reversed the direction of the question that is often asked of them regarding the possibility of behaving morally without God. Another way of framing this question is to ask, are there unique benefits or goods in secular ethical systems that religious systems do not, or cannot have? Or, more provocatively, are there unique harms or evils that religious systems bring? Answering in the affirmative to both questions, the New Atheist movement that began in the early 2000s exemplifies this reversal of the religious claim that one needs God to be moral. Popular New Atheist Christopher Hitchens (1949–2011) has his own version of this critique and was fond of issuing it in the form of a challenge during his public debates. He would ask his interlocutor (and often the audience) to name a morally good claim or action uttered or committed by a believer that could not be uttered or committed by a nonbeliever. Hitchens stated that no one has ever come up with anything. Any good thing that a religious person can do, a nonbeliever can do, and with good secular reasons. The same cannot be said of the second part of the challenge—that is, to name a morally horrible claim or action committed by a believer that a nonbeliever could not claim or commit. He stated that it would not take much time to come up with a list of such atrocities. According to Hitchens (2007b), religiously motivated evils such as genital mutilation and suicide terrorism simply do not find justification within secular circles. The criticism is that not only does religion not help the world's people to do what is good, but that it also makes a unique contribution in justifying and motivating certain evils. And, as Hitchens was fond of saying, religion adds to such evils by enabling the perpetrator to commit these heinous actions with a sense of self-righteousness that comes from (assumed) divine approval. Although not a conclusive (or philosophically sophisticated) argument by any means, such challenges succeed in problematizing the often dogmatically asserted religious mantra that religious belief is necessary for moral motivation and action.

RELIGION ETHICS AS OBSTACLE TO MORAL DEVELOPMENT

Accompanying and supporting this type of secular critique, such thinkers often put forth the standard grocery list of atrocities committed by religious people or groups. The historical litany of religious bloodshed, enslavement, bigotry, heresy hunting, and the like is detailed with a particular emphasis on the religious teaching and modes of authority that are central to such actions. The Crusades are but one historical instance of this most indictable mixture of scriptural justification, authoritarian mandate, and the blind allegiance of the faithful. Furthermore, secular ethicists are quick to point out that the Bible and the Qur'an themselves record, and frequently detail, the divine sanctioning of such atrocities. By itself, this tactic often has a profound effect on the reader and serves as a caution against thinking too simplistically about the relationship between religion and morality. Yet, a deeper criticism is called for. Are there identifiable features of religion that are centrally (and even causally) linked to certain moral ills? Hitchens and Richard Dawkins (1941–) believe so and are particularly critical of the authoritarian, top-down, dogmatic approach to ethics that they take to be so central to many religious ethical systems. In *The God Delusion* (2006), Dawkins goes as far as to equate certain forms of religious upbringing and education (particularly the authoritarian dogmatism and teaching of eternal damnation) with child abuse. Secular ethicists claim that these religious modes of ethics subvert natural moral development and are inherently harmful to broader childhood growth and improvement. They champion moral autonomy and see the demand for obedience and the emphasis on authority as inimical to healthy moral development. Such claims have some support from developmental psychology. As eminent psychologist Lawrence Kohlberg (1927–1987) writes in *The Philosophy of Moral Development* (1981) and others have pointed out, moral reasoning based on such factors correspond to early and underdeveloped stages of moral development.

For them, at its best, religion can give people bad reasons for doing good things. And, all too often, through authoritarianism and fear tactics, they give people bad reasons for doing bad things. Sam Harris (1967–) and others have attempted to account for this more sinister role that religion plays in some of the evils of the world by claiming that such motivations stem from features that are at the very core of religion. In addition to the authoritarianism and theological exclusivism (i.e., only our kind of people are spiritually valued by God), religion causes an erosion of our otherwise-rational capacities for critical thinking and analysis. For Harris, a foundational irrationality to many religious beliefs (coupled with a corresponding religious mandate to believe) requires a subversion of common sense and even moral judgments. He likens these beliefs to a mental illness that is corrupting of people's abilities to reason and think clearly. And, in morality, this has had disastrous consequences. Harris states,

> Most people of faith are perfectly sane, of course, even those who commit atrocities on account of their beliefs. But what is the difference between a man who believes that God will reward him with seventy-two virgins if he kills a score of Jewish teenagers, and one who believes that creatures from Alpha Centauri are beaming him messages of world peace through his hair dryer? ... To be ruled by ideas for which you have no evidence (and which therefore cannot be justified in conversation with other human beings) is generally a sign that something is seriously wrong with your mind ... And so, while religious people are not generally mad, their core beliefs absolutely are. (2004, 72)

Following Dawkins, Harris and others from the New Atheist camp see religion functioning as a type of mind virus that corrupts many human capacities and instead favors authoritarianism, dogmatic certainty, and distrust or even hatred of religious others, among other things. This type of criticism of religious ethics is probably the most severe. The claim is that religion generally (or even inherently, as with the model of the mind virus) works against morality and proper moral development. It supplants and suppresses the natural tools of morality (critical thinking and a general humanism), replacing them with irrational and dogmatic dictates. According to such thinkers, it is in this way that one cannot be truly moral with God, gods, or religion.

SECULAR ETHICS AND MORAL IMPROVEMENT

Beyond these types of polemics against religious ethics, there is literature dealing with the qualitative experience of secular individuals as they navigate their ethical lives apart from religion. Zuckerman explains in *Faith No More* (2011) that the possibility of having a deeper

Chapter 17: Secularism and Morality

and more meaningful ethical orientation apart from religion is seen at this subjective level in the accounts that many ex-believers give of the moral clarity and awareness that accompanied their leaving traditional religious modes of ethics. For many who once held to moral beliefs informed by their faith and have now moved on to secular modes of morality, a type of ethical liberation often is experienced. This liberation is not the nihilist anarchic vision that they had been taught would be the result of leaving the fold. Rather, it is the liberty to cultivate and live out their values as morally alive and autonomous beings. It is a freedom to truly develop their values as they engage with and experience the world. And, rather than their transition being into a state of confusion and moral depravity, they report a greater clarity, a more authentic moral drive and a greater commitment to moral causes. After looking at many cases of those who have transitioned from religious to secular ways of life in *Faith No More*, sociologist Zuckerman explains that not only are postreligious moral lives possible but also, "I would take it a step farther and argue that morality actually *improves* after individuals undergo a transition from being religious to secular. As many apostates emphatically explained to me, their own personal morality was sharpened, enhanced, and ultimately became more mature once religion was left behind" (2011, 122). Zuckerman goes on to address a bit of the experiential texture of this transition. Many of the specific moral claims stayed the same, especially on significant issues like stealing or lying. But, what changed was their moral motivation. Rather than being motivated out of an authoritarian duty to a divine ruler or fear of divine or priestly damnation or condemnation, they were more aware of their feelings of concern for how such actions would affect people. They engaged in their moral lives with empathy and a more holistic sense of participating in the creation of a world that was a better place to live. Or, in words that will be used shortly, their whole moral orientation went from being *vertical* to more *horizontal—this worldly* rather than *otherworldly*. And, this is essentially at the core of the humanist ethos. The view is that when one transitions from more vertical systems of moral authority and motivation, one is truly free to engage with the world around without artificial imposition from a higher power. One is free to cultivate empathy and compassion and to develop one's own, morally autonomous sense of morality that is grounded in the reality of one's experiences in the world rather than simply given to him or her by divine fiat and enforced through the coercive and corrosive power of religious authority and fear.

To be clear, not all nonreligious people have had this same experience of moral liberation and enlightenment. For some, there is no great revelation but rather a gradual passing away of certain habits and views and an equally gradual development of new habits and views. And it is quite possible that some succumb to the type of nihilistic atheism that their religious leaders had warned them of. But the academic research so far indicates that secular people not only are leading meaningful, moral lives, but also often do so with even greater clarity, conviction, and depth than they did while they were religious.

SECULAR HUMANISM: A BRIEF INTRODUCTION

In many ways, the ethical system of secular humanism is an elucidation and construction of a completely horizontal ethical worldview. It fleshes out the details of an ethical system that places humanity front and center and rejects the reality and significance of the vertical dimension so often claimed by religious ethical systems. As with religions, there are numerous species and subspecies of secular humanism, each with its own particular emphases. Some are more focused on formulating concrete ethical principles. Others promote a broadly naturalistic worldview and a scientific and even scientistic (the belief that science is the only method for determining truth) approach to grounding ethics and solving ethical problems. A handful of features seem to be present in most versions. The Council for Secular Humanism offers a four-dimensional model of secular humanism that is fairly representative of the contemporary landscape. As stated, secular humanism is defined as follows: (1) a comprehensive, nonreligious life stance, (2) a naturalistic philosophy, (3) a cosmic outlook rooted in science, and (4) a consequentialist ethical system. Secular humanism is rooted in the belief that people's lives are the only ones that they have, the physical world is all that there is, and science and reason are the best tools for understanding the world and figuring out how to live. Humans have evolved the capacity for moral agency and should apply it in a truly global (considering the effects of our actions on everything in the universe) and often consequentialist (doing that which has the best overall balance of good consequences over bad ones) way. Many nonreligious people find this way of framing one's moral life to be empowering, liberating, and also morally convicting. The mantra of making the world better for all of its inhabitants often emerges in the secular humanist approach. Religious ethicists find much to be critical of in this account, focusing on its failure to truly ground ethics in a transcendent source. Furthermore, as with the emerging science of ethics movement, secular humanism faces the problem of overcoming the is-ought fallacy (i.e., how it is possible to derive a moral ought from merely understanding what is). Also known as the fact-value distinction, the claim is that no amount of facts can determine how one should value those facts. These and other issues in contemporary secular ethics will be addressed at the end of the chapter.

DOES ONE NEED GOD, GODS, OR RELIGION TO GROUND MORALITY?

This is a question that is similar in form to the previous question about whether one needs god(s) to be moral, but it goes a bit deeper. It is more of a metaethical or theoretical question about the origin and nature of morality. One common but less academic way that this question emerges is in the question that many budding skeptics have encountered at a family gathering as their least favorite aunt asks them some form of "So, if you're an atheist, where do you get your morality from?" Stated in this way, it is not generally meant to invite serious philosophical contemplation and discussion. But it reflects the philosophical concern in metaethics of finding a solid source or ground to secure and validate morality. It is interesting to note that this particular question has become something of an obsession among contemporary secular ethicists. Philip Kitcher (1947–), Patricia Churchland (1943–), Michael Shermer (1954–), and several of the New Atheists have all attempted to provide an account of a secular ground for morality. Although these philosophical questions might not seem as important or interesting as the more pragmatic questions about the benefits and harms of religious and secular ethics, they emerge in the wake of such discussions. It might help to think of them as the philosophical underpinnings of such debates. From a secular perspective, if God, gods, and religion are removed as what accounts for the origin and truth of morality, what is to take their place? Are individual humans, societies, or nature more generally, the originators and metaphysical ground of people's values and also what make their moral statements true? If morality is grounded in humanity or even in nature, this seems to be a varied and ever-changing foundation. Theories like ethical subjectivism (grounding morality and moral truth in individual subjective viewpoints) and cultural relativism (grounding morality and moral truth in social or cultural groups) attempt to answer such metaethical

RELIGION: BEYOND RELIGION

307

Chapter 17: Secularism and Morality

challenges. And, they run into a flurry of criticisms as they seem to fail to provide a fixed, robust, or solid foundation for ethics.

BRIDGING THE MORAL GAP

A proponent of the position that the nature of morality requires a transcendent source, Yale philosopher John Hare (1949–), has written extensively on the metaphysical need to have morality grounded in a God. As a fundamental starting point, he describes the human experience of the "gap between the moral demand on us and our natural capacities to live by it" (Hare 1996, 1). For Hare, this moral gap is one that philosophers have been addressing for centuries and have been unable to account for a solution to, apart from God. The fundamental view is that humans have (or should have) a universal awareness of the moral law. For Hare, one feature of the awareness of this moral law is that it is not attainable by humanity. In essence, humans understand that the moral law is binding and that it is not within their power to achieve its demands. On this view, the gap is a real, metaphysical gulf that demands an explanation and hopefully a way out. And, for Hare and other theistic philosophers, only God, or some similar transcendent reality, can serve as the ultimate metaphysical ground for this moral law. Furthermore, only God can provide a practical, moral solution for our lives. The argument here is both philosophical and theological. Philosopher Huw Parri Owen (1926–1996) elaborates on some of the features of morality that require or demand a theistic explanation and foundation. These include things such as the personal and obligatory nature of moral claims, inherent human dignity, the need for a solution to the ought-can paradox. Furthermore, in "Why Morality Implies the Existence of God" (2000), Owen highlights three specific moral terms that demand a personal and divine foundation: (1) reverence, this would not make sense if morality were just a secular formula; (2) responsibility, inherently involves the idea of other people to whom it is due; and (3) guilt, only the existence of a divine lawgiver could make sense of our feelings of guilt (Owen 2000). There is a rich tradition in philosophy of religion of inferring God's existence from the existence of morality. In its various forms, the argument first details various fundamental features of our moral lives and shows how they constitute a real, metaphysical order of reality. They then attempt to show that a supernatural, personal being and lawgiver is the best explanation for this reality and is even metaphysically required to make sense of and ultimately ground them.

THE MORAL PROOF FOR GOD'S EXISTENCE

Some philosophers of religion have even developed this intuition and belief into a species of formal argument for the existence of God. Immanuel Kant (1724–1804) offered a version of this in the eighteenth century, and many contemporary philosophers have expanded this into something of a theistic proof. Indeed, both Hare and Owen attempt to reason from morality to God. But, the theistic proof approach goes beyond the inductive approach addressed in the previous section and claims that God's existence can be deductively proven. Such an argument would have the following form:

1. If objective moral laws exist, then God exists.

2. Objective moral laws exist.

3. Therefore, God exists.

As both of the two premises are contestable, much work must be done to argue for the reality of this objective moral law and the connection that this has with God. A number of secular thinkers (e.g., Harris, Shermer, and Steven Pinker [1954–]) confirm the truth of premise two but deny the logical implication of God's existence as stated in premise one. They believe that objective moral laws exist but can be grounded naturalistically apart from any appeal to God or the supernatural. In their view, the theist unfairly smuggles in metaphysical and theological premises in their understanding of the objective moral law in such a way that it necessitates the existence of this personal, supernatural lawgiver.

A SECULAR REJOINDER

By way of a secular critique, what sense can be made of both the claim that morality needs God as a metaphysical ground or even the stronger claim that the very existence of the moral law (or some other feature of morality) deductively proves the existence of God? Generally speaking, secular philosophers, and a lot of theistic ones for that matter, simply do not find these types of arguments convincing. This criticism is simply to deny that morality has a metaphysical dimension. Many empiricist and naturalistic philosophers believe that one can explain all of the alleged features of morality in terms of natural phenomena. Claiming divine origins for morality is at best superfluous and at worst a distraction from understanding and appreciating the real nature of morality. Unlike a more comprehensive evolutionary, genetic, social, and neurobiological account of morality, the divine source perspective is completely impotent in terms of explanatory power. The criticism here is that it is a clever (or not-so-clever) intellectual sleight of hand argument. Rather than getting to work and trying to explain the complicated business of human reality via the methodologies of the sciences, social sciences, and philosophy, God is invoked as the necessary ultimate explanation and origin of morality to stop such explanatory endeavors. In short, it is yet another species of the "god of the gaps" argument. This line of reasoning has been used through the history of Western religion and argues that phenomena that are complex or generally hard to explain must be the handiwork of God. These arguments are usually about religious institutions maintaining their influence, power, and control over the masses and are aimed at halting serious intellectual investigation. Historically, "god of the gaps" arguments have been used to explain mental illness, communicable diseases, planetary motion, and, of course, human origins. And, although it is important to have an account of the origins and even the philosophical ground for ethics, the appeal to the supernatural simply does no serious work. It does not deliver on its promise to explain or ground ethics. It is merely another in a long line of failed or pseudo-explanations.

To flesh this out, scientists and philosophers have been busy attempting to provide more serious and explanatorily efficacious account of the nature of morality. Recall Owen's claims that theism best explains some of the personal features (e.g., reverence, responsibility, and guilt) of our experience with the moral law. Secular critics point out that offering naturalistic explanations of these and other features of moral experience has been going on for more than a century. Whether it is historical figures like Sigmund Freud (1856–1939) and David Émile Durkheim (1858–1917) or contemporary theorists like Yale psychologist Paul Bloom (1963–), many accounts have been given for both how and why we feel guilt, responsibility, and even reverence relative to moral norms. Bloom's work *Just Babies: The Origins of Good and Evil* (2013) is particularly intriguing as he has traced the origins of some of our most basic natural moral instincts (of both altruism and bigotry) to infancy and has determined these instincts to have both genetic and social components. His work, and the work of his wife, Karen Wynn (1962–), the director of the Infant Cognition Center (a.k.a. the Baby Lab) at Yale University, demonstrates the ways in which some of our moral sense is

Chapter 17: Secularism and Morality

The Garden of Earthly Delights, *triptych by Hieronymus Bosch, c. 1490–1510. The three panels depict the Garden of Eden, a teeming scene of nude humans and fantastical animals, and hell. The central panel has been interpreted both as a moral warning against temptation—suggesting religious ethics—and a vision of a wild, liberated party—suggesting hedonistic secular ethics.* WORLD HISTORY ARCHIVE/ALAMY.

hardwired and also how, as we develop, our natural moral sense is socially and culturally conditioned. In various tests, infants act in ways that show an inclination towards justice, kindness, compassion (i.e., by preferring a puppet who performs such actions versus a puppet that doesn't). Of particular interest is his work on the developmental origins of the hostility to strangers and our inclinations toward prejudice and even bigotry. As infants develop into childhood, they learn complex systems of cultivating and mitigating various hard-wired tendencies of thought and behavior. All of these tendencies have deep sociobiological origins, and for Bloom and other scientists, our ability to successfully deal with them involves understanding how they developed in the first place. As with the theories of Jean Piaget (1896–1980) and Lawrence Kohlberg (1927–1987), Bloom has shown how the fields of developmental and evolutionary psychology can be utilized to explain the origin, nature, and function of humanity's moral experience. They account for the depth and the power of our experience of moral norms. They address both what is hard-wired and what is socially constructed and do this without appealing to an external, supernatural source.

Churchland's work in *Braintrust: What Neuroscience Tells Us about Morality* (2011) on the evolutionary development of morality focuses on the neurobiological origins of mammalian sociability. Through this evolutionary sense, Churchland locates the neurological structures and processes involved in the mammalian tendencies to develop strong empathy and group-belonging and to form attachments. Churchland is able to explain many of the features of our moral lives that Owen and others highlight, grounding them in our evolving mammalian and human natures rather than in abstract metaphysical principles or indeed in God. In addition to the research into the genetic, social, and neurobiological origins of morality, primatologist Frans De Waal (1948–) has demonstrated that many moral traits such as empathy and compassionate cooperation exist in our nearest primate relatives. Furthermore, in *Primates and Philosophers* (2006), De Waal and coauthors have shown how particular values such as justice, fairness, and reciprocity are exhibited by many primates and by other mammals as well. De Waal discusses one of these prominent studies with research collaborator Sarah Brosnan wherein a pair of chimpanzees would each be rewarded with a food item after performing a basic task. As De Waal explains in *The Bonobo and the Atheist* (2013), the researchers observed a startling phenomenon: chimpanzees were more likely to refuse their own high-value reward (a grape) if the other chimpanzee received a lower value reward (a carrot) than if they both received grapes. De Waal concludes, "Fairness and justice are therefore best looked at as ancient capacities. They derive from a need to preserve harmony in the face of resource competition" (2013, 234). De Wall discusses this study as a direct refutation of philosophers who challenged earlier primate research that merely showed the desire of chimps to be equally compensated relative to their peers. The skeptical philosophical challenge stated that such studies would only succeed in showing a true moral sense of justice and fairness in primates if they would voluntarily give up their own reward.

Such naturalistic accounts of the origin and nature of morality might not completely explain all of the features that religious ethicists believe point to a divine source, but secular ethicists believe that this will eventually happen. Seeing the significance of moral awareness and experience in infants, neurobiology, evolutionary and developmental psychology, and elsewhere, secular thinkers claim that we get a clearer sense of the powerful role morality plays in humanity. The deep sense of responsibility, guilt, and even reverence come into clearer focus and even seem inevitable given morality's embeddedness in the human experience. The secular response to the alleged moral gap is that the fields of the sciences, social sciences, and philosophy ultimately give more accurate and satisfying accounts of the nature of morality than claims of divine origin. For such thinkers, the appeal to metaphysics is both premature and unnecessary.

At this point, there is ultimately a standoff of sorts between certain religious and secular ethicists. For secular ethicists (and even for some moderate religious thinkers), many of the features of morality that seem to involve or even necessitate the reality of God for some theistic philosophers are seen to have clear, naturalistic causes, and explanations. The standoff often involves a difference in presuppositions and starting points. Whereas many religious ethicists are open to (and often looking for) supernatural explanation, many secularists begin with a strict naturalism that does not admit to such metaphysical speculation. As both sides look at the varied phenomena of people's ethical lives, the character and nature of explanation is fundamentally different. One side sees divine reality in human experience and the other side precludes this as a viable option via their naturalistic modes of explanation.

ASSESSING RELIGIOUS ETHICS

PROBLEMS WITH RELIGIOUS THEORIES OF ETHICS:
TWO HORNS OF THE *EUTHYPHRO DILEMMA*

One common way to frame the two most prominent religious theories of ethics in the West, divine command and natural law, is to utilize a paradox employed by Socrates (470–399

Chapter 17: Secularism and Morality

Socrates and Euthyphro. *As recounted by Plato, the philosopher Socrates asked the diviner Euthyphro "whether the holy is beloved by the gods because it is holy, or holy because it is beloved of the gods." This logical problem has come to be known as the* Euthyphro Dilemma. **COPYRIGHT © JOLYON TROSCIANKO.**

BCE) in his interaction with Euthyphro regarding the relationship between the Greek gods and piety. In this dialogue, Plato (427–347 BCE) details the dilemma via Socrates's query, "The point which I should first wish to understand is whether the pious or holy is beloved by the gods because it is holy, or holy because it is beloved of the gods" (Plato 2013). Plato raises a logical problem in considering the relationship between the gods and what is pious or holy.

And, as Paul Woodruff (1943–) writes in "Plato's Shorter Ethical Works" (2014), although these terms are not perfect synonyms for morality (piety might be best understood as a type of virtue that involves reverence, keeping of oaths, helping the weak, observing commitments to family, and respecting the gods), this paradox has wide application. Philosophers have applied the general logical formulation of this dilemma to the question of the relationship between the God of the Abrahamic faiths and moral law or commandments. A reformulation for this context would be: "Are God's commandments (think of the Ten Commandments or Jesus's admonitions) moral because he commands them? or does God command them because they are moral?"

In other words, is God's act of commanding these things what makes them moral? Or, are these things moral prior (at least logically) to God's commanding them? Generally speaking, the *Euthyphro Dilemma* challenges the religious ethicists with taking on one of two options (or horns), each corresponding to one of the dominant theories of religious ethics and each with its own set of problems. If one takes on the first horn, namely, that God's commanding things is what make them moral, this corresponds to divine command ethics. And, this view runs into the criticisms that God's commands then appear to be: (1) arbitrary, (2) relative, and (3) often immoral and logically contradictory. If one takes the second horn, that God commands things because they are already moral, this often corresponds to a type of natural law ethics. This view also runs into several problems: (1) it presupposes an independent moral standard beyond God (making God, in some ways, unnecessary), and (2) if God is still claimed as the foundation, defining and explaining morality becomes circular.

In addressing divine command ethics, God's commands are charged with being arbitrary because if there is no morality beyond God's commands, there can be no moral criteria, reasons, or evidences for such commands. God simply commands what God does apart from any reasons or considerations. There can be no reason why God commands for or against murder, cheating, or adultery. But, this makes morality arbitrary in an essential way and works against many people's intuitions that there have to be some reasons or grounds for calling something moral or immoral. Some theists are fine with the arbitrariness and even circularity of this arrangement, but others, who hold to doctrines like divine rationality, struggle to make sense of how this is possible and how and why, if it is the case that God's commanding something is what makes it moral, one can call such commandments good in any meaningful way.

There are also problems with the seemingly intractable and progressive relativism built into divine command ethics. There is an initial relativism in merely getting clear on which god(s) and which traditions are the sources of such commands. As critics point out, what could be more relative than picking a particular god and a particular tradition out of the thousands of religions in the world? And, even if one settles on a particular tradition, there is then the relativism of settling on the sources and interpretations of such divine commands. Are there foundational texts? Founders? Prophets? Authoritative interpreters? In any given tradition, there are often multiple such sources, and the battle over interpretation inherently involves a perspectival relativism. Think here of the ways in which the scriptures are invoked on both sides of major social issues (e.g., civil rights, abortion, euthanasia, and same-sex marriage). Assuming that this relativism can be overcome and one picks a deity, say the God of the Abrahamic traditions and even a single source (i.e., the Bible), there is now the problem of morality being relative to God's commandments at any given point in time. The God of the Bible commands different things to different groups of people at different periods in history (e.g., kosher laws, animal sacrifice, and in the case of Abraham, the killing of children). This particular feature of divine command ethics makes it difficult to hold to any robust notion of moral truth. There is only truth at a given time for a given person or people, but God's commands in themselves can have no universal, objective truth. These charges of relativism are particularly troubling given that the fundamental benefit of religious theories of ethics, like divine command, is that they provide an objective, perfect, and unchanging ground for ethics.

Furthermore, the deeper problem for divine command theory lies in the commands themselves. There seem to be contradictions and changes in the moral dictates of the scriptures and in other alleged sources of divine commands. An even deeper indictment, and one that is made by many secular ethicists is not just that there are contradictions in the divine commands but that the morality of many of these claims is atrocious and our recognizing this implies, necessarily, a moral standard independent of God.

One way to avoid some of these problems and paradoxes of the first horn, is to take on the second horn. This perspective corresponds to natural law ethics and holds that God issues commandments because they are moral. On this view, moral law comes before God's commandments and serves as a system of checks and balances for them. The Catholic Church teaches a version of this doctrine that was thoroughly articulated by Medieval Christian theologian St. Thomas Aquinas (1225–1274). He offers a version of this natural law perspective with his claim that the moral laws that humans come to understand and with which God's commandments are consistent are rooted in the Eternal Law, which is in the very mind of God. Philosopher Brian Davies (1951–) elaborates in his *Thomas Aquinas's Summa Theologiae: A Guide and Commentary*, "Aquinas identifies eternal law with God … The idea seems to be that what is good for God's creatures can be thought of as a rule of measure in God's mind before it is in creatures as governed by divine providence" (2014, 214). On such a view, the ultimate moral law exists in the mind of God and all of creation is imbued with this reality. For Aquinas, much of this morality is revealed through natural reason. In utilizing our capacity for reason in discerning right from wrong, human beings are discovering natural law, which, as Davies points out, is an act of participation (*participatio*) in God's eternal law. When God occasionally issues commandments (divine law), these are both consistent with the eternal law and natural law. On this view, God's commandments do not become moral in the act of commanding them, they are moral

Chapter 17: Secularism and Morality

because they are consistent with and emanate from the very mind of God. Nor are these commandments commanded because they possess certain moral properties independent from God. Aquinas's view thus seems to avoid both horns of the *Euthyphro Dilemma*.

Still, there seems to be a lingering paradox here. For even if we ground morality in God's nature, one could still ask what makes that nature good? A familiar circularity emerges here. If God's commands are good because they stem from God's nature, how do we know that these are in fact good things unless we presuppose the goodness of God? Of course, if we begin with a belief in the essential goodness of God, it might follow that the things that this God commands are good, but this is question begging. As Kai Nielsen (1926–) points out, we need to have an independent criterion of morality before we can make the assessment that God is a being worth following. In his *Ethics without God*, he states that a religious moralist who claims to ground his morality in the will of God, "must believe and thus be prepared to make the moral claim that there exists a being whom he deems to be perfectly good or worthy of worship and whose will should always be obeyed. But to do this he must have a moral criterion (a standard for what is morally good) that is independent of God's will" (1990, 61). Nielsen goes on to say that the claim that God's will is good is logically dependent on some distinct criterion of morality such that one can make a legitimate, non-question-begging assessment that this God is good and worthy of being worshipped and followed. Nielsen's critique here is focused on divine command ethics, but the logical problem of grounding morality in God's nature without having an independent criterion of goodness plagues natural law theory as well. In essence, natural law theory is saying that natural laws are moral because they are grounded in a perfectly moral being. But, this is only a meaningful statement if we can first assess how and why the being in question is indeed perfectly moral, and this requires an independent measure or criterion for moral goodness. This type of criticism is difficult to escape and is a powerful indictment of both divine command and natural law ethics. Secular ethicists generally have seen this as exposing the reality that God cannot be seen as the source of ethics without invoking insuperable logical problems. Both horns of the *Euthyphro Dilemma* are claimed to be insurmountable and the rational ethicist must thus abandon the possibility of having God as the source of ethics.

PRACTICAL PROBLEMS WITH RELIGIOUS ETHICS

As mentioned earlier, beyond the more theoretical or philosophical objections to religious ethical systems, there is also a practical, ethical objection: many of the core religious commandments and values are themselves rotten. Even if there were some noncircular way for God to be the source of morality and that this way was theologically and philosophically viable, one still has to take a look at the specific commandments. The criticism is that the commandments are both inconsistent with each other and even when consistent, they represent a morality that many cannot reconcile with their most basic moral intuitions and beliefs. This claim also has theoretical implications as it invokes a separate, external standard of ethics.

A cursory reading of the Bible or the Qur'an quickly reveals moral commandments that are at odds with these basic moral intuitions about the world. It is hard to make moral sense of biblical commandments like the mandate for a woman to be stoned to death on her father's doorstep if or when she is believed to not be a virgin upon getting married (Deut 22:13–21). Other crimes deserving of stoning also seem particularly problematic: for being a wizard or witch (Lev 20:27), for disobeying one's parents (Deut 21:18–21), for touching Mt. Sinai (Exod 19:13), and for adultery (Deut 22:23–24). Not only do the punishments seem excessive and probably immoral in their own right, but many of the moral infractions themselves seem to invert our basic moral sensibilities. Consider the case of a rape victim in the New American Standard Bible:

> [28]If a man finds a girl who is a virgin, who is not engaged, and seizes her and lies with her and they are discovered, [29]then the man who lay with her shall give to the girl's father fifty *shekels* of silver, and she shall become his wife because he has violated her; he cannot divorce her all his days. (Deut 22:28–29)

There are many debates about the precise meaning of this passage and whether or not the seized woman is indeed a rape victim. That said, the entire way that this passage treats the value and dignity of women is an affront to the most basic moral convictions about gender equality and human dignity more generally. The fact that the debt for violating the woman is owed to her father evidences a brutal patriarchy wherein women are the property of men. Furthermore, the fact that the man's punishment includes being forced to marry the woman that he violated, without consideration for the reality that the woman might not desire this betrothal is further evidence of a brutally patriarchal ethic in which women's interests are not considered in any fundamental way. When many read these and dozens of other passages in the Bible and the Qur'an, they encounter a moral universe that is not their own.

The New Testament adds some new dimensions to the moral character of God but still presents an ethical world that is foreign to most people. By way of example, consider Jesus's reaffirmation of the duty to keep all of the Jewish law (parts of which were just discussed) in Matthew 5:17–20, and his admonition for slaves to accept the lashes that they deserve, with a seemingly kind caveat that masters will be held responsible if they beat their slaves too hard (Luke 12:45–48). Other passages present further moral conundrums as seen in Luke 14:26: "If anyone comes to Me, and does not hate his own father and mother and wife and children and brothers and sisters, yes, and even his own life, he cannot be My disciple." Jesus also introduces (or at least reaffirms) the idea of an eternal place of suffering. The teachings of the Apostle Paul in the Epistles represent another series of challenges as they seem to be at odds with some of the things that Jesus teaches and also support more conservative teachings on gender, sexuality, and slavery.

The point is not to enumerate and analyze all of the moral teachings of Jesus (or the rest of the Bible) but merely to point out, again, that the ethical world described in the scriptures and affirmed and taught by Jesus often cuts against many people's moral intuitions. In short, even if the logical problems addressed in the *Euthyphro Dilemma* could be overcome, the moral commands, claims, and values present in religious sources are often themselves immoral. They represent a less-evolved, brutal, and frequently tribal ethos. And, in light of Nielsen's criticism, the fact that we can recognize this demonstrates the reality of a prior and independent source of morality. Philosopher Walter Sinnott-Armstrong (1955–) is particularly clear on this point. He has argued persuasively that morality is fundamentally independent of, and prior to, religion. He represents a growing trend in academic philosophical secularism of challenging the alleged connection between morality and religion. He pushes for reframing this discussion, purging it of the *de facto* assumption, even among many secularists, that morality without religion is somehow a provocative proposal standing in need of defense. He states, "there is really no question of morality without God. There is just plain morality" (2009, xi).

CONSTRUCTING AND ASSESSING SECULAR ETHICS

So, where does one go from here? As secular philosophers and ethicists have analyzed, exposed, and compared the problems, both theoretical and practical, with traditional

Chapter 17: Secularism and Morality

religious approaches to ethics, what do they propose as a substitute? Many secular philosophers have struggled with this very question, finding it difficult to articulate a moral theory that does not suffer from many of the same types of philosophical and practical pitfalls as religious theories. Referencing Churchill's famous comment about democracy, philosopher Kitcher states, "the idea of a religious foundation for ethics is the worst available theory of the ethical life-except for all of its rivals" (2014, 31).

Yet, there are many attempts at constructing a secular ethic. As one can imagine, the options are limitless. In many ways, the modern history of moral philosophy is a testimony to this very objective. From Kant's deontology to the ethical pragmatism of John Dewey (1859–1952), to the contemporary attempts by Shermer and Harris to ground a universal, normative, secular ethic in notions of human flourishing and progress, the past few hundred years of ethics has largely consisted of attempts to construct secular models of ethics. The term *secular* is merely meant to denote theories that do not appeal to god or religious concepts in articulating their system of ethics. And, in this sense, most of the theories of ethics are secular. Introductory texts on ethical theory are great for getting a sense of the variety of secular approaches (and some are included in the bibliography). Outside of certain religious philosophical circles, it is largely seen as unacceptable to appeal to divine authority, religious traditions, or scriptures in developing an ethical theory or system. The goal in this section is to look at a couple of approaches that are secular in a further sense. They are theories that have been developed as direct responses to, and criticisms of, religious theories of ethics. The first attempts to explain and ground morality apart from appeal to religion, and generally holds religious ethics to be inherently flawed, philosophically confused, and even morally backward. The second is a species of secular humanism that addresses these concerns but has a more modest assessment of the prospects of grounding or proving ethics in a secular framework.

A SCIENCE OF ETHICS

In an emerging movement in the twenty-first century, numerous philosophers, scientists, and others have begun to advocate for a new science of ethics. Some of these figures are also secular humanists. And, although different methodologies and even different moral values are advocated by many of these figures, they generally converge in agreement on a couple of major points: (1) there are moral facts about the world, (2) these moral facts or values can be determined through the application of broadly scientific tools, and (3) the is-ought fallacy can be overcome. The attempt to ground morality in a naturalistic metaphysic is a particularly significant hallmark of much of the science of ethics movement. The view is that objective, well-grounded ethical norms can be discovered through science.

Harris, Pinker, and Shermer are all vocal proponents of this secular science of ethics movement and have each written tomes devoted to their particular version. They have similar starting points and take a broadly evolutionary perspective on what grounds the science of morality. Evolution shows us that conscious beings (and all organic life for that matter) are directed toward survival, well-being, and flourishing. For Harris, questions about morality are ultimately questions about the well-being of such conscious creatures. Furthermore, this well-being is a scientifically discernable and measurable reality. He states, "Values, therefore, translate into facts that can be scientifically understood" (Harris 2011, 1). For the science of ethics movement, this transition from facts to values is the pivotal point. For its critics, it is also the focal point for attack. Harris maintains that we can assess the morality of the actions of a person, society, or even religious teachings by the measurable outcomes that they have on the well-being of conscious creatures. Harris is particularly interested in measuring effects at the level of the brain (2011). And, he admits that there

316   MACMILLAN INTERDISCIPLINARY HANDBOOKS

Chapter 17: Secularism and Morality

may be many ways to achieve well-being, much like there are many ways of being healthy. But, all such attempts can be assessed in a scientific way. Cultures, religions and subjective preferences do not get a free pass when it comes to ethical claims or mandates. All actions can and must be tested for their outcome relative to the well-being of those conscious beings that are affected. Of this project, Harris states, "But if questions affect human well-being then they do have answers, whether or not we can find them. And just admitting this—just admitting that there are right and wrong answers to the question of how humans flourish—will change the way we talk about morality, and will change our expectations of human cooperation in the future" (2010). As mentioned earlier, Harris is critical of both secularists and religious thinkers who have accepted the fact-value or is-ought distinction. As with the rest of his science of ethics colleagues, he sees this as a key presupposition that must be deconstructed for this secular and scientific moral age to commence.

Shermer, a historian of science and well-known skeptic, states his conception of the science of ethics quite clearly, "Morality involves how we think and act toward other moral agents in terms of whether our thoughts and actions are right or wrong with regard to their *survival and flourishing*. By *survival* I mean the instinct to live, and by *flourishing* I mean having adequate sustenance, safety, shelter, bonding, and social relation for physical and mental health" (2015, 11). Shermer is not as much concerned with the complexities of neurobiology. The innate biological drive to survive itself becomes the measure of the ethical. Those things that facilitate or enhance this drive are *de facto* ethical, and those things that work against it are unethical. As with Harris, the science of ethics then fundamentally lies in the utilitarian measurement of these enhancements and detriments to flourishing and survival. With this clear ethical goal in mind, the science amounts to something more like tabulating. To be sure, a rather complex, qualitative calculus may evolve to accommodate the numerous types and pathways to flourishing and happiness (or as Harris might say, to various peaks and valleys of this complicated moral landscape). But, in principle, this is a utilitarian project that can provide real, substantive answers to the moral questions and problems of our day. Rather than debating about what some holy book says or what someone's deeply held personal or cultural beliefs are, people should actually look to the world and measure the real-life effects of one's actions.

THE IS-OUGHT (A.K.A. FACT-VALUE) FALLACY

The is-ought fallacy is the most significant philosophical challenge to purely naturalistic, secular theories of ethics. The claim is that it is fallacious to derive an ought, or moral judgment, merely from what is. As many philosophers in the science of ethics movement point out, the specter of this fallacy is what has kept thinkers from even attempting any type of objective or realist account of ethics within a secular, naturalistic framework. Harris and Shermer offer fairly lengthy discussions of this problem, but Churchland's discussion of this problem is particularly enlightening. She focuses on the historical nature of Enlightenment philosopher David Hume's (1711–1776) introduction of this problem and attempts to dismantle its hold on people's thinking. She points out that Hume's point is fundamentally about the limits of formal, deductive arguments and not about the impossibility of moving from *is* facts to values in all cases. In formal deductive arguments, the conclusions follow necessarily from the premises. For example—

1. All penguins are flightless birds.
2. Chilly Willy is a penguin.
3. Therefore, Chilly Willy is a flightless bird.

Chapter 17: Secularism and Morality

In this simple deductive proof, the conclusion follows necessarily from the two stated premises. No inference or probability is involved. If the premises are true, the conclusions must be true. Within this framework, it is impossible to deductively prove an ought statement. Moral statements are ought statements that are interpretive judgments one makes based on certain facts, experiences, or other variables. But, they can never be deductively proven or determined by the facts. Put crudely, a judgment is different than a fact. One might be able to offer reasons, facts, and evidences in support of one's ethical judgments, but these only probabilify one's conclusion and can never serve as deductive proof. This process of induction is categorically different than deduction.

In full view of this logical point, Churchland points to a much more open conception of the relationship between facts and values. She writes, "In a much broader sense of 'infer' than *derive* you can infer (*figure out*) what you ought to do, drawing on knowledge, perception, emotions, and understanding, and balancing considerations against each other" (Churchland 2011, 6). It might be true that one cannot derive an *ought* from an *is* in a deductive sense, but this deductive sense is too narrow and does not do justice to the real and practical ways in which we can, and do, derive morality from our experiences in the world. Furthermore, facts about our neurobiology and our evolutionary development more generally form the framework for our moral thinking and action (e.g., the tendency to care for our kin, the ability to recognize others' psychological states, problem-solving in a social context, and learning social practices. For Churchland, these interconnected brain processes inform the navigation of our moral lives. Understanding these features of our humanity, we can begin a science of ethics and can at least discuss which actions or behaviors work best with these attributes or best serve our goals as human beings. For Churchland, "the routine rejection of scientific approaches to moral behavior based on Hume's warning against deriving ought from is seems unfortunate, especially as the warning is limited to deductive inferences.... The truth seems to be that the values rooted in the circuitry for caring—for well-being of self, offspring, mates, kin and others—shape social reasoning about many issues" (2011, 8).

It is clear that a deeper understanding of evolutionary psychology, sociobiology, and neurology of moral belief and practice will be of great value as moral philosophy develops in the years and decades to come. There can be both philosophical and practical benefits to acquiring this new knowledge. A richer knowledge of why we believe and behave in the ways that we do and when and how the structures of the brain have evolved to serve us in navigating our moral worlds is essential to understanding our own humanity. Furthermore, such an understanding will undoubtedly be of service in many pragmatic ways. It can be of great use in helping to construct more effective systems of moral education, provide more common ground or common methods for settling moral differences, and even aid in cultivating moral character.

A criticism emerges at this point: there is no necessity to what will happen even if one agrees with many of the findings and methods of the science of ethics. As with all advancements in scientific and practical understanding, its moral worth lies in the hands of those who utilize it and is judged by the uses to which it is put. Understanding the neuroscience of ethics is indeed valuable but it does not necessarily make us more moral. In the service of a government or regime with malevolent goals, it may well serve to facilitate a more rapid and insidious indoctrination program. Indeed, many of this past century's discoveries in social psychology have served just those ends.

The point is not to say that these things will happen but merely to point out that knowledge about ethics (and the biological or neurological bases of it) is categorically different than the practice of being ethical. This brings the discussion back to a lingering trace of the is-ought fallacy. Churchland is right in showing that there are ways of bridging this gap in a practical sense. Scientists and philosophers may very well be able to locate reasons and evidences for claiming that this or that moral norm is more connected with our neurobiology or fits better with our evolutionary trajectory. But, there is ultimately no necessity to valuing these facts in any particular way. One might merely say, "Yes, I grant that not harming you fits better with the evidence of the evolution of our species and that it would even contribute to my own flourishing (so defined) ... but I simply do not care." Or consider a less morally loaded case: an ascetic. They simply do not define or value well-being and flourishing in the same way as others do. They do not desire happiness, comfort, or the trappings of modern life. Indeed, for them, these very things are the obstacles to living a truly moral life. Is it possible to settle who is right about this through appealing to certain facts about nature?

A MODEST SECULAR HUMANISM

One contemporary thinker who takes the religious ethicists' concerns seriously and attempts to construct a secular humanist ethic while recognizing the depth of the is-ought fallacy is philosopher Kitcher. Kitcher articulates a version of secular humanism that avoids the extreme antireligious sentiment of the new atheists but maintains the criticisms of traditional religious morality. For Kitcher, the challenge is to construct an intellectually honest version of secular humanism that does not pretend to solve all of the philosophical problems of ethics and can admit its shortcomings but still provide normative guidance for our moral lives. He summarizes his goal, couched within his criticism of some of the more scientistic and antitheistic approaches to ethics that are so common in secular literature in the twenty-first century. He states,

> However forceful or well-informed or eloquent the voices of atheism may be, however convincing their denunciations of the devastating effects of religious intolerance, mere denial leaves human need unaddressed: the fully secular life cries out for orientation. Nor is it enough to extend the atheistic critique with a hymn to the glory of scientific understanding. Listening to the choir of contemporary atheists, it is easy to sympathize with William James's pithy characterization of the fervent unbeliever: "He who believes in No God and worships him." (Kitcher 2014, 1)

Kitcher's book, *Life after Faith: The Case for Secular Humanism*, is an attempt to construct a robust, yet modest secular ethic that answers the questions of philosophy but without the confidence and dogmatism that he finds in contemporary atheist literature. In this text, Kitcher takes a broadly evolutionary approach in accounting for the origin and nature of our morality. Our ancestors were faced with real problems regarding survival and how to get along and in the process cultivated responsiveness and a mutuality that gave way to more codified systems of morality. Rather than solve all of the philosophical problems of ethics, Kitcher attempts to account for what ethics actually is, in a descriptive, evolutionary sense. We continue to face problems and struggle with the cultivation of the same capacities of understanding, caring for, and responding to each other. For Kitcher, this is just the ethical project of humanity. And, although he does not think that you can provide an explicit, universal standard for measuring ethics, he does believe that we can see ethical progress in human history. It involves the increased capacity to problem solve relative to the major issues of the day. Kitcher does not ultimately solve the is-ought fallacy nor does he provide a universal metaphysical ground for ethics. Rather, he attempts to give a descriptive account of what ethics actually is by looking at how and why humans developed this moral sense and began the ethical project. In a sense, his goal is a pragmatic one that attempts to dissolve some of the traditional philosophical questions that have haunted the discussion of ethics (and much of this chapter).

RELIGION: BEYOND RELIGION

Chapter 17: Secularism and Morality

Summary

This chapter has explored a handful of the philosophical issues that emerge in the analysis of secularism and morality. The first issue involved the meaning and use of the words *secularism*, *morality*, *religion*, and related terms. It is clear that this discussion has deep conceptual and ethical dimensions.

The chapter next dealt with the traditional problems in moral philosophy involving the possibility of being moral apart from God, gods, or religion and the issue of grounding morality apart from such religious foundations. Secularists claim that it is possible to do both things and often maintain that there are even unique philosophical and practical benefits to doing so. Furthermore, they often claim that religious systems do not succeed in providing the clear, objective foundation for ethics that they promise. Religious ethical systems have philosophical and practical flaws. Many religious ethicists still hold that secular ethical systems cannot adequately bridge the gap between the demands of the moral law, and account for its nature without a transcendent, metaphysical source. Furthermore, they claim that secular attempts to ground morality naturalistically fatally suffer from the is-ought fallacy. Secularists counter that current research in the areas of developmental and evolutionary psychology, neurobiology, and primatology is helping to provide a practical and more realistic foundation for ethics. They also claim that the is-ought fallacy can be overcome to a large degree through a more nuanced understanding of the relationship between facts and values. It is clear throughout this debate, that a standoff is rooted in deeply held presuppositions and philosophical starting points.

In view of this seeming stalemate, philosophers like Kitcher offer a type of modest secular humanism that affirms the values of a more horizontal, compassionate, global ethic. This maintains the secular criticism of religious ethics but does not promise to solve all of the problems of ethics through science or reason. It simply offers a compelling moral vision for the world. In conclusion, this chapter should serve as a solid starting point for an investigation of the concepts, issues, and complications of secularism and morality. Rather than attempting to solve all of these discussions and debates, it hopefully will encourage readers to join them and develop their own contributions to this most lively area of academic discourse.

Bibliography

Amarasingam, Amarnath. *Religion and the New Atheism A Critical Appraisal.* Leiden, the Netherlands: Brill, 2010.

Amesbury, Richard. "Rethinking 'Religion and Politics': Reflections on the Reception and Import of Talal Asad's Genealogies of Religion." *Bulletin for the Study of Religion* 43, no. 1 (2014): 2–7.

Asad, Talal. *Formations of the Secular: Christianity, Islam, Modernity.* Stanford, CA: Stanford University Press, 2003.

Asad, Talal. *Genealogies of Religion: Discipline and Reasons of Power in Christianity and Islam.* Baltimore, MD: Johns Hopkins University Press, 1993.

Asad, Talal. "Thinking about Religion, Belief and Politics with Talal Asad." YouTube. 2008. https://www.youtube.com/watch?v=L5YgAM6yO4E.

Ayer, Alfred J. *Language, Truth, and Logic.* New York: Dover Publications, 1952.

Barker, Dan. *Godless: How an Evangelical Preacher Became One of America's Leading Atheists.* Berkeley, CA: Ulysses Press, 2008.

Baron-Cohen, Simon. *The Science of Evil: On Empathy and the Origins of Cruelty.* New York: Basic Books, 2011.

Berlinerblau, Jacques. *How to Be Secular: A Call to Arms for Religious Freedom.* Boston: Houghton Mifflin Harcourt, 2012.

Bloom, Paul. *Just Babies: The Origins of Good and Evil.* New York: Crown, 2013.

Boss, Judith. *Ethics for Life: A Text with Readings*, 5th ed. New York: McGraw-Hill, 2011.

Brickhouse, Thomas C., and Nicholas D. Smith. *Plato's Socrates*. New York: Oxford University Press, 1994.

Bstan-'dzin-rgya-mtsho. *Beyond Religion: Ethics for a Whole World*. Boston: Houghton Mifflin Harcourt, 2011.

Buckley, Michael J. *At the Origins of Modern Atheism*. New Haven, CT: Yale University Press, 1987.

Calhoun, Craig J., Mark Juergensmeyer, and Jonathan VanAntwerpen, eds. *Rethinking Secularism*. Oxford: Oxford University Press, 2011.

Churchland, Patricia Smith. *Braintrust: What Neuroscience Tells Us about Morality*. Princeton, NJ: Princeton University Press, 2011.

D'Arms, Justin, and Daniel Jacobson. *Moral Psychology and Human Agency: Philosophical Essays on the Science of Ethics*. Oxford: Oxford University Press, 2014.

Davies, Brian. *Philosophy of Religion: A Guide and Anthology*. Oxford: Oxford University Press, 2000.

Davies, Brian. *Thomas Aquinas's Summa Theologiae: A Guide and Commentary*. Oxford: Oxford University Press, 2014.

Davis, Stephen T. *God, Reason and Theistic Proofs: How Do We Prove the Existence of God?* Edinburgh: Edinburgh University Press, 1997.

Dawkins, Richard. *The God Delusion*. Boston: Houghton Mifflin, 2006.

De Waal, F. B. M. *The Bonobo and the Atheist: In Search of Humanism among the Primates*. New York: Norton, 2013.

De Waal, F. B. M., Stephen Macedo, Josiah Ober, and Robert Wright. *Primates and Philosophers: How Morality Evolved*. Princeton, NJ: Princeton University Press, 2006.

Dennett, D. C. *Breaking the Spell: Religion As a Natural Phenomenon*. New York: Viking, 2006.

Dennett, Daniel. "Daniel Dennett—The Scientific Study of Religion." Point of Inquiry. December 12, 2011. http://www.pointofinquiry.org/daniel_dennett_the_scientific_study_of_religion/.

Falcioni, Ryan. "Is God a Hypothesis? The New Atheism, Contemporary Philosophy of Religion, and Philosophical Confusion." In *Religion and the New Atheism: A Critical Appraisal*, edited by Amarnath Amarasingam, 203–224. Leiden, the Netherlands: Brill, 2010.

Flew, Antony, and Alasdair C. MacIntyre. *New Essays in Philosophical Theology*. London: SCM Press, 1955.

Flew, Antony, and Roy Abraham Varghese. *There Is a God: How the World's Most Notorious Atheist Changed His Mind*. New York: HarperOne, 2007.

Garcia, Arturo. "Rick Santorum: Let's Call Secularism a Religion So It Can Be Banned from the Classroom." RawStory. http://www.rawstory.com/2014/09/rick-santorum-lets-call-secularism-a-religion-so-it-can-be-banned-from-the-classroom/.

Garcia, Robert K., and Nathan L. King. *Is Goodness without God Good Enough? A Debate on Faith, Secularism, and Ethics*. Lanham, MD: Rowman & Littlefield, 2009.

Geertz, Clifford. *Available Light: Anthropological Reflections on Philosophical Topics*. Princeton, NJ: Princeton University Press, 2000.

Hare, J. E. *The Moral Gap: Kantian Ethics, Human Limits, and God's Assistance*. Oxford: Clarendon Press, 1996.

Harris, Sam. *The End of Faith: Religion, Terror, and the Future of Reason*. New York: Norton, 2004.

Harris, Sam. *Letter to a Christian Nation*. New York: Knopf, 2006.

Harris, Sam. *The Moral Landscape: How Science Can Determine Human Values*. New York: Free Press, 2010.

Harris, Sam. "Science Can Answer Moral Questions | TED Talk | TED.com." *TED: Ideas Worth Spreading*. March 2010. http://www.ted.com/talks/sam_harris_science_can_show_what_s_right?language=en.

Hitchens, Christopher. *God Is Not Great: How Religion Poisons Everything*. New York: Twelve, 2007.

Hitchens, Christopher, and Alister McGrath. "'Poison or Cure: Religious Belief in the Modern World' Christopher Hitchens Debates Alister McGrath." FORA.tv. October 11, 2007. http://library.fora.tv/2007/10/11/Christopher_Hitchens_Debates_Alister_McGrath.

Jacoby, Susan. *Freethinkers: A History of American Secularism*. New York: Metropolitan Books, 2004.

Kitcher, Philip. *Life after Faith: The Case for Secular Humanism*. New Haven, CT: Yale University Press, 2014.

Kohlberg, Lawrence. *The Philosophy of Moral Development: Moral Stages and the Idea of Justice*. San Francisco: Harper & Row, 1981.

Lindsay, Ronald A. *The Necessity of Secularism: Why God Can't Tell Us What to Do*. Durham, NC: Pitchstone, 2014.

Martin, Michael. *The Cambridge Companion to Atheism*. New York: Cambridge University Press, 2007.

Miller, Alexander. *Contemporary Metaethics: An Introduction*, 2nd ed. Cambridge, UK: Polity Press, 2013.

Nielsen, Kai. *Ethics without God*, rev. ed. Amherst, NY: Prometheus, 1990.

Owen, Huw Parri. "Why Morality Implies the Existence of God." In *Philosophy of Religion: A Guide and Anthology*, edited by Brian Davies, 646–658. Oxford: Oxford University Press, 2000.

Chapter 17: Secularism and Morality

Pals, Daniel L. *Eight Theories of Religion*. New York: Oxford University Press, 2006.

Peterson, Michael, and William Hasker. *Reason and Religious Belief: An Introduction to the Philosophy of Religion,* 4th ed. Oxford: Oxford University Press, 2009.

Phillips, Dewi Zephaniah. *Faith and Philosophical Enquiry*. New York: Schocken Books, 1971.

Phillips, Dewi Zephaniah. *Interventions in Ethics*. Albany: State Univ. of New York Press, 1992.

Phillips, Dewi Zephaniah. *Religion and Friendly Fire: Examining Assumptions in Contemporary Philosophy of Religion*. Aldershot, UK: Ashgate, 2004.

Phillips, Dewi Zephaniah. *Religion and the Hermeneutics of Contemplation*. Cambridge: Cambridge University Press, 2001.

Phillips, Dewi Zephaniah. *Wittgenstein and Religion*. New York: St. Martin's Press, 1993.

Pigliucci, Massimo. *Answers for Aristotle: How Science and Philosophy Can Lead Us to a More Meaningful Life*. New York: Basic Books, 2012.

Pinker, Steven. *The Better Angels of Our Nature: Why Violence Has Declined*. New York: Viking, 2011.

Plato. *Euthyphro*. Translated by Benjamin Jowett. Project Gutenberg, 2008. January 15, 2013. http://www.gutenberg.org/files/1642/1642-h/1642-h.htm.

"Religion in America: U.S. Religious Data, Demographics and Statistics—Pew Research Center." Pew Research Center's Religion & Public Life Project. http://www.pewforum.org/religious-landscape-study/.

Shermer, Michael. *The Moral Arc: How Science and Reason Lead Humanity Toward Truth, Justice, and Freedom*. New York: Henry Holt, 2015.

Shermer, Michael. *The Science of Good and Evil: Why People Cheat, Gossip, Care, Share, and Follow the Golden Rule*. New York: Times Books, 2004.

Sinnott-Armstrong, Walter. *Morality without God?* Oxford: Oxford University Press. 2009.

Sproul, Robert Charles. *What Is Reformed Theology? Understanding the Basics*. Grand Rapids, MI: Baker Books, 2005.

Stark, Rodney. "Secularization, R.I.P." *Sociology of Religion* 60, no. 3 (1999): 249–273. doi:10.2307/3711936.

Stephen, Law. *Humanism: A Very Short Introduction*. Oxford: Oxford University Press, 2011.

Swinburne, Richard. "What Difference Does God Make to Morality?" In *Is Goodness without God Good Enough? A Debate on Faith, Secularism, and Ethics*, edited by Robert K. Garcia and Nathan L. King, 151–165. Lanham, MD: Rowman & Littlefield, 2009.

Swatos, William H., and Kevin J. Christiano. "Secularization Theory: The Course of a Concept." *Sociology of Religion* 60, no. 3 (1999): 209–228. doi:10.2307/3711934.

Taylor, Charles. *A Secular Age*. Cambridge, MA: Belknap Press of Harvard University Press, 2007.

"Thinking about Religion, Belief and Politics with Talal Asad." YouTube. https://www.youtube.com/watch?v=L5YgAM6yO4E.

"In U.S., Socialist Presidential Candidates Least Appealing." Gallup.com. http://www.gallup.com/poll/183713/socialist-presidential-candidates-least-appealing.aspx.

van der Veer, Peter. *The Modern Spirit of Asia: The Spiritual and the Secular in China and India*. Princeton, NJ: Princeton University Press, 2014.

Walters, Kerry S. *Atheism: A Guide for the Perplexed*. New York: Continuum, 2010.

Warner, Michael, Jonathan VanAntwerpen, and Craig J. Calhoun. *Varieties of Secularism in a Secular Age*. Cambridge, MA: Harvard University Press, 2010.

"What Is Secular Humanism?" Council for Secular Humanism. https://www.secularhumanism.org/index.php/3260.

Wittgenstein, Ludwig. *Philosophical investigations*. Oxford, UK: Basil Blackwell, 1967.

Wittgenstein, Ludwig, and Cyril Barrett. *Lectures and Conversations on Aesthetics, Psychology, and Religious Belief*. Berkeley: University of California Press, 1966.

Woodruff, Paul. "Plato's Shorter Ethical Works." Stanford Encyclopedia of Philosophy/Winter 2014. Stanford Encyclopedia of Philosophy. Accessed September 7, 2015. http://plato.stanford.edu/archives/win2014/entries/plato-ethics-shorter/.

"Worldwide, Many See Belief in God As Essential to Morality—Pew Research Center." Pew Research Center's Global Attitudes Project. Last modified 2014. http://www.pewglobal.org/2014/03/13/worldwide-many-see-belief-in-god-as-essential-to-morality/.

Zuckerman, Phil, "Atheism: Contemporary Numbers and Patterns." In *The Cambridge Companion to Atheism*, edited by Michael Martin, 47–65. New York: Cambridge University Press, 2007.

Zuckerman, Phil. *Faith No More: Why People Reject Religion*. New York: Oxford University Press, 2011.

Zuckerman, Phil. *Living the Secular Life: New Answers to Old Questions*. New York: Penguin Press, 2014.

Zuckerman, Phil. *Society without God: What the Least Religious Nations Can Tell Us About Contentment*. New York: New York University Press, 2008.

Chapter 17: Secularism and Morality

WEBSITES

Center for Inquiry. http://www.centerforinquiry.net/.

Council for Secular Humanism. https://www.secularhumanism.org/.

The Kenan Institute for Ethics (Duke University). http://kenan.ethics.duke.edu/.

McKoy Family Center for Ethics and Society (Stanford University). https://ethicsinsociety.stanford.edu/.

Pew Religious Landscape Study. http://www.pewforum.org/religious-landscape-study/.

Rationally Speaking Podcast. http://rationallyspeakingpodcast.org/.

Religion Dispatches. http://religiondispatches.org/.

Skeptic's Annotated Bible. http://skepticsannotatedbible.com/.

Stanford Encyclopedia of Philosophy. http://plato.stanford.edu/.

FILMS

The Invention of Lying. Dir. Ricky Gervais and Matthew Robinson. 2009. A humorous and satirical look at the nature of religious morality, authority, and the origins of religion more generally.

Jesus Camp. Dir. Heidi Ewing and Rachel Grady. 2006. A provocative documentary that examines the inner workings of a particular evangelical Christian summer camp for children. It gives an insider perspective on this phenomenon of training Christian children to be cultural and spiritual warriors for Christ. It succeeds in showing the effects of this particular brand of Christianity on children.

Monty Python's Life of Brian. Dir. Terry Jones. 1979. A modern classic. An entertaining piece of religious satire that succeeds in challenging many of the sacred cows of religion. The story follows a young Jewish man, Brian, who happens to be born on the same day as Jesus and is ultimately mistaken for being the Messiah.

Religulous. Dir. Larry Charles. 2008. A humorous and oftentimes uncomfortable comedic documentary by Bill Maher (1956–). He explores, challenges, and ridicules the varieties of religious belief and practice, with an eye for the extreme and absurd.

RELIGION: BEYOND RELIGION

CHAPTER 18

Atheism, Pacifism, and Anarchism

Andrew Fiala
Professor of Philosophy
California State University, Fresno

This chapter asks whether in going beyond religion we also move beyond war and the state. The question of this chapter is: how is atheism connected to pacifism and anarchism? As we shall see, there are varieties of atheism, pacifism, and anarchism. No necessary or absolute connection between these three ideas exists. Nevertheless, for some, the dream of a world beyond religion accompanies a vision of a world beyond wars and states.

Let's begin in an unlikely place: a recent book by the prominent religious figure Tenzin Gyatso (1935–), the current Dalai Lama. Despite his status of a global religious leader, the Dalai Lama published a book provocatively titled *Beyond Religion*, which argues that we should develop a secular ethic. The book contends that war is "outdated and illogical" (2011, 87). Futhermore, nationalism has kept people apart. *Beyond Religion* concludes with an explanation that humanity is outgrowing its old-fashioned faith in violence and nationalism. As a result, the Dalai Lama argues, "the oneness and interdependence of humanity are increasingly taken for granted" (186). He conjoins a critique of religion with a critique of nationalism and war. Although the Dalai Lama and the Tibetan people he leads have suffered much at the hands of the Chinese who invaded Tibet and forced him into exile, he continues to advocate for nonviolence. He has written that war could conceivably be justified, but "violence begets violence. And violence means only one thing: suffering" (1999, 201).

We can debate the degree to which the Dalai Lama fits exactly into the antireligion, antiwar, and antistate category, but Buddhism does provide a useful source for a critique of religion, war, and states. After all, the first moral precept of Buddhist ethics is nonviolence (or *ahimsa*) and Buddhism holds that much of the suffering of life is caused by our attachment to the institutions and structures of political, military, and religious life. One cure for suffering is to see that the things we kill and die for are often illusory goods. From a Buddhist perspective, nations, states, and military honors are merely constructed goods without deep or lasting significance; our attachment to these goods—along with our attachment to religious hierarchies and icons—is a source of suffering because defense of these goods leads to violence and unhappiness. Despite the fact that much of Buddhism is heavily ritualized and religious, Buddhism is nontheistic, and Buddhist philosophy questions attachment to religious ritual.

Gary Snyder (1930–), an American poet and interpreter of Asian thought, has described what he calls Buddhist anarchism. In an essay from 1961, Snyder imagined a

325

Chapter 18: Atheism, Pacifism, and Anarchism

"cultural and economic revolution that moves clearly toward a free, international, classless society." He continues:

> It means resisting the lies and violence of governments and their irresponsible employees. Fighting back with civil disobedience, pacifism, poetry, poverty—and violence if it comes to a matter of clobbering some rampaging redneck or shoving a scab off the pier. Defending the right to smoke pot, eat peyote, be polygamous, polyandrous, or queer—and learning from the hip fellaheen peoples of Asia and Africa, attitudes and techniques banned by the Judaeo-Christian West. Respecting intelligence and learning, but not as greed or means to personal power. Working on one's own responsibility, no dualism of ends and means—never the agent of an ideology—but willing to join in group action.... I see it as a kind of committed disaffiliation: "Buddhist Anarchism." (2009, 242–243)

In going beyond religion as traditionally conceived in the West, we find experimentation with non-Western ideas, openness to alternative social organization and ways of life, and opposition to traditional structures of political and military power. Such thinking came alive in the counterculture of the 1960s—which Snyder helped to inspire. Atheistic, anarchistic, pacifistic ways of thinking continue to live in a variety of ways in the contemporary world.

ATHEISM, ANARCHISM, AND PACIFISM: CONCEPTUAL CLARIFICATIONS

No absolute, rigid, and necessary connections exist among atheism, anarchism, and pacifism. However, a strong affinity thrums throughout these skeptical points of view. Let's begin by clarifying these concepts.

- *Atheism* is the denial of belief in a God or gods, and a general opposition to religion and religious institutions.

- *Pacifism* is a commitment to peace and nonviolence, which includes rejection of war, militarism, and violence.

- *Anarchism* is opposition to structures of political authority, including the legitimacy of nation-states.

Atheists, anarchists, and pacifists share a critical skepticism of hierarchical institutions, unjustified power, and the tyranny of prevailing opinion. They also share an optimistic hope about our ability to live well without religions, wars, and states. This trio of values is connected by their humanism and by their generally critical perspective on authority, institutional hierarchies, social conservatism, and power and violence. However, important differences exist among atheists, pacifists, and anarchists. For example, some pacifists and anarchists are religious. Some atheists and anarchists are militant. Some nations have enforced state-sponsored atheism. We should admit that there is no single way of uniting critical perspectives on states, wars, and churches. However, pacifists, anarchists, and atheists commonly share skepticism in the faith in states, wars, and religion, especially when these institutions violate personal autonomy. They also claim that these institutions often create bad and immoral outcomes. Finally, they believe a happy world without religion, wars, and states is possible.

Let's now extend these preliminary definitions.

ATHEISM

Atheism is often narrowly construed as a metaphysical commitment grounded in materialism and naturalism. *Materialism* claims that only matter exists, whereas *naturalism* contends that things can be explained and understood without appeal to supernatural or spiritual beings. However, atheism is not merely a metaphysical theory. Most atheists are not simply interested in denying the metaphysical claim that God exists. They are also often opposed to religious institutions. Thus atheists are also often anticlerical (opposed to the clergy), anti-ecclesiastical (opposed to churches), and secular (committed to a nonspiritual, humanistic worldview). Such opposition comes in a variety of forms. For some atheists, secularism is enough; they believe secular systems of government will reduce the cultural and political power of religious organizations, which is enough for them. Other atheists, however, are more militant in their rejection of religious ideas, feeling that churches and the clergy are pernicious and should be actively opposed. During the French Revolution, for example, some revolutionaries advocated active de-Christianization, which carried out the destruction of religious artifacts and aimed at establishing something like a cult of reason. A similar anti-ecclesiastical motif can be found in twentieth-century communism, which has sometimes been described as state-sponsored atheism. Clearly, defenders of state-sponsored atheism are not advocates of anarchism because they are deeply invested in the cohesion of a nation-state. Nor are militant antireligious activists who use violence to destroy religion sympathetic to pacifism.

Nonetheless, because the focus of atheistic critique is often the political and cultural power of the church and those who assert spiritual power, it is not surprising that some atheists are also opposed to other hierarchical institutions such as those found in military and political organizations. In the modern liberal Western world, atheists have often been committed to a secular ideal, which uses political means to limit the power of religion. *Secularism* calls for a firm distinction between political and religious authority, relegating religion to a private sphere of liberty, where individuals are free to believe or not believe. In societies where religious power is strong, atheists will often want to strengthen the political sphere in order to weaken the religious domination of the culture. Secular political systems can be supported by atheists and by a variety of religious believers, all sharing an interest in keeping religious power out of the political realm. However, some atheists may worry that even supposedly secular polities remain too closely tied to religious authority. Anarcho-atheists reject both political power and religious power as unjustified forms of authority and domination.

PACIFISM

Like atheism, pacifism is usually negatively defined by what it opposes or rejects. Usually pacifists reject war, and pacifism is often defined as antiwarism. Some pacifists extend their critique of violence to a rejection of all forms of violence, including the killing of animals. Pacifism also usually contains a positive affirmation of the power of nonviolence. Whereas atheism is a metaphysical commitment, pacifism is a moral one, focused on the proper means for moral action. So-called nonviolentism contends that only nonviolent means are justifiable and that violence is always wrong. For some, pacifism creates a way of life that culminates in explicit action—from conscientious refusal and civil disobedience to deliberate work on disarmament or other forms of antimilitarist protest. Pacifists tend to be critical of violence in all of its forms: both overt violence of war and structural or institutional violence, which is woven into the fabric of social institutions.

RELIGION: BEYOND RELIGION

Chapter 18: Atheism, Pacifism, and Anarchism

Wars often result from political and religious ideology. Thus pacifists may be sympathetic to antireligious and antipolitical points of view. Of course, many pacifists have been religious. However, religious pacifists have usually offered radical criticism of religious beliefs and institutions that too easily justify violence and war. Thus religious pacifists are often antinomian reformers, who offer a radical internal critique of those religious institutions that support violence. Many religious pacifists have explicitly affirmed a version of anarchism, holding that states and wars are systematically intertwined. Nonreligious pacifists will, however, reject the metaphysical commitments and idealism of religious pacifism. Atheistic pacifism proposes a moral commitment to nonviolence that is grounded in a humanistic approach to ethics and often criticizes the structural or institutional violence fostered by religious institutions. Some forms of atheistic pacifism hold that religious institutions hurt people physically (say through circumcision or other pernicious rituals), cause discrimination and inequality (through chauvinistic and hierarchical religious preferences), and damage people psychologically (perhaps by creating guilt and anxiety). A further argument claims that overt religious violence, including religious warfare and violence against women, is a serious historical problem.

ANARCHISM

Like atheism and pacifism, anarchism is also often defined negatively. Anarchists reject political institutions and structures of hierarchical authority, arguing that they cannot be justified. Some anarchists are actively involved in efforts to deconstruct political structures. Other anarchists opt out of the mainstream and seek to build separate societies, such as communes. For others, anarchism is more a philosophical idea than an agenda for political action. Philosophical anarchism is the claim that, in theory, states are not fully legitimate. However, some philosophical anarchists may pragmatically acknowledge the importance of political institutions. Anarchists are not merely skeptical rejectionists. They usually also envision a humane and organic conception of society developing outside of state structures, as voluntary associations and cooperative ventures working toward human flourishing. Anarchists are usually committed to human solidarity grounded in ethical concern. Anarchists have thus often been sympathetic to the concerns of *cosmopolitanism*, which holds that all people can and should be united by common ethical principles that transcend culture, politics, and religion.

In arguing that states lack legitimacy, anarchists critique the morality of political power. In many cases, anarchists have argued against traditional religious structures, too, maintaining that religious power should be subjected to the same moral critique as political power. When comparing anarchism with pacifism, however, it is important to remember that no absolute or necessary relationship exists between them despite the fact that they share much in common. Indeed, militant anarchists have argued that violence can be justified to oppose state power. However, other anarchists advocate only nonviolent means of resisting political power. A deep affinity lies between anarchist critiques of authority and pacifist critiques of structural violence. Pacifistic anarchists reject the use of violence to oppose state violence. Some anarchists have been religious, but the beliefs of religious anarchists are anti-ecclesiastic and antiauthoritarian. Atheistic anarchists reject both God and the state, holding that religious and political authority are each unjustifiable and that religious and political power often work in tandem to support one another. As can be seen, much variety distinguishes the positions within and among anarchism, pacifism, and atheism.

328   MACMILLAN INTERDISCIPLINARY HANDBOOKS

Nevertheless, some overlap occurs among atheism, pacifism, and anarchism as shown in Figure 18.1. A synthesis of these three ideas would focus on building a nonviolent community based in the human world (as opposed to a violent political structure grounded in religious belief). However, there may also be disconnection: one may be an atheist but not a pacifist or anarchist, and so on.

We also need to be aware of varying levels of commitment to these ideas. Some people are absolutely committed to one or all of these theories, whereas others have a less adamant and more pragmatic approach, acknowledging that in the short run we have to accommodate ourselves to a world that in many ways does not live up to our ideals. Absolute pacifism, for example, simply refuses to admit that violence can ever be justified. Absolute opposition to religion—what we might call absolute atheism—will claim that religion is always irrational and pernicious and ought to be opposed. A similar absolutism about

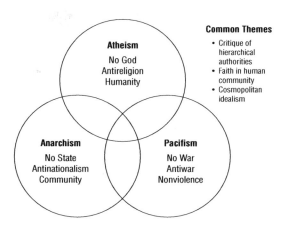

Figure 18.1. Distinguishing and common themes of atheism, anarchism, and pacifism. ANDREW FIALA. ADAPTED FROM ANDREW FIALA, 2016.

political reality—absolute anarchism—will claim that political life always results in a violation of autonomy and is therefore wrong. Absolutism in any of these forms, however, is difficult to support. Some religious and state organizations are more easily justified than others: democratic, tolerant, and ethically sensitive secular institutions are preferred over despotism. Moreover, it is possible that some limited forms of violence can be justified—an idea that fits with what is known as the just war theory.

A less absolutist approach to these issues would be grounded in empirical claims based on contingent facts. Contingent pacifism, for example, claims that wars are largely not justifiable given the ubiquity of weapons of mass destruction, the likelihood of collateral damage, and the past record of unjustified and horrible wars. However, a contingent pacifist would admit that in some limited cases, war could be justifiable. A similar sort of contingent and empirical approach is possible with regard to anarchism. A contingent anarchist may argue that political states could be justifiable in theory, but that contemporary states fail to live up to the standards of that theory. It is also possible to imagine a contingent form of atheism: perhaps a form of agnosticism that claims it is possible that God exists but that we cannot be sure, or that current religions fail to live up to the standards we might expect if God really did exist.

ANARCHISM, PACIFISM, AND ATHEISM IN POP CULTURE

Let's switch gears now and turn away from philosophical analysis to consider some ways that atheism, pacifism, and anarchism have entered popular consciousness. We mentioned in our discussion of Gary Snyder that the 1960s counterculture often supported anarchist, atheist, and pacifist ideals. Consider, for example, John Lennon's song "Imagine," released in 1971 at the height of anti-establishment activism. The song has continued to inspire those who dream of a world beyond religions, wars, and states. The song has subsequently been

Chapter 18: Atheism, Pacifism, and Anarchism

rerecorded and reissued in a variety of ways. For example, it was chosen as a theme song for the 2012 Summer Olympics in London, where it was sung by a children's choir. "Imagine" could well be the anthem of those who are sympathetic to the effort to unify atheism, anarchism, and pacifism. Lennon's simple lyrics ask us to imagine our world with no religion, no countries, and no war. Lennon's imagined world would leave human beings alone to live for today—without religions or nations or wars—"living life in peace." Lennon seems to realize that critics will claim he's a "dreamer." But he says he's not the only one who is enchanted by the dream of a world beyond religion, wars, and states—not the only one who is disenchanted by the chaos, hatred, and violence of a world torn apart by religious strife, political violence, domination, and power.

The last line of the song is a cosmopolitan dream of a world unified in peace, the pacifist ideal. The world can be united, the song suggests, when we overcome our old-fashioned allegiance to religions, states, and military power.

Some have characterized "Imagine" as sappy and trite. Critics complain that the melody is simple and boring, and they suspect that Lennon and the hippies he inspired were clueless utopian dreamers. Others who are more sympathetic to Lennon and his song may claim that this is not really an atheist anthem (there's no denying that Lennon was a pacifist ... and his anarchism is nearly as obvious). Some try to salvage a defense of God in the worldview in "Imagine," pointing out that Lennon imagines a world without "religion"—not a world without God.

We noted that Lennon's song went global with the 2012 Olympics. The Olympic dream also strives toward a world beyond war and beyond old-fashioned political allegiance and religious division. The Olympic ideal grew out of internationalist, pacifist, and secularist ideas developed in the late nineteenth century (Quanz 1993). The idealism of the Olympics (named *Olympism* by the founder of the modern games, Pierre de Coubertin) focuses on friendly competition, sportsmanship, and peaceful cosmopolitanism. It also looks beyond religious and political difference, toward a celebration of the embodied human spirit. Although there are neo-pagan elements in the idea of the Olympics (the ancient Olympics were dedicated to Zeus, for example), the modern Olympic ideal maintains that athletic competition and devotion to sport provides a hopeful way of moving beyond religion and nationalistic warfare.

Despite such hopeful idealism, atheists, anarchists, and pacifists often also give voice to a deep-seated cynicism about the status quo. One place to find this cynicism is in works of social satire and comedy. Consider, for example, Kurt Vonnegut (1922–2007), the author of *Slaughterhouse-Five*, one of the great antiwar books, and *Cat's Cradle*, which parodies religion. Vonnegut once explained, "I am a pacifist, I am an anarchist, I am a planetary citizen, and so on" (2009, 110). Vonnegut's work is routinely critical, to the point of cynicism. He is not hopeful about humanity's future, and he views wars, militarism, politics, and religion as serious impediments to human flourishing. In an interview, Vonnegut pointed out that religious people tended not to like his work. He replied of his critics: "They think it's the proper business of government to protect the reputation of God. All I can say is, 'Good luck to them, and good luck to the government, and good luck to God'" (96).

Vonnegut's anarchic mocking of religions, governments, and wars resonates with the work of other comedians and satirists. George Carlin (1937–2008) once wrote, "anarchy and comedy are a team" (2009, 285). In one of Carlin's most famous routines he flatly declares that religion is "bullshit."

When it comes to bullshit, big-time, major league bullshit, you have to stand in awe of the all-time champion of false promises and exaggerated claims: religion. No contest…. Religion easily has the greatest bullshit story ever told. (2001, 28)

Carlin also has a cynical critique of war. Carlin saw war as "dick-waving": "Since war is the ultimate competition, essentially men are killing one another in order to improve their genital self-esteem…. There's an unconscious need to project the national penis into the affairs of others. It's called 'fucking with people'" (2001, 242). Carlin concludes that there is no good reason to believe the authorities, who sell us religious stories, the ideology of war, and the myths of patriotism. He said:

My first rule: Never believe anything anyone in authority says. None of them. Government, police, clergy, the corporate criminals. None of them. And neither do I believe anything I'm told by the media, who, in the case of the Gulf War, functioned as little more than unpaid employees of the Defense Department, and who, most of the time, operate as an unofficial public relations agency for government and industry. (2001, 241)

Comedians and satirists find easy prey in the hypocrisies of religious, political, and military hierarchies. Musicians can easily sing about peace and harmony, but comedians and musicians are not supposed to offer complete theories or lead political or religious movements. They criticize and dream, point out flaws, and imagine new things.

ANARCHISM, PACIFISM, AND ATHEISM IN ART

One of the tasks of art is to create new possibilities for seeing the world in unique and inspiring ways. Indeed, a deep philosophical connection thrives between music, art, and peaceful anarchism. The American anarchist Josiah Warren (1798–1874) noted, in 1836, that although militaries and nations require subordination that is enforced by violence, "no subordination can be more perfect than that of an Orchestra; but it is all voluntary" (145). When musicians harmonize and coordinate their mutual activity, great art occurs. There is no need for war, military power, or police domination in the orchestra. Nor is there need of the threat of divine punishment. Art—like sport—can be seen as a model for atheistic, anarchistic, and pacifistic activity.

Artists, poets, and musicians have often been critical of religion, of states, and of war. Consider, for example, Oscar Wilde (1854–1900), whose anarchistic and atheistic tendencies were connected to a countercultural aesthetic and sympathy with pacifism. Wilde embraces a strong antiauthoritarianism and libertarianism that fit with the spirit of atheism and anarchism. He wrote: "Every man must be left quite free to choose his own work. No form of compulsion must be exercised over him…. Of course, authority and compulsion are out of the question. All association must be quite voluntary. It is only in voluntary associations that man is fine" (1900, 14–15). Wilde provides an interesting example because his own libertine behaviors eventually got him into serious trouble and he was imprisoned for indecency and sodomy in 1895. While in prison, he postulated that religion should be re-created by humans for humans. He concluded that he wanted to create a religion for agnostics, which he called "Confraternity of the Faithless" and explained as "an order for those who cannot believe" (2005, 98). One model for Wilde's imagined paradise can be found in Chinese Taoism. Wilde wrote a review of a translation of Chuang-Tzu in which

RELIGION: BEYOND RELIGION

Chapter 18: Atheism, Pacifism, and Anarchism

he sympathized with the Taoist longing for a Golden Age in which people lived in peace without government. Wilde sympathizes with the anarchism he found in Chuang-Tzu:

> All modes of government are wrong. They are unscientific because they seek to alter the natural environment of man; they are immoral because, by interfering with the individual, they produce the most aggressive forms of egotism; they are ignorant, because they try to spread education; they are self-destructive, because they engender anarchy. (1916, 339)

Wilde is well known for his paradoxical and whimsical statements, which fits with the spirit of Taoism, as well. He continues in this essay to offer agreement to the Taoist idea that humanity is naturally at peace, but that war is the result of an "artificial society" based on economic, political, and moral hierarchies (Wilde 1916, 340).

Another example is found in the work of Aldous Huxley (1894–1963), the author of *Brave New World*. That novel, published in 1932, can be read as a critique of both organized religion and the political structures of advanced civilization. As Huxley explained in his later book of essays, *Brave New World Revisited*, one of the problems of religion and politics is "over-organization," which violates individuality and liberty: "Physically and mentally, each one of us is unique. Any culture which, in the interests of efficiency or in the name of some political or religious dogma, seeks to standardize the human individual, commits an outrage against man's biological nature" (2004, 254). It is interesting to note that Aldous Huxley's grandfather, T. H. Huxley (1825–1895), popularized the term *agnosticism*, a philosophical skepticism that refuses to admit the truth of anything without proof (Huxley 1992). Antireligious ideas thus run deep in Huxley's family. Aldous Huxley experimented with alternative spirituality, for example through his use of mescaline, which opened "the doors of perception" (the title of a book he wrote, which went on to influence Jim Morrison and The Doors, who named their band after Huxley's book). Huxley viewed organized religion as a pale social construction, which got in the way of original spiritual experience. Indeed, he argued that religious and political power existed to prevent human beings from finding that primal source of spiritual experience through prohibitions on the use of psychedelic substances and through forced conformity of orthodox belief. It is clear that Huxley is skeptical of religious and political power. He thinks that in the Christian West, for example, religion has outlived its social function because it no longer binds people together in ethically appropriate ways while also preventing social progress. Pointing out some absurdities of religious sentiment, including the fact that religious leaders do not condemn warfare, he concludes, "If this is religion, then God deliver us from such criminal imbecility" (2012, 266). As a pacifist, he argued that the conjunction of religious and political power leads to war. He explained, for example, "the rise of war appears to be connected with the rise of self-conscious leaders, preoccupied with the ideas of personal domination and personal survival after death" (2012, 102). Civilization, from this point of view, is built on a hierarchical cult of prophet-kings who use war, religion, and political power to dominate others and enhance their own prestige.

Huxley's dystopian novel is a work of science fiction, as is much of the work of Kurt Vonnegut. Science fiction has often been critical of religion, states, and wars. Consider, as another example, the writings of Ursula K. Le Guin (1929–). In works such as *The Left Hand of Darkness* and *The Dispossessed*, Le Guin explores ideas about religion and politics with an atheistic, pacifistic, and anarchistic focus. *The Dispossessed*, for example, imagines an anarchist planet, an entire alternative world of peaceful anarchism. Le Guin's anarchism is

Chapter 18: Atheism, Pacifism, and Anarchism

not incidental to her work, nor is her critique of organized, patriarchal, Western religion. She claims as an inspiration the anarchist pacifism of Peter Kropotkin (1842–1941) and the Goodman brothers, Paul Goodman (1911–1972) and Percival Goodman (1904–1989). She locates her inspiration in Native American spirituality and, as with Wilde, in Taoism (Le Guin 2004).

Taoism also influenced Gary Snyder, the beatnik poet who has described Buddhism as a kind of anarchism, as noted previously. Snyder's work contains ideologies of anarchism, pacifism, and atheism. Snyder has explained:

> Anarchism should refer to the creation of nonstatist, natural societies as contrasted with legalistically organized societies, as alternative models for human organization. Not to be taken totally literally, but to be taken poetically as a direction toward the formation of better and more viable communities. Anarchism, in political history, does not mean chaos, it means self-government. So a truly anarchist society is a self-governing society. (1996)

Snyder grew up as an atheist (2010, 58). His interest in Taoism and Buddhism is ultimately antireligious. His work encourages us to get in touch with the earth and to stray beyond the confines of religions and states. In a recent essay on the problem of humanity's war against nature, Snyder argues in defense of the Asian ethic of *ahimsa* (nonviolence) and compassion. He laments our inhumanity to our fellow humans and our complete and utter disregard for the natural world. Although he does not reach an absolutist anarchist or antireligious conclusion, he calls for a radical shift in religion and politics that would transform political and religious organizations toward compassion and nonviolence, the same form of committed disaffiliation he outlined in the early 1960s. In the end, Snyder concludes, "what we ultimately need most is human beings who love the world" (2007, 70).

CONTEMPORARY MOVEMENTS

Poetry and music inspire and amuse; they don't make arguments or construct institutions. Hard-nosed realists will protest that all of this idealism is a silly remnant of a passing fad of utopian dreams. Hippies who imagine a world beyond religion, states, and wars should wise up, the realist will argue, and understand that the real world is structured by religious, political, and military power, and these things are never going away.

Yet, the anarchist, pacifist, and atheistic idealism of the 1960s has not faded away. Contemporary social movements continue the work of decentralization, cosmopolitanism, interfaith dialogue, nonreligion and secularism, antiwar activism, and resistance to the dominant political, religious, and military powers of the world. Feminists and queer theorists have criticized structures of power in religion, politics, and the military. People concerned with animal welfare and environmental ethics have offered similar critiques. Defenders of indigenous cultures have echoed such concerns. The idea that we need to move beyond religions, wars, and states has been articulated by academics in the ivory tower as well as by voices from the margins. The difficulty of resounding this message is the resistance of dominant powers.

Atheism, pacifism, and anarchism are skeptical ideas opposed to much of what we take for granted in the contemporary world. Someone who affirms atheism, pacifism, and anarchism would be opposed to just about everything we take for granted in the status quo.

RELIGION: BEYOND RELIGION

333

Chapter 18: Atheism, Pacifism, and Anarchism

Thus atheists, pacifists, and anarchists exist on the fringes or on the margins of mainstream society.

For that reason, some may think that the conjunction of atheism, pacifism, and anarchism creates an unholy trinity that is both dangerous and delusional. For many people (maybe most people), atheism, pacifism, and anarchism are naïve, utopian, and possibly also immoral. On the other hand, atheists, pacifists, and anarchists will claim that it is naïve and utopian to continue to put our faith in those old-fashioned ideas, ancient traditions, and decrepit institutions that often get in the way of progress.

At any rate, we should admit that atheism, pacifism, and anarchism are minority positions, and that a position that conjoins the three would have an even smaller number of adherents. Only about 23 percent of Americans admit to being religiously unaffiliated (so-called nones): 3.1 percent are atheist, 4 percent are agnostic, and 15.8 percent are "nothing in particular" (see Pew Forum poll, May 2015). Few people—the explicit atheists—flatly deny the existence of God. A few more are less assured (or agnostic) in their disavowal of knowledge about God, and a number more are disaffiliated: still believing in God, while turning away from organized religion. There may be problems in the reported numbers, because some atheists may be reluctant to affirm their position due to a negative social stigma.

A similar problem may occur with regard to affirmations of pacifism or anarchism: it is not socially acceptable to affirm such things. No comparable survey data exist on the numbers of pacifists or anarchists, but the numbers must be similarly low.

Consider, for example, the low number of people who belong to historic peace churches such as Amish, Quakers, Mennonites, Seventh Day Adventists, and others. These pacifist (and occasionally anarchist) traditions account for less than 5 percent of those who are religiously affiliated in the United States. Of course a number of people oppose war who do not self-identify as pacifists. To see that number we might consider those who showed up in antiwar protests in 2003, when the United States was planning to invade Iraq. However, mere opposition to a given war is not pacifism. Pacifism is a sustained commitment to peace and opposition to war. Absolute pacifists will have a moral problem with military service, taxation used to support militarism, and so on.

Anarchism is also obviously a minority view, on the margins. As with pacifism, the number of anarchists has not been surveyed adequately. However, we could take the Occupy Protests of 2011 as an example of anarchist activism. Although not all Occupy protesters would identify as anarchists, the populist and antiauthoritarian message of Occupy ("we are the 99%") as well as the decentralized way the movement was organized point in an anarchist direction. Despite these important events and well-known examples, the numbers participating in antiwar protests or in Occupy protests are still relatively low. Far more people turned out for the big Occupy marches than actually affirmed the position by occupying public spaces and living in the tent cities that sprang up around the world. Even among those who occupied these public spaces, the number of explicit anarchists was low.

Given the low numbers of people who identify as either atheist, anarchist, or pacifist, there must be an even smaller number who identify as each of these combined. So we must admit that arguments against religions, wars, and states, held together simultaneously, represent a minority view. However, those on the margin may argue that the fact of their marginalization provides an important argument: the mainstream of religious, military, and

334   MACMILLAN INTERDISCIPLINARY HANDBOOKS

Chapter 18: Atheism, Pacifism, and Anarchism

political culture creates the oppression and marginalization that the atheists, anarchists, and pacifists criticize.

COURAGEOUS HUMANISM OR MORONIC MISCHIEF

Atheists, anarchists, and pacifists are often mocked for being mean, malicious, mischievous, and moronic. Atheists and anarchists are often accused of *nihilism*, that is, of believing in nothing. (We might picture, here, the nihilists of the film *The Big Lebowski* (1998), who declare, "we believe in nothing.") Anarchists and atheists have also been caricatured as malevolent bomb-throwers who only want to destroy things. A related criticism charges that pacifists are either cowardly or stupid. Pacifists have been caricatured as naïve sheep led meekly and stupidly to slaughter. In fact, anarchists and atheists do not believe in nothing. Rather, they affirm human community. For example, pacifists such as Mahatma Gandhi (1869–1948) and Martin Luther King Jr. (1929–1968) affirmed the importance of courage and intelligent use of nonviolent social activism.

Behind the stereotypes is a real sustained and thoughtful effort to think critically about the justifications of much we take for granted. That form of criticism has deep roots in the world's philosophical traditions, which routinely argue against the injustice and oppression of states, religions, and wars. The courageous humanism of Socrates provides a model of critical thinking: the individual stands up to religious, military, and political authorities and asks "why?" We should note that although Socrates is an inspiration, he was not himself an atheist, anarchist, or pacifist, but it could be that his model of critical questioning opens the door toward such conclusions. We should also note again that the goal is not merely to be critical. Rather, atheists, pacifists, and anarchists have often affirmed a positive, humane, and ethically rich form of life beyond religion, wars, and states. The positive vision of the anarchist-pacifist-atheist is of a world where human beings live together in peace and harmony, without domination, oppression, and violence.

The humane and humanitarian vision of anarchism, pacifism, and atheism may be called *humanism*. Humanism has a long lineage, extending as far back as the ancient Greeks and Romans. In the Renaissance, humanism suggested a focus on human life in this world, as opposed to a focus on religion and the next life. In the nineteenth and twentieth centuries, humanism was associated with progressive reformers and radical revolutionaries who wanted to reconstruct society on a more humane basis. In the twentieth century, especially, *secular humanism* developed as an approach to life that is agnostic or atheistic and focused on using reason and ethics to improve human life. Humanists, including secular humanists, tend to oppose religious authority, to favor human liberty, and to prefer nonviolent methods of resolving social conflict. Although not all humanists are anarchists, pacifists, or atheists—humanists may be sympathetic to the idealism of the anarchists, pacifists, and atheists.

When anarchists speak of creating a society of voluntary associations and mutual cooperation, they are not nihilists. Instead, they affirm ethical relations, social connection, caring relations, and other humanistic and humane ideas. When pacifists speak of a world beyond war, where love and nonviolence replace hatred and violence, they are not immoral or nihilistic. Rather, they affirm a deeply humane vision of the possibility of human progress. Finally, when atheists insist that religion should be transformed away from divisive issues of theology and culturally specific differences in religion, they assert the need for

RELIGION: BEYOND RELIGION

335

Chapter 18: Atheism, Pacifism, and Anarchism

progress toward an inclusive vision of shared understanding. Atheists are not simply denying theism and leaving a vacuum. Rather, they offer human practices including art, dance, literature, philosophy, and science as a better means for understanding ourselves, our place in the universe, the origin of ethics, and the meaning of life.

HISTORICAL DEVELOPMENT

Atheism, pacifism, and anarchism are often understood as late historical developments. From this perspective, atheism grows out of the theology of theism; pacifism grows out of a moral critique of war and militarism; and anarchism develops out of a philosophical critique of political authority. It is likely that there have always been atheistic, pacifistic, and anarchic ideas, individuals, and groups. Perhaps our hunter-gatherer ancestors started out in small anarchic groups, without religious belief, and without organized violence. But once civilization began, religious, political, and military power became the norm. For thousands of years it was taken for granted that human beings should live subject to religious, political, and military hierarchy. A few individuals ventured criticism of such ideas, but atheism, anarchism, and pacifism only became full-fledged theoretical and practical ideas in the past few centuries.

No doubt religion has often been accompanied by political and military power. Consider that in the ancient world, political, religious, and military power was vested into one person: the pharaoh, emperor, or king. Moses is a good example. Moses was a prophet who spoke with God. He led his people out of bondage and with God's help fought off enemies, established political unity, and took his people to the edge of the promised land. He shared power with his brother Aaron and did not enter Israel. When Joshua ascended to the throne, he clearly united military, political, and religious power. The same story runs throughout the Old Testament in accounts of kings such as Saul and David. In other traditions, a similar story can be found. The Caesars in Rome united religious, political, and military power. Christians united political, religious, and military power in the reign of the popes and Holy Roman Emperors. Muhammad united religious, political, and military power. And so on. This story can be told over and over about other parts of the world, where priests, politicians, and generals share power.

Given this structure of unitary power behind the façade of civilization, we can see that if we move beyond religion we may also have to move beyond states and beyond war and military power. To reject one leg of the civilizational tripod is to risk tipping the whole thing over. Now it may not be necessary (or even possible) to unite atheism, anarchism, and pacifism in one all-embracing critique, but atheism, anarchism, and pacifism are three movements or ideas that have long been interrelated.

THE ANCIENT WORLD

The ancient Cynics and Epicureans had atheistic, pacifist, and anarchist sympathies. Building upon what they learned from Socrates, the Cynics stood apart from structures of social, religious, and political power. Unlike Plato and his followers, who believed that a philosopher-king was needed to save the world from injustice, Cynics such as Diogenes avoided political power and flouted social conventions. The Cynics took pains to deface the currency, which meant not only destroying (or even counterfeiting) money, but also more symbolically taking action to burst the bubbles of social and political convention. Diogenes purportedly claimed there was no need to worship or sacrifice to the gods, because if the gods were perfect, they needed nothing. This claim may not be explicit atheism, but it was clearly opposed to the religious practice of the time and indicates a practical sort of humanistic life beyond religion. The Epicureans provide another example of a tradition that was antipolitical, peaceful, and critical of religion. Epicurus counseled that we should avoid political life, retreat to private gardens, and seek to cultivate tranquility. Epicurus also said there was nothing to fear from the gods, because the gods—if there are any—were probably not concerned with the trivial affairs of human beings. Again, as with the Cynics, this claim may not be explicit atheism, but the Epicurean worldview is not impressed with political power or with religious myth.

Also in the anarchist, pacifist, atheist ballpark we might find the ancient Chinese Taoists and Mohists. We discussed Taoist influences on Oscar Wilde, Ursula Le Guin, and Gary Snyder previously. Although some forms of Taoism are close to animism, which sees spiritual powers at work in the natural world, philosophical Taoism contains nonreligious, peaceful, and anarchistic ideals. The idea of Tao (the *way* that guides the universe) is not a theistic idea. Rather, the way is a force or power in the natural order of things. Taoist works do speak of heavens and dragons and other spiritual beings, but the deep metaphysics of Taoism is focused on a naturalistic account of the Tao. The works of Chuang-Tzu and Lao-Tzu also contain cryptic hints about pacifist and anarchist ideas. These works teach "leaving things alone," "letting things be," and "nonaction," precepts beyond both political and military power. The Taoist way attempts to avoid conflict and the pitfalls of power. Chuang-Tzu and Lao-Tzu both appear to give advice to military and political leaders, but much of this advice consists in leaving things alone. Chuang-Tzu, for example, imagines a perfect ruler, who would be in tune with the Tao and would rule in peace and harmony. However, the difficulty is that there is no perfect ruler so the world contains war, injustice, and civil strife. Taoist sages exist on the periphery of society, such as in the woods and mountains, apart from religious, military, and political power. From the margins, they offer radical criticism of the status quo. Like the Epicureans and Cynics, they are reluctant to engage in politics or warfare. A related school of thought of the followers of Mozi, the so-called Mohists, appears to have been even more sincere in its pacifism. Chuang-Tzu describes the Mohists as follows: "They regarded it as no shame to suffer insult, but sought to put an end to strife among the people, to outlaw aggression, to abolish the use of arms, and to rescue the world from warfare" (1968, 368). Much more could be said about Chinese thought and about non-Western atheism, pacifism, and anarchism in general.

Before moving toward the modern period, we should note that some have suggested that Jesus himself could be interpreted from an anarchist and pacifist perspective. Indeed, the Mennonites and others argue that the historical Jesus decried political and military power. This interpretation took root in the writings of some of the American Transcendentalists, in the work of Leo Tolstoy (1828–1910), and in the work of contemporary thinkers such as John Howard Yoder (1927–1997), Jacques Ellul (1912–1994), and Vernard Eller (1927–2007). We'll turn to Tolstoy in a moment, but let's pause to consider the historical Jesus directly.

On the pacifist interpretation of Jesus, when Jesus says to turn the other cheek and to love our enemies he is offering a form of pacifism. Furthermore, the anarchist interpretation offers that when Jesus says his kingdom is not of this world and when he rejects Satan's offer of political power, he is telling us to avoid the constructs of political hierarchy and turn away

Chapter 18: Atheism, Pacifism, and Anarchism

from the power of this world. Now it would be a stretch to claim that Jesus was also an atheist, but some have made the point that if Jesus were to come back today he might well be an atheist. Richard Dawkins has argued this claim in an essay, "Atheists for Jesus" (2006). Dawkins suggests that Jesus would be appalled at the spread of religious hierarchy. There is no denying that Jesus is opposed to religion as a hierarchy superseding the precepts he espoused in the New Testament, at least as it was practiced by the Pharisees and other Jews. Although it is too much to claim that Jesus is an atheist, he did urge his followers to move beyond rigid and legalistic religion, and he taught ideals that go beyond violence and beyond faith in political authority.

THE NINETEENTH AND TWENTIETH CENTURIES

In more contemporary times, anarchists have often also been atheists, as in the case of Pierre-Joseph Proudhon (1809–1865), Mikhail Bakunin (1814–1876), and Emma Goldman (1869–1940). Proudhon is the first person who explicitly avowed *anarchism*. As he put it in *What Is Property?* (first published 1840): "The government of man by man (under whatever name it be disguised) is oppression. Society finds its highest perfection in the union of order with anarchy" (1876, 286). Proudhon argues that all forms of social organization violate liberty and defy common sense. This argument leads him to roundly criticize both political and religious authority. He wrote in *The Philosophy of Poverty* (first published 1846):

> Forget your faith, and through wisdom become an atheist.... God is not angry with those who are led by reason to deny him, any more than he is anxious for those who are led by faith to worship him; and in the state of your conscience, the surest course for you is to think nothing about him. Do you not see that it is with religion as with governments, the most perfect of which would be the denial of all? (1888, 41)

Proudhon may be advancing a sort of agnosticism here that is not full-fledged atheism, but his point is that religious and political ideology prevents us from actualizing the good in this world. We are too caught up in ideology about God and political life to do what is right. The solution is to reject both religion and the political system. He concludes:

> The first duty of man, on becoming intelligent and free, is to continually hunt the idea of God out of his mind and conscience. For God, if he exists, is essentially hostile to our nature, and we do not depend at all upon his authority. We arrive at knowledge in spite of him, at comfort in spite of him, at society in spite of him; every step we take in advance is a victory in which we crush Divinity. (448)

Proudhon was a socialist revolutionary, whose ideas were criticized by Karl Marx. Although Marx was also a critic of religion (which he called the opium of the people), Marx was not an anarchist. Marxism emphasized a state-centered communism led by the dictatorship of the proletariat. Proudhon also imagined a world beyond war, where militarism would fade away along with faith in nation-states. Marx was not a pacifist: he advocated violent revolution. One of Marx's communist colleagues was Mikhail Bakunin, who eventually broke away from Marx because of the authoritarian tendencies of revolutionary Marxism. Bakunin's focus was liberty and emancipation, which culminate in atheism and anarchism. Bakunin's most famous book is *God and the State* (written in 1871). In that book, Bakunin argues against both religious and political power: both God and the state are viewed as antithetical to human liberty and flourishing. Bakunin's anarchism is

338   MACMILLAN INTERDISCIPLINARY HANDBOOKS

Chapter 18: Atheism, Pacifism, and Anarchism

based on the ideal of emancipating humans from oppression by the state and by religion. He maintains that political power is grounded in religious power. As he puts it, "the State is consecrated by the Church" (24). Thus if we turn against the state, we must also turn against religion, and vice versa. With regard to God, Bakunin famously said that "if God existed, it would be necessary to abolish him" (28). This idea builds upon Voltaire (1694–1778), who once quipped that if God did not exist, it would be necessary to invent him. Voltaire's point was that God and the church offer a safety valve, which provides release and hope for downtrodden humanity. Bakunin argues in reverse that this safety valve prevents us from understanding the cause of our misery, which is oppression by governments and churches, and from taking action to fight back against that misery and its source. Bakunin concluded, "If God is, man is a slave; now, man can and must be free; then, God does not exist" (25). From Bakunin's perspective, in order to begin working for true human emancipation, we must overthrow both God and the state.

Similar ideas are found in the work of the American anarchist Emma Goldman. Like Bakunin, whom she quotes, Goldman argued that religion kept human beings in bondage. Theism keeps things "static and fixed," she argued, but "the philosophy of atheism expresses the expansion and growth of the human mind" (1998, 245). Goldman makes the connection between anarchism and the rejection of militarism more clear. She wrote that militarism is wrong and that anarchists are the only serious critics of militarism. One of the significant problems of militarism is that soldiers are trained to become mechanical killers. The cold brutality of military power is a concern for her. She wrote:

> The military spirit is the most merciless, heartless and brutal in existence. It fosters an institution for which there is not even a pretense of justification. The soldier, to quote Tolstoy, is a professional man-killer. He does not kill for the love of it, like a savage, or in a passion, like a homicide. He is a cold-blooded, mechanical, obedient tool of his military superiors. (52)

Now, even though Goldman condemns political and organized violence, she did not condemn individual acts of terrorism used against the state. Along with Marx and Bakunin, she imagined a revolution. In this regard, we might argue that her pacifism was inconsistent.

As indicated in the previous quote, Goldman developed some of her thinking from Tolstoy. Tolstoy developed his Christian anarchist-pacifism from his reading of the Bible. Tolstoy explained in *What I Believe* (written in 1884) that the central message of the Gospels was "resist not evil." Tolstoy suggests that this means "resist not evil at any time." Also, "Never employ force, never do what is contrary to love; and if men still offend you, employ no force against force" (1902, 19). This nonresistant pacifism is also a form of anarchism because law courts and political hierarchy employ force, as does the military. Tolstoy turns his back on both political and military power. Tolstoy, of course, remained religious, but he also criticized religious hierarchy and the hypocrisy of religions that support military and political power. As a result, he was excommunicated from the Russian Orthodox Church.

Tolstoy was influenced by some American Transcendentalist authors who preceded him in offering a countercultural view of religion with pacifist and anarchist underpinnings. Among these authors was Adin Ballou (1803–1890), an American Christian pacifist and anarchist whose work also influenced Henry David Thoreau (1817–1862). In his book *Christian Non-Resistance* (1846), Ballou defends the idea of "conscientious withdrawal" from government (7–8). Such ideas led Thoreau to write his essay "Civil Disobedience" (published in 1849). Thoreau and his mentor, Ralph Waldo Emerson (1803–1882), were not anarchists, pacifists, or atheists per se, but their ideas align with these ideals. Emerson offered a radical

RELIGION: BEYOND RELIGION

339

Chapter 18: Atheism, Pacifism, and Anarchism

critique of traditional religion. In his "Divinity School Address" (1838), Emerson suggested that traditional Christianity worships the dead corpse of God, instead of a God that is alive and present. He claimed that all religions are merely "forms," and he urged his audience to "go alone" without church or creed: "refuse the good models, even those which are sacred in the imagination of men, and dare to love God without mediator or veil" (2000, 75).

Thoreau had a similar view of religion and political life, which explains his effort to live on the margins in his experience at Walden Pond and in other adventures in the wilderness. Thoreau was also critical of American militarism. He famously called soldiers "wooden men" in his essay on civil disobedience. In this same milieu there are other influential authors and activists, such as Amos Bronson Alcott (1799–1888), who was jailed for civil disobedience before Thoreau. We might also note the abolitionist William Lloyd Garrison (1805–1879), who once said, "civil government—a government upheld by military power—is not justified among Christians" (1971, 332).

Tolstoy was impressed by the American Transcendentalists, but his own work had an influence on American anarchists such as Emma Goldman and Jane Addams (1860–1935). Addams agreed with Tolstoy's critique of war and political power. She even met Tolstoy in person on a visit to Russia. Addams's own religiosity led beyond creeds and sects toward social activism and a life of service. Her interpretation of Jesus is significant. She wrote:

> Jesus had no set of truths labeled Religious. On the contrary, his doctrine was that all truth is one, that the appropriation of it is freedom. His teaching had no dogma to mark it off from truth and action in general. He himself called it a revelation—a life. (1912, 122)

Like Tolstoy and the Transcendentalists, Addams thought that Jesus had an antireligious message, one wholly of service and love. She maintained that this message is what early Christianity was all about:

> That Christianity has to be revealed and embodied in the line of social progress is a corollary to the simple proposition, that man's action is found in his social relationships in the way in which he connects with his fellows; that his motives for action are the zeal and affection with which he regards his fellows. By this simple process was created a deep enthusiasm for humanity; which regarded man as at once the organ and the object of revelation; and by this process came about the wonderful fellowship, the true democracy of the early Church, that so captivates the imagination. The early Christians were preëminently nonresistant. They believed in love as a cosmic force. (122–123)

Addams's interpretation of Christianity, like Tolstoy's, was prosocial but antipolitical activism. Like Tolstoy, Addams develops an antireligious idea: religions pull us away from the social gospel of love. Even though Addams is not typically understood as an anarchist or as an atheist, she was intimately involved in anarchism. Indeed, the Russian anarchist Kropotkin stayed at her Hull House, and Addams was involved in political activity aimed at defending the rights of anarchists who had been arrested in Chicago. However, Addams did not focus on negative critique. Instead, she tried to build peace and social justice directly, across the nation and the world.

We could trace further connections here that would extend through Tolstoy's influence on Gandhi and Martin Luther King Jr. We might also consider Dorothy Day (1897–1980) and the pacifist-anarchism of the Catholic Worker movement as well as contemporary activism that is opposed to political authority and military, such as in the Christian Plowshares movement. All of these examples show the connection between pacifism and

Chapter 18: Atheism, Pacifism, and Anarchism

religion. We have also seen that some religious pacifists move in an even more explicitly anarchist direction. On its face, the connection between pacifism and atheism may not be obvious. Nonetheless, a number of notable pacifist-atheists have done important work, such as Albert Einstein (1879–1955), Bertrand Russell (1872–1970), and Linus Pauling (1901–1994). It may seem that anarchism tends in the direction of violence because anarchists want to overthrow social and political systems. However, peaceful, nonreligious anarchists, who reject violence, states, and wars want to live in peace, harmony, and liberty.

Summary

We have seen that authors and activists who discuss atheism, anarchism, and pacifism share much in common. The thread is a critique of institutions that tend to violate autonomy, that are grounded in conformity and obedience, and that are violent (both overtly and structurally). We have looked at a variety of sources for these ideas, both in Western literature and culture and in non-Western sources such as Buddhism and Taoism. The struggle to move beyond religions, wars, and states will likely continue, offering insight and hopeful idealism that the world would be better if only we could work our way beyond old-fashioned allegiance to hierarchical religions, rigid nation-states, and the various forms of overt and structural violence that plague our world. This idealism may be utopian dreaming in a world fixedly structured by religious, political, and military power, but it is useful to imagine a different world, where we live in peace and the world will be as one.

Bibliography

Addams, Jane. *Twenty Years at Hull-House*. New York: Macmillan, 1912.

Bakunin, Mikhail. *God and the State*. New York: Dover, 1970.

Ballou, Adin. *Christian Non-Resistance*. Oberlin, OH: Nonresistance.org, 2006. http://www.nonresistance.org /docs_pdf/Christian_Nonresistance.pdf.

Carlin, George. *Last Words*. New York: Simon and Schuster, 2009.

Carlin, George. *Napalm and Silly Putty*. New York: Hyperion, 2001.

Chuang Tzu. *Complete Works of Chuang Tzu*. New York: Columbia University Press, 1968.

Dalai Lama. *Beyond Religion: Ethics for a Whole World*. Boston: Houghton Mifflin Harcourt, 2011.

Dalai Lama. *Ethics for the New Millennium*. New York: Riverhead Books, 1999.

Dawkins, Richard. "Atheists for Jesus." 2006. http://old.richard dawkins.net/articles/20-atheists-for-jesus.

Emerson, Ralph Waldo. *The Essential Writings of Ralph Waldo Emerson*. New York: Modern Library, 2000.

Garrison, William Lloyd. *Garrison, A House Dividing Against Itself, 1836–1840*. Cambridge: Harvard University Press, 1971.

Goldman, Emma. *Red Emma Speaks,* 3rd ed. Amherst, NY: Humanity Books, 1998.

Huxley, Aldous. *Brave New World and Brave New World Revisited*. New York: Harper Perennial, 2004.

Huxley, Aldous. *Ends and Means*. New Brunswick, NJ: Transaction Publishing, 2012.

Huxley, Thomas Henry. *Agnosticism and Christianity and Other Essays*. New York: Prometheus Books, 1992.

Le Guin, Ursula. "Ursula Le Guin Q&A." *The Guardian* (February 9, 2004). http://www.theguardian.com/books/2004 /feb/09/sciencefictionfantasyandhorror.ursulakleguin.

Pew Forum. "Religious Landscape Survey." 2015. http://www .pewforum.org/religious-landscape-study/.

Proudhon, Pierre-Joseph. *System of Economical Contradictions or The Philosophy of Misery*. Boston: Benjamin Tucker, 1888.

Proudhon, Pierre-Joseph. *What Is Property?* Princeton: Benjamin Tucker, 1876.

RELIGION: BEYOND RELIGION

Chapter 18: Atheism, Pacifism, and Anarchism

Quanz, Dietrich R. "Civic Pacifism and Sports-Based Internationalism: Framework for the Founding of the International Olympic Committee." *OLYMPIKA: The International Journal of Olympic Studies* 2 (1993): 1–23.

Snyder, Gary. *Back on the Fire: Essays*. Berkeley, CA: Counterpoint, 2007.

Snyder, Gary. "Buddhist Anarchism." In *Anarchism: A Documentary History of Libertarian Ideas*, Vol. 2, edited by Robert Graham. Montreal, Canada: Black Rose Books, 2009. First published 1961.

Snyder, Gary. *The Etiquette of Freedom*. Berkeley, CA: Counterpoint Press, 2010.

Snyder, Gary. "Interview." *Paris Review* 141 (Winter 1996). http://www.theparisreview.org/interviews/1323/the-art-of-poetry-no-74-gary-snyder.

Tolstoy, Leo. *What I Believe: My Religion*. Christchurch, New Zealand: Free Age Press, 1902.

Vonnegut, Kurt. *Palm Sunday: An Autobiographical Collage*. New York: Random House, 2009.

Warren, Josiah. *The Practical Anarchist: Writings of Josiah Warren*. New York: Fordham University Press, 2011.

Wilde, Oscar. "De Profundis … Epistola: In Carcere Et Vinculis." In *The Complete Works of Oscar Wilde*. New York: Oxford University Press, 2000.

Wilde, Oscar. "The Great Creed of Inaction." In *The Prose of Oscar Wilde*. New York: Cosmopolitan, 1916.

Wilde, Oscar. *The Soul of Man*. London: Arthur Humphreys, 1900.

FILMS

The Big Lebowski. Dir. Joel Coen and Ethan Coen. 1998. "The Dude" is mistaken for a millionaire, and goes on a quest to fix the mistake along with his bowling pals.

CHAPTER 19

Humanistic Judaism and Secular Spirituality

Adam Chalom
Dean, North America
International Institute for Secular Humanistic Judaism,
Lincolnshire, IL

Can one be Jewish and a humanist? Can one be both secular and spiritual? A contradiction to some may be meaningful experience for others.

Humanistic Judaism has no monopoly on secular spirituality, but the two phenomena do share many features. The conceptual tension in both highlights the simple truth that lived human reality is neither pure logic nor pure language. The reality we experience is an encounter among the natural world; the power and limitations of logic and science; and actual human beings with personal histories, emotional attachments, and individual experiences. Both Humanistic Judaism and secular spirituality can challenge some nontheistic approaches, and these challenges clarify differences among various secular identities. Humanistic Judaism in particular is open to nonsupernatural inspiration from one's cultural or religious tradition; from ethnic community and identity; and from music, beauty, and other nonanalytic experiences— all potential sources or expressions of secular spirituality. Finally, when one stretches nontheistic philosophy beyond basic factual premises and conclusions to seek inspiration and meaning, as do both Humanistic Judaism and secular spirituality, issues concerning boundaries, definitions, and inclusivity/diversity arise. Humanistic Judaism's approach to these issues can be illuminating for similar challenges with secular spirituality.

Humanistic Jews are a double minority—Jewish in an overwhelmingly non-Jewish society (except in Israel) and humanists in a largely theistic world. American Jews' historic and persistent minority presence is problematic for those who would proclaim the United States a Christian nation. Likewise, Humanistic Judaism, with its congregations, rabbis, and tradition-inflected holiday and life-cycle celebrations, complicates a purely universalist or antireligion secularism that also questions ethnic diversity and claims that true Secular Humanism cannot draw on one's religious and cultural heritage. The same dynamic applies for secular spirituality—some reject it, others welcome it, and still others find some elements of value and reject others. Real life is complicated; why should philosophy and personal identity, even secular versions, be immune to the human condition?

Chapter 19: Humanistic Judaism and Secular Spirituality

THE SETTING FOR HUMANISTIC JUDAISM AND SECULAR SPIRITUALITY

Fully setting the stage for the emergence of Humanistic Judaism and secular spirituality is far beyond this work; however, there are important reasons both phenomena have appeared when and where they have. Many of the most significant steps away from traditional religious life during the last few centuries, both behavioral and intellectual, continue to be directly relevant to both. It must be recalled that "Secularization is an intellectual process … occurring among people who ponder issues of cause and effect, belief and evidence, teaching and experience. But it is also a behavioral process, not necessarily informed by philosophical consideration" (Gitelman 2009, 304). Activity on intellectual and behavioral levels has affected both Humanistic Judaism and secular spirituality.

As individual freedom increased in Western society over the past few centuries, religious authority has decreased. The excommunication of Baruch Spinoza (1632–1677) in 1656 by the Amsterdam Jewish community for challenging traditional Jewish theology produced significant personal and social dislocation, but the excommunication of Rabbi Mordecai Kaplan (1881–1983) in 1945 by the Union of Orthodox Rabbis for the same offense was ignored by the vast majority of contemporary Jews. This individual religious freedom is in some ways even more pronounced in the United States than in Europe or Israel; in the latter, some version of government-supported established religion persists, even if it is ignored by most of the population it claims to represent. The relative freedom of religious creativity in the United States has maintained some variety of religious identification compared with the mandatory approach—a 2015 *Times*/YouGov survey showed that, despite the established Church of England, 42 percent of Britons said they had "no religion" and only 49 percent were Christian (Jordan 2015), whereas a 2010 Israel Central Bureau of Statistics report showed at least 40 percent of Israeli Jews self-identified as "secular." By comparison, in the United States, "the number of religiously unaffiliated adults remained below 10 percent from the 1970s through the early 1990s" (Pew Research Center 2012), although this group has increased in the past 2 decades to 23 percent of the population, including 32 percent of those under 30 years old (Pew Research Center 2013).

Individual freedom to secularize also creates a space between the religious and the secular, which has led to both a proliferation of religious sects and denominations and eclectic individual expressions of nontraditional identities. As one Buddhist of Jewish origin describes himself in Rodger Kamenetz's *The Jew in the Lotus* (1994), "I have Jewish roots and Buddhist wings." Alternatively, consider the self-labeled *spiritual, but not religious*:

> Many of the country's 46 million unaffiliated adults are religious or spiritual in some way. Two-thirds of them say they believe in God (68%). More than half say they often feel a deep connection with nature and the earth (58%), while more than a third classify themselves as "spiritual" but not "religious" (37%), and one-in-five (21%) say they pray every day. (Lipka 2005)

In a society in which organized religion no longer holds the monopoly on belief in God or everyday prayer, a monopoly on spirituality is similarly hard to maintain.

Secularizing Western society has also profoundly secularized Jews. Their demographic profile in Pew's 2013 "Portrait of Jewish Americans" is a virtual secular checklist: 58 percent of American Jews are college educated (compared with 29% for the general population), 66 percent have incomes more than $75,000 (29% for the general population), 49 percent are

344   MACMILLAN INTERDISCIPLINARY HANDBOOKS

politically liberal (21% for the general population), and "the vast majority of Jews live either in urban areas (49%) or in the suburbs (47%). Just 4 percent of US Jews reside in rural areas, compared with about one-in-five Americans overall." All of these characteristics—college education, affluence, liberalism, and urbanization—are strongly correlated with increasingly secular behavior and beliefs.

It comes as no surprise then that Pew also showed that similar proportions of the general population and Jewish millennials identified as "Jews of no religion" (JNR): when asked their religion, they did not reply "Jewish," but when asked "Aside from religion, do you consider yourself Jewish or partly Jewish," they said, "yes." In general, Jews are secular in both belief and behavior: 23 percent say they do not believe in a God or universal spirit compared with 7 percent of the general population, and "roughly one-quarter of Jews say religion is very important in their lives, compared with more than half of Americans overall. Similarly, a quarter of Jews say they attend religious services at least once or twice a month, compared with 50% among the general population" (Pew Research Center 2013). These are not only the results from JNR—16 percent of "Jews by religion" (JBR) do not believe in God, one-third say religion is not important in their lives, and 30 percent seldom or never attend religious services. JBR and JNR overwhelmingly describe being Jewish as important to them, but it is clear that being Jewish is more complicated than simply a religious identity. The same is true for the 40 percent of Israeli Jews who are secular.

There are many intellectual reasons for increasing secularization in society over the past few centuries beyond urbanization and higher education: the tremendous explosion of knowledge of the natural world and human history, increasing lifespans and control of human conditions through medical science, and political and philosophical emphasis on the importance and self-sovereignty of the individual, to name just three. Each of these developments casts doubt on traditional religious factual and historical claims and made a this-worldly (rather than supernatural) approach to life and inspiration more plausible. However, this secularization has not eliminated from secularized individuals the need of those of Jewish heritage to identify as Jewish or the need of those wanting inspiration (or *spirituality*) to seek it or to create the experience for themselves.

HUMANISTIC JUDAISM—FOUNDING AND EVOLUTION

In 1963, eight families and a Reform rabbi who had been raised in a Conservative Jewish congregation in the ethnic Jewish neighborhoods of Detroit started a suburban Detroit congregation named The Birmingham Temple. Founded as a Reform synagogue, it soon evolved into the first congregation of Humanistic Judaism. The Birmingham Temple initially maintained language invoking God in its liturgy and educational program, attempting to redefine the term as signifying "the best in people." Within several months, the community came to agree that if they did not believe in the personal, interventionist, omniscient being described in the prayer book and the Hebrew Bible, then they would be more honest to their values by saying clearly what they did believe. If they believed that people healed the sick, created justice in the world, and responded to the realities of life by creating societies and ethics, then why should they give credit anywhere else? Where Reconstructionist Judaism had expressed such humanistic sentiments through reinterpretation but did not thoroughly change the Hebrew liturgy, Humanistic Judaism took the next step to be fully humanistic, in any language.

RELIGION: BEYOND RELIGION

Chapter 19: Humanistic Judaism and Secular Spirituality

The results of the departure from God belief, language, and imagery were manifold. New holiday and life-cycle ceremonies needed to be developed. Jewish history needed to be reconceptualized as the result of human actions and social forces rather than divine providence or punishment, and its content needed to be reevaluated based on archaeological and scientific evidence. Furthermore, the need to balance among a secular approach to life, acculturation to non-Jewish society and a continued Jewish identity required new answers beyond Covenant and the Chosen People.

These theoretical issues were grappled with in the context of practical challenges: the congregation and its rabbi, Sherwin Wine, became infamous for their "heresy" of removing God from their Sabbath and holiday services—a January 1965 profile of Wine as "The Atheist Rabbi" in *Time Magazine* only added to their notoriety. Because of this, finding regular meeting space became challenging as the congregation grew, so they finally built their own building by 1970, which was later expanded twice. In the main meeting room, the congregation placed an artistic rendering of the Hebrew *adam* (humanity) where a Torah scroll would have traditionally been found, and the Torah scroll was set in the congregation's library—here the Torah was an important ancient book with a place of honor (unable to be checked out), but it was still treated as a book by human authors.

Humanistic Judaism faced controversy precisely because of their boundary-crossing identity. Previous generations of secularized Jews had generally taken one of three options:

1. Some joined universalist and cosmopolitan identities through politics (e.g., socialism or communism) or philosophy (e.g., Ethical Culture founded by Felix Adler [1851–1933] who trained as a Reform rabbi before moving away from Jewish identity). They and later universalist humanists of Jewish background such as Howard Radest (1928–2014; Ethical Culture), Paul Kurtz (1925–2012; Council for Secular Humanism), or David Silverman (1966–; American Atheists) challenged Humanistic Judaism by asking "How can you be a real humanist if you maintain a particularist identity as a Jew and continue that particularism to future generations?"

2. Some secularized Jews maintained an ethnic and cultural Jewish identity separate from or in opposition to religious Judaism—some focused on Yiddish language and culture, often combined with socialist political activism, whereas others identified with modern Hebrew and Zionism. In the United States in 1934, 20,000 Jewish children received some variety of secular Jewish education distributed among communist, socialist, centrist, and Labor Zionist organizations; this was 10 percent of American Jewish children receiving any Jewish education at that time (Fishman 2009, 72). These organizations and their post–McCarthy era heirs challenged Humanistic Judaism by saying, "Secular and Jewish, fine. How can you be truly secular when you have a congregation, a rabbi, services, and the trappings of Jewish religion?"

3. Although they were personally secular, some secularized Jews continued (and continue today) to identify with the religious culture and memories of their upbringing and to accept the dominant American post–World War II paradigm of Jew as a religious identity (as in Will Herberg's famous 1955 study *Protestant—Catholic—Jew: An Essay in American Religious Sociology*). Thus, they joined suburban Reform or even Conservative congregations, or they attempted to "reconstruct" what they meant when they recited traditional prayers to be more consistent with secular philosophy and science. They challenged Humanistic Judaism by asking, "Who are you to change our tradition of thousands of years? Being Jewish is all about synagogues, talking to God

346　　MACMILLAN INTERDISCIPLINARY HANDBOOKS

(even a god in which one does not believe), and the ritual *sancta* passed down by Jewish tradition."

Despite these challenges, which are explored further below, enough people in the metropolitan Detroit area and beyond found the message of Humanistic Judaism compelling in its first decade to create an Association of Humanistic Rabbis (1968) and the Society for Humanistic Judaism (1969) to support existing communities and to sponsor new ones. By the 1980s, connections with the aforementioned secular Jewish world (and specifically a partnership with the Congress of Secular Jewish Organizations) led to a Leadership Conference of Secular and Humanistic Jews (1982); an International Institute for Secular Humanistic Judaism (IISHJ) to train new leadership and serve as an intellectual center for the movement (1985); and an International Federation of Secular Humanistic Jews (1986) to connect like-minded individuals and communities in Israel, Europe, and elsewhere. As of 2015, there were more than forty Secular and Humanistic Jewish communities in North America as well as dozens of Secular Humanistic Jewish leaders (also called *madrikh/madrikha* or *vegvayzer*) and rabbis trained by the IISHJ in North America and Israel. Over the past 50 years, thousands of individuals and families have identified with this philosophy and participated in the lived experience that flows from its basic principles and practices.

THE POWER OF WORDS

At a November 2011 Kol Hadash Humanistic Congregation Shabbat service, the audience was polled as to how many of them had ever had a *spiritual experience* (without defining the concept in advance). Some said "Yes," others said "No." When those who accepted the label were asked what they meant by *spiritual experience*, they mentioned examples such as the birth of a child or a striking experience of natural beauty. When the rejectionists were asked if they had experienced such events as emotionally meaningful, the reply was "Of course." The point, Rabbi Binyamin Biber explained, is that both groups experienced and valued these moments, but they had different vocabulary for similar experiences.

This disagreement over terminology is no oddity to those familiar with the secular movement. Consider the various terms for nontheistic identities deployed by movement organizations (italics added for emphasis): American *Atheists*, American *Humanist* Association, Military Association of *Atheists and Freethinkers*, The *Brights*, *Secular* Coalition for America, Council for *Secular Humanism*, Black *Nonbelievers*, and Foundation *Beyond Belief* as well as Congress of *Secular Jewish* Organizations, Society for *Humanistic Judaism*, International Institute for *Secular Humanistic Judaism*, and even *Ex-Muslims* of North America. Partisans from each faction may insist theirs is the most effective term, although individuals often join multiple organizations and accept multiple labels; former Pentecostal minister Jerry DeWitt says (and shares on social media), "Skepticism is my nature. Freethought is my methodology. Agnosticism is my conclusion. Atheism is my opinion. Humanitarianism is my motivation." This exploration will confine itself to providing parameters for the current topic as well as suggesting avenues for further study.

HUMANISM FOR HUMANISTIC JEWS

Like any school of philosophy, as Fred Edwords explains in "What is Humanism?" (2008), there are many definitions of humanism, from the Renaissance-era pursuit of all human

Chapter 19: Humanistic Judaism and Secular Spirituality

knowledge to an emphasis on human power and responsibility with or without a simultaneous de-emphasis or denial of divine agency or existence. The American Humanist Association defines humanism concisely as "a progressive philosophy of life that, without supernaturalism, affirms our ability and responsibility to lead ethical lives of personal fulfillment that aspire to the greater good of humanity." Most statements describing humanism go on to enumerate extensions and implications of this basic approach that emphasize the importance of reason, science, and human observation to understand reality; the dignity and value of every human being and thus the importance of human rights and personal autonomy; and more. What these statements have in common is an emphasis on human action, human needs, human knowledge, human self-reliance, and mutual responsibility.

In theory, a philosophy of life could be combined with any variety of ethnic identities because principles such as those described above can be equally valid and meaningful in English, French, or Swahili. However, sometimes the universalist impulse of humanism conflicts with human diversity: among their online "Affirmations of Humanism," the Council for Secular Humanism includes "We attempt to transcend divisive parochial loyalties based on race, religion, gender, nationality, creed, class, sexual orientation, or ethnicity, and strive to work together for the common good of humanity." Needless to say, a continued Jewish identity could fit into these rejected categories. A debate over the wisdom of having separate organizations for Black Nonbelievers, LGBT Humanists, or Ex-Muslims has also taken place within the freethought movement.

For Humanistic Jews, the pursuit of rational philosophy certainly leads to and reinforces humanistic conclusions regarding the importance of self-reliance and responsibility, an approach to ethics that considers real-life consequences rather than authoritarian traditional demands, and an emphasis on the worth of every person. At the same time, their understanding of Jewish history and Jewish experience is also a significant basis for their humanism. Jews traditionally saw themselves as the Chosen People, around whom all history revolved. If they followed God's commandments, then they did well; if they sinned, then they were punished with conquest, expulsion, suffering, and death. The scale, depth, and injustice of Jewish suffering, particularly in light of the Holocaust, provoke a different reading of that same history by Humanistic Judaism:

> If Jewish history has any message, it is the demand for human self-reliance. In an indifferent universe there is no help from destiny. Either we assume responsibility for our fate or no one will. A world without divine guarantees and divine justice is a little bit frightening. But it is also the source of human freedom and human dignity. (Wine cited in Rowens 2003, 56)

This reading of their particular Jewish history provides Humanistic Jews with universal philosophical conclusions about the nature of the universe.

Everyone comes from somewhere, and millions of personally secular individuals remain connected to their ethnic and religious heritage in various ways. Just as one may be both patriotically American and connected to diverse ethnic languages and countries of origin, so too may one hold universalist philosophical beliefs while maintaining a connection to family and peoplehood. Morris Schappes, a former communist himself, put it well:

> Universal history is the sum total of group histories (tribe, people, nationality...), seen in their interconnections. Similarly, there is no simply "human" experience that can give rise simply to "human values." For all these thousands of years all

348   MACMILLAN INTERDISCIPLINARY HANDBOOKS

human experience has been cast in the form of the limited group. An "internationalist," thus, is not one who lives in an "internation" in outer space, far far out. He is an American internationalist, a Polish internationalist, a Ghanaian or an Indian internationalist. They may converge, but they converge from different points. We here may be American Jewish internationalists. But to omit the American or the Jewish is to strip the "internationalist" of vital, concrete meaning. (Schappes [1966] 2003, 267)

In other words, an abiding Jewish connection is not a betrayal of one's Humanism; it is both a reflection of the human reality of family and ethnic origins and a means to appreciate human diversity.

Few would argue that a loving attachment to one's family is a barrier to broader human sympathies; a positive sense of roots and self-identity is psychologically healthy. Of course, just as one educates one's children to be self-confident but not egotistical, a humanistic ethnic or religious identity is on guard against chauvinism and parochialism. Every culture and religion is a response to the human experience, and one may better appreciate human diversity from one's own people's particular perspective. Rather than homogenize everything into a bland version of WASP (White Anglo Saxon Protestant) culture, an open ethnicity can be true to its roots while celebrating, respecting, and learning from other particular cultures.

JUDAISM FOR HUMANISTIC JEWS

The Humanism of Humanistic Judaism is learned from the Jewish experience. Yet the question remains: why bother with a Humanistic Jewish fusion beyond the intense ethnicity of immigrant generations?

Is Judaism a religion defined by set doctrine, practices, scriptures, and supernatural belief? There is certainly a diverse religious phenomenon called Judaism that has evolved greatly over 2500 years and appears today in both organized denominations and widely diverging individual and communal expressions; this Judaism could be reasonably compared to varieties of Christianity or Islam.

However, the description *Jewish* is broader than Christian or Muslim, encompassing music, food, art, language, humor, literature, and many other human creations more commonly identified as culture. Pew's 2013 survey of Jewish Americans showed that only 15 percent agreed that being Jewish was mainly a matter of religion whereas more than 60 percent claimed it was mainly a matter of ancestry or culture. For Humanistic Jews, this latter approach is what they mean by *Judaism*.

Bible is Judaism, Talmud is Judaism, everyday life is Judaism, Jewish history is Judaism, Jewish poetry is Judaism, Jewish customs are Judaism, Jewish food is Judaism, Jewish jokes are Judaism; just as religion is Judaism. But you cannot argue that Judaism equals the religious beliefs of Jews; first, because these beliefs were and are different, even mutually contradictory; and second, because religion was and is just one aspect of Jewish existence; today, for many Jews, it is not even that. Judaism, then, is everything that the Jewish people in their very long history have produced. Judaism is Jewish civilization, Judaism is Jewish culture. (Bauer 1995, xiv)

As a response to the human experience, Jewish civilization may be legitimately explored for humanistic insight and inspiration, just as others may explore their own heritage.

The issue is also clearer in other Jewish languages—the equivalent terms to *Judaism* are *Yiddishkeit* (Yiddish, literally "Jewish-ness") or *Yahadut* (Hebrew, also "Jewish-ness"). In

Chapter 19: Humanistic Judaism and Secular Spirituality

both cases, the suffixes *-keit* or *-ut* often refer to a quality of being, an identity, more than a system belief as suggested by the English *-ism*. *Hellenism* as the culture and civilization of the Greeks may be a better parallel to *Judaism* than *theism* or *Mormonism*.

This understanding of *Judaism* is the answer to both the secular Jewish and the traditionalist critiques described above. Because Jewish religious culture was created by people, elements of it may be rejected or accepted depending on whether they provide meaning and value. Like anything made by human beings, Jewish religious culture can be flawed and thus improvable by later generations. If a rabbi as expert teacher and pastoral counselor or a congregation as mutual support and opportunity for communal learning and celebration work, then keeping them does not betray one's secular Jewish commitment.

> Congregations, Shabbat meetings and holiday celebration were not the sole possession of theistic people. Bar mitsvas [sic] and confirmations were not, of necessity, attached to prayers and Torah readings. Religion was more than the worship of God. It was, in the broadest sense, a philosophy of life turned into the morality and celebrations of an organized community. (Wine 1988)

Just as Judaism itself historically changed from animal sacrifice to verbal prayers and religious law observance, and from national identity to religious culture, so too can Jewish institutions and ceremonies adapt to new circumstances and beliefs.

At the same time, a secular approach to Jewish civilization does not privilege Jewish religion above and beyond other Jewish culture or the past over the present—contemporary Jewish poetry or wisdom can be more inspiring and praiseworthy than some Bible passages, such as those concerning the objectionable treatment of women, homosexuality, or non-Jews. If the key elements of Jewish tradition were not given by God to Moses on Mount Sinai, but instead were part of a larger cultural matrix of human creativity, new possibilities are opened. This creativity has not been unique to Secular Humanistic Judaism—secular Zionists in Israel also reinterpreted traditional Jewish holiday and life-cycle celebrations and continue to do so through the Kibbutz Institute for Holidays and Jewish Culture and other institutions.

If one accepts that Judaism, or at least Jewish identity, can be understood as ethnicity and culture, then several implications follow. If Judaism is a culture created by people, then it was created in response to specific circumstances. Considering the agendas behind the authors of the Bible or the prayer book is legitimate, even required, to explore possible meanings of the texts. It also means that Jewish culture learned from and adopted elements of its surrounding cultures, from language (Yiddish from Middle German written in Hebrew letters) to Jewish holiday traditions such as the Passover *afikomen* (the last piece of unleavened bread eaten at the festival meal, the name of which derives from the Greek *epikomen* for "dessert"). Of course, human culture evolves tremendously over centuries of migration and history as well as changing beliefs and values. If contemporary Jews do not believe what earlier generations did, then they have the right and even the duty to express their values through their cultural creativity: "Cautious, piecemeal reform does not serve consistency well. Life is too short to be the prisoner of foolish contradictions. We do not exist to fit the forms of the past. The forms of the past exist to serve our needs and the needs of future generations. Sometimes only bold action will enable us to make things right" (Wine 1988).

General philosophical descriptions or even clear philosophical statements such as the five Core Principles of the Society for Humanistic Judaism only go so far—experiencing a

350   MACMILLAN INTERDISCIPLINARY HANDBOOKS

Humanistic Jewish wedding or Shabbat celebration provides a clearer demonstration of this approach to lived Jewish life (e.g., reading a description of the rules of basketball compared with attending a game). The Humanistic Jewish bar/bat mitzvah as a coming-of-age ceremony that emphasizes growing maturity and self-responsibility is an evolution of the traditional rite, but the focus of the presentation is on a subject of relevance and interest to the student—rather than an assigned portion of the Torah, the student chooses a passage from the Torah or other Hebrew literature, or else a topic or an individual from the wide sweep of the Jewish experience, to research and present at one's celebration. Yom Kippur is reoriented from the traditional seeking of divine forgiveness after asking for and giving forgiveness to one's fellow to renewed emphasis on both interpersonal relations and the importance of being able to forgive oneself.

Although organized Humanistic Judaism represents a fraction of the Jews in the world who might agree with its message and philosophical approach, it nevertheless serves as an important and plausible option for secularized Jews and a potential model for other ethnic or religiously based humanisms, which could broaden the appeal of the secular movement in new directions. "I sometimes like to describe myself as a *faithful atheist*. I am an atheist, since I believe neither in God nor in any supernatural power, and yet I am faithful, since I acknowledge my place within a specific history, tradition and community, namely the Greco-Judeo-Christian values of the Western World" (Comte-Sponville 2007, loc. 402). Sherwin Wine explained in 2007 at a conference on "The New Humanism" that many individuals are neither wounded by religion nor are yet aware secularists—they have been unconsciously secularized even if they accept religious labels. "It isn't religion that is the issue; they are part of a culture, an historic culture, whether it's Jewish culture, Christian culture, Muslim culture … they're not prepared to reject it." A positive relationship with their religious and cultural heritage could be a humanism they would accept, as have Humanistic Jews.

SECULAR FOR SECULAR SPIRITUALITY

Similar to Humanistic Judaism, secular spirituality evokes vehement condemnation and passionate defense. The battle again turns on definitions: is *secular* merely noninstitutional, freelance, but still allowing supernaturalism, or does it strictly limit matters to this natural world alone? Is *spirituality* talking to the spirit world or uplifting the human spirit, and is there such a thing as the spirit apart from mind and body?

There are many understandings of the term *secular*, depending on the context. In Jacques Berlinerblau's *How to Be Secular: A Call to Arms for Religious Freedom* (2012), the emphasis is on secularist politics, an expression of the separation of religion and government. In Secular Humanism, the emphasis is on *secular* as the opposite, even opponent, of *religious*, differentiating secular humanists from religious humanists, focusing exclusively on the natural world rather than the supernatural and being opposed to religious authority structures. Ironically, this parallels usage in the Catholic Church, which differentiates between secular priests and religious priests: secular priests are engaged in the work of this world serving their diocese (and are thus also called diocesan priests) whereas the religious priests focus on supernatural matters of prayer and theology.

In Jewish life, a similar diversity of meanings appears: *veltlekh* (Yiddish for "secular") can be understood as either "worldly" (i.e., cosmopolitan) or "this-worldly" (as opposed to "supernatural"). And the Hebrew *khiloni* often refers to one of two groups: the non-Orthodox, nonobservant of Jewish law, not generally participating in synagogue life, and the

Chapter 19: Humanistic Judaism and Secular Spirituality

antireligious, who emphasize both the separation of religion and government and philosophic naturalism.

When it comes to secular spirituality, the governmental aspect to secular is largely irrelevant, unless one considers political activism for one's favorite cause to be a spiritually uplifting experience (more on this in "Ethics, Activism, and Human Connection"). The natural world focus of secular is largely agreed upon throughout the various nontheistic approaches and organizations: widespread disbelief in miracles; a personal afterlife or spirits; or in magical healing, auras, or other unproven phenomena. The two points of contention when it comes to the secular in secular spirituality are

1. Anti-institutional: Some are comfortable with many of the structures common to religion, such as Unitarian Universalist Humanists, the so-called "atheist church" Sunday Assembly, Humanist chaplaincies at universities, and Humanistic Judaism. Others strongly reject anything that smacks of religious origins or structures, be they responsive readings, clergy titles, guided meditations, or the very terms *church*, *synagogue*, or *congregation*.

2. Naturalism demanding evaluation: Many of the examples of secular spirituality detailed below are nonanalytic experiences whereas those who identify as secular are much more comfortable in the rational, analytic mode they see as the only valid method of evaluating human experience: "Scientists generally start with an impoverished view of spiritual experience, assuming it must be a grandiose way of describing ordinary states of mind—parental love, artistic inspiration, awe at the beauty of the night sky" (Harris 2014, 7).

Thus, the challenge is for the promoter of secular spirituality to be simultaneously nonsupernatural and rational and yet also open to the many human experiences beyond words and analysis. The gap can be bridged: "The landscape of human experience includes deeply transformative insights about the nature of one's own consciousness, and yet it is obvious that these psychological states must be understood in the context of neuroscience, psychology, and related fields" (Harris 2014, 7). In other words, the experiences claimed to be secular spirituality can be analyzed by the tools of science, but they can also be deeply influential as personally transformative emotional moments.

SPIRITUALITY FOR SECULAR SPIRITUALITY

Sigfried Gold, reviewing atheist writer Sam Harris's *Waking Up: A Guide to Spirituality Without Religion* (2014), noted Harris's challenge: "many in his audience can be expected to have a positive hostility to his suggestion that they suffer a malady whose indicated treatment is spirituality, rationally approached or otherwise." Many in the secular and nontheistic worlds have emerged from lives of deep faith and religious devotion; thus, they reject the term *spirituality* as inherently problematic:

> I use the terms *spiritual* and *spirituality* defensively, that is to say, only when someone with whom I have to be in conversation or written exchange uses them. I am otherwise allergic to them. My allergy stems from the fact that they are used to account for alleged realities that are beyond the ability of the senses to perceive. (Cook 2003, 141)

Such allergens include spiritualism (communication with the dead); the spirit world (afterlife or supernatural beings); and, as Harris admits, "to walk the aisles of any 'spiritual' bookstore is to confront the yearning and credulity of our species by the yard" (Harris

2014, 6). A substantial portion of Harris's book focuses on debunking manipulative gurus, spiritual leaders, and unsubstantiated claims of supernatural experience—perhaps confirming Harris's secularist credentials as he simultaneously advocates a broader understanding of what is secularly kosher.

For the author of *The Little Book of Atheist Spirituality*, spirituality is at the heart of what it means to be human; thus, it is a key component to any secular identity:

> The human spirit is far too important a matter to be left up to priests, mullahs or spiritualists. It is our noblest part, or rather our highest function, the thing that makes us not only different from other animals (for we are animals as well), but greater than and superior to them.... Renouncing religion by no means implies renouncing spiritual life. (Comte-Sponville 2007, loc. 1593)

Those secular individuals who object to spirituality might say that renouncing the spiritual is exactly what they intended by renouncing religion. For them, any use of *spirituality*, however qualified, is hopelessly tainted by its connection to supernatural understandings of the word *spirit*.

One can certainly differentiate between supernatural and natural spirituality—the former attempts meaningful human connection with a realm beyond this life and this world, whereas the latter "seems to suggest comfort, connection, support, guidance, peace, and, most importantly, happiness—all ideas that are easily reconciled with their secular lives ... in their connections to something greater than themselves and within themselves" (Cousens 2003, 2). Thus, a natural spirituality might pass the secular test, even if discomfort with use of the term persists—one is not committing a secular thought crime by pursuing the supernatural, although one may be skirting the edges of acceptable secular vocabulary.

Psychologist Abraham Maslow (1908–1970) chose alternative terminology, referring instead to peak experiences: "the parental experience, the mystic or oceanic, or nature experience, the aesthetic perception, the creative moment, the therapeutic or intellectual insight, the orgasmic experience, certain forms of athletic fulfillment, etc." (Maslow [1968] 1999). These moments are essential to Maslow's hierarchy of needs, which culminates in self-actualization as the foundation of his self-termed humanistic psychology. Three decades before, Sigmund Freud (1856–1939) had rejected an oceanic feeling as the basis of religious belief, but (prefiguring critics of secular spirituality) Freud admitted that "I cannot discover this 'oceanic' feeling in myself. It is not easy to deal scientifically with feelings" (Freud [1929] 1961, 12). The emotional experience Maslow describes is what is often meant by secular spirituality, which still challenges those who insist on always thinking scientifically.

A more productive path may be to consider three means of experiencing meaningful moments: rational, antirational, and nonrational. A rational analysis considers why one felt this way, what physical effects it had on the body and brain, or the psychological impact of such an experience. An antirational response puts the ultimate explanation beyond any scientific or natural realm into an unknowable world of supernatural spirits and religious belief. A nonrational stance, although nonanalytic, could also be appropriate for a secular person: the nonrational response focuses on experiencing the experience without analyzing in the moment; hearing the symphony without marking beats or key changes, suspending analysis for aesthetic enjoyment. "A true spiritual practitioner is someone who has discovered that it is possible to be at ease in the world for no reason, if only for a few moments at a time, and that such ease is synonymous with transcending the apparent boundaries of the self" (Harris 2014, 17).

Chapter 19: Humanistic Judaism and Secular Spirituality

TRANSCENDENCE AND INSPIRATION: BASIC HUMAN NEEDS

Does a secular spirituality create an experience of transcendence? Is it inspirational? Again, one may differentiate between supernatural and natural transcendence, a feeling of being part of something larger than oneself, beyond the individual self. For the religiously inclined, transcendence is inevitably a mystical connection with God, angels, spirits, and the supernatural. For the secular or naturalistic, transcendence can be achieved in natural ways through community, family, nature, or activism as well as through individual meditation and experience. One would be hard put today to argue that *inspiration* may only be understood in a supernatural way, despite the term's origins.

The subjective, emotional experience of religious and secular transcendence may be more similar than either side would choose to admit: "The [two] states are phenomenologically indistinguishable, with the qualification that the [religiously] trained mystics report experiences conforming more closely to the specific religious cosmology to which they are accustomed" (Deikman [1966] 1980, 242). In other words, Jewish mystics generally do not meet Mohammed, and Muslim Sufis tend not to meet the Holy Spirit. Although this coincidence may undermine any religious claims from the experience, it also suggests a shared human biology that does not require theology. The oneness felt with God or the universe was "a consequence of a deautomatization of the psychological structures that organize, limit, select, and interpret perceptual stimuli.... Cognition is inhibited in favor of perception; the active intellectual style is replaced by a receptive perceptual mode" (Deikman [1966] 1980, 247–248). By intentionally avoiding the brain's natural tendency to analyze, human perception changes: religious mystics interpret this experience in light of preexisting beliefs whereas secular individuals more likely interpret their experience in naturalistic ways; for example, if they feel gratitude at a family gathering, "Our gratitude toward who and what makes our coming together possible can give us a profound feeling of belonging to each other and to the universe, and a sense of strength in doing so" (Aronson 2008, 63).

The simple reason that such experiences have appeared in many human cultures across time and space is the fact that feeling part of something larger than our individual self appears to be a deeply rooted human need. Many accounts of World War II concentration camps such as Viktor Frankl's *Man's Search for Meaning* ([1959] 2014) describe the survival value of believing in a cause, having someone else to care for, the determination to bear witness to future generations—double rations could be less important than these personally transcendent commitments.

The author of *Religion for Atheists* believes that, "Those of us who hold no religious or supernatural beliefs still require regular, ritualized encounters with concepts such as friendship, community, gratitude and transcendence" (de Botton 2012, 298). Likewise, a life without inspiration is difficult to imagine. If the goal of philosophical humanism is to respond to the human condition, then human needs for inspiration and transcendence may be met in a secular way rather than denied or suppressed.

PATHS TO SECULAR SPIRITUALITY

Just as Humanistic Judaism may be more clearly demonstrated through specific example than theoretical definitions, so too is the concept of secular spirituality better defined through explanation of various paths to secular spiritual experiences. Few of those who connect with the concept find meaning in all of these paths, but many of those who are secular recognize at least some of these experiences as meaningful and inspirational, whether or not they accept the label *spiritual.*

SECULAR CONNECTIONS TO RELIGIOUS TRADITIONS

For Humanistic Judaism in particular, the sense of cultural transcendence evoked by symbols and rituals of one's cultural past is an important route to personal inspiration. Using the Hanukah menorah one's great-grandfather brought to America from Europe, hearing the intentionally anachronistic sound of the *shofar* ("ram's horn") blast at the Jewish New Year, seeing one's grandchildren getting married under a *huppah* ("wedding canopy") and breaking a glass at the end—these experiences transcend time and personality to help one feel connected to both the past and the future. Supernatural origins and associations are unnecessary: "religious images, myths and ceremonies become precious to us not because we believe in their divine origin, but because our spirit is moved by their human beauty. They evoke in us such poetic feelings and thoughts that we consider them humanistic sanctities" (Zhitlowsky [1911] 1995, 93). As human rather than divine creations, the feeling of cultural continuity evoked by a symbol combined with the family continuity of heirlooms and the community solidarity of collective celebration can uplift the human spirit in a secular key.

INDIVIDUAL MEDITATION

Although Judaism can be understood as a culture and a religion, Buddhism is often pointed to as personal meditative practice that can be either religious or secular. Calm breathing, internal focus, and relaxing the analytical mind certainly have health benefits, as Harris points out in *Waking Up* (2014), but "The goal is to come out of the trance of discursive thinking and to stop reflexively grasping at the pleasant and recoiling from the unpleasant, so that we can enjoy a mind undisturbed by worry, merely open like the sky, and effortlessly aware of the flow of experience in the present" (Harris 2014, 39). To be sure, there are those secular individuals for whom meditation is a meaningful experience, and there are those who would find sitting still without thinking, doing, or analyzing to be almost torture. Both advocates and skeptics of secular meditation would likely appreciate the pretension-skewering humor of parodies such as the YouTube video "F*ck That: A Guided Meditation," in which images of waves and calm language of oneness and transcendence are interrupted by vulgarity and barely contained anger and hostility—precisely what meditation is supposed to counteract.

The challenge is that for all of the emphasis on words in both Jewish culture and in organized nontheism—blogs, magazines, books, articles, lectures, conferences, debates—learning how to be silent together has proven to be more challenging. Why be silent when one could be learning or sharing one's knowledge? Sometimes, "In the face of reality, silence is more appropriate. The silence of sensation. The silence of attention ... a prayer that is addressed to no one and asks for nothing. The silence of contemplation" (Comte-Sponville 2007, loc. 1693). This silence is neither rational nor antirational; it is a nonrational experience.

THE NATURAL WORLD

For secular individuals who focus their search for knowledge and meaning on this life and the natural world, experiences with nature are often a significant source of secular

Chapter 19: Humanistic Judaism and Secular Spirituality

spirituality: "More than half [of 'nones'] say they often feel a deep connection with nature and the earth (58%)" (Lipka 2005). And rather than seeing this connection with nature as a contradiction of one's commitment to science and rationality, advocates for secular spirituality insist that their practice is a natural outgrowth of their emphasis on materialism: "If everything is immanent, then so is the spirit. If everything is natural, then so is spirituality. Far from precluding spiritual life, this makes it possible. We are *in* and *of* the world. Spirit is part of nature" (Comte-Sponville 2007, loc. 1664).

It may even be the case that the availability of powerful nature experiences can have a secularizing effect, providing an alternative route to meeting that basic human need for inspiration. Areas in the United States with greater natural amenities such as lakes, hills, and water features show lower rates of religious affiliation, serving as "a spiritual resource that supplies a portion of the population's spiritual needs" (Ferguson and Tamburello 2015). This also helps explain why religious affiliation rates in the Western United States are lower than other regions—more readily available natural experiences. Walks in nature, paying attention to the changing seasons, standing in silence before awe-inspiring views—all of these experiences uplift the human spirit and reaffirm a commitment to naturalism and secularism. "The universe is our home; the celestial vault is our horizon; eternity is here and now. This moves me far more than the Bible or the Koran. It astonishes me far more than miracles (if I believed in them)" (Comte-Sponville 2007, loc. 1733).

Popularizers of science from Carl Sagan (1934–1996) to Neil deGrasse Tyson (1958–) have understood well the power of inspiration to spark scientific inquiry and the sense of wonder and awe that can motivate it. One may experience the beauty of a starry night or map the stars at different moments, but both are secular approaches to nature. Even if one does not see a god's hand behind the circumstances of our individual existence, our knowledge and our experience of the natural world facilitate a natural transcendence.

> From the patterning of our DNA derived from our parents to the firing of the hundred billion neurons in our brain to the cultural and historical conditioning of the twentieth century to the education and upbringing given to us to all the experiences we have ever had and choices we have ever made: these have conspired to configure the unique trajectory that culminates in this present moment. (Batchelor 1997, 82)

Even without a divine, an emotional response of gratitude or wonder can be secularly appropriate.

Advocates for secular spirituality are clear that any feeling of oneness with the entire universe is a function of our perception rather than a material reality, and they are often careful to distinguish themselves from the cosmic claims of religious mysticism. Harris is explicit on this: "It is quite possible to lose one's sense of being a separate self and to experience a kind of boundless, open awareness—to feel, in other words, at one with the cosmos. This says a lot about the possibilities of human consciousness, but it says nothing about the universe at large" (Harris 2014, 43).

ART, BEAUTY, AND CULTURE

Just as natural beauty can inspire awe, wonder, and emotional experience, so too can creations of the human hand and mind:

> Aware that beauty enriches our lives, evokes the most powerful emotions, and inspires the noblest ambitions—aware, that is, that beauty causes the spirit to

356   MACMILLAN INTERDISCIPLINARY HANDBOOKS

soar—we naturally wish to cultivate beauty and the appreciation of beauty.... It is clear that, absent belief in God, you are nevertheless a spiritual person. Unless you have no use for music, literature, drama, or dance, unless you are oblivious to the genius of Shakespeare and Chopin and the talent of Michael Jordan, unless you are indifferent to the majesty of a mountain range or the spectacle of a starry sky. (Friedman 2003, 108)

One of the reasons that secularized Jews and those from other religious traditions remain involved in religious congregations despite theological doubt is the aesthetic beauty they find in the liturgical or architectural experience.

It may even be the case that, as society secularized, artistic culture was a potential substitute for the content and form of religious aesthetics: "One would be able to have meaning unburdened by superstition. The maxims of Marcus Aurelius, the poetry of Boccaccio, the operas of Wagner and the paintings of Turner could be secular society's new sacraments" (de Botton 2012, 106). Aesthetics is surely an area where personal taste dictates, and thus what one secular person would find spiritually uplifting another might find boring or bland; it is also clear that there is nothing necessarily theological about finding inspiration from beauty or from a beautifully crafted narrative.

HISTORY AND ROOTS

One's connection with the sweep of the human experience is not limited to aesthetic cultural productions. Visits to Stonehenge or the cave paintings at Lascaux are powerful not only because of the raw beauty of human artistic production preserved there, but also because of the historical transcendence of a shared humanity across thousands of years—a relief image of a hand is tremendously moving because of both its artistry and its humanity.

Archaeology is a careful, exacting science as one extracts layers of sediment and civilization. Yet the knowledge that humans like oneself built that coliseum, or that ancient synagogue, or that floor mosaic that survived 2000 years to be rediscovered provides a natural transcendence. "For many Jews their spirituality arises from their sense of connection to generations of ancestors—a sense of solidarity with the past and with time. The pleasure of roots gives us an experience of immortality, of continuity beyond our all-too-brief personal existence" (Wine "Spirituality" 2003, 181). Even if individual immortality is rejected, feeling one's roots as part of an extended and ancient cultural or human family can still be a secular spiritual experience.

ETHICS, ACTIVISM, AND HUMAN CONNECTION

Many secular individuals, both past and present, have found their spirits uplifted by their participation in life-changing causes for social improvement. Such activism could also be a bridge beyond parochialism toward the

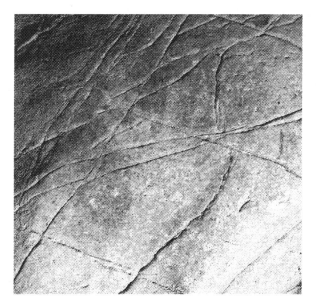

Relief image of a hand from a prehistoric cave. Images such as this one are tremendously moving not only because of their artistry but because they impart a sense of shared humanity across thousands of years. COPYRIGHT © ROBERTO ONTAÑÓN PEREDO.

Chapter 19: Humanistic Judaism and Secular Spirituality

universalist side of secularism. A century ago, "the essence of the Yiddishist socialists' activism was to go beyond solidarity with their own narrow set.... Ideological stances created spiritual connections to the past and future, but the social activism, the concrete and routine work of the movement, created spiritual bonds to all of oppressed, un-free humanity" (Silver 2003, 94). If there are no angels of rescue, then humanity is the only conscious force available to improve the human condition. However, such activity can go beyond community building, ethical enlightened self-interest, or living out one's values to true inspirational experience. An activist secular spirituality may be the antidote to the accusation that individual contemplative spirituality is both selfish and inhumane: "Transcendent experiences that focus only on nature and the universe to the exclusion of other people are morally dangerous. A healthy spirituality is not so transcendent that human affairs become unimportant" (Wine "Spirituality" 2003, 183). Ethical activism and personal contemplation are not mutually exclusive, but rather two different routes to secular spiritual experience.

Secularists today tend to be more skeptical of grand causes than they were in the early twentieth century, when international socialism drew thousands (and secularized thousands more). However, even causes on a smaller scale such as social and racial justice or same-sex marriage equality could fit the same spiritual niche that other causes did for previous generations: "secular Yiddishist socialists ... may have felt unconnected to God, but their movement was replete with connections that gave their lives meaning and purpose" (Silver 2003, 86). If one seeks a feeling of being part of something larger than oneself, political and social activism can often fit that need for community and, through its overarching values and ideals, a natural transcendence.

However, transcending the individual human condition can also happen through developing personal connections with others, which is one reason for the emergence of secular communities in the early twenty-first century, building on twentieth-century models such as Humanistic Judaism.

> The fully ethical condition emerges when my own humanity touches and actively builds connections with the other. It arises when I experience the joy of the human bond, when we sing together and celebrate together, and when we work together under the inspiration of justice to serve the good of humanity. It emerges, even more, when I enter into the life of a person who is down and enable him or her to think well of him or herself. It emerges when I express myself to another with support, empathy, and caring. (Chuman 2003, 61)

The power of the interpersonal connection, whether in a relationship of support and assistance, romantic connection, a deep personal bond, or a caring community, requires no theology and no supernaturalism to be personally transformative.

Is it secularly controversial to describe movies or biographies or interpersonal interactions as "a triumph of the human spirit?" There will be some who disagree on the use of "the S word," but even the most atheistic audience will instantly know what one means. At the end of the 1989 film "Jesus of Montreal" (spoiler alert), the main character who has been both acting the part of Jesus in a passion play and experiencing odd echoes of the Jesus story in his own life is crushed by his cross and dies. In their grief, his friends donate his body for what good it can do. The lame walk, the blind see, and the sick are healed. Medical miracles all, but also inspirational examples of the power of human interconnection and mutual need—a triumph of the human spirit, even after death.

Summary

Like poetry and philosophy, religion is an everlasting branch on the tree of human culture. Its leaves may wither and fall, but others sprout in their place. The source of religion is an eternal well-spring—the yearning of the human soul for a better and more beautiful world. As Ludwig Feuerbach put it: "God is a tear that human beings weep over their own destiny." And the wellsprings of such tears will never dry up. (Zhitlowsky [1909] 1995, 93)

Humanistic Judaism and secular spirituality are two sides of the same phenomenon—the meeting in secular fashion of human needs that previous generations addressed through religion. The need for roots, the need for personal and family identity, the need for inspiration, the need to feel more than an isolated individual—all of these emotional and psychological needs need not be denied or rejected as in conflict with a self-aware secular identity. As Harris explains concisely, "There is more to understanding the human condition than science and secular culture generally admit" (Harris 2014, 5–6).

At their most insistent, advocates for secular spirituality claim that their version of spiritual experience is not only an appropriate substitute for religion, but that it reinforces their secularism. As Comte-Sponville put it in *The Little Book of Atheist Spirituality* (2007), "When you feel 'at one with the All,' you need nothing more. Why would you need a God? The universe suffices. Why would you need a church? The world suffices. Why would you need faith? Experience suffices" (loc. 1786). Likewise, participants in Humanistic Judaism feel that their understandings of both the historical Jewish experience and their contemporary open Jewish identity reinforce both their nontheistic secularism and their respect for human diversity.

Whatever labels one prefers for these experiences—transcendence, spirituality, inspiration, or more prosaic versions such as "feeling part of something greater than oneself"—human reality includes these nonrational emotions and expressions. The question is whether one's secularism is broad enough to incorporate the positive side of this deeply rooted (in both culture and biology) human phenomenon. It is not only a matter of accommodating one's secularism to pesky human limitations; it is also an opportunity.

When we feel insignificant in the midst of a vast and overwhelming universe but feel significant as a part of a single nature evolving through the ages; when we feel insignificant as a lonely and mortal individual but feel significant as part of a centuries long chain of family love; when we see ourselves as powerless fighting the forces of evil alone but see ourselves as powerful when joined together with others in a movement of political idealism—we experience the wonder of natural transcendence. (Wine "Spirituality" 2003, 181)

From such wonder, better worlds and better lives may be made.

Bibliography

American Humanist Association. "Humanism and its Aspirations." http://americanhumanist.org/humanism/humanist_manifesto_iii.

Aronson, Ronald. *Living without God: New Directions for Atheists, Agnostics, Secularists and the Undecided.* Berkeley, CA: Counterpoint, 2008.

Chapter 19: Humanistic Judaism and Secular Spirituality

Batchelor, Stephen. *Buddhism without Beliefs: A Contemporary Guide to Awakening*. New York: Riverhead Books, 1997.

Bauer, Yehuda. "Introduction." In *Judaism in a Secular Age: An Anthology of Secular Humanistic Jewish Thought*, edited by Renee Kogel and Zev Katz, xiii–xlix. Jersey City, NJ: Ktav, 1995.

Berlinerblau, Jacques. *How to Be Secular: A Call to Arms for Religious Freedom*. Boston: Houghton Mifflin Harcourt, 2012.

Chalom, Adam. "Beyond *Apikorsut*: A Judaism for Secular Jews." In *Religion or Ethnicity? Jewish Identities in Evolution*, edited by Zvi Gitelman, 286–302. New Brunswick, NJ: Rutgers University Press, 2009.

Chuman, Joseph. "The Spirituality of Ethics." In *Secular Spirituality: Passionate Search for a Rational Judaism*, edited by M. Bonnie Cousens, 49–62. Farmington Hills, MI: IISHJ/Milan Press, 2003.

Comte-Sponville, André. *The Little Book of Atheist Spirituality*. New York: Viking, 2007. Citations are from Kindle edition (New York: Penguin, 2007) by location.

Cook, Harry. "The Embrace of Ambiguity and the Courage to Doubt." In *Secular Spirituality: Passionate Search for a Rational Judaism*, edited by M. Bonnie Cousens, 137–157. Farmington Hills, MI: IISHJ/Milan Press, 2003.

Cousens, Bonnie. "Introduction." In *Secular Spirituality: Passionate Search for a Rational Judaism*, edited by M. Bonnie Cousens, 1–9. Farmington Hills, MI: IISHJ/Milan Press, 2003.

de Botton, Alain. *Religion for Atheists: A Non-Believer's Guide to the Uses of Religion*. New York: Vintage, 2012.

Deikman, Arthur J. "Deautomatization and the Mystic Experience." http://www.deikman.com/deautomat.html. Originally published in *Psychiatry* 29 (1966): 324–338; reprinted in and cited from *Understanding Mysticism*, edited by Richard Woods. New York: Image Books, 1980.

Edwords, Fred. "What Is Humanism." American Humanist Association, 2008. http://americanhumanist.org/Humanism/What_is_Humanism.

Ferguson, Todd W., and Jeffrey A. Tamburello. "The Natural Environment as a Spiritual Resource: A Theory of Regional Variation in Religious Adherence." *Sociology of Religion*. 2015. http://socrel.oxfordjournals.org/content/early/2015/07/21/socrel.srv029.full.

Fishman, David E. "Yiddish Schools in America and the Problem of Secular Jewish Identity." In *Religion or Ethnicity? Jewish Identities in Evolution*, edited by Zvi Gitelman, 69–89. New Brunswick, NJ: Rutgers University Press, 2009.

Frankl, Viktor. *Man's Search for Meaning*. Boston: Beacon Press, 2014. First published 1959.

Freud, Sigmund. *Civilization and its Discontent*. Translated by James Strachey. New York: Norton, 1961. First published 1929.

Friedman, Daniel. "Art and Nature: Beauty and Spirituality." In *Secular Spirituality: Passionate Search for a Rational Judaism*, edited by M. Bonnie Cousens, 99–108. Farmington Hills, MI: IISHJ/Milan Press, 2003.

Gitelman, Zvi. "Conclusion: The Nature and Viability of Jewish Religious and Secular Identities." In *Religion or Ethnicity? Jewish Identities in Evolution*, edited by Zvi Gitelman, 303–322. New Brunswick, NJ: Rutgers University Press, 2009.

Gold, Sigfried. "Atheist Spirituality." *eSkeptic*, September 10, 2014. http://www.skeptic.com/eskeptic/14-09-10/.

Harris, Sam. *Waking Up: A Guide to Spirituality without Religion*. New York: Simon & Schuster, 2014.

Herberg, Will. *Protestant—Catholic—Jew: An Essay in American Religious Sociology*. Chicago: University of Chicago Press, 1955.

Jordan, William. "A Third of British Adults Don't Believe in a Higher Power." YouGov UK, February 12, 2015. https://yougov.co.uk/news/2015/02/12/third-britishadults-dont-believe-higher-power/.

"Judaism: The Atheist Rabbi." *Time Magazine*. January 29, 1965. http://content.time.com/time/magazine/article/0,9171,839200,00.html.

Kamenetz, Rodger. *Jew in the Lotus: A Poet's Rediscovery of Jewish Identity in Buddhist India*. San Francisco: HarperSanFrancisco, 1994.

Liebman, Charles, and Yaakov Yagdar. "Secular-Jewish Identity and the Condition of Secular Judaism in Israel." In *Religion or Ethnicity? Jewish Identities in Evolution*, edited by Zvi Gitelman, 149–170. New Brunswick, NJ: Rutgers University Press, 2009.

Lipka, Michael. "A Closer Look at America's Rapidly Growing Religions 'Nones.'" May 13, 2005. http://www.pewresearch.org/fact-tank/2015/05/13/a-closer-look-at-americas-rapidly-growing-religious-nones/.

Maslow, Abraham. *Religions, Values and Peak Experience*. Columbus: Ohio State University Press, 1964.

Maslow, Abraham. *Toward a Psychology of Being*, 3rd ed. New York: Wiley, 1999. First published 1968.

Pew Research Center. "Nones on the Rise." October 9, 2012. http://www.pewforum.org/2012/10/09/nones-on-the-rise/.

Pew Research Center. "A Portrait of Jewish Americans." October 1, 2013. http://www.pewforum.org/files/2013/10/jewish-american-full-report-for-web.pdf.

Reuters. "Losing Faith: Atheism Rising in Britain, Poll Suggests." February 12, 2015. http://www.rt.com/uk/231811-uk-atheism-report-decline/.

Rowens, Marilyn. "Reflections on a Life of Courage." In *A Life of Courage: Sherwin Wine and Humanistic Judaism*, edited by Dan Cohn-Sherbok, Marilyn Rowens, and Harry Cook, 49–73. Farmington Hills, MI: IISHJ/Milan Press, 2003.

Schappes, Morris. "A Secular View of Jewish Life." In *Judaism in a Secular Age: An Anthology of Secular Humanistic Jewish Thought*, edited by Renee Kogel and Zev Katz, 264–269. Jersey City, NJ: Ktav, 1995. First published 1966.

Silver, Mitchell. "Rethinking Jewish Secularism." In *Secular Spirituality: Passionate Search for a Rational Judaism*, edited by M. Bonnie Cousens, 79–98. Farmington, Hills, MI: IISHJ/Milan Press, 2003.

Wine, Sherwin. "The Rabbi Writes." *The Jewish Humanist* (The Birmingham Temple newsletter), January 1988.

Wine, Sherwin. "Secular Spirituality." In *Secular Spirituality: Passionate Search for a Rational Judaism*, edited by M. Bonnie Cousens, 177–184. Farmington Hills, MI: IISHJ/ Milan Press, 2003.

Wine, Sherwin. *Staying Sane in a Crazy World: A Guide to Rational Living.* Birmingham, MI: Center for New Thinking, 1995.

Ynet. "Israel 2010: 42% of Jews are Secular." May 18, 2010. Available from http://www.ynetnews.com/articles /0,7340,L-3890330,00.html.

Zhitlowsky, Chaim. "Death and Rebirth of Gods and Religion." Translated by Max Rosenfeld. In *Judaism in a Secular Age: An Anthology of Secular Humanistic Jewish Thought*, edited by Renee Kogel and Zev Katz, 90–95. Jersey City, NJ: Ktav, 1995. First published 1909.

Zhitlowsky, Chaim. "The National Poetic Rebirth of the Jewish People." Translated by Max Rosenfeld. In *Judaism in a Secular Age: An Anthology of Secular Humanistic Jewish Thought*, edited by Renee Kogel and Zev Katz, 90–95. Jersey City, NJ: Ktav, 1995. First published 1911.

FILMS

F*ck That: A Guided Meditation. Dir. Jason Headley. 2015. A modern parody of meditation in which images of waves and calm language of oneness and transcendence are interrupted by anger and vulgarity. https://www.youtube .com/watch?v=HEBRKkxDqK8.

Jesus of Montreal. Dir. Denys Arcand. 1989. Staging a passion play leads to real-life events echoing the drama, with tragic results.

The Powers of Ten. Dir. Charles and Ray Eames. 1977. Two documentary films exploring the power of scale larger and smaller to depict everything from the universe to subatomic particles. https://www.youtube.com/watch?v =0fKBhvDjuy0.

Secular Spirituality: Passionate Search for a Rational Judaism. Produced by International Institute for Secular Humanistic Judaism. 2001. Conference on varieties of secular spirituality with a particular emphasis on their applicability to Secular Humanistic Judaism. https://www.youtube.com/playlist ?list=PLyHcweASuE69lqtcmrYa08g41sDczyy0K.

Sherwin Wine at 'The New Humanism' Conference. Harvard Humanist Chaplaincy. 2007. Presentation by the founder of Humanistic Judaism on both the movement and its relationship to other aspects of secular identity. Parts I–V available online beginning from https://www.youtube .com/watch?v=cEzfvGo64Tg.

CHAPTER 20

Naturalism and Well-Being

Thomas W. Clark
Director, Center for Naturalism, Somerville, MA
Research Associate, Institute for Behavioral Health, Brandeis University,
Waltham, MA

Conceptions of human flourishing vary, but there are requirements for well-being that nearly everyone would endorse: meeting basic physical and emotional needs; having opportunities for learning, mastery, and self-expression; being a valued member of a secure community; and finding one's place in the ultimate scheme of things. These domains of well-being reflect the complexity and variety of human motivations, not all of which, unfortunately, find fulfillment in every life.

Because it speaks to all of these domains—material, psychological, social, and existential—a worldview can inform the full range of human flourishing. Naturalism is a science-based worldview that situates us in an impersonal cosmos, with no god in charge and no apparent purpose. Although this austere vision of the human condition might seem bereft of resources for well-being, this chapter will argue the opposite: naturalism is a rich, rewarding, and (importantly) true understanding of reality that offers ethical and spiritual wisdom, psychological stability, and practical guidance.

This chapter does not aim to justify naturalism as a worldview, although some remarks in its defense will be forthcoming, and it will be contrasted favorably with other worldviews. Rather, the aim of this chapter is to show how naturalism can contribute to a conception of human flourishing that is widely, although not universally, accepted. Naturalism has ethically positive and politically progressive implications in its support for human rights for all human beings, whatever their gender, race, sexual orientation, or religious persuasion. It has humanitarian implications for criminal and social justice policies and for our understanding of addiction and behavioral health. It affords greater latitude for personal self-expression and autonomy than do many faith-based worldviews while providing a satisfying perspective on the existential questions of meaning and purpose in life.

However, it should be emphasized that naturalism is not the only route to such goods. Adherents of supernaturalist religions, as well as naturalistic variants of Buddhism (and those who hold no worldview at all) may reach roughly similar conclusions about human flourishing, albeit from different premises. Nevertheless, naturalism is unique in using the scientific understanding of ourselves and our place in the cosmos to address the many-faceted question of how to find fulfillment in life.

Worldview naturalism obviously goes beyond atheism (the denial that gods exist) or agnosticism (having no definite view about gods' existence) by presenting a comprehensive

363

Chapter 20: Naturalism and Well-Being

Whirlpool Galaxy. *Naturalism is a science-based understanding of reality that posits an impersonal cosmos, with no god and no apparent purpose. Though austere, this vision of the human condition does offer ethical and spiritual wisdom.* UNIVERSAL HISTORY ARCHIVE/GETTY IMAGES.

picture of reality and the human condition that can serve as a guide to living a meaningful life. Although it has close affinities with secular humanism, which takes naturalism as its metaphysics (secular humanists usually have no truck with the supernatural), naturalism is perhaps less parochial in its orientation. It draws greater attention to the global impersonal picture—the natural cosmos and its causal laws—that sets the stage for, and ultimately shapes the human drama. Human beings are but one among trillions of natural phenomena, and naturalism should not be confused with the Transcendentalism of Ralph Waldo Emerson (1836) and Henry David Thoreau (1854), which asserts that communion with untrammeled nature (think forests and glades) affords us access to a higher, true reality. Worldview naturalism sets up no deep dichotomy between human culture and commerce and the natural world from which they spring; nor does it suppose that experiences, however transcendent, necessarily reveal truths about the world.

THE QUEST FOR FLOURISHING

The personal quest for flourishing comes naturally to us. From birth onward, we seek out rewarding activities and states of affairs and avoid pain and discomfort, whether physical or emotional. Therefore, it is safe to say that whatever your projects and interests might be, from the mundane to the spiritual, their pursuit participates in your quest for flourishing. Of course, we do not always make the achievement of personal well-being our top priority because we are also concerned with the well-being of our family, friends, community, nation, and sometimes even the planet. Nevertheless, we engage in larger spheres of ethical concern because it matters to us as particular individuals. To want a safe, secure, and rewarding social environment is part of our selfish motivational endowment, which usually makes the quest for human flourishing a communal project.

DIMENSIONS OF WELL-BEING

The dimensions of personal well-being range from the satisfaction of basic material and emotional needs—food, shelter, and security—to exploring the possibilities of our physical, aesthetic, and intellectual potential. Some satisfactions are consummatory, driven by biological appetites; others are a matter of companionship, learning, mastery, long-range achievement, and the quest for the deepest meanings in life. Abraham Maslow's "hierarchy of needs" is an oft-cited guide to these dimensions, a central point being that unless basic needs are met first, other sorts of well-being may be unobtainable (Maslow 1943). The multiplicity of dimensions of well-being means that the human animal has huge, diverse potential for flourishing, and therefore for the denial of such flourishing. We are bequeathed, like it or not, with a life, and with the desire to make the most of it. We are often thwarted in this quest.

REQUIREMENTS FOR WELL-BEING

To flourish anywhere near our potential, we must bring a host of resources to bear: material sustenance, education, social and technical skills, the physical and social infrastructure of communities, and ideally a set of goals and purposes that endow our lives with meanings beyond the pursuit of momentary satisfactions. Because the dimensions of human well-being encompass all that we creatures are—material, psychological, social, and existential—a coherent worldview that addresses these dimensions can help us live a fulfilling, meaningful life. Naturalism is such a worldview (Clark 2007a).

WORLDVIEW NATURALISM

Simply put, a worldview is how we take ourselves to be situated in the widest possible context, the context of existence itself, of all that there is. Necessarily, we take our worldview to be at least an approximation to the truth of our global situation, including the truth about what sorts of creatures we fundamentally are.

TRADITIONAL SUPERNATURALISM

The dominant worldviews these days are religious in the traditional supernatural, dualistic sense: there exists a god (Christianity, Islam, Judaism) or gods (Hinduism) with powers of creation and control that transcend our ordinary earthly powers. Nature is real enough, but there is also a supernatural, perhaps immaterial, realm that exists beyond it that supplies us with morality, meaning, and life everlasting. As much as some traditional religions may affirm the importance of our material lives on Earth, they nevertheless divide reality into the natural and supernatural and posit that we have two natures: body and soul (Moreland 2009).

THE NATURALIST ALTERNATIVE

Naturalism begs to differ with traditional religious dualism. Taking science as the most trustworthy route to knowledge, naturalists see no good evidence for the claim that either we or existence as a whole are of two categorically different natures. What science reveals instead is a vast, interconnected, multilayered, diversely populated, and yet single realm in which all phenomena partake of the same basic constituents. This realm we simply call nature. There seems no reason to suppose, given scientific observations thus far, that there exists another, supernatural realm that operates according to different laws or that contains radically different phenomena (Ritchie 2008). Applied to ourselves, naturalism holds that we too are of a single, physical nature. We are naturally evolved, material creatures whose remarkable capacities for thought, feeling, cooperation, and ethical concern derive from our materially based endowments (Richards 2000).

APPEARANCE VERSUS REALITY: PUTTING EPISTEMOLOGY FIRST

We can apply the tenets of worldview naturalism—its understanding of how we can best know (science) and how things ultimately are (a single natural world)—to the project of

Chapter 20: Naturalism and Well-Being

human well-being in the domains mentioned above: practical, ethical, and existential. To start, well-being arguably requires a reasonably good grasp of how things are as opposed to how they might seem or how we might want them to be. Worldview naturalism gets its initial grip on us by respecting the crucial distinction between appearance and reality.

COGNITIVE FALLIBILITY

As creatures wanting to survive and prosper in a complex world, we need a reasonably accurate picture of our environment to guide successful behavior. We have sensory and cognitive capacities with which to construct perceptual and conceptual models of the world, which we then use to make predictions. However, often enough, we do not get things exactly right, and sometimes we are drastically off of the mark. We are often deceived about reality given our cognitive limitations and motivational biases. Thus arises the commonsense distinction between how things appear to us versus how they actually are. The project of knowing, of epistemology, is to make our models more accurate.

THE RISE OF SCIENCE

In the twenty-first century, we are the beneficiaries of great progress in the epistemological project that, afforded by the scientific method, gradually refined over the last four hundred years. The basic idea is simple enough: in deciding what is likely to be true about the world, do not trust authority, revelation, sacred books, or traditional wisdom, but look to the world itself. Neither trust your intuitions, hopes, or fears; instead, look to the publicly available evidence for and against a claim (e.g., the probability of a tornado tomorrow or the best cure for cancer).

Naturalists say that this method for deciding what is true applies to all factual questions about the world, from the mundane to the cosmological. Because nature is of a piece, including ourselves and our cultures, there is not another way of knowing that works better in certain domains. This puts naturalism directly at odds with traditional religious claims that certain questions, such as our true nature and the origins of life and the universe, find more truthful answers in faith and scripture (Coyne 2015). The conflict between science and religion is on full display in *Inherit the Wind* (1960), a dramatic recounting of the 1925 Scopes "Monkey Trial" on teaching evolution in Tennessee (science loses, but religion is taken down a peg).

THE RATIONAL REQUIREMENT FOR EVIDENCE

The scientific, empirical method has been extraordinarily successful in giving us useful knowledge. A primary contribution that science-based naturalism makes to well-being is to insist that we track the truth of our situation, whatever the scale of our inquiry. The advisory is straightforward: whether it is your personal health, or the health of the planet, stick to publicly available evidence as a guide to action. Your hopes, fears, prejudices, personality quirks, politics, and commercial interests are not good reflections of the facts; they are, more probably, biases (Shermer 1997). You may not like what the evidence shows (say you are diagnosed with cancer), but the chances are you will like the outcomes of evidence-based action (chemotherapy) better than faith-based alternatives (prayer). To stick with the best objective evidence in forming beliefs—empiricism—is simply to be maximally rational in acting on your own and others' behalf.

366   MACMILLAN INTERDISCIPLINARY HANDBOOKS

COGNITIVE HUMILITY AND RESPONSIBILITY

The rational allegiance to empiricism not only makes us more effective agents, it keeps us from getting too cocksure and inflexible in our opinions. The naturalist's commitment to public evidence leads to cognitive humility and openness to correction. As it might be put, the naturalist always maintains the right to be wrong should the facts turn against her. This has great psychological advantages: one's identity is less wrapped up in being right—an enervating and unattractive use of personal resources—and more in being true to the best method of deciding what is true. The commitment to evidence means that revising one's long-held view of, say, climate change or genetically modified organisms, can be seen as a virtue and a strength, not a defeat or admission of weakness. Moreover, as interdependent social beings, it is arguably our cognitive responsibility to model reality as accurately as we can. To flout the demand for good evidence can put us individually and collectively at risk: we may well be acting on the basis of ignorance and wishful thinking, not facts (Clifford 1877). However, being a good empiricist is not easy. In the film *Contact* (1997), a scientist is forced to admit that she does not have sufficient evidence to prove that she has encountered an advanced species elsewhere in the Milky Way, although she is convinced that the encounter took place.

RESILIENCE

Naturalists imagine, with some justification, that their commitment to empiricism makes them less susceptible to delusion and wishful thinking. In turn, this inoculates them against the disappointments that would otherwise follow when cherished beliefs are debunked. To be reality based in one's convictions leaves one less vulnerable to cognitive disruption and more emotionally stable should the facts require changing one's mind. By being less factually wrong in the first place, and more open to correction when proven wrong, naturalists can access a nondefensive psychological resilience and flexibility unavailable to those wedded to beliefs that must be defended no matter what the cost.

HUMAN NATURE: WHO ARE WE, ESSENTIALLY?

The science-based, empirical conclusion about human nature is that we are entirely natural, physical beings, the product of unguided evolution. This has profound implications for our conceptions of self and personhood, challenging traditional notions of soul, agency, and free will. However, when understood correctly, the naturalistic revolution in our self-concept gives us many advantages in the quest for human flourishing.

PHYSICALISM

As natural beings, we are entirely physical beings. Despite how it might feel, there is no empirical evidence for anything categorically nonphysical about us, such as an immaterial soul. Our capacities for thought and consciousness are materially based in the brain and body, our stable personalities are likewise functions of complex patterns of neural connections that persist over a lifetime. The brain, linked via sensory and perceptual systems to the body and outside world, gives rise to our conscious experience and effectively controls behavior, putting the soul out of a job (Flanagan 2002, Metzinger 2010). Therefore, the natural world is not merely physical; it is astonishingly, fantastically physical in what it

Chapter 20: Naturalism and Well-Being

manages to accomplish in the human form (Crick 1995). However, this is not to say that the so-called "hard problem" of consciousness—how certain brain processes bring about subjective experience—has been definitively solved (Chalmers 1995). Indeed, sentience might not need a biological brain as its physical substrate, an unsettling possibility explored in the films *Her* (2013) and *Ex Machina* (2015).

CAUSATION AND HUMAN AGENCY

The science-driven project of naturalizing ourselves is rapidly picking up steam; in the process, some long-standing beliefs about human agency are coming under pressure. In particular, the naturalist's challenge to the soul calls into question the widespread belief that human beings are causal exceptions to nature, that we have a contracausal free will (often called libertarian free will) that transcends natural laws (Oerton 2012, Wegner 2002). This denial is a radical departure from the dualist view of ourselves that has held sway for millennia. That we are fully caused creatures, as science strongly suggests, and are in no sense ultimately self-caused are among the most profound and far-reaching tenets of worldview naturalism.

In proceeding through this chapter, keep in mind that any randomness or indeterminism that might play a role in explaining behavior cannot add to human powers of origination and control. By definition, random, uncaused, or undetermined events are not produced by our desires or intentions, so we cannot take credit or blame for them. Nor can anyone be their own cause: one would have to first exist to bring oneself into being—a logical impossibility.

CONNECTION, COMPASSION, AND CONTROL

Before delving into the details of how naturalism can inform human well-being, an overview is in order. Although naturalism defeats pretensions of our being little gods, situated above nature, it has definite compensations that fall into three basic categories that speak to universal human needs.

CONNECTION

First, under naturalism we find ourselves completely at home on the planet, in the solar system, and in the cosmos, alienated in no respect from what has given rise to us. Our intensely personal projects participate in something vastly larger, the origins, scope, and ultimate destiny of which may forever elude our understanding. Although it puts us in our natural place, so to speak, this realization can add dimensions of significance and wonder to life that rival and perhaps surpass standard religious reassurances of salvation and the life hereafter. Naturalism affords us, in all aspects of our being, a deep connection to all that exists.

We are also causally connected: to the past, to our current situation, and to the future as our lives play out. These connections conform to deterministic and probabilistic natural laws described by science, whether at the physical, chemical, biological, or behavioral level. Each of us is an unfolding natural process, a moment-to-moment expression of all of the conditions that constitute us and surround us. Nothing about us escapes causal connection to the world, nor, equally, is the world insulated from our individual causal contributions to the unfolding of events.

COMPASSION

Because a person's character, thoughts, and actions do not transcend the cause and effect laws that science reveals, we are all equally products of our genetic endowments and our environments. Because you did not ultimately create yourself in any respect, you cannot take ultimate credit (or blame) for who you are, as some supernatural notions of human nature would have it. There are no privileged souls or spirits that are somehow more deserving than others. But for the luck of the draw in your genes and upbringing, you would be the criminal, the homeless person, or the billionaire. This insight leads us to become more accepting, compassionate, and sympathetic toward ourselves and others and less likely to harbor feelings of resentment, anger, envy, or contempt. As Baruch Spinoza said about causal determinism: "This doctrine ... teaches us to hate no one, to disesteem no one, to mock no one, to be angry at no one, and to envy no one..." (Spinoza [1677] 1996, 68).

CONTROL

By understanding that you are fully caused, and the ways in which you are caused, you gain control and power over yourself. We are not passive puppets of determinism because human beings have causal powers just as much as the conditions that shaped them, often more. However, instead of supposing you can simply choose to be other than you are, you understand that self-change and effective action flow from concrete causal factors. Create the right conditions, then self-change and self-efficacy will follow, whether your project is losing weight or becoming a Fortune 500 CEO.

Naturalism also makes us wiser in creating conditions that foster cooperation and social harmony. Because attitudes and actions always result from causes, not from a mysterious uncontrollable free will, we can learn to control those causes in service to our collective well-being. Understanding causation in behavior translates into becoming more effective at work, in family and social situations, and especially in efforts on behalf of planetary sustainability, which may well require significant behavioral change on all of our parts. Thus, to connection and compassion, we can add increased control as a benefit of adopting a worldview that locates us entirely within the natural causal nexus.

THE MORAL PSYCHOLOGY OF NATURALISM

Having covered in general terms some advantages naturalism affords in the quest for well-being, there are many specific benefits in domains of ethics, social policy, personal autonomy, and existential concerns. In arriving at these benefits, the route often traveled is to address worries that arise in taking a completely causal view of ourselves and then to point out the advantages of embracing it.

MORALITY SURVIVES

Primary among these concerns is a worry about morality and responsibility: if (any randomness aside) human beings are fully determined in who they become and what they do, then how can we justly credit and blame them for their actions? If indeed no one could have done other than what they did in an actual situation (as opposed to hypothetical situations), then is everything forgiven, excused, or permitted?

Chapter 20: Naturalism and Well-Being

Not at all. Our basic sense of right and wrong is a natural endowment given to us by evolution; therefore, even in the absence of a divine law giver, most of us are strongly motivated to observe and maintain ethical norms (Greene 2013). As described by ethologist Franz de Waal (2013), human morality has clear precursors among primates such as bonobos and chimpanzees. Humans of course enjoy more complex social arrangements, with greater opportunities for cooperation and cheating; therefore, they have correspondingly more nuanced moral intuitions. However, there is little doubt that our moral sense is genetically encoded, although there is considerable cultural variability in its expression (Pinker 2008).

Moral rules, rewards, and sanctions are necessary to guide behavior to the good, so there is no "get-out-of-jail-free" card that follows from causal determinism. Just because we have behaved badly in the past does not mean we will in the future: we can be caused—determined—to behave better (Clark 2006). Nor are we required to automatically forgive or excuse transgressions against us, something that is psychologically impossible and perhaps dangerous if the transgressor remains unrepentant and likely to reoffend (McCullough 2008).

BLAME AND ADMIRATION: THE MITIGATION RESPONSE

These reassurances in hand, there are distinct moral and practical advantages to the naturalistic realization that we are not first causes, that character and behavior are entirely the result of circumstances that ultimately we did not choose. First, we become more reality based in our expectations of ourselves and others. We cannot any longer suppose that, as a situation played out, someone could have done otherwise, although we might wish they had. Nor can we suppose people are fundamentally to blame for their character: individuals are fully caused to become good or bad. Unsurprisingly, this realization reduces recrimination, resentment, unproductive anger, and blame—emotions that are incited and amplified by seeing others as first causes (Waller 2011).

Likewise, we are much less likely to stand in worshipful awe of the talented and successful. As much as we admire their achievements, we can see they were, finally, lucky in their genetic and environmental circumstances. Because the psychological effect of putting human agents in a causal context is to mitigate or dampen reactive attitudes, such as resentment and hero worship, this could be called the mitigation response. Appreciating the fact that there is a full causal story behind each and every human being and their choices and actions (even if we cannot know all of the details) can help maintain equanimity and poise in a world that supplies us with endless emotional provocations. This counts as a substantial contribution to our well-being, one proposed by none other than the Buddha, who taught the thesis of dependent origination (what we think of as cause and effect). His insight, the basis for Buddhist principles of compassion and acceptance, is now reinforced by naturalism (Clark 2007a 24–25).

SELF-COMPASSION AND ACCEPTANCE

The mitigation response can also serve us well by modulating our self-directed attitudes and emotions. Because we cannot suppose that we could have done otherwise as a situation played itself out, this helps to limit unproductive self-blame, recrimination, and feelings of worthlessness. This is not to say that emotions such as regret, guilt, and shame are never appropriate because they prompt us to make amends and strengthen our resolve to do better next time. Without them we would all be heartless and shameless psychopaths. However,

Chapter 20: Naturalism and Well-Being

the mitigation response prevents these emotions from overtaking and incapacitating us; self-compassion can replace self-recrimination.

Likewise, for pride and self-aggrandizement, we cannot, under naturalism, suppose that our successes are the expression of a self-made will, talent, or capacity for hard work. All of these qualities have ultimately been given to us, although we might experience making sustained effort as purely self-originated. Still, we can celebrate our accomplishments, but without the smugness or superiority generated by supposing we were anything but lucky in our circumstances. The gratitude and humility generated by taking a causal, naturalistic view of one's good fortune is a more attractive and more secure basis for one's identity than self-centered pride.

SCIENCE AND SOLIDARITY: THE CASE FOR UNIVERSAL HUMAN RIGHTS

The foundation for compassion afforded by naturalism has far-reaching implications for human rights. Because there are no superior, especially deserving souls (there are no souls, period), no one can claim a special privilege or worth that justifies special treatment. There is no empirical justification for supposing that any class of individuals deserves greater rights or opportunities for well-being than other classes.

NO SCIENTIFIC BASIS FOR DISCRIMINATION

Discriminatory policies, such as withholding equal rights to women in patriarchal societies, often find justification in nonempirical beliefs (e.g., in the natural inferiority and subservience of females to males). In contrast, science cannot justify special privileges supposedly owed those ranked higher in a social hierarchy, or belonging to particular groups, whether of gender, race, sexual orientation, ethnicity, nationality, religious affiliation, or other denomination. Progress in human rights has been driven by dismantling ideological and religious justifications for discrimination by showing them to have no factual basis. There is no evidence to support the claim that whites deserve greater opportunity or success than blacks or Latinos, or that men have a greater claim to self-actualization than women, although such claims have historically been rather common and are still made in some cultures. Furthermore, any departure from science in deciding what is true about human relations has the potential to lend support to social discrimination. Faith, scripture, intuition, and revelation, when untethered to evidence, can provide fertile ground for the belief that we are not equally deserving of a good life.

As scientific empiricism—the basis for naturalism—gains popularity as a guide to reality, the discriminatory social practices built on nonempirical beliefs will be deprived of their rationales, making the presumption of equal and universal rights more and more the norm (Shermer 2015). Whatever biological and cultural differences exist among genders, races, and nationalities, there are no scientific grounds for supposing that members of out-groups, or low-status members of in-groups, deserve not to have their human needs met or not to develop their full potential by according them the same rights as others. To the extent that these rights depend on being free from religious or ideological dictates, the acceptance of naturalism works to support their affirmation.

RELIGION: BEYOND RELIGION

371

Chapter 20: Naturalism and Well-Being

AN EQUAL OPPORTUNITY WORLDVIEW

The upshot is that science-based naturalism accords greater numerical opportunity for human flourishing than do some non-naturalistic worldviews because it extends the basic rights necessary for such flourishing across the board. There are no chosen people, as there are under some versions of traditional religions, racist ideologies such as Nazism or white supremacy, and social Darwinism (the pseudoscientific supposition that economic winners deserve to win and losers lose). Under naturalism there is no reason that you—whatever your race, class, or religion—do not deserve a full measure of well-being so long as you respect the same rights to well-being for those of other groups. Therefore, naturalism is an equal opportunity worldview, supporting the ideal of universal human flourishing.

CRIMINAL JUSTICE

Having seen its global egalitarian implications, we can next consider benefits conferred by adopting social policies consistent with naturalism. Two policy domains stand out as especially relevant: criminal and social justice. Taking a thoroughly cause and effect view of human agents cuts against certain justifications for punishment and social inequality, helping to produce a less punitive, more equitable society—one that increases opportunities for personal and collective flourishing (Clark 2004).

AGAINST RETRIBUTION

How might our attitudes toward criminal offenders change were we to take on the science-based view that they could not have acted otherwise, given their genetics, upbringing, and the situation in which they committed a crime? Arguably, we would see that they were, ultimately, unlucky in their biological, environmental, and situational circumstances; but for our good luck, we too might be standing in the dock. Given his circumstances, a murderer could not have been or acted otherwise, in which case causal responsibility for the crime is distributed to factors outside (but still including) the individual. This realization helps to undercut a primary motivation for punishment: that the offender deserves to suffer because he could have acted otherwise but simply chose not to.

This retributive rationale for punishment—that suffering is deserved and so should be inflicted whether or not it produces any benefit to the offender or society—is deprived of its main psychological support once we realize that the offender is in no sense self-created but rather the outcome of a largely deterministic causal chain. We cannot any longer single out the agent as ultimately blameworthy and thus deserving of suffering; rather, he is only the most proximate cause of the offense. This in turn triggers the mitigation response: our retributive emotions are attenuated by seeing that the offender could not have done otherwise; instead, a host of historical and situational factors determined the criminal and the crime.

FORGIVENESS AND RECONCILIATION

Our retributive inclinations are natural enough, but we need not give them pride of place in our emotional economy. Indeed, the benefits of giving up retribution are potentially far-reaching. Having appreciated the causal factors that explain the offender, we are more likely to rise above the desire for revenge, a desire that diminishes us by its narrow, aggressive drive for vindication and its need for another's suffering. Having let go of this desire, when we see signs that the offender truly regrets the harm he has done, we are in a far better position to forgive. Forgiveness then opens up the possibility for reconciliation and reintegration of the offender into the community as well as the opportunity for victims to recover their equanimity, compassion, and self-control in service to ends more productive than retaliation (McCullough 2008).

CRIMINAL JUSTICE REFORM

Questioning retribution can also play a central role in criminal justice reform. Prison conditions, especially in the United States, are often designed to maximize degradation and deprivation on the grounds that offenders are simply getting what they deserve (for instance, when raped, beaten, or held in solitary confinement). However, when punishment is shorn of its retributive rationale, its aims are limited to deterrence, rehabilitation, restitution, public safety, and moral reform. If so, then the infliction of harms, deprivation, and death on wrongdoers can only be justified by whether it serves these aims. And often it does not: harsh prison conditions are far more likely to further damage inmates than impart any moral or social improvement. Nor are they effective in deterring those with little to lose (every crime committed constitutes a failure of deterrence), but are more likely to foster criminality and legitimize aggression. Renouncing the punitive excesses justified by retribution, and reforming the criminal justice system to focus on rehabilitation, reform, and community restoration, not meting out just deserts, will benefit both the offender and the community to which he will likely return (Clark 2005, Gilligan 2001). However, such reforms must always respect the autonomy and basic human rights of wrongdoers, lest the cure of rehabilitation prove worse than the disease of crime—a point vividly made in Stanley Kubrick's film *A Clockwork Orange* (1971).

GETTING SMART ON CRIME

A third benefit of accepting that wrongdoers are fully caused in their character and behavior is that we become smarter on crime, seeking to prevent it by addressing criminogenic conditions. There is no essential mystery about why criminal and moral offenses occur, only a deficit of knowledge and attention to their causes, a deficit encouraged by the myth that human beings somehow transcend causation in their character and choices. Give up that myth and then wrongdoing becomes a failure, not of an individual's uncaused will, but of our (caused) collective will to investigate and remediate the determinants of crime. And indeed, we can be caused to become more proactive in crime prevention by promoting the science-based insight that behavior and will themselves are fully caused. Seeing that individuals are completely a function of biological and environmental conditions will allow us to move beyond retribution and access the economic and social benefits of taking a public health, prevention-oriented approach to crime, as opposed to the punitive, after-the-fact approach currently in place.

SOCIAL INEQUALITY

The naturalistic insight that there are no privileged or special persons, only the luck of the draw in our determinants, can also help to shape attitudes and policies related to social justice and inequality. Exposing the myth of the ultimately self-made self draws attention to the actual causes of success and failure in life.

Chapter 20: Naturalism and Well-Being

THE CAUSES OF SUCCESS

On a deterministic understanding of behavior, we can see that the economically successful achieved what they did as a function of fortunate genetic endowment, upbringing, education, and connections. This is not to discount the importance of capacities for hard work and self-discipline in reaching one's goals, only to say that such capacities are also ultimately bequeathed us by our biological and environmental circumstances; they are not self-created virtues. Nor does this insight diminish the social value of an individual's success or our appreciation of someone's talent, genius, and originality; it simply places them in the broader context in which they originated. Admiration remains, but it is conditioned by the knowledge that the talented and successful are, ultimately, lucky in their endowments and advantages. As strange as it might sound, they do not ultimately deserve their riches or success, although they certainly deserved, like the rest of us, the opportunity to succeed.

POVERTY AND THE AMERICAN DREAM

Likewise, we can understand the failure to get ahead not as a failure of an ultimately self-chosen self, but as the outcome of a host of formative and situational causes. There is no deep puzzle about poverty; rather, there are a host of socioeconomic conditions that were they addressed, would increase social mobility and grant the opportunity to flourish to many more individuals. In many cases, we do not know the full causal story, of course, but admitting there is such a story challenges the presumption that somehow the poor deserve to be poor and that they could and should have succeeded given the disadvantaged conditions they faced.

The myth of the so-called American dream is exactly this presumption: that everyone has an equal shot at success; if you do not make it you have got no one but yourself to blame, whatever your situation. This ethos of ultimate personal responsibility diverts attention from the myriad causes that shape a person and his or her prospects, and it drives the conclusion that individuals deeply merit their economic status. Unsurprisingly, this helps to justify laissez faire social policies, which take inequality to reflect the just outcomes of self-willed choices. Challenge the myth of self-creation and the justification for inequality as deserved collapses, clearing the way for policies that support community development, education, job training, and other requirements for individual advancement. Ironically, the American dream will be more likely to be realized if the self-made self is called into question.

NATURALISM AND PROGRESSIVE POLICY

It will not have escaped the reader's notice that naturalism as presented here lends support to what many might consider liberal, progressive policies in criminal and social justice (this partisanship continues in the section, "Maximizing Autonomy" in other policy domains). This is because liberals, more than conservatives, are by nature more likely to be receptive to evidence that contradicts beliefs that restrict rights and opportunities to supposedly privileged, "deserving" groups. Liberals, as characterized by the Big Five scale of personality dimensions, a well-validated psychometric instrument (Goldberg 1992), exhibit more "openness to experience" than do conservatives; therefore, they are more exploratory and less resistant to change than conservatives. By contrast, conservatives exhibit more "conscientiousness," a trait associated with a need for structure, order, and stability (Carney et al. 2008).

Conservative social policies are often (not always) grounded in traditional beliefs about human nature and social hierarchies that have little or no empirical basis (for instance, belief

374   MACMILLAN INTERDISCIPLINARY HANDBOOKS

Chapter 20: Naturalism and Well-Being

in the ultimately self-made self that deeply deserves its economic lot in life). Those who are more evidence-based in their worldview—those more open to what science has to say—will tend to reject such beliefs and the policies they help justify, ending up on the liberal side of the political spectrum (Mooney 2012). Therefore, it is no coincidence that according to a 2009 Pew Research Center poll, only six percent of scientists identified themselves as Republicans (5), and that institutions of higher learning, friendly to fact-based research, lean liberal in their politics.

This is not to say that all naturalists are liberals; laissez faire libertarians, not infrequently found among atheist and skeptic groups, usually make no appeal to the supernatural in arguing for shrinking the social safety net. This suggests that one needs an inclination toward empathy, as well as openness to empiricism, to end up a liberal.

MAXIMIZING AUTONOMY

Because it challenges the restrictions on the freedoms of conscience and belief often associated with supernatural religions and nonempirical ideologies, naturalism liberates reason to explore the world, constrained only by the demand for evidence. By discounting traditional religious justifications for prohibitions on certain behaviors, it expands the available options when facing momentous choices in life: who to partner with; whether to reproduce; when and how to die; and, beyond the personal, what sorts of creatures we might want to become and in what sort of world. Therefore, naturalism can help maximize personal and collective autonomy.

CHALLENGING AUTHORITY

Science mounts a powerful challenge to the argument from authority in justifying beliefs: nothing is true simply because a religious leader or text claims it to be so, but only because the collective enterprise of fact-finding and theory-building makes it the most plausible conclusion. This immediately frees us from any requirement to believe what has been handed to us—by a church, political party, or other presumptive authority—as a supposedly incontrovertible take on reality. We can, and should, be skeptical of pronouncements about the existence of souls, gods, miracles, contracausal free will, the paranormal, divine laws and purposes, and life after death. As a song in the George Gershwin musical *Porgy and Bess* (1934) memorably puts it, "The things that you're liable, to read in the Bible, it ain't necessarily so." When the supernatural and the laws and injunctions based on nonempirical beliefs about the world are discounted, restrictions on behavior associated with such beliefs are no longer tenable.

SEX, MARRIAGE, BIRTH, AND DEATH

Freedom from nonempirical claims about what is true and morally permissible benefits us by widening the available choices for personal fulfillment. Although some traditional religions still hold that homosexuality is sinful and "unnatural," there is no naturalistic justification for discrimination against gays or transsexuals. Thus, marriage and other rights are extended to those of all sexual orientations, a dramatic expansion of personal liberties for a significant proportion of humanity. By discounting religious prohibitions on contraception and abortion, but taking any secular, evidence-based arguments against them seriously (Clark 2007b, Wenz 1992), we are freer to choose if and when to bring a

RELIGION: BEYOND RELIGION

375

Chapter 20: Naturalism and Well-Being

child into being, to correct or prevent birth defects as technology allows, and to end unwanted pregnancies before a person comes into existence. Because under naturalism there is no divinely ordained requirement for us to suffer in pain or irreversible dementia (such as caused by Alzheimer's disease) until death finally comes, we gain in autonomy at the end of life, more able to choose the time and manner of our passing.

TRANSHUMANISM

Because there is no inviolable soul or immaterial essence that defines a human being, and because as a species we are the result of natural selection, not God's plan, there is no supernaturally derived prohibition against taking control of our biological destiny. We are free to decide, collectively, whether or not to reengineer our bodies, perhaps melding with machines to suit our desires and ambitions (More and Vita-More 2013). Of course, there is equally no requirement that we must undertake any such Promethean transhumanist transformation. However, because the option is there, this too adds to our freedom. Such freedom is perhaps not an unmixed blessing, given that we cannot foresee all of the consequences of embarking on our redesign; however, the naturalist insists that it is better to grapple with tough questions than to take refuge in illusory limitations. Taking responsibility for our own nature is among the most daunting challenges presented by naturalism, and it adds a dimension of interest to life missing from some traditional worldviews.

NATURALISM AND THE PLURALIST STATE

Because naturalism makes no appeal to otherworldly or sectarian justifications for policies concerning what we can or cannot do, it is broadly consistent with the requirement, characteristic of liberal democracies such as the United States, that there be secular, this-world justifications for such policies. This means that naturalism is by nature friendly to pluralist societies that permit holding a wide range of worldviews, unlike some of its theistic and nonempirical rivals in the marketplace of belief. Indeed, the rise of the pluralist state is closely linked to science's challenge to the ideological justifications for authoritarian regimes that prohibit freedom of religion (Dacey 2008). If you value the separation of church and state, diversity of belief, the right to self-government, the due process of secular—not religious or sectarian—law, and equal protection under that law, then you have an ally in naturalism. But of course, the pluralist state, properly conceived, will not make naturalism itself a required belief, because that would limit the freedom of conscience prized by so many naturalists and supernaturalists alike.

ADDICTION AND BEHAVIORAL HEALTH

Human beings are vulnerable creatures, subject to a myriad of diseases and disorders that compromise well-being. Behavioral disorders such as addiction and obesity, and mental illnesses such as depression, schizophrenia, and obsessive compulsive disorder (OCD), are often stigmatized as personal failures of will and self-control. If we suppose choices and actions are not fully determined, then we can (and often will) hold the victims of such disorders as ultimately responsible for their plight, affording them little sympathy or support. We will also tend to ignore the actual genesis of addiction and mental illness, which lies in a person's history, biology and environment; such ignorance slows the pace of discovering effective cures and interventions.

Chapter 20: Naturalism and Well-Being

THE PHYSICAL BASIS OF ADDICTION

On a fully naturalistic view of ourselves, there is a physical, brain- and behavior-based explanation of how someone becomes addicted to alcohol, tobacco, cocaine, heroin, marijuana, or any other psychoactive substance. There is no nonphysical component of the human animal that somehow escapes being at the effect of the conditions in which addiction takes hold, even in making the first voluntary choice to use a drug (Heyman 2009). This means that if you had more or less the same biochemical vulnerability to addiction as the alcoholic next door, and had been in more or less his circumstances (e.g., a family culture of drinking), you too might be obsessed with finding your next beer. This realization necessarily undermines the supposition that addicts could simply have chosen not to become addicted, given their circumstances, and therefore morally deserve their suffering and stigmatization. Because under naturalism they deserve no such thing, the proper and natural response is compassion: there but for chance and causality go you. In turn, compassion opens the motivational door to effective action on behalf of those unlucky enough to have fallen prey to addiction.

PREVENTION AND CURE

The physicalist understanding of behavioral disorders, although by no means complete, holds great promise for their prevention and cure. For example, obesity is now at epidemic levels in the United States and rising in many parts of the world, but research on its environmental and biological determinants is gradually giving us the tools to combat it. What has become clear is that levels of eating and exercise are fully a function of a person's learned behavior, their immediate environment, and any inherited predispositions. Willpower is also a factor here, so long as we do not suppose the will is independent of its own determinants, physical and situational (Baumeister and Tierney 2011). We can strengthen the will to lose weight more effectively once we accept that it has sufficient causes. Therefore, the key to physical fitness is to first understand the mechanics of food- and exercise-related behavior and then modify the home, school, work, and community environments to produce the healthy behavior we want. Human beings can become smart behavioral self-modifiers once it is acknowledged that all behavior, and all motivation, have their causes.

DESIGNING FREEDOM

A reassurance is in order here: the intentional design of environments to produce healthy behavior, whether with respect to fitness, food, drugs, gambling, sex, or other potential causes of disordered behavior, is in no sense a limitation of our freedom so long as the design process is responsive to input from those affected. In the long run, individuals are far freer when they are not burdened (literally) by excess weight or (figuratively) by gambling debts, although some public policies—regulations, taxes, cash incentives, zoning—might intentionally limit or "nudge" their behavioral choices in certain (healthy) directions (Thaler and Sunstein 2008). The smart design of environments, in light of accepting that behavior is fully caused, is simply to assert our real, natural autonomy and self-control (Waller 1998) in service to better public health, a necessary condition for increased freedom and well-being.

THE FATE OF THE PLANET

In the second decade of the twenty-first century, we face looming threats, mostly of our own making, to the stability of global civilization and thus the well-being of billions of human

Chapter 20: Naturalism and Well-Being

beings alive and yet to be born, not to mention the very survival of other species. These include the environmental threats of climate change and resource depletion as well as the threat of ideologically motivated conflict, all of which could result in mass dislocation and destruction (and already have to some extent). How might worldview naturalism contribute to the long-term sustainability of our planet and the peaceful resolution of disputes between worldviews themselves?

PLANETARY RESPONSIBILITY

Concerning the environment, naturalism heightens our concern for planetary well-being because it holds that this world is all we have: there is no supernatural realm that awaits us in the hereafter. Moreover, there is no divinity looking out for us, so the fate of the planet and its life forms depends primarily on us. Thus, humans are charged with the responsibility for securing their own well-being—a daunting but highly motivating challenge, one that can generate global solidarity by giving us a transnational common cause. Because naturalists hew to science, not faith, in deciding what is true, they are also much more likely to accept the empirically based consensus about overpopulation, the scarcity of resources such as food and water, the reality of climate change, and the contribution of humans to global warming. Attuned to the scientific evidence, naturalists are in a good position to appreciate the actual risks to the planet and, with the help of science-based technologies, take effective action to sustain resources and mitigate the effect of rising seas and temperatures.

GENETIC MODIFICATION

In the debate about genetically modified organisms (GMOs) and their potential to contribute to food supplies, naturalists have no reason to think there is anything untoward about the intentional manipulation of genes in designing more productive, pest-resistant crops so long as any environmental risks are researched and minimized. There is no scientific justification for rejecting GMOs as unnatural or intrinsically inferior to conventionally produced hybrids. What matters, again, is the evidence for their safety, productivity, resource efficiency, transportability, nutritive value, and palatability. If these tests are passed, then the potential of GMOs such as golden rice to contribute to human well-being, at a fundamental, necessary level, should be tapped (Golden Rice Project, Silver 2006).

IDEOLOGICAL CONFLICT

Unlike climate change, there is little disagreement about the reality of regional and global conflict driven by ideological—often religious—differences. Humans are by nature tribal creatures, prone to discriminate against out-groups competing for territory and resources, and only relatively recently has the rise of science and the secular state, along with increases in economic security, managed in some cases to overcome sectarian strife and forge a pluralist détente (Greene 2013).

One prescription for reducing sectarianism over the long haul, and thus the prospects for a more peaceful, flourishing global culture, is to promote science and naturalism itself. As seen previously, a naturalistic worldview is maximally inclusive and antitribalistic because it understands human differences as simply variations on a common theme. Because there are no chosen people or tribes that science can discern, the naturalist cannot suppose she merits a special place on the planet. Because there are no gods for the naturalist, there is no religiously driven mandate to marginalize, enslave, or perhaps even kill nonbelievers. Were

MACMILLAN INTERDISCIPLINARY HANDBOOKS

we, impossibly, all to become naturalists, then there would still exist other sources of potential conflict—political, territorial, and economic—but not the sometimes deadly conviction that nonbelievers deserve to suffer for their disbelief.

NONDEMONIZATION

The naturalist can also see that, but for lucky circumstances of birth and upbringing, she herself might subscribe to a faith, a superstition, or a pseudoscientific justification for discrimination. Thus, she is not in a position to demonize antinaturalists as self-created, willful deniers of empirical truths, but understands that they are, at least for the time being, psychologically unable to simply drop their delusions and falsehoods. This understanding constrains the methods by which naturalists will seek to change hearts and minds—not by propaganda or decree, but by education; improving economic security; and establishing secular, inclusive institutions of government and trade that can compete with sectarian regimes for popular support. These means are consistent with human flourishing as the naturalist (and those of many other persuasions) see it—creating a culture that minimizes conflict; maximizes opportunities for growth, autonomy, and self-expression for all individuals; and secures a sustainable world on behalf of generations yet to come, not just ourselves.

MEANING AND PURPOSE

In considering the resources of naturalism for well-being, this chapter has addressed the personal, interpersonal, social, and planetary contexts. There remains, finally, the cosmic perspective, the ultimate context in which humans might flourish. Naturalism is by no means hostile to consideration of the existential questions of life's meaning and purpose—the traditional concerns of religion and spirituality—but it does frame them rather differently.

NATURALISTIC SPIRITUALITY AND RELIGIOUS NATURALISM

It is a commonplace that atheists are at a disadvantage to theists when it comes to the question of life's meaning because on atheists' view there exists no meaning-giver (God or gods), just the purposeless play of physical phenomena. Evolution just happened to give rise to human beings, creatures that often want there to be a guiding goal to life, something that could redeem the suffering we endure and take the sting from the finality of death. Given these desires, it would be good if we could reconcile ourselves to the human condition as seen by science, to accept and perhaps even enjoy the truth that there is no God, no creator, and that the cosmos exists for no apparent reason, with no end in mind.

Naturalism can respond to the existential concerns sparked by science, offering what could be called a naturalistic spirituality (Clark 2002). Although there are no spirits or otherworldly phenomena involved, it counts as a spirituality because it addresses the same questions and emotions as do traditional supernatural religions, questions evoked by confronting the rather strange and startling fact that we exist at all, and only contingently, apparently. Likewise, religious naturalism is not the oxymoron it might seem, but an increasingly available option for those who confront the mystery of existence from a scientific orientation (Goodenough 2000, Murry 2006, Religious Naturalist Association).

RELIGION: BEYOND RELIGION

Chapter 20: Naturalism and Well-Being

NATURALISTIC RE-ENCHANTMENT

As mentioned at the outset, naturalism situates us firmly in the cosmos as fully natural phenomena, albeit of a rather curious sort: motivated, intelligent, self-aware, and sentient agents. In effect, we are nature become cognizant of itself, a bit of minded, person-constituting physicality cooked up by impersonal evolution. Looked at this way, we can appreciate ourselves as rather amazing natural contrivances, privileged to have the capacity for understanding and perspective-taking, although this very capacity burdens us with difficult existential questions. Just as we can marvel at the sheer scale of the cosmos depicted by science, we can marvel at what mere atoms and molecules, left to their own devices over billions of years, have produced in us. This perspective helps to re-enchant the physical world while remaining true to science: atoms and molecules are not so "mere" after all (Goodenough 2000, Raymo 1998).

The epic story of the universe, and our place in it, is perhaps best told in the classic PBS television series "Cosmos," hosted by Carl Sagan and reprised by Neil deGrasse Tyson for the Fox Network. The art film *The Tree of Life* (2011) includes an extended, visually spectacular sequence that captures the grand sweep of cosmic and terrestrial evolution.

EXISTENTIAL ASTONISHMENT

We of course did not ask for any of this—we simply find ourselves present in the cosmos, which according to naturalism exists precisely for no discernible reason. Therefore, we exist, ultimately, for no discernible reason. But strangely enough, the naturalistic subtraction of ultimate meaning and purpose can generate a genuinely spiritual response to the human condition. Although it takes a little getting used to, appreciating the sheer unguided facticity of the cosmos can be the gateway to existential wonder and amazement. It is not as if existence as a whole is meaningless (i.e., to project our parochial demand for meaning onto it, and find it rebuffed); rather, it altogether escapes the meaningful-meaningless distinction—it just is. Seeing that we cannot expect nature to have a meaning, we are left, finally, existentially astonished—to be alive and aware, participants in a grand mystery that necessarily transcends any ascription of purpose (Clark 2002, Comte-Sponville 2007).

LOCAL MEANING

But as meaning-seeking creatures we can't live day-to-day on a diet of existential astonishment. Naturalists, like everyone else, are bequeathed the normal complement of human needs, which predominate most of the time in driving behavior. And it is the satisfaction of these needs, including needs for community, exploration, mastery, and understanding, that actually solves the problem of local (as opposed to ultimate) meaning. We do not, as a matter of fact, need an ultimate purpose to make life worth living, so long as we have opportunities to flourish in all (or at least many) of the dimensions of being human. Arguably, it is the very diversity of our desires, of possible projects, and their possible—not certain—fulfillment, that makes life such an interesting, if sometimes frustrating, prospect.

EXISTENTIAL FREEDOM AND CONTROL

Because it challenges any supernaturally or ideologically derived mandate for how we must live, naturalism maximizes our freedom to pursue these needs and projects, perhaps even to the point of modifying our motives themselves (Stanovich 2004). Are there some desires we would be better off not having? Naturalists can raise this question whereas many supernaturalists are barred from even contemplating such a possibility given scriptural

380   MACMILLAN INTERDISCIPLINARY HANDBOOKS

Chapter 20: Naturalism and Well-Being

constraints. Not that everything is permitted, of course, because there is nearly universal agreement on moral maxims derived from the golden rule, a rule that naturalists also accept. However, within these ethical constraints, naturalism offers a latitude of action unavailable to those bound by traditional religious or ideological worldviews (Kitcher 2014). As citizens of an unsupervised cosmos, the range of exploration open to us is limited only by our foresight and technological prowess.

NATURALIST COMMUNITY

Just as adherents of traditional religions form communities of belief within which to find companionship and express their philosophy of life, so too can naturalists. Secular alternatives to church, such as Sunday Assembly and Ethical Culture (New York Society for Ethical Culture), offer rituals, observances, inspirational talks and music, all without any reference to the supernatural. Of course, not everyone wants or needs this sort of community, but for those who do there are increasing opportunities to join with like-minded naturalists (humanist, free-thought, and atheist groups are usually friendly to naturalism) to explore and celebrate what it means to be a citizen of the cosmos. For those who have lost their faith and their religious network, naturalist groups and congregations can help replace the personal connections so important to human well-being (De Botton 2013).

FACING DEATH

When facing the personal extinction of death, perhaps the toughest existential challenge, naturalists cannot look forward to a life everlasting, but they can be reassured that they do not face the onset of eternal nothingness or blackness either. Consciousness cannot witness its own extinction, so as the philosopher Epicurus observed long ago, nonexistence cannot be a subjective fact. In which case, what should one anticipate at death? The particular individual ends, but it is fair to say that experience will not, given that other sentient beings exist and will come into being. Therefore, one should, perhaps, anticipate the continuation of experience, just not in the context of being the person that dies. Naturalists can understand death as the ultimate adventure in the transformation of consciousness: the radical refreshment of subjectivity (Clark 1994). As in other aspects of naturalistic spirituality mentioned previously, naturalism trades security, in this case the unattainable security of personal immortality, for open-ended excitement—of being a transitory participant in, and witness to, the natural order (Watts 1968).

Summary

This chapter has argued that worldview naturalism has considerable resources to offer in the quest for human flourishing. But of course, the vision of flourishing articulated here is to some extent influenced by naturalism itself and its central commitments. Most central is the naturalist's commitment to cognitive responsibility and openness, to being guided by observational evidence when deciding what is true—empiricism. Science is the most formal expression of empiricism, but one need not be a scientist to be a naturalist, only adhere to the proposition that all factual claims require sufficient evidence. Naturalists aspire more to truth than security.

Chapter 20: Naturalism and Well-Being

Adherence to empiricism, applied consistently, leads to the denial of the supernatural, leaving only the natural world as our home. This is the central factual claim of naturalism. As natural creatures, we discover ourselves fully within the causal nexus of natural laws described by science at the physical, chemical, biological, and psychological levels. While seeing our complete connection to nature challenges some long-standing notions of human agency, it offers us increased control over our circumstances while providing a basis for compassion, self-acceptance, equanimity, and resilience. Naturalism also challenges claims that certain classes of human beings deserve to flourish more than others; therefore, it supports the goal of universal well-being.

The connection, compassion, and control offered by naturalism are directly applicable to those domains—material, psychological, social, and existential—that encompass the multiplicity of human needs driving the quest for a fulfilled life. Naturalism is by no means the only worldview that can contribute to the quest, but its firm commitment to science as a guide to reality distinguishes it from traditional religions and nonempirical philosophies and ideologies. Although it cannot satisfy desires for personal immortality, ultimate purpose, or a benign divinity, naturalism can serve us well as we seek to flourish in the lives given us by nature here in the cosmos.

Bibliography

Aronson, Ronald. *Living without God: New Directions for Atheists, Agnostics, Secularists, and the Undecided.* Berkeley, CA: Counterpoint, 2008.

Baumeister, Roy F., and John Tierney. *Willpower: Rediscovering the Greatest Human Strength.* New York: Penguin, 2011.

Carney, Dana R., John T. Jost, Samuel D. Gosling, et al. "The Secret Lives of Liberals and Conservatives: Personality Profiles, Interaction Styles, and the Things They Leave Behind." *Political Psychology* 29, no. 6 (2008): 807–840.

Carrier, Richard. *Sense and Goodness without God: A Defense of Metaphysical Naturalism.* Bloomington, IN: AuthorHouse, 2005.

Clark, Thomas W. "Crime and Causality: Do Killers Deserve to Die?" *Free Inquiry* 25, no. 2 (2005). http://www.naturalism.org.

Clark, Thomas W. "Death, Nothingness and Subjectivity." *The Humanist* 54, no. 6 (1994): 15–20. Reprinted in *The Experience of Philosophy*, 6th ed., edited by Daniel Kolak and Ray Martin. Oxford: Oxford University Press, 2005. http://www.naturalism.org.

Clark, Thomas W. *Encountering Naturalism: A Worldview and Its Uses.* Somerville, MA: Center for Naturalism, 2007a.

Clark, Thomas W. "Facing Facts: Policy Implications of the Humanist Commitment to Science." In *Toward a New Political Humanism*, edited by Barry F. Seidman and Neil J. Murphy, 343–354. Amherst, NY: Prometheus Books, 2004. http://www.naturalism.org.

Clark, Thomas W. "Faith in Hiding: Are There Secular Grounds for Banning Abortion?" *The Humanist*, July–August, 2007b. http://www.naturalism.org.

Clark, Thomas W. "Holding Mechanisms Responsible." *Medical Ethics* 13, no. 3 (2006): 10–11. http://www.naturalism.org.

Clark, Thomas W. "Spirituality without Faith." *The Humanist* 62, no. 1 (2002). http://www.naturalism.org.

Clifford, William K. "The Ethics of Belief." *Contemporary Review*, 1877. Reprinted in William K. Clifford, *Lectures and Essays*, edited by Leslie Stephen and Frederick Pollock. London: Macmillan, 1886. http://people.brandeis.edu/~teuber/Clifford_ethics.pdf.

Comte-Sponville, Andre. *The Little Book of Atheist Spirituality.* New York: Penguin, 2007.

Coyne, Jerry. *Faith vs. Fact: Why Science and Religion are Incompatible.* New York, Viking, 2015.

Crick, Francis. *The Astonishing Hypothesis: The Scientific Search for the Soul.* New York: Simon and Schuster, 1994.

Dacey, Austin. *The Secular Conscience: Why Belief Belongs in Public Life.* Amherst, NY: Prometheus Books, 2008.

De Botton, Alain. *Religion for Atheists: A Non-Believer's Guide to the Uses of Religion.* New York: Vintage, 2013.

de Waal, Franz. *The Bonobo and the Atheist: In Search of Humanism Among the Primates*. New York: Norton, 2013.

Emerson, Ralph Waldo. *Nature*. Boston: James Munroe and Company, 1836. http://www.emersoncentral.com/nature .htm.

Flanagan, Owen. *The Problem of the Soul: Two Visions of the Mind and How to Reconcile Them*. New York: Basic Books, 2002.

Flanagan, Owen. *The Really Hard Problem: Meaning in a Material World*. Cambridge, MA: MIT Press, 2007.

Gilligan, James. *Preventing Violence*. New York: Thames & Hudson, 2001.

Goldberg, L. R. "The Development of Markers for the Big-Five Factor Structure." *Psychological Assessment* 4 (1992): 26–42.

Goodenough, Ursula. *The Sacred Depths of Nature*. New York: Oxford University Press, 2000.

Greene, Joshua. *Moral Tribes: Emotion, Reason, and the Gap Between Us and Them*. New York: Penguin Press, 2013.

Heyman, Gene M. *Addiction: A Disorder of Choice*. Cambridge, MA: Harvard University Press, 2009.

Kitcher, Philip. *Life After Faith: The Case for Secular Humanism*. New Haven, CT: Yale University Press, 2014.

Maslow, Abraham H. "A Theory of Human Motivation." *Psychological Review* 50, no. 4 (1943): 370–396.

McCullough, Michael. *Beyond Revenge: The Evolution of the Forgiveness Instinct*. Hoboken, NJ: Wiley, 2008.

Metzinger, Thomas. *The Ego Tunnel: The Science of Mind and the Myth of the Self*. New York: Basic Books, 2010.

Mooney, Chris. *The Republican Brain: The Science of Why They Deny Science and Reality*. Hoboken, NJ: Wiley, 2012.

More, Max, and Natasha Vita-More, eds. *The Transhumanist Reader: Classical and Contemporary Essays on the Science, Technology and Philosophy of the Human Future*. Oxford: Wiley-Blackwell, 2013.

Moreland, J. P. *The Recalcitrant Imago Dei: Human Persons and the Failure of Naturalism*. London: SCM Press, 2009.

Murry, William R. *Reason and Reverence: Religious Humanism for the 21st Century*. Cambridge MA: Skinner House, 2006.

Oerton, Richard T. *The Nonsense of Free Will: Facing Up to a False Belief*. Leicestershire, UK: Matador, 2012.

Pew Research Center. "Public Praises Science; Scientists Fault Public, Media." 2009. http://www.people-press.org /2009/07/09/public-praises-science-scientists-fault-public -media/.

Pinker, Steven. "The Moral Instinct." *The New York Times Magazine*, January 13, 2008. http://www.nytimes.com /2008/01/13/magazine/13Psychology-t.html.

Raymo, Chet. *Skeptics and True Believers: The Exhilarating Connection between Science and Religion*. New York: Walker and Company, 1998.

Richards, Janet R. *Human Nature after Darwin: A Philosophical Introduction*. London: Routledge, 2000.

Ritchie, Jack. *Understanding Naturalism*. Stocksfield, UK: Acumen, 2008.

Shermer, Michael. *The Moral Arc: How Science and Reason Lead Humanity toward Truth, Justice, and Freedom*. New York: Henry Holt, 2015.

Shermer, Michael. *Why People Believe Weird Things*. New York: Henry Holt, 1997.

Silver, Lee M. *Challenging Nature: The Clash of Science and Spirituality at the New Frontiers of Life*. New York: Ecco, 2006.

Spinoza, Baruch. *Ethics*. New York: Penguin, 1996. First published 1677.

Stanovich, Keith. *The Robot's Rebellion: Finding Meaning in the Age of Darwin*. Chicago: University of Chicago Press, 2004.

Thaler, Richard H., and Cass R. Sunstein. *Nudge: Improving Decisions about Health, Wealth, and Happiness*. New Haven, CT: Yale University Press, 2008.

Thoreau, Henry David. *Walden; or, Life in the Woods*. Boston: Tichnor and Fields, 1854.

Waller, Bruce N. *Against Moral Responsibility*. Cambridge, MA: MIT Press, 2011.

Waller, Bruce N. *The Natural Selection of Autonomy*. Albany: SUNY Press, 1998.

Watts, Alan. *The Wisdom of Insecurity: A Message for an Age of Anxiety*. New York: Vintage Books, 1968.

Wegner, Daniel. *The Illusion of Conscious Will*. Cambridge, MA: MIT Press, 2002.

Wenz, Peter. *Abortion Rights as Religious Freedom*. Philadelphia: Temple University Press, 1992.

WEBSITES

deGrasse Tyson, Neil. "Cosmos: A Spacetime Odyssey." http://www.haydenplanetarium.org/tyson/.

Golden Rice Project. http://www.goldenrice.org/. The Golden Rice Project won the 2015 Patents for Humanity Award, awarded by the White House Office of Science and Technology Policy and the US Patent and Trademark Office.

Chapter 20: Naturalism and Well-Being

Naturalism.Org. http://www.naturalism.org. A source for articles, reviews, and other materials related to worldview naturalism.

New York Society for Ethical Culture. http://www.nysec.org/.

Religious Naturalist Association. http://religious-naturalist -association.org/.

Sunday Assembly. https://sundayassembly.com/.

FILMS

A Clockwork Orange. Dir. Stanley Kubrick. 1971. A dystopian crime drama based on Anthony Burgess's novel, which portrays the downsides of therapeutic cures for wrongdoers.

Contact. Dir. Robert Zemeckis. 1997. Adaptation of Carl Sagan's science fiction novel about encountering an alien intelligence.

Ex Machina. Dir. Alex Garland. 2015. A science fiction drama exploring the possibility, and possible dangers, of creating artificial intelligence, consciousness, and personhood.

Her. Dir. Spike Jonze. 2013. A story set in the near future about the perils of falling in love with a smart and rapidly evolving computer operating system.

Inherit the Wind. Dir. Stanley Kramer. 1960. A film adaptation of the play concerning the 1925 Scopes "Monkey Trial" on teaching evolution in Tennessee.

The Matrix (trilogy). Dir. Lana and Andrew Wachowski. 1999–2003. Science fiction series involving themes of machine intelligence, consciousness, virtual reality, fate, and free will.

Porgy and Bess. Dir. Otto Preminger and Rouben Mamoulian. 1959. Musical based on the opera by George Gershwin (score), Ira Gershwin and Dubose Heyward (libretto), 1935. An inspiring and sometimes irreverent hard-luck love story plays out in Charleston, South Carolina.

The Tree of Life. Dir. Terrence Malick. 2011. Depicts a boy's poignant coming of age in Texas, told against a backdrop of cosmic and terrestrial evolution.

Glossary

A

A First Cause. Also known as the cosmological argument, states that because everything that exists has a cause, the universe must have had a cause: God. Does not say, however, what caused God.

Absolute Anarchism. The claim that political authority always results in a violation of autonomy and therefore is wrong.

Absolute Atheism. The claim that religion is always irrational and pernicious and ought to be opposed.

Absolute Pacifism. The refusal to admit that violence can ever be justified, usually because of fundamental moral principles.

Accommodationism. The constitutional doctrine that the US Supreme Court ought to allow for state and religious organizations to support one another rather than maintain a strict wall of separation between them.

Advanced Secularity. Societies in which a majority of individuals are secular and in which religion has a weak, if any, role in public discourse.

Age Cohort. A similarly aged generational group as defined in demographics, statistics, and other social scientific research.

Aggregate- or Macro-Level Analysis. A way of thinking about social phenomena as a comparison of different social systems (states or societies).

Agnostic. A person who believes that it is impossible to attain definitive knowledge of something; in religion, it often implies the belief that it is impossible to know whether there is a god or not.

Agnosticism. The philosophical conviction that one cannot know if there is or is not a God.

Ahimsa. A Sanskrit term, relevant in Hinduism, Jainism, and Buddhism, referring to a principle of nonviolence or reverence for life.

Anarchism. Opposition to structures of political authority, including denial of the legitimacy of nation-states.

Anarcho-Atheism. Rejection of both political power and religious power as unjustified forms of authority and domination.

Anticlerical. Opposed to clergy (religious leaders such as priests, ministers, etc.), usually on the basis of assumed abuse of power, perceived malfeasance, or alleged undue privilege.

Anticlericalism. Movements or ideologies opposed to the power, influence, or abuse of the clergy (religious leaders).

Anti-ecclesiastical. Opposed to church structures—such as church governance boards, priestly councils, authoritative clerical bodies—or religious organizations.

Antiwarism. A form of pacifism that is focused primarily on the claim that war is immoral.

Apatheists. Those who have no opinion about God's existence and are neither religious nor outspoken atheists, but rather are indifferent to or uninterested in religion.

Apocalypse. Any revelation, prophecy, or vision of the end of the world or current world order.

Apostasy. The rejection of one's previously held religious beliefs.

Apostate. A person who has rejected or abandoned his or her religious faith, affiliation, or beliefs. There are countless reasons and/or occurrences which impel people to reject their religion, but the most common one is a simple loss of faith: the claims of religion no longer seem rational.

GLOSSARY

Atheism. The philosophical conviction that there is no God.

Atheist. A person who does not believe in the existence of God or gods.

Atheologians. Philosophers who argue against the existence of God and put forth and defend various critiques of theism.

Atheology. Explores varieties of disbelief in religions, explains how atheists justify and encourage non-religious views, and defends their secular engagement with religion and religious aspects of society.

Attitude. A psychological evaluation held by an individual of a person, object, or idea.

Axiology. The philosophical study of the nature of values and value judgments. Axiology is also used as a collective term for ethics and aesthetics—philosophical fields that depend crucially on notions of worth, or the foundation for these fields—and is thus similar to value theory and meta-ethics.

B

Behavior. A generic term for any observable or measurable action of an organism.

Belief Abstraction. Mental strategy of forming and preserving feelings or convictions by extracting common patterns out of frequent experiences.

Belief Affirmation. Mental strategy of preserving feelings or convictions by strengthening endorsement of other existing mental frameworks.

Belief Assimilation. Mental strategy of preserving feelings or convictions by incorporating any new knowledge into preexisting knowledge structures.

Belief Replacement Hypothesis. An idea or theory predicting that one set of preexisting belief or beliefs can be replaced by a psychologically satisfying equivalent.

Belief System. A set of mutually supportive feelings or convictions. *See also* Worldviews.

Blasphemy. Expressing disrespect, contempt, or defiance toward God or sacred scriptures or sacred things.

C

Civic Atheology. The philosophical position that greater justice and social harmony is achieved by reducing God-belief in society and insulating politics from religious control.

Civic Republicans. Among the founding generation of the United States, those who believed that political life depended on virtue and that religion was a useful way to make (or keep) people virtuous; it was not necessarily the truth of religion that mattered but rather its value in directing people toward the public good.

Civic Theology. The religious position that a god ensures that society conforms to civil order, and everyone in society should be properly religious.

Civil Rights. Authority and privileges possessed by individuals as citizens whom good government must respect and protect.

Cognitive Biases. Common limitations to observation, judgment, and inference built into human cognitive abilities that evolutionarily survived because of limited utility but that fail to be fully rational by logical standards.

Cognitive Psychology. The study of the mind that examines mental and thought processes, such as attention, perception, learning, memory, and judgment.

Comparative Analysis. A type of research design that looks at similarities and differences across and within units (especially countries) at a single point in time.

Confessional Parties. Political groups centrally organized around religious identity for the purpose of advocating for their religious values and/or members within a national context.

Contingent Anarchism. Admits that political states could be justifiable in theory, but concludes that contemporary states fail to live up to the standards of the best political theory.

Contingent Pacifism. Rejects violence and war because of unforeseen circumstances of the world, such as weapons of mass destruction, while admitting that some wars, in theory, could be justified.

Correlational Method. In theology, identified with Paul Tillich's (1886–1965) attempt to correlate the problems of existence with the answers offered by Christianity.

Cosmopolitanism. The idea that all people can and should be united by common ethical principles that transcend culture, politics, and religion.

386   MACMILLAN INTERDISCIPLINARY HANDBOOKS

Creationism. The belief that God made the world and all living things, including humans, through divine magic; rejects the evidence supporting Darwinian evolution.

Cross-Sectional (Study). A family of research methods that examines individuals of varying ages at a single point in time.

Cultural Defense. The mechanisms employed to strengthen the sense of community when a group of people is threatened or their religious identity is challenged.

Cultural Psychology. The study of the mind that examines the impact of customs, tradition, and social practices on individual thought and action.

Cultural Religion. Identification with a religion and participation in its traditions and rituals without holding supernatural beliefs.

D

Death of God. A theological movement, predominantly of Protestant origins during the 1950s and 1960s, arguing that the religious life in modern times can benefit from ceasing to be concerned about God's existence and focusing on divine immanence within religious communities.

Deism. The belief, popular among some elites at the American founding, that God is no longer active in the world and that the Bible is not evidence of his revelation; belief that reason and nature alone are sufficient to demonstrate the existence of God.

Deontology. The ethical theory prioritizing moral duties and their authoritative obligations despite self-interest, tradition, interpersonal relations, future consequences, and other matters.

Dependent Origination. The thesis in Buddhism that all phenomena exist in relation to one another; there are no causally independent, self-created events or objects.

Dependent Variable. The outcome or effect of a phenomenon (cause). A change in a variable that is caused by a change in a preceding variable. For example, the religious affiliation of parents tends to determine the religious affiliation of their children. In such a dynamic, the children's religious affiliation is the dependent variable.

Determinism. The position that—given current conditions and natural laws—there is a single possible next state of affairs.

Developmental Psychology. The study of the mind that examines changes in thought and action that occur across an individual's life span.

Discontented Unbeliever (Hypothesis). The prediction that lack of acceptance of something as true is a manifestation or expression of a wider psychological maladjustment.

Dogmatism. The arrogant, stubborn assertion of opinion or belief, often in the face of contrary evidence.

Dualism. The idea that reality contains two sorts of substances, physical versus nonphysical, or that reality is split between two realms or forces, such as the natural versus the supernatural, true versus false, light versus dark, or spirit versus body.

Dynamic (Beliefs). A description of the quality of something that is characterized by continuous change, activity, or progress.

E

Efficacy. A description of something that has the power or capacity to produce a desired effect.

Empirical. In scientific methodology, the approach to testing theories through the collection of data accumulated through observation and experience.

Empiricism. The position that all knowledge comes from sensory experience and that observational evidence is the best basis for factual claims.

Epistemology. The branch of philosophy concerned with what we can know.

Established Church. A religion endorsed and sponsored by a particular state.

Establishment Clause. The portion of the First Amendment that forbids the federal government from instituting or supporting religion.

Ethics. The study of human morality, values, and virtues, and the creation of moral theories and the analysis of their justifications; the systematic construction and defense of what is right and what is wrong.

Ethnocentrism. A perspective that privileges the views, values, and experiences of a particular race or group of people while judging others as inferior or unnatural; the explicit or unconscious belief that one's own race or group of people is superior; the tendency to view one's

GLOSSARY

own race or group of people as the comparison standard for judgment.

Evangelicalism. A worldwide Protestant movement within Christianity that emphasizes the supremacy of the Gospels and the need of acceptance of Jesus Christ as one's personal savior for salvation.

Event Sampling Methodology (ESM). A family of research tools and procedures that assesses individual responses during a researcher-determined time period (or sampling frame). ESM typically features a list of all those within a population who can be questioned, observed, or studied, and may include individuals, households or institutions.

Evil. The normative category for an event or a deed that is both morally unjustifiable (never indifferent or good) and inexcusable (anything good that might result cannot minimize or legitimate the original act).

Evolutionary Psychology. The study of cognition and behavior through the categories of evolutionary biology.

Experimental Existential Psychology. The study of the mind that tests the impact of human confrontation with abstract questions regarding the nature of their reality and/or their state of being.

Experimental Methods. A family of research tools and procedures that examines the causal impact of researcher-manipulated variables on other outcome measures.

Explicit (Cognition). Any psychological processes that occur in awareness or consciousness. Refers to unconscious influences such as knowledge, perception, or memory, that influence a person's behavior, even though that person has no conscious awareness whatsoever of those influences.

F

Faith. In religious contexts, a devotion to the sacred with trusting confidence that one's fidelity can culminate in hoped-for results; belief in something without sufficient evidence for that belief.

Feminist Theory. Seeks to critique patriarchy and investigate the nature of women's inequality and presents philosophical and speculative analyses to mitigate oppression.

Fluid Compensation (Beliefs). A description of mental coping processes that attempt to preserve or maintain the integrity of existing mental representations through processes of assimilation, accommodation, affirmation, abstraction, or assembly of information.

Free Exercise Clause. The portion of the First Amendment that prohibits the federal government from limiting or denying people's right to openly practice their religion.

Free Will. Acting in accordance with one's own character, motives, and intentions; not being fully determined in one's actions, such that one could have acted otherwise in an actual situation.

Freethinker. A person who rejects authority and dogma, especially in religious thinking, in favor of rational inquiry and speculation.

Freethought. An intellectual rebellion, often within a movement of thought and literature, against a traditional authority (usually religious or political), challenging that authority's control over orthodoxy and its right to dominate society.

Fundamentalism. A conservative religious movement emphasizing intense commitment to literally interpreted religious principles held to be foundational to the religious tradition.

G

God. According to various world religions, such as Judaism and Christianity, this is a magical, invisible, incorporeal, all-powerful, all-knowing, all-benevolent deity who created everything and is the source of all time, space, life, and morality.

H

Hell. A fiery realm where souls are condemned to suffering for eternity for various transgressions deemed unforgiveable by a given religion's deity.

Heterogeneous. Something that consists of dissimilar elements or parts.

Human Dignity. The status of individuals guaranteeing that they must receive full moral and legal regard and respect, and protection from degradation and humiliation.

Human Rights. Those rights to specifiable conditions (such as life or liberty) or possessions (such as property or education), held by all individuals, obligating all others to aid in their promotion, or at least to avoid their obstruction.

Humanism. A life philosophy that rejects all supernatural claims and rests instead on reason and empirical evidence.

Humanist. A person who primarily defines his or her beliefs in terms of concern for the interests and welfare of people; people who place their hopes for the betterment of the world in humanity, rather than a deity.

I

Ideology. A set of doctrines or beliefs that are shared by the members of a social group or that form the basis of a political, religious, national, or economic vision.

Impiety. A lack of reverence or respect for God or religious authorities.

Implicit (Cognition). Any psychological processes that occur outside of awareness or consciousness.

Incorporation. The constitutional doctrine by which the US Supreme Court began selectively applying particular provisions in the Bill of Rights to the states via the Due Process Clause of the Fourteenth Amendment; before incorporation, provisions in the Bill of Rights applied only to the federal government.

Independent Variable. The cause or explanation of a phenomenon (outcome). A variable that, when it changes, produces a change in a related variable. For example, the religious affiliation of parents tends to determine the religious affiliation of their children. In such a dynamic, the parent's religious affiliation is the independent variable.

Individual or Micro-Level Analysis. A way of thinking about social phenomena as a comparison of distinct differences; studies that use survey data based on population samples are an example of this type of analysis.

Individualism. A value system or beliefs emphasizing the importance of personal choice and freedoms (over obligation to others).

L

Laïcité. A French form of secularism that insists on the absence of religion in government affairs and the absence of government in religious affairs.

Lived Secularity. The experiences, values, attitudes, beliefs, and behaviors of nonreligious individuals.

Longitudinal Analysis. A type of research design that monitors changes within units (e.g., individuals, groups, or countries) over a period of time.

Longitudinal Methods. A family of research designs that assesses the same individuals over an extended period of time.

M

Magical Thinking. Accepting accounts of events that involve the unnatural intervention of other-worldly spirits or powers to explain events deemed impossible by common sense or science.

Materialism. A philosophical conviction that the world consists only of physical matter and that no spiritual substances or beings exist.

Meaning Maintenance. The psychological process of preserving preexisting understandings of the human condition.

Meaning Making. The psychological process of extracting personal significance or understanding of the human condition.

Mental (Process). A generic term for any internal psychological action or series of actions that is indirectly inferred from behavior.

Metaperception. The general psychological process of perceiving another person's way of thinking or seeing things.

Moral Atheology. Critiques of religious institutions, practices, and personal commitments toward God on the basis of normative values that all humanity should respect, such as human dignity and human rights.

Moral Theology. The religious position that a god is necessary to ensure a natural and human orientation toward goodness, and that proper religiosity is essential to ethical conduct.

Morality. Principles and values concerning the distinction between right and wrong, good and bad, or just and unjust.

Motivation. Referring to psychological goals or objectives. The reasons for acting a particular way or the desire and willingness to pursue a given course of action.

GLOSSARY

Multidimensional. A measurement assumption implying that a psychological variable or concept can be assessed on multiple properties or quantitative aspects.

Mutual Constitution (Model). Cultural psychological theory predicting that individuals and their cultures each influence one another in a cyclical manner.

N

Natural Laws. Causal regularities discovered by science that enable prediction and control of events.

Natural Theology. A model of God that argues for God's existence on the grounds of reason and the order of the natural world.

Naturalism. The idea that things can be explained and understood without appeal to supernatural or spiritual beings; the science-based hypothesis that the world not made or caused by people exhausts reality and that nothing beyond that reality exists.

Neuroscience. The study of the impact of brain and nervous system functioning on human thought and action.

New Atheism. A social and political movement begun in the 2000s publicly critiquing belief in God or gods and advocating for the replacement of religion with disbelief in God or gods and secular traditions.

Nihilism. Belief in nothing; the rejection of all moral beliefs and principles.

No-Atheists-in-Foxholes (Hypothesis). The prediction that in situations of extreme stress, typified by the wartime bunker or foxhole, people abandon disbelief and embrace theism.

Nones. People who do not identify with a religious tradition.

Nonpreferentialism. The constitutional doctrine that as long as a state action does not favor one religion over another (or over nonreligion), then the action may be constitutional. Advanced by Justice William Rehnquist (1924–2005), it became a theoretical alternative to the US Supreme Court's separationist approach.

Nonreligion. Any beliefs or belief systems that are defined by their difference to organized beliefs in God or gods.

Nonresistance. A radical form of pacifism that emphasizes turning the other cheek and avoiding resistance to wrongdoing.

Nonviolentism. The idea that only means without physical or destructive force are justifiable and that physical or destructive force is always wrong.

Numinal Theology. The religious position that something divine is needed to fully explain experiences of the holy or the spiritual, which is radically unlike ordinary perception and awareness (like the mystical) while conveying no information (unlike revelation).

O

Objective Religiosity. Participation, membership, or identification with an organized group that holds a shared set of beliefs in God or gods.

Ontology. A branch of philosophy concerned with the fundamental nature of being itself, including questions of "what is a thing?" and "what is existence?"

Operational Definition. The scientific approach to defining a concept by its measurable or observable qualities.

Organizational or Meso-Level Analysis. The study and comparison of groups formed for particular purposes that exist above the individual and the family, but below the state and its institutions—for example, studies of the internal structure and workings of religious groups that change over time to adapt to modern society.

Original Intent. The practice of trying to judge constitutionality based on what one believes the American founders meant while writing the US Constitution.

Overdetermined. Quality describing any outcome that occurs when multiple causes decide or dictate a single-observed effect.

P

Pacifism. The commitment to peace and nonviolence; opposition to war, militarism, and violence.

Paranormal. Not to be identified with the supernatural, paranormal is a term that was developed by English and French intellectuals at the end of the nineteenth century to refer to extraordinary events that still lie beyond our present scientific understandings but presumably can eventually be understood.

Pedagogical Atheology. Instruction for children and young adults explaining why faith, religion, and quasi-religious beliefs should be regarded with skepticism.

Personality Psychology. The study of the mind that examines individual or internal patterns in thought and action.

Phenomenology. A methodology focusing on the observation of experience as it presents itself to the experiencer.

Philosophical Anarchism. The claim that, as a matter of theory, states are not fully legitimate.

Physicalism. An interpretation that advances the idea that there exist only mathematical patterns as tracked and predicted by physics.

Pluralism. Tolerance or recognition of a variety of beliefs, worldviews, and lifestyles.

Political Secularism. The most prominent form of secularism that advocates for the separation of church and state.

Practical Atheology. Offers persuasive discussions about atheism by emphasizing logic, science, moral and civic norms, and secular wisdom.

Praxiology. The philosophical study of human ethics.

Priming. The psychological research approach of presenting a mental concept in an initial setting that prepares or predisposes the use of that concept in a subsequent setting.

Promethean. Daring to challenge conventional views and practices; revolutionary.

Psychological Dimension. A measurement assumption of the existence of an underlying quantitative continuum in a trait or attribute of the mind.

Psychometrics. The psychological study and practice of mental measurement techniques.

Puritans. Members of a group of English Protestants during the sixteenth and seventeenth centuries who sought to regulate and control Christian behavior within society.

R

Rationalism. A philosophical enterprise that seeks to transform intellectual uncertainty into the foundations for obtaining certainty; the belief that opinions and actions should be based on reason and empirical knowledge rather than faith or emotion.

Rationalist Atheology. Applies logical thinking based on fact and reason to skeptically reject arguments for supernatural and transcendent deities, leaving unbelief as the more reasonable alternative.

Reactive Attitudes. Emotion-laden responses triggered by how we perceive others, such as (negatively) resentment, anger, and contempt, and (positively) gratitude, admiration, and forgiveness.

Religion. Any life orientation through a commitment to an ultimate concern via symbol, language, and behavior that addresses the human desire for meaning and grapples with the perennial questions of human existence: Who are we? What are we? Where are we? Why are we?

Religiosity. The individual experience of faith, including practice, belief, and identity.

Religious Criticism. The shaming of people who hold shared beliefs in God or gods and institutions organized around those beliefs for deviating from, or violating, significant moral norms (such as rights) or important social rules (such as laws).

Religious Ethics. Accounts for morality and our moral responsibilities by appealing to divine matters, such as a God's divine providence, plans, wishes, or commands.

Religious Nones. A collective term for different types of nonbelievers unaffiliated with any particular religion (e.g., atheists, agnostics, unaffiliated), including those who, when asked what their religion is, state "none."

Retribution. Inflicting punishment or suffering on the grounds that it is deserved, independent of any benefit or consequence that might result.

S

Science. The systematic study of the structure and behavior of the physical and natural world through observation and experiment.

Scientific Atheology. Applies systematic methods and knowledge to skeptically reject arguments for supernatural and transcendent deities, leaving unbelief as the more reasonable alternative. *See also* Science.

Scientific Evidence. Observations of things and events acquired through systematic methods that justify the

GLOSSARY

inclusion of those observed matters in a natural worldview. Some kinds of evidence, formulated as propositional statements or measurements, can empirically test hypotheses trying to predict experimental outcomes. *See also* Science.

Secular. Nonreligious; committed to a nonspiritual, humanistic, or naturalistic worldview; someone who does not hold supernatural beliefs, does not engage in religious rituals, and is not affiliated with a religious group.

Secular Ethics. Accounts for morality and our moral responsibilities by grounding them in worldly matters, such as humanity's evolution into highly sociable people or humanity's long-term welfare.

Secular Humanism. An optimistic belief in the potential of humans to solve problems and make the world a better, safer, and more just place by championing a set of affirmative values, ideas, and ideals, such as the separation of church and state, tolerance, reason, science, and human rights.

Secular Studies. The study of nonreligious people, groups, thought, and cultural expressions, past and present.

Secularism. Ideologies and movements that are either explicitly nonreligious or antireligious or that seek to limit religion's influence in society and disabuse people of their religious faith; a normative, ideological position that espouses the separation of government and religion or advocates for government neutrality concerning religion.

Secularity. The absence of religious beliefs, religious practices, or religious influence in the public space.

Secularization. A term describing the historical process by which supernatural beliefs decline, participation in religious activities drops, and religion plays a diminishing role in institutions exerting power and authority.

Self-Labeling. The technique of asking individuals to define or describe their psychological qualities.

Semiotics. The study of symbols and their interpretation.

Skepticism. Refrain from credulity or conviction when insufficient reasons justify belief; active doubt.

Social Cognition. The subfield of psychology focusing on how people think about and react to their environment and how it is influenced by others.

Social Ethics. Examines the conventional rules, laws, and moral norms of a society to strengthen their positive influence on the lives of all members; goals can include the expansion of freedoms, the devotion to virtues, and the delivery of justice.

Social Justice. The goal of liberation theology in which justice is conceived of in terms of the equitable distribution of wealth, opportunities, and privileges within a society.

Social Psychology. The study of the mind that examines the influence of groups and other environmental factors on individual thought and action.

Social Significance of Religion. The importance of religious beliefs and actions to institutions and the individual.

Structural or Institutional Violence. Violence that is woven into the fabric of social institutions, which, in turn, are unjust and cause harm.

Supernatural. That which presumably exists but is impervious to scientific observation or empirical verification; deities or forces that exist outside of nature and are not bound by the limits of the physical universe.

T

Teleology. The philosophical study of purpose or design in living things.

Theistic Rationalism. According to historian Gregg L. Frazer (1956–), a hybrid belief system of the American founders that combined elements of natural religion, Christianity, and rationalism.

Theology. Any systematic thinking about God (or gods) and all things in relation to God (or gods).

Theory of Evolution. A scientific, empirically supported account for the development of life on earth, based on the dynamics of random mutation and natural selection.

Toleration. The capacity of the majority of a society to extend moral status, legal protection, and a measure of civil equality to weaker subgroups regarded as objectionable or immoral.

Transcendentalism. A nineteenth-century religious and philosophic movement whose adherents believed in the inherent goodness of nature—including humans—and in the inevitable corruption of human institutions over time; involved critiques of authority and praise for individual poetic genius and spiritual experience.

Transhumanism. A philosophical and technoscientific movement that enthusiastically takes up the future of being human, particularly via technological and medical advancements that will increase longevity, well-being, cognition, and other human capacities.

Type, Typology, Typological. The process of arranging or grouping things into classifications using specifiable criteria.

U

Utilitarianism. Doctrine that actions are right if they are profitable or beneficial for the majority of society; the theory that moral decisions should be based on what will produce the greatest good for the greatest number.

V

Value. The psychological process of perceiving the quality of an object in terms of utility, esteem, or desire; describes things that individuals or cultures hold in high regard.

Variable. A characteristic that changes across units (individuals, organizations, states). Any factor, trait, or condition that can exist in differing amounts or types. For example, the religious affiliation of parents tends to determine the religious affiliation of their children. In such a dynamic, the parent's religious affiliation can be considered a variable—as can the children's religious affiliation.

Vicarious Religion. The type of affiliation of people who do not want to participate regularly in an organized practice of a shared belief, but who still want that organized practice to remain for the potential future use of themselves, others, and the nation as a whole.

W

Well-Being. The psychological perception of satisfaction, happiness, and good quality of life.

Worldview. A belief system involving personal assumptions of an individual about the nature of society, which structures the individual's understanding of his or her existence.

Z

Zealotry. The expression of excessive enthusiasm or fanaticism in beliefs.

Index

The index is alphabetized in word-by-word order. Page references in **boldface** indicate chapter topics; page references in *italics* indicate photographs and illustrations. Tables and figures are indicated by *t* or *f*, respectively.

A

Abbott, Henry, 171
Abdalla, Ulil Abshar, 82
Abington School District v. Schempp (1963), 178
Abolitionism, 174, 177
Abortion, 188, 196, 375–376
Abuse, 104, 305
Academic left, 292–293
Acceptance, 370–371
Accommodationism, 180–182
Activism, 357–358
Addams, Jane, 340
Addiction, 376–377
Adler, Felix, 346
Advertising
    American Humanist Association, *98*
    belief used in, 62–66
    New Atheist, 286–287, *287*
Aesthetics, 356–357
"Affirmations of Humanism," 348
Afghanistan, 206, 214
"Against Rationalization" (Hitchens), 285
Agency, belief and, 65–66, 368
Agnosticism
    vs. apostasy, 74
    defined, 8–10, 150
    education and, 142
    ethnic diversity in, 135
    political party affiliations, 137
Agora (movie), 123
Agostini v. Felton, 181
Ahearne, Jeremy, 214

Ahimsa, 333
Ahlquist, Jessica, 193
Ahmadiyya movement, 86
Akin, Murat, 213
Al Qaeda, 206, 214
Albania, 215
Alcott, Amos Bronson, 340
Algerian War of Independence, 205
Ali, Ayaan Hirsi, 6, 82, 86, 286
Alienation, 74
Allen, Danielle, 169
Altemeyer, Robert, 253
Altizer, Thomas, 265, 291
Altmeyer, Robert, 248–249
Amazing Conversions (Altemeyer and Hunsberger), 253
American Anti-Slavery Society, 174
American Atheist magazine, 125, 156
American Atheists, 156
American Federation of Labor, 176
American Humanist Association. *See* Humanist Association
American Mosaic Project Survey, 289
American National Election Studies, 27–28
American Nones (Kosmin, Keysar, Cragun, and Navarro-Rivera), 142
American Party, 174
American Protestant Association, 174
American Religious Identification Survey (ARIS), 130, 133
American Tract Society, 174
American Trends Panel, 289
American Values Atlas (AVA), 131–133, 132*t*, 136–137
Amis, Martin, 285
Anabaptists, 168
Analytic thinking, 232
"Analytic Thinking Promotes Religious Disbelief" (Gervais and Norenzayan), 253–254

Anarchism, **325–342**
    absolute *vs.* contingent, 329
    in art, 331–333
    contemporary social movements, 333–335
    defined, 326, 328–329
    history of, 336–341
    humanism in, 335–336
    overlap with atheism and pacifism, 329, 329*f*
    in pop culture, 329–331
Anderson, Benedict, 66
Anderson, Pippa, 297
Animism, 55
Anthropology, 55–58, 62
Antinoff, Steve, 296–297
Anti-Saloon Society, 174
Antisectarianism, 169–170
Antiwar activism, 219
Anxiety, religion-based, 104
Apatheism, 40, 232
Apostasy, **71–91**
    consequences of, 80–85
    defined, 10–12, 71–72
    female, 126
    laws on, 187
    life cycle and, 106–107
    nature and features of, 72–80
    paths to, 106–107
    politicization of, 11
    Saudi Arabia, 4
    as social psychological process, 85–88
    sociology of, 73–75
    types of, 75–80
Apostate, 10–12
Applewhite, Marshall, 87
Aquinas, Thomas, 268–269, 313–314
Arab Spring, 63
Areligion, defined, 13
Arik, Hulya, 210

395

ARIS. *See* American Religious Identification Survey (ARIS)
Aristotle, 264
"Arrantly Absent: Atheism in Psychological Science from 2001 to 2012" (Brewster, et al.), 242
Art, 356–357
Asad, Talal, 58, 189, 217
Aspirational marketing, 64
Aspirational nominalist, 60
Assisted suicide, 188, 376
Association of Humanistic Rabbis, 347
Ataturk, Kemal, 193, 210
Atheism, **325–342**
    absolute, 329
    vs. agnosticism, 9–10
    alternative terms for, 14–15
    anarchism and pacifism and, 325–342
    vs. apostasy, 74
    in art, 331–333
    awakening in, 295
    awareness of, 152, 155
    community, 107, 147, 149–161
    concealability of, 234–235
    contemporary movements in, 333–335
    Dawkins, Richard on, 283
    defined, 6–8, 112, 326, 327
    diversity in, 296
    education and, 136, 142
    ethnic diversity in, 135
    gender gap in, 286
    growth of and distrust of, 229–230
    historical analysis, 121–125
    history of, 336–341
    humanism in, 335–336
    in mainstream society, 152–156
    mind-blind, 232
    moral development and, 230–231, 235
    negative, 7
    negative connotations of, 42
    New, 15, 281–300
    organization, 95
    as other, 6–8
    overlap with pacifism and anarchism, 329, 329f
    paths to, 106–107
    political party affiliation, 137–138
    in pop culture, 329–331
    in popular culture, 151

positive, 7, 10, 151–152
    proactive, 41–43, 51
    rituals, 158–159
    secularity paradox, 37, 39–41
    spiritual, 296–297
    stigma of, 50, 225–239, 257–258
        U.S., 75
    terms extending, 15
    typologies, 7, 231–233
    values of, 150–152
    women, 111–128
Atheism+, 15
"Atheism, Gender, and Sexuality" (Brewster), 111–112
"Atheism: Contemporary Numbers and Patterns" (Zuckerman), 302
Atheist
    coming out as, 106–107, 152–153, 160–161, 248
    defined, 6–7
    distrust of, 153, 228–230, 235, 248
    emotional reactions to, 227–228
    as empty signifier, 8
    everyday, 127
    family life, 104
    identity, 88, 152–155
        Finland, 295
        Harris, Sam, on, 283
    Jefferson, Thomas, as, 173
    Jesus as, 338
    public perception of, 75
    as reminder of mortality, 231
    stereotypes of, 226–231, 234–236
Atheist Awakening (Cimino and Smith), 88
Atheist Bus Campaign, 286–287, *287,* 288
The Atheist Bus Campaign: Global Manifestations and Responses (Bullivant and Tomlins), 287
Atheist Community of the University of Ottawa, 157–158
Atheist Forums, 155
Atheist Shoes, *226,* 226–227
Atheistic Humanism (Flew), 275
Atheists: A Groundbreaking Study of America's Nonbelievers (Hunsberger and Altemeyer), 248–249
"Atheists as 'Other': Moral Boundaries and Cultural Membership in American Society" (Edgell, Gerteis, and Hartmann), 124, 149, 153
"Atheists for Jesus" (Dawkins), 338

Atheology, **263–279**
    complete, 273–275
    defined, 263, 264
    freethought, religious criticism, and, 265–268
    models of, 271–272
    philosophers of, 263–264
    theology and, 264–265
    types of, 268–271
Augustine, 19
Authoritarianism, 193, 203–204, 249, 250, 305, 306
Authority, 26–27, 375–376
Autonomy, 326, 375–376
Aweism, 114
Azande, 56–57

B

Ba'athism, 207, 208, 209, 218–219
Bäckström, Anders, 46
Badawi, Raif, 82
Bakunin, Mikhail, 338–339
Ballou, Adin, 339
Baptism, in belonging, 46
Barbershops, Bibles, and BET (Harris-Lacewell), 134–135
Barlow, Philip, 134
Barndt, Will, 165–184
Barrett, Justin, 105
Basil the Great, 80, *80*
Bataille, Georges, 265
Bauman, Zygmunt, 293
Beck, Ulrich, 65
Beckford, James A., 149
"Becoming an Atheist in America: Constructing Identity and Meaning from the Rejection of Theism" (Smith), 153
Becoming an Ex (Ebaugh), 87
"Becoming Muslim: The Development of a Religious Identity" (Peek), 78
Behzti (Dishonour), 187
Being and Time (Heidegger), 274
Belief
    anthropological views, 55–58
    apostasy and, 78–79
    case studies, 62–66
    conditions of, 302
    defined by disbelief, 88
    identity and, 54
    language of, 59–62
    life span changes in, 244
    meaning and, 56–57

INDEX

Belief, *continued*
   multidimensional analysis of, 61–62
   politics of, 66–67
   pressure for, 233–234
   psychological research on, 245–248
   rationality and, 58–59
   research methods on, 246–248
   scholarly disagreement over, 54–59
   secularity and, 94–95
   secularization of, **53–69**
   self-reported, 233–234
   worldview systems, 250–253
Belief replacement hypothesis, 252
"Believing without belonging" thesis, 33, 54
Bellah, Robert, 34, 149
Belonging
   apostasy and, 77
   baptism in, 46
   believing without, 33, 54
   church, secularity paradox with, 37, 38, 43–49
   secularity and, 94–95
"Belonging, Behaving, and Believing: Assessing the Role of Religion on Presidential Approval" (Olson and Warber), 27
Benedict XVI, Pope, 198, 285
Bengston, Vern, 97
Berger, Peter, 20, 23, 32, 56, 291
Berkeley, George, 264
Berlinerblau, Jacques, 3–4, 295, 351
Besant, Annie, 113, 121, 126
Beyer, Peter, 32
"Beyond Belief: Atheism, Agnosticism, and Theistic Certainty in the United States" (Sherkat), 152
Beyond Good and Evil (Nietzsche), 273
Beyond Religion (Dalai Lama), 325
Bhargava, Rajeev, 194
Bhat, Shakeel Ahmad, 292
Biber, Binyamin, 347
Bible Belt, 160–161
The Big Lebowski (movie), 335
Big Society agenda, 198
Bilgin, Pinar, 215
"Bill for Establishing Religious Freedom" (Jefferson), 170, 178
Bill of Rights, 171, 177–179
The Birmingham Temple, 345–346
Birth control, 188, 375–376

Black, Hugo, 177–178
Black Church, 134–135, 174
"Black Churches and Civic Traditions" (Harris), 174
Black Lives Matter movement, 143
Blackham, Harold, 272
Blame, 370
Blasphemy, 86, 187, 225–226
Blessing, Kimberly, 84
Bloom, Paul, 309–310
Bluemke, Matthias, 247
Bonaparte, Napoleon, 192
The Bonobo and the Atheist (De Waal), 311
Bosch, Hieronymus, *310*
Bosnia, 217
Boss, Judith, 303
Botton, Alain de, 297
Bowen, John, 213, 214
Bradfield v. Roberts (1899), 177
Bradlaugh, Charles, 126, 272
Braintrust: What Neuroscience Tells Us about Morality (Churchland), 310–311
Branding, belief and, 62–66
Brave New World (Huxley), 332
Brave New World Revisited (Huxley), 332
Breaking the Spell: Religion as a Natural Phenomenon (Dennett), 284, 293
Brewster, Melanie E., 111–112, 242
Bright, 14–15
Brinkerhoff, Merlin B., 76–77, 78–79, 83, 87
Brint, Steven, 149
British Humanist Association. *See* Humanist Association
Bromley, David, 11, 72, 73
Brooks, Clem, 27
Brosnan, Sarah, 311
Brown, Andrew, 293
Brown, Callum, 49, 115–116
Bruce, Steve, 20, 38
   cultural defense theory, 48
   on erosion of supernatural, 49
   on indifference, 51
   on negative connotations of atheism, 42
   on secularization, 66
Bruno, Giordano, 267–268
Bryan, William Jennings, 175
Buddhism, 264
   anarchism, 325–326
   compassion and acceptance, 370

Harris, Sam, on, 283
New Atheism and, 296–297
nonviolence, 325
as secular, 96
Bullivant, Stephen, 112, 287
Burhani, Ahmad Najib, 86
Burwell v. Hobby Lobby Stores, Inc. (2014), 182
Bush, George H. W., 225
Bush, George W., 181–182, 198, 288

C

Calvert, Cecil, Lord Baltimore, 168
Calvert, Jane E., 169
Campbell, Colin, 12–13
Campbell, David, 215
Cancer Research UK, 57
Capitalism
   belief in service of, 53, 62–66
   universality from, 65
Caplovits, David, 75, 79, 81, 89
Cardinal Newman Society, 158
Carlin, George, 241, 330–331
Casanova, José, 29, 291
"Casting of the Bonds of Organized Religion" (Brinkerhoff and Mackie), 78–79
Catholic Education Daily, 158
Catholic Worker movement, 340
Catholicism
   apostasy, 82–83, 89
   atheism and, 158
   charitable organizations, 174
   colonial America, 168
   Democratic Party and, 27, 27f
   demographics, 133, 134
   education levels in, 135
   ethnic diversity in, 134–135, 138–140
   France, 191–192
   on militant secularism, 198
   moral law in, 313–314
   political party affiliations, 136–137
   secularization in, 25
   sentiment against, 174
   Sweden, 3
Cat's Cradle (Vonnegut), 330
Catto, Rebecca, 76
Causation, 368, 369
Cavanaugh, William, 191, 206, 215
Center for Secular Inquiry, 159
Center of Religion and Public Life Project, 135

INDEX

Central Intelligence Agency, 22
Chalom, Adam, 343–361
Chandler, Russell, 30
Charity, 173–174, 198
Charlie Hebdo, 86, 187, 203, 204, 213, 291
The Charter of Privileges (Penn), 168–169
Chaves, Mark, 20, 22, 26–27
Child-rearing approaches, 101–103
    See also Family life
China, 193, 215, 331–332, 333, 337
Chomsky, Noam, 288
Christian Coalition, 180
Christian Non-Resistance (Ballou), 339
Christian Plowshares movement, 340
Christianity
    anarchism and pacifism in, 337–338
    apostasy, 72–73
    belief in, 57–58
    early, called atheism, 7
    ethics in, 311–315
    feminization of, 118–119
    great apostasy, 72
    New Atheism on, 282–283
    Turkey, 216
    as values, 48–49
"Christians as Believers" (Ruel), 57–58
Chuang-Tzu, 331–332, 337
Chuman, Joseph, 358
Church, State, and Original Intent (Drakeman), 173
Church attendance
    adolescent withdrawal from, 59–62
        decline, 25–26
        self-reported, 233–234
Church belonging, 37, 38, 43
Church of England, 29, 66, 194
    See also United Kingdom
Church of Latter Days Saints. *See* Mormonism
Church of Sweden, 44–45
Church of the Holy Trinity v. United States (1892), 176–177
"The Church of the Non-Believers" (Wolf), 281, 282
Churchland, Patricia, 307, 310–311, 317–318
Cicero, 117–118
Cimino, Richard, 88, 95, 107, 152, 159, 295

Citizens United v. FEC (2010), 182
Civic atheology, 266–267, 271
Civic life, 172–175
Civic theology, 267
"Civil Disobedience" (Thoreau), 339
Civil religion, 34
Civil Religion and the Presidency (Pierard and Linder), 34
Civil rights, 212–213
Civil rights movement, 179, 197
Civil War, 174
Clark, Thomas W., 363–384
A Clockwork Orange (movie), 373
Closing the Gate: Race, Politics, and the Chinese Exclusion Act (Gyory), 139–140
Coca-Cola, 63–64, 65
Cognitive fallibility, 366
Cognitive humility, 367
Cognitive psychology, 244
Cognitive style, 250
Coles, Robert, 105
Collective beliefs, 2, 47
Collective cultures, 245
Collective effervescence, 56
Communism, 193, 203, 211, 294
Community, **147–163**
    acceptance of atheism and, 152–156
    anarchism, pacifism and, 335–336
    apostasy and, 74–75, 78–79
    atheist, 107, 150–161
    church as, in secular countries, 48
    conflict and, 158
    defined, 148–152
    modern and traditional, 155–156
    naturalist, 381
    New Atheist, 290, 296–297
    secular, 97–98, *98*
    secular Jewish, 347
    spirituality in, 357–358
    types, 149
    well-being and, 368
Community (television show), 241
"'Community' in the Sociology of Religion" (Beckford), 149
Comparative Constitutions Project, 23
Compassion, 369
Comte, Auguste, 14, 20, 273, 291
Comte-Sponville, André, 297, 351, 353, 355, 356, 359
Conflict, **203–221**
    academic literature on, 214–216

community and, 158
Middle East, 207–212
naturalism on ideological, 378–379
political tradition on, 218
religiously inspired, 186–187
suppression of dissent, 215–216
western Europe, 212–214
See also War
"Confraternity of the Faithless" (Wilde), 331–332
Confucianism, 264
Congress of Secular Jewish Organizations, 347
Conjunction fallacy, 228–229
Connection, 368
    See also Community
Consciousness, 367–368, 381
Conservatism
    diversity and, 136–138
    ethnicity and, 130, 142–143
    ethno-national-religious, 66
    naturalism and, 374–375
    political parties and, 175–176
    See also Political party affiliation
Constitute Project, 23, 24
Construct validity, 97
Context
    of atheism, 8
    of belief, 61–62
    of community, 149
    evolution of, 114
    morality and, 302–303, 307–308
    of New Atheism, 293–294
    for nonreligion, 12
    of nonreligion, 244–245
    psychological research on, 247–248
    religion defined by, 2
    religious rise and, 66
    return of religion and, 186
    Scotland, 50–51
    Sweden, 50–51
    of women and nonbelief, 117–118, 121–125
"Continuity Thinking and the Problem of Christian Culture" (Robbins), 58
Conversion
    apostasy and, 87–88
    deconversion, 87–88, 126–127
    defined, 79
    psychology of, 244
Copts, 217
Cornwell, John, 287–288

Corporations, civil rights of, 182
Cosmopolitanism, 328
"Cosmos" (television show), 380
Cottrell, C. A., 227
Council for Secular Humanism, 5,
   272, 307, 348
Cox, Daniel, 131, 135, 136,
   137–138
Cragun, Ryan T., 1–16, 301
Creationism, 157, 288
Credibility enhancing displays, 232
Criminal justice, 144, 372–373
Croce, Benedetto, 273
Crockett, Alasdair, 33, 54
Crusades, 304
Cudworth, Ralph, 264, 265
Cults, 73, 86–87
Cultural defense, 48
Cultural identity
   family life, 96
   Jewish, 346–351, 355
   psychology of nonreligion and,
     245
   religion in, 44–49, 60
   rituals and ceremonies, 99–100
   women and, 121
   See also Identity
Cultural relativism, 307–308
Cultural religion, 45, 47
Cynics, 336–337

D

Dalai Lama, 325
Danbury Baptists Association, 172
Danish Cartoons crisis, 86, 187
Darwin, Charles, 273, 281, 296
Darwin Day, 159
Davie, Grace
   on atheism and secularity levels,
     40
   on belief and belonging, 54, 55,
     77
   "believing without belonging"
     thesis, 33
   on church ritual, 47
   on European exceptionalism, 32
   on methodology, 39
   on religiosity of women, 114
Davies, Brian, 313–314
Dawkins, Richard, 241, 283
   agnostic atheism of, 10
   Atheist Bus Campaign, 286–287,
     287
   on Bush, George W., 288

on Darwin, Charles, 296
on enemies of science, 293
incomplete atheology of, 274
influence of, 287–288
on Jesus as atheist, 338
Krauss, Lawrence, and, 285
on morality, 304–305
national context of, 293–294
on negative force of religion, 196
on privileging of religion, 5
social media use, 290
on stigma of atheism, 289
values promoted by, 150–151
See also New Atheism
Day, Abby, 53–69
Day, Dorothy, 340
De Botton, Alain, 354, 357
De Waal, Franz, 311, 370
Death of God movement, 265
"Debating the Role of Religion in
   War" (Hassner), 205–206
Declaration of Independence, 169
Declining religious authority thesis,
   26–28
Decolonization, 193, 203
Deconversion, 87–88, 126–127
Defectors, 11
"Defining Normative Islam" (Epken-
   hans), 212
Deikman, Arthur J., 354
Deism, 170
Demerath, Jay, 45
Democracy
   compatibility of Islam, 216–217
   fairness and, 196–197
   liberal, 212–213
   public sphere religion and,
     187–188, 195
*The Democratic Virtues of the Chris-
tian Right* (Shields), 180
Demographic transformation, 131
Demographics
   age, 133
   apostasy and, 76
   of belief, 61–62
   of diversity, 129–145, 132*t*, 140*t*
   family life, 97
   gender, 117
   Jewish, 344–345
   of nones, 117, 248–249
   of nonreligion, 248
   of secularity, 140*t*
   secularization by, 21, 21*f*,
     106–107, 107–108
Demonization, 379

Dennett, Daniel, 13, 284, 293, 296
   See also New Atheism
"Denominations as Dual Structures:
   An Organizational Analysis"
   (Chaves), 25
Deontology, 316
Dependent origination thesis, 370
Derrida, Jacques, 265
Descartes, René, 58
The Desecularization of the World
   (Berger), 32
Deserters, 11
Developmental psychology, 244,
   256–257, 305, 310
DeWeese, James, 193
Dewey, John, 273–274, 316
DeWitt, Jerry, 347
Dialogues Concerning Natural Religion
   (Hume), 263–264
Diderot, Denis, 267
"Dimensions of Religious Defection"
   (Mauss), 77–78
Diogenes, 336–337
Disaffection, 74
Disaffiliates, 11, 87
"Disaffiliation: Some Notes on Fall-
   ing from the Faith" (Brinkerhoff
   and Burke), 76–77
Disbelief, 253–255, 254*t*
"Discovering Atheism: Heterogeneity
   in Trajectories to Atheist Identity
   and Activism" (LeDrew), 154–155
Discrimination, **225–239**, 371–372
   See also Stigma
Disengagers, 11
Disgust, 227–228
The Dispossessed (Le Guin),
   332–333
Dissent and dissenters
   colonial America, 168–169
   early American, 173
   suppression of, 215–216
Distrust of atheists, 153, 228–230,
   235, 248
Diversity and secularism, **129–145**
   atheism, 295
   colonial America, 169
   demographic characteristics,
     133–138
   humanism, 348
   of nonbelievers, 249
   race, 138–143
   separation of church and state
     and, 179–180
Divine right, 190, 191

INDEX

"Divinity School Address" (Emerson), 340
Dobbelaere, Karel, 20, 22, 25, 29
Dobson, James, 180
Dones, 12
The Doors, 332
Doré, Gustave, *81*
Dorres-Worter, Paula, 124
Dorrien, Gary, 176
Doubters, 243
Douglas, Mary, 57
Drakeman, Donald L., 173, 178
Draulans, Veerle, 26
Dropouts, religious, 11
Dualism, 365
Duck Dynasty, 229–230
Durkheim, Émile
    on belief, 56, 57
    on community, 149, 158
    definition of religion, 1
    on morality, 309
    on secularization, 20, 291
    on social cohesion, 44
    on social functions of religion, 77, 158
Dyer, Mary, 3

E

Ebaugh, Helen, 87
Eccles, Janet, 76
Economist Intelligence Unit, 22
Economy and Society (Weber), 59
Edgell, Penny, 75, 84, 124, 149, 158
Education
    demographics of, 135–136, 140*t*
    early American, 173–174
    ethnicity and, 135–136, 139, 141–142
    of Jews, 344–345
    link with secularization, 21, 22*f*
    secular family life, 101–103
    separation of church and state in, 178–179
Edwords, Fred, 347–348
Egypt
    Coca-Cola ads, 63
    conflict, 207–210, 209
    Copts, 217
    Muslim Brotherhood, 66, 203, 209
Einstein, Albert, 341
Eisenhower, Dwight D., 179
Eller, Vernand, 337
Ellis, Jenny, 288

Ellul, Jacques, 337
Emerson, Ralph Waldo, 339–340, 364
Emotional apostasy, 78
Empiricism, Huxley, Thomas, on, 9–10
The End of Faith: Religion, Terror, and the Future of Reason (Harris), 5, 282–283
Engel v. Vitale (1962), 178
Engelke, Matthew, 100–101
Enlightenment
    atheology, 273
    ethnocentrism, 198
    Hitchens, Christopher, on, 285
    humanism, 13–14
    origins of secularism, 190–194
    on religious freedom, 3
    separation of church and state, 170
    view of self, 245
Environmental design, 377
Epicureanism, 336–337
Epicurus, 264, 267, 273, 337, 381
Epistemology, 365–367
Epkenhans, Tim, 212
Epstein, Greg, 152
Equality, 195–198, 373–375
ESPN The Magazine, 152–153
Esposito, Jessica, 242
"Establishment and Disestablishment at the Founding" (McConnell), 167
Establishment clause, 177–178, 178–179
Ethical Culture, 346, 381
Ethics
    assessing religious, 311–315
    cosmopolitan, 328
    defining, 303
    family life in instilling, 101–105
    vs. morality, 303
    naturalism and, 273, 369–371
    science of, 316–317
    secular, constructing, 315–319
    of secular humanists, 151–152
    in secularism, 196
    spirituality and, 357–358
    war and, 204
    well-being and, 364–365
    See also Pacifism
Ethics for Life: A Text with Readings (Boss), 303
Ethics without God (Nielsen), 314
Ethnic identity

church as community, 48
    Jewish, 345, 346–347, 348–351
    religious conflict and, 218
Ethnic nominalist, 60
Ethnicity and secularism, **129–145**
    demographics of, 132*t*, 133–138
    emotional reactions to, 227–228
    humanism and, 348–349
    party preference and, 142–143
    United States, 130–133
Ethnocentrism, 189, 198
Eurobarometer, 25, 26, 28
Europe: The Exceptional Case: Parameters of Faith in the Modern World (Davie), 32
European Convention on Human Rights, 194
European Court of Human Rights, 198
European exceptionalism, 32
European Values Survey, 25, 28
Europe's Encounter with Islam: The Secular and the Postsecular, 215
Euthanasia, 188, 376
Euthyphro Dilemma, 311–314, *312*
Evangelicalism
    backlash, 302
    demographics, 133
    education levels in, 135
    ethnic diversity in, 134–135, 139–140
    political party and, 175–176
    on separation of church and state, 179–180
    Turkey, 216
Evans, Pippa, 147
Evans-Pritchard, Edward Evans, 56–57
Everson v. Board of Education (1947), 177–178
Evil, problem of, 270–271
Evolution, 157, 273
    Dawkins, Richard, on, 283
    Harris, Sam, on, 283
    of morality, 316–317, 318, 319
    New Atheism on, 281
    Scopes trial, 175, *176,* 366
Evolutionary psychology
    of disbelief, 251, 253–254
    on morality, 310
    on natural religion, 105–106
Ex Machina (movie), 368
Excommunication, 82–83, 344
Existentialist atheism, 296
Existentialist theology, 265

Exiters, 10–12
Experience and Nature (Dewey), 273–274
L'expérience intérieure (Bataille), 265
Experimental existential psychology, 252

F

Fact-value fallacy, 316, 317–319
Faith, 58
Faith No More (Zuckerman), 78, 305–306
Faith-based initiatives, 181–182, 198
Faktizität und Geltung (Between Facts and Norms) (Habermas), 275
Falcioni, Ryan, 301–323
"The Fall and Rise of Religion in International Relations History and Theory" (Shah and Philpott), 217
Falwell, Jerry, 179–180
Family life, **93–110**
    atheism and, 154
    defining, 94–96
    research areas, 98–108
    research methodologies, 96–98
    rituals and rites of passage, 98–101
    women in, 116–118, 120–121, 126
Family Research Council, 180
Farage, Nigel, 66–67
Farias, Miguel, 245, 246, 249, 252
Fatah, 203
Fate, 57
Fatwa, 81–82, 187
"F*ck That: A Guided Meditation," 355
Fear, 226, 227
Federal Council of Churches, 176
Felt belief, 61–62, 63
Female Missionary Society for the Poor, 174
Feminism, 83, **111–128**
    anarchism and pacifism, 333
    on family life, 94
    respectability and, 120–121
Feuerbach, Ludwig, 359
Fiala, Andrew, 325–342
Filosofia come scienza dello spirit (Croce), 273
Finke, Roger, 23, 40, 47
Finland, 289–290, 294, 295
Firebaugh, Glenn, 21
First Amendment, 171, 192–193

Fitzgerald, Timothy, 189
"The Five 'A's of Meaning Maintenance" (Proulx and Inzlicht), 256
Flew, Antony, 275
Flippen, Douglas, 158
Focus on the Family, 180
Forbidden Fruit: The Ethics of Humanism (Kurtz), 275
Forgiveness, 372–373
Formations of the Secular (Asad), 217
Fortuyn, Pim, 291
Foster, Arian, 152–153
Four Horsemen roundtable, 282
Fox, Jonathan, 23
"Foxhole Atheism, Revisited" (Jong, Halberstadt, and Bluemke), 247
Frame of Government of Pennsylvania (Penn), 168–169
Framed by Gender (Ridgeway), 111
France
    groups legally favored in, 4
    laïcité, 193–194, 213–214
    religious conflicts, 213–214, 291
    Revolution, 23–24, 191, 327
    secularism, 23–24, 191–192
Frankl, Victor, 354
Franklin, Benjamin, 171
Frazer, Gregg L., 170
Frederick William III, King of Prussia, 124
Free exercise clause, 177
Free Inquiry magazine, 272
Free love, 120–121
Free speech, 186–187
Freedom
    apostasy as, 81
    existential, 380–381
    from religious ethics, 305–306
    secularism in ensuring, 195–196
Freedom House, 22
Freedom of religion
    community and, 160–161
    safe expression of, 96
    secularism as, 3–4
Freethinkers, 14, 112, 121, 150
Freethinkers: A History of American Secularism (Jacoby), 118, 192
Freethought, 14, 265–268, 348
    respectability and, 120–121
    women in, 113, 114, 116–117, 118–119
Freethought Society of America, 125
Freud, Sigmund, 20, 296, 309, 353
Friedman, Daniel, 356–357

Fundamentalism
    backlash, 302
    reversibility of secularization, 32
    on separation of church and state, 179–180
    violence and, 206
Funerals, 99, 100–101

G

Gallie, Walter B., 217
Gandhi, Mahatma, 335, 340
The Garden of Earthly Delights (Bosch), *310*
Garneau, Christopher, 160–161
Garrison, William Lloyd, 340
The Gay Science (Nietzsche), 273
Gaylor, Annie Laurie, 118
Geertz, Clifford, 39
Geiger, Elizabeth, 242
Geisert, Paul, 14
"Gemeinschaft Revisited: A Critique and Reconstruction of the Community Concept" (Brint), 149
Gender, **111–128**
    apostasy and, 76
    atheism and, 286
    diversity and secularity, 133, 134
    nonbelief and, 249
    religiosity and, 114–118
Genealogies of Religion (Asad), 58
General Social Survey, 25, 27, 50, 83–84, 150
A General Theory of Secularization (Martin), 32
Generation X, 131
Genetic engineering, 376, 378
Germany, church tax, 196
Gershwin, George, 375
Gerteis, Joseph, 75, 84, 149, 158
Gervais, Ricky, 151, 227, 241
Gervais, Will M., 153, 225–239, 251
    on distrust of atheists, 228–229
    on levels of disbelief, 234
    on priming, 257
    typology of nonbelief, 253–254
Giddens, Anthony, 64, 65
Ginzberg, Lori D., 127
Global Atheist Census, 286
Globalization, **53–69**
    backlash against secularization and, 32
    link with secularization, 22, 22*f*
    religious neutrality and, 199

INDEX

"Globalization and Religious Nationalism: Self, Identity, and the Search for Ontological Security" (Kinnvall), 29–30

God
defining, 265
vs. Judeo-Christian, 6
morality based on, 307–309
theological arguments for, 268–269

God and the Grounding of Morality (Nielsen), 275

God and the State (Bakunin), 338–339

The God Delusion (Dawkins), 150–151, 283, 289
influence of, 286
on morality, 305
on privileging of religion, 5

God Is Back: How the Global Rise of Faith Is Changing the World (Micklethwait and Wooldridge), 291

God Is Dead: Secularization in the West (Bruce), 20

God Is Not Great (Hitchens), 284–285

God of the gaps, 309

God's Own Party (Williams), 175

Godwin, Benjamin, 263

Gogh, Theo van, 291
secularization, 204

Goldman, Emma, 338, 339, 340

Good without God: What a Billion Nonreligious People Do Believe (Epstein), 152

Goodman, Paul, 333

Goodman, Percival, 333

Google Ngrams, 23, 24

Gorbachev, Mikhail, 211

Government
Locke on, 165–166, *166*
origins of secularism, 190–194
religion in control by, 4–5
secularization of, 5

Graham, Billy, 179

Grayling, A. C., 285

Great apostasy, 72

Greece v. Galloway (2014), 182

Greek Orthodox Church, 30

Green, John Clifford, 130

Green, Martin, 248

Grim, Brian, 23

Guilt, 104, 308, 370–371

Gustav Vasa, King of Sweden, 3

Gutkowski, Stacey, 203

Gyatso, Tenzin, 325

Gyory, Andrew, 139–140

H

Habermas, Jürgen, 66, 196–197, 216, 275

Hadaway, Kirk, 83–84

Halberstadt, Jamin, 247

Haldeman-Julius, Emanuel, 272

Halman, Loek, 26

Ham, Ken, 157

Hamas, 203

Hammer, Joseph H., 11–12

Happiness, 83–84

Hare, John, 308

Harley, Brian, 21

Harris, Frederick C., 174

Harris, Sam, 282–283
incomplete atheology of, 274
irreligious writings, 13
on meditation, 99, 355
on morality, 305, 316–317
national context and, 293
on negative force of religion, 196
on privileging of religion, 5
on religious brainwashing, 106
social media use, 290
on spirituality, 296–297, 352–353, 356, 359
on women in atheism, 116
See also New Atheism

Harris-Lacewell, Melissa Victoria, 134–135

Hartmann, Douglas, 75, 84, 149, 158

Hassner, Ron, 205–206

Hatch, Nathan, 173

Health, 376–377

Heaven's Gate, 87

Heelas, Paul, 40, 114

Hegel, G. W. F., 267–268

Heidegger, Martin, 267–268, 274, 275

Hein v. Freedom from Religion Foundation (2007), 181–182

Hepburn, Katherine, 113

Her (movie), 368

Herberg, Will, 346

Heresy, 7, 85–86

Heretic (Ali), 86

Hervieu-Léger, Danièle, 45

Hierarchy of needs, 353, 364

Hill, Peter C., 246

Historical analysis
of apostasy, 75–76
Jewish, 348–349
of secularization, 23–24
of women and nonbelief, 117–118, 121–125

Hitchens, Christopher, 241, 284–285
diversity of atheism and, 296
on Islamic rage boy, 292
on morality, 304–305
negative connotations of atheism, 42
politics of, 288
See also New Atheism

Hobbes, Thomas, 264, 267

Hobby Lobby, 182

Hoesly, Dusty, 100

Holidays
community and, 158–159
family life and, 98–99, 103
Jewish, 346, 350
secularization of, 99

"Holistic Individualism in the Age of Aquarius" (Faris and Lalljee), 249

Holocaust, 348

Holy Roman Emperor, 336

Holyoake, George Jacob, 3, 188

Homosexuality, 196, 203
as apostasy, 89
emotional reactions to, 227
legislation on, 187–188
naturalism on, 375

Honor killing, 121

Hood, Ralph W., 246

Hoover, Herbert, 175

"How Secular Is Europe?" (Halman and Draulans), 26

How to Be Secular: A Call to Arms for Religious Freedom (Berlinerblau), 3–4, 351

Hoxha, Enver, 215

Hubbard, L. Ron, 87

Human Development Index, 26

Human nature, 367–368

Human rights
atheology on, 271
criminal justice and, 372–373
inclusivist secularism and, 193–194
naturalism on, 371–372
public sphere and religion, 187–188
religious freedom, 3
secularism for, 195–196

The Human Tradition (Blackham), 272

Humanism
in atheism, anarchism, pacifism, 326, 335–336
atheology and, 265
defined, 13–14, 347–348
morality and, 306–307
natural secularity, 105–106
pedagogical atheology and, 271–272
war and, 219

Humanism as a Philosophy (Lamont), 274

"Humanism in Daily Life: Practical Aspects in Secular Living," 156

Humanist Association, 4, 14
ad campaigns, *98*
Atheist Bus Campaign, 286–287, *287*
atheology, 272
ceremonies, 100–101
definition of humanism, 348
ethics of, 151–152
families in, 97–98
family life and, 95
values in, 155–156
worldview education, 102

Humanist Ceremonies, 159

Humanist Hub, 152

"A Humanist Manifesto," 14

"The Humanist Manifesto III," 151–152

Humanist Society, 43

Humanistic Judaism, **343–361**

Hume, David, 263–264, 296, 317, 318

Hunsberger, Bruce, 74–75, 248–249, 253

Hurd, Shakman, 215

Huxley, Aldous, 332

Huxley, Thomas Henry, 9–10, *10,* 332

Hwang, Karen, 84, 104

Hypatia of Alexandria, *122,* 122–123

I

Ibrahim, Mariam, 82

Identity
in advertising, 62–66
apostasy and, 74–75, 78–79, 88
belief in, 54, 62–66
family formation and, 107–108
family *vs.* individual, 106–107

gender, 111
Harris, Sam, on atheist, 283
Jewish, 344, 346–347, 348–349, 349–351
morality in, 303
New Atheism, 289–290
political party affiliation and, 175–176
public sphere religion and, 197–198
rationality in, 58–59
religion in cultural, 42, 43–49
religious nationalism, 29–30
secular, 105–106
war and, 203, 204

"Identity Crisis: Greece, Orthodoxy, and the European Union" (Molokotos-Liederman), 30

Igarashi, Hitoshi, 187

"Imagine" (Lennon), 329–330

Imagined Communities (Anderson), 66

Imaging There's No Heaven: How Atheism Helped Create the Modern World (Stephens), 125

Immigration, 144

Imperialism, 193

In Defense of Secular Humanism (Kurtz), 275

Income, 136, 374
demographics of, *140t*
ethnicity and, 141–142
of Jews, 344–345

Incorporation Doctrine, 177–178

InCREDulous atheism, 232

India, 194, 217

Indifference, 51
apatheism, 40, 232
secularity as, 39–41
women, 126

Indigenous cultures, 333

Individualism
colonial America, 169
rights *vs.* government control, 4
in secularism, 245
secularization, 6
valued by nonbelievers, 249

Industrialization, 22, *22f*

Infant Cognition Center, 309–310

Infidel, 86, 112

Infidel Feminism (Schwartz), 111

Ingersoll, Robert G., 126, 272

Inglehart, Ronald, 26, 31, 115, 186, 199

Inherit the Wind (movie), 366

Inspiration, 355–356

International comparisons, 21–22, *22f*

International Federation of Secular Humanistic Jews, 347

International Humanist and Ethical Union, 5

International Religious Freedom Data Set, 23, 24

International Social Survey Program, 25, 28, 38

Internet
atheist communities, 107, 155–156
family life resources, 96
research methodologies, 97, 98

Interpersonal connection, 358

"Intraorganizational Power and Internal Secularization in Protestant Denominations" (Chaves), 25

Inzlicht, Michael, 256

Iran, 206
conflict in, 207–208
family life secularity, 93–94
Islamic revolution, 291

Iraq, 214, 288, 334

Irreligion, defined, 12–13

"Is Atheism Only for the Upper Class?" (Cox), 135

Isidore of Seville, 85

Islam
apostasy, 72–73, 81–82
backlash in, 302
blasphemy, 86
Central Asia, 210–212
clothing laws, 192, 213–214, 215
compatibility with democratic values, 216–217
ethics, 311–315
France, 192, 213–214
freethought in, 264
heresies, 86
identity, 204
jihadist, 206, 214, 218
New Atheism on, 282–283, 289
political and military power in, 336
religious freedom and, 4
return of religion, 186, 291
secularization backlash, 32, 206
stereotypes of, 292
suppression of, 215–216
as threat, 211–212, 213–214
Turkey, 207–210
in wars, 203

INDEX

Islamic rage boy, 292
Islamic State (ISIS), 32, 186–187, 209
Is-ought fallacy, 316, 317–319
Israel, 203, 208, 209, 218, 344

J

Jacobs, Janet, 87
Jacoby, Susan, 118, 192
Jainism, 264
James, William, 302
Jefferson, Thomas, 169
  accused of atheism, 173
  in disestablishment, 170
  First Amendment, 171
  on religious freedom, 3, 178
  secularism, 192
  on separation of church and state, 172
Jenkins, Philip, 32
Jerry Springer the Opera, 187
Jesus, as anarchist and pacifist, 337–338, 340
The Jew in the Lotus (Kamenetz), 344
Jews and Judaism, 208, 209, **343–361**
  ethnic diversity and, 138–139
  family life, 99
  humanistic, 344–351
  paths to secular, 354–358
  rituals, 99
Jillette, Penn, 151, 230
Jones, Bob, 179
Jones, Jim, 87
Jones, Robert P., 131, 136, 137–138
Jones, Sanderson, 297
Jong, Jonathan, 247
Jörð (Norse goddess), 7
Judas Iscariot, 80
Judeo-Christian privileging, 6–7
Juergensmeyer, Mark, 206
Julian, Roman Emperor, 80, *80*
Just Babies: The Origins of Good and Evil (Bloom), 309–310
Jyllands-Posten, 86, 187, 291

K

Kahneman, D., 228–229
Kamenetz, Rodger, 344
Kant, Immanuel, 308, 316
Kapferer, Jean-Noël, 62
Kaplan, Mordecai, 344
Kasselstrand, Isabella, 37–52

Kehl-Bodrogi, Krisztina, 211
Kelly, Kate, 83
Kennedy, Anthony, 181
Kennedy, John F., 179
Kepel, Gilles, 291
Kettell, Steven, 185–201
Keysar, Ariela, 117, 130
Khalid, Adeeb, 210, 211
Khomeini, Ayatollah, 82, 187, 208
Kibbutz Institute for Holidays and Jewish Culture, 350
King, Martin Luther Jr., 143, 176, 335, 340
Kinnvall, Catarina, 29–30
Kirkley, Evelyn, 116, 119
Kitcher, Philip, 307, 316, 319
Know-Nothing Party, 174
Kohlberg, Lawrence, 305, 310
Kol Hadash Humanistic Congregation, 347
Koltko-Rivera, Mark E., 251
Kosmin, Barry, 94–95, 130
Krauss, Lawrence M., 285
Kropotkin, Peter, 333
Ku Klux Klan, 175
Kubrick, Stanley, 373
Kurtz, Paul, 272, 275, 346
Kuru, Ahmet, 193, 216

L

Lacroix, Paul, *80*
Laïcité, 213–214
"Laïcité: A Parallel French Cultural Policy (2002–2007)" (Ahearne), 214
"Laïcité and Multiculturalism" (Akin), 213
Laïcité model, 193–194
Laissez faire policies, 374
Lalljee, Mansur, 249
Lamont, Corliss, 274
Lao-Tzu, 337
Lascaux cave paintings, 357, *357*
The Last Temptation of Christ (movie), 187
Law, Harriet Teresa, 113, 114
Law on the Separation of the Churches and State (1905), 192
Lay leadership, 25
Le Guin, Ursula K., 332–333, 337
Leaders, religion determined by, 58
Leadership Conference of Secular and Humanistic Jews, 347
Leave-takers, 73, 79

Leaving Islam: Apostates Speak Out (Warraq), 82
Lebanon, 217
Lectures on the Atheistic Controversy (Godwin), 263
LeDrew, Stephen, 107, 154–155
Lee, L., 243
Lee, Lois, 12, 112
Lee v. Weisman (1992), 181
The Left Hand of Darkness (Le Guin), 332
Leland, John, 171
Lemon, Edward, 212
Lemon v. Kurtzman, 178–179
Lennon, John, 329–330
Letter to a Christian Nation: A Challenge of Faith (Harris), 293
Levinas, Emmanuel, 265
Lewin, Kurt, 244
Liberal Islamic Network, 82
Liberal theology, 265
Liberalism
  as apostasy, 82
  diversity and, 136–138
  ethnicity and, 130, 142–143
  Jewish, 344–345
  naturalism and, 374–375
  nonreligion and, 250
  political parties and, 175–176
  See also Political party affiliation
Life after Faith: The Case for Secular Humanism (Kitcher), 319
Life magazine, 125
The Life of Brian (movie), 187
The Life of Reason: The Phases of Human Progress (Santayana), 273
Linder, Robert, 34
Lipka, Michael, 356
Literacy, 21, 22f
Little Blue Books, 272
The Little Book of Atheist Spirituality (Comte-Sponville), 353, 359
Lived secularity, **37–52**
  atheism paradox and, 37, 39–41
  church belonging and, 43–49
  defined, 37
  methodology for studying, 39
  northern Europe, 38
  opinions on atheism and, 41–43
  Scotland and Sweden, 40–4150–51
  studying, 39
  United States, 49–50
Living the Secular Life (Zuckerman), 114

404   MACMILLAN INTERDISCIPLINARY HANDBOOKS

Locke, John, 113, 165–166, *166,* 170

Logic, 9–10, 13–14, 272
See also Rationality

Love, Poverty and War: Journeys and Essays (Hitchens), 285

Loveland, Matthew, 147–163

Luckmann, Thomas, 20, 22

Lucretius, 264, 273

Luther, Martin, 3

Lutheranism
colonial America, 168
Finland, 294
Sweden, 3, 289–290

Lynch v. Donnelly (1984), 180

M

MacIntyre, Alasdair, 265

Mackey, James P., 263

Mackie, Marlene, 76–77, 78–79, 83, 87

MacManus, Christopher, 65

Madison, James, 170, 171, 178

Maher, Bill, 151, 241, 286

Mainline churches, 132–137

"Make.Believe" ad campaign, 65

Malinowski, Bronislaw, 64

Manning, Christel, 93–110

Man's Search for Meaning (Frankl), 354

Manza, Jeff, 27

Marginal belief, 60

Marginalization
of atheists, 158
backlash against secularization and, 32
of church in secular societies, 43–44
of religion, 198

Martin, David, 32, 48, 293

Martin, Emma, 114

Martin, Michael, 268

Martineau, Harriet, 126

Maru, Jaynita, 241–261

Marx, Karl, 20, 263, 273, 291, 296, 338

Maslow, Abraham, 353, 364

Materialism, 263–264, 267–268, 273, 327

Mattathias, 80, *81*

Mauss, Armand, 77–78, 82

Mavelli, Luca, 215

McCollum v. Board of Education (1948), 178

McConnell, Michael W., 167, 168

McCreight, Jen, 15

McEwan, Ian, 285

McGowen, Dale, 96

McGrath, Alister, 284

McGuire, Meredith B., 19

Meaning
apostasy and, 84
belief and, 56–57
experiencing, 353
family life, 93
humanism on, 13
naturalism on, 363–364, 379–381
nonbelief and, 256
spirituality and, 353
worldview in making, 251–253

Meaning-maintenance theory, 252–253

"Mediating Conflict in the Rasht Valley, Tajikistan" (Lemon), 212

Meditation, 99, 355

"Megachurches of Atlanta" (Miller), 29

"Memorial and Remonstrance against Religious Assessments" (Madison), 170, 178

Mennonites, 337–338

Mental health, 257

Mentalizing, 232

Meslier, Jean, 7

Meyer, Birgit, 23

Micklethwait, John, 291

Middle East conflicts, 207–212

Military chaplaincy, 219

Mill, John Stuart, 273

Millennials, 107–108

Miller, Donald, 29

Mind perception, 232

Mind-blind atheism, 232

Mirabaud, 263

The Missionary Position: Mother Teresa in Theory and Practice (Hitchens), 284

Mitigation response, 370–371

Modernization
causal link with secularization, 21–22
conflict theories and, 207
defined, 21
inevitability of secularization and, 6
measurement of, 22, 26
New Atheism and, 293
as progress, 64

religious repression in, 203–204
restlessness in, 65
secularization thesis on, 19, 20*f,* 20–21, 65–66, 291
Turkey, 209–210

Mohism, 337

Monnier, Ricki, 268

Montaigne, Michel de, 267

Moore, Sean E., 241–261, 254*t*

Moors, Annelies, 23

Moral atheology, 266–267, 268, 270–271

Moral development, 309–311
atheists as lacking, 230–231, 235
atheology on, 271–272
religion as obstacle to, 304–305
secular ethics and, 305–307

Moral gap, 308

Moral Majority, 179–180

Moral psychology, 369–371

Moral theology, 267

Morality, **301–323**
assessing religious, 311–315
atheism associated with lack of, 229–231
atheology on, 266–267, 268, 270–271
defining, 302–303
family life in, 101–106
god as grounds for, 307–311
motivation in, 306
as natural phenomenon, 309–311, 370
in naturalism, 369–371
nonreligious, 249–250
in primates, 235
secular, constructing, 315–319
secular humanist, 306–307, 319
in secularism, 196
terminology, 301–303
women and, 120–121, 124

"A More Perfect Union" (Obama), 182

Mormonism, 73, 82, 83, 89, 178

Morrison, Jim, 332

Morsi, Mohammed, 209

Mortality, 231, 381

Moses, 336

Mozi, 337

Mubarak, Hosni, 209

Muhammad, 336

Muhlenberg, Henry, 171

Muñoz, Vincent Phillip, 180, 181

Muslim Board of Uzbekistan, 211–212

INDEX

Muslim Brotherhood, 66, 203, 208, 209
Myth, 64, 206
The Myth of American Individualism (Shain), 169

N

Najle, Maxine B., 225–239, 234
Nasrin, Taslima, 113–114
Natal nominalist, 60
Nation states, 4, 190–194
    See also Anarchism
National Association of Evangelicals, 179
National Election Studies, 25
National Liberation Front, 205
National September 11 Memorial and Museum, 192–193
National Survey of Religious Identification (NSRI), 129, 130
Nationalism
    Arab, 208–212
    civil religion in, 34
    problems from, 325
    return of religion in, 186
    secularization backlash and, 29–30, 206
    violence and, 206
    war and, 203–204, 208–212, 218
    women and, 121
    See also Anarchism
Native American spirituality, 333
Nativism movements, 32
Natural law, 312–314, 316–317
Natural theology, 267
Naturalism, 270, **363–384**
    appearance *vs.* reality in, 365–367
    atheism and, 327
    autonomy and, 375–376
    compassion and, 369
    connection in, 368
    control and, 369
    criminal justice and, 372–373
    defined, *364*, 363
    fate of the planet and, 377–379
    on human nature, 367–368
    on inequality, 373–375
    meaning and purpose in, 379–381
    morality and, 369–371
    secular spirituality, 352
    as worldview, 365

Naturalism and Religion (Nielsen), 275
Nature, awe of, 114, 355–356
Navarro-Rivera, Juhem, 117, 129–145, 131, 136, 137–138
Needham, Rodney, 57
Neoplatonism, 122–123
Neuberg, S. L., 227
Neuroscience
    on human nature, 367–368
    of morality, 310–311, 317, 318
    of nonreligion, 244, 247–248
The New Abolition (Dorrien), 176
New Atheism, 15, **281–300**
    active opposition in, 253
    contexts, 293–294
    definition of, 281
    Four Horsemen in, 282–286
    future of, 294–297
    gender gap in, 286
    incomplete atheology of, 274
    media coverage, 288, 290, 293–294
    morality in, 307
    on negative force of religion, 196, 304–305
    openness in, 152, 155
    political dimensions, 288–290
    reception and dissemination of, 286–288
    rituals and ceremonies, 99
    sociological interpretations, 290–293
    values, 150–151
    women in, 116
    See also Atheism
"The New Atheism and the Formation of the Imagined Secularist Community" (Cimino and Smith), 152
The New Atheism: Taking a Stand for Science and Reason (Stenger), 285
New religious movements, as apostasy, 83, 86–87
Newton, Isaac, 273
The Next Christendom: The Coming of Global Christianity (Jenkins), 32
Nielsen, Kai, 275, 314, 315
Nietzsche, Friedrich Wilhelm, 20, 273, 296
Nihilism, 335–336
Nominal religion, 60
Nonbelief
    atheist women defining, 113–114
    defined, 15

diversity in, 249
gender differences, 114–118
psychological functions of, 251–252
public perceptions of, 257–258
stigma toward, 50
typology of, 253–256
Nones
    atheist awakening and, 295
    demographics of, 248–249
    ethnic diversity of, 141
    families, 95, 97
    female, **111–128**
    Jewish, 344–345
    meaning-making by, 252
    political party affiliations, 137–138
    psychology of, 250–253
    rites and rituals, 43
Nonpreferentialism doctrine, 180–181
Nonreligion
    defined, 12, 112, 243
    ethnicity and, 129–145
    vs. low religiosity, 246
    morality and, 303–304
    organized, 118–119
    psychology of, 241–261
    researching, 117–118
    self-reported, 244
    typologies, 253–255, 254*t*
Nonreligion and Secularity Research Network, 242
Nonviolence, 325, 327–328, 333, 335–336
    See also Pacifism
Norenzayan, Ara, 153, 228–229, 251, 253–254, 257
Norris, Pippa, 26, 31, 115, 186, 199
North Atlantic Treaty Organization, 214
Northern Ireland, 217
Numinal theology, 267
Nyad, Diana, 114
Nye, Bill, 157

O

Obama, Barack, 182
Objective religiosity, 44
Occupy Protests, 334
O'Hair, Madalyn Murray, 113, 125, *125*
Oklahoma Atheists, 160–161
Olson, Laura, 27

Olympic Games, 330
Olympism, 330
Omi, Michael, 138
On Heresies (Isidore of Seville), 85
On the Genealogy of Morals
  (Nietzsche), 273
Openly Secular Campaign, 151, 157
Ordain Women, 83
Orestes (Roman governor), 123
Organization theory, 24–25
Orientalism, 213
Orthodoxy, 7, 243
Other, **1–16**
  agnosticism and agnostics, 8–10
  apostates and exiters, 10–12, 84
  atheism and atheists, 6–8, 124,
    153, 158
  in community, 149
  humanism, 13–14
  less common terms, 14–15
  negative force of religion, 196
  New Atheism and, 291–292
  nonreligion, irreligion, and
    areligion, 12–13
  secular and secularity, 2–3
  secularism, 3–5
  secularization, 5–6
Ottoman Empire, 207–210
Our Declaration (Allen), 169
Outsiders, 77
Owen, Huw Parri, 308, 309

P

Pacifism, **325–342**
  absolute *vs.* contingent, 329
  in art, 331–333
  contemporary social movements,
    333–335
  defined, 326, 327–328
  history of, 336–341
  humanism in, 335–336
  overlap with atheism and anar-
    chism, 329, 329*f*
  in pop culture, 329–331
Paganism, 7
Paine, Thomas, 3
Pakistan, 214
Palestine, 203, 209, 218
*Parenting Beyond Belief: On Raising
  Ethical, Caring Kids Without Religion* (McGowen), 96
Patrikios, Stratos, 19–36
Pauling, Linus, 341
Peace of Westphalia, 191, 215

Pedagogical atheology, 271–272
Peek, Lori, 78
Peirce, Charles, 267–268
Pemberton, John, 63
Penn, William, 168–169
Pentecostalism, 139
Peoples Temple, 87
Performative belief, 61–62, 63
Personality, 249–250, 374
"Personality and Group Factors in the
  Making of Atheists" (Vetter and
  Green), 248
Personality psychology, 244–245
Pew Research Center
  on age, 133
  on gender, 134
  on increase in unaffiliated, 50,
    131
  on Judaism, 349
  on religious freedom laws, 187
  on scientists and political
    affiliation, 375
  secularization data, 25, 28
  self-reports, 253
  U.S. Christian population data,
    34
Philosophical atheology, 272
The Philosophy of Humanism
  (Lamont), 274
The Philosophy of Moral Development
  (Kohlberg), 305
The Philosophy of Poverty (Proudhon),
  338
*Philosophy of the Practical: Economic
  and Ethic* (Croce), 273
Philpott, Daniel, 217
Physicalism, 367–368
Piaget, Jean, 310
Pierard, Richard, 34
Piety, 312
Pinker, Steven, 316
Pitt, Brad, 152
Planetary responsibility, 377–379
*Planting Seeds: Practicing Mindfulness
  with Children* (Thich Nhat Hanh),
  96
Plantinga, Alvin, 265
Plato, 19, 264, 312
"Plato's Shorter Ethical Works"
  (Woodruff), 312
Pledge of allegiance, 193
Pluralism, 31–32, 102, 195, 199, 376
Political legitimacy, 190–191
Political participation
  atheists banned from, 225–226

civil religion and, 34
  community and, 155–156
  ethnicity and, 143–144
  link with secularization, 22, 22*f*
  religious cleavage and, 27–28
  religious tests for, 192
  secular community and, 159–161
Political party affiliation
  Catholics, 27, 27*f*
  demographics of, 140*t*
  early American, 173, 174–175
  ethnicity and, 130, 142–143
  by religion, 136–138
  secularization effect on, 27, 27*f*
  Turkey, 193
  twentieth century, 175–176,
    179–181
Politics
  of belief, 66–67
  identity, 289–290
The Politics of Religious Apostasy
  (Bromley), 11
Polity, 22
Polygamy, 178
Poor relief, 173–174
Porgy and Bess (Gershwin), 375
*The Portable Atheist: Essential Read-
  ings for the Nonbeliever* (Hitchens),
  296
Postindustrial society, 115–116
Postmodern theology, 265
Postsecular, 66, 199
Postsecularism, 199, 206
Poverty, 374
Power, 115, 326
Practical atheology, 272
Practice, embodied, 56
Prebish, Charles, 30
Prejudice against atheists, 225–226
  See also Stigma
Prejudice-reducing techniques,
  234–235
Primates, morality in, 235, 311, 370
Primates and Philosophers (De Waal),
  311
Primitive, belief as, 55, 67
Primitive Culture (Tylor), 55
Privileging of religion, 4–5, 195–196
  apostasy, 11–12
  colonial America, 167–171
  Hitchens, Christopher, on,
    284–285
  Judaism, 350
  Judeo-Christian, 6–7
  New Atheism on, 295

INDEX

Product lifecycle, 64
Profane, 56
"Professionalization and Secularization in the Belgian Catholic Pillar" (Dobbelaere), 25
Progress, 64–65, 150–151
Prohibition movement, 174, 175, 176
Propositional belief, 55, 61–62
Protection of Individuals with Regard to the Processing of Personal Data (Greece), 30
Protestant Reformation, 23–24, 190–192
Protestant—Catholic—Jew: An Essay in American Religious Sociology (Herberg), 346
Protestantism
  civil rights and, 179
  demographics, 132–133, 134
  education levels in, 135
  ethnic diversity in, 134–135, 138–140
  megachurches, 29
  social gospel, 175–176
Proudhon, Pierre-Joseph, 338
Proulx, Travis, 256
Psychological coercion, 181
Psychology
  on moral development, 305
  on religion as natural, 105–106
  spirituality and, 353
"The Psychology of Atheism" (Farias), 245
Psychology of secularity, **241–261**
  academic interest in, 242
  applications and extensions of, 256–258
  approaches to, 243–245
  definitions in, 242–248
  findings on, 248–250
  framework for, 250–253
  nonbeliever typologies in, 253–256
  research methods, 245–248
Psychometric approaches, 246
Public Religion Research Institute (PRRI), 131, 136–137
Public Religions in the Modern World (Casanova), 291
Public speaking, gender and, 120
Public/private spheres, **185–201**
  arguments for and against secularism in, 194–198
  gendered, 115–118

origins of secularism, 190–194
return of religion, 185–188
women and nonreligion, 118–119
See also Family life
Puritans, 3, 166, 167, 168, 173
Purpose, 379–381
Putnam, Robert D., 166

Q

Quack, Johannes, 12
Quaker Constitutionalism and the Political Thought of John Dickinson (Calvert), 169
Quaker Party, 169
Quakers, 3, 167, 168–169
Qualitative research, 97
Quantitative research, 96–97
Queer theory, 333

R

Race. *See* Ethnicity and secularism
Racial Formation in the United States (Omi and Winant), 138
Racism, 144
  See also Ethnicity and secularism
Radest, Howard, 346
Radical Humanism (Roy), 274–275
Radical theology, 265
Rahnema, Saeed, 207–208
Rape, 315
Rasht Valley conflict (2008–2011), 212
Rational choice theory, 31–32, 121
Rational Mothers and Infidel Gentlemen (Kirkley), 116
Rationalism, theistic, 170
Rationalist atheology, 266–269, 268–269
Rationality
  as atheist value, 150–151
  belief and, 54, 58–59, 67
  Euthyphro Dilemma and, 312–314
  humanism on, 13–14
  morality and, 305
  multidimensional, 196–197
  in naturalism, 366
  secular Judaism, 348–349
Rawls, John, 195
Reagan, Ronald, 180
Reason Rally (2012), 88
"Reasons to Believe" ad campaign, 63–64

Reconciliation, 372–373
Reconstructionist Judaism, 345
"Red Harlot of Infidelity" (Ginzberg), 127
Reformation, 23–24, 190–192
Regnerus, Mark D., 59–62
Rehabilitation, 372–373
Rehnquist, William, 180–181
Reinventing American Protestantism (Miller), 29
Relativism, 307–308, 313
Relax It's Just God: How and Why to Talk to Your Kids about Religion When You're Not Religious (Russell), 96
Religion
  alternatives to, 95
  anthropological views of, 55
  benefits on children, 103–105
  civil, 34
  contentious nature of scholarship on, 11–12
  critical thinking and, 305
  criticism of, 265–268
  cultural, 45, 47
  as default identity, 154
  definitions, 1–2, 188–189
  family life and, 95, 99–100
  feminization of, 118–119
  function of in society, 19
  government control through, 4
  idealized past, 31–32
  imposed, 106
  levels of analysis, 22–28
  media publicization of, 290
  morality and, 303–304, 305–307
  natural basis of, 105–106
  as negative social force, 196
  as organizational phenomenon, 24–25
  political and military power and, 336
  as private *vs.* public, 165–166
  privatization of, 291
  privileging of, 4–5, 167–169, 284–285
  as public good, 173–175, 177, 197–198
  respectability and, 120–121
  return of, 185–188, 199, 288, 291–292
  schismatic, 73
  secular, 38
  separation of from society, 22–24
  social significance of, 38, 43

408   MACMILLAN INTERDISCIPLINARY HANDBOOKS

Religion, *continued*
   in societies and states, 22–24
   substantive *vs.* functional, 19–20, 30–31
   substitutes for, 30–31
   transform *vs.* decline, 54
   vicarious, 39
Religion, Media, and the Public Sphere (Meyer and Moors), 23
Religion and Globalization (Beyer), 32
Religion and Public Life in the Midwest (Barlow and Silk), 134
Religion and State Data Set, 23, 24
Religion and the Culture Wars (Green), 130
"Religion and the Five Factors of Personality" (Saroglou), 250
Religion for Atheists (de Botton), 354
Religion in a Free Market (Kosmin and Keysar), 130
"Religion in Britain: Neither Believing nor Belonging" (Voas and Crockett), 33
Religion in Britain Since 1945: Believing without Belonging (Davie), 54
Religion in Public Life Project, 131
   See also Pew Research Center
"Religion in the Public Sphere," 66
Religion Is Not So Strong Here (Kehl-Bodrogi), 211
Religion: The Social Context (McGuire), 19
Religiosity
   apostasy and, 76–77
   assessing, 54
   health and, 284
   historical analysis, 121–125
   objective, 44–49
   self-reported, 233–234, 244
   women, 114–119
"The Religiosity of Women in the Modern West" (Walter and Davie), 114
Religious awakenings, 73
Religious cleavage, 27–28
Religious economy approach, 31–32
"The Religious Factor in US Presidential Elections, 1960–1992" (Manza and Brooks), 27
Religious Landscape Surveys, 133
Religious Liberty and the American Supreme Court (Muñoz), 180
The Religious Significance of Atheism (Ricoeur), 265

Religulous (film), 286
Renaissance, 13
Reproductive rights, 188, 196, 375–376
Repudiation, 74
Research methodology, 39, 96–98, 150–151, 246–248
"Research Note: Talking about a Revolution" (Lee), 243
Resilience, 367
Respectability, 120–121
"Retreat and Return of the Secular in Iran" (Rahnema), 207–208
Retribution, 372
"Retrospective Accounts of Religious Disaffiliation in the United States" (Vargas), 152
Return-of-religion thesis, 185–188, 199
   New Atheism and, 288, 291–292
The Revenge of God: The Resurgence of Islam, Christianity and Judaism in the Modern World (Kepel), 291
Reverence, 308
Reynolds, George, 178
Reynolds v. United States (1879), 176–177, 178
Reza Shah, 208
Ricoeur, Paul, 265
Ridgeway, Cecilia L., 111
Rig Veda, 264
Riis, Ole, 41
"The Rise and Fall of Secularism in the Arab World" (Salem), 207
Rising Tide: Gender Equality and Cultural Change around the World (Norris and Inglehart), 115
Rites of passage, 39
   in community, 159
   family life, 98–101
   in secular societies, 43, 47
   women in, 116
Ritualist apostate, 76–77
Rituals and ceremonies
   atheist community and, 158–159
   in community, *148*
   family life, 98–101
   Jewish, 350–351
   naturalist, 381
   in secular societies, 43, 45–47
   secularizing, 99–100
   women in, 116
Robbins, Joel, 58
Robertson, Pat, 180
Robertson, Phil, 229–230
Robinson, Matthew A., 242

Roof, Wade, 83–84
Roosevelt, Franklin Delano, 175
Rose, Ernestine L., 120, *123,* 123–125
Rose, William, 124
Rosie, Michael, 48
Roy, M. N., 274–275
Ruel, Malcolm, 57–58
Runciman, Walter Garrison, 117
Rushdie, Salman, 82, 86, 187, 285
Russell, Bertrand, 341
Russell, Wendy, 96
Russian Orthodox Church, 211

S

Sacred, 56–57
Sacred and Secular: Religion and Politics Worldwide (Norris and Inglehart), 26, 186
Sadat, Anwar, 209
SADUM, 211
Sagan, Carl, 356, 380
Salem, Paul, 207
Same-sex marriage, 89, 144, 187–188
Sandil, Riddhi, 242
Santayana, George, 273
Sarkozy, Nicolas, 214
Saroglou, Vassilis, 250
Sartre, Jean-Paul, 263, 296
The Satanic Verses (Rushdie), 82, 187
Satisfaction, 83–84, 257
   See also Well-being
Saudi Arabia, 4, 226
Scale content, 246
Scalia, Antonin, 181, 225
Scandinavia
   atheism and gender in, 286
   atheism identity in, 289–290
   lived secularity, 37–52
   New Atheism, 294
   rituals and ceremonies, 99
   societal health, 84–85, 159–160
Schappes, Morris, 348–349
Schism, 73, 86
Schwartz, Laura, 111, 117, 121
Science
   atheology and, 273
   on human nature, 367–368
   human rights and, 371–372
   humanism on, 13–14
   link with secularization, 21, 22f
   New Atheism and, 292–293
   New Atheism on, 15
   truth in, 366

INDEX

Science and Philosophy (Roy), 274–275
Science fiction, 332–333
Scientific atheology, 266–267, 268, 269–270
Scientific method, 150–151, 366
Scientology, 87
Scopes, John, 175, *176, 366*
Scorsese, Martin, 187
Scotland
  Christianity as values in, 48–49
  church as community, 48
  lived secularity, 37
  secularity context, 50–51
Second Great Awakening, 73, 172–173, 177
Sectarianism, 378–379
Secular
  definition of, 2–3, 112, 217–218
  neutrality of term, 3
  vs. nonreligion, 12
  vs. unchurched, 54, 61–62
A Secular Age (Taylor), 191, 245, 302
Secular Coalition for America, 4
Secular humanism, 14, 150, 151–152, 306–307, 319, 335
  See also Humanism
Secular identity, 105–108
Secular Student Alliance, 156–161
Secular studies, 264
Secularism
  arguments for and against, 194–198
  assertive, 216
  on authority, 327
  backlash against, 206–207
  community and, 147–163
  definition of, 3–5, 188–190, 217–218, 302
  ethnic diversity and, 129–145
  exclusivist, 190, 191–192, 195–196
  illiberal, 193
  inclusivist, 190, 193–194
  militant, 198
  morality and, 301–323
  New Atheism and, 295
  origins of, 190–194
  passive, 216
  political party affiliations, 136–138
  religion and the public sphere, 185–201
  values in, 150–152
  violence reduced by, 216–217

war and, 203–221
Secularism and Nonreligion journal, 242
Secularism and State Policies toward Religion: The United States, France, and Turkey (Kuru), 193, 216
Secularist organization, 4–5
Secularity
  advanced, 37
  affirmative *vs.* passive, 95
  in belief, behavior, and belonging, 94–95
  definition of, 2–3, 94, 189, 243
  degrees of, 95
  family life, 93–110
  hostility toward religion, 51
  as ideology, 243
  impact on children, 103–105
  as indifference, 39–41
  life cycle changes in, 105–107
  lived, 37–52
  as natural, 105–106
  neutrality of term, 3
  psychology of, 241–261
  safe expression of, 93–94, 96
  sequence of, 93–94
  war and, 203–221
  of women, 111–128
Secularization, **19–36**, 21*f*, 22*f*
  age comparisons, 21, 21*f*
  atheism as requisite for secularization, 42
  backlash against, 28, 29, 206–207, 302
  basic idea of, 20*f*, 20–21
  of belief, **53–69**
  causal links, 21–22
  country comparisons, 21, 21*f*
  declining religious authority thesis, 26–28
  definition, 5–6, 38
  definition of, 189, 217–218
  education and, 135–136
  as erosion of supernatural, 49
  family life, 93–94
  gender differences, 114–118
  levels of analysis, 22–28
  macro level, 22–24, 29–30
  meso level, 24–25, 29
  micro level, 25–28, 29
  psychological motives for, 244
  return of religion and, 185–188, 199, 288, 291–292
  reversibility and nonlinearity of, 32

societal health, 84–85
"Secularization as Declining Religious Authority" (Chaves), 26–27
Secularization thesis
  based on idealized religious past, 31–32
  basic idea of, 20–21
  critiques of, 28–33
  defined, 19
  internal, 24–25
  macro-level analysis, 22–24
  return of religion and, 185–188
  U.S. as exception, 28–29, 31–32
"Security, Secularism and Gender: The Turkish Military's Security Discourse in Relation to Political Islam" (Arik), 210
"The Securityness of Secularism? The Case of Turkey" (Bilgin), 215
Self-report methods, 233–234, 244, 246–247
  on nonbelief, 255–256
  problems with, 253
  on spirituality, 344
Separation of church and state, 22–24, **165–184**
  colonial America, 167–169
  constitutionalism, 176–177
  disestablishment, 169–171
  dislike of atheists and, 225
  early American, 172–177
  France, 213–214
  future of, 181–183
  as market mechanism, 31–32
  religion as private *vs.* public, 165–166
  religious participation decline and, 182–183
  secularism defined as, 3–5, 188–190
  Supreme Court on, 176–179, 180–182, 192–193
  Treaties of Westphalia on, 191
  twentieth century, 179–181
Sexuality
  naturalism on, 375–376
  women and respectability, 120–121
  See also Homosexuality
Shah, Timothy Samuel, 217
Shain, Barry Allen, 169
Sharia law, 4
Shariff, Azim F., 153, 228–229
Sharples, Eliza, 113
Sherine, Ariane, 286–287, *287*

410   MACMILLAN INTERDISCIPLINARY HANDBOOKS

Sherkat, Darren, 71, 74, 152, 154
Shermer, Michael, 307, 316, 317
Sherrow, Fred, 75, 79, 81, 89
Shields, Jon, 180
The Shifting Religious Identity of Latinos in the United States, 135
Shook, John R., 40, 263–279
Silk, Mark, 134
Silver, Mitchell, 358
Silverman, David, 346
Simulated social contact, 234–235
Singh, Jasit, 60
Sinnott-Armstrong, Walter, 315
"The Six Types of Nonbelief: A Qualitative and Quantitative Study of Type and Narrative" (Silver, et al.), 254–255
Skeggs, Beverly, 64
Skeptics and skepticism, 150
    Atheism+ on, 15
    defined, 14
    history of, 264
Sky Television, 64–65
Slaughterhouse-Five (Vonnegut), 330
Smith, Al, 175
Smith, Christopher, 88, 95
    atheist awakening, 295
    ritual, 159
    secularist identity, 107, 152
Smith, Jesse M., 50, 71–91, 106–107, 153–155
Smith, Joseph, 73
Smith, Wilfred Cantwell, 57
Snow, C. P., 292–293
Snyder, Gary, 325–326, 333
"So You Believe in Atheists?" (Gervais, Shariff, and Norenzayan), 153
Social apostasy, 77–78
Social capital, 197–198
Social Cleavages and Political Change (Manza and Brooks), 27
Social cohesion, 44
Social Darwinism, 372
Social gospel, 175–176
Social justice, 271, 373–375
Social learning theory, 74–75
Social media, community in, 152, 155–156, 290
Social movements, 174–175, 333–335
Social psychology, 244–245
Social sciences
    on apostasy, 73–75
    on belief, 53, 55
    on community, 149, 153–155

on gender and nonreligion, 117–118
    New Atheism and, 290–293
    return of religion and, 185–186
Social significance of religion, 38, 43
Socialism, 358
Socialization, 78, 79
Society
    apostasy and health of, 84–85
    atheology on, 267–268
    function of religion in, 19
    health of and secularism, 84–85, 159–160, 230–231, 303–304
    negative influences of religion on, 196
    religion and health of, 303–307
    religion as control in, 4–5
    religion separated from, 22–24
    See also Secularization
Society for Humanistic Judaism, 347, 350–351
Society of Separationists, 125
Society without God (Zuckerman), 152, 196, 303
Socioeconomic status
    demographics of, 140t
    ethnicity and, 135–136, 139, 141–142
Socrates, 7, 311–312, *312*
Sony Corporation, 64–66
Southern Baptist Convention, 134–135, 179
Southern Christian Leadership Conference, 176
Sovereignty, 190–191
Soviet Union, 193, 206, 211, 294
Spencer, Herbert, 273
Spinoza, Baruch, 267–268, 344, 369
Spiritual Administration for the Muslims of Central Asia and Kazakhstan, 211
The Spiritual Revolution: Why Religion Is Giving Way to Spirituality (Heelas and Woodhead), 114
Spiritualism, 113, 352–353
Spirituality
    atheism and, 296–297
    defined, 351–352
    naturalist, 379–381
    paths to, 354–358
    secular, 343–361
Sports as religion, 30
St. Vincent de Paul Society, 174
Stalwarts, 79
Stanton, Elizabeth Cady, 118

Stark, Rodney, 40, 47
"States, Religious Diversity, and the Crisis of Secularism" (Bhargava), 194
Stem cell research, 188
Stenger, Victor J., 285
Stephens, Mitchell, 125
Stereotype of atheism, 227–231, 234–236
Stigma, **225–239**
    of apostasy, 81–82
    of atheism, 50, 75, 152–156
    atheist stereotypes and, 226–231
    coming out and, 106–107, 152–153, 160–161, 248
    consequences of, 233–234
    New Atheism and, 287–288, 289–290
    of pacifism and anarchism, 334
    self-reports and, 253
    toward nonreligiosity, 243, 257–258
    women and disbelief, 111–127
Subjectivism, 307–308
Sunday Assembly, 97–98, 147, *148,* 297, 381
    community in, 155
    family life, 101–102
    ritual and ceremony in, 159
Supernatural
    atheists who believe in, 253
    Durkheim on, 56–57
    humanism on, 13–14
    vs. naturalism, 6
    New Atheism on, 15, 296–297
    religion based on, 2
    spirituality and, 353
Supernaturalism, 365
Supreme Court (U.S.), 176–179, 180–182, 192–193
Sweden
    attitudes toward church, 43–49
    lived secularity, 37
    secularity context, 50–51
    state religion established, 3
Switchers, religious, 12, 79
Symbolic boundaries theory, 158
Syria, 207, 208, 218–219
Systeme de la nature (System of Nature) (Mirabaud), 263

T

Taira, Teemu, 281–300
Tajikistan, 210–211, 212

INDEX

Taliban, 214
Taoism, 331–332, 333, 337
Taylor, Charles, 38, 191, 245, 302
Technology, 22, 22f
Temperance movement, 174
Ten Commandments, 193, 312–314
Terrorism, 203, 204, 206
　　atheism as, 226
　　civil rights and, 212–213
　　Hitchens, Christopher, on, 285
　　New Atheism on, 282–283
　　religiously inspired, 186–187, 217
　　return of religion and, 291–292
　　United Kingdom, 214
Theism, 9, 106
Theistic rationalism, 170
Theology, 267
　　See also Atheology
Theorie des kommunikativen Handelns (Theory of Communicative Action) (Habermas), 275
The Theory of Vision (Berkeley), 264
Theos, 288
There Is No God (Williamson and Yancey), 76
Thich Nhat Hanh, 96
Third culture, 292–293
Thirty Years' War (1618–1648), 190–191, 206, 215
Thiry, Paul-Henry, Baron d'Holbach, 263
Thomas, Clarence, 181
Thomas Aquinas's Summa Theologiae: A Guide and Commentary (Davies), 313–314
Thoreau, Henry David, 339–340, 364
Thurmond, Strom, 179
Thus Spoke Zarathustra (Nietzsche), 273
Tillich, Paul, 267–268
Time magazine, 291, 346
Tocqueville, Alexis de, 166, 173
Tokyo Telecommunications Engineering Corporation, 64
Tolstoy, Leo, 337, 339–340
Tomlins, Steven, 157–158, 287
Tonga, 245
Tönnies, Ferdinand, 149
Totem, 56
Toynbee, Polly, *287*
Transcendence
　　from art, beauty, culture, 356–357, *357*

in atheology, 267–268
　　naturalist, 380
　　spirituality and, 353–354
　　See also Spirituality
The Transcendental Temptation: A Critique of Religion and the Paranormal (Kurtz), 275
Transcendentalism, 337, 339–340, 364
Transhumanism, 376
Treaties of Westphalia, 191, 215
A Treatise on Social Theory (Runciman), 117–118
Treaty of Peace and Friendship of Tripoli, 172
The Tree of Life (movie), 380
The True Intellectual System of the Universe (Cudworth), 264, 265
Truth, rationality and, 59
Trzebiatowska, Marta, 111–128
Tschannen, Olivier, 20
Tunisia, 209
Turkey, secularism in, 193, 203, 207–210, 215, 216
Turney, Bryan, 81
Tversky, A., 228–229
2012 Pre-Election American Values Survey (Jones, Cox, and Navarro-Rivera), 131
Two Treatises of Government and A Letter Concerning Toleration (Locke), 165–166
Tylor, Edward Burnett, 55
Tyson, Neil deGrasse, 356, 380

U

"Ulama and the State of Uzbekistan" (Khalid), 210, 211
Ulrich, Laurel Thatcher, 121
Unbeliever, defined, 15, 121
The Unbelievers (film), 285
Unchurched, 54, 61–62
Unitarian Universalist Association, 97–98, 102
United Kingdom
　　apostasy in, 77
　　atheist identity in, 289, 293–294
　　Big Society agenda, 198
　　court cases on public sphere religion, 198
　　freethought, 116–117
　　idealized religious past, 31
　　inclusivist secularism, 194

politics of belief, 66–67
　　privileging of religion in, 195
　　religious conflict, 214
　　secularization, 29
　　Sky Television, 64–65
United Nations
　　Human Development Index, 26
　　measurements of modernity, 22
　　secularization data, 23
United States of America
　　apostasy, 75
　　colonial, 5, 167–169
　　Constitution
　　　　Bill of Rights, 171, 177–179
　　　　on disestablishment, 169–171
　　　　First Amendment, 171, 192–193
　　　　groups favored in, 4
　　cults, 87
　　dislike of atheists, 225–228
　　diversity and secularism, 129–145
　　Founders, *166,* 169–171
　　freedom of religion, 3
　　freethought, 116
　　humanism, 14
　　privileging of religion in, 195–196
　　Revolution, 191
　　Second Great Awakening, 172–173
　　secularism, 192–193
　　secularity in, 49–50
　　secularization thesis and, 28–29, 31–32, 33–34
　　separation of church and state, 22–24, 31–32, 165–184
　　social health, 160–161
Universal Declaration of Human Rights, 3
Universal Life Church, 100
Universalism, 348–349, 357–358
Unmatched count technique, 234
Urbanization, 22, 22f
US Census Bureau, 129, 136
Utopianism, 118, 334
Uzbekistan, 210–212

V

Values
　　aspirational nominalists, 60
　　atheology on, 268

Values, *continued*
    Christianity as, 48–49
    community, 150–152, 155–156
    democratic, 216–217
    of nonreligious, 249–250
    psychological research on,
      247–248
    religion in the public sphere and,
      187–188
    of secularism, 245
    See also Ethics
Vargas, Nicholas, 152
Vetter, Geo B., 248
Vicarious religion, 39
Violence, religiously inspired,
    186–187, 196, **203–221**
    Hitchens, Christopher, on, 285
    morality and, 304–305
    naturalism on, 378–379
    New Atheism on, 282–283
    secularism and reducing, 216–217
    toward atheists, 233
    See also Pacifism
Virginia Declaration of Rights
    (1776), 192
Voas, David, 33, 54
Voltaire, 3, 267–268, 285, 339
Volunteerism, 173–174, 198
Vonnegut, Kurt, 330, 332

W

Wahhabism, 208, 211
Waite, Morrison Remick, 178
*Waking Up: A Guide to Spirituality
    Without Religion* (Harris), 283,
    352–353
Waliyat Sinai, 209
Walker, Barbara G., 113
Wallace v. Jaffree (1985), 180–181
Walter, Tony, 114
War, **203–221, 325–342**
    academic literature on,
      214–216
    Middle East, 207–212
    political tradition on, 218
    research on religion and,
      205–207
    research on secularism and, 205
    sources of, 327–328
    suppression of dissent, 215–216
War on terror, 186, 207, 212–214
Warber, Adam, 27
Warner, Stephen, 54, 55
Warraq, Ibn, 82

Warren, Josiah, 331
Washington, George, 170
Weber, Max
    definition of religion, 2
    on ethnic membership, 60
    on meaning, 56
    on rationalization, 59
    on secularization, 6, 20, 291
Webster's Dictionary, 71
Weddings, 43, 100
Weil, Simone, 265
Welfare state, 21–22, 22*f*, 47
Well-being, 84–85, 257, **363–384**
    appearance *vs.* reality in,
      365–366
    dimensions of, 364
    quest for, 364–365
What I Believe (Tolstoy), 339–340
"What is Humanism?" (Edwords),
    347–348
What Is Property? (Proudhon), 338
White House Office of Faith-Based
    and Community Initiatives,
    181–182
Whitehead, A. N., 267–268
"Why Morality Implied the Existence
    of God" (Owen), 308, 309
Wilde, Oscar, 331–332, 337
Williams, Daniel K., 175
Williams, Roger, 168, 169, 172
Williams, William, 31
Williamson, David, 76
Wilson, Bryan, 20, 38, 44, 65–66,
    291
Winant, Howard, 138
Wine, Sherwin, 346, 350, 358, 359
Winfrey, Oprah, 114
Winter solstice, 159
Winthrop, John, 168
Witchcraft, 56–57
Wolf, Gary, 15, 281, 282
Women and secularity, **111–128**
    invisibility of, 112
    nonbelief, 113–114
    organized nonreligion, 118–119
    researching, 117–118
    respectability and, 120–121
    terminology, 112–113
    United States, 141
Women Without Superstition (Gaylor),
    120
Women's rights, 196
    Atheism+ on, 15
    freethinking and, 120–121

public sphere religion and,
    187–188
Rose, Ernestine, on, 124–125
Woodhead, Linda, 114, 293
Woodruff, Paul, 312
Woodstock for Atheists, 88
Wooldridge, Adrian, 291
"Working Schemas and Normative
    Models in French Governance of
    Islam" (Bowen), 213, 214
World Bank, 22
"A World of Atheism: Global
    Demographics" (Keysar and
    Navarro-Rivera), 117
*A World Survey of Religion and the
    State* (Fox), 23
World Trade Center, 192–193
World Values Study, 25, 26
World Values Survey, 28
World War I veterans, 248
World's Christian Fundamentals
    Association, 175
Worldview education, 102–103
Worldviews, 197–198
    atheology on, 272
    conflict and, 218–219
    defined, 365
    naturalism, 363–384
    nonbeliever, 256
    psychology of, 250–251,
      252–253
Wright, Frances, 113, 118, 263
Wynn, Karen, 309–310

Y

Yale University, secularization of, 5
Yamane, David, 20
Yancey, George, 76
YHWH, 6
Yoder, John Howard, 337
Young, Brigham, 178
Young Men's Christian Association,
    176
Young Men's Missionary Society,
    174

Z

Zenk, Thomas, 281
Zhitlowsky, Chaim, 355, 359
Zionism, 208, 346, 350
Zito, George, 85
Zuckerman, Phil
    on apostasy, 74, 75, 78
    on aweism, 114

INDEX

Zuckerman, Phil, *continued*
    on church attendance, 50
    on ethics and child-rearing, 104
    on growth of nonreligious, 88
    methodology for studying
      secularity, 39
    on moral improvement, 305–306

    on positive feelings about religion
      of atheists, 42
    on religious indifference,
      40–41
    on rise of secularism, 302
    on social health and secularism,
      159–160, 196

    on social significance of religion,
      38, 84
    on societal health, 84
    on U.S. secularization, 152

Zwischen Naturalismus und Religion
    (Between Naturalism and Religion)
    (Habermas), 275